D0856907

WITHDRAWN

WITHDRAWN

DIODORUS OF SICILY

V

LCL 384

DIODORUS OF SICILY

THE LIBRARY OF HISTORY
BOOKS XII.41–XIII

WITH AN ENGLISH TRANSLATION BY

C. H. OLDFATHER

HARVARD UNIVERSITY PRESS
CAMBRIDGE, MASSACHUSETTS
LONDON, ENGLAND

First published 1950
Reprinted 1962, 1976, 1994, 2000

LOEB CLASSICAL LIBRARY® is a registered trademark
of the President and Fellows of Harvard College

ISBN 0-674-99422-1

Printed in Great Britain by St Edmundsbury Press Ltd,
Bury St Edmunds, Suffolk, on acid-free paper.
Bound by Hunter & Foulis Ltd, Edinburgh, Scotland.

CONTENTS

THE LIBRARY OF HISTORY
OF
DIODORUS OF SICILY

BOOK XII

ΔΙΟΔΩΡΟΥ

ΤΟΥ ΣΙΚΕΛΙΩΤΟΥ
ΒΙΒΛΙΟΘΗΚΗΣ ΙΣΤΟΡΙΚΗΣ

ΒΙΒΛΟΣ ΔΩΔΕΚΑΤΗ

41. Αἰτίαι μὲν οὖν τοῦ Πελοποννησιακοῦ πολέμου τοιαῦταί τινες ὑπῆρξαν ὡς Ἔφορος ἀνέγραψε. τῶν δ᾽ ἡγουμένων πόλεων τοῦτον τὸν τρόπον εἰς πόλεμον ἐμπεσουσῶν, Λακεδαιμόνιοι μὲν μετὰ τῶν Πελοποννησίων συνεδρεύσαντες ἐψηφίσαντο πολεμεῖν τοῖς Ἀθηναίοις, καὶ πρὸς τὸν Περσῶν βασιλέα πρεσβεύσαντες παρεκάλουν συμμαχεῖν αὐτοῖς, καὶ τοὺς κατὰ τὴν Σικελίαν καὶ Ἰταλίαν συμμάχους διαπρεσβευσάμενοι διακοσίαις τριή-
2 ρεσιν ἔπεισαν βοηθεῖν, αὐτοὶ δὲ μετὰ τῶν Πελοποννησίων τὰς πεζὰς δυνάμεις διατάξαντες καὶ τἄλλα τὰ πρὸς τὸν πόλεμον ἡτοιμασμένοι πρῶτοι τοῦ πολέμου κατήρξαντο. κατὰ γὰρ τὴν Βοιωτίαν ἡ τῶν Πλαταιέων πόλις αὐτόνομος ἦν καὶ συμμα-
3 χίαν εἶχε πρὸς Ἀθηναίους. ἐν ταύτῃ τῶν πολιτῶν τινες καταλῦσαι τὴν αὐτονομίαν βουλόμενοι διελέχθησαν τοῖς Βοιωτοῖς, ἐπαγγελλόμενοι τὴν

2

THE LIBRARY OF HISTORY

OF

DIODORUS OF SICILY

BOOK XII

41. Now the causes of the Peloponnesian War were in general what I have described, as Ephorus has recorded them. And when the leading states had become embroiled in war in this fashion, the Lacedaemonians, sitting in council with the Peloponnesians, voted to make war upon the Athenians, and dispatching ambassadors to the king of the Persians, urged him to ally himself with them, while they also treated by means of ambassadors with their allies in Sicily and Italy and persuaded them to come to their aid with two hundred triremes ; and for their own part they, together with the Peloponnesians, got ready their land forces, made all other preparations for the war, and were the first to commence the conflict. For in Boeotia the city of the Plataeans was an independent state and had an alliance with the Athenians.[1] But certain of its citizens, wishing to destroy its independence, had engaged in parleys with the Boeotians, promising that they would range

[1] The fuller account of the following incident is in Thucydides, 2. 2 ff.

πόλιν ὑπὸ τὴν τῶν Θηβαίων τάξειν συντέλειαν
καὶ παραδώσειν αὐτοῖς τὰς Πλαταιάς, ἐὰν αὐτοὶ
4 στρατιώτας πέμψωσι τοὺς βοηθοῦντας. διὸ καὶ
τῶν Βοιωτῶν ἀποστειλάντων στρατιώτας ἐπιλέκτους τριακοσίους νυκτός, οἱ προδόται τούτους
παρεισαγαγόντες ἐντὸς τῶν τειχῶν κυρίους τῆς
5 πόλεως ἐποίησαν. οἱ δὲ Πλαταιεῖς βουλόμενοι τὴν
πρὸς Ἀθηναίους συμμαχίαν διαφυλάττειν, τὸ μὲν
πρῶτον ὑπολαβόντες πανδημεὶ τοὺς Θηβαίους παρεῖναι, διεπρεσβεύσαντο πρὸς τοὺς κατειληφότας
τὴν πόλιν καὶ παρεκάλουν συνθέσθαι σπονδάς· ὡς
δ' ἡ νὺξ παρῆλθε, κατανοήσαντες ὀλίγους ὄντας,
συνεστράφησαν καὶ περὶ τῆς ἐλευθερίας ἐκθύμως
6 ἠγωνίζοντο. γενομένης δὲ τῆς μάχης ἐν ταῖς
ὁδοῖς, τὸ μὲν πρῶτον οἱ Θηβαῖοι διὰ τὰς ἀρετὰς
προεῖχον καὶ πολλοὺς τῶν ἀνθισταμένων ἀνήρουν·
τῶν δ' οἰκετῶν καὶ τῶν παίδων ἀπὸ τῶν οἰκιῶν
βαλλόντων τὰς κεραμῖδας καὶ κατατιτρωσκόντων
τοὺς Θηβαίους ἐτράπησαν· καὶ τινὲς μὲν αὐτῶν
ἐκπεσόντες ἐκ τῆς πόλεως διεσώθησαν, τινὲς δὲ
εἰς οἰκίαν τινὰ καταφυγόντες ἠναγκάσθησαν παρα-
7 δοῦναι σφᾶς αὐτούς. οἱ δὲ Θηβαῖοι παρὰ τῶν ἐκ
τῆς μάχης διασωθέντων πυθόμενοι τὰ συμβεβηκότα,
παραχρῆμα πανδημεὶ κατὰ σπουδὴν ὥρμησαν.
διὰ δὲ τὸ παράδοξον ἀνετοίμων ὄντων τῶν κατὰ
τὴν χώραν, πολλοὶ μὲν ἀνῃρέθησαν, οὐκ ὀλίγοι δὲ
ζῶντες συνελήφθησαν, ἅπασα δ' ἡ χώρα ταραχῆς
καὶ διαρπαγῆς ἔγεμεν.

42. Οἱ δὲ Πλαταιεῖς διαπρεσβευσάμενοι πρὸς
τοὺς Θηβαίους ἠξίουν ἀπελθεῖν ἐκ τῆς χώρας αὐτῶν
καὶ ἀπολαβεῖν τοὺς αἰχμαλώτους. διὸ καὶ τῆς

that state under the confederacy [1] organized by the 431 B.C.
Thebans and hand Plataea over to them if they would
send soldiers to aid in the undertaking. Consequently, when the Boeotians dispatched by night
three hundred picked soldiers, the traitors got them
inside the walls and made them masters of the city.
The Plataeans, wishing to maintain their alliance with
the Athenians, since at first they assumed that the
Thebans were present in full force, began negotiations with the captors of the city and urged them to
agree to a truce ; but as the night wore on and they
perceived that the Thebans were few in number,
they rallied *en masse* and began putting up a vigorous
struggle for their freedom. The fighting took place
in the streets, and at first the Thebans held the upper
hand because of their valour and were slaying many
of their opponents ; but when the slaves and children
began pelting the Thebans with tiles from the houses
and wounding them, they turned in flight ; and some
of them escaped from the city to safety, but some
who found refuge in a house were forced to give
themselves up. When the Thebans learned the outcome of the attempt from the survivors of the battle,
they at once marched forth in all haste in full force.
And since the Plataeans who dwelt in the rural
districts were unprepared because they were not
expecting the attack, many of them were slain and
not a small number were taken captive alive, and the
whole land was filled with tumult and plundering.

42. The Plataeans dispatched ambassadors to the
Thebans demanding that they leave Plataean territory
and receive their own captives back. And so, when

[1] The Boeotian League, which had been revived after
Athens lost her dominating position in Central Greece in the
battle of Coroneia in 447 B.C. (cp. chap. 6).

συνθέσεως ταύτης γεγενημένης οἱ μὲν Θηβαῖοι
τοὺς αἰχμαλώτους ἀπολαβόντες καὶ τὴν λείαν
ἀποδόντες εἰς τὰς Θήβας ἀπηλλάγησαν· οἱ δὲ
Πλαταιεῖς πρὸς μὲν Ἀθηναίους ἔπεμψαν πρέσβεις
περὶ βοηθείας, αὐτοὶ δὲ τὰ πλεῖστα ἐκόμισαν εἰς
2 τὴν πόλιν. οἱ δὲ Ἀθηναῖοι πυθόμενοι τὰ περὶ τὰς
Πλαταιάς, παραχρῆμα ἐξέπεμψαν τοὺς ἱκανοὺς
στρατιώτας· οὗτοι δὲ κατὰ σπουδὴν παραγενόμενοι, καὶ μὴ φθάσαντες τοὺς Θηβαίους, τὰ λοιπὰ
τῶν ἀπὸ τῆς χώρας κατεκόμισαν εἰς τὴν πόλιν,
καὶ τέκνα καὶ γυναῖκας καὶ τὸν ὄχλον ἀθροίσαντες
ἐξαπέστειλαν εἰς τὰς Ἀθήνας.
3 Οἱ δὲ Λακεδαιμόνιοι κρίναντες καταλελύσθαι τὰς
σπονδὰς ὑπὸ τῶν Ἀθηναίων, δύναμιν ἀξιόλογον
ἤθροισαν ἔκ τε τῆς Λακεδαίμονος καὶ παρὰ τῶν
4 ἄλλων Πελοποννησίων. συνεμάχουν δὲ τότε[1] Λακεδαιμονίοις Πελοποννήσιοι μὲν πάντες πλὴν Ἀρ-
γείων· οὗτοι δ' ἡσυχίαν εἶχον· τῶν δ' ἐκτὸς τῆς
Πελοποννήσου Μεγαρεῖς, Ἀμβρακιῶται, Λευκάδιοι,
Φωκεῖς, Βοιωτοί, Λοκροὶ τῶν μὲν πρὸς Εὔβοιαν
ἐστραμμένων οἱ πλείους, τῶν δ' ἄλλων Ἀμφισσεῖς.
5 τοῖς δ' Ἀθηναίοις συνεμάχουν οἱ τὴν παράλιον
τῆς Ἀσίας οἰκοῦντες Κᾶρες καὶ Δωριεῖς καὶ Ἴω-
νες καὶ Ἑλλησπόντιοι καὶ νησιῶται πάντες πλὴν
τῶν ἐν Μήλῳ καὶ Θήρᾳ κατοικούντων, ὁμοίως δὲ
καὶ οἱ ἐπὶ Θρᾴκης πλὴν Χαλκιδέων καὶ Ποτι-
δαιατῶν· πρὸς δὲ τούτοις Μεσσήνιοι μὲν οἱ τὴν
Ναύπακτον οἰκοῦντες καὶ Κερκυραῖοι. τούτων

---

[1] τότε] τοῖς Wurm.

---

[1] Thucydides (2. 5. 7) says that the Plataeans persuaded the
Thebans to withdraw from their territory and that they then
slew the Theban captives.

this had been agreed upon, the Thebans received their captives back,[1] restored the booty they had taken, and returned to Thebes. The Plataeans dispatched ambassadors to the Athenians asking for aid, while they themselves gathered the larger part of their possessions into the city. The Athenians, when they learned of what had taken place in Plataea, at once sent a considerable body of soldiers ; these arrived in haste, although not before the Thebans, and gathered the rest of the property from the countryside into the city, and then, collecting both the children and women and the rabble,[2] sent them off to Athens.

The Lacedaemonians, deciding that the Athenians had broken the truce,[3] mustered a strong army from both Lacedaemon and the rest of the Peloponnesians. The allies of the Lacedaemonians at this time were all the inhabitants of the Peloponnesus with the exception of the Argives, who remained neutral ; and of the peoples outside of the Peloponnesus the Megarians, Ambraciotes, Leucadians, Phocians, Boeotians, and of the Locrians,[4] the majority of those facing Euboea, and the Amphissians of the rest. The Athenians had as allies the peoples of the coast of Asia, namely, the Carians, Dorians, Ionians, and Hellespontines, also all the islanders except the inhabitants of Melos and Thera, likewise the dwellers in Thrace except the Chalcidians and Potidaeans, furthermore the Messenians who dwelt in Naupactus and the Cercyraeans. Of these, the Chians, Lesbians,

[2] Thucydides (2. 6. 4) calls these " the least efficient of the men."

[3] The thirty-year truce concluded in 446 B.C. (chap. 7).

[4] Those facing Euboea were the Opuntian Locrians, those on the Corinthian Gulf the Ozolian.

ναυτικὸν παρείχοντο Χῖοι, Λέσβιοι, Κερκυραῖοι,[1]
αἱ δ' ἄλλαι πᾶσαι πεζοὺς στρατιώτας ἐξέπεμπον.
σύμμαχοι μὲν οὖν ἀμφοτέροις ὑπῆρχον οἱ προει-
ρημένοι.

6 Λακεδαιμόνιοι δὲ δύναμιν ἀξιόλογον προχειρισάμενοι τὴν ἡγεμονίαν ἔδωκαν Ἀρχιδάμῳ τῷ
βασιλεῖ. οὗτος δὲ μετὰ τῆς δυνάμεως ἐνέβαλεν
εἰς τὴν Ἀττικήν, τοῖς δὲ φρουρίοις προσβολὰς
ἐποιεῖτο καὶ τῆς χώρας πολλὴν ἐδῄωσε. τῶν δ'
Ἀθηναίων παροξυνομένων διὰ τὴν τῆς χώρας
καταδρομήν, καὶ βουλομένων παρατάξασθαι τοῖς
πολεμίοις, Περικλῆς στρατηγὸς ὢν καὶ τὴν ὅλην
ἡγεμονίαν ἔχων παρεκάλει τοὺς νέους ἡσυχίαν
ἔχειν, ἐπαγγελλόμενος ἄνευ κινδύνων ἐκβαλεῖν
7 τοὺς Λακεδαιμονίους ἐκ τῆς Ἀττικῆς. πληρώσας
οὖν ἑκατὸν τριήρεις καὶ δύναμιν ἀξιόλογον εἰς τὰς
ναῦς ἐνθέμενος, καὶ στρατηγὸν ἐπιστήσας Καρκίνον
καὶ ἑτέρους τινάς, ἐξέπεμψεν εἰς τὴν Πελοπόννησον.
οὗτοι δὲ πολλὴν τῆς παραθαλαττίου χώρας πορθήσαντες καί τινα τῶν φρουρίων ἑλόντες κατεπλήξαντο τοὺς Λακεδαιμονίους· διὸ καὶ τὴν ἐκ τῆς
Ἀττικῆς δύναμιν ταχέως μεταπεμψάμενοι πολλὴν
8 ἀσφάλειαν τοῖς Πελοποννησίοις[2] παρείχοντο. τούτῳ δὲ τῷ τρόπῳ τῆς Ἀττικῆς ἐλευθερωθείσης, ὁ
μὲν Περικλῆς ἀποδοχῆς ἐτύγχανε παρὰ τοῖς πολί-

[1] τούτων . . . Κερκυραῖοι added by Wesseling from Thuc.
2. 9. 5.
[2] So the MSS.; πολεμίοις Hermann, followed by Wurm,
Dindorf, Bekker, Vogel.

---

[1] There is a lacuna in the Greek ; the preceding words of
the sentence are taken from Thucydides, 2. 9. 5.

and Cercyraeans furnished ships,[1] and all the rest sup- 431 B.C.
plied infantry. The allies, then, on both sides were
as we have listed them.

After the Lacedaemonians had prepared for service
a strong army, they placed the command in the hands
of Archidamus their king. He invaded Attica with
his army, made repeated assaults upon its fortified
places, and ravaged a large part of the countryside.
And when the Athenians, being incensed because of
the raiding of their countryside, wished to offer battle
to the enemy, Pericles, who was a general [2] and held
in his hands the entire leadership of the state, urged
the young men to make no move, promising that
he would expel the Lacedaemonians from Attica
without the peril of battle. Whereupon, fitting out
one hundred triremes and putting on them a strong
force of men, he appointed Carcinus general over
them together with certain others and sent them
against the Peloponnesus. This force, by ravaging
a large extent of the Peloponnesian territory along the
sea and capturing some fortresses, struck terror into
the Lacedaemonians; consequently they speedily re-
called their army from Attica and thus provided a
large measure of safety to the Peloponnesians.[3] In
this manner Athens was delivered from the enemy,
and Pericles received approbation among his fellow

[2] The ten generals were the most important Athenian
magistrates of this period, and Pericles, elected every year as
one of the ten, acted as their president.

[3] Many editors (see critical note) read " enemy " for
" Peloponnesians," thereby making the Athenians the ones
who were made safe. But there is no reason to emend the
text. The fleet dispatched by Pericles was ravaging the territory of many of Sparta's Peloponnesian allies; cp. the
following chapter, and Thucydides, 2. 25, 30.

9

DIODORUS OF SICILY

ταις, ὡς δυνάμενος στρατηγεῖν καὶ τοῖς Λακεδαιμονίοις διαπολεμεῖν.

43. Ἐπ' ἄρχοντος δ' Ἀθήνησιν Ἀπολλοδώρου
Ῥωμαῖοι κατέστησαν ὑπάτους Μάρκον Γεγάνιον
καὶ Λούκιον Σέργιον. ἐπὶ δὲ τούτων ὁ τῶν Ἀθηναίων στρατηγὸς οὐ διέλιπε τὴν μὲν χώραν τῶν
Πελοποννησίων λεηλατῶν καὶ καταφθείρων, τὰ δὲ
φρούρια πολιορκῶν· προσγενομένων δὲ αὐτῷ πεντήκοντα τριήρων ἐκ τῆς Κερκύρας, πολὺ μᾶλλον ἐπόρθει τὴν Πελοποννησίων χώραν, καὶ μάλιστα τῆς
παραθαλαττίου τὴν καλουμένην Ἀκτὴν ἐδῄου καὶ
2 τὰς ἐπαύλεις ἐνεπύριζε. μετὰ δὲ ταῦτα πλεύσας ἐπὶ
Μεθώνην τῆς Λακωνικῆς, τήν τε χώραν κατέσυρε
καὶ τῇ πόλει προσβολὰς ἐποιεῖτο. ἔνθα δὴ Βρασίδας ὁ Σπαρτιάτης, νέος μὲν ὢν τὴν ἡλικίαν, ἀλκῇ
δὲ καὶ ἀνδρείᾳ διαφέρων, ὁρῶν τὴν Μεθώνην κιν-
δυνεύουσαν ἐκ βίας ἁλῶναι, παραλαβών τινας τῶν
Σπαρτιατῶν διὰ μέσου τῶν πολεμίων ἐσκεδασ-
μένων ἐτόλμησε διεκπερᾶσαι, καὶ πολλοὺς ἀνελὼν
3 παρεισέπεσεν εἰς τὸ χωρίον. γενομένης δὲ πολιορκίας, καὶ τοῦ Βρασίδου λαμπρότατα κινδυνεύσαν-
τος, Ἀθηναῖοι μὲν οὐ δυνάμενοι τὸ χωρίον ἑλεῖν
ἀπεχώρησαν πρὸς τὰς ναῦς, Βρασίδας δὲ διασε-
σωκὼς τὴν Μεθώνην διὰ τῆς ἰδίας ἀρετῆς καὶ
ἀνδρείας ἀποδοχῆς ἔτυχε παρὰ τοῖς Σπαρτιάταις.
διὰ δὲ τὴν ἀνδραγαθίαν ταύτην φρονηματισ-
θείς, πολλάκις ἐν τοῖς ὕστερον χρόνοις παραβόλως
ἀγωνιζόμενος μεγάλην δόξαν ἀνδρείας ἀπηνέγκατο.
4 Ἀθηναῖοι δὲ περιπλεύσαντες εἰς τὴν Ἠλείαν τήν

---

[1] The eastern coast between Argolis and Laconia.
[2] The single able general the Peloponnesians produced in

citizens as having the ability to perform the duties of
a general and to fight it out with the Lacedaemonians.

43. When Apollodorus was archon in Athens, the
Romans elected as consuls Marcus Geganius and
Lucius Sergius. During this year the general of the
Athenians never ceased plundering and harrying the
territory of the Peloponnesians and laying siege to
their fortresses ; and when there were added to his
command fifty triremes from Cercyra, he ravaged all
the more the territory of the Peloponnesians, and in
particular he laid waste the part of the coast which is
called Actê ¹ and sent up the farm-buildings in flames.
After this, sailing to Methonê in Laconia, he both
ravaged the countryside and made repeated assaults
upon the city. There Brasidas ² the Spartan, who
was still a youth in years but already distinguished
for his strength and courage, seeing that Methonê
was in danger of capture by assault, took some
Spartans, and boldly breaking through the hostile
forces, which were scattered, he slew many of them
and got into the stronghold. In the siege which
followed Brasidas fought so brilliantly that the
Athenians found themselves unable to take the stronghold and withdrew to their ships, and Brasidas, who
had saved Methonê by his individual bravery and
valour, received the approbation of the Spartans. And
because of this hardihood of his, Brasidas, having
become inordinately proud, on many subsequent
occasions fought recklessly and won for himself a
great reputation for valour. And the Athenians,
sailing around to Elis, ravaged the countryside and

this ten-year war. For his further career see below, chaps. 62,
67-68, 74.

τε χώραν ἐπόρθουν καὶ Φειὰν¹ χωρίον Ἠλείων ἐπολιόρκουν. ἐκβοηθησάντων δὲ τῶν Ἠλείων, μάχῃ
τε ἐνίκησαν καὶ πολλοὺς ἀποκτείναντες τῶν πο-
5 λεμίων εἷλον τὰς Φειὰς κατὰ κράτος. μετὰ δὲ
ταῦτα τῶν Ἠλείων πανδημεὶ παραταξαμένων ἀπεκρούσθησαν εἰς τὰς ναῦς· εἶτ' ἀποπλεύσαντες εἰς
τὴν Κεφαλληνίαν, καὶ τοὺς ταύτην κατοικοῦντας
εἰς τὴν συμμαχίαν προσαγαγόμενοι τὸν εἰς τὰς
Ἀθήνας πλοῦν ἐποιήσαντο.

44. Μετὰ δὲ ταῦτα Ἀθηναῖοι στρατηγὸν προχειρισάμενοι Κλεόπομπον ἐξαπέστειλαν μετὰ νεῶν
τριάκοντα, προστάξαντες τήν τε Εὔβοιαν παραφυ-
λάττειν καὶ Λοκροῖς πολεμεῖν. ὁ δ' ἐκπλεύσας τήν
τε παραθαλάττιον τῆς Λοκρίδος ἐδῄωσε καὶ πόλιν
Θρόνιον ἐξεπολιόρκησε, τοῖς δ' ἀντιταξαμένοις τῶν
Λοκρῶν συνάψας μάχην ἐνίκησε περὶ πόλιν Ἀλό-
πην. ἔπειτα τὴν προκειμένην τῆς Λοκρίδος νῆσον,
ὀνομαζομένην Ἀταλάντην, ἐπιτείχισμα τῆς Λοκρίδος κατεσκεύασε, πολεμῶν πρὸς τοὺς ἐγχωρίους.
2 Ἀθηναῖοι δ' ἐγκαλοῦντες Αἰγινήταις ὡς συνηργηκόσι
Λακεδαιμονίοις ἀνέστησαν αὐτοὺς ἐκ τῆς πόλεως,
ἐκ δὲ τῶν πολιτῶν οἰκήτορας ἐκπέμψαντες κατεκληρούχησαν τήν τε Αἴγιναν καὶ τὴν χώραν.
3 Λακεδαιμόνιοι δὲ τοῖς ἐκπεπτωκόσιν Αἰγινήταις
ἔδωκαν οἰκεῖν τὰς καλουμένας Θυρέας διὰ τὸ
καὶ τοὺς Ἀθηναίους δεδωκέναι τοῖς ἐκ Μεσσήνης
ἐκβληθεῖσι κατοικεῖν Ναύπακτον. Ἀθηναῖοι δὲ
Περικλέα μετὰ δυνάμεως ἐξέπεμψαν πολεμήσοντα
τοῖς Μεγαρεῦσιν. οὗτος δὲ πορθήσας τὴν χώραν

¹ So Palmer, from Thuc. 2. 25. 3: φεράν P, φερίαν v.

laid siege to Pheia, a stronghold of the Eleians. The Eleians who came out to its defence they defeated in battle, slaying many of their opponents, and took Pheia by storm. But after this, when the Eleians *en masse* offered them battle, the Athenians were driven back to their ships, whereupon they sailed off to Cephallenia, where they brought the inhabitants of that island into their alliance, and then voyaged back to Athens. 430 B.C.

44. After these events the Athenians chose Cleopompus general and sent him to sea with thirty ships under orders both to keep careful guard over Euboea and to make war upon the Locrians. He, sailing forth, ravaged the coast of Locris and reduced by siege the city of Thronium, and the Locrians who opposed him he met in battle and defeated near the city of Alopê.[1] Following this he made the island known as Atalantê, which lies off Locris, into a fortress on the border of Locris for his operations against the inhabitants of that country. Also the Athenians, accusing the Aeginetans of having collaborated with the Lacedaemonians, expelled them from their state, and sending colonists there from their own citizens they portioned out to them in allotments both the city of Aegina and its territory. To the Aeginetan refugees the Lacedaemonians gave Thyreae,[2] as it is called, to dwell in, because the Athenians had also once given Naupactus as a home for the people whom they had driven out of Messenê.[3] The Athenians also dispatched Pericles with an army to make war upon the Megarians. He plundered their territory, laid

[1] Thronium and Alopê are in Opuntian Locris facing the northern tip of Euboea.
[2] In northern Laconia near the border of Argolis.
[3] Cp. Book 11. 84. 7.

καὶ τὰς κτήσεις αὐτῶν λυμηνάμενος μετὰ πολλῆς
ὠφελείας ἐπανῆλθεν εἰς τὰς Ἀθήνας.

45. Λακεδαιμόνιοι δὲ μετὰ Πελοποννησίων καὶ
τῶν ἄλλων συμμάχων ἐνέβαλον εἰς τὴν Ἀττικὴν τὸ
δεύτερον. ἐπιπορευόμενοι δὲ τὴν χώραν ἐδενδρο-
τόμουν καὶ τὰς ἐπαύλεις ἐνεπύριζον, καὶ πᾶσαν
σχεδὸν τὴν γῆν ἐλυμήναντο πλὴν τῆς καλουμένης
Τετραπόλεως· ταύτης δ' ἀπέσχοντο διὰ τὸ τοὺς
προγόνους αὐτῶν ἐνταῦθα κατῳκηκέναι καὶ τὸν
Εὐρυσθέα νενικηκέναι τὴν ὁρμὴν ἐκ ταύτης ποιη-
σαμένους· δίκαιον γὰρ ἡγοῦντο τοῖς εὐηργετηκόσι
τοὺς προγόνους παρὰ τῶν ἐκγόνων τὰς προσηκού-
2 σας εὐεργεσίας ἀπολαμβάνειν. οἱ δ' Ἀθηναῖοι
παρατάξασθαι μὲν οὐκ ἐτόλμων, συνεχόμενοι δ'
ἐντὸς τῶν τειχῶν ἐνέπεσον εἰς λοιμικὴν περί-
στασιν· πολλοῦ γὰρ πλήθους καὶ παντοδαποῦ
συνερρυηκότος εἰς τὴν πόλιν διὰ τὴν στενοχωρίαν
εὐλόγως εἰς νόσους ἐνέπιπτον, ἕλκοντες ἀέρα δι-
3 εφθαρμένον. διόπερ οὐ δυνάμενοι τοὺς πολεμίους
ἐκβαλεῖν ἐκ τῆς χώρας, πάλιν ναῦς πολλὰς ἐξέπεμπον εἰς Πελοπόννησον στρατηγὸν ἐπιστήσαντες
Περικλέα. οὗτος δὲ πολλὴν χώραν τῆς παραθαλαττίου δῃώσας καί τινας πόλεις πορθήσας,
ἐποίησεν ἀπελθεῖν ἐκ τῆς Ἀττικῆς τοὺς Λακε-
4 δαιμονίους. μετὰ δὲ ταῦθ' οἱ Ἀθηναῖοι, τῆς μὲν
χώρας δεδενδροκοπημένης τῆς δὲ νόσου πολλοὺς

---

[1] " Four-city." This was the north-eastern part of Attica
containing the four demes of Marathon, Oenoë, Probalinthus,
and Tricorythus, forming an administrative unit.

[2] The Athenians had been the only people of Greece to
offer a home to the Heracleidae, in Tricorythus of the Tetrapolis ; cp. Book 4. 57.

waste their possessions, and returned to Athens with
much booty.

45. The Lacedaemonians together with the Peloponnesians and their other allies invaded Attica for
a second time. In their advance through the country
they chopped down orchards and burned the farm-
buildings, and they laid waste almost the entire land
with the exception of the region known as the
Tetrapolis.[1] This area they spared because their
ancestors had once dwelt there and had gone forth
from it as their base on the occasion when they had
defeated Eurystheus; for they considered it only fair
that the benefactors of their ancestors should in turn
receive from their descendants the corresponding
benefactions.[2] As for the Athenians, they could not
venture to meet them in a pitched battle, and being
confined as they were within the walls, found themselves involved in an emergency caused by a plague ;
for since a vast multitude of people of every description had streamed together into the city, there was
good reason for their falling victim to diseases as they
did, because of the cramped quarters, breathing air
which had become polluted.[3] Consequently, since
they were unable to expel the enemy from their
territory, they again dispatched many ships against
the Peloponnesus, appointing Pericles general. He
ravaged a large part of the territory bordering on the
sea, plundered some cities, and brought it about that
the Lacedaemonians withdrew from Attica. After
this the Athenians, now that the trees of their countryside had been cut down and the plague was carrying

[3] The detailed description of this plague, whose symptoms
resemble more those of typhus than of any other disease, is in
Thucydides, 2. 47 ff.

διαφθειρούσης, ἐν ἀθυμίᾳ καθειστήκεσαν, καὶ τὸν
Περικλέα νομίζοντες αἴτιον αὐτοῖς γεγονέναι τοῦ
πολέμου δι᾽ ὀργῆς εἶχον. διόπερ ἀποστήσαντες
αὐτὸν τῆς στρατηγίας καὶ μικράς τινας ἀφορμὰς
ἐγκλημάτων λαβόντες, ἐζημίωσαν αὐτὸν ὀγδοήκον-
5 τα ταλάντοις. μετὰ δὲ ταῦτα πρεσβείας ἀποστείλαντες Λακεδαιμονίοις ἠξίουν καταλύσασθαι τὸν
πόλεμον· ὡς δὲ οὐδεὶς αὐτοῖς προσεῖχεν, ἠναγκάζοντο πάλιν τὸν Περικλέα στρατηγὸν αἱρεῖσθαι.

Ταῦτα μὲν οὖν ἐπράχθη κατὰ τοῦτον τὸν ἐνιαυτόν.

46. Ἐπ᾽ ἄρχοντος δ᾽ Ἀθήνησιν Ἐπαμείνονος[1]
Ῥωμαῖοι κατέστησαν ὑπάτους Λεύκιον Παπίριον
καὶ Αὖλον Κορνήλιον Μακερῖνον. ἐπὶ δὲ τούτων ἐν
μὲν ταῖς Ἀθήναις Περικλῆς ὁ στρατηγὸς ἐτελεύτησεν, ἀνὴρ γένει καὶ πλούτῳ, πρὸς δὲ τούτοις
δεινότητι λόγου καὶ στρατηγίᾳ πολὺ προέχων τῶν
πολιτῶν.

2   Ὁ δὲ δῆμος φιλοτιμούμενος κατὰ κράτος ἑλεῖν
τὴν Ποτίδαιαν, ἐξαπέστειλεν Ἅγνωνα στρατηγὸν
ἔχοντα τὴν δύναμιν ἣν πρότερον εἶχε Περικλῆς.
οὗτος δὲ μετὰ παντὸς τοῦ στόλου καταπλεύσας
εἰς τὴν Ποτίδαιαν παρεσκευάσατο τὰ πρὸς τὴν
πολιορκίαν· μηχανάς τε γὰρ παντοδαπὰς παρεσκεύ-
ασε πολιορκητικὰς καὶ ὅπλων καὶ βελῶν πλῆθος,
ἔτι δὲ σίτου δαψίλειαν ἱκανὴν πάσῃ τῇ δυνάμει.
προσβολὰς δὲ ποιούμενος συνεχεῖς καθ᾽ ἑκάστην

---

[1] So Palmer : Ἐπαμινώνδου.

[1] Thucydides (2. 65. 3) mentions only " a fine " ; Plutarch
(*Pericles*, 35) states that estimates of the fine varied from
fifteen to fifty talents ; according to Plato (*Gorg.* 516 A) the
charge was embezzlement. The scholia on Aristophanes,

off great numbers, were plunged into despondency 430 B.C.
and became angry with Pericles, considering him to
have been responsible for their being at war. Consequently they removed him from the generalship,
and on the strength of some petty grounds for accusation they imposed a fine upon him of eighty talents.[1]
After this they dispatched embassies to the Lacedaemonians and asked that the war be brought to an
end ; but when not a man paid any attention to them,
they were forced to elect Pericles general again.

These, then, were the events of this year.

46. When Epameinon was archon in Athens, the 429 B.C.
Romans elected as consuls Lucius Papirius and Aulus
Cornelius Macerinus. This year in Athens Pericles
the general died, a man who not only in birth and
wealth, but also in eloquence and skill as a general,
far surpassed his fellow citizens.

Since the people of Athens desired for the glory of
it to take Potidaea by storm,[2] they sent Hagnon there
as general with the army which Pericles had formerly
commanded. He put in at Potidaea with the whole
expedition and made all his preparations for the
siege ; for he had made ready every kind of engine
used in sieges, a multitude of arms and missiles, and
an abundance of grain, sufficient for the entire army.
Hagnon spent much time making continuous assaults

Clouds, 859, explain that Pericles entered in his accounts
an expenditure εἰς τὰ δέοντα (" for necessary purposes "),
which the Lacedaemonians interpreted as being for bribes
and accordingly punished some of their leading men. Also
mentioned is the charge that the gold on Athena's statue was
not of the weight charged ; but Pheidias removed and
weighed it, disproving the allegation.

[2] An Athenian army had been before the city for four
years ; cp. chap. 34.

17

ἡμέραν διέτριβε πολὺν χρόνον, οὐ δυνάμενος ἑλεῖν
3 τὴν πόλιν. οἱ μὲν γὰρ πολιορκούμενοι διὰ τὸν ἐκ
τῆς ἁλώσεως φόβον ἐρρωμένως ἠμύνοντο καὶ ταῖς
ὑπεροχαῖς τῶν τειχῶν πεποιθότες ἐπλεονέκτουν
τοὺς ἐκ τοῦ λιμένος· ἡ δὲ[1] νόσος τοὺς πολιορκοῦντας
συνέχουσα πολλοὺς ἀνῄρει, καὶ τὸ στρατόπεδον
4 ἀθυμία κατεῖχεν. ὁ δ᾽ Ἅγνων εἰδὼς τοὺς Ἀθηναίους δεδαπανηκότας εἰς τὴν πολιορκίαν πλείω
τῶν χιλίων ταλάντων καὶ χαλεπῶς διακειμένους πρὸς
τοὺς Ποτιδαιάτας διὰ τὸ πρώτους ἀποστῆναι πρὸς
τοὺς Λακεδαιμονίους, ἐφοβεῖτο λῦσαι τὴν πολι-
ορκίαν· διόπερ ἠναγκάζετο διακαρτερεῖν καὶ τοὺς
στρατιώτας ἀναγκάζειν παρὰ δύναμιν βίαν προσ-
5 άγειν τῇ πόλει. ἐπεὶ δὲ τῶν πολιτῶν πολλοὶ
διεφθείροντο κατὰ τὰς προσβολὰς καὶ κατὰ τὴν
ἐκ τοῦ λοιμοῦ νόσον, ἀπολιπὼν μέρος τῆς δυνάμεως
ἐπὶ τῆς πολιορκίας ἀπέπλευσεν εἰς τὰς Ἀθήνας,
ἀποβεβληκὼς τῶν στρατιωτῶν πλείους τῶν χιλίων.
6 ἀπελθόντων δὲ τούτων οἱ Ποτιδαιᾶται, τοῦ τε
σίτου παντελῶς ἐκλιπόντος καὶ τῶν κατὰ τὴν
πόλιν ἀθυμούντων, ἐπεκηρυκεύσαντο πρὸς τοὺς πολιορκοῦντας περὶ διαλύσεως. ἀσμένως δὲ κἀκεί-
νων προσδεξαμένων διαλύσεις ἐποιήσαντο τοιαύτας,
ἀπελθεῖν ἐκ τῆς πόλεως ἅπαντας τοὺς Ποτιδαιάτας, ἄλλο μὲν μηθὲν λαβόντας, ἔχοντας δὲ τοὺς
7 μὲν ἄνδρας ἱμάτιον ἕν, τὰς δὲ γυναῖκας δύο. γενομένων δὲ τούτων τῶν σπονδῶν οἱ μὲν Ποτιδαιᾶται πάντες μετὰ γυναικῶν καὶ τέκνων ἐξέλιπον
τὴν πατρίδα κατὰ τὰς συνθήκας, καὶ παρελθόντες εἰς τοὺς ἐπὶ Θρᾴκης Χαλκιδεῖς παρ᾽ αὐτοῖς

---

[1] So the MSS.; ἐπλεονέκτουν, ἡ δ᾽ ἐκ τοῦ λοιμοῦ νόσος
Vogel.

every day, but without the power to take the city. 429 B.C.
For on the one side the besieged, spurred on by their
fear of capture, were putting up a sturdy resistance
and, confiding in the superior height of the walls,
held the advantage over the Athenians attacking
from the harbour, whereas the besiegers were dying
in large numbers from the plague and despondency
prevailed throughout the army. Hagnon, knowing
that the Athenians had spent more than a thousand
talents on the siege and were angry with the
Potidaeans because they were the first to go over to
the Lacedaemonians, was afraid to raise the siege ;
consequently he felt compelled to continue it and to
compel the soldiers, beyond their strength, to force
the issue against the city. But since many Athenian
citizens were being slain in the assaults and by the
ravages of the plague, he left a part of his army to
maintain the siege and sailed back to Athens, having
lost more than a thousand of his soldiers. After
Hagnon had withdrawn, the Potidaeans, since their
grain supply was entirely exhausted and the people
in the city were disheartened, sent heralds to the
besiegers to discuss terms of capitulation. These
were received eagerly and an agreement to cessation
of hostilities was reached on the following terms :
All the Potidaeans should depart from the city, taking
nothing with them, with the exception that men
could have one garment and women two. When this
truce had been agreed upon, all the Potidaeans
together with their wives and children left their
native land in accordance with the terms of the compact and went to the Chalcidians in Thrace among

κατῴκησαν· οἱ δ' Ἀθηναῖοι τῶν πολιτῶν εἰς χιλίους οἰκήτορας ἐξέπεμψαν εἰς τὴν Ποτίδαιαν, καὶ
τήν τε πόλιν καὶ τὴν χώραν κατεκληρούχησαν.

47. Ἀθηναῖοι δὲ Φορμίωνα στρατηγὸν προχειρισάμενοι μετὰ εἴκοσι τριήρων ἐξαπέστειλαν. οὗτος
δὲ περιπλεύσας τὴν Πελοπόννησον εἰς Ναύπακτον
κατῆρε, καὶ θαλαττοκρατῶν τοῦ Κρισαίου κόλπου
διεκώλυσε ταύτῃ πλεῖν τοὺς Λακεδαιμονίους. Λακεδαιμόνιοι δὲ δύναμιν ἀξιόλογον ἐξέπεμψαν μετ'
Ἀρχιδάμου τοῦ βασιλέως· οὗτος δὲ παρελθὼν τῆς
Βοιωτίας εἰς Πλαταιὰς ἐστρατοπέδευσε.[1] μελλόντων δ' αὐτῶν δῃοῦν τὴν χώραν καὶ παρακαλούντων
τοὺς Πλαταιεῖς ἀποστῆναι τῶν Ἀθηναίων, ὡς οὐ
προσεῖχον αὐτοῖς, ἐπόρθησε τὴν χώραν καὶ τὰς κατ'
2 αὐτὴν κτήσεις ἐλυμήνατο. μετὰ δὲ ταῦτα τὴν πόλιν περιτειχίσας ἤλπιζε τῇ σπάνει τῶν ἀναγκαίων
καταπονήσειν τοὺς Πλαταιεῖς· οὐδὲν δ' ἧττον καὶ
μηχανὰς προσάγοντες καὶ διὰ τούτων σαλεύοντες
τὰ τείχη καὶ προσβολὰς ἀδιαλείπτως ποιούμενοι
διετέλουν. ἐπεὶ δὲ οὐδὲ διὰ τῶν προσβολῶν
ἠδύναντο χειρώσασθαι τὴν πόλιν, ἀπολιπόντες τὴν
ἱκανὴν φυλακὴν ἐπανῆλθον εἰς Πελοπόννησον.
3 Ἀθηναῖοι δὲ στρατηγοὺς καταστήσαντες Ξενο-
φῶντα καὶ Φανόμαχον ἀπέστειλαν ἐπὶ Θρᾴκην
μετὰ στρατιωτῶν χιλίων. οὗτοι δὲ παραγενηθέντες εἰς Σπάρτωλον[2] τῆς Βοττικῆς ἔτεμον τὴν
χώραν καὶ τὸν σῖτον ἐν χλόῃ διέφθειραν. προσ-

---

[1] So Dindorf: ἐστράτευσε.
[2] So Palmer (Thuc. 2. 79. 2): Πάκτωλον.

---

[1] At about the centre of the north side of the Gulf of
Corinth.

whom they made their home ; and the Athenians 429 B.C.
sent out as many as a thousand of their citizens to
Potidaea as colonists and portioned out to them in
allotments both the city and its territory.

47. The Athenians elected Phormio general and
sent him to sea with twenty triremes. He sailed
around the Peloponnesus and put in at Naupactus,
and by gaining the mastery of the Crisaean Gulf [1]
prevented the Lacedaemonians [2] from sailing in those
parts. And the Lacedaemonians sent out a strong
army under Archidamus their king, who marched
into Boeotia and took up positions before Plataea.
Under the threat of ravaging the territory of the
Plataeans he called upon them to revolt from the
Athenians, and when they paid no attention to him,
he plundered their territory and laid waste their
possessions everywhere. After this he threw a wall
about the city, in the hope that he could force the
Plataeans to capitulate because of lack of the neces-
sities of life ; at the same time the Lacedaemonians
continued bringing up engines with which they kept
shattering the walls and making assaults without
interruption. But when they found themselves unable to take the city through their assaults, they left
an adequate guard before it and returned to the
Peloponnesus.

The Athenians appointed Xenophon and Phano-
machus generals and sent them to Thrace with a
thousand soldiers. When this force arrived at
Spartolus [3] in the territory of Botticê, it laid waste
the land and cut the grain in the first growth. But

---

[2] Specifically the Corinthians, the leading naval allies of
the Lacedaemonians.

[3] In the Thracian Chalcidicê near Olynthus.

βοηθησάντων δὲ τοῖς Βοττιαίοις Ὀλυνθίων, ἡττήθησαν ὑπὸ τούτων μάχῃ· ἀνῃρέθησαν δὲ τῶν
Ἀθηναίων οἵ τε στρατηγοὶ καὶ τῶν στρατιωτῶν
4 οἱ πλείους. ἅμα δὲ τούτοις πραττομένοις Λακεδαιμόνιοι πεισθέντες ὑπὸ Ἀμβρακιωτῶν ἐστράτευσαν εἰς Ἀκαρνανίαν. ἡγούμενος δὲ τούτων
Κνῆμος εἶχε στρατιώτας πεζοὺς χιλίους καὶ ναῦς
ὀλίγας· προσλαβόμενος δὲ καὶ παρὰ τῶν συμμάχων
στρατιώτας τοὺς ἱκανοὺς ἧκεν εἰς τὴν Ἀκαρνανίαν
καὶ κατεστρατοπέδευσε πλησίον πόλεως τῆς ὀνο-
5 μαζομένης Στράτου. οἱ δὲ Ἀκαρνᾶνες συστραφέντες καὶ τοῖς πολεμίοις ἐνεδρεύσαντες πολλοὺς
ἀπέκτειναν, καὶ συνηνάγκασαν τὸν Κνῆμον ἀπαγαγεῖν τὴν δύναμιν εἰς τοὺς ὀνομαζομένους Οἰνιάδας.
48. Περὶ δὲ τοὺς αὐτοὺς χρόνους Φορμίων ὁ
τῶν Ἀθηναίων στρατηγὸς ἔχων εἴκοσι τριήρεις
περιέτυχε ναυσὶ Λακεδαιμονίων ἑπτὰ πρὸς ταῖς
τετταράκοντα. ναυμαχήσας δὲ πρὸς ταύτας τήν
τε στρατηγίδα ναῦν τῶν πολεμίων κατέδυσε καὶ
τῶν ἄλλων πολλὰς ἄπλους ἐποίησε, δώδεκα δὲ
αὐτάνδρους εἷλε, τὰς δὲ λοιπὰς μέχρι τῆς γῆς
κατεδίωξεν. οἱ δὲ Λακεδαιμόνιοι παρ᾽ ἐλπίδας
ἡττηθέντες ταῖς ὑπολειφθείσαις ναυσὶν ἔφυγον εἰς
Πάτρας τῆς Ἀχαίας. αὕτη μὲν οὖν ἡ ναυμαχία
συνέστη περὶ τὸ Ῥίον καλούμενον. οἱ δ᾽ Ἀθηναῖοι τρόπαιον στήσαντες καὶ τῷ Ποσειδῶνι περὶ[1]
τὸν πορθμὸν[2] ναῦν καθιερώσαντες ἀπέπλευσαν εἰς

---

[1] περὶ] τῷ περὶ Wurm.   [2] So Palmer : ἰσθμόν.

[1] In southern Acarnania.

the Olynthians came to the aid of the Bottiaeans and 429 B.C.
defeated them in battle ; and there were slain of
the Athenians both the generals and the larger part
of the soldiers.   And while this was taking place,
the Lacedaemonians, yielding to the request of the
Ambraciotes, made a campaign against Acarnania.
Their leader was Cnemus and he had a thousand foot-
soldiers and a few ships.   To these he added a considerable number of soldiers from their allies and
entered Acarnania, pitching his camp near the city
known as Stratus.   But the Acarnanians gathered
their forces and, laying an ambush, slew many of the
enemy, and they forced Cnemus to withdraw his
army to the city called Oeniadae.[1]

48. During the same time Phormio, the Athenian
general, with twenty triremes fell in with forty-seven
Lacedaemonian warships.   And engaging them in
battle he sank the flag-ship of the enemy and put
many of the rest of the ships out of action, capturing
twelve together with their crews and pursuing the
remaining as far as the land.[2]   The Lacedaemonians,
after having suffered defeat contrary to their expectations, fled for safety with the ships which were left
them to Patrae in Achaea.   This sea battle took place
off Rhium,[3] as it is called.   The Athenians set up a
trophy, dedicated a ship to Poseidon at the strait,[4]
and then sailed off to the city of Naupactus, which

[2] Phormio's famous manœuvring in this battle is described
in Thucydides, 2. 83-84.

[3] A cape at the entrance of the Corinthian Gulf.

[4] The Greek, which reads " at the Isthmus," must be
defective, for Thucydides' (2. 84. 4) account makes it certain
that the ship was dedicated near the scene of the battle ; the
emendation of Wurm (see critical note) would have the
dedication made " to Poseidon the patron god of the Isthmus."

2 πόλιν συμμαχίδα Ναύπακτον. Λακεδαιμόνιοι δ'
ἑτέρας ναῦς ἐξέπεμψαν εἰς τὰς Πάτρας. αὗται
δὲ προσλαβόμεναι τὰς ἐκ τῆς ναυμαχίας περι-
λελειμμένας τριήρεις ἠθροίσθησαν εἰς τὸ Ῥίον·
εἰς τὸν αὐτὸν δὲ τόπον καὶ τὸ πεζὸν στρατόπεδον
τῶν Πελοποννησίων κατήντησε καὶ πλησίον τοῦ
3 στόλου κατεστρατοπέδευσε. Φορμίων δὲ τῇ προ-
γεγενημένῃ νίκῃ φρονηματισθεὶς ἐτόλμησεν ἐπιθέσθαι ταῖς πολεμίαις ναυσὶν οὔσαις πολλαπλασίαις·
καί τινας αὐτῶν καταδύσας καὶ τῶν ἰδίων ἀπο-
βαλὼν ἀμφίδοξον ἔσχε τὴν νίκην. μετὰ δὲ ταῦτα
Ἀθηναίων ἀποστειλάντων εἴκοσι τριήρεις, οἱ Λακεδαιμόνιοι φοβηθέντες ἀπέπλευσαν εἰς τὴν Κόρινθον, οὐ τολμῶντες ναυμαχεῖν.

Ταῦτα μὲν οὖν ἐπράχθη κατὰ τοῦτον τὸν ἐνιαυτόν.

49. Ἐπ' ἄρχοντος δ' Ἀθήνησι Διοτίμου Ῥωμαῖοι μὲν ὑπάτους κατέστησαν Γάιον Ἰούλιον
καὶ Πρόκλον Οὐεργίνιον Τρίκοστον, Ἠλεῖοι δ'
ἤγαγον Ὀλυμπιάδα ὀγδόην πρὸς ταῖς ὀγδοήκοντα,
καθ' ἣν ἐνίκα στάδιον Σύμμαχος Μεσσήνιος ἀπὸ
2 Σικελίας. ἐπὶ δὲ τούτων Κνῆμος ὁ τῶν Λακεδαιμονίων ναύαρχος ἐν τῇ Κορίνθῳ διατρίβων
ἔκρινε τὸν Πειραιᾶ καταλαβέσθαι. ἐπυνθάνετο
γὰρ μήτε ναῦς ἐν αὐτῷ καθειλκυσμένας ὑπάρχειν
μήτε στρατιώτας εἶναι τεταγμένους ἐπὶ τῆς φυ-
λακῆς· τοὺς γὰρ Ἀθηναίους ἀμελῶς ἔχειν περὶ
τῆς τούτου φυλακῆς διὰ τὸ μηδαμῶς ἐλπίζειν
3 τολμῆσαί τινας καταλαβέσθαι τὸν τόπον. διόπερ
ἐν τοῖς Μεγάροις καθελκύσας τὰς νενεωλκημένας
τεττάρακοντα τριήρεις νυκτὸς ἔπλευσεν εἰς τὴν
Σαλαμῖνα· προσπεσὼν δ' ἀπροσδοκήτως εἰς τὸ

was in their alliance. The Lacedaemonians sent other
ships to Patrae. These ships joined to themselves
the triremes which had survived the battle and
assembled at Rhium, and also the land force of the
Peloponnesians met them at the same place and
pitched camp near the fleet. And Phormio, having
become puffed up with pride over the victory he had
just won, had the daring to attack the ships of the
enemy, although they far outnumbered his [1] ; and
some of them he sank, though losing ships of his own,
so that the victory he won was equivocal. After this,
when the Athenians had dispatched twenty triremes,[2]
the Lacedaemonians sailed off in fear to Corinth, not
daring to offer battle.

These, then, were the events of this year.

49. When Diotimus was archon in Athens, the
Romans elected as consuls Gaius Julius and Proculus
Verginius Tricostus, and the Eleians celebrated the
Eighty-eighth Olympiad, that in which Symmachus
of Messenê in Sicily won the " stadion." In this
year Cnemus, the Lacedaemonian admiral, who was
inactive in Corinth, decided to seize the Peiraeus.
He had received information that no ships in the
harbour had been put into the water for duty and no
soldiers had been detailed to guard the port ; for
the Athenians, as he learned, had become negligent
about guarding it because they by no means expected
any enemy would have the audacity to seize the
place. Consequently Cnemus, launching forty triremes which had been hauled up on the beach at
Megara, sailed by night to Salamis, and falling

---

[1] Thucydides (2. 86. 4) states that there were seventy-seven
ships against Phormio's twenty.
[2] These were reinforcements from Athens.

φρουριον τῆς Σαλαμῖνος τὸ καλούμενον Βουδόριον,
τρεῖς ναῦς ἀπέσπασε καὶ τὴν ὅλην Σαλαμῖνα
4 κατέδραμε. τῶν δὲ Σαλαμινίων πυρσευσάντων
τοῖς κατὰ τὴν Ἀττικήν, οἱ μὲν Ἀθηναῖοι δόξαντες
τὸν Πειραιᾶ κατειλῆφθαι ταχέως ἐξεβοήθουν μετὰ
πολλῆς ταραχῆς· γνόντες δὲ τὸ γεγονός, ταχέως
πληρώσαντες ναῦς ἱκανὰς ἔπλεον εἰς τὴν Σαλαμῖνα.
5 οἱ δὲ Πελοποννήσιοι τῆς ἐπιβολῆς διαψευσθέντες
ἀπέπλευσαν ἐκ τῆς Σαλαμῖνος εἰς τὴν οἰκείαν. οἱ
δ᾽ Ἀθηναῖοι, τῶν πολεμίων ἀποπεπλευκότων, τῆς
μὲν Σαλαμῖνος ἐπιμελεστέραν φυλακὴν ἐποιήσαντο
καὶ κατέλιπον φρουροὺς τοὺς ἱκανούς, τὸν δὲ
Πειραιᾶ κλείθροις καὶ φυλακαῖς ἱκαναῖς διαλαβόντες
ὠχύρωσαν.

50. Περὶ δὲ τοὺς αὐτοὺς χρόνους Σιτάλκης ὁ τῶν
Θρᾳκῶν βασιλεὺς παρειλήφει μὲν βασιλείαν ὀλίγην
χώραν, διὰ δὲ τὴν ἰδίαν ἀνδρείαν καὶ σύνεσιν ἐπὶ
πολὺ τὴν δυναστείαν ηὔξησεν, ἐπιεικῶς μὲν ἄρχων
τῶν ὑποτεταγμένων, ἀνδρεῖος δ᾽ ὢν ἐν ταῖς μάχαις
καὶ στρατηγικός, ἔτι δὲ τῶν προσόδων μεγάλην
ποιούμενος ἐπιμέλειαν. τὸ δὲ τέλος ἐπὶ τοσοῦτον
δυνάμεως προῆλθεν, ὥστε χώρας ἄρξαι πλείστης
τῶν πρὸ αὐτοῦ βασιλευσάντων κατὰ τὴν Θρᾴκην.
2 ἡ μὲν γὰρ παραθαλάττιος αὐτῆς ἀπὸ τῆς Ἀβδηρι-
τῶν χώρας τὴν ἀρχὴν ἔχουσα διέτεινε μέχρι τοῦ
Ἴστρου ποταμοῦ, ἀπὸ δὲ θαλάττης εἰς τὸ μεσό-
γειον πορευομένῳ τοσοῦτον εἶχε διάστημα, ὥστε
πεζὸν εὔζωνον ὁδοιπορῆσαι ἡμέρας δέκα τρεῖς.
τηλικαύτης δὲ χώρας βασιλεύων ἐλάμβανε προσ-

---

[1] Used to block the entrance; cp. Book 18. 64. 4.

unexpectedly on the fortress on Salamis called 428 B.C.
Boudorium, he towed away three ships and overran
the entire island. When the Salaminians signalled
by beacon-fires to the inhabitants of Attica, the
Athenians, thinking that the Peiraeus had been
seized, quickly rushed forth in great confusion to its
succour ; but when they learned what had taken
place, they quickly manned a considerable number
of warships and sailed to Salamis. The Peloponnesians, having been disappointed in their main
design, sailed away from Salamis and returned home.
And the Athenians, after the retreat of the enemy,
in the case of Salamis gave it a more vigilant guard
and left on it a considerable garrison, and the Peiraeus
they strengthened here and there with booms ¹ and
adequate guards.

50. In the same period Sitalces, the king of the
Thracians, had succeeded to the kingship of a small
land indeed but nonetheless by his personal courage
and wisdom he greatly increased his dominion,
equitably governing his subjects, playing the part of
a brave soldier in battle and of a skilful general, and
furthermore giving close attention to his revenues.
In the end he attained to such power that he ruled
over more extensive territory than had any who had
preceded him on the throne of Thrace. For the coastline of his kingdom began at the territory of the
Abderites and stretched as far as the Ister ² River,
and for a man going from the sea to the interior the
distance was so great that a man on foot travelling
light required thirteen days for the journey. Ruling as
he did over a territory so extensive he enjoyed annual

² Abdera was on the Nestus River facing the Aegean Sea ;
the Ister is the Danube.

ὁδοὺς καθ᾽ ἕκαστον ἐνιαυτὸν πλείω χιλίων ταλάν-
3 των. κατὰ δὲ τοὺς ὑποκειμένους καιροὺς ἔχων
πόλεμον ἤθροισεν ἐκ τῆς Θρᾴκης στρατιώτας
πεζοὺς μὲν πλείους τῶν δώδεκα μυριάδων ἱππεῖς
δὲ πεντακισμυρίους. ἀναγκαῖον δ᾽ ἐστὶ τοῦ πολέμου τούτου προεκθέσθαι τὰς αἰτίας, ἵνα σαφὴς
ὁ περὶ αὐτοῦ λόγος ὑπάρξῃ τοῖς ἀναγινώσκουσι.

Σιτάλκης τοίνυν πρὸς Ἀθηναίους φιλίαν συν-
θέμενος ὡμολόγησεν αὐτοῖς συμμαχήσειν τὸν ἐπὶ
Θρᾴκης πόλεμον· διόπερ βουλόμενος τοὺς Χαλκιδεῖς σὺν τοῖς Ἀθηναίοις καταπολεμῆσαι, παρ-
4 εσκευάζετο δύναμιν ἀξιόλογον. ἅμα δὲ καὶ πρὸς
Περδίκκαν τὸν βασιλέα τῶν Μακεδόνων ἀλλοτρίως
διακείμενος, ἔκρινε κατάγειν ἐπὶ τὴν Μακεδονικὴν
βασιλείαν Ἀμύνταν τὸν Φιλίππου. δι᾽ ἀμφοτέρας
οὖν τὰς προειρημένας αἰτίας ἦν ἀναγκαῖον αὐτῷ
συστήσασθαι δύναμιν ἀξιόλογον. ὡς δ᾽ αὐτῷ τὰ
πρὸς τὴν στρατείαν εὐτρεπῆ κατεσκεύαστο, προ-
ήγαγε τὴν δύναμιν ἅπασαν, καὶ διελθὼν τὴν Θρᾴκην
5 ἐνέβαλεν εἰς τὴν Μακεδονίαν. οἱ δὲ Μακεδόνες
τὸ μέγεθος τῆς δυνάμεως καταπλαγέντες παρατάξασθαι μὲν οὐκ ἐτόλμησαν, ἐκκομίσαντες δὲ
τόν τε σῖτον καὶ τῶν χρημάτων ὅσα δυνατὸν ἦν
εἰς τὰ καρτερώτατα φρούρια, μένοντες ἐν τούτοις
6 ἡσυχίαν εἶχον. οἱ δὲ Θρᾷκες καταγαγόντες τὸν
Ἀμύνταν ἐπὶ τὴν βασιλείαν τὸ μὲν πρῶτον διὰ
λόγων καὶ πρεσβειῶν ἐπειρῶντο προσάγεσθαι τὰς
πόλεις, ὡς δ᾽ οὐδεὶς αὐτοῖς προσεῖχεν, εὐθὺς τῷ
πρώτῳ φρουρίῳ προσβαλόντες κατὰ κράτος εἷλον.
7 μετὰ δὲ ταῦτά τινες τῶν πόλεων καὶ τῶν φρουρίων

---

[1] In 431 B.C. The war described below opened two years
later.

revenues of more than a thousand talents; and when 428 B.C.
he was waging war in the period we are discussing
he mustered from Thrace more than one hundred and
twenty thousand infantry and fifty thousand cavalry.
But with respect to this war we must set forth its
causes, in order that the discussion of it may be clear
to our readers.

Now Sitalces, since he had entered into a treaty of
friendship with the Athenians,[1] agreed to support
them in their war in Thrace; and consequently, since
he desired, with the help of the Athenians, to subdue
the Chalcidians, he made ready a very considerable
army. And since he was at the same time on bad
terms with Perdiccas, the king of the Macedonians,
he decided to bring back Amyntas, the son of Philip,
and place him upon the Macedonian throne.[2] It was
for these two reasons, therefore, as we have described
them, that he was forced to raise an imposing army.
When all his preparations for the campaign had been
made, he led forth the whole army, marched through
Thrace, and invaded Macedonia. The Macedonians,
dismayed at the great size of the army, did not dare
face him in battle, but they removed both the grain
and all the property they could into their most powerful strongholds, in which they remained inactive.
The Thracians, after placing Amyntas upon the
throne, at the outset made an effort to win over the
cities by means of parleys and embassies, but when
no one paid any attention to them, they forthwith
made an assault on the first stronghold and took it by
storm. After this some of the cities and strongholds

[2] Perdiccas had driven his brother Philip from the kingdom, and Philip had taken refuge at the court of Sitalces;
cp. Thucydides, 2. 95.

διὰ τὸν φόβον ἑκουσίως ὑπετάγησαν. πορθήσαντες δὲ πᾶσαν τὴν Μακεδονίαν καὶ πολλῆς ὠφελείας κύριοι γενόμενοι μετέβησαν ἐπὶ τὰς Ἑλληνίδας πόλεις τὰς τῶν Χαλκιδέων.

51. Τοῦ δὲ Σιτάλκου περὶ ταῦτα διατρίβοντος Θετταλοὶ καὶ Ἀχαιοὶ καὶ Μάγνητες καὶ οἱ ἄλλοι πάντες Ἕλληνες ὅσοι κατῴκουν μεταξὺ Μακεδονίας καὶ Θερμοπυλῶν, συνεφρόνησαν καὶ δύναμιν ἀξιόλογον κοινῇ συνεστήσαντο· εὐλαβοῦντο γὰρ μήποτε τοσαύταις μυριάσιν οἱ Θρᾷκες ἐμβάλωσιν αὐτῶν 2 εἰς τὴν χώραν καὶ κινδυνεύσωσι ταῖς πατρίσι. τὸ δ' αὐτὸ καὶ τῶν Χαλκιδέων ποιησάντων, Σιτάλκης, πυθόμενος τοὺς Ἕλληνας ἁδρὰς δυνάμεις συνηθροικέναι καὶ τοὺς στρατιώτας ὑπὸ τοῦ χειμῶνος ἐνοχλουμένους ἐννοούμενος,[1] πρὸς μὲν τὸν Περδίκκαν διαλυσάμενος ἐπιγαμίας ἐποιήσατο, τὰς δὲ δυνάμεις ἀπήγαγεν εἰς τὴν Θρᾴκην.

52. Ἅμα δὲ τούτοις πραττομένοις Λακεδαιμόνιοι μὲν παραλαβόντες τοὺς ἐκ Πελοποννήσου συμμάχους εἰσέβαλον εἰς τὴν Ἀττικήν, ἔχοντος τὴν ἡγεμονίαν Ἀρχιδάμου τοῦ βασιλέως, τὸν δὲ σῖτον ἐν τῇ χλόῃ διέφθειραν, καὶ τὴν χώραν δῃώ-2 σαντες ἐπανῆλθον εἰς τὰς πατρίδας. οἱ δ' Ἀθηναῖοι παρατάξασθαι μὲν οὐ τολμῶντες, ὑπὸ δὲ τῆς νόσου καὶ τῆς σιτοδείας πιεζόμενοι, κακὰς περὶ τοῦ μέλλοντος ἐλάμβανον ἐλπίδας.

Ταῦτα μὲν οὖν ἐπράχθη κατὰ τοῦτον τὸν ἐνιαυτόν.

53. Ἐπ' ἄρχοντος δ' Ἀθήνησιν Εὐκλείδου Ῥωμαῖοι κατέστησαν ἀντὶ τῶν ὑπάτων χιλιάρχους τρεῖς, Μάρκον Μάνιον, Κόιντον Σουλπίκιον Πραι-

---

[1] ἐννοούμενος added by Bezzel.

submitted to them of their own accord through fear. 428 B.C.
And after plundering all Macedonia and appro-
priating much booty the Thracians turned against
the Greek cities in Chalcidicê.

51. While Sitalces was engaged in these operations,
the Thessalians, Achaeans, Magnesians, and all the
other Greeks dwelling between Macedonia and Ther-
mopylae took counsel together and united in raising
a considerable army ; for they were apprehensive
lest the Thracians with all their myriads of soldiers
should invade their territory and they themselves
should be in peril of losing their native lands. Since
the Chalcidians made the same preparations, Sitalces,
having learned that the Greeks had mustered strong
armies and realizing that his soldiers were suffering
from the hardships of the winter, came to terms with
Perdiccas, concluded a connection by marriage with
him,[1] and then led his forces back to Thrace.

52. While these events were taking place, the
Lacedaemonians, accompanied by their allies of the
Peloponnesus, invaded Attica under the command of
Archidamus their king, destroyed the grain, which
was in its first growth, ravaged the countryside, and
then returned home. The Athenians, since they did
not dare meet the invaders in the field and were
distressed because of the plague and the lack of provisions, had only bleak hopes for the future.

These, then, were the events of this year.

53. When Eucleides was archon in Athens, the 427 B.C.
Romans elected in place of consuls three military
tribunes, Marcus Manius, Quintus Sulpicius Prae-

---

[1] Seuthes, a nephew of Sitalces and his successor on he
throne, married Stratonicê, Perdiccas' sister (Thucydides, 2.
101. 6).

τέξτατον, Σερούιον[1] Κορνήλιον Κόσσον. ἐπὶ δὲ
τούτων κατὰ τὴν Σικελίαν Λεοντῖνοι, Χαλκιδέων
μὲν ὄντες ἄποικοι συγγενεῖς δὲ Ἀθηναίων, ἔτυχον
ὑπὸ Συρακοσίων πολεμούμενοι. πιεζόμενοι δὲ τῷ
πολέμῳ, καὶ διὰ τὴν ὑπεροχὴν τῶν Συρακοσίων
κινδυνεύοντες ἁλῶναι κατὰ κράτος, ἐξέπεμψαν
πρέσβεις εἰς τὰς Ἀθήνας, ἀξιοῦντες τὸν δῆμον
βοηθῆσαι τὴν ταχίστην καὶ τὴν πόλιν ἑαυτῶν ἐκ
2 τῶν κινδύνων ῥύσασθαι. ἦν δὲ τῶν ἀπεσταλμένων
ἀρχιπρεσβευτὴς Γοργίας ὁ ῥήτωρ, δεινότητι λόγου
πολὺ προέχων πάντων τῶν καθ' ἑαυτόν. οὗτος
καὶ τέχνας ῥητορικὰς πρῶτος ἐξεῦρε καὶ κατὰ
τὴν σοφιστείαν τοσοῦτο τοὺς ἄλλους ὑπερέβαλεν,
ὥστε μισθὸν λαμβάνειν παρὰ τῶν μαθητῶν μνᾶς
3 ἑκατόν. οὗτος οὖν καταντήσας εἰς τὰς Ἀθήνας
καὶ παραχθεὶς εἰς τὸν δῆμον διελέχθη τοῖς Ἀθηναίοις περὶ τῆς συμμαχίας, καὶ τῷ ξενίζοντι τῆς
λέξεως ἐξέπληξε τοὺς Ἀθηναίους ὄντας εὐφυεῖς
4 καὶ φιλολόγους. πρῶτος γὰρ ἐχρήσατο τοῖς τῆς
λέξεως σχηματισμοῖς περιττοτέροις καὶ τῇ φιλο-
τεχνίᾳ διαφέρουσιν, ἀντιθέτοις καὶ ἰσοκώλοις καὶ
παρίσοις καὶ ὁμοιοτελεύτοις καί τισιν ἑτέροις
τοιούτοις, ἃ τότε μὲν διὰ τὸ ξένον τῆς κατασκευῆς
ἀποδοχῆς ἠξιοῦτο, νῦν δὲ περιεργίαν ἔχειν δοκεῖ
καὶ φαίνεται καταγέλαστα πλεονάκις καὶ κατα-
5 κόρως τιθέμενα. τέλος δὲ πείσας τοὺς Ἀθηναίους
συμμαχῆσαι τοῖς Λεοντίνοις, οὗτος μὲν θαυμασθεὶς
ἐν ταῖς Ἀθήναις ἐπὶ τέχνῃ ῥητορικῇ τὴν εἰς
Λεοντίνους ἐπάνοδον ἐποιήσατο.

54. Ἀθηναῖοι δὲ καὶ πάλαι μὲν ἦσαν ἐπιθυμηταὶ
τῆς Σικελίας διὰ τὴν ἀρετὴν τῆς χώρας, καὶ τότε

----

[1] So Dindorf : Σερούλιον.

textatus, and Servius Cornelius Cossus. This year in 427 B.C. Sicily the Leontines, who were colonists from Chalcis but also kinsmen of the Athenians, were attacked, as it happened, by the Syracusans. And being hard-pressed in the war and in danger of having their city taken by storm because of the superior power of the Syracusans, they dispatched ambassadors to Athens asking the Athenian people to send them immediate aid and save their city from the perils threatening it. The leader of the embassy was Gorgias the rhetorician, who in eloquence far surpassed all his contemporaries. He was the first man to devise rules of rhetoric and so far excelled all other men in the instruction offered by the sophists that he received from his pupils a fee of one hundred minas.[1] Now when Gorgias had arrived in Athens and been introduced to the people in assembly, he discoursed to them upon the subject of the alliance, and by the novelty of his speech he filled the Athenians, who are by nature clever and fond of dialectic, with wonder. For he was the first to use the rather unusual and carefully devised structures of speech, such as anti-thesis, sentences with equal members or balanced clauses or similar endings, and the like, all of which at that time was enthusiastically received because the device was exotic, but is now looked upon as laboured and to be ridiculed when employed too frequently and tediously. In the end he won the Athenians over to an alliance with the Leontines, and after having been admired in Athens for his rhetorical skill he made his return to Leontini.

54. For some time past the Athenians had been covetous of Sicily because of the fertility of its land,

[1] Some 1800 dollars, 360 pounds sterling.

δ' ἀσμένως προσδεξάμενοι τοὺς τοῦ Γοργίου λόγους ἐψηφίσαντο συμμαχίαν ἐκπέμπειν τοῖς Λεοντίνοις, πρόφασιν μὲν φέροντες τὴν τῶν συγγενῶν χρείαν καὶ δέησιν, τῇ δ' ἀληθείᾳ τὴν νῆσον 2 σπεύδοντες κατακτήσασθαι. καὶ γὰρ οὐ πολλοῖς ἔτεσι πρότερον τῶν τε Κορινθίων καὶ τῶν Κερκυραίων διαπολεμούντων μὲν πρὸς ἀλλήλους φιλοτιμηθέντων δ' ἀμφοτέρων συμμάχους λαβεῖν τοὺς Ἀθηναίους, προέκρινεν ὁ δῆμος συμμαχεῖν τοῖς Κερκυραίοις διὰ τὸ τὴν Κέρκυραν εὐφυῶς κεῖσθαι 3 πρὸς τὸν εἰς Σικελίαν πλοῦν. καθόλου γὰρ οἱ Ἀθηναῖοι κατακτησάμενοι τὴν τῆς θαλάττης ἡγεμονίαν καὶ μεγάλας πράξεις ἐπιτελεσάμενοι συμμάχων τε πολλῶν εὐπόρουν καὶ δυνάμεις μεγίστας ἐκέκτηντο[1] καὶ χρημάτων τε πλῆθος ἕτοιμον παρέλαβον, μετακομίσαντες ἐκ Δήλου τὰ κοινὰ χρήματα τῶν Ἑλλήνων, ὄντα πλείω τῶν μυρίων ταλάντων, ἡγεμόσι τε μεγάλοις καὶ διὰ στρατηγίαν δεδοκιμασμένοις ἐχρήσαντο, καὶ διὰ τούτων ἁπάντων ἤλπιζον καταπολεμήσειν μὲν τοὺς Λακεδαιμονίους, πάσης δὲ τῆς Ἑλλάδος τὴν ἡγεμονίαν περιπεποιημένοι ἀνθέξεσθαι τῆς Σικελίας. 4 Διὰ ταύτας οὖν τὰς αἰτίας ψηφισάμενοι βοηθεῖν τοῖς Λεοντίνοις ἐξέπεμψαν εἰς τὴν Σικελίαν ναῦς εἴκοσι καὶ στρατηγοὺς[2] Λάχητα καὶ Χαροιάδην. οὗτοι δὲ πλεύσαντες εἰς τὸ Ῥήγιον προσελάβοντο ναῦς εἴκοσι παρὰ τῶν Ῥηγίνων καὶ τῶν ἄλλων[3] Χαλκιδέων ἀποίκων. ἐντεῦθεν δ' ὁρμώμενοι τὸ

---

[1] So Reiske : δυνάμεις ἐπιτελεσάμενοι μεγίστας ἐκέκτηντο πόλεις.
[2] στρατηγοὺς omitted P, Vogel.
[3] ἄλλων suggested by Vogel (Thuc. 3. 86).

and so at the moment, gladly accepting the proposals 427 B.C. of Gorgias, they voted to send an allied force to the Leontines, offering as their excuse the need and request of their kinsmen, whereas in fact they were eager to get possession of the island. And indeed not many years previously, when the Corinthians and Cercyraeans were at war with one another and both were bent upon getting the Athenians as allies,[1] the popular Assembly chose the alliance with the Cercyraeans for the reason that Cercyra was advantageously situated on the sea route to Sicily. For, speaking generally, the Athenians, having won the supremacy of the sea and accomplished great deeds, not only enjoyed the aid of many allies and possessed powerful armaments, but also had taken over a great sum of ready money, since they had transferred from Delos to Athens the funds of the confederacy of the Greeks,[2] which amounted to more than ten thousand talents ; they also enjoyed the services of great commanders who had stood the test of actual leadership ; and by means of all these assets it was their hope not only to defeat the Lacedaemonians but also, after they had won the supremacy over all Greece, to lay hands on Sicily.

These, then, were the reasons why the Athenians voted to give aid to the Leontines, and they sent twenty ships to Sicily and as generals Laches and Charoeades. These sailed to Rhegium, where they added to their force twenty ships from the Rhegians and the other Chalcidian colonists. Making Rhegium their base they first of all overran the islands of the

---

[1] Cp. chap. 33.   [2] The Confederacy of Delos.

μὲν πρῶτον τὰς Λιπαραίων νήσους κατέδραμον
διὰ τὸ συμμαχεῖν τοὺς Λιπαραίους τοῖς Συρακοσίοις, μετὰ δὲ ταῦτα ἐπὶ Λοκροὺς πλεύσαντες
καὶ πέντε νεῶν Λοκρίδων κυριεύσαντες, Μύλας[1]
5 φρούριον ἐπολιόρκησαν. ἐπιβοηθησάντων δὲ τῶν
πλησιοχώρων Σικελιωτῶν τοῖς Μυλαίοις ἐγένετο
μάχη, καθ' ἣν Ἀθηναῖοι νικήσαντες ἀπέκτειναν
μὲν πλείους τῶν χιλίων, ἐζώγρησαν δὲ οὐκ ἐλάττους τῶν ἑξακοσίων· εὐθὺς δὲ καὶ τὸ φρούριον
ἐκπολιορκήσαντες κατέσχον.

6 Τούτων δὲ πραττομένων κατέπλευσαν νῆες
τετταράκοντα ἃς ἀπέστειλεν ὁ δῆμος, κρίνων
γενναιότερον ἅπτεσθαι τοῦ πολέμου· ἡγεῖτο δ'
αὐτῶν Εὐρυμέδων καὶ Σοφοκλῆς. ἀθροισθεισῶν
δὲ τῶν τριήρων εἰς ἕνα τόπον ἀξιόλογος ἤδη στόλος κατεσκεύαστο, συγκείμενος ἐκ τριήρων ὀγδοή-
7 κοντα. τοῦ δὲ πολέμου χρονίζοντος οἱ Λεοντῖνοι
διαπρεσβευσάμενοι πρὸς τοὺς Συρακοσίους διε-
λύθησαν. διόπερ αἱ μὲν τῶν Ἀθηναίων τριήρεις
ἀπέπλευσαν εἰς τὴν οἰκείαν, οἱ δὲ Συρακόσιοι τοῖς
Λεοντίνοις μεταδόντες τῆς πολιτείας ἅπαντας Συρακοσίους ἐποίησαν, καὶ τὴν πόλιν φρούριον ἀπέδειξαν
τῶν Συρακοσίων.

Καὶ τὰ μὲν κατὰ τὴν Σικελίαν ἐν τούτοις ἦν.

55. Κατὰ δὲ τὴν Ἑλλάδα Λέσβιοι μὲν ἀπέστησαν ἀπὸ τῶν Ἀθηναίων· ἐνεκάλουν γὰρ αὐτοῖς,
ὅτι βουλομένων συνοικίζειν πάσας τὰς κατὰ τὴν
Λέσβον πόλεις εἰς τὴν Μυτιληναίων πόλιν διεκώ-

---

[1] Μύλας added by Cluver (Thuc. 3. 90. 2).

---

[1] The group of small volcanic islands west of the toe of
Italy ; cp. Book 5. 7.

Liparaeans [1] because they were allies of the Syra- 427 B.C.
cusans, and after this they sailed to Locri,[2] where
they captured five ships of the Locrians, and then laid
siege to the stronghold of Mylae.[3] When the neighbouring Sicilian Greeks came to the aid of the
Mylaeans, a battle developed in which the Athenians
were victorious, slaying more than a thousand men
and taking prisoner not less than six hundred ; and
at once they captured and occupied the stronghold.

While these events were taking place there arrived
forty ships which the Athenian people had sent,
deciding to push the war more vigorously ; the commanders were Eurymedon and Sophocles. When all
the triremes were gathered into one place, a fleet of
considerable strength had been fitted out, consisting
as it did of eighty triremes. But since the war was
dragging on, the Leontines entered into negotiations
with the Syracusans and came to terms with them.
Consequently the Athenian triremes sailed back
home, and the Syracusans, granting the Leontines
the right of citizenship, made them all Syracusans and
their city a stronghold of the Syracusans.

Such were the affairs in Sicily at this time.

55. In Greece the Lesbians revolted from the
Athenians ; for they harboured against them the complaint that, when they wished to merge all the cities
of Lesbos with the city of the Mytilenaeans,[4] the

---

[2] Epizephyrian Locris on the east shore of the toe of Italy.
[3] On the north coast of Sicily west of Messenê.
[4] By this union of the island (*sunoikismos*) the separate
governments of the different cities would have been dissolved
and the inhabitants would all have become citizens of Mitylenê, the capital and seat of rule ; just as, traditionally under
Theseus, the governments of the several cities of Attica were
put down and Athens became the city-state of the entire area.

2 λῦσαν. διὸ καὶ πρὸς Λακεδαιμονίους ἀποστείλαντες πρεσβευτὰς καὶ συμμαχίαν συνθέμενοι συν-
εβούλευον τοῖς Σπαρτιάταις ἀντέχεσθαι τῆς κατὰ
θάλατταν ἡγεμονίας· πρὸς ταύτην δὲ τὴν ἐπιβολὴν
ἐπηγγείλαντο πολλὰς τριήρεις εἰς τὸν πόλεμον παρ-
3 έξεσθαι. ἀσμένως δὲ τῶν Λακεδαιμονίων ὑπακουσάντων καὶ περὶ τὴν κατασκευὴν τῶν τριήρων
γινομένων, Ἀθηναῖοι φθάσαντες αὐτῶν τὴν παρασκευὴν παραχρῆμα δύναμιν ἐξέπεμψαν εἰς τὴν
Λέσβον, πληρώσαντες ναῦς τετταράκοντα καὶ
στρατηγὸν προχειρισάμενοι Κλεινιππίδην. οὗτος
δὲ προσλαβόμενος βοήθειαν παρὰ τῶν συμμάχων
4 κατέπλευσεν εἰς Μυτιλήνην. γενομένης δὲ ναυμαχίας οἱ μὲν Μυτιληναῖοι λειφθέντες συνεκλεί-
σθησαν εἰς πολιορκίαν, τῶν δὲ Λακεδαιμονίων
ψηφισαμένων βοηθεῖν τοῖς Μυτιληναίοις καὶ παρα-
σκευαζομένων στόλον ἀξιόλογον, ἔφθασαν Ἀθηναῖοι
ναῦς ἄλλας σὺν ὁπλίταις χιλίοις ἀποστείλαντες εἰς
5 Λέσβον. τούτων δ' ἡγούμενος Πάχης ὁ Ἐπικλή-
ρου καταντήσας εἰς τὴν Μυτιλήνην, καὶ τὴν προ-
ϋπάρχουσαν δύναμιν παραλαβών, περιετείχισε τὴν
πόλιν καὶ συνεχεῖς προσβολὰς ἐποιεῖτο οὐ μόνον
κατὰ γῆν, ἀλλὰ καὶ κατὰ θάλατταν.
6 Λακεδαιμόνιοι δὲ ἐξαπέστειλαν εἰς τὴν Μυτιλήνην
τριήρεις μὲν τετταράκοντα πέντε καὶ στρατηγὸν
Ἀλκίδαν, εἰς δὲ τὴν Ἀττικὴν εἰσέβαλον μετὰ τῶν
συμμάχων· ἐπελθόντες δὲ τοὺς παραλελειμμένους
τόπους τῆς Ἀττικῆς καὶ δῃώσαντες τὴν χώραν
7 ἐπανῆλθον εἰς τὴν οἰκείαν. Μυτιληναῖοι δὲ τῇ
σιτοδείᾳ καὶ τῷ πολέμῳ πιεζόμενοι καὶ στασιάζοντες πρὸς ἀλλήλους, καθ' ὁμολογίαν παρέδωκαν
8 τὴν πόλιν τοῖς πολιορκοῦσιν. ἐν δὲ ταῖς Ἀθήναις

Athenians had prevented it. Consequently, after ^{427 b.c.} dispatching ambassadors to the Peloponnesians and concluding an alliance with them, they advised the Spartans to make an attempt to seize the supremacy at sea, and toward this design they promised to supply many triremes for the war. The Lacedaemonians were glad to accept this offer, but while they were busied with the building of the triremes, the Athenians forestalled their completion by sending forthwith a force against Lesbos, having manned forty ships and chosen Cleinippides as their commander, He gathered reinforcements from the allies and put in at Mytilenê. In a naval battle which followed the Mytilenaeans were defeated and enclosed within a siege of their city. Meanwhile the Lacedaemonians had voted to send aid to the Mytilenaeans and were making ready a strong fleet, but the Athenians forestalled them by sending to Lesbos additional ships along with a thousand hoplites. Their commander, Paches the son of Epiclerus, upon arriving at Mytilenê, took over the force already there, threw a wall about the city, and kept launching continuous assaults upon it not only by land but by sea as well.

The Lacedaemonians sent forty-five triremes to Mytilenê under the command of Alcidas, and they also invaded Attica together with their allies ; here they visited the districts of Attica which they had passed by before, ravaged the countryside, and then returned home. And the Mytilenaeans, who were distressed by lack of food and the war and were also quarrelling among themselves, formally surrendered the city to the besiegers. While in Athens the people

39

τοῦ δήμου βουλευομένου πῶς χρὴ προσενέγκασθαι
τοῖς Μυτιληναίοις, Κλέων ὁ δημαγωγός, ὠμὸς
ὢν τὸν τρόπον καὶ βίαιος, παρώξυνε τὸν δῆμον,
ἀποφαινόμενος δεῖν τοὺς Μυτιληναίους αὐτοὺς
μὲν ἡβηδὸν ἅπαντας ἀποκτεῖναι, τέκνα δὲ καὶ
9 γυναῖκας ἐξανδραποδίσασθαι. τέλος δὲ πεισθέν-
των τῶν Ἀθηναίων κατὰ τὴν γνώμην τε τοῦ
Κλέωνος ψηφισαμένων, ἀπεστάλησαν εἰς τὴν
Μυτιλήνην οἱ τὰ δοχθέντα τῷ δήμῳ δηλώσοντες
10 τῷ στρατηγῷ. τοῦ δὲ Πάχητος ἀναγνόντος τὸ
ψήφισμα ἦλθεν ἐναντίον τῷ προτέρῳ ἕτερον. ὁ
δὲ Πάχης γνοὺς τὴν μετάνοιαν τῶν Ἀθηναίων
ἐχάρη, καὶ τοὺς Μυτιληναίους συναγαγὼν εἰς ἐκκλησίαν ἀπέλυσε τῶν ἐγκλημάτων, ἅμα δὲ καὶ
τῶν μεγίστων φόβων. Ἀθηναῖοι δὲ τῆς Μυτιλήνης
τὰ τείχη περιελόντες τὴν Λέσβον ὅλην πλὴν τῆς
Μηθυμναίων χώρας κατεκληρούχησαν.

Ἡ μὲν οὖν Λεσβίων ἀπόστασις ἀπ᾽ Ἀθηναίων
τοιοῦτον ἔσχε τὸ τέλος.

56. Περὶ δὲ τοὺς αὐτοὺς χρόνους Λακεδαιμόνιοι
τὰς Πλαταιὰς πολιορκοῦντες περιετείχισαν τὴν πόλιν καὶ στρατιώταις πολλοῖς παρεφύλαττον. χρονιζούσης δὲ τῆς πολιορκίας καὶ τῶν Ἀθηναίων
μηδεμίαν ἐξαποστελλόντων βοήθειαν, οἱ πολιορκούμενοι σιτοδείᾳ τε συνείχοντο καὶ τῶν πολιτῶν
2 ἐν ταῖς προσβολαῖς πολλοὺς ἀπεβεβλήκεσαν. ἀπορουμένων δ᾽ αὐτῶν καὶ βουλευομένων περὶ τῆς
σωτηρίας, τοῖς μὲν πολλοῖς ἐδόκει τὴν ἡσυχίαν
ἄγειν, τοῖς δ᾽ ἄλλοις ὡς διακοσίοις οὖσιν ἔδοξε

---

[1] Among Athenian colonists. Thucydides (3. 50. 2) states

were deliberating on what action they should take
against the Mytilenaeans, Cleon, the leader of the
populace and a man of cruel and violent nature,
spurred on the people, declaring that they should slay
all the male Mytilenaeans from the youth upward and
sell into slavery the children and women. In the end
the Athenians were won over and voted as Cleon had
proposed, and messengers were dispatched to Mytilenê to make known to the general the measures
decreed by the popular assembly. Even as Paches
had finished reading the decree a second decree
arrived, the opposite of the first. Paches was glad
when he learned that the Athenians had changed their
minds, and gathering the Mytilenaeans in assembly
he declared them free of the charges as well as of
the greatest fears. The Athenians pulled down the
walls of Mytilenê and portioned out in allotments [1]
the entire island of Lesbos with the exception of the
territory of the Methymnaeans.

Such, then, was the end of the revolt of the Lesbians
from the Athenians.

56. About the same time the Lacedaemonians who
were besieging Plataea threw a wall about the city
and kept a guard over it of many soldiers. And as the
siege dragged on and the Athenians still sent them
no help, the besieged not only were suffering from
lack of food but had also lost many of their fellow
citizens in the assaults. While they were thus at a
loss and were conferring together how they could be
saved, the majority were of the opinion that they
should make no move, but the rest, some two hundred
in number, decided to force a passage through the

that the Lesbians arranged to work the allotments as renters,
paying the colonists a fixed rental.

νυκτὸς βιάσασθαι τοὺς φύλακας καὶ διεκπεσεῖν εἰς
3 τὰς Ἀθήνας. τηρήσαντες οὖν ἀσέληνον νύκτα τοὺς
μὲν ἄλλους ἔπεισαν εἰς θάτερα μέρη προσβάλ-
λειν τῷ περιτειχίσματι, αὐτοὶ δ' ἑτοιμασάμενοι
κλίμακας, καὶ τῶν πολεμίων παραβοηθούντων ἐν
τοῖς ἀπεστραμμένοις μέρεσι τῶν τειχῶν, αὐτοὶ
διὰ τῶν κλιμάκων ἔτυχον ἀναβάντες ἐπὶ τὸ τεῖχος, καὶ τοὺς φύλακας ἀποκτείναντες διέφυγον
4 εἰς τὰς Ἀθήνας. τῇ δ' ὑστεραίᾳ Λακεδαιμόνιοι
μὲν παροξυνθέντες ἐπὶ τῷ δρασμῷ τῶν ἀπελη-
λυθότων ἐκ τῆς πόλεως, προσέβαλον τῇ πόλει τῶν
Πλαταιέων καὶ πᾶσαν εἰσεφέροντο σπουδὴν βίᾳ
χειρώσασθαι τοὺς πολιορκουμένους· οἱ δὲ Πλαταιεῖς καταπλαγέντες καὶ διαπρεσβευσάμενοι παρ-
5 έδωκαν ἑαυτούς τε καὶ τὴν πόλιν τοῖς πολεμίοις. οἱ
δ' ἡγεμόνες τῶν Λακεδαιμονίων καθ' ἕνα τῶν
Πλαταιέων προσκαλούμενοι ἐπηρώτων τί ἀγαθὸν
πεποίηκε τοῖς Λακεδαιμονίοις, ἑκάστου δὲ ὁμο-
λογοῦντος μηδὲν εὐηργετηκέναι, πάλιν ἐπηρώτων
εἴ τι κακὸν ἔδρασαν τοὺς Σπαρτιάτας· οὐδενὸς δ'
6 ἀντιλέγοντος, πάντων κατέγνωσαν θάνατον. διὸ
καὶ τοὺς ἐγκαταλειφθέντας ἅπαντας ἀνεῖλον καὶ
κατασκάψαντες ἐμίσθωσαν τὴν χώραν αὐτῶν. Πλαταιεῖς μὲν οὖν τὴν πρὸς Ἀθηναίους συμμαχίαν
βεβαιοτάτην τηρήσαντες ἀδίκως ταῖς μεγίσταις συμφοραῖς περιέπεσον.

57. Ἅμα δὲ τούτοις πραττομένοις ἐν τῇ Κερκύρᾳ
μεγάλη συνέστη στάσις καὶ φιλοτιμία διὰ τοιαύτας
αἰτίας. ἐν τῷ περὶ Ἐπίδαμνον πολέμῳ πολλοὶ
Κερκυραίων αἰχμάλωτοι γενόμενοι καὶ καταβλη-
θέντες εἰς τὴν δημοσίαν φυλακὴν ἐπηγγείλαντο
τοῖς Κορινθίοις παραδώσειν τὴν Κέρκυραν, ἐὰν

guards by night and make their way to Athens. And 427 b.c.
so, on a moonless night for which they had waited,
they persuaded the rest of the Plataeans to make an
assault upon one side of the encircling wall; they themselves then made ready ladders, and when the enemy
rushed to defend the opposite parts of the walls,
they managed by means of the ladders to get up on
the wall, and after slaying the guards they made their
escape to Athens. The next day the Lacedaemonians,
provoked at the flight of the men who had got away
from the city, made an assault upon the city of the
Plataeans and strained every nerve to subdue the
besieged by storm; and the Plataeans in dismay sent
envoys to the enemy and surrendered to them both
themselves and the city. The commanders of the
Lacedaemonians, summoning the Plataeans one by
one, asked what good deed he had ever performed for
the Lacedaemonians, and when each confessed that
he had done them no good turn, they asked further if
he had ever done the Spartans any harm; and when
not a man could deny that he had, they condemned
all of them to death. Consequently they slew all
who still remained, razed the city to the ground, and
farmed out its territory. So the Plataeans, who had
maintained with the greatest constancy their alliance
with the Athenians, fell unjust victims to the most
tragic fate.

57. While these events were taking place, in
Cercyra bitter civil strife and contentiousness arose
for the following reasons. In the fighting about
Epidamnus [1] many Cercyraeans had been taken
prisoner and cast into the state prison, and these men
promised the Corinthians that, if the Corinthians set

---

[1] Cp. chap. 31.

2 αὐτοὺς ἀπολύσωσιν. ἀσμένως δὲ τῶν Κορινθίων προσδεξαμένων τοὺς λόγους, οἱ Κερκυραῖοι προσποιηθέντες λύτρα διδόναι διηγγυήθησαν ὑπὸ[1] τῶν

3 προξένων ἱκανῶν τινων ταλάντων ἀφεθέντες. καὶ τηροῦντες τὴν[2] τῶν ὡμολογημένων πίστιν, ὡς κατήντησαν εἰς τὴν πατρίδα, τοὺς δημαγωγεῖν εἰωθότας καὶ μάλιστα τοῦ πλήθους προΐστασθαι συλλαβόντες ἀπέσφαξαν. καταλύσαντες δὲ τὴν δημοκρατίαν, μετ᾿ ὀλίγον χρόνον[3] Ἀθηναίων βοηθησάντων τῷ δήμῳ, οἱ μὲν Κερκυραῖοι τὴν ἐλευθερίαν ἀνακτησάμενοι κολάζειν ἐπεβάλοντο τοὺς τὴν ἐπανάστασιν πεποιημένους· οὗτοι δὲ φοβηθέντες τὴν τιμωρίαν κατέφυγον ἐπὶ τοὺς τῶν θεῶν βωμοὺς καὶ ἱκέται τοῦ δήμου καὶ τῶν θεῶν ἐγέ-

4 νοντο. οἱ δὲ Κερκυραῖοι διὰ τὴν πρὸς θεοὺς εὐσέβειαν τῆς μὲν τιμωρίας αὐτοὺς ἀπέλυσαν, ἐκ τῆς πόλεως δὲ ἐξέπεμψαν. οὗτοι δὲ πάλιν νεωτερίζειν ἐπιβαλόμενοι καὶ τειχίσαντες ἐν τῇ νήσῳ χωρίον ὀχυρὸν ἐκακοποίουν τοὺς Κερκυραίους.

Ταῦτα μὲν οὖν ἐπράχθη κατὰ τοῦτον τὸν ἐνιαυτόν.

58. Ἐπ᾿ ἄρχοντος δ᾿ Ἀθήνησιν Εὐθύνου[4] Ῥωμαῖοι κατέστησαν ἀντὶ τῶν ὑπάτων χιλιάρχους τρεῖς, Μάρκον Φάβιον, Μάρκον Φαλίνιον, Λεύκιον Σερουίλιον. ἐπὶ δὲ τούτων Ἀθηναῖοι χρόνον τινὰ τῆς νόσου τῆς λοιμικῆς ἀνειμένοι πάλιν εἰς τὰς

2 αὐτὰς[5] συμφορὰς ἐνέπεσον· οὕτω γὰρ ὑπὸ τῆς

---

[1] So Rhodoman : ἀπό.
[2] ὑπὸ after τὴν deleted by Reiske.
[3] κατέλυσάν τε τὴν δ., μετ᾿ ὀλίγον δὲ χρόνον Reiske.
[4] So Dindorf : Εὐθυδήμου.   [5] αὐτὰς added by Reiske.

them free, they would hand Cercyra over to them. 427 B.C.
The Corinthians gladly agreed to the proposals, and
the Cercyraeans, after going through the pretence of
paying a ransom, were released on bail of a considerable sum of talents furnished by the proxeni.[1] Faithful to their promises the Cercyraeans, as soon as they
had returned to their native land, arrested and put to
death the men who had always been popular leaders
and had acted as champions of the people. They also
put an end to the democracy; but when, a little
after this time, the Athenians came to the help of
the popular party, the Cercyraeans, who had now
recovered their liberty, undertook to mete out
punishment to the men responsible for the revolt
against the established government. These, in fear of
the usual punishment, fled for refuge to the altars of
the gods and became suppliants of the people and
of the gods. And the Cercyraeans, out of reverence
for the gods, absolved them from that punishment
but expelled them from the city. But these exiles,
undertaking a second revolution, fortified a strong
position on the island, and continued to harass the
Cercyraeans.

These, then, were the events of this year.

58. When Euthynes was archon in Athens, the 426 B.C.
Romans elected in place of consuls three military
tribunes, Marcus Fabius, Marcus Falinius, and Lucius
Servilius. In this year the Athenians, who had
enjoyed a period of relief from the plague,[2] became
involved again in the same misfortunes; for they

---

[1] Proxeni were citizens of one city chosen by another city
to look after the interests of its citizens who were residing,
sojourning, or doing business there; they were a sort of
consul in the modern sense.

[2] Cp. chap. 45.

νόσου διετέθησαν, ὥστε τῶν στρατιωτῶν ἀποβαλεῖν πεζοὺς¹ μὲν ὑπὲρ τοὺς τετρακισχιλίους,
ἱππεῖς δὲ τετρακοσίους, τῶν δ' ἄλλων ἐλευθέρων
τε καὶ δούλων ὑπὲρ τοὺς μυρίους. ἐπιζητούσης
δὲ τῆς ἱστορίας τὴν² τῆς περὶ τὴν νόσον δεινότητος
αἰτίαν, ἀναγκαῖόν ἐστιν ἐκθέσθαι ταῦτα.

3 Προγεγενημένων ἐν τῷ χειμῶνι μεγάλων ὄμβρων
συνέβη τὴν γῆν ἔνυδρον γενέσθαι, πολλοὺς δὲ καὶ
τῶν κοίλων τόπων δεξαμένους πλῆθος ὕδατος
λιμνάσαι καὶ σχεῖν στατὸν ὕδωρ παραπλησίως
τοῖς ἑλώδεσι τῶν τόπων, θερμαινομένων δ' ἐν τῷ
θέρει τούτων καὶ σηπομένων συνίστασθαι παχείας
καὶ δυσώδεις ἀτμίδας, ταύτας δ' ἀναθυμιωμένας
διαφθείρειν τὸν πλησίον ἀέρα· ὅπερ δὴ καὶ ἐπὶ
τῶν ἑλῶν τῶν νοσώδη διάθεσιν ἐχόντων ὁρᾶται
4 γινόμενον. συνεβάλετο δὲ πρὸς τὴν νόσον καὶ ἡ
τῆς προσφερομένης τροφῆς κακία· ἐγένοντο γὰρ
οἱ καρποὶ κατὰ τοῦτον τὸν ἐνιαυτὸν ἔνυγροι παντελῶς καὶ διεφθαρμένην ἔχοντες τὴν φύσιν. τρίτην
δὲ αἰτίαν συνέβη γενέσθαι τῆς νόσου τὸ μὴ πνεῦσαι
τοὺς ἐτησίας, δι' ὧν ἀεὶ κατὰ τὸ θέρος ψύχεται
τὸ πολὺ τοῦ καύματος· τῆς δὲ θερμασίας ἐπίτασιν
λαβούσης καὶ τοῦ ἀέρος ἐμπύρου γενομένου, τὰ
σώματα τῶν ἀνθρώπων μηδεμιᾶς ψύξεως γενομένης
5 λυμαίνεσθαι συνέβαινε. διὸ καὶ τὰ νοσήματα τότε
πάντα καυματώδη συνέβαινεν εἶναι διὰ τὴν ὑπερβολὴν τῆς θερμασίας. διὰ δὲ ταύτην τὴν αἰτίαν
οἱ πλεῖστοι τῶν νοσούντων ἔρριπτον ἑαυτοὺς εἰς
τὰ φρέατα καὶ τὰς κρήνας ἐπιθυμοῦντες αὐτῶν
6 καταψύξαι τὰ σώματα. οἱ δ' Ἀθηναῖοι διὰ τὴν

---

¹ πεζοὺς added by Dindorf.
² τὴν added by Eichstädt.

were so seriously attacked by the disease that of their 426 B.C.
soldiers they lost more than four thousand infantry
and four hundred cavalry, and of the rest of the
population, both free and slave, more than ten thousand. And since history seeks to ascertain the cause
of the malignancy of this disease, it is our duty to
explain these matters.

As a result of heavy rains in the previous winter the
ground had become soaked with water, and many
low-lying regions, having received a vast amount of
water, turned into shallow pools and held stagnant
water, very much as marshy regions do ; and when
these waters became warm in the summer and grew
putrid, thick foul vapours were formed, which, rising
up in fumes, corrupted the surrounding air, the very
thing which may be seen taking place in marshy
grounds which are by nature pestilential. Contributing also to the disease was the bad character of the
food available ; for the crops which were raised that
year were altogether watery and their natural quality
was corrupted. And a third cause of the disease
proved to be the failure of the etesian[1] winds to blow,
by which normally most of the heat in summer is
cooled ; and when the heat intensified and the air
grew fiery, the bodies of the inhabitants, being without anything to cool them, wasted away. Consequently all the illnesses which prevailed at that time
were found to be accompanied by fever, the cause of
which was the excessive heat. And this was the
reason why most of the sick threw themselves into the
cisterns and springs in their craving to cool their
bodies. The Athenians, however, because the disease

---

[1] That is, the " annual " winds, blowing from the north-
west in summer.

ὑπερβολὴν τῆς νόσου τὰς αἰτίας τῆς συμφορᾶς ἐπὶ
τὸ θεῖον ἀνέπεμπον. διὸ καὶ κατά τινα χρησμὸν
ἐκάθηραν τὴν νῆσον Δῆλον, Ἀπόλλωνος μὲν οὖσαν
ἱεράν, δοκοῦσαν δὲ μεμιάνθαι διὰ τὸ τοὺς τετελευ-
7 τηκότας ἐν αὐτῇ τεθάφθαι. ἀνασκάψαντες οὖν
ἁπάσας τὰς ἐν τῇ Δήλῳ θήκας μετήνεγκαν εἰς
τὴν Ῥήνειαν καλουμένην νῆσον, πλησίον ὑπάρχουσαν τῆς Δήλου. ἔταξαν δὲ καὶ νόμον μήτε
τίκτειν ἐν τῇ Δήλῳ μήτε θάπτειν. ἐποίησαν δὲ
καὶ πανήγυριν τὴν τῶν Δηλίων, γεγενημένην μὲν
πρότερον, διαλιποῦσαν δὲ πολὺν χρόνον.

59. Τῶν δ᾽ Ἀθηναίων περὶ ταῦτ᾽ ἀσχολουμένων
Λακεδαιμόνιοι τοὺς Πελοποννησίους παραλαβόντες
κατεστρατοπέδευσαν περὶ τὸν ἰσθμόν, διανοούμενοι
πάλιν εἰς τὴν Ἀττικὴν εἰσβαλεῖν· σεισμῶν δὲ
μεγάλων γινομένων δεισιδαιμονήσαντες ἀνέκαμψαν
2 εἰς τὰς πατρίδας. τηλικούτους δὲ τοὺς σεισμοὺς
συνέβη γενέσθαι κατὰ πολλὰ μέρη τῆς Ἑλλάδος,
ὥστε καὶ πόλεις τινὰς ἐπιθαλαττίους ἐπικλύσασαν
τὴν θάλατταν διαφθεῖραι, καὶ κατὰ τὴν Λοκρίδα
χερρονήσου καθεστώσης ῥῆξαι μὲν τὸν ἰσθμόν,
ποιῆσαι δὲ νῆσον τὴν ὀνομαζομένην Ἀταλάντην.
3 Ἅμα δὲ τούτοις πραττομένοις Λακεδαιμόνιοι
τὴν Τραχῖνα καλουμένην ᾤκισαν καὶ μετωνόμασαν
4 Ἡράκλειαν διὰ τοιαύτας τινὰς αἰτίας. Τραχίνιοι
πρὸς Οἰταίους ὁμόρους ὄντας ἔτη πολλὰ διεπολέμουν καὶ τοὺς πλείους τῶν πολιτῶν ἀπέβαλον.
ἐρήμου δ᾽ οὔσης τῆς πόλεως ἠξίωσαν Λακεδαιμονίους ὄντας ἀποίκους ἐπιμεληθῆναι τῆς πόλεως.

---

[1] An ancient festival of the Ionian Amphictyony, held in
honour of Apollo and Artemis. Cp. Thucydides, 3. 104.

was so severe, ascribed the causes of their misfortune 426 B.C.
to the deity. Consequently, acting upon the command of a certain oracle, they purified the island of
Delos, which was sacred to Apollo and had been
defiled, as men thought, by the burial there of the
dead. Digging up, therefore, all the graves on Delos,
they transferred the remains to the island of Rheneia,
as it is called, which lies near Delos. They also passed
a law that neither birth nor burial should be allowed
on Delos. And they also celebrated the festival
assembly,[1] the Delia, which had been held in former
days but had not been observed for a long time.

59. While the Athenians were busied with these
matters, the Lacedaemonians, taking with them the
Peloponnesians, pitched camp at the Isthmus [2] with
the intention of invading Attica again ; but when
great earthquakes took place, they were filled with
superstitious fear and returned to their native lands.
And so severe in fact were the shocks in many parts
of Greece that the sea actually swept away and
destroyed some cities lying on the coast, while in
Locris the strip of land forming a peninsula was torn
through and the island known as Atalantê [3] was
formed.

While these events were taking place, the Lacedaemonians colonized Trachis, as it was called, and
renamed it Heracleia,[4] for the following reasons. The
Trachinians had been at war with the neighbouring
Oetaeans for many years and had lost the larger
number of their citizens. Since the city was deserted,
they thought it proper that the Lacedaemonians, who
were colonists from Trachis, should assume the care of

---

[2] Of Corinth.   [3] Opposite Opus in Opuntian Locris.
       [4] At the head of the Malian Gulf.

οἱ δὲ καὶ διὰ τὴν συγγένειαν καὶ διὰ τὸ τὸν
Ἡρακλέα, πρόγονον ἑαυτῶν ὄντα, ἐγκατῳκηκέναι
κατὰ τοὺς ἀρχαίους χρόνους ἐν τῇ Τραχῖνι,
5 ἔγνωσαν μεγάλην αὐτὴν ποιῆσαι πόλιν. διὸ καὶ
Λακεδαιμονίων μὲν καὶ τῶν Πελοποννησίων τετρακισχιλίους οἰκήτορας ἐκπεμψάντων, καὶ παρὰ[1]
τῶν ἄλλων Ἑλλήνων τοὺς βουλομένους μετέχειν
τῆς ἀποικίας προσεδέξαντο· οὗτοι δ᾽ ἦσαν οὐκ
ἐλάττους τῶν ἑξακισχιλίων. διὸ καὶ τὴν Τραχῖνα
μυρίανδρον ποιήσαντες, καὶ τὴν χώραν κατα-
κληρουχήσαντες, ὠνόμασαν τὴν πόλιν Ἡράκλειαν.
60. Ἐπ᾽ ἄρχοντος δ᾽ Ἀθήνησι Στρατοκλέους ἐν
Ῥώμῃ ἀντὶ τῶν ὑπάτων χιλίαρχοι τρεῖς κατεστάθησαν, Λεύκιος Φούριος, Σπόριος Πινάριος καὶ
Γάιος Μέτελλος.[2] ἐπὶ δὲ τούτων Ἀθηναῖοι μὲν
Δημοσθένη προχειρισάμενοι στρατηγὸν μετὰ νεῶν
τριάκοντα καὶ στρατιωτῶν ἱκανῶν ἐξαπέστειλαν.
οὗτος δὲ προσλαβόμενος παρὰ τῶν Κερκυραίων
τριήρεις πεντεκαίδεκα καὶ παρὰ τῶν Κεφαλ-
λήνων καὶ Ἀκαρνάνων καὶ Μεσσηνίων τῶν ἐν
Ναυπάκτῳ στρατιώτας ἔπλευσεν ἐπὶ τὴν Λευκάδα.
δηώσας δὲ τὴν χώραν τῶν Λευκαδίων ἀπέπλευσεν ἐπὶ τὴν Αἰτωλίαν καὶ πολλὰς αὐτῶν κώμας
ἐπόρθησε. τῶν δὲ Αἰτωλῶν συστραφέντων ἐπ᾽ αὐτὸν ἐγένετο μάχη, καθ᾽ ἣν Ἀθηναῖοι λειφθέντες
2 εἰς Ναύπακτον ἀπεχώρησαν. οἱ δὲ Αἰτωλοὶ
διὰ τὴν νίκην ἐπαρθέντες, καὶ προσλαβόμενοι
Λακεδαιμονίων τρισχιλίους στρατιώτας, στρατεύσαντες ἐπὶ Ναύπακτον, κατοικούντων ἐν αὐτῇ
3 τότε Μεσσηνίων, ἀπεκρούσθησαν. μετὰ δὲ ταῦτα

---

[1] τε after παρὰ deleted by Vogel.
[2] καὶ Γάιος Μέτελλος omitted PAL.

it. And the Lacedaemonians, both because of their 426 B.C.
kinship and because Heracles, their ancestor, in
ancient times had made his home in Trachis, decided
to make it a great city. Consequently the Lacedaemonians and the Peloponnesians sent forth four
thousand colonists and accepted any other Greeks
who wished to have a part in the colony ; the latter
numbered not less than six thousand. The result
was that they made Trachis a city of ten thousand inhabitants, and after portioning out the territory in
allotments they named the city Heracleia.

60. When Stratocles was archon in Athens, in 425 B.C
Rome in place of consuls three military tribunes were
elected, Lucius Furius, Spurius Pinarius, and Gaius
Metellus.[1] This year the Athenians chose Demosthenes general and sent him forth with thirty ships
and an adequate body of soldiers. He added to his
force fifteen ships from the Cercyraeans and soldiers
from the Cephallenians, Acarnanians, and the
Messenians in Naupactus, and then sailed to Leucas.
After ravaging the territory of the Leucadians he
sailed to Aetolia and plundered many of its villages.
But the Aetolians rallied to oppose him and there was
a battle in which the Athenians were defeated, whereupon they withdrew to Naupactus. The Aetolians,
elated by their victory, after adding to their army
three thousand Lacedaemonian soldiers, marched
upon Naupactus, which was inhabited at the time by
Messenians, but were beaten off. After this they

[1] These names are badly confused. They should be
L. Pinarius Mamercinus Rufus, L. Furius Medullinus Fusus,
and Sp. Postumius Albus Regillensis.

51

στρατεύσαντες ἐπὶ τὴν ὀνομαζομένην Μολυκρίαν
εἷλον τὴν πόλιν. ὁ δὲ τῶν Ἀθηναίων στρατηγὸς
Δημοσθένης εὐλαβούμενος μὴ καὶ τὴν Ναύπακτον
ἐκπολιορκήσωσι, χιλίους ὁπλίτας ἐξ Ἀκαρνανίας
μεταπεμψάμενος ἀπέστειλεν εἰς τὴν Ναύπακτον.
4 Δημοσθένης δὲ περὶ τὴν Ἀκαρνανίαν διατρίβων
περιέτυχεν Ἀμπρακιώταις χιλίοις στρατοπεδεύουσι,
πρὸς οὓς συνάψας μάχην σχεδὸν πάντας ἀνεῖλε.
τῶν δ' ἐκ τῆς Ἀμπρακίας ἐπεξελθόντων πανδημεί,
πάλιν ὁ Δημοσθένης τοὺς πλείους αὐτῶν ἀπέκτει-
5 νεν, ὥστε τὴν πόλιν σχεδὸν ἔρημον γενέσθαι. ὁ
μὲν οὖν Δημοσθένης ᾤετο δεῖν ἐκπολιορκῆσαι τὴν
Ἀμπρακίαν, ἐλπίζων διὰ τὴν ἐρημίαν τῶν ἀμυνομένων ῥᾳδίως αὐτὴν αἱρήσειν. οἱ δ' Ἀκαρνᾶνες
φοβούμενοι μὴ τῆς πόλεως Ἀθηναῖοι κυριεύσαντες
βαρύτεροι πάροικοι γένωνται τῶν Ἀμπρακιωτῶν,
6 οὐκ ἔφασαν ἀκολουθεῖν. στασιαζόντων δ' αὐτῶν,
οἱ μὲν Ἀκαρνᾶνες διαλυσάμενοι τοῖς Ἀμπρακιώταις συνέθεντο τὴν εἰρήνην εἰς ἔτη ἑκατόν,
Δημοσθένης δ' ἐγκαταλειφθεὶς ὑπὸ τῶν Ἀκαρνάνων ἀπέπλευσε σὺν ταῖς εἴκοσι ναυσὶν εἰς Ἀθήνας.
Ἀμπρακιῶται δὲ μεγάλῃ συμφορᾷ περιπεπτωκότες
παρὰ τῶν Λακεδαιμονίων φρουρὰν μετεπέμψαντο,
φοβούμενοι τοὺς Ἀθηναίους.

61. Δημοσθένης δὲ στρατεύσας ἐπὶ Πύλον ἐπεβάλετο τοῦτο τὸ χωρίον τειχίσαι κατὰ τῆς Πελοποννήσου[1]· ἔστι γὰρ ὀχυρόν τε διαφερόντως καὶ

---

[1] So Reiske: τὴν Πελοπόννησον.

---

[1] About five miles south-west of Naupactus.
[2] The reader may refer to the detailed account of the

52

marched upon the city called Molycria [1] and captured 425 B.C.
it. But the Athenian general, Demosthenes, being
concerned lest the Aetolians should reduce by siege
Naupactus also, summoned a thousand hoplites from
Acarnania and sent them to Naupactus. And Demosthenes, while tarrying in Acarnania, fell in with a
thousand Ambraciotes, who were encamped there,
and joining battle with them he destroyed nearly the
entire force. And when the men of Ambracia came
out against him *en masse*, again Demosthenes slew
the larger number of them, so that their city became
almost uninhabited. Demosthenes then believed that
he should take Ambracia by storm, hoping that he
would have an easy conquest because the city had no
one to defend it. But the Acarnanians, fearing lest,
if the Athenians became masters of the city, they
should be harder neighbours to deal with than the
Ambraciotes, refused to follow him. And since they
were thus in disagreement, the Acarnanians came to
terms with the Ambraciotes and concluded with them
a peace of one hundred years, while Demosthenes,
being left in the lurch by the Acarnanians, sailed back
with his twenty ships to Athens. The Ambraciotes,
who had experienced a great disaster, sent for a
garrison of Lacedaemonians, since they stood in fear
of the Athenians.

61. Demosthenes now led an expedition against
Pylos,[2] intending to fortify this stronghold as a threat
to the Peloponnesus ; for it is an exceptionally strong

following campaign in Thucydides, 4. 3-23, 26-40. In the
Bay of Navarino, on which Pylos lies, occurred the famous
naval Battle of Navarino between the allied British, Russian,
and French fleet and the Turkish. The victory of the allied
fleet, 20th October 1827, decided the issue of the Greek war of
independence.

κείμενον ἐν τῇ Μεσσηνίᾳ, τῆς δὲ Σπάρτης[1] ἀπέχον
σταδίους τετρακοσίους. ἔχων δὲ τότε καὶ ναῦς
πολλὰς καὶ στρατιώτας ἱκανούς, ἐν εἴκοσιν ἡμέραις
ἐτείχισε τὴν Πύλον. Λακεδαιμόνιοι δὲ πυθόμενοι
τὸν τειχισμὸν τῆς Πύλου συνήγαγον δύναμιν ἀξιό-
2 λογον οὐ μόνον πεζὴν ἀλλὰ καὶ ναυτικήν. διὸ καὶ
τριήρεσι μὲν ἐπὶ τὴν Πύλον ἔπλευσαν τετταράκοντα
πέντε καλῶς κατεσκευασμέναις, πεζοῖς δὲ ἐστράτευσαν μυρίοις καὶ δισχιλίοις, αἰσχρὸν ἡγούμε-
νοι τοὺς τῇ Ἀττικῇ δῃουμένῃ μὴ τολμήσαντας
βοηθεῖν ἐν Πελοποννήσῳ χωρίον[2] τειχίζειν καὶ
3 καταλαμβάνεσθαι. οὗτοι μὲν οὖν ἡγουμένου Θρα-
συμήδους πλησίον τῆς Πύλου κατεστρατοπέδευσαν.
ἐμπεσούσης δὲ ὁρμῆς τῷ πλήθει πάντα κίνδυνον
ὑπομένειν καὶ βίᾳ χειρώσασθαι τὴν Πύλον, τὰς
μὲν ναῦς ἀντιπρώρους ἔστησαν τῷ στόματι τοῦ
λιμένος, ὅπως διὰ τούτων ἐμφράξωσι τὸν εἴσπλουν
τῶν πολεμίων, πεζῇ δ᾽ ἐκ διαδοχῆς προσβάλλοντες
τῷ τείχει καὶ φιλοτιμίαν τὴν μεγίστην εἰσφερό-
4 μενοι θαυμασίους ἀγῶνας συνεστήσαντο. εἰς δὲ
τὴν νῆσον τὴν καλουμένην Σφακτηρίαν, παρατετα-
μένην δ᾽ ἐπὶ μῆκος καὶ ποιοῦσαν εὔδιον τὸν λιμένα,
διεβίβασαν τοὺς ἀρίστους τῶν Λακεδαιμονίων καὶ
τῶν συμμάχων. τοῦτο δ᾽ ἔπραξαν φθάσαι βουλόμενοι τοὺς Ἀθηναίους προκαταλαβέσθαι τὴν
νῆσον, εὐφυῶς σφόδρα κειμένην πρὸς τὴν πολιορ-
5 κίαν. διημερεύοντες δ᾽ ἐν[3] ταῖς τειχομαχίαις καὶ
κατατιτρωσκόμενοι διὰ τὴν ἀπὸ τοῦ τείχους ὑπεροχὴν οὐκ ἔληγον τῆς βίας· διὸ πολλοὶ μὲν αὐτῶν

[1] So Palmer : Μεσσηνίας.
[2] So Dindorf : χώραν.
[3] δ᾽ ἐν Wesseling : δέ.

place, situated in Messenia and four hundred stades 425 b.c.
distant from Sparta. Since he had at the time both
many ships and an adequate number of soldiers,
in twenty days he threw a wall about Pylos. The
Lacedaemonians, when they learned that Pylos had
been fortified, gathered together a large force, both
infantry and ships. Consequently, when they set sail
for Pylos, they not only had a fleet of forty-five fully
equipped triremes but also marched with an army of
twelve thousand soldiers ; for they considered it to
be a disgraceful thing that men who were not brave
enough to defend Attica while it was being ravaged
should fortify and hold a fortress in the Peloponnesus.
Now these forces under the command of Thrasymedes
pitched their camp in the neighbourhood of Pylos.
And since the troops were seized by an eager desire
to undergo any and every danger and to take Pylos
by storm, the Lacedaemonians stationed the ships
with their prows facing the entrance to the harbour
in order that they might use them for blocking the
enemy's attempt to enter, and assaulting the walls
with the infantry in successive waves and displaying
all possible rivalry, they put up contests of amazing
valour. Also to the island called Sphacteria, which
extends lengthwise to the harbour and protects it
from the winds, they transported the best troops of
the Lacedaemonians and their allies. This they did
in their desire to forestall the Athenians in getting
control of the island before them, since its situation
was especially advantageous to the prosecution of the
siege. And though they were engaged every day in
the fighting before the fortifications and were suffering wounds because of the superior height of the wall,
they did not relax the violence of their fighting ; as a

ἀπέθνησκον, οὐκ ὀλίγοι δὲ κατετραυματίζοντο πρὸς
6 τόπον ὠχυρωμένον βιαζόμενοι. οἱ δὲ Ἀθηναῖοι
προκατειλημμένοι χωρίον καὶ φύσει καρτερόν, καὶ
βελῶν τε πλήθη καὶ τῶν ἄλλων τῶν χρησίμων
πολλὴν ἔχοντες ἀφθονίαν, ἐκθύμως ἠμύνοντο·
ἤλπιζον γὰρ κρατήσαντες τῆς ἐπιβολῆς πάντα τὸν
πόλεμον περιαγαγεῖν εἰς τὴν Πελοπόννησον καὶ
δῃώσειν ἀνὰ μέρος τὴν χώραν τῶν πολεμίων.

62. Τῆς δὲ πολιορκίας ἀνυπέρβλητον τὴν σπουδὴν ἐχούσης παρ' ἀμφοτέροις, καὶ τῶν Σπαρτιατῶν
βίαν προσαγόντων τοῖς τείχεσι, πολλοὶ μὲν ἄλλοι
κατὰ τὰς ἀνδραγαθίας ἐθαυμάσθησαν, μεγίστης
2 δὲ ἀποδοχῆς ἔτυχε Βρασίδας. τῶν γὰρ τριηράρχων οὐ τολμώντων προσαγαγεῖν τῇ γῇ τὰς
τριήρεις διὰ τὴν χαλεπότητα τῶν τόπων, τριήρ-
αρχος ὢν ἐβόα καὶ παρεκελεύετο τῷ κυβερνήτῃ
μὴ φείδεσθαι τοῦ σκάφους, ἀλλὰ καὶ βίᾳ προσ-
άγειν τῇ γῇ τὴν τριήρη· αἰσχρὸν γὰρ εἶναι τοῖς
Σπαρτιάταις τῆς μὲν ψυχῆς ἀφειδεῖν ἕνεκα τῆς
νίκης, τῶν δὲ σκαφῶν φείδεσθαι καὶ περιορᾶν
3 Ἀθηναίους κρατοῦντας τῆς Λακωνικῆς. τέλος δὲ
συναναγκάσαντος τὸν κυβερνήτην προσαγαγεῖν τὴν
ναῦν, ἡ μὲν τριήρης ἐπώκειλεν, ὁ δὲ Βρασίδας
ἐπιβὰς ἐπὶ τὴν τῆς νεὼς ἐπιβάθραν ἐκ ταύτης
ἠμύνατο τὸ πλῆθος τῶν ἐπ' αὐτὸν συνδραμόντων
Ἀθηναίων. καὶ τὸ μὲν πρῶτον τοὺς προσιόντας
πολλοὺς ἀπέκτεινε, μετὰ δὲ ταῦτα πολλῶν ἐπ'
αὐτὸν ἐπιφερομένων βελῶν πολλοῖς περιέπιπτεν
4 ἐναντίοις τραύμασι. τέλος δὲ διὰ τῶν τραυμάτων
αἵματος ἐκχυθέντος πολλοῦ, καὶ διὰ τοῦτο λιπο-
ψυχήσαντος αὐτοῦ, ὁ μὲν βραχίων προέπεσεν ἐκ

consequence, many of them were slain and not a few ^{425 B.C.} were wounded as they pressed upon a position which had been fortified. The Athenians, who had secured beforehand a place which was also a natural stronghold and possessed large supplies of missiles and a great abundance of everything else they might need, kept defending their position with spirit ; for they hoped that, if they were successful in their design, they could carry the whole war to the Peloponnesus and ravage, bit by bit, the territory of the enemy.

62. Both sides displayed unsurpassable energy in the siege, and as for the Spartans in their assaults upon the walls, while many others were objects of wonder for their deeds of valour, the greatest acclaim was won by Brasidas. For when the captains of the triremes lacked the courage to bring the ships to land because of the rugged nature of the shore, he, being himself the commander of a trireme, called out in a loud voice to the pilot, ordering him not to spare the vessel but to drive the trireme at full speed to the land ; for it would be disgraceful, he cried, for Spartans to be unsparing of their lives as they fought for victory, and yet to spare their vessels and to endure the sight of Athenians holding the soil of Laconia. And finally he succeeded in forcing the pilot to drive the ship forward and, when the trireme struck the shore, Brasidas, taking his stand on the gangway, fought off from there the multitude of Athenians who converged upon him. And at the outset he slew many as they came at him, but after a while, as numerous missiles assailed him, he suffered many wounds on the front of his body. In the end he suffered much loss of blood from the wounds, and as he lost consciousness his arm ex-

τῆς νεώς, ἡ δ᾽ ἀσπὶς περιρρυεῖσα καὶ πεσοῦσα εἰς
τὴν θάλατταν ὑποχείριος ἐγένετο τοῖς πολεμίοις.
5 μετὰ δὲ ταῦτα οὗτος μὲν πολλοὺς τῶν πολεμίων
νεκροὺς σωρεύσας αὐτὸς ἡμιθανὴς ἐκ τῆς νεὼς
ὑπὸ τῶν ἰδίων ἀπηνέχθη, τοσοῦτον τοὺς ἄλλους
ὑπερβαλόμενος ἀνδρείᾳ, ὥστε τῶν ἄλλων τοὺς
ἀποβαλόντας τὴν ἀσπίδα θανάτῳ κολάζεσθαι, τοῦτον δ᾽ ἐπὶ τῇ αὐτῇ αἰτίᾳ ἀπενέγκασθαι δόξαν.
6 Οἱ μὲν οὖν Λακεδαιμόνιοι συνεχεῖς προσβολὰς
ποιούμενοι τῇ Πύλῳ, καὶ πολλοὺς ἀποβαλόντες
στρατιώτας, ἔμενον καρτερῶς ἐν τοῖς δεινοῖς.
θαυμάσαι δ᾽ ἄν τις τῆς τύχης τὸ παράδοξον καὶ
τὴν ἰδιότητα τῆς τῶν[1] περὶ τὴν Πύλον διαθέσεως.
7 Ἀθηναῖοι μὲν γὰρ ἐκ τῆς Λακωνικῆς ἀμυνόμενοι
τοὺς Σπαρτιάτας ἐκράτουν, Λακεδαιμόνιοι δὲ τὴν
ἰδίαν χώραν πολεμίαν[2] ἔχοντες ἐκ τῆς θαλάττης
προσέβαλλον τοῖς πολεμίοις, καὶ τοῖς μὲν πεζῇ
κρατοῦσι θαλαττοκρατεῖν συνέβαινε, τοῖς δὲ κατὰ
θάλατταν πρωτεύουσι τῆς γῆς ἀπείργειν τοὺς
πολεμίους.

63. Χρονιζούσης δὲ τῆς πολιορκίας, καὶ τῶν
Ἀθηναίων ταῖς ναυσὶν ἐπικρατησάντων καὶ σῖτον
εἰς τὴν γῆν εἰσκομίζειν κωλυόντων, ἐκινδύνευον οἱ
κατειλημμένοι ἐν τῇ νήσῳ τῷ λιμῷ διαφθαρῆναι.

---

[1] τῶν added by Capps.
[2] πολεμίαν added by Hertlein from Thuc. 4. 12. 3.

---

[1] The inscription on a shield found in the Agora excavations
states that it was taken by the Athenians from Lacedaemonians at Pylos (Shear in *Hesperia*, 6 (1937), 347-348). It
must have originally belonged to the collection of shields taken

tended over the side of the ship and his shield,[1] slip- 425 B.C.
ping off and falling into the sea, came into the hands
of the enemy.   After this Brasidas, who had built up
a heap of many corpses of the enemy, was himself
carried off half-dead from the ship by his men, having
surpassed to such a degree all other men in bravery
that, whereas in the case of all other men those who
lose their shields are punished with death, he for that
very reason won for himself glory.

Now the Lacedaemonians, although they kept
making continuous assaults upon Pylos and had lost
many soldiers, remained steadfast in the fierce
struggles.   And one may well be amazed at the
strange perversity of Fortune and at the singular
character of her ordering of what happened at Pylos.
For the Athenians, defending themselves from a base
on Laconian soil, were gaining the mastery over the
Spartans, whereas the Lacedaemonians, regarding
their own soil as the enemy's, were assaulting the
enemy from the sea as their base ; and, as it happened, those who were masters of the land in this
case controlled the sea, and those who held first place
on the sea were beating off an attack on land which
they held.

63. Since the siege dragged on and the Athenians,
after their victory [2] with their ships, were preventing
the conveyance of food to the land, the soldiers caught
on the island [3] were in danger of death from starva-

---

at Pylos which Pausanias (1. 15. 4) saw suspended as trophies
in the Stoa Poikilê, although the cistern in which it was
found had been filled before the third century B.C.   No
doubt the captured shield of the Spartan captain occupied
a central place in this collection.
   [2] Over the Spartan fleet ; cp. Thucydides, 4. 14.
   [3] Sphacteria.

59

2 διόπερ οἱ Λακεδαιμόνιοι φοβηθέντες περὶ τῶν
ἀπειλημμένων ἐν τῷ νήσῳ, πρεσβείας ἀπέστειλαν
εἰς τὰς Ἀθήνας περὶ τῆς καταλύσεως τοῦ πολέμου·
οὐ συγκατατιθεμένων δ' αὐτῶν ἠξίουν ἀλλαγὴν
ποιήσασθαι τῶν ἀνδρῶν καὶ λαβεῖν τοὺς ἴσους
τῶν Ἀθηναίων τῶν ἑαλωκότων· ἀλλ' οὐδὲ τοῦτο
συνεχώρησαν οἱ Ἀθηναῖοι. διόπερ οἱ πρέσβεις
παρρησίαν ἤγαγον ἐν ταῖς Ἀθήναις ὡς ὁμολογοῦ-
σι Λακεδαιμονίους κρείττους εἶναι, μὴ βουλόμενοι
3 τὴν ἀντίδοσιν τῶν αἰχμαλώτων ποιήσασθαι. οἱ
δ' Ἀθηναῖοι τῇ σπάνει τῶν ἀναγκαίων καταπονή-
σαντες τοὺς ἐν τῇ Σφακτηρίᾳ παρέλαβον αὐτοὺς
καθ' ὁμολογίαν. ἦσαν δ' οἱ παραδόντες αὐτοὺς
Σπαρτιᾶται μὲν ἑκατὸν εἴκοσι, τῶν δὲ συμμάχων
4 ἑκατὸν ὀγδοήκοντα. οὗτοι μὲν οὖν ὑπὸ Κλέωνος
τοῦ δημαγωγοῦ στρατηγοῦντος τότε δεθέντες
ἤχθησαν εἰς τὰς Ἀθήνας· ὁ δὲ δῆμος ἐψηφίσατο
αὐτοὺς φυλάττειν, ἐὰν βούλωνται Λακεδαιμόνιοι
λῦσαι τὸν πόλεμον, ἐὰν δὲ προκρίνωσι τὸ πολεμεῖν,
5 τότε πάντας τοὺς αἰχμαλώτους ἀποκτεῖναι. μετὰ
δὲ ταῦτα τῶν ἐν Ναυπάκτῳ κατῳκισμένων Μεσσηνίων μεταπεμψάμενοι τοὺς ἀρίστους καὶ τῶν ἄλλων
συμμάχων τοὺς ἱκανοὺς προσθέντες, τούτοις παρέδωκαν τὴν Πύλον φρουρεῖν· ἐνόμιζον γὰρ τοὺς
Μεσσηνίους διὰ τὸ πρὸς τοὺς Σπαρτιάτας μῖσος
ἐκθυμότατα κακοποιήσειν τὴν Λακωνικήν, ὁρμω-
μένους ἐξ ὀχυροῦ χωρίου.

Καὶ τὰ μὲν κατὰ τὴν Πύλον ἐν τούτοις ἦν.

64. Ἀρταξέρξης δ' ὁ τῶν Περσῶν βασιλεὺς

---

[1] The Lacedaemonians would get back the Spartans upon
Sphacteria.

tion. Consequently the Lacedaemonians, fearing for 425 B.C. the men left on the island, sent an embassy to Athens to discuss the ending of the war. When no agreement was being reached, they asked for an exchange of men,[1] the Athenians to get back an equal number of their soldiers now held prisoner ; but not even to this would the Athenians agree. Whereupon the ambassadors spoke out frankly in Athens, that by their unwillingness to effect an exchange of prisoners the Athenians acknowledged that Lacedaemonians were better men than they. Meanwhile the Athenians wore down the bodily strength of the Spartans on Sphacteria through their lack of provisions and accepted their formal surrender. Of the men who gave themselves up one hundred and twenty were Spartans and one hundred and eighty were of their allies. These, then, were brought by Cleon the leader of the populace, since he held the office of general when this took place, in chains to Athens ; and the people voted to keep them in custody in case the Lacedaemonians should be willing to end the war, but to slay all the captives if they should decide to continue it. After this they sent for select troops from the Messenians who had been settled in Naupactus,[2] joined to them an adequate force from their other allies, and turned over to them the garrisoning of Pylos ; for they believed that the Messenians, by reason of their hatred of the Spartans, would show the greatest zeal in harrying Laconia by forays, once they were operating from a strong position as their base.

Such were the events about Pylos in this year.

64. Artaxerxes, the king of the Persians, died[3]

[2] Cp. Book 11. 84. 7-8.
[3] In the spring of 424 B.C.

ἐτελεύτησεν ἄρξας ἔτη τετταράκοντα, τὴν δ᾽ ἀρχὴν διαδεξάμενος Ξέρξης ἐβασίλευσεν ἐνιαυτόν.

Κατὰ δὲ τὴν Ἰταλίαν Αἴκλων ἀποστάντων ἀπὸ Ῥωμαίων κατὰ τὸν πόλεμον αὐτοκράτορα μὲν Αὖλον Ποστούμιον, ἵππαρχον δὲ Λεύκιον Ἰούλιον 2 ἐποίησαν. οὗτοι δὲ μετὰ πολλῆς δυνάμεως ἀξιολόγου στρατεύσαντες εἰς τὴν τῶν ἀφεστηκότων χώραν τὸ μὲν πρῶτον τὰς κτήσεις ἐπόρθησαν, μετὰ δὲ ταῦτα Αἴκλων ἀντιταχθέντων ἐγένετο μάχη, καθ᾽ ἣν ἐνίκησαν οἱ Ῥωμαῖοι, καὶ πολλοὺς μὲν τῶν πολεμίων ἀνεῖλον, οὐκ ὀλίγους δ᾽ ἐζώ- 3 γρησαν, λαφύρων δὲ πολλῶν ἐκυρίευσαν. μετὰ δὲ τὴν μάχην οἱ μὲν ἀφεστηκότες διὰ τὴν ἧτταν καταπεπληγμένοι τοῖς Ῥωμαίοις ὑπετάγησαν, ὁ δὲ Ποστούμιος δόξας καλῶς διῳκηκέναι τὰ κατὰ τὸν πόλεμον, κατήγαγε τὸν εἰωθότα θρίαμβον. ἴδιον δέ τι καὶ παντελῶς ἄπιστόν φασι πρᾶξαι τὸν Ποστούμιον· κατὰ γὰρ τὴν μάχην τὸν υἱὸν αὐτοῦ διὰ τὴν προθυμίαν προεκπηδῆσαι τῆς ὑπὸ[1] τοῦ πατρὸς δεδομένης τάξεως· τὸν δὲ πατέρα τηροῦντα τὸ πάτριον ἔθος τὸν υἱὸν ὡς λελοιπότα τὴν τάξιν ἀποκτεῖναι.

65. Τούτου δὲ τοῦ ἔτους διελθόντος Ἀθήνησι μὲν ἦν ἄρχων Ἴσαρχος, ἐν δὲ τῇ Ῥώμῃ καθεισήκεσαν ὕπατοι Τίτος Κοΐντιος καὶ Γάιος Ἰούλιος, παρὰ δὲ Ἠλείοις Ὀλυμπιὰς ἤχθη ἐνάτη καὶ ὀγδοηκοστή, καθ᾽ ἣν ἐνίκα στάδιον Σύμμαχος τὸ δεύτερον. ἐπὶ δὲ τούτων Ἀθηναῖοι στρατηγὸν καταστήσαντες Νικίαν τὸν Νικηράτου, καὶ παραδόντες αὐτῷ τριήρεις μὲν ἑξήκοντα, ὁπλίτας δὲ τρισχιλίους, προσέταξαν πορθῆσαι τοὺς Λακεδαιμονίων συμ-

---

[1] τῆς ὑπὸ added by Rhodoman.

after a reign of forty years, and Xerxes succeeded to the throne and ruled for a year.

In Italy, when the Aequi revolted from the Romans, in the war which followed Aulus Postumius was made Dictator and Lucius Julius was named Master of the Horse. And the Romans, having marched against the territory of the rebels with a large and strong army, first of all plundered their possessions, and when the Aequi later drew up against them, a battle ensued in which the Romans were victorious, slaying many of the enemy, taking not a few captive, and capturing great quantities of booty. After the battle the revolters, being broken in spirit because of the defeat, submitted themselves to the Romans, and Postumius, because he had conducted the war brilliantly, as the Romans thought, celebrated the customary triumph. And Postumius, we are told, did a peculiar thing and altogether unbelievable; for in the battle his own son in his eagerness leaped forward from the station assigned him by his father, and his father, preserving the ancient discipline, had his son executed as one who had left his station.

65. At the close of this year, in Athens the archon was Isarchus and in Rome the consuls elected were Titus Quinctius and Gaius Julius, and among the Eleians the Eighty-ninth Olympiad was celebrated, that in which Symmachus [1] won the " stadion " for the second time. This year the Athenians chose as general Nicias, the son of Niceratus, and assigning to him sixty triremes and three thousand hoplites, they ordered him to plunder the allies of the Lacedae-

---

[1] Of Messenê; cp. chap. 49. 1.

2 μάχους. οὗτος δ' ἐπὶ πρώτην τὴν Μῆλον πλεύσας
τήν τε χώραν ἐδήωσε καὶ τὴν πόλιν ἐφ' ἱκανὰς
ἡμέρας ἐπολιόρκησεν· αὕτη γὰρ μόνη τῶν Κυκλά-
δων νήσων διεφύλαττε τὴν πρὸς Λακεδαιμονίους
3 συμμαχίαν, ἄποικος οὖσα τῆς Σπάρτης. ὁ δὲ
Νικίας, γενναίως ἀμυνομένων τῶν Μηλίων οὐ δυνάμενος ἑλεῖν τὴν πόλιν, ἀπέπλευσεν εἰς Ὠρωπὸν
τῆς Βοιωτίας. ἐνταῦθα δὲ τὰς ναῦς ἀπολιπὼν
παρῆλθεν εἰς τὴν τῶν Ταναγραίων χώραν μετὰ
τῶν ὁπλιτῶν, καὶ κατέλαβεν ἐνταῦθα δύναμιν
ἑτέραν[1] Ἀθηναίων, ἧς ἐστρατήγει Ἱππόνικος ὁ
4 Καλλίου. συνελθόντων δὲ εἰς ταὐτὸ τῶν στρατοπέδων ἀμφοτέρων, οὗτοι μὲν ἐπεπορεύοντο τὴν
χώραν πορθοῦντες, τῶν δὲ Θηβαίων ἐκβοηθούντων
συνάψαντες αὐτοῖς μάχην οἱ Ἀθηναῖοι καὶ πολλοὺς
ἀνελόντες ἐνίκησαν.

5 Μετὰ δὲ τὴν μάχην οἱ μεθ' Ἱππονίκου στρατιῶται τὴν εἰς Ἀθήνας ἐπάνοδον ἐποιήσαντο,
Νικίας δὲ παρελθὼν ἐπὶ τὰς ναῦς παρέπλευσεν
ἐπὶ τὴν Λοκρίδα, καὶ τὴν παραθαλάττιον χώραν
πορθήσας προσελάβετο παρὰ τῶν συμμάχων τριήρεις τετταράκοντα, ὥστε τὰς πάσας ἔχειν αὐτὸν
ναῦς ἑκατόν· καταλέξας δὲ καὶ πεζοὺς στρατιώτας
οὐκ ὀλίγους, καὶ δύναμιν ἀξιόλογον συστησάμενος,
6 ἔπλευσεν ἐπὶ τὴν Κόρινθον. ἀποβιβάσαντος δ'
αὐτοῦ τοὺς στρατιώτας, καὶ τῶν Κορινθίων ἀντιταχθέντων, οἱ Ἀθηναῖοι δυσὶ μάχαις ἐνίκησαν
καὶ πολλοὺς τῶν πολεμίων ἀνελόντες τρόπαιον
ἔστησαν. ἐτελεύτησαν δ' ἐν τῇ μάχῃ τῶν Ἀθηναίων εἰς ὀκτώ, τῶν δὲ Κορινθίων πλείους τῶν
7 τριακοσίων. ὁ δὲ Νικίας πλεύσας εἰς Κρομ-

---

[1] So Eichstädt: ἑτέρων.

monians.   He sailed to Melos as the first place, where 424 B.C.
he ravaged their territory and for a number of days
laid siege to the city ; for it was the only island
of the Cyclades which was maintaining its alliance
with the Lacedaemonians, being a Spartan colony.
Nicias was unable to take the city, however, since the
Melians defended themselves gallantly, and he then
sailed to Oropus ¹ in Boeotia.   Leaving his ships
there, he advanced with his hoplites into the territory
of the Tanagraeans, where he fell in with another
Athenian force which was commanded by Hipponicus,
the son of Callias.   When the two armies had united,
the generals pressed forward, plundering the land ;
and when the Thebans sallied forth to the rescue, the
Athenians offered them battle, in which they inflicted
heavy casualties and were victorious.

After the battle the soldiers with Hipponicus made
their way back to Athens, but Nicias, returning to his
ships, sailed along the coast to Locris, and when he
had laid waste the country on the coast, he added to
his fleet forty triremes from the allies, so that he
possessed in all one hundred ships.   He also enrolled
no small number of soldiers and gathered together
a strong armament, whereupon he sailed against
Corinth.   There he disembarked the soldiers, and
when the Corinthians drew up their forces against
them, the Athenians gained the victory in two
battles, slew many of the enemy, and set up a trophy.
There perished in the fighting eight Athenians and
more than three hundred Corinthians.²   Nicias then

¹ Oropus was always debatable territory between Attica
and Boeotia.
² Thucydides (4. 44. 6) states that two hundred and twelve
Corinthians died, and of the Athenians " somewhat fewer
than fifty."

μυῶνα τήν τε χώραν ἐδήωσε καὶ τὸ φρούριον
ἐχειρώσατο. εὐθὺς δ' ἐπαναζεύξας καὶ τειχίσας
φρούριον ἐν τῇ Μεθώνῃ, φυλακὴν κατέλιπε τὴν
τὸ χωρίον ἅμα φυλάξουσαν καὶ τὴν ἐγγὺς χώραν
δηώσουσαν· αὐτὸς δὲ τὴν παραθαλάττιον πορθήσας
ἐπανῆλθεν εἰς τὰς Ἀθήνας.

8 Μετὰ δὲ ταῦτα ἐπὶ Κύθηρα ναῦς ἀπέστειλαν
ἑξήκοντα καὶ δισχιλίους ὁπλίτας, ὧν εἶχε τὴν
στρατηγίαν Νικίας μετ' ἄλλων τινῶν. οὗτος δὲ
στρατεύσας ἐπὶ τὴν νῆσον καὶ προσβολὰς ποιησάμενος παρέλαβε τὴν πόλιν καθ' ὁμολογίαν. ἐν
δὲ τῇ νήσῳ καταλιπὼν φρουρὰν ἐξέπλευσεν εἰς
τὴν Πελοπόννησον καὶ τὴν παραθαλάττιον χώραν
9 ἐδήωσε. καὶ Θυρέας μὲν κειμένας ἐν τοῖς μεθ-
ορίοις τῆς Λακωνικῆς καὶ τῆς Ἀργείας ἐκπολι-
ορκήσας ἐξηνδραποδίσατο καὶ κατέσκαψε, τοὺς
δ' ἐν αὐτῇ κατοικοῦντας Αἰγινήτας καὶ τὸν φρούρ-
αρχον Τάνταλον Σπαρτιάτην ζωγρήσας ἀπήγαγεν
εἰς τὰς Ἀθήνας. οἱ δὲ Ἀθηναῖοι τὸν μὲν Τάνταλον
δήσαντες ἐφύλαττον μετὰ τῶν ἄλλων αἰχμαλώτων
καὶ τοὺς Αἰγινήτας.

66. Ἅμα δὲ τούτοις πραττομένοις Μεγαρεῖς
θλιβόμενοι τῷ πολέμῳ τῷ πρὸς τοὺς Ἀθηναίους
καὶ τῷ πρὸς τοὺς φυγάδας. . . . διαπρεσβευομένων
δὲ πρὸς ἀλλήλους περὶ τούτων, τῶν πολιτῶν τινες
ἀλλοτρίως ἔχοντες πρὸς τοὺς φυγάδας ἐπηγγείλαντο πρὸς τοὺς Ἀθηναίων στρατηγοὺς προδώσειν
2 τὴν πόλιν. οἱ δὲ στρατηγοί, Ἱπποκράτης τε καὶ

---

[1] In Megaris.
[2] Strabo states that the correct name was Methana (in
Argolis; cp. Thucydides, 4. 45).
[3] The large island off the south-eastern tip of Laconia.

sailed to Crommyon,[1] ravaged its territory, and 424 B.C.
seized its stronghold. Then he immediately removed
from there and built a stronghold near Methonê,[2] in
which he left a garrison for the twofold purpose of
protecting the place and ravaging the neighbouring
countryside ; then Nicias plundered the coast and
returned to Athens.

After these events the Athenians sent sixty ships
and two thousand hoplites to Cythera,[3] the expedition being under the command of Nicias and certain
other generals. Nicias attacked the island, hurled
assaults upon the city, and received its formal surrender. And leaving a garrison behind on the island
he sailed off to the Peloponnesus and ravaged the territory along the coast. And Thyreae, which lies on the
border between Laconia and Argolis, he took by siege,
making slaves of its inhabitants, and razed it to the
ground ; and the Aeginetans, who inhabited the city,
together with the commander of the garrison, Tantalus the Spartan, he took captive and carried off to
Athens. And the Athenians fettered Tantalus and
kept him under guard together with the other
prisoners, as well as the Aeginetans.

66. While these events were taking place the
Megarians were finding themselves in distress because of their war with the Athenians on the one
hand and with their exiles on the other hand. And
while representatives [4] were exchanging opinions regarding the exiles, certain citizens [5] who were hostile
to the exiles approached the Athenian generals with
the offer to deliver the city to them. The generals.

[4] From the different parties in the city.
[5] These represented the party of the masses   cp. Thucydides, 4. 66.

Δημοσθένης, συνθέμενοι περὶ τῆς προδοσίας, ἐξέπεμψαν νυκτὸς στρατιώτας ἑξακοσίους εἰς τὴν
πόλιν, καὶ οἱ συνθέμενοι παρεδέξαντο τοὺς Ἀθηναίους ἐντὸς τειχῶν. καταφανοῦς δὲ τῆς προδοσίας γενομένης κατὰ τὴν πόλιν, καὶ τοῦ πλήθους
σχιζομένου κατὰ τὴν αἵρεσιν, καὶ τῶν μὲν συμμαχούντων τοῖς Ἀθηναίοις, τῶν δὲ βοηθούντων τοῖς
Λακεδαιμονίοις, ἐκήρυξέ τις ἀφ' ἑαυτοῦ τοὺς βουλομένους τίθεσθαι τὰ ὅπλα μετὰ Ἀθηναίων καὶ
3 Μεγαρέων. διόπερ τῶν Λακεδαιμονίων ἐγκατα-
λείπεσθαι μελλόντων ὑπὸ τῶν Μεγαρέων, συνέβη
τοὺς φρουροῦντας τὰ μακρὰ τείχη καταλιπεῖν, εἰς
δὲ τὴν καλουμένην Νίσαιαν, ἥπερ ἐστὶν ἐπίνειον
4 τῶν Μεγαρέων, καταφυγεῖν. περιταφρεύσαντες δὲ
αὐτὴν οἱ Ἀθηναῖοι ἐπολιόρκουν· μετὰ δὲ ταῦτα ἐκ
τῶν Ἀθηνῶν τεχνίτας προσλαβόμενοι περιετείχισαν τὴν Νίσαιαν. οἱ δὲ Πελοποννήσιοι φοβούμενοι μὴ κατὰ κράτος ἁλόντες ἀναιρεθῶσι, παρέδοσαν
τὴν Νίσαιαν τοῖς Ἀθηναίοις καθ' ὁμολογίαν.

Καὶ τὰ μὲν κατὰ τοὺς Μεγαρέας ἐν τούτοις ἦν.
67. Βρασίδας δὲ δύναμιν ἱκανὴν ἀναλαβὼν ἔκ τε
Λακεδαίμονος καὶ παρὰ τῶν ἄλλων Πελοποννησίων
ἀνέζευξεν ἐπὶ Μέγαρα. καταπληξάμενος δὲ τοὺς
Ἀθηναίους, τούτους μὲν ἐξέβαλεν ἐκ τῆς Νισαίας,
τὴν δὲ πόλιν τῶν Μεγαρέων ἐλευθερώσας ἀπο-
κατέστησεν εἰς τὴν τῶν Λακεδαιμονίων συμμαχίαν·
αὐτὸς δὲ μετὰ τῆς δυνάμεως διὰ Θετταλίας τὴν
πορείαν ποιησάμενος ἧκεν εἰς Δῖον τῆς Μακεδο-
2 νίας. ἐκεῖθεν δὲ παρελθὼν εἰς Ἄκανθον συνεμάχησε
τοῖς Χαλκιδεῦσι. καὶ πρώτην μὲν τὴν Ἀκανθίων

---

[1] Thucydides (4. 68. 3) says he was the Athenian herald.

Hippocrates and Demosthenes, agreeing to this be- 424 B.C.
trayal, sent by night six hundred soldiers to the city,
and the conspirators admitted the Athenians within
the walls. When the betrayal became known
throughout the city and while the multitude were
divided according to party, some being in favour of
fighting on the side of the Athenians and others of
aiding the Lacedaemonians, a certain man,[1] acting
on his own initiative, made the proclamation that any
who so wished could take up arms on the side of the
Athenians and Megarians. Consequently, when the
Lacedaemonians were on the point of being left in
the lurch by the Megarians, it so happened that the
Lacedaemonian garrison of the long walls[2] abandoned them and sought safety in Nisaea, as it is called,
which is the sea-port of the Megarians. The Athenians thereupon dug a ditch about Nisaea and put it
under siege, and then, bringing skilled workmen from
Athens, they threw a wall about it. And the Peloponnesians, fearing lest they should be taken by storm and
put to death, surrendered Nisaea to the Athenians.

Such, then, were the affairs of the Megarians at
this time.

67. Brasidas, taking an adequate force from Lacedaemon and the other Peloponnesian states, advanced
against Megara. And striking terror into the
Athenians he expelled them from Nisaea, and then
he set free the city of the Megarians and brought it
back into the alliance of the Lacedaemonians. After
this he made his way with his army through Thessaly
and came to Dium in Macedonia. From there he
advanced against Acanthus and associated himself
with the cause of the Chalcidians. The city of the

[2] These connected Megara with its harbour.

πόλιν τὰ μὲν καταπληξάμενος, τὰ δὲ καὶ λόγοις
φιλανθρώποις πείσας ἐποίησεν ἀποστῆναι τῶν
Ἀθηναίων· ἔπειτα πολλοὺς καὶ τῶν ἄλλων τῶν
ἐπὶ Θράκης κατοικούντων προετρέψατο κοινωνεῖν[1]
3 τῆς τῶν Λακεδαιμονίων συμμαχίας. μετὰ δὲ
ταῦτα Βρασίδας βουλόμενος ἐνεργότερον ἅψασθαι
τοῦ πολέμου, μετεπέμπετο στρατιώτας ἐκ τῆς
Λακεδαίμονος, σπεύδων ἀξιόλογον συστήσασθαι
δύναμιν· οἱ δὲ Σπαρτιᾶται βουλόμενοι τῶν Εἱλώτων τοὺς κρατίστους ἀπολέσθαι, πέμπουσιν ἐξ
αὐτῶν τοὺς μάλιστα πεφρονηματισμένους χιλίους,
νομίζοντες ἐν ταῖς μάχαις τοὺς πλείστους αὐτῶν
4 κατακοπήσεσθαι. ἔπραξαν δέ τι καὶ ἄλλο βίαιον
καὶ ὠμόν, δι᾽ οὗ ταπεινώσειν ὑπελάμβανον τοὺς
Εἵλωτας· ἐκήρυξαν γὰρ ἀπογράφεσθαι τῶν Εἱλώτων τοὺς ἀγαθόν τι πεποιηκότας τῇ Σπάρτῃ, καὶ
τούτους κρίναντες ἐλευθερώσειν ἐπηγγείλαντο· ἀπο-
γραψαμένων δὲ δισχιλίων, τούτους μὲν προσέταξαν
τοῖς κρατίστοις ἀποκτεῖναι κατ᾽ οἶκον ἑκάστου.
5 σφόδρα γὰρ εὐλαβοῦντο μήποτε καιροῦ δραξάμε-
νοι καὶ μετὰ τῶν πολεμίων ταχθέντες εἰς κίνδυνον
ἀγάγωσι τὴν Σπάρτην. οὐ μὴν ἀλλὰ τῷ Βρασίδᾳ παραγενομένων χιλίων Εἱλώτων, ἔκ τε συμμάχων στρατολογηθέντων συνέστη δύναμις ἀξιόχρεως.

68. Διὸ καὶ θαρρήσας τῷ πλήθει τῶν στρατιωτῶν ἐστράτευσεν ἐπὶ τὴν καλουμένην Ἀμφίπολιν.
ταύτην δὲ τὴν πόλιν πρότερον μὲν ἐπεχείρησεν
οἰκίζειν Ἀρισταγόρας ὁ Μιλήσιος, φεύγων Δαρεῖον
2 τὸν βασιλέα τῶν Περσῶν· ἐκείνου δὲ τελευτή-

---

[1] μετὰ after κοινωνεῖν deleted by Rhodoman.

Acanthians was the first which he brought, partly 424 B.C. through fear and partly through kindly and persuasive arguments, to revolt from the Athenians; and afterwards he induced many also of the other peoples of Thrace to join the alliance of the Lacedaemonians. After this Brasidas, wishing to prosecute the war more vigorously, proceeded to summon soldiers from Lacedaemon, since he was eager to gather a strong army. And the Spartans, wishing to destroy the most influential among the Helots, sent him a thousand of the most high-spirited Helots, thinking that the larger number of them would perish in the fighting. They also committed another violent and savage act whereby they thought to humble the pride of the Helots: They made public proclamation that any Helots who had rendered some good service to Sparta should give in their names, and promised that after passing upon their claims they would set them free; and when two thousand had given in their names, they then commanded the most influential citizens to slay these Helots, each in his own home. For they were deeply concerned lest the Helots should seize an opportune moment to line up with the enemy and bring Sparta into peril. Nevertheless, since Brasidas had been joined by a thousand Helots and troops had been levied among the allies, a satisfactory force was assembled.

68. Brasidas, confiding in the multitude of his soldiers, now advanced with his army against the city known as Amphipolis. This city Aristagoras of Miletus at an earlier time had undertaken to found as a colony,[1] when he was fleeing from Darius, the king of the Persians; after his death the colonists

---

[1] In 497 B.C.; cp. Herodotus, 5. 126.

σαντος, καὶ τῶν οἰκητόρων ἐκπεσόντων ὑπὸ
Θρᾳκῶν τῶν ὀνομαζομένων Ἠδωνῶν, μετὰ ταῦτα
ἔτεσι δυσὶ πρὸς τοῖς τριάκοντα Ἀθηναῖοι μυρίους
οἰκήτορας εἰς αὐτὴν ἐξέπεμψαν. ὁμοίως δὲ καὶ
τούτων ὑπὸ Θρᾳκῶν διαφθαρέντων περὶ Δράβη-
σκον, διαλιπόντες ἔτη δύο πάλιν ἀνεκτήσαντο τὴν
3 πόλιν Ἅγνωνος[1] ἡγουμένου. περιμαχήτου δ' αὐτῆς πολλάκις γεγενημένης, ἔσπευδεν ὁ Βρασίδας
κύριος γενέσθαι τῆς πόλεως. διὸ καὶ στρατεύσας
ἐπ' αὐτὴν ἀξιολόγῳ δυνάμει, καὶ στρατοπεδεύσας
πλησίον τῆς γεφύρας, τὸ μὲν πρῶτον εἷλε τὸ προ-
άστειον τῆς πόλεως, τῇ δ' ὑστεραίᾳ καταπληξάμενος τοὺς Ἀμφιπολίτας παρέλαβε τὴν πόλιν καθ'
ὁμολογίαν, ὥστ' ἐξεῖναι τῷ βουλομένῳ τὰ ἑαυτοῦ
λαβόντα ἀπελθεῖν ἐκ τῆς πόλεως.

4 Εὐθὺς δὲ καὶ τῶν πλησιοχώρων πόλεων πλείονας
προσηγάγετο, ἐν αἷς ἦσαν ἀξιολογώταται Οἰσύμη[2]
καὶ Γαληψός, ἀμφότεραι Θασίων ἄποικοι, καὶ Μύρ-
κινον, Ἠδωνικὸν πολισμάτιον. ἐπεβάλετο δὲ καὶ
ναυπηγεῖσθαι τριήρεις πλείους ἐπὶ τῷ Στρυμόνι ποταμῷ, καὶ στρατιώτας ἔκ τε Λακεδαίμονος καὶ
5 παρὰ τῶν ἄλλων συμμάχων μετεπέμπετο. κατεσκεύαζε δὲ καὶ πανοπλίας πολλάς, καὶ τοῖς ἀόπ-
λοις τῶν νέων ἀνεδίδου ταύτας, καὶ βελῶν καὶ
σίτου καὶ τῶν ἄλλων ἀπάντων παρασκευὰς ἐποιεῖτο. ὡς δ' αὐτῷ πάντα παρεσκεύαστο, ἀνέζευξεν
ἐκ τῆς Ἀμφιπόλεως μετὰ τῆς δυνάμεως, καὶ
παραγενόμενος εἰς τὴν καλουμένην Ἀκτὴν κατεστρατοπέδευσεν. ἐν ταύτῃ δ' ὑπῆρχον πέντε πόλεις,
ὧν αἱ μὲν Ἑλληνίδες ἦσαν, Ἀνδρίων ἄποικοι, αἱ

---

[1] So Wesseling, from Thuc. 4. 102. 3: Ἀπίωνος.
[2] So Valesius, from Thuc. 4. 107. 3: Σύμη.

were driven out by the Thracians who are called 424 B.C
Edones, and thirty-two years after this event the
Athenians dispatched ten thousand colonists to the
place. In like manner these colonists also were
utterly destroyed by Thracians at Drabescus,[1] and
two years later [2] the Athenians again recovered the
city, under the leadership of Hagnon. Since the city
had been the object of many a battle, Brasidas was
eager to master it. Consequently he set out against
it with a strong force, and pitching his camp near the
bridge,[3] he first of all seized the suburb of the city
and then on the next day, having struck terror into
the Amphipolitans, he received the formal surrender
of the city on the condition that anyone who so wished
could take his property and leave the city.

Immediately after this Brasidas brought over to his
side a number of the neighbouring cities, the most
important of which were Oesymê and Galepsus, both
colonies of the Thasians, and also Myrcinus, a small
Edonian city. He also set about building a number
of triremes on the Strymon River and summoned
soldiers from both Lacedaemon and the rest of the
allies. Also he had many complete suits of armour
made, which he distributed among the young men
who possessed no arms, and he gathered supplies of
missiles and grain and everything else. And when
all his preparations had been made, he set out from
Amphipolis with his army and came to Actê,[4] as it is
called, where he pitched his camp. In this area there
were five cities, of which some were Greek, being

---

[1] Cp. Book 11. 70. 5.
[2] Twenty-nine years later, according to Thucydides,
4. 102. 3.
[3] Over the Strymon River and not far from the city.
[4] The region about Mt. Athos.

δὲ εἶχον ὄχλον βαρβάρων διγλώττων Βισαλτικόν.
6 ταύτας δὲ χειρωσάμενος ἐστράτευσεν ἐπὶ πόλιν
Τορώνην, ἄποικον μὲν Χαλκιδέων, κατεχομένην δὲ
ὑπ᾿ Ἀθηναίων. προδιδόντων δέ τινων τὴν πόλιν,
ὑπὸ τούτων εἰσαχθεὶς νυκτὸς ἐκράτησε τῆς Τορώνης ἄνευ κινδύνων.

Τὰ μὲν οὖν κατὰ τὸν Βρασίδαν μέχρι τούτου
προέβη κατὰ τοῦτον τὸν ἐνιαυτόν.

69. Ἅμα δὲ τούτοις πραττομένοις περὶ τὸ
Δήλιον ἐγένετο παράταξις κατὰ τὴν Βοιωτίαν[1]
Ἀθηναίων πρὸς Βοιωτοὺς διὰ τοιαύτας τινὰς αἰτίας.
τῶν Βοιωτῶν τινες δυσαρεστούμενοι τῇ τότε πολι-
τείᾳ καὶ σπεύδοντες δημοκρατίας ἐν ταῖς πόλεσι
καταστῆσαι, διελέχθησαν περὶ τῆς ἰδίας προαιρέσεως τοῖς Ἀθηναίων στρατηγοῖς Ἱπποκράτει καὶ
Δημοσθένει, καὶ κατεπηγγέλλοντο παραδώσειν τὰς
2 ἐν τῇ Βοιωτίᾳ πόλεις. ἀσμένως δὲ τῶν Ἀθηναίων
προσδεξαμένων, περί τε τῶν κατὰ τὴν ἐπίθεσιν
διοικήσεων διελομένων τῶν στρατηγῶν τὴν δύναμιν, Δημοσθένης μὲν τὸ πλεῖστον τοῦ στρατεύματος ἀναλαβὼν ἐνέβαλεν εἰς τὴν Βοιωτίαν, καὶ
καταλαβὼν τοὺς Βοιωτοὺς προνενοημένους τὴν
προδοσίαν, ἄπρακτος ἀπῆλθεν, Ἱπποκράτης δὲ
πανδημεὶ τοὺς Ἀθηναίους ἀγαγὼν ἐπὶ τὸ Δήλιον
κατελάβετο τὸ χωρίον, καὶ φθάσας τὴν ἔφοδον
τῶν Βοιωτῶν ἐτείχισε τὸ Δήλιον. τοῦτο δὲ τὸ
χωρίον κεῖται μὲν πλησίον τῆς Ὠρωπίας καὶ τῶν
3 ὅρων τῆς Βοιωτίας· Παγώνδας δ᾿ ὁ τῶν Βοιωτῶν ἔχων τὴν στρατηγίαν ἐξ ἁπασῶν τῶν κατὰ
τὴν Βοιωτίαν πόλεων μεταπεμψάμενος στρατιώτας

---

[1] κατὰ τὴν Βοιωτίαν deleted by Vogel.

colonies from Andros, and the others had a populace 424 B.C. of barbarians of Bisaltic [1] origin, which were bilingual. After mastering these cities Brasidas led his army against the city of Toronê, which was a colony of the Chalcidians but was held by Athenians. Since certain men were ready to betray the city, Brasidas was by night admitted by them and got Toronê in his power without a fight.

To such a height did the fortunes of Brasidas attain in the course of this year.

69. While these events were happening, at Delium in Boeotia a pitched battle took place between the Athenians and the Boeotians for the following reasons. Certain Boeotians, who were restive under the form of government which obtained at the time and were eager to establish democracies in the cities, discussed their policy with the Athenian generals, Hippocrates and Demosthenes, and promised to deliver the cities of Boeotia into their hands. The Athenians gladly accepted this offer and, having in view the arrangements for the attack, the generals divided their forces : Demosthenes, taking the larger part of the army, invaded Boeotia, but finding the Boeotians already informed of the betrayal he withdrew without accomplishing anything ; Hippocrates led the popular levy of the Athenians against Delium, seized the place, and threw a wall about it before the approach of the Boeotians. The town lies near the territory of Oropus and the boundary of Boeotia.[2] Pagondas, who commanded the Boeotians, having summoned soldiers from all the cities of Boeotia, came

[1] A Thracian tribe.
[2] Oropus was the last city of Attica on the coast before the border of Boeotia. Delium lay near the coast in the territory of Tanagra.

ἧκε πρὸς τὸ Δήλιον μετὰ πολλῆς δυνάμεως· εἶχε
γὰρ στρατιώτας πεζοὺς μὲν οὐ πολὺ λείποντας
4 τῶν δισμυρίων, ἱππεῖς δὲ περὶ χιλίους. οἱ δ'
Ἀθηναῖοι τῷ πλήθει μὲν ὑπερεῖχον τῶν Βοιωτῶν,
ὡπλισμένοι δὲ οὐχ ὁμοίως τοῖς πολεμίοις· ἄφνω
γὰρ καὶ συντόμως ἐξεληλύθεσαν ἐκ τῆς πόλεως,
καὶ διὰ τὴν σπουδὴν ὑπῆρχον ἀπαράσκευοι.

70. Ἀμφοτέρων δὲ προθύμως ὡρμημένων παρετάχθησαν αἱ δυνάμεις τόνδε τὸν τρόπον. παρὰ
τοῖς Βοιωτοῖς ἐτάχθησαν ἐπὶ τὸ δεξιὸν κέρας Θηβαῖοι, ἐπὶ δὲ τὸ εὐώνυμον Ὀρχομένιοι, τὴν δὲ
μέσην ἀνεπλήρουν φάλαγγα Βοιωτοί· προεμά-
χοντο δὲ πάντων οἱ παρ' ἐκείνοις ἡνίοχοι καὶ
παραβάται καλούμενοι, ἄνδρες ἐπίλεκτοι τριακό-
σιοι. Ἀθηναῖοι δὲ διατάττοντες ἔτι τὴν δύναμιν
2 ἠναγκάσθησαν συνάψαι μάχην. γενομένης δὲ
τῆς παρατάξεως ἰσχυρᾶς, τὸ μὲν πρῶτον οἱ τῶν
Ἀθηναίων ἱππεῖς ἀγωνιζόμενοι λαμπρῶς ἠνάγκασαν φυγεῖν τοὺς ἀντιστάντας ἱππεῖς· μετὰ δὲ
ταῦτα τῶν πεζῶν διαγωνισαμένων οἱ ταχθέντες
κατὰ τοὺς Θηβαίους Ἀθηναῖοι βιασθέντες ἐτράπησαν, οἱ δὲ λοιποὶ τοὺς ἄλλους Βοιωτοὺς τρεψάμενοι καὶ συχνοὺς ἀνελόντες ἐφ' ἱκανὸν τόπον
3 ἐδίωξαν. οἱ δὲ Θηβαῖοι, διαφέροντες ταῖς τῶν
σωμάτων ῥώμαις, ἐπέστρεψαν ἀπὸ τοῦ διωγμοῦ,
καὶ τοῖς διώκουσι τῶν Ἀθηναίων ἐπιπεσόντες
φυγεῖν ἠνάγκασαν· ἐπιφανεῖ δὲ μάχῃ νικήσαντες

---

[1] This designation is probably derived from that of an
originally wealthy class who were able to provide their own
chariots for warfare, like the Roman " Knights," who could
furnish horses. The three hundred are what were known
later as the " Sacred Band " of the Thebans which was drawn
up, not as here before the whole Theban line, but many men

to Delium with a great army, since he had little less 424 B.C.
than twenty thousand infantry and about a thousand
cavalry. The Athenians, although superior to the
Boeotians in number, were not so well equipped as
the enemy ; for they had left the city hurriedly and on
short notice, and in such haste they were unprepared.

70. Both armies advanced to the fray in high
spirits and the forces were disposed in the following
manner. On the Boeotian side, the Thebans were
drawn up on the right wing, the Orchomenians on
the left, and the centre of the line was made up of
the other Boeotians ; the first line of the whole army
was formed of what they called " charioteers and
footmen," [1] a select group of three hundred. The
Athenians were forced to engage the enemy while
still marshalling their army. A fierce conflict ensued
and at first the Athenian cavalry, fighting brilliantly,
compelled the opposing cavalry to flee ; but later,
after the infantry had become engaged, the Athenians
who were opposed to the Thebans were overpowered
and put to flight, although the remaining Athenians
overcame the other Boeotians, slew great numbers of
them, and pursued them for some distance. But the
Thebans, whose bodily strength was superior, turned
back from the pursuit, and falling on the pursuing
Athenians forced them to flee ; and since they had
won a conspicuous victory,[2] they gained for them-

deep on one wing (cp. Plutarch, *Pelopidas*, 18 ff.). Thucydides (4. 93. 4) states that in his battle " the Thebans were
marshalled in ranks twenty-five shields deep," a statement
which cannot have been true of the whole Theban contingent.

[2] Delium was the greatest battle of the Archidamian War ;
Socrates participated in it and his life was saved by Alcibiades (Plato, *Symp.* 221 A-c); Socrates had saved Alcibiades
at Potidaea in 432 B.C. (*Symp.* 220 E).

4 μεγάλην ἀπηνέγκαντο δόξαν πρὸς ἀνδρείαν. τῶν
δ' Ἀθηναίων οἱ μὲν εἰς Ὠρωπόν, οἱ δὲ εἰς τὸ
Δήλιον κατέφυγον, τινὲς δὲ πρὸς τὴν θάλατταν
διέτειναν πρὸς τὰς ἰδίας ναῦς, ἄλλοι δὲ κατ'
ἄλλους ὡς ἔτυχε τόπους διεσπάρησαν. ἐπιγενομένης δὲ τῆς νυκτὸς ἔπεσον τῶν μὲν Βοιωτῶν οὐ
πλείους τῶν πεντακοσίων, τῶν δ' Ἀθηναίων
πολλαπλάσιοι τούτων. εἰ μὲν οὖν ἡ νὺξ μὴ προ-
κατέλαβεν, οἱ πλεῖστοι τῶν Ἀθηναίων ἂν ἐτελεύ-
τησαν· αὕτη γὰρ μεσολαβήσασα τὰς τῶν διωκόντων
5 ὁρμὰς διέσωσε τοὺς φεύγοντας. ὅμως δὲ τοσοῦτο
πλῆθος τῶν ἀναιρεθέντων ἦν, ὥστε τοὺς Θηβαίους
ἐκ τῆς τῶν λαφύρων τιμῆς τήν τε στοὰν τὴν μεγάλην ἐν ἀγορᾷ κατασκευάσαι καὶ χαλκοῖς ἀνδριᾶσι
κοσμῆσαι, τοὺς δὲ ναοὺς καὶ τὰς κατὰ τὴν ἀγορὰν
στοὰς τοῖς ὅπλοις τοῖς ἐκ τῶν σκύλων προσηλωθεῖσι
καταχαλκῶσαι· τήν τε τῶν Δηλίων πανήγυριν ἀπὸ
τούτων τῶν χρημάτων ἐνεστήσαντο ποιεῖν.

6 Μετὰ δὲ τὴν μάχην οἱ μὲν Βοιωτοὶ τῷ Δηλίῳ
προσβολὰς ποιησάμενοι κατὰ κράτος εἷλον τὸ
χωρίον· τῶν δὲ φρουρούντων τὸ Δήλιον οἱ πλείους
μὲν μαχόμενοι γενναίως ἀπέθανον, διακόσιοι δὲ
ἥλωσαν· οἱ δὲ λοιποὶ κατέφυγον εἰς τὰς ναῦς, καὶ
διεκομίσθησαν μετὰ τῶν ἄλλων εἰς τὴν Ἀττικήν.
Ἀθηναῖοι μὲν οὖν ἐπιβουλεύσαντες τοῖς Βοιωτοῖς
τοιαύτῃ συμφορᾷ περιέπεσον.

71. Κατὰ δὲ τὴν Ἀσίαν Ξέρξης ὁ βασιλεὺς ἐτελεύτησεν ἄρξας ἐνιαυτόν, ὡς δ' ἔνιοι γράφουσι,
μῆνας δύο· τὴν δὲ βασιλείαν διαδεξάμενος ὁ
ἀδελφὸς Σογδιανὸς ἦρξε μῆνας ἑπτά. τοῦτον δ'
ἀνελὼν Δαρεῖος ἐβασίλευσεν ἔτη δεκαεννέα.

----

[1] The Athenian losses were less than a thousand in addi-

selves great fame for valour. Of the Athenians some 424 B.C.
fled for refuge to Oropus and others to Delium;
certain of them made for the sea and the Athenian
ships; still others scattered this way and that, as
chance dictated. When night fell, the Boeotian dead
were not in excess of five hundred, the Athenian many
times that number.[1] However, if night had not inter-
vened, most of the Athenians would have perished,
for it broke the drive of the pursuers and brought
safety to those in flight. Even so the multitude of
the slain was so great that from the proceeds of the
booty the Thebans not only constructed the great
colonnade in their market-place but also embellished
it with bronze statues, and their temples and the
colonnades in the market-place they covered with
bronze by the armour from the booty which they
nailed to them; furthermore, it was with this money
that they instituted the festival called Delia.[2]

After the battle the Boeotians launched assaults
upon Delium and took the place by storm[3]; of the
garrison of Delium the larger number died fighting
gallantly and two hundred were taken prisoner; the
rest fled for safety to the ships and were transported
with the other refugees to Attica. Thus the
Athenians, who devised a plot against the Boeotians,
were involved in the disaster we have described.

71. In Asia King Xerxes died after a reign of one
year, or, as some record, two months; and his brother
Sogdianus succeeded to the throne and ruled for seven
months. He was slain by Darius, who reigned nineteen years.

tion to light-armed troops and baggage carriers (Thucydides,
4. 101). [2] Held at Delium.
[3] A " flame-thrower " was used in the assault upon the
walls; cp. Thucydides, 4. 100.

2 Τῶν δὲ συγγραφέων Ἀντίοχος ὁ Συρακόσιος
τὴν τῶν Σικελικῶν ἱστορίαν εἰς τοῦτον τὸν ἐνιαυτὸν
κατέστρεψεν, ἀρξάμενος ἀπὸ Κωκάλου τοῦ Σικανῶν βασιλέως, ἐν βίβλοις ἐννέα.

72. Ἐπ᾽ ἄρχοντος δ᾽ Ἀθήνησιν Ἀμεινίου Ῥωμαῖοι μὲν κατέστησαν ὑπάτους Γάιον Παπίριον
καὶ Λεύκιον Ἰούνιον. ἐπὶ δὲ τούτων Σκιωναῖοι μὲν
καταφρονήσαντες τῶν Ἀθηναίων διὰ τὴν περὶ τὸ
Δήλιον ἧτταν, ἀπέστησαν πρὸς τοὺς Λακεδαιμονίους καὶ τὴν πόλιν παρέδωκαν Βρασίδᾳ τῷ
στρατηγοῦντι τῶν ἐπὶ Θράκης Λακεδαιμονίων.

2 Ἐν δὲ τῇ Λέσβῳ μετὰ τὴν ἅλωσιν τῆς Μυτιλήνης ὑπ᾽ Ἀθηναίων οἱ πεφευγότες ἐκ τῆς ἁλώσεως
πολλοὶ τὸν ἀριθμὸν ὄντες καὶ πάλαι μὲν ἐπεχείρουν
κατελθεῖν εἰς τὴν Λέσβον, τότε δὲ συστραφέντες
Ἄντανδρον κατέλαβον, κἀκεῖθεν ὁρμώμενοι διεπολέμουν τοῖς κατέχουσι τὴν Μυτιλήνην Ἀθηναίοις.

3 ἐφ᾽ οἷς παροξυνθεὶς ὁ δῆμος τῶν Ἀθηναίων ἐξέπεμψε στρατηγοὺς μετὰ δυνάμεως ἐπ᾽ αὐτοὺς
Ἀριστείδην καὶ Σύμμαχον. οὗτοι δὲ καταπλεύσαντες εἰς τὴν Λέσβον καὶ προσβολὰς ποιησάμενοι
συνεχεῖς εἷλον τὴν Ἄντανδρον, καὶ τῶν φυγάδων
τοὺς μὲν ἀπέκτειναν, τοὺς δ᾽ ἐκ τῆς πόλεως ἐξέβαλον, αὐτοὶ δὲ φρουρὰν ἀπολιπόντες τὴν φυλάξουσαν τὸ χωρίον ἀπέπλευσαν ἐκ τῆς Λέσβου.

4 μετὰ δὲ ταῦτα Λάμαχος ὁ στρατηγὸς ἔχων δέκα
τριήρεις ἔπλευσεν εἰς τὸν Πόντον, καὶ καθορμισθεὶς
εἰς Ἡράκλειαν περὶ τὸν ποταμὸν τὸν ὀνομαζόμενον
Κάλητα[1] πάσας τὰς ναῦς ἀπέβαλε· μεγάλων γὰρ
ὄμβρων καταρραγέντων, καὶ τοῦ ποταμοῦ βίαιον

---

[1] So Palmer (Thuc. 4. 75. 2): Κάχητα.

Of the historians Antiochus of Syracuse concluded 424 B.C. with this year his history of Sicily, which began with Cocalus,[1] the king of the Sicani, and embraced nine Books.

72. When Ameinias was archon in Athens, the 423 B.C. Romans elected as consuls Gaius Papirius and Lucius Junius. In this year the people of Scionê, holding the Athenians in contempt because of their defeat at Delium, revolted to the Lacedaemonians and delivered their city into the hands of Brasidas, who was in command of the Lacedaemonian forces in Thrace.

In Lesbos, after the Athenian seizure of Mytilenê, the exiles, who had escaped the capture in large numbers, had for some time been trying to return to Lesbos, and they succeeded at this time in rallying and seizing Antandrus,[2] from which as their base they then carried on war with the Athenians who were in possession of Mytilenê. Exasperated by this state of affairs the Athenian people sent against them as generals Aristeides and Symmachus with an army. They put in at Lesbos and by means of sustained assaults took possession of Antandrus, and of the exiles some they put to death and others they expelled from the city; then they left a garrison to guard the place and sailed away from Lesbos. After this Lamachus the general sailed with ten triremes into the Pontus and anchored at Heracleia,[3] on the river Cales, as it is called, but he lost all his ships; for when heavy rains fell, the river brought down so

[1] Cp. Book 4. 78 f.
[2] On the south coast of the Troad, some fifteen miles from Lesbos.
[3] More accurately, with Thucydides, 4. 75. 2, " in the territory of Heracleia," since the city lay on the Lycus, not the Cales, River.

τὴν καταφορὰν τοῦ ῥεύματος ποιησαμένου, τὰ σκάφη κατά τινας τραχεῖς τόπους προσπεσόντα τῇ
γῇ διεφθάρη.

5 Ἀθηναῖοι δὲ πρὸς Λακεδαιμονίους σπονδὰς ἐνι-
αυσίους ἐποιήσαντο κατὰ ταύτας τὰς ὁμολογίας,
ὥστ᾽ ἔχειν ἑκατέρους ὧν τότε κύριοι καθειστήκεσαν. συνιόντες δὲ πολλάκις εἰς λόγους ᾤοντο
δεῖν καταλῦσαι τὸν πόλεμον καὶ εἰς τέλος παύσασθαι τῆς πρὸς ἀλλήλους φιλοτιμίας· Λακεδαιμόνιοι
δὲ ἔσπευδον ἀπολαβεῖν τοὺς ἐν τῇ Σφακτηρίᾳ γε-
6 νομένους αἰχμαλώτους. τῶν δὲ σπονδῶν τὸν εἰρημένον τρόπον συντελεσθεισῶν, περὶ μὲν τῶν ἄλλων
αὐτοῖς ὁμολογούμενα πάντα ὑπῆρξε, περὶ δὲ τῆς
Σκιώνης ἠμφισβήτουν ἀμφότεροι. γενομένης δὲ
μεγάλης φιλοτιμίας τὰς σπονδὰς κατελύσαντο, περὶ
δὲ τῆς Σκιώνης διεπολέμουν πρὸς ἀλλήλους.

7 Κατὰ δὲ τοῦτον τὸν χρόνον καὶ Μένδη πόλις
πρὸς τοὺς Λακεδαιμονίους ἀπέστη καὶ τὴν φιλοτιμίαν τὴν ὑπὲρ τῆς Σκιώνης ἰσχυροτέραν ἐποίησε.
διὸ καὶ Βρασίδας μὲν ἐκ τῆς Μένδης καὶ τῆς
Σκιώνης ἀποκομίσας τέκνα καὶ γυναῖκας καὶ
τἆλλα τὰ χρησιμώτατα φρουραῖς ἀξιολόγοις ἠσφα-
8 λίσατο τὰς πόλεις, Ἀθηναῖοι δὲ παροξυνθέντες
ἐπὶ τοῖς γεγονόσιν ἐψηφίσαντο πάντας τοὺς Σκιωναίους, ὅταν ἁλῶσιν, ἡβηδὸν ἀποσφάξαι, καὶ
δύναμιν ἐξέπεμψαν ἐπ᾽ αὐτοὺς ναυτικὴν τριήρων
πεντήκοντα· τούτων δὲ τὴν στρατηγίαν εἶχε
9 Νικίας καὶ Νικόστρατος. οὗτοι δὲ πλεύσαντες
ἐπὶ πρώτην τὴν Μένδην ἐκράτησαν τῆς πόλεως

violent a current that his vessels were driven on certain rocky places and broken to pieces on the bank.

The Athenians concluded a truce with the Lacedaemonians for a year, on the terms that both of them should remain in possession of the places of which they were masters at the time. They held many discussions and were of the opinion that they should stop the war and put an end to their mutual rivalry; and the Lacedaemonians were eager to recover their citizens who had been taken captive at Sphacteria. When the truce had been concluded on the terms here mentioned, they were in entire agreement on all other matters, but both of them laid claim to Scionê.[1] And so bitter a controversy followed that they renounced the truce and continued their war against each other over the issue of Scionê.

At this time the city of Mendê [2] also revolted to the Lacedaemonians and made the quarrel over Scionê the more bitter. Consequently Brasidas removed the children and women and all the most valuable property from Mendê and Scionê and safeguarded the cities with strong garrisons, whereupon the Athenians, being incensed at what had taken place, voted to put to the sword all the Scionaeans from the youth upward, when they should take the city, and sent a naval force of fifty triremes against them, the command of which was held by Nicias and Nicostratus. They sailed to Mendê first and conquered it with the aid of certain men who betrayed

[1] This city, on the promontory of Pallenê, revolted to Brasidas before it had learned of the signing of the truce, but in fact two days, as was later reckoned, after its signing (Thucydides, 4. 120 ff.).

[2] On the Thermaic Gulf west of Scionê.

προδόντων τινῶν αὐτήν· τὴν δὲ Σκιώνην περιετείχισαν, καὶ προσκαθήμενοι τῇ πολιορκίᾳ συνεχεῖς
10 προσβολὰς ἐποιοῦντο. οἱ δ' ἐν τῇ Σκιώνῃ φρου-
ροί, πολλοὶ μὲν τὸν ἀριθμὸν ὄντες, εὐπορίαν δ'
ἔχοντες βελῶν καὶ σίτου καὶ τῆς ἄλλης παρασκευῆς, ῥᾳδίως ἠμύνοντο τοὺς Ἀθηναίους, καὶ
στάσιν ὑπερδέξιον ἔχοντες πολλοὺς κατετίτρωσκον.
Ταῦτα μὲν οὖν ἐπράχθη κατὰ τοῦτον τὸν ἐνιαυτόν.

73. Μετὰ δὲ ταῦτα Ἀθήνησι μὲν ἦρχεν Ἀλκαῖος,
ἐν Ῥώμῃ δὲ ὑπῆρχον ὕπατοι Ὀπίτερος Λουκρήτιος
καὶ Λεύκιος Σέργιος Φιδηνιάτης. ἐπὶ δὲ τούτων
Ἀθηναῖοι τοῖς Δηλίοις ἐγκαλοῦντες ὅτι λάθρα
πρὸς Λακεδαιμονίους συντίθενται συμμαχίαν, ἐξέβαλον αὐτοὺς ἐκ τῆς νήσου καὶ τὴν πόλιν αὐτοὶ
κατέσχον. τοῖς δ' ἐκπεσοῦσι Δηλίοις Φαρνιάκης
ὁ σατράπης ἔδωκεν οἰκεῖν πόλιν Ἀδραμύτιον.
2   Οἱ δ' Ἀθηναῖοι προχειρισάμενοι στρατηγὸν Κλέ-
ωνα τὸν δημαγωγόν, καὶ δόντες ἀξιόλογον δύναμιν
πεζήν, ἐξέπεμψαν εἰς τοὺς ἐπὶ Θράκης τόπους. οὗτος δὲ πλεύσας εἰς Σκιώνην, κἀκεῖθεν προσλαβόμενος στρατιώτας ἐκ τῶν πολιορκούντων τὴν πόλιν,
ἀπέπλευσε καὶ κατῆρεν εἰς Τορώνην· ἐγίνωσκε
γὰρ τὸν μὲν Βρασίδαν ἐκ τούτων τῶν τόπων
ἀπεληλυθότα, πρὸς δὲ τῇ Τορώνῃ τοὺς ἀπολε-
λειμμένους στρατιώτας οὐκ ὄντας ἀξιομάχους.
3   πλησίον δὲ τῆς Τορώνης καταστρατοπεδεύσας καὶ
πολιορκήσας ἅμα κατὰ γῆν καὶ κατὰ θάλατταν,
εἷλε κατὰ κράτος τὴν πόλιν, καὶ τοὺς μὲν παῖδας
καὶ τὰς γυναῖκας ἠνδραποδίσατο, αὐτοὺς δὲ καὶ
τοὺς τὴν πόλιν φρουροῦντας αἰχμαλώτους λαβών,
δήσας ἀπέστειλεν εἰς τὰς Ἀθήνας· τῆς δὲ πόλεως

it; then they threw a wall about Scionê, settled 423 B.C. down to a siege, and launched unceasing assaults upon it. But the garrison of Scionê, which was strong in numbers and abundantly provided with missiles and food and all other supplies, had no difficulty in repulsing the Athenians and, because they held a higher position, in wounding many of their men.

Such, then, were the events of this year.

73. The next year Alcaeus was archon in Athens 422 B.C. and in Rome the consuls were Opiter Lucretius and Lucius Sergius Fideniates. During this year the Athenians, accusing the Delians of secretly concluding an alliance with the Lacedaemonians, expelled them from the island and took their city for their own. To the Delians who had been expelled the satrap Pharniaces gave the city of Adramytium [1] to dwell in.

The Athenians elected as general Cleon, the leader of the popular party, and supplying him with a strong body of infantry sent him to the regions lying off Thrace. He sailed to Scionê, where he added to his force soldiers from the besiegers of the city, and then sailed away and put in at Toronê; for he knew that Brasidas had gone from these parts and that the soldiers who were left in Toronê were not strong enough to offer battle. After encamping near Toronê and besieging the city both by land and by sea, he took it by storm, and the children and women he sold into slavery, but the men who garrisoned the city he took captive, fettered them, and sent them to Athens.

[1] On the coast of Asia Minor north-east of Lesbos.

ἀπολιπὼν τὴν ἱκανὴν φρουρὰν ἐξέπλευσε μετὰ τῆς
δυνάμεως, καὶ κατῆρε τῆς Θρᾴκης ἐπὶ Στρυμόνα
ποταμόν. καταστρατοπεδεύσας δὲ πλησίον πόλεως
Ἠϊόνος, ἀπεχούσης ἀπὸ τῆς Ἀμφιπόλεως σταδίους
ὡς τριάκοντα, προσβολὰς ἐποιεῖτο τῷ πολίσματι.

74. Πυθόμενος δὲ τὸν Βρασίδαν μετὰ δυνάμεως
διατρίβειν περὶ πόλιν Ἀμφίπολιν, ἀνέζευξεν ἐπ᾽
αὐτόν. ὁ δὲ Βρασίδας ὡς ἤκουσε προσιόντας
τοὺς πολεμίους, ἐκτάξας τὴν δύναμιν ἀπήντα τοῖς
Ἀθηναίοις· γενομένης δὲ παρατάξεως μεγάλης,
καὶ τῶν στρατοπέδων ἀγωνισαμένων ἀμφοτέρων
λαμπρῶς, τὸ μὲν πρῶτον ἰσόρροπος ἦν ἡ μάχη,
μετὰ δὲ ταῦτα παρ᾽ ἑκατέροις τῶν ἡγεμόνων
φιλοτιμουμένων δι᾽ ἑαυτῶν κρῖναι τὴν μάχην,
συνέβη πολλοὺς τῶν ἀξιολόγων ἀνδρῶν ἀναιρε-
θῆναι, τῶν στρατηγῶν αὐτοὺς καταστησάντων
εἰς τὴν μάχην καὶ ὑπὲρ τῆς νίκης ἀνυπέρβλητον
2 φιλοτιμίαν εἰσενεγκαμένων. ὁ μὲν οὖν[1] Βρασίδας
ἀριστεύσας καὶ πλείστους ἀνελὼν ἡρωικῶς κατέστρεψε τὸν βίον· ὁμοίως δὲ καὶ τοῦ Κλέωνος ἐν
τῇ μάχῃ πεσόντος, ἀμφότεραι μὲν αἱ δυνάμεις
διὰ τὴν ἀναρχίαν ἐταράχθησαν, τὸ τέλος δ᾽ ἐνίκησαν οἱ Λακεδαιμόνιοι καὶ τρόπαιον ἔστησαν.
οἱ δ᾽ Ἀθηναῖοι τοὺς νεκροὺς ὑποσπόνδους ἀνελόμενοι καὶ θάψαντες ἀπέπλευσαν εἰς τὰς Ἀθήνας.
3 εἰς δὲ τὴν Λακεδαίμονα παραγενομένων τινῶν ἐκ
τῆς μάχης καὶ τὴν Βρασίδου νίκην ἅμα καὶ τελευτὴν ἀπαγγειλάντων, ἡ μήτηρ τοῦ Βρασίδου πυνθα-
νομένη περὶ τῶν πραχθέντων κατὰ τὴν μάχην
ἐπηρώτησε, ποῖός τις γέγονεν ἐν τῇ παρατάξει
Βρασίδας· τῶν δ᾽ ἀποκριναμένων ὅτι πάντων

[1] οὖν added by Dindorf.

Then, leaving an adequate garrison for the city, he 422 B.C. sailed away with his army and put in at the Strymon River in Thrace. Pitching camp near the city of Eïon, which is about thirty stades distant from Amphipolis, he launched successive assaults upon the town.

74. Cleon, learning that Brasidas and his army were tarrying at the city of Amphipolis, broke camp and marched against him. And when Brasidas heard of the approach of the enemy, he formed his army in battle-order and went out to meet the Athenians. A fierce battle ensued, in which both armies engaged brilliantly, and at first the fight was evenly balanced, but later, as the leaders on both sides strove to decide the battle through their own efforts, it was the lot of many important men to be slain, the generals injecting themselves into the battle and bringing into it a rivalry for victory that could not be surpassed. Brasidas, after fighting with the greatest distinction and slaying a very large number, ended his life heroically ; and when Cleon also, after displaying like valour, fell in the battle, both armies were thrown into confusion because they had no leaders, but in the end the Lacedaemonians were victorious and set up a trophy. The Athenians got back their dead under a truce, gave them burial, and sailed away to Athens. And when certain men from the scene of the battle arrived at Lacedaemon and brought the news of Brasidas' victory as well as of his death, the mother of Brasidas, on learning of the course of the battle, inquired what sort of a man Brasidas had shown himself to be in the conflict. And when she was told that of all the Lacedaemonians he was the

Λακεδαιμονίων ἄριστος, εἶπεν ἡ μήτηρ τοῦ τετελευτηκότος ὅτι Βρασίδας ὁ υἱὸς αὐτῆς ἦν ἀγαθὸς
ἀνήρ, πολλῶν μέντοι γε ἑτέρων καταδεέστερος.
4 τῶν δὲ λόγων τούτων διαδοθέντων κατὰ τὴν πόλιν
οἱ ἔφοροι δημοσίᾳ τὴν γυναῖκα ἐτίμησαν, ὅτι προ-
έκρινε τὸν τῆς πατρίδος ἔπαινον τῆς τοῦ τέκνου
δόξης.
5 Μετὰ δὲ τὴν εἰρημένην μάχην ἔδοξαν οἱ Ἀθηναῖοι τοῖς Λακεδαιμονίοις συνθέσθαι σπονδὰς πεν-
τηκονταετεῖς ἐπὶ τοῖσδε· τοὺς μὲν αἰχμαλώτους
παρ' ἀμφοτέροις ἀπολυθῆναι, τὰς δὲ πόλεις ἀπο-
6 δοῦναι τὰς κατὰ πόλεμον ληφθείσας. ὁ μὲν οὖν
Πελοποννησιακὸς πόλεμος, διαμείνας μέχρι τῶν
ὑποκειμένων καιρῶν ἔτη δέκα, τὸν εἰρημένον
τρόπον κατελύθη.

75. Ἐπ' ἄρχοντος δ' Ἀθήνησιν Ἀριστίωνος Ῥωμαῖοι κατέστησαν ὑπάτους Τίτον Κοΐντιον καὶ
Αὖλον Κορνήλιον Κόσσον. ἐπὶ δὲ τούτων ἄρτι
τοῦ πολέμου τοῦ Πελοποννησιακοῦ καταλελυμέ-
νου πάλιν ταραχαὶ καὶ κινήσεις πολεμικαὶ συν-
έβησαν κατὰ τὴν Ἑλλάδα διὰ τοιαύτας τινὰς
2 αἰτίας. Ἀθηναῖοι καὶ Λακεδαιμόνιοι κοινῇ μετὰ
τῶν συμμάχων πεποιημένοι σπονδὰς καὶ διαλύσεις,
χωρὶς τῶν συμμαχίδων πόλεων συνέθεντο συμμαχίαν. τοῦτο δὲ πράξαντες εἰς ὑπόνοιαν ἦλθον
ὡς ἐπὶ καταδουλώσει τῶν ἄλλων Ἑλλήνων ἰδίᾳ[1]
3 πεποιημένοι συμμαχίαν. διόπερ αἱ μέγισται τῶν
πόλεων διεπρεσβεύοντο πρὸς ἀλλήλας καὶ συνδιε-
λέγοντο περὶ ὁμονοίας καὶ συμμαχίας κατὰ τῶν
Ἀθηναίων καὶ Λακεδαιμονίων. ἦσαν δὲ προ-
εστῶσαι πόλεις ταύτης αἱ δυνατώταται τέτταρες,
Ἄργος, Θῆβαι, Κόρινθος, Ἦλις.

best, the mother of the dead man said, " My son 422 B.C.
Brasidas was a brave man, and yet he was inferior to
many others." When this reply passed throughout
the city, the ephors accorded the woman public
honours, because she placed the fair name of her
country above the fame of her son.

After the battle we have described the Athenians
decided to make a truce of fifty years with the
Lacedaemonians, upon the following terms : The
prisoners with both sides were to be released and each
side should give back the cities which had been taken
in the course of the war. Thus the Peloponnesian
War, which had continued up to that time for ten
years, came to an end in the manner we have
described.

75. When Aristion was archon in Athens, the 421 B.C.
Romans elected as consuls Titus Quinctius and Aulus
Cornelius Cossus. During this year, although the
Peloponnesian War had just come to an end, again
tumults and military movements occurred throughout
Greece, for the following reasons. Although the
Athenians and Lacedaemonians had concluded a truce
and cessation of hostilities in company with their
allies, they had formed an alliance without consultation with the allied cities. By this act they fell under
suspicion of having formed an alliance for their private
ends, with the purpose of enslaving the rest of the
Greeks. As a consequence the most important of
the cities maintained a mutual exchange of embassies
and conversations regarding a union of policy and an
alliance against the Athenians and Lacedaemonians.
The leading states in this undertaking were the four
most powerful ones, Argos, Thebes, Corinth, and Elis.

---

¹ So Dindorf; omitted JK, ἰδίαν other MSS.

4 Εὐλόγως δ' ὑπωπτεύθησαν αἱ πόλεις συμφρονεῖν
κατὰ τῆς Ἑλλάδος διὰ τὸ προσγεγράφθαι ταῖς
κοιναῖς συνθήκαις· ἐξεῖναι Ἀθηναίοις καὶ Λακεδαιμονίοις, ὅπερ ἂν δοκῇ ταύταις ταῖς πόλεσι,
προσγράφειν ταῖς συνθήκαις καὶ ἀφαιρεῖν ἀπὸ τῶν
συνθηκῶν. χωρὶς δὲ τούτων Ἀθηναῖοι μὲν διὰ
ψηφίσματος ἔδωκαν δέκα ἀνδράσιν ἐξουσίαν ἔχειν
βουλεύεσθαι περὶ τῶν τῇ πόλει συμφερόντων· τὸ
παραπλήσιον δὲ καὶ τῶν Λακεδαιμονίων πεποιη-
κότων φανερὰν συνέβη γενέσθαι τῶν δύο πόλεων
5 τὴν πλεονεξίαν. πολλῶν δὲ πόλεων ὑπακουουσῶν
πρὸς τὴν κοινὴν ἐλευθερίαν, καὶ τῶν μὲν Ἀθηναίων
καταφρονουμένων διὰ τὴν περὶ τὸ Δήλιον συμφοράν, τῶν δὲ Λακεδαιμονίων τεταπεινωμένων τῇ
δόξῃ διὰ τὴν ἅλωσιν τῶν ἐν τῇ Σφακτηρίᾳ νήσῳ,
πολλαὶ πόλεις συνίσταντο, καὶ προῆγον τὴν τῶν
6 Ἀργείων πόλιν ἐπὶ τὴν ἡγεμονίαν. εἶχε[1] γὰρ ἡ
πόλις αὕτη μέγα ἀξίωμα διὰ τὰς παλαιὰς πράξεις·
πρὸ γὰρ τῆς Ἡρακλειδῶν κατηλύσεως[2] ἐκ τῆς
Ἀργείας ὑπῆρξαν σχεδὸν ἅπαντες οἱ μέγιστοι τῶν
βασιλέων· πρὸς δὲ τούτοις πολὺν χρόνον εἰρήνην
ἔχουσα προσόδους μεγίστας ἐλάμβανε, καὶ πλῆθος οὐ μόνον χρημάτων εἶχεν, ἀλλὰ καὶ ἀνδρῶν.
7 οἱ δ' Ἀργεῖοι νομίζοντες αὐτοῖς συγχωρηθήσε-
σθαι τὴν ὅλην ἡγεμονίαν, ἐπέλεξαν τῶν πολιτῶν
χιλίους τοὺς νεωτέρους καὶ μάλιστα τοῖς τε σώμασιν ἰσχύοντας καὶ ταῖς οὐσίαις· ἀπολύσαντες δὲ
αὐτοὺς καὶ τῆς ἄλλης λειτουργίας καὶ τροφὰς
δημοσίας χορηγοῦντες προσέταξαν γυμνάζεσθαι

---

[1] So Dindorf: ἔχει.   [2] So Wesseling: καταλύσεως.

[1] See chap. 63.   [2] See Book 4. 57 ff.

There was good reason to suspect that Athens and Lacedaemon had common designs against the rest of Greece, since a clause had been added to the compact which the two had made, namely, that the Athenians and Lacedaemonians had the right, according as these states may deem it best, to add to or subtract from the agreements. Moreover, the Athenians by decree had lodged in ten men the power to take counsel regarding what would be of advantage to the city ; and since much the same thing had also been done by the Lacedaemonians, the selfish ambitions of the two states were open for all to see. Many cities answered to the call of their common freedom, and since the Athenians were disdained by reason of the defeat they had suffered at Delium and the Lacedaemonians had had their fame reduced because of the capture of their citizens on the island of Sphacteria,[1] a large number of cities joined together and selected the city of the Argives to hold the position of leader. For this city enjoyed a high position by reason of its achievements in the past, since until the return of the Heracleidae [2] practically all the most important kings had come from the Argolis, and furthermore, since the city had enjoyed peace for a long time, it had received revenues of the greatest size and had a great store not only of money but also of men. The Argives, believing that the entire leadership was to be conceded to them, picked out one thousand of their younger citizens who were at the same time the most vigorous in body and the most wealthy, and freeing them also from every other service to the state and supplying them with sustenance at public expense, they had them undergo continuous training and exer-

συνεχεῖς μελέτας. οὗτοι μὲν οὖν διὰ τὴν χορηγίαν καὶ τὴν συνεχῆ μελέτην ταχὺ τῶν πολεμικῶν ἔργων ἀθληταὶ κατεστάθησαν.

76. Λακεδαιμόνιοι δὲ ὁρῶντες ἐπ' αὐτοὺς συνισταμένην τὴν Πελοπόννησον καὶ προορώμενοι τὸ μέγεθος τοῦ πολέμου, τὰ κατὰ τὴν ἡγεμονίαν ὡς ἦν δυνατὸν ἠσφαλίζοντο. καὶ πρῶτον μὲν τοὺς μετὰ Βρασίδα κατὰ τὴν Θρᾴκην ἐστρατευμένους Εἵλωτας ὄντας χιλίους ἠλευθέρωσαν, μετὰ δὲ ταῦτα τοὺς ἐν τῇ Σφακτηρίᾳ νήσῳ ληφθέντας αἰχμαλώτους Σπαρτιάτας ἀτιμίᾳ περιβεβληκότες, ὡς τὴν Σπάρτην ἀδοξοτέραν πεποιηκότας, ἀπ-
2 έλυσαν τῆς ἀτιμίας. ἀκολούθως δὲ τούτοις τοῖς κατὰ τὸν πόλεμον ἐπαίνοις καὶ τιμαῖς προετρέποντο τὰς προγεγενημένας ἀνδραγαθίας ἐν τοῖς μέλλουσιν ἀγῶσιν ὑπερβάλλεσθαι· τοῖς τε συμμάχοις ἐπιεικέστερον προσεφέροντο, καὶ ταῖς φιλανθρωπίαις τοὺς ἀλλοτριωτάτους αὐτῶν ἐθερά-
3 πευον. Ἀθηναῖοι δὲ τοὐναντίον τῷ φόβῳ βουλόμενοι καταπλήξασθαι τοὺς ἐν ὑποψίᾳ ἀποστάσεως ὄντας, παράδειγμα πᾶσιν ἀνέδειξαν τὴν ἐκ τῶν Σκιωναίων τιμωρίαν· ἐκπολιορκήσαντες γὰρ αὐτοὺς καὶ πάντας ἡβηδὸν κατασφάξαντες, παῖδας μὲν καὶ γυναῖκας ἐξηνδραποδίσαντο, τὴν δὲ νῆσον οἰκεῖν παρέδοσαν τοῖς Πλαταιεῦσιν, ἐκπεπτωκόσι δι' ἐκείνους ἐκ τῆς πατρίδος.
4 Περὶ δὲ τοὺς αὐτοὺς χρόνους κατὰ τὴν Ἰταλίαν Καμπανοὶ μεγάλῃ δυνάμει στρατεύσαντες ἐπὶ Κύμην ἐνίκησαν μάχῃ τοὺς Κυμαίους καὶ τοὺς[1]

---

[1] τοὺς added by Dindorf.

---

[1] Scionê was a *cherso-nesos* (" near-island ").
[2] See chap. 56.

cise. These young men, therefore, by reason of the 421 B.C.
expense incurred for them and their continuous training, quickly formed a body of athletes trained to
deeds of war.

76. The Lacedaemonians, seeing the Peloponnesus uniting against them and foreseeing the
magnitude of the impending war, began exerting
every possible effort to make sure their position of
leadership. And first of all the Helots who had
served with Brasidas in Thrace, a thousand in all,
were given their freedom ; then the Spartans, who
had been taken prisoner on the island of Sphacteria
and had been disgraced on the ground that they had
diminished the glory of Sparta, were freed from their
state of disgrace. Also, in pursuance of the same
policy, by means of the commendations and honours
accorded in the course of the war they were incited
to surpass in the struggles which lay before them the
deeds of valour they had already performed ; and
toward their allies they conducted themselves more
equitably and conciliated the most unfavourably disposed of them with kindly treatment. The Athenians,
on the contrary, desiring to strike with fear those
whom they suspected of planning secession, displayed
an example for all to see in the punishment they
inflicted on the inhabitants of Scionê ; for after reducing them by siege, they put to the sword all of
them from the youth upwards, sold into slavery the
children and women, and gave the island [1] to the
Plataeans to dwell in, since they had been expelled
from their native land on account of the Athenians.[2]

In the course of this year in Italy the Campanians
advanced against Cymê with a strong army, defeated
the Cymaeans in battle, and destroyed the larger part

93

πλείους τῶν ἀντιταχθέντων κατέκοψαν. προσκαθεζόμενοι δὲ τῇ πολιορκίᾳ καὶ πλείους προσβολὰς
ποιησάμενοι κατὰ κράτος εἷλον τὴν πόλιν. διαρπάσαντες δ' αὐτὴν καὶ τοὺς καταληφθέντας ἐξανδραποδισάμενοι τοὺς ἱκανοὺς οἰκήτορας ἐξ αὐτῶν
ἀπέδειξαν.

77. Ἐπ' ἄρχοντος δ' Ἀθήνησιν Ἀστυφίλου Ῥωμαῖοι κατέστησαν ὑπάτους Λεύκιον Κοΐντιον καὶ
Αὖλον Σεμπρώνιον, Ἠλεῖοι δ' ἤγαγον Ὀλυμπιάδα
ἐνενηκοστήν, καθ' ἣν ἐνίκα στάδιον Ὑπέρβιος
Συρακόσιος. ἐπὶ δὲ τούτων Ἀθηναῖοι μὲν κατά
τινα χρησμὸν Δηλίοις ἀπέδοσαν τὴν νῆσον, καὶ
κατῆλθον εἰς τὴν πατρίδα οἱ τὸ Ἀδραμύτιον
2 οἰκοῦντες Δήλιοι. τῶν δὲ Ἀθηναίων οὐκ ἀπο-
δόντων Λακεδαιμονίοις τὴν Πύλον, πάλιν αἱ
πόλεις αὗται πρὸς ἀλλήλας διεφέροντο καὶ πολε-
μικῶς εἶχον. ἃ δὴ πυθόμενος ὁ δῆμος τῶν
Ἀργείων ἔπεισε τοὺς Ἀθηναίους φιλίαν συνθέσθαι
3 πρὸς τοὺς Ἀργείους. αὐξομένης δὲ τῆς διαφορᾶς,
οἱ μὲν Λακεδαιμόνιοι τοὺς Κορινθίους ἔπεισαν
ἐγκαταλιπεῖν τὴν κοινὴν σύνοδον καὶ συμμαχεῖν
τοῖς Λακεδαιμονίοις. τοιαύτης δὲ ταραχῆς γενομένης καὶ ἀναρχίας οὔσης, τὰ κατὰ τὴν Πελοπόννησον ἐν τούτοις ἦν.

4 Ἐν δὲ τοῖς ἐκτὸς τόποις Αἰνιᾶνες καὶ Δόλοπες
καὶ Μηλιεῖς συμφρονήσαντες δυνάμεσιν ἀξιολόγοις
ἐστράτευσαν ἐπὶ τὴν Ἡράκλειαν τὴν ἐν Τραχῖνι.[1]
ἀντιταχθέντων δὲ τῶν Ἡρακλεωτῶν καὶ μάχης
γενομένης ἰσχυρᾶς, ἡττήθησαν οἱ τὴν Ἡράκλειαν

---

[1] So Dindorf: Τραχινίᾳ.

[1] Cp. chap. 73. 1.   [2] See chap. 75 at end.

of the opposing forces.   And settling down to a siege, 421 B.C
they launched a number of assaults upon the city and
took it by storm.   They then plundered the city, sold
into slavery the captured prisoners, and selected
an adequate number of their own citizens to settle
there.

77. When Astyphilus was archon in Athens, the 420 B.C.
Romans elected as consuls Lucius Quinctius and
Aulus Sempronius, and the Eleians celebrated the
Ninetieth Olympiad, that in which Hyperbius of
Syracuse won the " stadion." This year the Athenians, in obedience to a certain oracle, returned
their island to the Delians, and the Delians who
were dwelling in Adramytium [1] returned to their
native land.   And since the Athenians had not returned the city of Pylos to the Lacedaemonians, these
cities were again at odds with each other and hostile.
When this was known to the Assembly of the Argives,
that body persuaded the Athenians to close a treaty
of friendship with the Argives.   And since the quarrel
kept growing, the Lacedaemonians persuaded the
Corinthians to desert the league of states [2] and ally
themselves with the Lacedaemonians.   Such being
the confusion that had arisen together with a lack
of leadership, the situation throughout the Peloponnesus was as has been described.

In the regions outside,[3] the Aenianians, Dolopians,
and Melians, having come to an understanding,
advanced with strong armaments against Heracleia
in Trachis.   The Heracleians drew up to oppose them
and a great battle took place, in which the people of

[3] Since the following three tribes are of southern Thessaly,
apparently Diodorus does not consider that area to be a part
of Greece proper.

κατοικοῦντες. πολλοὺς δ' ἀποβαλόντες στρατιώτας καὶ συμφυγόντες ἐντὸς τῶν τειχῶν,
μετεπέμψαντο βοήθειαν παρὰ τῶν Βοιωτῶν. ἀποστειλάντων δ' αὐτοῖς τῶν Θηβαίων χιλίους ὁπλίτας
ἐπιλέκτους, μετ' αὐτῶν ἠμύνοντο τοὺς ἐπεστρα-
τευκότας.

5 Ἅμα δὲ τούτοις πραττομένοις Ὀλύνθιοι μὲν
στρατεύσαντες ἐπὶ πόλιν Μηκύβερναν, φρουρου-
μένην ὑπ' Ἀθηναίων, τὴν μὲν φρουρὰν ἐξέβαλον,
αὐτοὶ δὲ τὴν πόλιν κατέσχον.

78. Ἐπ' ἄρχοντος δ' Ἀθήνησιν Ἀρχίου Ῥωμαῖοι
κατέστησαν ὑπάτους Λεύκιον Παπίριον Μουγιλανὸν
καὶ Γάιον Σερουίλιον Στροῦκτον. ἐπὶ δὲ τούτων
Ἀργεῖοι μὲν ἐγκαλέσαντες τοῖς Λακεδαιμονίοις
ὅτι τὰ θύματα οὐκ ἀπέδοσαν τῷ Ἀπόλλωνι τῷ
Πυθαεῖ,[1] πόλεμον αὐτοῖς κατήγγειλαν· καθ' ὃν δὴ
χρόνον Ἀλκιβιάδης ὁ στρατηγὸς τῶν Ἀθηναίων
2 ἐνέβαλεν εἰς τὴν Ἀργείαν ἔχων δύναμιν. τούτους
δὲ οἱ Ἀργεῖοι παραλαβόντες ἐστράτευσαν ἐπὶ
Τροιζῆνα, πόλιν σύμμαχον Λακεδαιμονίων, καὶ
τὴν μὲν χώραν λεηλατήσαντες, τὰς δὲ ἐπαύλεις
ἐμπρήσαντες, ἀπηλλάγησαν εἰς τὴν οἰκείαν. οἱ
δὲ Λακεδαιμόνιοι παροξυνθέντες ἐπὶ τοῖς εἰς τοὺς
Τροιζηνίους παρανομήμασιν ἔγνωσαν διαπολεμεῖν
πρὸς Ἀργείους· διὸ καὶ δύναμιν ἀθροίσαντες
3 ἐπέστησαν ἡγεμόνα Ἆγιν τὸν βασιλέα. οὗτος δὲ
μετὰ τῆς δυνάμεως ἐστράτευσεν ἐπὶ τοὺς Ἀργείους
καὶ τὴν μὲν χώραν ἐδῄωσε, πλησίον δὲ τῆς πόλεως
ἀγαγὼν τὴν δύναμιν προεκαλεῖτο τοὺς πολεμίους

---

[1] So Oldfather (Paus. 2. 35, 36): Πυθίῳ.

Heracleia were defeated. Since they had lost many 420 B.C.
soldiers and had sought refuge within their walls, they
sent for aid from the Boeotians. The Thebans dispatched to their help a thousand picked hoplites, with
whose aid they held off their adversaries.

While these events were taking place, the Olynthians dispatched an army against the city of
Mecyberna[1] which had an Athenian garrison, drove
out the garrison, and themselves took possession of
the city.

78. When Archias was archon in Athens, the 419 B.C.
Romans elected as consuls Lucius Papirius Mugilanus
and Gaius Servilius Structus. In this year the
Argives, charging the Lacedaemonians[2] with not
paying the sacrifices to Apollo Pythaeus,[3] declared
war on them; and it was at this very time that
Alcibiades, the Athenian general, entered Argolis
with an army. Adding these troops to their forces,
the Argives advanced against Troezen, a city which
was an ally of the Lacedaemonians, and after plundering its territory and burning its farm-buildings they
returned home. The Lacedaemonians, being incensed at the lawless acts committed against the
Troezenians, resolved to go to war against the
Argives; consequently they mustered an army and
put their king Agis in command. With this force
Agis advanced against the Argives and ravaged their
territory, and leading his army to the vicinity of the

[1] Situated a short distance east of Olynthus.
[2] The Epidaurians, not the Lacedaemonians (see Thucydides, 5. 53); but Diodorus frequently uses the term " Lacedaemonian " in a wide sense to refer to any ally of Sparta.
[3] The temple is likely the one in Asinê, which was the only
building spared by the Argives when they razed that city
(cp. Pausanias, 2. 36. 5; Thucydides, 5. 53. 1).

4 εἰς¹ μάχην. οἱ δ' Ἀργεῖοι προσλαβόμενοι στρατιώτας παρὰ μὲν Ἠλείων τρισχιλίους, παρὰ δὲ
Μαντινέων οὐ πολὺ λειπομένους τούτων, προῆγον
ἐκ τῆς πόλεως τὸ στρατόπεδον. μελλούσης δὲ
παρατάξεως γίνεσθαι, οἱ στρατηγοὶ παρ' ἀμφοτέροις διαπρεσβευσάμενοι τετραμηνιαίους ἀνοχὰς
5 συνέθεντο. ἐπανελθόντων δὲ τῶν στρατοπέδων
ἀπράκτων εἰς τὴν οἰκείαν, δι' ὀργῆς εἶχον αἱ
πόλεις ἀμφότεραι τοὺς συνθεμένους τὰς σπονδὰς
στρατηγούς. διόπερ οἱ μὲν Ἀργεῖοι τοῖς λίθοις
βάλλοντες τοὺς ἡγεμόνας ἀποκτείνειν ἐπεχείρησαν, καὶ μόγις μεταξὺ² πολλῆς δεήσεως τὸ ζῆν συνεχώρησαν, τὴν δ' οὐσίαν αὐτῶν δημεύσαντες
6 κατέσκαψαν τὰς οἰκίας. οἱ δὲ Λακεδαιμόνιοι τὸν
Ἆγιν ἐπεβάλοντο μὲν κολάζειν, ἐπαγγειλαμένου
δ' αὐτοῦ διὰ τῶν καλῶν ἔργων διορθώσασθαι τὴν
ἁμαρτίαν, μόγις συνεχώρησαν, εἰς δὲ τὸν λοιπὸν
χρόνον ἑλόμενοι δέκα ἄνδρας τοὺς συνετωτάτους,
παρακατέστησαν συμβούλους καὶ προσέταξαν μηδὲν
ἄνευ τῆς τούτων γνώμης πράττειν.

79. Μετὰ δὲ ταῦτα Ἀθηναίων ἀποστειλάντων
κατὰ θάλατταν εἰς Ἄργος³ ὁπλίτας μὲν χιλίους
ἐπιλέκτους, ἱππεῖς δὲ διακοσίους, ὧν ἐστρατήγουν
Λάχης καὶ Νικόστρατος· συνῆν δὲ τούτοις καὶ
Ἀλκιβιάδης ἰδιώτης ὢν διὰ τὴν φιλίαν τὴν πρὸς
Ἠλείους καὶ Μαντινεῖς· συνεδρευσάντων δὲ πάντων,
ἔδοξε τὰς μὲν σπονδὰς ἐᾶν χαίρειν, πρὸς δὲ τὸν
2 πόλεμον ὁρμῆσαι. διὸ καὶ τοὺς ἰδίους ἕκαστος
στρατηγὸς παρώρμησε πρὸς τὸν ἀγῶνα, καὶ πάντων προθύμως ὑπακουσάντων, ἐκτὸς τῆς πόλεως
κατεστρατοπέδευσαν. ἔδοξεν οὖν αὐτοῖς πάντων

¹ τὴν after εἰς deleted by Hertlein.

city he challenged the enemy to battle.   The Argives, 419 B.C.
adding to their army three thousand soldiers from the
Eleians and almost as many from the Mantineians,
led out their forces from the city.   When a pitched
battle was imminent, the generals conducted negotiations with each other and agreed upon a cessation
of hostilities for four months.   But when the armies
returned to their homes without accomplishing
anything, both cities were angry with the generals
who had agreed upon the truce.   Consequently the
Argives hurled stones at their commanders and began
to menace them with death ; only reluctantly and
after much supplication their lives were spared, but
their property was confiscated and their homes razed
to the ground.   The Lacedaemonians took steps to
punish Agis, but when he promised to atone for his
error by worthy deeds, they reluctantly let him off,
and for the future they chose ten of their wisest men,
whom they appointed his advisers, and they ordered
him to do nothing without learning their opinion.

79. After this the Athenians dispatched to Argos
by sea a thousand picked hoplites and two hundred
cavalry, under the command of Laches and Nicostratus ; and Alcibiades also accompanied them,
although in a private capacity, because of the friendly
relations he enjoyed with the Eleians and Mantineians ; and when they were all gathered in council,
they decided to pay no attention to the truce but to
set about making war.   Consequently each general
urged on his own troops to the conflict, and when they
all responded eagerly, they pitched camp outside
the city.   Now they agreed that they should march

---

² So Capps : μετά.
³ So Reiske : αὐτούς.

πρῶτον στρατεύειν ἐπ' Ὀρχομενὸν τῆς Ἀρκαδίας. διὸ καὶ παρελθόντες εἰς Ἀρκαδίαν, προσκαθεζόμενοι τῇ πόλει καθ' ἡμέραν ἐποιοῦντο προσβολὰς 3 τοῖς τείχεσι. χειρωσάμενοι δὲ τὴν πόλιν κατεστρατοπέδευσαν πλησίον Τεγέας, κεκρικότες καὶ ταύτην πολιορκῆσαι. τῶν δὲ Τεγεατῶν ἀξιούντων τοὺς Λακεδαιμονίους βοηθῆσαι κατὰ τάχος, οἱ Σπαρτιᾶται παραλαβόντες τοὺς ἰδίους πάντας καὶ τοὺς συμμάχους ἧκον ἐπὶ τὴν Μαντίνειαν, νομίζοντες ταύτης πολεμουμένης ἀρθήσεσθαι τὴν τῆς 4 Τεγέας πολιορκίαν. οἱ δὲ Μαντινεῖς τοὺς συμμάχους παραλαβόντες, καὶ αὐτοὶ πανδημεὶ στρατεύσαντες, ἀντετάχθησαν τοῖς Λακεδαιμονίοις. γενομένης δὲ μάχης ἰσχυρᾶς, οἱ μὲν ἐπίλεκτοι τῶν Ἀργείων, χίλιοι τὸν ἀριθμὸν ὄντες, γεγυμνασμένοι δὲ καλῶς τὰ κατὰ τὸν πόλεμον, ἐτρέψαντο τοὺς ἀντιτεταγμένους πρῶτοι, καὶ διώκοντες πολὺν 5 ἐποίουν φόνον. οἱ δὲ Λακεδαιμόνιοι τἆλλα μέρη τοῦ στρατεύματος τρεψάμενοι καὶ πολλοὺς ἀνελόντες ὑπέστρεψαν ἐπ' αὐτοὺς ἐκείνους,[1] καὶ τῷ πλήθει κυκλώσαντες ἤλπιζον κατακόψειν ἅπαντας. 6 τῶν δὲ λογάδων[2] τῷ μὲν πλήθει πολὺ λειπομένων, ταῖς δ' ἀνδραγαθίαις προεχόντων, ὁ μὲν βασιλεὺς τῶν Λακεδαιμονίων προαγωνιζόμενος ἐνεκαρτέρησε τοῖς δεινοῖς, καὶ πάντας ἂν ἀνεῖλεν· ἔσπευδε γὰρ τοῖς πολίταις ἀποδοῦναι τὰς ἐπαγγελίας, καὶ μέγα τι κατεργασάμενος διορθώσασθαι τὴν γεγενημένην ἀδοξίαν· οὐ μὴν εἰάθη γε τὴν προαίρεσιν ἐπιτελέσαι. Φάραξ γὰρ ὁ Σπαρτιάτης, εἷς ὢν τῶν συμβούλων, ἀξίωμα δὲ μέγιστον ἔχων ἐν τῇ Σπάρτῃ,

---

[1] οἱ after ἐκείνους deleted by Reiske.
[2] So Rhodoman (Thuc. 5. 67. 2): λοχαγῶν.

first of all against Orchomenus in Arcadia; and 419 B.C.
so, advancing into Arcadia, they settled down to the
siege of the city and made daily assaults upon its
walls. And after they had taken the city, they
encamped near Tegea, having decided to besiege
it also. But when the Tegeatans called upon the
Lacedaemonians for immediate aid, the Spartans
gathered all their own soldiers and those of their allies
and moved on Mantineia, believing that, once Mantineia was attacked in the war, the enemy would raise
the siege of Tegea.[1] The Mantineians gathered their
allies, and marching forth themselves *en masse*,
formed their lines opposite the Lacedaemonians. A
sharp battle followed, and the picked troops of the
Argives, one thousand in number, who had received
excellent training in warfare, were the first to put to
flight their opponents and made great slaughter of
them in their pursuit. But the Lacedaemonians,
after putting to flight the other parts of the army
and slaying many, wheeled about to oppose the
Argives and by their superior numbers surrounded
them, hoping to destroy them to a man. Now
although the picked troops of the Argives, though
in numbers far inferior, were superior in feats of
courage, the king of the Lacedaemonians led the
fight and held out firmly against the perils he encountered; and he would have slain all the Argives
—for he was resolved to fulfil the promises he had
made to his fellow citizens and wipe out, by a great
deed, his former ill repute—but he was not allowed
to consummate that purpose. For Pharax the
Spartan, who was one of the advisers of Agis and
enjoyed the highest reputation in Sparta, directed

[1] Presumably in order to bring aid to the Mantineians.

διεκελεύετο τοῖς λογάσι¹ δοῦναι δίοδον, καὶ μὴ
πρὸς ἀπεγνωκότας τὸ ζῆν διακινδυνεύοντας πεῖραν
7 λαβεῖν ἀτυχούσης ἀρετῆς. ὅθεν ἠναγκάσθη κατὰ
τὴν ἀρτίως ῥηθεῖσαν ἐπιταγὴν δοῦναι διέξοδον κατὰ
τὴν τοῦ Φάρακος γνώμην. οἱ μὲν οὖν χίλιοι τὸν
εἰρημένον τρόπον ἀφεθέντες διελθεῖν διεσώθησαν,
οἱ δὲ Λακεδαιμόνιοι μεγάλῃ μάχῃ νικήσαντες καὶ
τρόπαιον στήσαντες ἀπῆλθον εἰς τὴν οἰκείαν.

80. Τοῦ δ' ἐνιαυσίου χρόνου διεληλυθότος Ἀθήνησι μὲν ἦρχεν Ἀντιφῶν, ἐν Ῥώμῃ δ' ἀντὶ τῶν
ὑπάτων χιλίαρχοι τέτταρες κατεστάθησαν, Γάιος
Φούριος καὶ Τίτος Κοΐντιος, ἔτι δὲ Μάρκος Ποστούμιος καὶ Αὖλος Κορνήλιος. ἐπὶ δὲ τούτων
Ἀργεῖοι καὶ Λακεδαιμόνιοι διαπρεσβευσάμενοι πρὸς
ἀλλήλους εἰρήνην ἐποιήσαντο καὶ συμμαχίαν συν-
2 έθεντο. διόπερ οἱ Μαντινεῖς ἀποβαλόντες τὴν ἀπὸ
τῶν Ἀργείων βοήθειαν ἠναγκάσθησαν ὑποταγῆναι
τοῖς Λακεδαιμονίοις. περὶ δὲ τοὺς αὐτοὺς χρόνους
ἐν τῇ πόλει τῶν Ἀργείων οἱ κατ' ἐκλογὴν κεκρι-
μένοι τῶν πολιτῶν χίλιοι συνεφώνησαν, καὶ τὴν
μὲν δημοκρατίαν ἔγνωσαν καταλύειν, ἀριστοκρατίαν
3 δ' ἐξ αὐτῶν καθιστάναι. ἔχοντες δὲ πολλοὺς συν-
εργοὺς διὰ τὸ προέχειν τῶν πολιτῶν ταῖς οὐσίαις
καὶ ταῖς ἀνδραγαθίαις, τὸ μὲν πρῶτον συλλαβόντες
τοὺς δημαγωγεῖν εἰωθότας ἀπέκτειναν, τοὺς δ' ἄλλους καταπληξάμενοι κατέλυσαν τοὺς νόμους καὶ
δι' ἑαυτῶν τὰ δημόσια διῴκουν. διακατασχόντες
δὲ ταύτην τὴν πολιτείαν μῆνας ὀκτὼ κατελύθησαν,

¹ So Reiske: ἀρκάσι.

him to leave a way of escape for the picked men and 419 B.C.
not, by hazarding the issue against men who had
given up all hope of life, to learn what valour is when
abandoned by Fortune. So the king was compelled,
in obedience to the command recently given him,[1] to
leave a way of escape even as Pharax advised. So
the Thousand, having been allowed to pass through
in the manner described, made their way to safety,
and the Lacedaemonians, having won the victory in
a great battle, erected a trophy and returned home.

80. When this year had come to an end, in Athens 418 B.C.
the archon was Antiphon, and in Rome in place of
consuls four military tribunes were elected, Gaius
Furius, Titus Quinctius, Marcus Postumius, and
Aulus Cornelius. During this year the Argives and
Lacedaemonians, after negotiations with each other,
concluded a peace and formed an alliance. Consequently the Mantineians, now that they had lost the
help of the Argives, were compelled to subject themselves to the Lacedaemonians. And about the same
time in the city of the Argives the Thousand who had
been selected out of the total muster of citizens came
to an agreement among themselves and decided to
dissolve the democracy and establish an aristocracy
from their own number. And having as they did
many to aid them, because of the prominent position
their wealth and brave exploits gave them, they first
of all seized the men who had been accustomed to
be the leaders of the people and put them to death,
and then, by terrorizing the rest of the citizens, they
abolished the laws and were proceeding to take the
management of the state into their own hands. They
maintained this government for eight months and

[1] Cp. chap. 78. 6.

τοῦ δήμου συστάντος ἐπ' αὐτούς· διὸ καὶ τούτων
ἀναιρεθέντων ὁ δῆμος ἐκομίσατο τὴν δημοκρατίαν.

4 Ἐγένετο δὲ καὶ ἑτέρα κίνησις κατὰ τὴν Ἑλλάδα·
καὶ Φωκεῖς γὰρ πρὸς Λοκροὺς διενεχθέντες παρατάξει ἐκρίθησαν διὰ τὴν οἰκείαν ἀνδρείαν· ἐνίκησαν
γὰρ Φωκεῖς ἀνελόντες Λοκρῶν πλείους χιλίων.

5 Ἀθηναῖοι δὲ Νικίου στρατηγοῦντος εἷλον δύο
πόλεις, Κύθηρα καὶ Νίσαιαν· τήν τε Μῆλον ἐκπολιορκήσαντες πάντας[1] ἡβηδὸν ἀπέσφαξαν, παῖδας
δὲ καὶ γυναῖκας ἐξηνδραποδίσαντο.

6 Καὶ τὰ μὲν κατὰ τοὺς Ἕλληνας ἐν τούτοις ἦν.
κατὰ δὲ τὴν Ἰταλίαν Φιδηνᾶται μέν, παραγενομένων εἰς τὴν πόλιν αὐτῶν πρέσβεων ἐκ τῆς Ῥώμης,

7 ἐπὶ μικραῖς αἰτίαις ἀνεῖλον τούτους. ἐφ' οἷς οἱ
Ῥωμαῖοι παροξυνθέντες ἐψηφίσαντο πολεμεῖν, καὶ
προχειρισάμενοι δύναμιν ἀξιόλογον εἵλοντο δικτά-
τωρα Ἄνιον Αἰμίλιον καὶ μετὰ τούτου κατὰ τὸ

8 ἔθος Αὖλον Κορνήλιον ἵππαρχον. ὁ δ' Αἰμίλιος
παρασκευασάμενος τὰ πρὸς τὸν πόλεμον, ἀνέζευξε
μετὰ τῆς δυνάμεως ἐπὶ τοὺς Φιδηνάτας. ἀντιτα-
ξαμένων δὲ τῶν Φιδηνατῶν ἐγένετο μάχη ἐπὶ
πολὺν χρόνον ἰσχυρά, καὶ πολλῶν παρ' ἀμφοτέροις
πεσόντων ἰσόρροπος ὁ ἀγὼν ἐγένετο.

81. Ἐπ' ἄρχοντος δ' Ἀθήνησιν Εὐφήμου ἐν
Ῥώμῃ κατεστάθησαν ἀντὶ τῶν ὑπάτων χιλίαρχοι
Λεύκιος Φούριος, Λεύκιος Κοΐντιος, Αὖλος Σεμ-
πρώνιος. ἐπὶ δὲ τούτων Λακεδαιμόνιοι μετὰ τῶν
συμμάχων στρατεύσαντες εἰς τὴν Ἀργείαν Ὑσιὰς

---

[1] πάντας suggested by Vogel (ch. 76. 3).

then were overthrown, the people having united 418 B.C.
against them ; and so these men were put to death
and the people got back the democracy.

Another movement also took place in Greece. The
Phocians also, having quarrelled with the Locrians,
settled the issue in pitched battle by virtue of their
own valour. For the victory lay with the Phocians,
who slew more than one thousand Locrians.

The Athenians under the command of Nicias seized
two cities, Cythera and Nisaea [1] ; and they reduced
Melos by siege, slew all the males from the youth
upward, and sold into slavery the children and
women.[2]

Such were the affairs of the Greeks in this year.
In Italy the Fidenates, when ambassadors came to
their city from Rome, put them to death for trifling
reasons. Incensed at such an act, the Romans voted
to go to war, and mobilizing a strong army they
appointed Anius Aemilius Dictator and with him,
following their custom, Aulus Cornelius Master of
Horse. Aemilius, after making all the preparations
for the war, marched with his army against the
Fidenates. And when the Fidenates drew up their
forces to oppose the Romans, a fierce battle ensued
which continued a long time ; heavy losses were
incurred on both sides and the conflict was indecisive.

81. When Euphemus was archon in Athens, in 417 B.C
Rome in place of consuls military tribunes were
elected, Lucius Furius, Lucius Quinctius, and Aulus
Sempronius. In this year the Lacedaemonians and
their allies took the field against Argolis and captured

---

[1] The loss of Cythera was a blow to the Spartans, that of
Nisaea to the Megarians.
[2] Melos was destroyed in 416 B.C.

χωρίον εἷλον, καὶ τοὺς ἐνοικοῦντας ἀποκτείναντες
τὸ μὲν φρούριον κατέσκαψαν, αὐτοὶ δὲ πυθόμενοι
τοὺς Ἀργείους ᾠκοδομηκέναι τὰ μακρὰ τείχη μέχρι τῆς θαλάττης, ἐπελθόντες τὰ κατεσκευασμένα
τείχη κατέσκαψαν, καὶ τὴν εἰς τὴν οἰκείαν ἐπάνοδον
ἐποιήσαντο.

2 Ἀθηναῖοι δ᾽ ἑλόμενοι στρατηγὸν Ἀλκιβιάδην,
καὶ δόντες αὐτῷ ναῦς εἴκοσι, προσέταξαν συγκατα-
σκευάσαι τοῖς Ἀργείοις τὰ κατὰ τὴν πολιτείαν·
ἔτι γὰρ ἦσαν ἐν ταραχαῖς διὰ τὸ πολλοὺς ὑπολελεῖ-
3 φθαι τῶν¹ τὴν ἀριστοκρατίαν αἱρουμένων. ὁ δ᾽
οὖν Ἀλκιβιάδης καταντήσας εἰς τὴν τῶν Ἀργείων
πόλιν, καὶ συνεδρεύσας μετὰ τῶν τὴν δημοκρατίαν προκρινόντων, ἐπέλεξε τῶν Ἀργείων τοὺς μάλιστα δοκοῦντας τὰ τῶν Λακεδαιμονίων αἱρεῖσθαι·
μεταστησάμενος δὲ τούτους ἐκ τῆς πόλεως, καὶ
συγκατασκευάσας βεβαίως τὴν δημοκρατίαν, ἀπέπλευσεν εἰς τὰς Ἀθήνας.

4 Τούτου δὲ τοῦ ἔτους λήγοντος Λακεδαιμόνιοι
μετὰ πολλῆς δυνάμεως ἐμβαλόντες εἰς τὴν Ἀργείαν, καὶ πολλὴν τῆς χώρας δῃώσαντες, τοὺς
φυγάδας τῶν Ἀργείων κατῴκισαν εἰς Ὀρνεάς·
ἐπιτειχίσαντες δὲ τοῦτο τὸ χωρίον ἐπὶ τῆς Ἀργείας,
καὶ φρουροὺς τοὺς ἱκανοὺς ἀπολιπόντες, προσ-
5 έταξαν κακοποιεῖν τοὺς Ἀργείους. ἀπελθόντων
δὲ τῶν Λακεδαιμονίων ἐκ τῆς Ἀργείας, Ἀθηναῖοι
μὲν συμμαχίαν ἐξέπεμψαν τοῖς Ἀργείοις τριήρεις
τετταράκοντα, ὁπλίτας δὲ χιλίους καὶ διακοσίους·
οἱ δ᾽ Ἀργεῖοι μετὰ τῶν Ἀθηναίων στρατεύσαντες

---

¹ τῶν added by Reiske.

the stronghold of Hysiae,[1] and slaying the inhabitants 417 B.C. they razed the fortress to the ground ; and when they learned that the Argives had completed the construction of the long walls clear to the sea,[2] they advanced there, razed the walls that had been finished, and then made their way back home.

The Athenians chose Alcibiades general, and giving him twenty ships commanded him to assist the Argives in establishing the affairs of their government ; for conditions were still unsettled among them because many still remained of those who preferred the aristocracy. So when Alcibiades had arrived at the city of the Argives and had consulted with the supporters of the democracy, he selected those Argives who were considered to be the strongest adherents of the Lacedaemonian cause ; these he removed from the city,[3] and when he had assisted in establishing the democracy on a firm basis, he sailed back to Athens.

Toward the end of the year the Lacedaemonians invaded Argolis with a strong force, and after ravaging a large part of the country they settled the exiles from Argos in Orneae [4] ; this place they fortified as a stronghold against Argolis, and leaving in it a strong garrison, they ordered it to harass the Argives. But when the Lacedaemonians had withdrawn from Argolis, the Athenians dispatched to the Argives a supporting force of forty triremes and twelve hundred hoplites. The Argives then advanced against Orneae

[1] In Argolis near the Laconian border.
[2] The walls were to connect Argos and the sea. This was an enormous undertaking and the walls were certainly not yet completed (cp. below and Thucydides, 5. 82. 5).
[3] They were distributed among the islands of the Athenian Empire.
[4] In north-west Argolis on the border of Phlius.

ἐπὶ τὰς Ὀρνεὰς τήν τε πόλιν κατὰ κράτος εἷλον καὶ τῶν φρουρῶν καὶ φυγάδων οὓς μὲν ἀπέκτειναν, οὓς δ' ἐξέβαλον ἐκ τῶν Ὀρνεῶν.

Ταῦτα μὲν οὖν ἐπράχθη κατὰ τὸ πεντεκαιδέκατον ἔτος τοῦ Πελοποννησιακοῦ πολέμου.

82. Τῷ δ' ἑκκαιδεκάτῳ παρὰ μὲν Ἀθηναίοις ἦν ἄρχων Ἀρίμνηστος, ἐν Ῥώμῃ δ' ἀντὶ τῶν ὑπάτων χιλίαρχοι κατεστάθησαν τέτταρες, Τίτος Κλαύδιος καὶ Σπόριος Ναύτιος, ἔτι δὲ Λούκιος Σέντιος καὶ Σέξτος Ἰούλιος. ἐπὶ δὲ τούτων παρὰ μὲν Ἠλείοις ἤχθη Ὀλυμπιὰς πρώτη πρὸς ταῖς ἐνενήκοντα, καθ' ἣν ἐνίκα στάδιον Ἐξαίνετος Ἀκραγαντῖνος.

2 Βυζάντιοι δὲ καὶ Χαλκηδόνιοι παραλαβόντες Θρᾷκας ἐστράτευσαν εἰς τὴν Βιθυνίαν πολλοῖς πλήθεσι, καὶ τήν τε χώραν ἐπόρθησαν καὶ πολλὰ τῶν μικρῶν πολισματίων ἐκπολιορκήσαντες ἐπετελέσαντο πράξεις ὠμότητι διαφερούσας· πολλῶν γὰρ αἰχμαλώτων κρατήσαντες ἀνδρῶν τε καὶ γυναικῶν καὶ παίδων ἅπαντας ἀπέσφαξαν.

3 Περὶ δὲ τοὺς αὐτοὺς χρόνους κατὰ τὴν Σικελίαν Ἐγεσταῖοι πρὸς Σελινουντίους ἐπολέμησαν περὶ χώρας ἀμφισβητησίμου, ποταμοῦ τὴν χώραν τῶν 4 διαφερομένων πόλεων ὁρίζοντος. Σελινούντιοι δὲ διαβάντες τὸ ῥεῖθρον τὸ μὲν πρῶτον τῆς παραποταμίας βίᾳ κατέσχον, μετὰ δὲ ταῦτα καὶ τῆς προσκειμένης χώρας πολλὴν ἀποτεμόμενοι κατε- 5 φρόνησαν τῶν ἠδικημένων. οἱ δ' Ἐγεσταῖοι παροξυνθέντες τὸ μὲν πρῶτον διὰ τῶν λόγων πείθειν ἐπεβάλοντο μὴ ἐπιβαίνειν τῆς ἀλλοτρίας γῆς· ὡς δὲ οὐδεὶς αὐτοῖς προσεῖχεν, ἐστράτευσαν ἐπὶ τοὺς κατέχοντας τὴν χώραν, καὶ πάντας ἐκβαλόντες ἐκ τῶν 6 ἀγρῶν αὐτοὶ τὴν χώραν κατέσχον. γενομένης δὲ

together with the Athenians and took the city by 417 B.C.
storm, and of the garrison and exiles some they put
to death and others they expelled from Orneae.

These, then, were the events of the fifteenth year
of the Peloponnesian War.

82. In the sixteenth year of the War Arimnestus 416 B.C.
was archon among the Athenians, and in Rome in
place of consuls four military tribunes were elected,
Titus Claudius, Spurius Nautius, Lucius Sentius, and
Sextus Julius. And in this year among the Eleians
the Ninety-first Olympiad was celebrated, that in
which Exaenetus of Acragas won the "stadion."
The Byzantines and Chalcedonians, accompanied by
Thracians, made war in great force against Bithynia,
plundered the land, reduced by siege many of the
small settlements, and performed deeds of exceeding
cruelty; for of the many prisoners they took, both
men and women and children, they put all to the
sword.

About the same time in Sicily war broke out between the Egestaeans and the Selinuntians from a
difference over territory, where a river divided the
lands of the quarrelling cities. The Selinuntians,
crossing the stream, at first seized by force the land
along the river, but later they cut off for their own a
large piece of the adjoining territory, utterly dis-
regarding the rights of the injured parties. The
people of Egesta, aroused to anger, at first endeavoured to persuade them by verbal arguments not to
trespass on the territory of another city; however,
when no one paid any attention to them, they
advanced with an army against those who held the
territory, expelled them all from their fields, and
themselves seized the land. Since the quarrel be-

διαφορᾶς μεγάλης ἀμφοτέραις ταῖς πόλεσι, στρατιώτας ἀθροίσαντες διὰ τῶν ὅπλων ἐποιοῦντο τὴν κρίσιν. διόπερ ἀμφοτέρων παραταξαμένων ἐγένετο
μάχη καρτερά, καθ' ἣν Σελινούντιοι νικήσαντες
7 ἀπέκτειναν τῶν Ἐγεσταίων οὐκ ὀλίγους. οἱ δ'
Ἐγεσταῖοι ταπεινωθέντες καὶ καθ' ἑαυτοὺς οὐκ
ὄντες ἀξιόμαχοι, τὸ μὲν πρῶτον Ἀκραγαντίνους
καὶ Συρακοσίους ἔπειθον συμμαχῆσαι· ἀποτυχόν-
τες δὲ τούτων ἐξέπεμψαν πρεσβευτὰς εἰς τὴν
Καρχηδόνα, δεόμενοι βοηθῆσαι· οὐ προσεχόντων
δ' αὐτῶν, ἐζήτουν τινὰ διαπόντιον συμμαχίαν· οἷς
συνήργησε ταὐτόματον.

83. Λεοντίνων γὰρ ὑπὸ Συρακοσίων ἐκ τῆς πόλεως μετῳκισμένων καὶ τὴν πόλιν καὶ τὴν χώραν
ἀποβεβληκότων, οἱ φυγάδες αὐτῶν συστραφέντες
ἔκριναν πάλιν τοὺς[1] Ἀθηναίους προσλαβέσθαι συμ-
2 μάχους, ὄντας συγγενεῖς. περὶ δὲ τούτων κοινο-
λογησάμενοι τοῖς Ἐγεσταίοις[2] συνεφρόνησαν καὶ
κοινῇ πρέσβεις ἐξέπεμψαν πρὸς Ἀθηναίους, ἀξιοῦντες μὲν βοηθῆσαι ταῖς πόλεσιν αὐτῶν ἀδικουμέ-
ναις, ἐπαγγειλάμενοι δὲ συγκατασκευάσειν αὐτοῖς
3 τὰ κατὰ τὴν Σικελίαν πράγματα. παραγενομένων
οὖν εἰς τὰς Ἀθήνας τῶν πρέσβεων, καὶ τῶν μὲν
Λεοντίνων τὴν συγγένειαν προφερομένων καὶ τὴν προ-
υπάρχουσαν συμμαχίαν, τῶν δ' Ἐγεσταίων ἐπαγ-
γελλομένων χρημάτων τε πλῆθος δώσειν εἰς τὸν
πόλεμον καὶ συμμαχήσειν κατὰ τῶν Συρακοσίων,
ἔδοξε τοῖς Ἀθηναίοις ἐκπέμψαι τινὰς τῶν ἀρίστων

---

[1] τοὺς Dindorf : αὐτούς.
[2] Ἐγεσταίοις σ. καὶ Post : ἔθνησιν οἷς σ.

tween the two cities had become serious, the two
parties, having mustered soldiers, sought to bring
about the decision by recourse to arms. Consequently, when both forces were drawn up in
battle-order, a fierce battle took place in which the
Selinuntians were the victors, having slain not a few
Egestaeans. Since the Egestaeans had been humbled
and were not strong enough of themselves to offer
battle, they at first tried to induce the Acragantini
and the Syracusans to enter into an alliance with
them. Failing in this, they sent ambassadors to
Carthage to beseech its aid. And when the Carthaginians would not listen to them, they looked about
for some alliance overseas ; and in this, chance came
to their aid.

83. For since the Leontines had been forced by
the Syracusans to leave their city for another place
and had thus lost their city and their territory,[1] those
of them who were living in exile got together and
decided once more to take the Athenians, who were
their kinsmen, as allies. When they had conferred
with the Egestaeans on the matter and come to
an agreement, the two cities jointly dispatched ambassadors to Athens, asking the Athenians to come
to the aid of their cities, which were victims of ill
treatment, and promising to assist the Athenians in
establishing order in the affairs of Sicily. When,
now, the ambassadors had arrived in Athens, and the
Leontines stressed their kinship and the former
alliance and the Egestaeans promised to contribute
a large sum of money for the war and also to fight as
an ally against the Syracusans, the Athenians voted
to send some of their foremost men and to investigate

[1] See chaps. 53 f.

ἀνδρῶν καὶ διασκέψασθαι τὰ κατὰ τὴν νῆσον καὶ
4 τοὺς Ἐγεσταίους. παραγενομένων οὖν τούτων εἰς
τὴν Ἔγεσταν, οἱ μὲν Ἐγεσταῖοι χρημάτων πλῆθος
ἐπέδειξαν, τὰ μὲν οἴκοθεν, τὰ δὲ παρὰ τῶν
5 ἀστυγειτόνων χρησάμενοι φαντασίας ἕνεκεν. ἀν-
ελθόντων[1] δὲ τῶν πρέσβεων καὶ τὴν εὐπορίαν τῶν
Ἐγεσταίων ἀπαγγειλάντων, συνῆλθεν ὁ δῆμος
περὶ τούτων. προτεθείσης δὲ τῆς βουλῆς περὶ τοῦ
στρατεύειν ἐπὶ Σικελίαν, Νικίας μὲν ὁ Νικηράτου,
θαυμαζόμενος ἐπ' ἀρετῇ παρὰ τοῖς πολίταις, συν-
6 εβούλευε μὴ στρατεύειν ἐπὶ Σικελίαν· μὴ γὰρ δυνατὸν ὑπάρχειν ἅμα τε Λακεδαιμονίοις διαπολεμεῖν
καὶ δυνάμεις μεγάλας ἐκπέμπειν διαποντίους, καὶ
τῶν Ἑλλήνων μὴ δυναμένους κτήσασθαι τὴν ἡγεμονίαν ἐλπίζειν τὴν μεγίστην τῶν κατὰ τὴν οἰκουμένην νήσων περιποιήσασθαι, καὶ Καρχηδονίους
μέν, ἔχοντας μεγίστην ἡγεμονίαν καὶ πολλάκις
ὑπὲρ τῆς Σικελίας πεπολεμηκότας, μὴ δεδυνῆσθαι
κρατῆσαι τῆς νήσου, τοὺς δὲ Ἀθηναίους, πολὺ λειπομένους τῇ δυνάμει τῶν Καρχηδονίων, δορίκτητον
ποιήσασθαι τὴν κρατίστην τῶν νήσων.

84. Πολλὰ δὲ καὶ ἄλλα διαλεχθέντος αὐτοῦ[2] τῆς
προκειμένης ὑποθέσεως οἰκεῖα, τῆς ἐναντίας γνώμης
προεστηκὼς Ἀλκιβιάδης, ἐπιφανέστατος Ἀθηναίων, ἔπεισε τὸν δῆμον ἐπανελέσθαι τὸν πόλεμον·
ἦν γὰρ ὁ ἀνὴρ οὗτος δεινότατος μὲν εἰπεῖν τῶν
πολιτῶν, εὐγενείᾳ δὲ καὶ πλούτῳ καὶ στρατηγίᾳ
2 διωνομασμένος. εὐθὺς οὖν ὁ δῆμος στόλον ἀξιό-

---

[1] So Dindorf: ἀπελθόντων; Vogel suggests ἐπανελθόντων.
[2] περὶ after αὐτοῦ deleted by Reiske.

the situation on the island and among the Egestaeans. 416 B.C.
When these men arrived at Egesta, the Egestaeans
showed them a great sum of money which they had
borrowed partly from their own citizens and partly
from neighbouring peoples for the sake of making a
good show.[1]   And when the envoys had returned and
reported on the wealth of the Egestaeans, a meeting
of the people was convened to consider the matter.
When the proposal was introduced to dispatch an
expedition to Sicily, Nicias the son of Niceratus, a
man who enjoyed the respect of his fellow citizens
for his uprightness, counselled against the expedition to Sicily.   They were in no position, he declared,
at the same time both to carry on a war against
the Lacedaemonians and to send great armaments
overseas ; and so long as they were unable to secure
their supremacy over the Greeks, how could they
hope to subdue the greatest island in the inhabited
world ? even the Carthaginians, he added, who possessed a most extensive empire and had waged war
many times to gain Sicily, had not been able to subdue
the island, and the Athenians, whose military power
was far less than that of the Carthaginians, could not
possibly win by the spear and acquire the most
powerful of the islands.

84. After Nicias had set forth these and many other
considerations appropriate to the proposal before the
people, Alcibiades, who was the principal advocate of
the opposite view and a most prominent Athenian,
persuaded the people to enter upon the war ; for this
man was the ablest orator among the citizens and was
widely known for his high birth, wealth, and skill as
a general.   At once, then, the people got ready a

[1] For this display see Thucydides, 6. 46.

χρεων κατεσκεύασε, τριάκοντα μὲν τριήρεις παρὰ
τῶν συμμάχων λαβών, ἰδίας δ' ἑκατὸν καταρτίσας.
3 ταύτας δὲ κοσμήσας πᾶσι τοῖς εἰς πόλεμον χρησί-
μοις κατέλεξεν ὁπλίτας εἰς πεντακισχιλίους, στρατηγοὺς δὲ τρεῖς ἐχειροτόνησεν ἐπὶ ταύτην τὴν
στρατηγίαν, Ἀλκιβιάδην καὶ Νικίαν καὶ Λάμαχον.
4 Ἀθηναῖοι μὲν οὖν περὶ ταῦτα ἦσαν. ἡμεῖς δὲ
παρόντες ἐπὶ τὴν ἀρχὴν τοῦ πολέμου τοῦ συστάντος
Ἀθηναίοις καὶ Συρακοσίοις, κατὰ τὴν ἐν ἀρχῇ
πρόθεσιν τὰς ἑπομένας πράξεις εἰς τὴν ἑχομένην
βίβλον κατατάξομεν.

strong fleet, taking thirty triremes from their allies 416 B.C. and equipping one hundred of their own. And when they had fitted these ships out with every kind of equipment that is useful in war, they enrolled some five thousand hoplites and elected three generals, Alcibiades, Nicias, and Lamachus, to be in charge of the campaign.

Such were the matters with which the Athenians were occupied. And as for us, since we are now at the beginning of the war between the Athenians and the Syracusans, pursuant to the plan we announced at the beginning of this Book [1] we shall assign to the next Book the events which follow.

[1] Cp. chap. 2. 3.

BOOK XIII

Τάδ' ἔνεστιν ἐν τῇ τρισκαιδεκάτῃ τῶν
Διοδώρου βίβλων

Στρατεία Ἀθηναίων ἐπὶ Συρακοσίους μεγάλαις δυνάμεσι πεζικαῖς τε καὶ ναυτικαῖς.

Κατάπλους Ἀθηναίων εἰς Σικελίαν.

Κατάκλησις Ἀλκιβιάδου τοῦ στρατηγοῦ καὶ φυγὴ
εἰς Λακεδαίμονα.

Ὡς Ἀθηναῖοι διαπλεύσαντες εἰς τὸν μέγαν λιμένα τῶν
Συρακοσίων κατελάβοντο τοὺς περὶ τὸ Ὀλύμπιον τόπους.

Ὡς Ἀθηναῖοι τὰς Ἐπιπολὰς καταλαβόμενοι καὶ μάχῃ
νικήσαντες ἐξ ἀμφοτέρων τῶν μερῶν ἐπολιόρκησαν τὰς
Συρακούσας.

Ὡς Λακεδαιμονίων καὶ Κορινθίων πεμψάντων βοήθειαν
ἐθάρρησαν οἱ Συρακόσιοι.

Μάχη Συρακοσίων καὶ Ἀθηναίων καὶ νίκη Ἀθηναίων
μεγάλη.

Μάχη τοῖς αὐτοῖς καὶ νίκη Συρακοσίων.

Ὡς Συρακόσιοι τῶν Ἐπιπολῶν κρατήσαντες ἠνάγκασαν
τοὺς Ἀθηναίους εἰς μίαν ἐλθεῖν παρεμβολὴν τὴν πρὸς
τῷ Ὀλυμπίῳ.

Ὡς ναυτικὴν δύναμιν οἱ Συρακόσιοι κατασκευάσαντες
ναυμαχεῖν διέγνωσαν.

CONTENTS OF THE THIRTEENTH BOOK
OF DIODORUS

119

Ὡς Ἀθηναῖοι Λαμάχου τοῦ στρατηγοῦ τελευτήσαντος καὶ Ἀλκιβιάδου μετακληθέντος, ἀντὶ τούτων στρατηγοὺς ἔπεμψαν Εὐρυμέδοντα καὶ Δημοσθένην ἔχοντας δύναμιν καὶ χρήματα.

Διάλυσις σπονδῶν ὑπὸ Λακεδαιμονίων καὶ πόλεμος πρὸς Ἀθηναίους ὁ Πελοποννησιακὸς λεγόμενος.

Ναυμαχία Συρακοσίων καὶ Ἀθηναίων καὶ νίκη Ἀθηναίων, καὶ ἅλωσις φρουρίων ὑπὸ Συρακοσίων καὶ κατὰ γῆν νίκη.

Ναυμαχία πάσαις ταῖς ναυσὶν ἐν τῷ μεγάλῳ λιμένι καὶ νίκη Συρακοσίων.

Κατάπλους ἐξ Ἀθηνῶν Δημοσθένους καὶ Εὐρυμέδοντος μετὰ δυνάμεως ἀξιολόγου.

Μάχη μεγάλη περὶ τὰς Ἐπιπολὰς καὶ νίκη Συρακοσίων.

Δρασμὸς τῶν Ἀθηναίων καὶ ἅλωσις τῆς πάσης δυνάμεως.

Ὡς Συρακόσιοι συνελθόντες εἰς ἐκκλησίαν προέθηκαν βουλὴν πῶς χρηστέον τοῖς αἰχμαλώτοις.

Οἱ ῥηθέντες λόγοι πρὸς ἑκάτερον μέρος τῆς ὑποθέσεως.

Τὰ ψηφισθέντα τοῖς Συρακοσίοις περὶ τῶν αἰχμαλώτων.

Ὡς Ἀθηναίων πταισάντων περὶ Σικελίαν πολλοὶ τῶν συμμάχων ἀπέστησαν.

Ὡς ὁ δῆμος τῶν Ἀθηναίων ἀθυμήσας παρεχώρησε τῆς δημοκρατίας καὶ τετρακοσίοις ἀνδράσι τὴν πολιτείαν ἐπέτρεψαν.

Ὡς Λακεδαιμόνιοι ταῖς ναυμαχίαις τοὺς Ἀθηναίους ἐνίκησαν.

CONTENTS OF THE THIRTEENTH BOOK

Ὡς Συρακόσιοι τοὺς ἀνδραγαθήσαντας κατὰ τὸν πόλεμον ἀξιολόγοις δωρεαῖς ἐτίμησαν.

Ὡς Διοκλῆς νομοθέτης αἱρεθεὶς ἔγραψε τοὺς νόμους Συρακοσίοις.

Ὡς Συρακόσιοι τοῖς Λακεδαιμονίοις δύναμιν ἀξιόλογον ἔπεμψαν.

Ὡς Ἀθηναῖοι τὸν τῶν Λακεδαιμονίων ναύαρχον καταναυμαχήσαντες Κύζικον ἐξεπολιόρκησαν.

Ὡς Λακεδαιμονίων ἐξ Εὐβοίας πεντήκοντα ναῦς ἀποστειλάντων ἐπὶ βοήθειαν τοῖς ἡττημένοις, ἅπασαι περὶ τὸν Ἄθω μετὰ τῶν ἀνδρῶν διεφθάρησαν ὑπὸ τοῦ χειμῶνος.

Ἀλκιβιάδου κάθοδος καὶ στρατηγία.

Πόλεμος Αἰγεσταίοις καὶ Σελινουντίοις περὶ τῆς ἀμφισβητουμένης χώρας.

Ναυμαχία Ἀθηναίων καὶ Λακεδαιμονίων περὶ τὸ Σίγειον καὶ νίκη Ἀθηναίων.

Ὡς Λακεδαιμόνιοι τὸν Εὔριπον χώσαντες τὴν Εὔβοιαν ἤπειρον ἐποίησαν.

Περὶ τῆς ἐν Κορκύρᾳ γενομένης στάσεως καὶ σφαγῆς.

Ὡς Ἀλκιβιάδης καὶ Θηραμένης ἐνίκησαν Λακεδαιμονίους ἅμα πεζῇ καὶ κατὰ θάλατταν ἐπιφανέστατα.

Ὡς Καρχηδόνιοι μεγάλας δυνάμεις διαβιβάσαντες ἐν Σικελίᾳ Σελινοῦντα καὶ Ἱμέραν κατὰ κράτος εἷλον.

Ὡς εἰς τὸν Πειραιέα καταπλεύσας μετὰ πολλῶν λαφύρων μεγάλης ἔτυχεν ἀποδοχῆς Ἀλκιβιάδης.

CONTENTS OF THE THIRTEENTH BOOK

Ὡς Ἆγις ὁ βασιλεὺς μεγάλῃ δυνάμει τὰς Ἀθήνας πολιορκεῖν ἐπιβαλόμενος ἐξέπεσεν.

Ἀλκιβιάδου φυγὴ καὶ κτίσις Θέρμων ἐν Σικελίᾳ.

Ναυμαχία Συρακοσίων πρὸς Καρχηδονίους καὶ νίκη Συρακοσίων.

Περὶ τῆς ἐν Ἀκράγαντι εὐδαιμονίας καὶ τῶν ἐν αὐτῇ κατασκευασμάτων.

Ὡς Καρχηδόνιοι τριάκοντα μυριάσι στρατεύσαντες εἰς Σικελίαν ἐπολιόρκησαν Ἀκράγαντα.

Ὡς Συρακόσιοι παραλαβόντες τοὺς συμμάχους μυρίοις στρατιώταις ἐβοήθουν τοῖς Ἀκραγαντίνοις.

Ὡς τετρακισμυρίων Καρχηδονίων ἀπαντησάντων ἐνίκησαν οἱ Συρακόσιοι καὶ πλείους τῶν ἑξακισχιλίων κατέκοψαν.

Ὡς Καρχηδονίων τὰς ἀγορὰς παραιρουμένων οἱ Ἀκραγαντῖνοι διὰ τὴν σπάνιν τῆς τροφῆς ἠναγκάσθησαν ἐκλιπεῖν τὴν πατρίδα.

Ὡς Διονύσιος στρατηγὸς αἱρεθεὶς ἐτυράννησε τῶν Συρακοσίων.

Ὡς Ἀθηναῖοι ἐν Ἀργινούσαις ἐπιφανεστάτῃ ναυμαχίᾳ νικήσαντες τοὺς στρατηγοὺς ἀδίκως ἐθανάτωσαν.

Ὡς Ἀθηναῖοι μεγάλῃ ναυμαχίᾳ λειφθέντες ἠναγκάσθησαν ἐφ᾽ οἷς δυνατὸν ἦν συνθέσθαι τὴν εἰρήνην, καὶ οὕτως ὁ Πελοποννησιακὸς πόλεμος κατελύθη.

Ὡς Καρχηδόνιοι λοιμικῇ νόσῳ περιπεσόντες ἠναγκάσθησαν συνθέσθαι τὴν εἰρήνην πρὸς Διονύσιον τὸν τύραννον.

CONTENTS OF THE THIRTEENTH BOOK

ΒΙΒΛΟΣ ΤΡΙΣΚΑΙΔΕΚΑΤΗ

1. Εἰ μὲν ὅμοια τοῖς ἄλλοις ἱστορίαν ἐπραγμα-
τευόμεθα, σχεδὸν ἦν ἐν τῷ προοιμίῳ περί τινων
διαλεχθέντας ἐφ' ὅσον ἦν εὔκαιρον, οὕτως ἐπὶ τὰς
συνεχεῖς πράξεις μεταβιβάζειν τὸν λόγον· ὀλίγον
γὰρ χρόνον ἀπολαβόντες τῇ γραφῇ, τὴν ἀναστροφὴν
ἂν εἴχομεν τὸν ἀπὸ τῶν προοιμίων καρπὸν προσ-
2 λαμβάνεσθαι· ἐπεὶ δὲ ἐν ὀλίγαις βίβλοις ἐπηγγει-
λάμεθα μὴ μόνον τὰς πράξεις ἐφ' ὅσον ἂν δυνώμεθα
γράψειν, ἀλλὰ καὶ περιλήψεσθαι χρόνον πλείονα
τῶν[1] χιλίων καὶ ἑκατὸν ἐτῶν, ἀναγκαῖόν ἐστι τὸν
πολὺν λόγον τῶν προοιμίων παραπέμψαντας ἐπ'
αὐτὰς ἔρχεσθαι τὰς πράξεις, τοῦτο μόνον προ-
ειπόντας, ὅτι κατὰ μὲν τὰς προηγουμένας ἓξ
βίβλους ἀνεγράψαμεν τὰς ἀπὸ τῶν Τρωικῶν
πράξεις ἕως εἰς τὸν ὑπὸ τῶν Ἀθηναίων ψηφισθέντα
πόλεμον ἐπὶ Συρακοσίους, εἰς ὃν ἀπὸ Τροίας
3 ἁλώσεως ἐστὶν ἔτη ἑπτακόσια ἑξήκοντα ὀκτώ[2]· ἐν
ταύτῃ δὲ προσαναπληροῦντες τὸν συνεχῆ χρόνον
ἀρξόμεθα μὲν ἀπὸ τῆς ἐπὶ Συρακοσίους στρατείας
καταλήξομεν δ' ἐπὶ τὴν ἀρχὴν τοῦ δευτέρου
πολέμου Καρχηδονίοις πρὸς Διονύσιον τὸν Συρακοσίων τύραννον.

γράψειν . . . τῶν omitted by PFKM.
[2] ὀκτὼ added by Wesseling.

126

BOOK XIII

1. If we were composing a history after the manner of the other historians, we should, I suppose, discourse upon certain topics at appropriate length in the introduction to each Book and by this means turn our discussion to the events which follow ; surely, if we were picking out a brief period of history for our treatise, we should have the time to enjoy the fruit such introductions yield. But since we engaged ourselves in a few Books not only to set forth, to the best of our ability, the events but also to embrace a period of more than eleven hundred years, we must forgo the long discussion which such introductions would involve and come to the events themselves, with only this word by way of preface, namely, that in the preceding six Books we have set down a record of events from the Trojan War to the war which the Athenians by decree of the people declared against the Syracusans,[1] the period to this war from the capture of Troy embracing seven hundred and sixty-eight years ; and in this Book, as we add to our narrative the period next succeeding, we shall commence with the expedition against the Syracusans and stop with the beginning of the second war between the Carthaginians and Dionysius the tyrant of the Syracusans.[2]

---

[1] *i.e.* from 1184 B.C. to 415 B.C.
[2] The Book covers the years 415–404 B.C.

2. Ἐπ' ἄρχοντος γὰρ Ἀθήνησι Χαβρίου Ῥωμαῖοι μὲν ἀντὶ τῶν ὑπάτων κατέστησαν χιλιάρχους τρεῖς, Λεύκιον Σέργιον, Μάρκον Παπίριον, Μάρκον Σερουίλιον. ἐπὶ δὲ τούτων Ἀθηναῖοι ψηφισάμενοι τὸν πρὸς Συρακοσίους πόλεμον τάς τε ναῦς ἐπεσκεύασαν καὶ χρήματα συναγαγόντες μετὰ πολλῆς σπουδῆς ἅπαντα τὰ πρὸς τὴν στρατείαν παρεσκευάζοντο. ᾑρημένοι δὲ τρεῖς στρατηγούς, Ἀλκιβιάδην, Νικίαν, Λάμαχον, αὐτοκράτορας αὐτοὺς 2 κατέστησαν ἁπάντων τῶν κατὰ τὸν πόλεμον. τῶν δὲ ἰδιωτῶν οἱ ταῖς οὐσίαις εὐποροῦντες τῇ προθυμίᾳ τοῦ δήμου χαρίζεσθαι βουλόμενοι τινὲς μὲν ἰδίας τριήρεις κατεσκεύασαν, τινὲς δὲ χρήματα δώσειν εἰς τὰς τροφὰς τῆς δυνάμεως ἐπηγγέλλοντο· πολλοὶ δὲ καὶ τῶν δημοτικῶν πολιτῶν καὶ ξένων, ἔτι δὲ συμμάχων, ἑκουσίως προσιόντες τοῖς στρατηγοῖς διεκελεύοντο καταγράφειν ἑαυτοὺς εἰς τοὺς στρατιώτας. οὕτως ἅπαντες μεμετεωρισμένοι ταῖς ἐλπίσιν ἐξ ἑτοίμου κατακληρουχεῖν ἤλπιζον τὴν Σικελίαν.

3 Ἤδη δὲ τοῦ στόλου παρεσκευασμένου, τοὺς ἑρμᾶς τοὺς κατὰ τὴν πόλιν παμπληθεῖς ὄντας συνέβη ἐν μιᾷ νυκτὶ περικοπῆναι. ὁ μὲν οὖν δῆμος, οὐχ ὑπὸ τῶν τυχόντων νομίσας γεγενῆσθαι τὴν πρᾶξιν, ἀλλ' ὑπὸ[1] τῶν προεχόντων ταῖς δόξαις ἐπὶ τῇ καταλύσει τῆς δημοκρατίας, ἐμισοπονήρει καὶ τοὺς πράξαντας ἐζήτει μεγάλας δωρεὰς προ-

---

[1] So Schäfer: ἀπό.

---

[1] The principal sources for this famous incident are Thucydides, 6. 27-29, 53, 60-61; Plutarch, *Alcibiades*, 18-21, and especially Andocides, *On the Mysteries*. The

2. When Chabrias was archon in Athens, the _{415 B.C.} Romans elected in place of consuls three military tribunes, Lucius Sergius, Marcus Papirius, and Marcus Servilius. This year the Athenians, pursuant to their vote of the war against the Syracusans, got ready the ships, collected the money, and proceeded with great zeal to make every preparation for the campaign. They elected three generals, Alcibiades, Nicias, and Lamachus, and gave them full powers over all matters pertaining to the war. Of the private citizens those who had the means, wishing to indulge the enthusiasm of the populace, in some instances fitted out triremes at their own expense and in others engaged to donate money for the maintenance of the forces ; and many, not only from among the citizens and aliens of Athens who favoured the democracy but also from among the allies, voluntarily went to the generals and urged that they be enrolled among the soldiers. To such a degree were they all buoyed up in their hopes and looking forward forthwith to portioning out Sicily in allotments.

And the expedition was already fully prepared when it came to pass that in a single night the statues of Hermes which stood everywhere throughout the city were mutilated.[1] At this the people, believing that the deed had not been done by ordinary persons but by men who stood in high repute and were bent upon the overthrow of the democracy, were incensed at the sacrilege and undertook a search for the perpetrators, offering large rewards to anyone who

faces of the statues were mutilated, and perhaps also τὰ αἰδοῖα (Aristophanes, *Lysistrata*, 1094). Andocides gives the names of those whose goods were confiscated and sold after the mutilation of the Hermae, and many of these are confirmed on a fragmentary inscription (*I.G.* i². 327, 332).

4 θεὶς τῷ μηνύσαντι. προσελθὼν δέ τις τῇ βουλῇ
τῶν ἰδιωτῶν ἔφησεν εἰς οἰκίαν μετοίκου τινὰς
ἑωρακέναι τῇ νουμηνίᾳ περὶ μέσας νύκτας εἰσιόν-
τας, ἐν οἷς καὶ τὸν Ἀλκιβιάδην. ἀνακρινόμενος
δ᾽ ὑπὸ τῆς βουλῆς πῶς νυκτὸς οὔσης ἐπεγίνωσκε
τὰς ὄψεις, ἔφησε πρὸς τὸ τῆς σελήνης φῶς ἑωρακέναι. οὗτος μὲν οὖν αὑτὸν ἐξελέγξας κατεψευ-
σμένος ἠπιστήθη,[1] τῶν δ᾽ ἄλλων οὐδ᾽ ἴχνος οὐδεὶς
τῆς πράξεως εὑρεῖν ἠδυνήθη.

5 Τριήρων μὲν ἑκατὸν τεσσαράκοντα ἑτοιμασμένων,
ὁλκάδων δὲ καὶ τῶν ἱππαγωγῶν, ἔτι δὲ τῶν τὸν
σῖτον καὶ τὴν ἄλλην παρασκευὴν κομιζόντων πο-
λύς τις ἀριθμὸς ἦν· ὁπλῖται δὲ καὶ σφενδονῆται,
πρὸς δὲ τούτοις ἱππεῖς[2] καὶ τῶν συμμάχων πλείους
τῶν ἑπτακισχιλίων ἐκτὸς τῶν ἐν τοῖς πληρώμασι.

6 τότε μὲν οὖν οἱ στρατηγοὶ μετὰ τῆς βουλῆς ἐν
ἀπορρήτῳ συνεδρεύοντες ἐβουλεύοντο πῶς χρὴ δι-
οικῆσαι τὰ κατὰ τὴν Σικελίαν, ἐὰν τῆς νήσου κρα-
τήσωσιν. ἔδοξεν οὖν αὐτοῖς Σελινουντίους μὲν
καὶ Συρακοσίους ἀνδραποδίσασθαι, τοῖς δ᾽ ἄλλοις
ἁπλῶς τάξαι φόρους οὓς κατ᾽ ἐνιαυτὸν οἴσουσιν
Ἀθηναίοις.

3. Τῇ δ᾽ ὑστεραίᾳ κατέβαινον οἱ στρατηγοὶ μετὰ
τῶν στρατιωτῶν εἰς τὸν Πειραιέα, καὶ συνη-
κολούθει πᾶς ὁ κατὰ τὴν πόλιν ὄχλος ἀναμὶξ
ἀστῶν τε καὶ ξένων, ἑκάστου τοὺς ἰδίους συγ-
2 γενεῖς τε καὶ φίλους προπέμποντος. αἱ μὲν οὖν
τριήρεις παρ᾽ ὅλον τὸν λιμένα παρώρμουν κεκοσμη-

---

[1] So Dindorf: ἐπιστεύθη PAF[2], εὑρήθη other MSS.
[2] Dindorf suggests τῶν τε πολιτῶν after ἱππεῖς.

---

[1] Probably the Diocleides mentioned by Andocides (*l.c.*
37 ff.), who gives the story in considerable detail.

would furnish information against them.   And a cer- 415 B.C.
tain private citizen,[1] appearing before the Council,
stated that he had seen certain men enter the house
of an alien about the middle of the night on the first
day of the new moon and that one of them was
Alcibiades.   When he was questioned by the Council
and asked how he could recognize the faces at night,
he replied that he had seen them by the light of the
moon.   Since, then, the man had convicted himself
of lying, no credence was given to his story, and
of other investigators not a man was able to discover a single clue to the deed.

One hundred and forty triremes were equipped,
and of transports and ships to carry horses as well as
ships to convey food and all other equipment there
was a huge number ; and there were also hoplites and
slingers as well as cavalry, and in addition more than
seven thousand men from the allies,[2] not including
the crews.   At this time the generals, sitting in secret
session with the Council, discussed what disposition
they should make of Sicilian affairs, if they should get
control of the island.   And it was agreed by them
that they would enslave the Selinuntians and Syracusans, but upon the other peoples they would merely
lay a tribute severally which they would pay annually
to the Athenians.

3. On the next day the generals together with the
soldiers went down to the Peiraeus, and the entire
populace of the city, citizens and aliens thronging
together, accompanied them, everyone bidding god-
speed to his own kinsmen and friends.   The triremes
lay at anchor over the whole harbour, embellished

[2] Or " slingers as well as more than seven thousand cavalry
from both the citizens and allies " ; see critical note.

μέναι τοῖς ἐπὶ ταῖς πρώραις ἐπισήμασι¹ καὶ τῇ
λαμπρότητι τῶν ὅπλων· ὁ δὲ κύκλος ἅπας τοῦ
λιμένος ἔγεμε θυμιατηρίων καὶ κρατήρων ἀργυρῶν,
ἐξ ὧν ἐκπώμασι χρυσοῖς ἔσπενδον οἱ τιμῶντες τὸ
θεῖον καὶ προσευχόμενοι κατατυχεῖν τῆς στρατείας.
3 ἀναχθέντες οὖν ἐκ τοῦ Πειραιέως περιέπλευσαν
τὴν Πελοπόννησον καὶ κατηνέχθησαν εἰς Κόρκυραν·
ἐνταῦθα γὰρ παραμένειν παρήγγελτο καὶ προσ-
αναλαμβάνειν τοὺς παροίκους τῶν συμμάχων.
ἐπεὶ δ' ἅπαντες ἠθροίσθησαν, διαπλεύσαντες τὸν
Ἰόνιον πόρον πρὸς ἄκραν Ἰαπυγίαν κατηνέχθησαν,
4 κἀκεῖθεν ἤδη παρελέγοντο τὴν Ἰταλίαν. ὑπὸ μὲν
οὖν Ταραντίνων οὐ προσεδέχθησαν, Μεταποντίνους
δὲ καὶ Ἡρακλεώτας παρέπλευσαν· εἰς δὲ Θουρίους
κατενεχθέντες πάντων ἔτυχον τῶν φιλανθρώπων.
ἐκεῖθεν δὲ καταπλεύσαντες εἰς Κρότωνα, καὶ
λαβόντες ἀγορὰν παρὰ τῶν Κροτωνιατῶν, τῆς τε
Λακινίας Ἥρας τὸ ἱερὸν παρέπλευσαν καὶ τὴν Διοσ-
5 κουριάδα καλουμένην ἄκραν ὑπερέθεντο. μετὰ δὲ
ταῦτα τὸ καλούμενόν τε Σκυλλήτιον² καὶ Λοκροὺς
παρήλλαξαν, καὶ τοῦ Ῥηγίου καθορμισθέντες ἐγγὺς ἔπειθον³ τοὺς Ῥηγίνους συμμαχεῖν· οἱ δὲ ἀπε-
κρίναντο βουλεύσεσθαι μετὰ τῶν ἄλλων Ἰταλιωτῶν.
4. Συρακόσιοι δ' ἀκούσαντες ἐπὶ τοῦ πορθμοῦ
τὰς δυνάμεις εἶναι τῶν Ἀθηναίων, στρατηγοὺς
κατέστησαν αὐτοκράτορας τρεῖς, Ἑρμοκράτην,
Σικανόν, Ἡρακλείδην, οἳ τοὺς στρατιώτας κατέγραφον καὶ πρέσβεις ἐπὶ τὰς κατὰ Σικελίαν πόλεις
ἀπέστελλον, δεόμενοι τῆς κοινῆς σωτηρίας ἀντι-
λαμβάνεσθαι· τοὺς γὰρ Ἀθηναίους τῷ μὲν λόγῳ

¹ So Hertlein : ἐπιστήμασι.   ² Σκυλλήτιον] Σκυλήτιον PA.
³ So Schäfer : ἔπεισαν.

with their insignia on the bows and the gleam of their 415 B.C.
armour ; and the whole circumference of the harbour
was filled with censers and silver mixing-bowls, from
which the people poured libations with gold cups,
paying honour to the gods and beseeching them to
grant success to the expedition. Now after leaving
the Peiraeus they sailed around the Peloponnesus and
put in at Corcyra, since they were under orders to
wait at that place and add to their forces the allies
in that region. And when they had all been assembled,
they sailed across the Ionian Strait and came to land
on the tip of Iapygia, from where they skirted along
the coast of Italy. They were not received by the
Tarantini, and they also sailed on past the Meta-
pontines and Heracleians ; but when they put in at
Thurii they were accorded every kind of courtesy.
From there they sailed on to Croton, from whose
inhabitants they got a market, and then they sailed
on past the temple of Hera Lacinia [1] and doubled the
promontory known as Dioscurias. After this they
passed by Scylletium, as it is called, and Locri, and
dropping anchor near Rhegium they endeavoured to
persuade the Rhegians to become their allies ; but
the Rhegians replied that they would consult with
the other Greek cities of Italy.

4. When the Syracusans heard that the Athenian
armaments were at the Strait,[2] they appointed three
generals with supreme power, Hermocrates, Sicanus,
and Heracleides, who enrolled soldiers and dispatched
ambassadors to the cities of Sicily, urging them to
do their share in the cause of their common liberty ;

[1] Cape Lacinium is at the extreme western end of the
Tarantine Gulf.
[2] Of Messina.

πρὸς Συρακοσίους ἐνίστασθαι τὸν πόλεμον, τῇ δ᾽
ἀληθείᾳ καταστρέψασθαι βουλομένους ὅλην τὴν
2 νῆσον. Ἀκραγαντῖνοι μὲν οὖν καὶ Νάξιοι συμμαχήσειν ἔφησαν Ἀθηναίοις, Καμαριναῖοι δὲ καὶ
Μεσσήνιοι τὴν μὲν εἰρήνην ἄξειν ὡμολόγησαν, τὰς
δ᾽ ὑπὲρ τῆς συμμαχίας ἀποκρίσεις ἀνεβάλοντο·
Ἱμεραῖοι δὲ καὶ Σελινούντιοι, πρὸς δὲ τούτοις
Γελῷοι καὶ Καταναῖοι, συναγωνιεῖσθαι τοῖς Συρακοσίοις ἐπηγγείλαντο. αἱ δὲ τῶν Σικελῶν
πόλεις τῇ μὲν εὐνοίᾳ πρὸς Συρακοσίους ἔρρεπον,
ὅμως δ᾽[1] ἐν ἡσυχίᾳ μένουσαι τὸ συμβησόμενον
ἐκαραδόκουν.
3 Τῶν δ᾽ Αἰγεσταίων οὐχ ὁμολογούντων δώσειν
πλέον τῶν τριάκοντα ταλάντων, οἱ στρατηγοὶ τῶν
Ἀθηναίων ἐγκαλέσαντες αὐτοῖς ἀνήχθησαν ἐκ
Ῥηγίου μετὰ τῆς δυνάμεως, καὶ κατέπλευσαν τῆς
Σικελίας εἰς Νάξον. δεξαμένων δ᾽ αὐτοὺς τῶν ἐν
τῇ πόλει φιλοφρόνως, παρέπλευσαν ἐκεῖθεν εἰς
4 Κατάνην. τῶν δὲ Καταναίων εἰς μὲν τὴν πόλιν
οὐ δεχομένων τοὺς στρατιώτας, τοὺς δὲ στρατηγοὺς ἐασάντων εἰσελθεῖν καὶ παρασχομένων
ἐκκλησίαν, οἱ στρατηγοὶ τῶν Ἀθηναίων περὶ συμ-
5 μαχίας διελέγοντο. δημηγοροῦντος δὲ τοῦ Ἀλκιβιάδου τῶν στρατιωτῶν τινες διελόντες πυλίδα
παρεισέπεσον εἰς τὴν πόλιν· δι᾽ ἣν αἰτίαν ἠναγκάσθησαν οἱ Καταναῖοι κοινωνεῖν τοῦ κατὰ τῶν
Συρακοσίων πολέμου.

5. Τούτων δὲ πραττομένων οἱ κατὰ τὴν ἰδίαν
ἔχθραν μισοῦντες τὸν Ἀλκιβιάδην ἐν Ἀθήναις,
πρόφασιν ἔχοντες τὴν τῶν ἀγαλμάτων περικοπήν,
διέβαλον αὐτὸν ἐν ταῖς δημηγορίαις ὡς συνωμοσίαν

---

[1] δ᾽ added by Eichstädt.

for the Athenians, they pointed out, while beginning 415 B. C. the war, as they alleged, upon the Syracusans, were in fact intent upon subduing the entire island. Now the Acragantini and Naxians declared that they would ally themselves with the Athenians; the Camarinaeans and Messenians gave assurances that they would maintain the peace, while postponing a reply to the request for an alliance; but the Himeraeans, Selinuntians, Geloans, and Catanaeans promised that they would fight at the side of the Syracusans. The cities of the Siceli, while tending to be favourably inclined toward the Syracusans, nevertheless remained neutral, awaiting the outcome.

After the Aegestaeans had refused to give more than thirty talents,[1] the Athenian generals, having remonstrated with them, put out to sea from Rhegium with their force and sailed to Naxos in Sicily. They were kindly received by the inhabitants of this city and sailed on from there to Catanê. Although the Catanaeans would not receive the soldiers into the city, they allowed the generals to enter and summoned an assembly of the citizens, and the Athenian generals presented their proposal for an alliance. But while Alcibiades was addressing the assembly, some of the soldiers burst open a postern-gate and broke into the city. It was by this cause that the Catanaeans were forced to join in the war against the Syracusans.

5. While these events were taking place, those in Athens who hated Alcibiades with a personal enmity, possessing now an excuse in the mutilation of the statues,[2] accused him in speeches before the Assembly

---

[1] Cp. Book 12. 83.   [2] Cp. chap. 2.

κατὰ τοῦ δήμου πεποιημένον. συνελάβετο[1] δ᾽
αὐτῶν ταῖς διαβολαῖς τὸ πραχθὲν παρὰ τοῖς ᾽Αρ-
γείοις· οἱ γὰρ ἰδιόξενοι συνθέμενοι καταλῦσαι τὴν
ἐν ῎Αργει δημοκρατίαν πάντες ὑπὸ τῶν πολιτῶν
2 ἀνῃρέθησαν. πιστεύσας οὖν ὁ δῆμος ταῖς κατ-
ηγορίαις καὶ δεινῶς ὑπὸ τῶν δημαγωγῶν παρ-
οξυνθείς, ἀπέστειλε τὴν Σαλαμινίαν ναῦν εἰς
Σικελίαν, κελεύων τὴν ταχίστην ἥκειν ᾽Αλκιβιάδην
ἐπὶ τὴν κρίσιν. παραγενομένης οὖν τῆς νεὼς εἰς
τὴν Κατάνην, ᾽Αλκιβιάδης, ἀκούσας τῶν πρέσβεων
τὰ δόξαντα τῷ δήμῳ, τοὺς συνδιαβεβλημένους
ἀναλαβὼν εἰς τὴν ἰδίαν τριήρη μετὰ τῆς Σαλα-
3 μινίας ἐξέπλευσεν. ἐπεὶ δ᾽ εἰς Θουρίους κατέπλευσεν, εἴτε καὶ συνειδὼς αὑτῷ τὴν ἀσέβειαν
ὁ ᾽Αλκιβιάδης εἴτε καὶ φοβηθεὶς τὸ μέγεθος τοῦ
κινδύνου, μετὰ τῶν συνδιαβεβλημένων διαδρὰς
ἐκποδὼν ἐχωρίσθη. οἱ δ᾽ ἐν τῇ Σαλαμινίᾳ νηὶ
παραγενόμενοι τὸ μὲν πρῶτον ἐζήτουν τοὺς περὶ
τὸν ᾽Αλκιβιάδην· ὡς δ᾽ οὐχ εὕρισκον, ἀποπλεύσαντες εἰς ᾽Αθήνας ἀπήγγειλαν τῷ δήμῳ τὰ πε-
4 πραγμένα. οἱ μὲν οὖν ᾽Αθηναῖοι παραδόντες
δικαστηρίῳ τοῦ τε ᾽Αλκιβιάδου καὶ τῶν ἄλλων
τῶν συμφυγόντων τὰ ὀνόματα δίκην ἐρήμην
κατεδίκασαν θανάτου. ὁ δ᾽ ᾽Αλκιβιάδης ἐκ τῆς
᾽Ιταλίας διαπλεύσας ἐπὶ Πελοπόννησον ἔφυγεν εἰς
Σπάρτην, καὶ τοὺς Λακεδαιμονίους παρώξυνεν
ἐπιθέσθαι τοῖς ᾽Αθηναίοις.

6. Οἱ δ᾽ ἐν Σικελίᾳ στρατηγοὶ μετὰ τῆς τῶν

---

[1] Vogel suggests συνεβάλετο.

[1] Cp. Thucydides, 6. 61.

of having formed a conspiracy against the democracy. Their charges gained colour from an incident that had taken place among the Argives ; for private friends [1] of his in that city had agreed together to destroy the democracy in Argos, but they had all been put to death by the citizens. Accordingly the people, having given credence to the accusations and having had their feelings deeply aroused by their dema- gogues, dispatched their ship, the Salaminia,[2] to Sicily with orders for Alcibiades to return with all speed to face trial. When the ship arrived at Catanê and Alcibiades learned of the decision of the people from the ambassadors, he took the others who had been accused together with him aboard his own trireme and sailed away in company with the Sala- minia. But when he had put in at Thurii, Alcibiades, either because he was privy to the deed of impiety or because he was alarmed at the seriousness of the danger which threatened him, made his escape to- gether with the other accused men and got away. The ambassadors who had come on the Salaminia at first set up a hunt for Alcibiades, but when they could not find him, they sailed back to Athens and reported to the people what had taken place. Accor- dingly the Athenians brought the names of Alcibiades and the other fugitives with him before a court of justice and condemned them in default [3] to death. And Alcibiades made his way across from Italy to the Peloponnesus, where he took refuge in Sparta and spurred on the Lacedaemonians to attack the Athenians.

6. The generals in Sicily sailed on with the arma-

---

[2] This was one of the two dispatch boats of the Athenian navy, the other being the Paralus.   [3] *i.e.* in their absence.

Ἀθηναίων δυνάμεως παραπλεύσαντες εἰς Αἴγε
σταν, Ὕκκαρα μὲν Σικελικὸν πολισμάτιον ἑλόντες
ἐκ τῶν λαφύρων συνήγαγον ἑκατὸν τάλαντα· κο
μισάμενοι δὲ καὶ τριάκοντα τάλαντα παρὰ τῶν
2 Αἰγεσταίων κατέπλευσαν εἰς Κατάνην. βουλό
μενοι δὲ τὸν πρὸς τῷ μεγάλῳ λιμένι τόπον Συρα
κοσίων[1] ἀκινδύνως καταλαβέσθαι, πέμπουσιν ἄνδρα
Καταναῖον, ἑαυτοῖς μὲν πιστὸν τοῖς δὲ Συρακοσίων
στρατηγοῖς πιθανόν, διακελευσάμενοι λέγειν τοῖς
ἡγεμόσι τῶν Συρακοσίων, ὅτι τινὲς Καταναίων
συστάντες βούλονται συχνοὺς τῶν Ἀθηναίων αὐλι
ζομένους ἀπὸ τῶν ὅπλων ἐν τῇ πόλει νυκτὸς
ἄφνω συλλαβόντες τὰς ἐν τῷ λιμένι ναῦς ἐμπρῆσαι·
πρὸς δὲ τὴν τούτων συντέλειαν ἀξιοῦν[2] τοὺς στρα
τηγοὺς ἐπιφανῆναι μετὰ δυνάμεως, μήποτε τῆς
3 ἐπιβολῆς ἀποτύχωσιν. ἐλθόντος δὲ τοῦ Καταναίου
πρὸς τοὺς ἡγεμόνας τῶν Συρακοσίων καὶ δηλώσαν
τος τὰ προειρημένα, πιστεύσαντες περὶ τούτων
οἱ στρατηγοὶ συνετάξαντο νύκτα καθ' ἣν ἐξάξουσι[3]
τὴν δύναμιν, καὶ τὸν ἄνθρωπον ἐξαπέστειλαν εἰς
τὴν Κατάνην.
4   Οἱ μὲν οὖν Συρακόσιοι κατὰ τὴν τεταγμένην νύ
κτα ἦγον τὸ στρατόπεδον ἐπὶ τὴν Κατάνην, οἱ δὲ
Ἀθηναῖοι παραπλεύσαντες εἰς τὸν μέγαν λιμένα
τῶν Συρακοσίων μετὰ πολλῆς ἡσυχίας τοῦ τε
Ὀλυμπίου κύριοι κατέστησαν καὶ πάντα τὸν
περικείμενον τόπον καταλαβόμενοι παρεμβολὴν
5 ἐποιήσαντο. οἱ δὲ στρατηγοὶ τῶν Συρακοσίων
ὡς ᾔσθοντο τὴν ἀπάτην, ταχέως ἀναστρέψαντες
προσέβαλον τῇ παρεμβολῇ τῶν Ἀθηναίων. ἐπ

---

[1] Συρακοσίων] Συρακουσῶν Dindorf.
[2] So Wurm : ἠξίουν.   [3] So Hertlein : ἐκτάξουσι.

ment of the Athenians to Aegesta and captured 415 B.C.
Hyccara, a small town of the Siceli, from the booty of
which they realized one hundred talents ; and after
receiving thirty talents in addition from the Aegestaeans they continued their voyage to Catanê. And
wishing to seize, without risk to themselves, the
position [1] on the Great Harbour of the Syracusans,
they sent a man of Catanê, who was loyal to themselves and was also trusted by the Syracusan generals,
with instructions to say to the Syracusan commanders
that a group of Catanaeans had banded together and
were ready to seize unawares a large number of
Athenians, who made it their practice to pass the
night in the city away from their arms, and set fire
to the ships in the harbour ; and he was to ask the
generals that, in order to effect this, they should
appear at the place with troops so that they might
not fail in their design. When the Catanaean went
to the commanders of the Syracusans and told them
what we have stated, the generals, believing his story,
decided on the night on which they would lead out
their troops and sent the man back to Catanê.

Now on the appointed night the Syracusans brought
the army to Catanê, whereupon the Athenians, sailing
down into the Great Harbour of the Syracusans in
dead silence, not only became masters of the Olympieum but also, after seizing the entire area about it,
constructed a camp. The generals of the Syracusans,
however, when they learned of the deceit which had
been practised on them, returned speedily and assaulted the Athenian camp. When the enemy came

---

[1] This was near the Olympieum (Thucydides, 6. 64. 2).
The reader is referred to the map at the back of the book,
which is based on the account of Thucydides.

ἐξελθόντων οὖν τῶν πολεμίων συνέστη μάχη, καθ᾽
ἣν οἱ Ἀθηναῖοι τετρακοσίους τῶν ἐναντίων ἀν-
6 ελόντες φυγεῖν ἠνάγκασαν τοὺς Συρακοσίους. οἱ
δὲ τῶν Ἀθηναίων στρατηγοὶ θεωροῦντες τοὺς
πολεμίους ἱπποκρατοῦντας, καὶ βουλόμενοι βέλτιον
τὰ πρὸς τὴν πολιορκίαν κατασκευάσασθαι, πάλιν
ἀπέπλευσαν εἰς τὴν Κατάνην. πέμψαντες δ᾽ εἰς
Ἀθήνας τινὰς ἔγραψαν πρὸς τὸν δῆμον ἐπιστολάς,
ἐν αἷς ἠξίουν ἱππεῖς ἀποστεῖλαι καὶ χρήματα·
πολυχρόνιον γὰρ ἔσεσθαι τὴν πολιορκίαν ὑπελάμβανον. οἱ δ᾽ Ἀθηναῖοι τριακόσια τάλαντα καὶ τῶν
ἱππέων τινὰς ἐψηφίσαντο πέμπειν εἰς τὴν Σικελίαν.
7 Τούτων δὲ πραττομένων Διαγόρας ὁ κληθεὶς
ἄθεος, διαβολῆς τυχὼν ἐπ᾽ ἀσεβείᾳ καὶ φοβηθεὶς
τὸν δῆμον, ἔφυγεν ἐκ τῆς Ἀττικῆς· οἱ δ᾽ Ἀθηναῖοι
τῷ ἀνελόντι Διαγόραν ἀργυρίου τάλαντον ἐπεκή-
ρυξαν.
8 Κατὰ δὲ τὴν Ἰταλίαν Ῥωμαῖοι πρὸς Αἴκους
πόλεμον ἔχοντες Λαβικοὺς ἐξεπολιόρκησαν.
Ταῦτα μὲν οὖν ἐπράχθη κατὰ τοῦτον τὸν ἐνιαυτόν.
7. Ἐπ᾽ ἄρχοντος δ᾽ Ἀθήνησι Τισάνδρου Ῥωμαῖοι μὲν ἀντὶ τῶν ὑπάτων χιλιάρχους κατέστησαν
τέτταρας, Πόπλιον Λουκρήτιον,[1] Γάιον Σερουίλιον,
Ἀγρίππαν Μενήνιον, Σπούριον Οὐετούριον. ἐπὶ
δὲ τούτων Συρακόσιοι πρέσβεις ἀποστείλαντες εἴς
τε Κόρινθον καὶ Λακεδαίμονα παρεκάλουν βοηθῆσαι καὶ μὴ περιορᾶν αὐτοὺς περὶ τῶν ὅλων κινδυ-
2 νεύοντας. συνηγορήσαντος δ᾽ αὐτοῖς Ἀλκιβιάδου
Λακεδαιμόνιοι μὲν ψηφισάμενοι βοηθεῖν τοῖς Συρακοσίοις στρατηγὸν εἵλοντο Γύλιππον, Κορίνθιοι

[1] Λουκρήτιον] Λοκρήτιον PA.

out to meet them, there ensued a battle, in which the 415 B.C. Athenians slew four hundred of their opponents and compelled the Syracusans to take to flight. But the Athenian generals, seeing that the enemy were superior in cavalry and wishing to improve their equipment for the siege of the city, sailed back to Catanê. And they dispatched men to Athens and addressed letters to the people in which they asked them to send cavalry and funds ; for they believed that the siege would be a long affair ; and the Athenians voted to send three hundred talents and a contingent of cavalry to Sicily.

While these events were taking place, Diagoras, who was dubbed " the Atheist," [1] was accused of impiety and, fearing the people, fled from Attica ; and the Athenians announced a reward of a talent of silver to the man who should slay Diagoras.

In Italy the Romans went to war with the Aequi and reduced Labici by siege.[2]

These, then, were the events of this year.

7. When Tisandrus was archon in Athens, the 414 B.C. Romans elected in place of consuls four military tribunes, Publius Lucretius, Gaius Servilius, Agrippa Menenius, and Spurius Veturius. In this year the Syracusans, dispatching ambassadors to both Corinth and Lacedaemon, urged these cities to come to their aid and not to stand idly by when total ruin threatened the Syracusans. Since Alcibiades supported their request, the Lacedaemonians voted to send aid to the Syracusans and chose Gylippus to be general, and

---

[1] He is said to have been a dithyrambic poet of Melos who was apparently accused of making blasphemous remarks about Athenian divinities (cp. Lysias, *Against Andocides*, 17 ff.).

[2] Cp. Livy, 4. 47.

δὲ πλείονας μὲν τριήρεις παρεσκευάζοντο πέμπειν,
τότε δὲ μετὰ Γυλίππου Πύθην μετὰ δύο τριήρων
3 προαπέστειλαν εἰς Σικελίαν. ἐν δὲ τῇ Κατάνῃ
Νικίας καὶ Λάμαχος οἱ τῶν Ἀθηναίων στρατηγοί,
παραγενομένων αὐτοῖς ἐξ Ἀθηνῶν ἱππέων μὲν
διακοσίων πεντήκοντα, ἀργυρίου δὲ ταλάντων
τριακοσίων, ἀναλαβόντες τὴν δύναμιν ἔπλευσαν εἰς
Συρακούσας. καὶ προσενεχθέντες τῇ πόλει νυκτὸς
ἔλαθον τοὺς Συρακοσίους καταλαβόμενοι τὰς Ἐπι-
πολάς. αἰσθόμενοι δ' οἱ Συρακόσιοι κατὰ τάχος
ἐβοήθουν, καὶ ἀποβαλόντες τῶν στρατιωτῶν τρια-
4 κοσίους εἰς τὴν πόλιν συνεδιώχθησαν. μετὰ δὲ
ταῦτα παραγενομένων τοῖς Ἀθηναίοις ἐξ Αἰγέστης
τριακοσίων μὲν ἱππέων, παρὰ δὲ τῶν Σικελῶν
ἱππέων διακοσίων πεντήκοντα, συνήγαγον ἱππεῖς
τοὺς πάντας ὀκτακοσίους. κατασκευάσαντες δὲ
περὶ τὸ Λάβδαλον ὀχύρωμα, τὴν πόλιν τῶν Συρακοσίων ἀπετείχιζον καὶ πολὺν φόβον τοῖς Συ-
5 ρακοσίοις ἐπέστησαν. διόπερ ἐπεξελθόντες ἐκ τῆς
πόλεως ἐπεχείρησαν διακωλύειν τοὺς οἰκοδομοῦντας
τὸ τεῖχος· γενομένης δ' ἱππομαχίας συχνοὺς ἀποβαλόντες ἐτράπησαν. οἱ δ' Ἀθηναῖοι τῷ μέρει τῆς
δυνάμεως τὸν ὑπερκείμενον τοῦ λιμένος τόπον κατελάβοντο, καὶ τὴν καλουμένην Πολίχνην τειχίσαντες
τό τε τοῦ Διὸς ἱερὸν περιεβάλοντο καὶ ἐξ ἀμφοτέρων τῶν μερῶν τὰς Συρακούσας ἐπολιόρκουν.
6 τοιούτων δὲ ἐλαττωμάτων περὶ τοὺς Συρακοσίους γενομένων ἠθύμουν οἱ κατὰ τὴν πόλιν· ὡς
δ' ἤκουσαν Γύλιππον εἰς Ἱμέραν καταπεπλευκέναι

the Corinthians made preparations to send a number 414 B.C. of triremes, but at the moment they sent in advance to Sicily, accompanying Gylippus, Pythes with two triremes. And in Catanê Nicias and Lamachus, the Athenian generals, after two hundred and fifty cavalry and three hundred talents of silver had come to them from Athens, took their army aboard and sailed to Syracuse. They arrived at the city by night and unobserved by the Syracusans took possession of Epipolae. When the Syracusans learned of this, they speedily came to its defence, but were chased back into the city with the loss of three hundred soldiers. After this, with the arrival for the Athenians of three hundred horsemen from Aegesta and two hundred and fifty from the Siceli, they mustered in all eight hundred cavalry. Then, having built a fort at Labdalum, they began constructing a wall about the city of the Syracusans and aroused great fear among the populace.[1] Therefore they advanced out of the city and endeavoured to hinder the builders of the wall; but a cavalry battle followed in which they suffered heavy losses and were forced to flee. The Athenians with a part of their troops now seized the region lying above the harbour and by fortifying Polichnê,[2] as it is called, they not only enclosed the temple of Zeus[3] but were also besieging Syracuse from both sides. Now that such reverses as these had befallen the Syracusans, the inhabitants of the city were disheartened; but when they learned that Gylippus had put in at Himera and was gathering

[1] This wall of circumvallation was to run from near Trogilus southward to the Great Harbour; see map.
[2] Thucydides (7. 4. 6) speaks of a *polichnê* (" hamlet ") near the Olympieum, which lay west of the centre of the Great Harbour.   [3] The Olympieum.

7 καὶ στρατιώτας ἀθροίζειν, πάλιν ἐθάρρησαν. ὁ
γὰρ Γύλιππος μετὰ τεττάρων τριήρων καταπλεύσας εἰς Ἱμέραν τὰς μὲν ναῦς ἐνεώλκησε, τοὺς
δ' Ἱμεραίους πείσας συμμαχεῖν τοῖς Συρακοσίοις,
παρά τε τούτων καὶ Γελῴων, ἔτι δὲ Σελινουντίων
καὶ Σικανῶν ἤθροιζε στρατιώτας. συναγαγὼν δὲ
τοὺς ἅπαντας τρισχιλίους μὲν πεζοὺς διακοσίους
δ' ἱππεῖς, διὰ τῆς μεσογείου παρῆγεν εἰς Συρακούσας.

8. Καὶ μετ' ὀλίγας ἡμέρας μετὰ τῶν Συρακοσίων ἐξήγαγε τὴν δύναμιν ἐπὶ τοὺς Ἀθηναίους.
γενομένης δὲ μάχης ἰσχυρᾶς Λάμαχος ὁ τῶν Ἀθηναίων στρατηγὸς μαχόμενος ἐτελεύτησε· πολλῶν δὲ
παρ' ἀμφοτέρων ἀναιρεθέντων ἐνίκησαν Ἀθηναῖοι.
2 μετὰ δὲ τὴν μάχην παραγενομένων τρισκαίδεκα
τριήρων ἐκ Κορίνθου, τοὺς ἐκ τῶν πληρωμά-
των ἀναλαβὼν ὁ Γύλιππος μετὰ τῶν Συρακοσίων
προσέβαλε τῇ παρεμβολῇ τῶν πολεμίων, καὶ τὰς
Ἐπιπολὰς ἐπολιόρκει. ἐξελθόντων δὲ τῶν Ἀθηναίων συνῆψαν μάχην οἱ Συρακόσιοι, καὶ πολλοὺς τῶν
Ἀθηναίων ἀποκτείναντες ἐνίκησαν, καὶ δι' ὅλης
τῆς Ἐπιπολῆς τὸ τεῖχος κατέσκαψαν· οἱ δ' Ἀθηναῖοι καταλιπόντες τὸν πρὸς ταῖς Ἐπιπολαῖς τόπον πᾶσαν τὴν δύναμιν εἰς τὴν ἄλλην παρεμβολὴν
μετήγαγον.
3 Τούτων δὲ πραχθέντων οἱ Συρακόσιοι μὲν
πρέσβεις ἀπέστειλαν εἰς Κόρινθον καὶ Λακεδαίμονα περὶ βοηθείας· οἷς ἀπέστειλαν Κορίνθιοι μετὰ
Βοιωτῶν μὲν καὶ Σικυωνίων χιλίους, Σπαρτιᾶται
4 δ' ἑξακοσίους· Γύλιππος δὲ περιπορευόμενος τὰς
κατὰ Σικελίαν πόλεις πολλοὺς προετρέπετο συμμαχεῖν, καὶ λαβὼν στρατιώτας παρά τε τῶν

soldiers, they again took heart. For Gylippus, having 414 B.C put in at Himera with four triremes, had hauled his ships up on shore, persuaded the Himeraeans to ally themselves with the Syracusans, and was gathering soldiers from them and the Geloans, as well as from the Selinuntians and the Sicani. And after he had assembled three thousand infantry in all and two hundred cavalry, he led them through the interior of the island to Syracuse.

8. After a few days Gylippus led forth his troops together with the Syracusans against the Athenians. A fierce battle took place and Lamachus, the Athenian general, died in the fighting; and although many were slain on both sides, victory lay with the Athenians. After the battle, when thirteen triremes had arrived from Corinth, Gylippus, after taking the crews of the ships, with them and the Syracusans attacked the camp of the enemy and sought to storm Epipolae. When the Athenians came out, they joined battle and the Syracusans, after slaying many Athenians, were victorious and they razed the wall throughout the length of Epipolê; at this the Athenians abandoned the area of Epipolae and withdrew their entire force to the other camp.

After these events the Syracusans dispatched ambassadors to Corinth and Lacedaemon to get help; and the Corinthians together with the Boeotians and Sicyonians sent them one thousand men and the Spartans six hundred. And Gylippus went about the cities of Sicily and persuaded many peoples to join the alliance, and after gathering three thou-

Ἰμεραίων καὶ Σικανῶν τρισχιλίους ἦγε διὰ τῆς
μεσογείου. πυθόμενοι δὲ οἱ Ἀθηναῖοι τὴν παρουσίαν αὐτῶν, ἐπιθέμενοι τοὺς ἡμίσεις ἀνεῖλον· οἱ
δὲ περιλειφθέντες διεσώθησαν εἰς Συρακούσας.
5 Ἐλθόντων δὲ τῶν συμμάχων οἱ Συρακόσιοι
βουλόμενοι καὶ τῶν κατὰ θάλατταν ἀγώνων ἀντι-
ποιεῖσθαι, τάς τε προϋπαρχούσας ναῦς καθείλκυσαν
καὶ ἄλλας προσκατασκευάσαντες ἐν τῷ μικρῷ
6 λιμένι τὰς ἀναπείρας ἐποιοῦντο. Νικίας δὲ ὁ τῶν
Ἀθηναίων στρατηγὸς ἀπέστειλεν εἰς Ἀθήνας ἐπιστολὰς ἐν αἷς ἐδήλου ὅτι πολλοὶ πάρεισι σύμμαχοι τοῖς Συρακοσίοις, καὶ διότι ναῦς οὐκ ὀλίγας
πληρώσαντες ναυμαχεῖν διέγνωσαν· κατὰ τάχος
οὖν ἠξίου τριήρεις τε πέμπειν καὶ χρήματα καὶ
στρατηγοὺς τοὺς συνδιοικήσοντας τὸν πόλεμον·
Ἀλκιβιάδου μὲν γὰρ πεφευγότος, Λαμάχου δὲ
τετελευτηκότος αὐτὸν μόνον ἀπολελεῖφθαι, καὶ
7 ταῦτ' ἀσθενῶς διακείμενον. οἱ δ' Ἀθηναῖοι μετ'
Εὐρυμέδοντος μὲν τοῦ στρατηγοῦ δέκα ναῦς ἀπέστειλαν εἰς Σικελίαν καὶ ἀργυρίου τάλαντα ἑκατὸν
τεσσαράκοντα περὶ τὰς χειμερινὰς[1] τροπάς· περὶ
δὲ τὴν ἐαρινὴν ὥραν παρεσκευάζοντο μέγαν στόλον
ἀποστέλλειν. διόπερ στρατιώτας τε πανταχόθεν
παρὰ τῶν συμμάχων κατέγραφον καὶ χρήματα
συνήθροιζον.
8 Κατὰ δὲ τὴν Πελοπόννησον οἱ Λακεδαιμόνιοι
παροξυνθέντες ὑπὸ Ἀλκιβιάδου τὰς σπονδὰς ἔλυσαν τὰς πρὸς Ἀθηναίους, καὶ ὁ πόλεμος οὗτος
διέμεινεν ἔτη δώδεκα.
9. Τοῦ δὲ ἔτους τούτου διελθόντος Κλεόκριτος
μὲν ἄρχων Ἀθηναίων ἦν, ἐν Ῥώμῃ δ' ἀντὶ τῶν

---

[1] So Wesseling, cp. Thuc. 7. 16. 2 : θερινάς.

sand soldiers from the Himeraeans and Sicani he led 414 B.C. them through the interior of the island. When the Athenians learned that these troops were near at hand, they attacked and slew half of them; the survivors, however, got safely to Syracuse.

Upon the arrival of the allies the Syracusans, wishing to try their hand also in battles at sea, launched the ships they already possessed and fitted out additional ones, giving them their trials in the small harbour. And Nicias, the Athenian general, dispatched letters to Athens in which he made known that many allies were now with the Syracusans and that they had fitted out no small number of ships and had resolved upon offering battle at sea; he therefore asked them to send speedily both triremes and money and generals to assist him in the conduct of the war, explaining that with the flight of Alcibiades and the death of Lamachus he was the only general left and at that was not in good health. The Athenians dispatched to Sicily ten ships with Eurymedon the general and one hundred and forty talents of silver, at the time of the winter solstice [1]; meantime they busied themselves with preparations to dispatch a great fleet in the spring. Consequently they were enrolling soldiers everywhere from their allies and gathering together money.

In the Peloponnesus the Lacedaemonians, being spurred on by Alcibiades, broke the truce with the Athenians, and the war which followed continued for twelve years.[2]

9. At the close of this year Cleocritus was archon 413 B.C. of the Athenians, and in Rome in place of consuls

---

[1] 22nd December.
[2] Ten years, 413-404 B.C. inclusive.

ὑπάτων χιλίαρχοι τέτταρες ὑπῆρχον, Αὖλος Σεμ-
πρώνιος καὶ Μάρκος Παπίριος, Κόιντος Φάβιος,
2 Σπόριος Ναύτιος. ἐπὶ δὲ τούτων Λακεδαιμόνιοι
μετὰ τῶν συμμάχων ἐνέβαλον εἰς τὴν Ἀττικήν,
Ἄγιδος¹ ἡγουμένου καὶ Ἀλκιβιάδου τοῦ Ἀθηναίου. καταλαβόμενοι δὲ χωρίον ὀχυρὸν Δεκέλειαν
φρούριον ἐποίησαν κατὰ τῆς Ἀττικῆς· διὸ καὶ
συνέβη τὸν πόλεμον τοῦτον Δεκελεικὸν προσα-
γορευθῆναι. Ἀθηναῖοι δὲ περὶ μὲν τὴν Λακω-
νικὴν τριάκοντα τριήρεις ἀπέστειλαν καὶ Χαρικλέα
στρατηγόν, εἰς δὲ τὴν Σικελίαν ἐψηφίσαντο πέμπειν
ὀγδοήκοντα μὲν τριήρεις, ὁπλίτας δὲ πεντακισ-
3 χιλίους. οἱ δὲ Συρακόσιοι κρίναντες ναυμαχεῖν
καὶ πληρώσαντες ὀγδοήκοντα τριήρεις ἐπέπλεον
τοῖς πολεμίοις. τῶν δὲ Ἀθηναίων ἑξήκοντα
ναυσὶν ἀνταναχθέντων, καὶ τῆς ναυμαχίας ἐνεργοῦ
γενομένης ἤδη, πάντες οἱ ἀπὸ τῶν φρουρίων
Ἀθηναῖοι κατέβησαν ἐπὶ τὴν θάλατταν· οἱ μὲν
γὰρ θεάσασθαι τὴν μάχην ἐπεθύμουν, οἱ δ᾽, εἴ τι
πταίσειαν ἐν τῇ ναυμαχίᾳ, βοηθήσειν τοῖς φεύ-
4 γουσιν ἤλπιζον. οἱ δὲ τῶν Συρακοσίων στρατηγοὶ προϊδόμενοι τὸ γινόμενον ἀπεστάλκεισαν τοὺς
κατὰ τὴν πόλιν ἐπὶ τὰ τῶν Ἀθηναίων ὀχυρώματα,
χρημάτων καὶ ναυτικῶν σκευῶν, ἔτι δὲ τῆς ἄλλης
παρασκευῆς ὑπάρχοντα πλήρη· ἃ δὴ καταλα-
βόντες² οἱ Συρακόσιοι παντελῶς ὑπ᾽ ὀλίγων τη-
ρούμενα κατέσχον³ καὶ τῶν ἀπὸ τῆς θαλάττης
5 προσβοηθούντων πολλοὺς ἀπέκτειναν. κραυγῆς δὲ
πολλῆς γενομένης περὶ τὰ φρούρια καὶ τὴν παρεμβολήν, οἱ ναυμαχοῦντες Ἀθηναῖοι καταπλαγέντες
ἐτράπησαν καὶ πρὸς τὸ λειπόμενον τῶν φρουρίων
ἔφυγον. τῶν δὲ Συρακοσίων ἀτάκτως διωκόντων

there were four military tribunes, Aulus Sempronius, 413 B.C.
Marcus Papirius, Quintus Fabius, and Spurius
Nautius. This year the Lacedaemonians together
with their allies invaded Attica, under the leadership
of Agis and Alcibiades the Athenian. And seizing
the stronghold of Deceleia they made it into a fortress
for attacks upon Attica, and this, as it turned out,
was why this war came to be called the Deceleian
War. The Athenians dispatched thirty triremes to
lie off Laconia under Charicles as general and voted
to send eighty triremes and five thousand hoplites to
Sicily. And the Syracusans, having made up their
minds to join battle at sea, fitted out eighty triremes
and sailed against the enemy. The Athenians put
out against them with sixty ships, and when the
battle was at its height, all the Athenians in the
fortresses went down to the sea ; for some were
desirous of watching the battle, while others hoped
that, in case of some reverse in the sea-battle, they
could be of help to those in flight. But the Syracusan
generals, foreseeing what really happened, had dispatched the troops in the city against the strongholds
of the Athenians, which were filled with money and
naval supplies as well as every other kind of equipment ; when the Syracusans found the strongholds
guarded by a totally inadequate number, they seized
them, and slew many of those who came up from the
sea to their defence. And since a great uproar arose
about the forts and the camp, the Athenians who
were engaged in the sea-battle turned about in dismay
and fled toward the last remaining fort. The Syra-

---

¹ Ἄγιδος δὲ P.
² καταλαμβάνοντες PAJL, Vogel, καταλαβόντες cet.
³ κατέσχον added by Post, διήρπασαν by Dindorf.

οἱ Ἀθηναῖοι πρὸς τὴν γῆν καταφεύγειν οὐ δυνάμενοι διὰ τὸ τοὺς Συρακοσίους δυεῖν φρουρίων
κυριεύειν, ἠναγκάσθησαν ἐξ ὑποστροφῆς πάλιν
6 ναυμαχῆσαι. τῶν δὲ Συρακοσίων λελυκότων τὰς
τάξεις καὶ κατὰ τὸν διωγμὸν διερριμμένων,[1]
ἀθρόαις ταῖς ναυσὶν ἐπιπλεύσαντες ἕνδεκα μὲν
κατέδυσαν, τὰς δὲ λοιπὰς ἕως τῆς Νήσου κατεδίωξαν. διαλυθείσης δὲ τῆς μάχης ἑκάτεροι τρόπαιον ἔστησαν, οἱ μὲν Ἀθηναῖοι τῆς ναυμαχίας,
οἱ δὲ Συρακόσιοι τῶν ἐπὶ τῆς γῆς κατωρθωμένων.

10. Τῆς δὲ ναυμαχίας τοιοῦτο τέλος λαβούσης,
οἱ μὲν Ἀθηναῖοι πυνθανόμενοι τὸν μετὰ Δημοσθένους στόλον ἐν ὀλίγαις ἡμέραις ἥξειν, ἔκριναν
μηκέτι διακινδυνεύειν ἕως ἂν ἡ δύναμις ἐκείνη
παραγένηται, οἱ δὲ Συρακόσιοι τοὐναντίον βουλόμενοι πρὶν ἐλθεῖν τὴν μετὰ Δημοσθένους στρατιὰν
περὶ τῶν ὅλων διακριθῆναι, καθ' ἡμέραν ἐπιπλέοντες[2] ταῖς τῶν Ἀθηναίων ναυσὶν ἐξήπτοντο τῆς
2 μάχης. συμβουλεύσαντος δ' αὐτοῖς Ἀρίστωνος τοῦ
Κορινθίου κυβερνήτου τὰς πρώρας τῶν νεῶν ποιῆσαι βραχυτέρας καὶ ταπεινοτέρας, πεισθέντες οἱ
Συρακόσιοι πολλὰ διὰ ταύτην τὴν αἰτίαν ἐν τοῖς
3 μετὰ ταῦτα κινδύνοις ἐπλεονέκτησαν. αἱ μὲν γὰρ
Ἀττικαὶ τριήρεις ἦσαν ἀσθενεστέρας ἔχουσαι τὰς
πρώρας καὶ μετεώρους· διὸ συνέβαινεν αὐτῶν τὰς
ἐμβολὰς τιτρώσκειν τοὺς ὑπερέχοντας τῆς θαλάττης τόπους, ὥστε τοὺς πολεμίους μὴ μεγάλοις
ἐλαττώμασι περιπίπτειν· αἱ δὲ τῶν Συρακοσίων
τὸν περὶ τὴν πρώραν τόπον ἰσχυρὸν ἔχουσαι καὶ
ταπεινόν, κατὰ τὰς τῶν ἐμβολῶν δόσεις μιᾷ

cusans pursued them without order, but the Athenians, 413 B.C. when they saw themselves unable to find safety on land because the Syracusans controlled two forts, were forced to turn about and renew the sea-battle. And since the Syracusans had broken their battle order and had become scattered in the pursuit, the Athenians, attacking with their ships in a body, sank eleven triremes and pursued the rest as far as the island.[1] When the fight was ended, each side set up a trophy, the Athenians for the sea-battle and the Syracusans for their successes on land.

10. After the sea-battle had ended in the manner we have described, the Athenians, learning that the fleet under Demosthenes would arrive within a few days, decided to run no more risks before that force should join them, whereas the Syracusans, on the contrary, wishing to reach a final decision before the arrival of Demosthenes and his army, kept sailing out every day against the ships of the Athenians and continuing the fight. And when Ariston the Corinthian pilot advised them to make the prows of their ships shorter and lower, the Syracusans followed his advice and for that reason enjoyed great advantage in the fighting which followed. For the Attic triremes were built with weaker and high prows, and for this reason it followed that, when they rammed, they damaged only the parts of a ship that extended above the water, so that the enemy suffered no great damage ; whereas the ships of the Syracusans, built as they were with the structure about the prow strong and low, would often, as they delivered their ram-

---

[1] *i.e.* of Ortygia.

---

[1] So Reiske: ἐρριμένων.
[2] So Wesseling: εἰσπλέοντες.

πολλάκις πληγῇ κατέδυον τὰς τῶν Ἀθηναίων τριήρεις.

4 Ἐπὶ μὲν οὖν συχνὰς ἡμέρας οἱ Συρακόσιοι τῇ παρεμβολῇ τῶν πολεμίων καὶ κατὰ γῆν καὶ κατὰ θάλατταν προσβάλλοντες οὐδὲν ἤνυον, τῶν Ἀθηναίων ἀγόντων ἡσυχίαν· ἐπειδὴ[1] δέ τινες τῶν τριηράρχων οὐκέτι δυνάμενοι καρτερεῖν τὴν τῶν Συρακοσίων καταφρόνησιν ἀντανήχθησαν τοῖς πολεμίοις ἐν τῷ μεγάλῳ λιμένι,[2] συνέστη πασῶν τῶν τριήρων ναυμαχία. οἱ μὲν οὖν Ἀθηναῖοι 5 ταχυναυτούσας ἔχοντες τριήρεις καὶ ταῖς κατὰ θάλατταν ἐμπειρίαις, ἔτι δὲ ταῖς τῶν κυβερνητῶν τέχναις προτεροῦντες, ἄπρακτον εἶχον τὴν ἐν τούτοις ὑπεροχήν, τῆς ναυμαχίας ἐν στενῷ τόπῳ γινομένης· οἱ δὲ Συρακόσιοι συμπλεκόμενοι καὶ τοῖς πολεμίοις οὐδεμίαν διδόντες ἀναστροφήν, τούς τε ἐπὶ τῶν καταστρωμάτων ἠκόντιζον καὶ λιθοβολοῦντες λιπεῖν ἠνάγκαζον τὰς πρῴρας, ἁπλῶς δὲ πολλαῖς τῶν ἐμπιπτουσῶν νεῶν ἐμβολὰς[3] διδόντες καὶ εἰς τὰς τῶν ἐναντίων ναῦς εἰσαλλόμενοι 6 πεζομαχίαν ἐν ταῖς ναυσὶ συνίσταντο. θλιβόμενοι δὲ πανταχόθεν οἱ Ἀθηναῖοι πρὸς φυγὴν ὥρμησαν· οἱ δὲ Συρακόσιοι διώξαντες ἑπτὰ μὲν τριήρεις κατέδυσαν πολλὰς δὲ ἀχρήστους ἐποίησαν.

11. Τῶν δὲ Συρακοσίων ἐπηρμένων ταῖς ἐλπίσι διὰ τὸ καὶ κατὰ γῆν καὶ κατὰ θάλατταν τοὺς πολεμίους νενικηκέναι, παρῆν Εὐρυμέδων καὶ Δημοσθένης, καταπεπλευκότες μὲν ἐξ Ἀθηνῶν μετὰ δυνάμεως πολλῆς, ἐν δὲ τῷ παράπλῳ παρὰ Θουρίων

---

[1] ἐπειδὴ MSS., Vogel, cp. chs. 66. 6, 99. 6; ἔπειτα Stephanus, cp. Thuc. 7. 40. 4.

[2] καὶ after λιμένι deleted by Wesseling.

ming blows, sink with one shock the triremes of the
Athenians.[1]

Now day after day the Syracusans attacked the
camp of the enemy both by land and by sea, but to no
effect, since the Athenians made no move ; but when
some of the captains of triremes, being no longer able
to endure the scorn of the Syracusans, put out against
the enemy in the Great Harbour, a sea-battle com-
menced in which all the triremes joined.   Now though
the Athenians had fast-sailing triremes and enjoyed
the advantage from their long experience at sea as
well as from the skill of their pilots, yet their superiority in these respects brought them no return since
the sea-battle was in a narrow area ; and the Syracusans, engaging at close quarters and giving the
enemy no opportunity to turn about to ram, not only
cast spears at the soldiers on the decks, but also, by
hurling stones, forced them to leave the prows, and in
many cases simply by ramming a ship that met them
and then boarding the enemy vessel they made it a
land-battle on the ship's deck.   The Athenians, being
pressed upon from every quarter, turned to flight ;
and the Syracusans, pressing in pursuit, not only sank
seven triremes but made a large number unfit for use.

11. At the moment when the hopes of the Syracusans had raised their spirits high because of their
victory over the enemy both by land and by sea,
Eurymedon and Demosthenes arrived, having sailed
there from Athens with a great force and gathered on
the way allied troops from the Thurians and Messa-

[1] Thucydides (7. 36) describes in considerable detail this
strengthening of the bow and its effect upon the tactics of the
fighting in the harbour.

---

³ ἐμβολὰς] ἐμβολαῖς PAHFK.

2 καὶ Μεσσαπίων προσειληφότες συμμαχίαν. ἦγον
δὲ τριήρεις πλείους τῶν ὀγδοήκοντα,[1] στρατιωτῶν
δὲ χωρὶς τῶν ἐν τοῖς πληρώμασι πεντακισχιλίους·
ὅπλα δὲ καὶ χρήματα, πρὸς δὲ τούτοις τὰ πρὸς
πολιορκίαν ὄργανα καὶ τὴν ἄλλην παρασκευὴν ἐν
στρογγύλοις πλοίοις ἐκόμιζον. δι' ἣν αἰτίαν οἱ
Συρακόσιοι πάλιν ἐταπεινοῦντο ταῖς ἐλπίσι, νομίζοντες μηκέτι ῥᾳδίως ἐξισωθῆναι τοῖς πολεμίοις
δυνήσεσθαι.

3 Δημοσθένης δὲ πείσας τοὺς συνάρχοντας ἐπιθέσθαι ταῖς Ἐπιπολαῖς, ἄλλως γὰρ οὐ δυνατὸν
ἦν ἀποτειχίσαι τὴν πόλιν, ἀναλαβὼν μυρίους μὲν
ὁπλίτας, ἄλλους δὲ τοσούτους ψιλούς, νυκτὸς
ἐπέθετο τοῖς Συρακοσίοις. ἀπροσδοκήτου δὲ
γενομένης τῆς ἐφόδου φρουρίων τέ τινων ἐκράτησαν καὶ παρεισπεσόντες ἐντὸς τοῦ τειχίσματος τῆς
4 Ἐπιπολῆς μέρος τι τοῦ τείχους κατέβαλον. τῶν
δὲ Συρακοσίων πανταχόθεν συνδραμόντων ἐπὶ τὸν
τόπον, ἔτι δὲ Ἑρμοκράτους μετὰ τῶν ἐπιλέκτων
ἐπιβοηθήσαντος, ἐξεώσθησαν οἱ Ἀθηναῖοι καὶ
νυκτὸς οὔσης διὰ τὴν ἀπειρίαν τῶν τόπων ἄλλοι
5 κατ' ἄλλους τόπους ἐσκεδάσθησαν. οἱ δὲ Συρακόσιοι μετὰ τῶν συμμάχων καταδιώξαντες, δισχιλίους
μὲν καὶ πεντακοσίους τῶν πολεμίων ἀποκτείναντες,
οὐκ ὀλίγους δὲ τραυματίας ποιήσαντες, πολλῶν ὅπ-
6 λων ἐκυρίευσαν. μετὰ δὲ τὴν μάχην Συρακόσιοι μὲν
Σικανὸν ἕνα τῶν στρατηγῶν μετὰ δώδεκα τριήρων ἀπέστειλαν εἰς τὰς ἄλλας πόλεις τήν τε νίκην
ἀπαγγελοῦντα τοῖς συμμάχοις καὶ βοηθεῖν ἀξιοῦντα.

12. Ἀθηναῖοι δέ, τῶν πραγμάτων αὐτοῖς ἐπὶ
τὸ χεῖρον ἐκβάντων καὶ διὰ τὸ τὸν περικείμενον
τόπον ὑπάρχειν ἑλώδη λοιμικῆς καταστάσεως εἰς

pians. They brought more than eighty triremes and 413 b.c.
five thousand soldiers, excluding the crews ; and they
also conveyed on merchant vessels arms and money
as well as siege machines and every other kind of
equipment. As a result the hopes of the Syracusans
were dashed again, since they believed that they
could not now readily find the means to bring themselves up to equality with the enemy.

Demosthenes persuaded his fellow commanders to
assault Epipolae, for it was impossible by any other
means to wall off the city, and taking ten thousand
hoplites and as many more light-armed troops, he
attacked the Syracusans by night. Since the assault
had not been expected, they overpowered some forts,
and breaking into the fortifications of Epipolê threw
down a part of the wall. But when the Syracusans ran
together to the scene from every quarter and
Hermocrates also came to the aid with the picked
troops, the Athenians were forced out and, it being
night, because of their unfamiliarity with the region
were scattered some to one place and others to
another. The Syracusans and their allies, pursuing
after them, slew two thousand five hundred of the
enemy, wounded not a few, and captured much
armour. And after the battle the Syracusans dispatched Sicanus, one of their generals, with twelve [1]
triremes to the other cities, both to announce the
victory to the allies and to ask them for aid.

12. The Athenians, now that their affairs had taken
a turn for the worse and a wave of pestilence had struck
the camp because the region round about it was

----

[1] Thucydides (7. 46) says fifteen.

----

[1] π (ὀγδοήκοντα) Stroth : τι P, τριακοσίων HL, τριακοσίων
δέκα cet.

τὸ στρατόπεδον ἐμπεσούσης, ἐβουλεύοντο πῶς δεῖ
2 χρῆσθαι τοῖς πράγμασιν. Δημοσθένης μὲν οὖν
ᾤετο δεῖν ἀποπλεῖν τὴν ταχίστην εἰς Ἀθήνας,
φάσκων αἱρετώτερον εἶναι πρὸς Λακεδαιμονίους
ὑπὲρ τῆς πατρίδος κινδυνεύειν ἢ καθημένους εἰς
Σικελίαν μηδὲν τῶν χρησίμων ἐπιτελεῖν· ὁ δὲ
Νικίας οὐκ ἔφη δεῖν αἰσχρῶς οὕτως ἐγκαταλιπεῖν
τὴν πολιορκίαν, καὶ τριήρων καὶ στρατιωτῶν ἔτι
δὲ χρημάτων εὐπορούντας· πρὸς δὲ τούτοις, ἐὰν
ἄνευ τῆς τοῦ δήμου γνώμης εἰρήνην ποιησάμενοι πρὸς τοὺς Συρακοσίους ἀποπλεύσωσιν εἰς τὴν
πατρίδα, κίνδυνον αὐτοῖς ἐπακολουθήσειν ἀπὸ τῶν
3 εἰωθότων τοὺς στρατηγοὺς συκοφαντεῖν. τῶν δὲ
εἰς τὸ συμβούλιον παρειλημμένων οἱ μὲν τῷ Δημοσθένει συγκατέθεντο περὶ τῆς ἀναγωγῆς, οἱ δὲ
τῷ Νικίᾳ τὴν αὐτὴν γνώμην ἀπεφαίνοντο· διόπερ
4 οὐδὲν σαφὲς ἐπικρίναντες ἐφ᾽ ἡσυχίας ἔμενον. τοῖς
δὲ Συρακοσίοις παραγενομένης συμμαχίας παρά
τε Σικελῶν[1] καὶ Σελινουντίων, ἔτι δὲ Γελῴων,
πρὸς δὲ τούτοις Ἱμεραίων καὶ Καμαριναίων, οἱ
μὲν Συρακόσιοι μᾶλλον ἐθάρρουν, οἱ δ᾽ Ἀθηναῖοι
περιδεεῖς ἐγίνοντο.[2] τῆς δὲ νόσου μεγάλην ἐπίτασιν λαμβανούσης πολλοὶ τῶν στρατιωτῶν ἀπέθνησκον, καὶ πάντες μετεμέλοντο διὰ τὸ μὴ πάλαι
5 τὸν ἀπόπλουν πεποιῆσθαι. διὸ καὶ τοῦ πλήθους
θορυβοῦντος, καὶ τῶν ἄλλων πάντων ἐπὶ τὰς ναῦς
ὁρμώντων, ὁ Νικίας ἠναγκάσθη συγχωρῆσαι περὶ
τῆς εἰς οἶκον ἀναγωγῆς. ὁμογνωμόνων δὲ ὄντων τῶν στρατηγῶν, οἱ στρατιῶται τὰ σκεύη
ἐνετίθεντο καὶ τὰς τριήρεις πληρώσαντες ἦρον
τὰς κεραίας· καὶ παρήγγειλαν οἱ στρατηγοὶ τοῖς
πλήθεσιν, ὅταν σημήνῃ, μηδένα τῶν κατὰ τὸ στρα-

marshy, counselled together how they should deal with the situation.   Demosthenes thought that they should sail back to Athens with all speed, stating that to risk their lives against the Lacedaemonians in defence of their fatherland was preferable to settling down on Sicily and accomplishing nothing worth while ; but Nicias said that they ought not to abandon the siege in so disgraceful a fashion, while they were well supplied with triremes, soldiers, and funds ; furthermore, he added, if they should make peace with the Syracusans without the approval of the Athenian people and sail back to their country, peril would attend them from the men who make it their practice to bring false charges against their generals.   Of the participants in the council some agreed with Demosthenes on putting to sea, but others expressed the same opinion as Nicias ; and so they came to no clear decision and took no action.   And since help came to the Syracusans from the Siceli, Selinuntians, and Geloans, as well as from the Himeraeans and Camarinaeans, the Syracusans were the more emboldened, but the Athenians became apprehensive.   Also, when the epidemic greatly increased, many of the soldiers were dying and all regretted that they had not set out upon their return voyage long since.   Consequently, since the multitude was in an uproar and all the others were eager to take to the ships, Nicias found himself compelled to yield on the matter of their returning home.   And when the generals were agreed, the soldiers began gathering together their equipment, loading the triremes, and raising the yard-arms ; and the generals issued orders to the multitude that at the signal not a man in the camp

---

¹ So Eichstädt : Σικελιωτῶν.   ² So Dindorf : ἐγένοντο.

τόπεδον ὑστερεῖν, ὡς ἀπολειφθησόμενον τὸν βραδύ-
6 νοντα. μελλόντων δ' αὐτῶν τῇ ὑστεραίᾳ πλεῖν,
ἐξέλιπεν ἡ σελήνη τῆς ἐπιούσης νυκτός. διόπερ ὁ
Νικίας, καὶ φύσει δεισιδαίμων ὑπάρχων καὶ διὰ
τὴν ἐν τῷ στρατοπέδῳ νόσον εὐλαβῶς διακείμενος,
συνεκάλεσε τοὺς μάντεις. τούτων δ' ἀποφηναμέ-
νων ἀναγκαῖον εἶναι τὰς εἰθισμένας τρεῖς ἡμέρας
ἀναβαλέσθαι τὸν ἔκπλουν, ἠναγκάσθησαν καὶ οἱ
περὶ τὸν Δημοσθένην συγκαταθέσθαι διὰ τὴν πρὸς
τὸ θεῖον εὐλάβειαν.

13. Οἱ δὲ Συρακόσιοι παρά τινων αὐτομόλων
πυθόμενοι τὴν αἰτίαν τοῦ ὑπερτεθεῖσθαι τὸν ἀπόπλουν, τάς τε τριήρεις πάσας ἐπλήρωσαν, οὔσας
ἑβδομήκοντα καὶ τέσσαρας, καὶ τὰς πεζὰς δυνάμεις
ἐξαγαγόντες προσέβαλον τοῖς πολεμίοις καὶ κατὰ
2 γῆν καὶ κατὰ θάλατταν. οἱ δ' Ἀθηναῖοι τριήρεις
πληρώσαντες ἓξ πρὸς ταῖς ὀγδοήκοντα, τὸ μὲν
δεξιὸν κέρας παρέδωκαν Εὐρυμέδοντι τῷ στρατηγῷ,
καθ' ὃ ἐτάχθη ὁ τῶν Συρακοσίων στρατηγὸς
Ἀγάθαρχος· ἐπὶ δὲ θατέρου μέρους Εὐθύδημος
ἐτέτακτο, καθ' ὃν ἀντετάξατο Σικανὸς τῶν Συρακοσίων ἡγούμενος· τῆς δὲ μέσης τάξεως εἶχε τὴν
ἡγεμονίαν παρὰ μὲν τοῖς Ἀθηναίοις Μένανδρος
παρὰ δὲ τοῖς Συρακοσίοις Πύθης ὁ Κορίνθιος.
3 ὑπερτεινούσης δὲ τῆς τῶν Ἀθηναίων φάλαγγος
διὰ τὸ πλείοσιν αὐτοὺς ἀγωνίζεσθαι τριήρεσιν,
οὐχ ἥκιστα καθ' ὃ πλεονεκτεῖν ἐδόκουν κατὰ τοῦτο
ἠλαττώθησαν. ὁ γὰρ Εὐρυμέδων ἐπιχειρήσας
περιπλεῖν τὸ κέρας τῶν ἐναντίων, ὡς ἀπεσπάσθη
τῆς τάξεως, ἐπιστρεψάντων ἐπ' αὐτὸν τῶν Συρακοσίων ἀπελήφθη πρὸς τὸν κόλπον τὸν Δάσκωνα

should be late, for he who lagged would be left behind. 413 b.c. But when they were about to sail on the following day, on the night of the day before, the moon was eclipsed.[1] Consequently Nicias, who was not only by nature a superstitiously devout man but also cautious because of the epidemic in the camp, summoned the soothsayers. And when they declared that the departure must be postponed for the customary three days,[2] Demosthenes and the others were also compelled, out of respect for the deity, to accede.

13. When the Syracusans learned from some deserters why the departure had been deferred, they manned all their triremes, seventy-four in number, and leading out their ground forces attacked the enemy both by land and by sea. The Athenians, having manned eighty-six triremes, assigned to Eurymedon, the general, the command of the right wing, opposite to which was stationed the general of the Syracusans, Agatharchus; on the other wing Euthydemus had been stationed and opposite to him was Sicanus commanding the Syracusans; and in command of the centre of the line were Menander for the Athenians and Pythes the Corinthian for the Syracusans. Although the Athenian line was the longer since they were engaging with a superior number of triremes, yet the very factor which they thought would work to their advantage was not the least in their undoing. For Eurymedon endeavoured to outflank the opposing wing; but when he had become detached from his line, the Syracusans turned to face him and he was cut off and forced into a bay

---

[1] 27th August, 413 b.c.
[2] " Thrice nine days," according to Thucydides, 7. 50. 4 ; " another full period of the moon," according to Plutarch, *Nicias*, 23. 6.

μὲν καλούμενον, ὑπὸ δὲ τῶν Συρακοσίων κατεχό-
4 μενον. κατακλεισθεὶς δ' εἰς στενὸν τόπον καὶ
βιασθεὶς εἰς τὴν γῆν ἐκπεσεῖν, αὐτὸς μὲν ὑπό τινος
τρωθεὶς καιρίᾳ πληγῇ τὸν βίον μετήλλαξεν, ἑπτὰ
5 δὲ ναῦς ἐν τούτῳ τῷ τόπῳ διεφθάρησαν. τῆς δὲ
ναυμαχίας ἤδη γινομένης ὅλοις τοῖς στόλοις, ὡς
διεδόθη λόγος τόν τε στρατηγὸν ἀνῃρῆσθαι καὶ
τινας ναῦς ἀπολωλέναι, τὸ μὲν πρῶτον αἱ μάλιστα
συνεγγίζουσαι ταῖς διεφθαρμέναις ναυσὶν ἐνέκλιναν,
μετὰ δὲ ταῦτα τῶν Συρακοσίων ἐπικειμένων καὶ
διὰ τὸ γεγονὸς εὐημέρημα θρασέως ἀγωνιζομένων,
βιασθέντες οἱ Ἀθηναῖοι πάντες φυγεῖν ἠναγκά-
6 σθησαν. γενομένου δὲ τοῦ διωγμοῦ πρὸς τὸ τε-
ναγῶδες μέρος τοῦ λιμένος, οὐκ ὀλίγαι τῶν τριήρων
ἐν τοῖς βράχεσιν ἐπώκειλαν. ὧν συμβαινόντων
Σικανὸς ὁ τῶν Συρακοσίων στρατηγὸς ταχέως
ὁλκάδα κληματίδων καὶ δάδων, ἔτι δὲ πίττης
πληρώσας, ἐνέπρησε τὰς ἐν τοῖς βράχεσι ναῦς
7 κυλινδουμένας. ὧν ἀναφθεισῶν οἱ μὲν Ἀθηναῖοι
ταχέως τήν τε φλόγα κατέσβεσαν καὶ ἀπὸ τῶν
νεῶν ἐρρωμένως ἠμύναντο τοὺς ἐπιφερομένους,
ἄλλην οὐδεμίαν εὑρίσκοντες σωτηρίαν· τὰ δὲ πεζὰ
στρατόπεδα παρεβοήθει παρὰ τὸν αἰγιαλὸν ἐφ'
8 ὃν αἱ ναῦς ἐξεπεπτώκεισαν. ἁπάντων δὲ καρτερῶς
ὑπομενόντων τὸν κίνδυνον, ἐπὶ μὲν τῆς γῆς ἐτράπησαν οἱ Συρακόσιοι, κατὰ θάλατταν δὲ προτερή-
σαντες ἀπέπλευσαν εἰς τὴν πόλιν. ἀπώλοντο δὲ
τῶν μὲν Συρακοσίων ὀλίγοι, τῶν δ' Ἀθηναίων
ἄνδρες μὲν οὐκ ἐλάττους δισχιλίων, τριήρεις δ'
ὀκτωκαίδεκα.

14. Οἱ δὲ Συρακόσιοι νομίζοντες μηκέτι τὸν
κίνδυνον εἶναι περὶ τῆς πόλεως, ἀλλὰ πολὺ μᾶλλον

called Dascon which was held by the Syracusans. Being hemmed in as he was into a narrow place, he was forced to run ashore, where some man gave him a mortal wound and he lost his life, and seven of his ships were destroyed in this place. The battle had now spread throughout both fleets, and when the word was passed along that the general had been slain and some ships lost, at first only those ships gave way which were nearest to those which had been destroyed, but later, as the Syracusans pressed forward and pushed the fight boldly because of the success they had won, the whole Athenian force was overpowered and compelled to turn in flight. And since the pursuit turned toward the shallow part of the harbour, not a few triremes ran aground in the shoals. When this took place, Sicanus, the Syracusan general, straightway filling a merchant ship with faggots and pine-wood and pitch, set fire to the ships which were wallowing in the shoals. But although they were put on fire, the Athenians not only quickly extinguished the flames but, finding no other means of safety, also vigorously fought off from their ships the men who were rushing against them; and the land forces ran to their aid along the beach on which the ships had run ashore. And since they all withstood the attack with vigour, on land the Syracusans were turned back, but at sea they won the decision and sailed back to the city. The losses of the Syracusans were few, but of the Athenians not less than two thousand men and eighteen triremes.

14. The Syracusans, believing that the danger no longer was the losing of their city but that, far

ἐνεστηκέναι τὸν ἀγῶνα περὶ τοῦ λαβεῖν τὸ στρατόπεδον μετὰ τῶν πολεμίων αἰχμάλωτον, ἀπέφρατ-
τον τὸ στόμα τοῦ λιμένος ζεῦγμα κατασκευάζοντες.
2 ἀκάτους τε γὰρ καὶ τριήρεις ἔτι δὲ στρογγύλας
ναῦς ἐπ' ἀγκυρῶν ὁρμίσαντες, καὶ σιδηραῖς ἀλύ-
σεσι διαλαμβάνοντες, ἐπὶ τὰ σκάφη γεφύρας ἐκ
σανίδων κατεσκεύασαν καὶ πέρας ἐν ἡμέραις τρισὶ
3 τοῖς ἔργοις ἐπέθηκαν.[1] οἱ δ' Ἀθηναῖοι θεωροῦντες
αὑτοῖς πάντοθεν τὴν σωτηρίαν ἀποκεκλεισμένην,
ἔκριναν ἁπάσας τὰς τριήρεις πληροῦν καὶ τῶν
πεζῶν τοὺς κρατίστους ἐμβιβάσαι, τῷ τε πλήθει
τῶν νεῶν καὶ τῇ τῶν ἀγωνιζομένων ὑπὲρ τῆς
σωτηρίας ἀπονοίᾳ καταπλήξειν[2] τοὺς Συρακοσίους.
4 διόπερ τοὺς ἐπὶ ταῖς ἡγεμονίαις τεταγμένους καὶ
τοὺς ἀρίστους ἐξ ὅλου τοῦ στρατεύματος ἐμβιβά-
σαντες τριήρεις μὲν ἐπλήρωσαν πέντε λειπούσας
τῶν ἑκατὸν εἴκοσι, τοὺς δὲ λοιποὺς ἐπὶ τῆς γῆς
ἔταξαν παρὰ τὸν αἰγιαλόν. οἱ δὲ Συρακόσιοι τὸ
μὲν πεζὸν στράτευμα πρὸ τῆς πόλεως ἔστησαν,
τριήρεις δὲ συνεπλήρωσαν ἑβδομήκοντα τέσσαρας·
συμπαρείποντό τε τὰς ὑπηρετικὰς ἔχοντες ναῦς
παῖδες ἐλεύθεροι, τοῖς τε ἔτεσιν ὄντες ὑπὸ τὴν τῶν
νεανίσκων ἡλικίαν καὶ συναγωνιζόμενοι μετὰ τῶν
5 πατέρων. τὰ δὲ περὶ τὸν λιμένα τείχη καὶ πᾶς ὁ
τῆς πόλεως ὑπερκείμενος τόπος ἔγεμε σωμάτων·
γυναῖκές τε γὰρ καὶ παρθένοι καὶ οἱ[3] ταῖς ἡλικίαις τὴν ἐν τῷ πολέμῳ χρείαν παρέχεσθαι μὴ
δυνάμενοι, τοῦ παντὸς πολέμου τὴν κρίσιν λαμ-
βάνοντος,[4] μετὰ πολλῆς ἀγωνίας ἐπεθεώρουν τὴν
μάχην.

15. Καθ' ὃν δὴ χρόνον Νικίας ὁ τῶν Ἀθηναίων
στρατηγὸς ἐπιβλέψας τὰς ναῦς καὶ τὸ μέγεθος τοῦ

more, the contest had become one for the capture 413 B.C.
of the camp together with the enemy, blocked off
the entrance to the harbour by the construction of
a barrier. For they moored at anchor both small
vessels and triremes as well as merchant-ships, with
iron chains between them, and to the vessels they
built bridges of boards, completing the undertaking
in three days.¹ The Athenians, seeing their hope of
deliverance shut off in every direction, decided to
man all their triremes and put on them their best
land troops, and thus, by means both of the multitude of their ships and of the desperation of the
men who would be fighting for their lives, eventually
to strike terror into the Syracusans.² Consequently
they put on board the officers and choicest troops
from the whole army, manning in this way one
hundred and fifteen triremes, and the other soldiers
they stationed on land along the beach. The Syracusans drew up their infantry before the city, and
fully manned seventy-four triremes ; and the triremes
were attended by free boys on small boats, who were
in years below manhood and were fighting at the side
of their fathers. And the walls about the harbour
and every high place in the city were crowded with
people ; for wives and maidens and all who, because
of age, could not render the service war demands,
since³ the whole war was coming to its decision, were
eyeing the battle with the greatest anguish of spirit.

15. At this time Nicias, the general of the Athenians, as he surveyed the ships and measured the

---

¹ συντέλειαν after ἐπέθηκαν omitted LM.
² Dindorf adds ἐλπίζοντες after καταπλήξειν.
³ ἐν after οἱ deleted by Hertlein.
⁴ So Reiske : λαμβάνοντες.

κινδύνου λογισάμενος, οὐκ ἐπέμεινεν ἐπὶ τῆς ἐν
τῇ γῇ τάξεως, ἀλλὰ καταλιπὼν τοὺς πεζοὺς ἐπί
τινα ναῦν ἀνέβη καὶ παρέπλει τὰς τριήρεις τῶν
Ἀθηναίων. ἕκαστον δὲ τῶν τριηράρχων ἐξ
ὀνόματος προσφωνῶν καὶ τὰς χεῖρας ἐκτείνων
ἐδεῖτο πάντων, εἰ καὶ¹ πρότερον,² τὸ νῦν ἀντιλα-
βέσθαι τῆς μόνης καταλελειμμένης ἐλπίδος· ἐν
γὰρ ταῖς τῶν ναυμαχεῖν μελλόντων ἀρεταῖς καὶ
ἑαυτῶν ἁπάντων καὶ τῆς πατρίδος κεῖσθαι τὴν
2 σωτηρίαν. καὶ τοὺς μὲν τέκνων ὄντας πατέρας
τῶν υἱῶν ὑπομιμνήσκων, τοὺς δ᾽ ἐνδόξων γεγονότας
πατέρων παρακαλῶν τὰς τῶν προγόνων ἀρετὰς
μὴ καταισχῦναι, τοὺς δ᾽ ὑπὸ τοῦ δήμου τετιμη-
μένους προτρεπόμενος ἀξίους φανῆναι τῶν στεφάνων, ἅπαντας δ᾽ ἀναμνησθέντας τῶν ἐν Σαλαμῖνι
τροπαίων ἠξίου μὴ καταρρῖψαι τῆς πατρίδος τὴν
περιβόητον δόξαν, μηδὲ αὐτοὺς ἀνδραπόδων τρόπον
παραδοῦναι τοῖς Συρακοσίοις.

3 Ὁ μὲν οὖν Νικίας τοιούτοις χρησάμενος λόγοις
πάλιν ἐπὶ τὴν ἰδίαν τάξιν ἐπανῆλθεν· οἱ δ᾽ ἐν ταῖς
ναυσὶ παιανίσαντες ἔπλεον καὶ φθάσαντες τοὺς
πολεμίους διέλυον τὸ ζεῦγμα. οἱ δὲ Συρακόσιοι
ταχέως ἐπαναχθέντες συνετάττοντο ταῖς τριήρεσι,
καὶ συμπλεκόμενοι τοῖς ἐναντίοις ἠνάγκασαν αὐτοὺς ἐπιστρέφειν ἀπὸ τοῦ ζεύγματος καὶ διαμά-
4 χεσθαι. ποιουμένων δὲ τὰς ἀνακρούσεις τῶν μὲν
ἐπὶ τὸν αἰγιαλόν, τῶν δ᾽ εἰς μέσον τὸν λιμένα,
τινῶν δὲ πρὸς τὰ τείχη, ταχέως ἀπ᾽ ἀλλήλων
διεσπάσθησαν αἱ τριήρεις ἅπασαι, καὶ χωρισθέντων
ἀπὸ τῶν κλείθρων πλήρης ἦν ὁ λιμὴν τῶν κατ᾽

---

¹ εἰ καὶ Dindorf, cp. Thuc. 7. 64. 2, 70. 7 : εἶναι.
² ἢ after πρότερον deleted by Vogel.

magnitude of the struggle, could not remain at his 413 B.C.
station on shore, but leaving the land troops he
boarded a boat and passed along the line of the
Athenian triremes. Calling each captain by name
and stretching forth his hands, he implored them all,
now if ever before, to grasp the only hope left to
them, for on the valour of those who were about to
join battle at sea depended the preservation both
of themselves, every man of them, and of their
fatherland. Those who were fathers of children he
reminded of their sons ; those who were sons of distinguished fathers he exhorted not to bring disgrace
upon the valorous deeds of their ancestors ; those
who had been honoured by their fellow citizens he
urged to show themselves worthy of their crowns ;
and all of them he reminded of the trophies erected
at Salamis and begged them not to bring to disrepute
the far-famed glory of their fatherland nor surrender
themselves like slaves to the Syracusans.

After Nicias had spoken to this effect, he returned
to his station, and the men of the fleet advanced
singing the paean and broke through the barrier of
boats before the enemy could prevent them. But
the Syracusans, putting quickly out to sea, formed
their triremes in battle order and coming to grips
with the enemy forced them to withdraw from the
barrier of boats and fight a pitched battle. And
as the ships backed water, some toward the beach,
others toward the middle of the harbour, and still
others in the direction of the walls, all the triremes
were quickly separated from each other, and after
they had got clear of the boom across its entrance

5 ὀλίγους ναυμαχούντων. ἔνθα δὴ παραβόλως ἀμφοτέρων περὶ τῆς νίκης ἀγωνιζομένων, οἱ μὲν
Ἀθηναῖοι τῷ τε πλήθει τῶν νεῶν θαρροῦντες καὶ
σωτηρίαν ἄλλην οὐχ ὁρῶντες θρασέως ἐκινδύνευον
καὶ τὸν ἐν τῇ μάχῃ θάνατον εὐγενῶς ὑπέμενον[1]·
οἱ δὲ Συρακόσιοι θεατὰς τῶν ἀγώνων ἔχοντες
γονεῖς καὶ παῖδας ἐφιλοτιμοῦντο πρὸς ἀλλήλους,
ἑκάστου βουλομένου δι᾽ ἑαυτοῦ τὴν νίκην περιγενέσθαι τῇ πατρίδι.

16. Διὸ καὶ πολλοὶ ταῖς τῶν ἐναντίων πρῴραις
ἐπιβάντες, τῆς οἰκείας νεὼς ὑφ᾽ ἑτέρας τρωθείσης,
ἐν μέσοις τοῖς πολεμίοις ἀπελαμβάνοντο. ἔνιοι
δὲ σιδηρᾶς χεῖρας ἐπιβάλλοντες ἠνάγκαζον τοὺς
2 ἀντιταττομένους ἐπὶ τῶν νεῶν πεζομαχεῖν. πολλάκις δὲ τὰς ἰδίας ἔχοντες ναῦς συντετριμμένας
εἰς τὰς τῶν ἐναντίων μεθαλλόμενοι, καὶ τοὺς μὲν
ἀποκτείνοντες, τοὺς δ᾽ εἰς τὴν θάλατταν προ-
ωθοῦντες ἐκυρίευον τῶν τριήρων. ἁπλῶς[2] δὲ καθ᾽
ὅλον τὸν λιμένα τῶν τ᾽ ἐμβολῶν ψόφος ἐγίνετο
καὶ βοὴ τῶν ἀγωνιζομένων ἐναλλὰξ ἀπολλυμένων.
3 ὅτε γὰρ ἀποληφθείη ναῦς ὑπὸ πλειόνων τριήρων
πανταχόθεν τυπτομένη τοῖς χαλκώμασι, τοῦ ῥεύματος εἰσπίπτοντος αὔτανδρος ὑπὸ τῆς θαλάττης κατεπίνετο. ἔνιοι δὲ καταδυομένων τῶν νεῶν
ἀποκολυμβῶντες τοῖς τε τόξοις κατετιτρώσκοντο
4 καὶ τοῖς δόρασι τυπτόμενοι διεφθείροντο. οἱ δὲ
κυβερνῆται θεωροῦντες τεταραγμένην τὴν μάχην,
καὶ πάντα τόπον ὄντα πλήρη θορύβου, καὶ πολλάκις
ἐπὶ μίαν ναῦν πλείους ἐπιφερομένας, οὔθ᾽ ὅτι
σημαίνοιεν εἶχον, μὴ τῶν αὐτῶν πρὸς ἅπαντα

---

[1] So Dindorf: ὑπομένοντες.
[2] So Vogel: ὅλως.

the harbour was full of ships fighting in small groups. 413 B.C.
Thereupon both sides fought with abandon for the
victory. The Athenians, cheered by the multitude
of their ships and seeing no other hope of safety,
carried on the fight boldly and faced gallantly their
death in battle, and the Syracusans, with their parents
and children as spectators of the struggle, vied with
one another, each man wishing the victory to come
to his country through his own efforts.

16. Consequently many leaped on the prows of the
hostile ships, when their own had been damaged by
another, and were isolated in the midst of their
enemies. In some cases they dropped grappling-
irons [1] and forced their adversaries to fight a land-
battle on their ships. Often men whose own ships
had been shattered leaped on their opponents' vessels,
and by slaying the defenders or pushing them into
the sea became masters of their triremes. In a word,
over the entire harbour came the crash of ship striking
ship and the cry of desperately struggling men slaying
and being slain. For when a ship had been inter-
cepted by several triremes and struck by their beaks
from every direction, the water would pour in and
it would be swallowed together with the entire crew
beneath the sea. Some who would be swimming away
after their ship had been sunk would be wounded
by arrows or slain by the blows of spears. The
pilots, as they saw the confusion of the battle, every
spot full of uproar, and often a number of ships con-
verging upon a single one, did not know what signal
to give, since the same orders were not suitable to all

---

[1] Thucydides (7. 65) states that these were a device of the
Athenians, against which the Syracusans covered the decks
of their ships with hides so that the grappling-irons would
not take hold.

συμφερόντων, οὔτε πρὸς τοὺς κελεύοντας τοὺς
ἐρέτας[1] ἐνεδέχετο βλέπειν διὰ τὸ πλῆθος τῶν
5 βελῶν. ἁπλῶς δὲ τῶν παραγγελλομένων οὐδεὶς
οὐδὲν ἤκουε τῶν σκαφῶν θραυομένων καὶ παρα-
συρομένων τῶν ταρσῶν, ἅμα δὲ καὶ τῇ κραυγῇ[2]
τῶν ναυμαχούντων καὶ τῶν ἀπὸ τῆς γῆς συμ-
6 φιλοτιμουμένων. τοῦ γὰρ αἰγιαλοῦ παντὸς τὸ
μὲν ὑπὸ τῶν πεζῶν τῶν Ἀθηναίων κατείχετο, τὸ
δ' ὑπὸ τῶν Συρακοσίων, ὥστ' ἐνίοτε τοὺς παρὰ
τὴν γῆν ναυμαχοῦντας συμμάχους ἔχειν τοὺς ἐπὶ
7 τῆς χέρσου στρατοπεδεύοντας. οἱ δ' ἐπὶ τῶν
τειχῶν ὅτε μὲν ἴδοιεν τοὺς ἰδίους εὐημεροῦντας,
ἐπαιάνιζον, ὅτε δ' ἐλαττουμένους, ἔστενον καὶ
μετὰ δακρύων τοῖς θεοῖς προσηύχοντο. ἐνίοτε
γάρ, εἰ τύχοι, τῶν Συρακοσίων τριήρων παρὰ τὰ
τείχη διαφθείρεσθαί τινας συνέβαινε, καὶ τοὺς
ἰδίους ἐν ὀφθαλμοῖς τῶν συγγενῶν ἀναιρεῖσθαι,
καὶ θεωρεῖν γονεῖς μὲν τέκνων ἀπώλειαν, ἀδελφὰς
δὲ καὶ γυναῖκας ἀνδρῶν καὶ ἀδελφῶν οἰκτρὰν
καταστροφήν.

17. Ἐπὶ πολὺν δὲ χρόνον πολλῶν ἀπολλυμένων
ἡ μάχη τέλος οὐκ ἐλάμβανεν· οὐδὲ γὰρ οἱ θλιβόμενοι πρὸς τὴν γῆν φεύγειν ἐτόλμων. οἱ μὲν γὰρ
Ἀθηναῖοι τοὺς ἀφισταμένους τῆς μάχης καὶ τῇ
γῇ προσπλέοντας ἠρώτων εἰ διὰ τῆς γῆς εἰς
Ἀθήνας πλεῦσαι νομίζουσιν, οἱ δὲ πεζοὶ τῶν
Συρακοσίων τοὺς προσπλέοντας ἀνέκρινον, διὰ
τί βουλομένων αὐτῶν εἰς τὰς τριήρεις ἐμβαίνειν
κωλύσαντες αὐτοὺς μάχεσθαι νῦν προδιδόασι τὴν
πατρίδα, καὶ εἰ διὰ τοῦτο ἔφραξαν τὸ στόμα τοῦ

---

[1] Vogel's suggestion for ἑτέρους of the MSS.
[2] So Wesseling : τῆς κραυγῆς.

situations, nor was it possible, because of the multitude of missiles, for the oarsmen to keep their eyes
upon the men who gave them their orders. In short,
not a man could hear any of the commands amid the
shattering of boats and the sweeping off of oars,[1] as
well as amid the uproar of the men in combat on the
ships and of their zealous comrades on land. For
of the entire beach a part was held by the Athenian
infantry and a part by the Syracusans, so that at
times the men fighting the sea-battle had as helpers,
when along the shore, the soldiers lined up on the
land. The spectators on the walls, whenever they
saw their own fighters winning, would sing songs of
victory, but when they saw them being vanquished,
they would groan and with tears offer prayers to the
gods. For now and then it happened that some
Syracusan triremes would be destroyed along the
walls and their crews slain before the eyes of their
kinsmen, and parents would witness the destruction
of their children, sisters and wives the pitiable end
of husbands and brothers.

17. For a long time, despite the many who were
dying, the battle would not come to an end, since not
even the men who were in desperate straits would
dare flee to the land. For the Athenians would ask
those who were breaking off the battle and turning
to the land, " Do you think to sail to Athens by
land ? " and the Syracusan infantry would inquire of
any who were bringing their ships towards them,
" Why, when we wanted to go aboard the triremes,
did you prevent us from engaging in the battle, if
now you are betraying the fatherland ? " " Was the
reason you blocked the mouth of the harbour that,

---

[1] As one ship brushed by another.

λιμένος, ὅπως κωλύσαντες τοὺς πολεμίους αὐτοὶ
φεύγωσιν ἐπὶ τὸν αἰγιαλόν, καὶ τοῦ τελευτᾶν
ὀφειλομένου πᾶσιν ἀνθρώποις ποῖον ζητοῦσι καλλίω
θάνατον ἢ τὸν ὑπὲρ τῆς πατρίδος, ἣν ἔχοντες
μάρτυρα τῶν ἀγώνων αἰσχρῶς ἐγκαταλείπουσιν.
2 τοιαῦτα δὲ τῶν ἀπὸ τῆς γῆς στρατιωτῶν ὀνειδι-
ζόντων τοῖς προσπλέουσιν, οἱ πρὸς τοὺς αἰγιαλοὺς
ἀποφεύγοντες πάλιν ἀνέστρεφον, καίπερ συντετριμμένας ἔχοντες τὰς ναῦς καὶ ὑπὸ τῶν τραυμά-
3 των καταβαρούμενοι. τῶν δὲ παρὰ τὴν πόλιν
κινδυνευόντων Ἀθηναίων ἐκβιασθέντων καὶ πρὸς
φυγὴν ὁρμησάντων, οἱ προσεχεῖς ἀεὶ τῶν Ἀθηναίων[1] ἐνέκλινον, καὶ κατ' ὀλίγον ἅπαντες ἐτράπη-
4 σαν. οἱ μὲν οὖν Συρακόσιοι μετὰ πολλῆς κραυγῆς
κατεδίωκον τὰς ναῦς ἐπὶ τὴν γῆν· τῶν δὲ Ἀθηναίων ὅσοι μὴ μετέωροι διεφθάρησαν, ἐπεὶ πρὸς τὰ
βράχη προσηνέχθησαν, ἐκπηδῶντες ἐκ τῶν νεῶν[2]
5 εἰς τὸ πεζὸν στρατόπεδον ἔφευγον. ὁ δὲ λιμὴν
πλήρης ἦν ὅπλων τε καὶ ναυαγίων, ὡς ἂν Ἀττι-
κῶν μὲν νεῶν ἀπολομένων ἑξήκοντα, παρὰ δὲ τῶν
Συρακοσίων ὀκτὼ μὲν τελέως διεφθαρμένων, ἑκ-
καίδεκα δὲ συντετριμμένων. οἱ δὲ Συρακόσιοι
τῶν τε τριήρων ὅσας δυνατὸν ἦν εἷλκον ἐπὶ τὴν
γῆν, καὶ τοὺς τετελευτηκότας πολίτας τε καὶ συμμάχους ἀνελόμενοι δημοσίας ταφῆς ἠξίωσαν.
18. Οἱ δ' Ἀθηναῖοι συνδραμόντες ἐπὶ τὰς τῶν
ἡγεμόνων σκηνὰς ἐδέοντο τῶν στρατηγῶν,[3] μὴ
τῶν νεῶν, ἀλλὰ τῆς ἑαυτῶν φροντίζειν σωτηρίας.
Δημοσθένης μὲν οὖν ἔφη δεῖν, λελυμένου τοῦ

---

[1] τῶν Ἀθηναίων deleted by Wesseling, Eichstädt.
[2] ἀπολομένων (from 3 ll. below) after νεῶν deleted by Dindorf.

after preventing the enemy from getting out, you might yourselves flee to the beach?" "Since it is the lot of all men to die, what fairer death do you seek than dying for the fatherland, which you are disgracefully abandoning though you have it as a witness of your fighting!" When the soldiers on the land hurled such upbraidings at the sailors who drew near, those who were fleeing for refuge to the beach would turn back again, even though their ships were shattered and they themselves were weighed down by their wounds. But when the Athenians who were engaged near the city had been thrust back and began to flee, the Athenians next in line gave way from time to time and gradually the whole host took to flight. Thereupon the Syracusans with great shouting pursued the ships to the land; and those Athenians who had not been slain out at sea, now that they had come to shallow water, leaped from the ships and fled to the land troops. And the harbour was full of arms and wreckage of boats, since of the Attic ships sixty were lost and of the Syracusan eight were completely destroyed and sixteen badly damaged. The Syracusans drew up on the shore as many of their triremes as they could, and taking up the bodies of their citizens and allies who had died, honoured them with a public funeral.

18. The Athenians thronged to the tents of their commanders and begged the generals to take thought, not for the ships, but for the safety of themselves. Demosthenes, accordingly, declared that, since the

---

[3] So Dindorf: στρατιωτῶν.

ζεύγματος, κατὰ τάχος πληροῦν τὰς τριήρεις,
καὶ ἀπροσδοκήτως ἐπιθεμένους ἐπηγγέλλετο ῥᾳδίως
2 κρατήσειν τῆς ἐπιβολῆς· Νικίας δὲ συνεβούλευε
καταλιπόντας τὰς ναῦς διὰ τῆς μεσογείου¹ πρὸς
τὰς συμμαχίδας πόλεις ἀναχωρεῖν. ᾧ πάντες
ὁμογνώμονες γενόμενοι τῶν νεῶν τινας ἐνέπρησαν
καὶ τὰ πρὸς τὴν ἀπαλλαγὴν παρεσκευάζοντο.
3 Φανεροῦ δ' ὄντος ὅτι τῆς νυκτὸς ἀναζεύξουσιν,
Ἑρμοκράτης συνεβούλευε τοῖς Συρακοσίοις ἐξάγειν τῆς νυκτὸς ἅπαν τὸ στρατόπεδον καὶ τὰς
4 ὁδοὺς ἁπάσας προκαταλαβέσθαι. οὐ πειθομένων
δὲ τῶν στρατηγῶν διὰ τὸ πολλοὺς μὲν τραυματίας
εἶναι τῶν στρατιωτῶν, πάντας δ' ὑπὸ τῆς μάχης
κατακόπους ὑπάρχειν τοῖς σώμασιν, ἀπέστειλέ
τινας τῶν ἱππέων ἐπὶ τὴν παρεμβολὴν τῶν Ἀθηναίων τοὺς ἐροῦντας, ὅτι προαπεστάλκασιν οἱ
Συρακόσιοι τοὺς τὰς ὁδοὺς καὶ τοὺς ἐπικαιροτάτους
5 τόπους προκαταληψομένους. ποιησάντων δὲ τῶν
ἱππέων τὸ προσταχθὲν ἤδη νυκτὸς οὔσης, οἱ μὲν
Ἀθηναῖοι νομίσαντες τῶν Λεοντίνων τινὰς εἶναι
τοὺς δι' εὔνοιαν ἀπηγγελκότας, διεταράχθησαν οὐ
μικρῶς καὶ τὴν ἀπαλλαγὴν ὑπερέθεντο· ὥπερ² εἰ
μὴ παρεκρούσθησαν, ἀσφαλῶς ἂν ἐχωρίσθησαν.
6 οἱ μὲν οὖν Συρακόσιοι τῆς ἡμέρας ὑποφωσκούσης
ἀπέστειλαν τοὺς προκαταληψομένους τὰ στενόπορα
τῶν ὁδῶν· οἱ δὲ τῶν Ἀθηναίων στρατηγοὶ διελό-
μενοι τοὺς στρατιώτας εἰς δύο μέρη, καὶ τὰ μὲν
σκευοφόρα καὶ τοὺς ἀρρώστους εἰς μέσον λαβόν-

---

¹ χώρας after μεσογείου deleted by Vogel.
² So Wesseling : ὅπερ.

barrier of boats had been broken, they should straight- 413 B.C. way man the triremes, and he expressed the belief that, if they delivered an unexpected attack, they would easily succeed in their design.[1] But Nicias advised that they leave the ships behind and withdraw through the interior to the cities which were their allies. This plan was agreed to by all, and they burned some of the ships and made preparations for the retreat.

When it was evident that the Athenians were going to withdraw during the night, Hermocrates advised the Syracusans to lead forth their entire army in the night and seize all the roads beforehand. And when the generals would not agree to this, both because many of the soldiers were wounded and because all of them were worn-out in body from the fighting, he sent some of the horsemen to the camp of the Athenians to tell them that the Syracusans had already dispatched men to seize in advance the roads and the most important positions. It was already night when the horsemen carried out these orders, and the Athenians, believing that it was men from Leontini who out of goodwill had brought them the word, were not a little disturbed and postponed the departure. If they had not been deceived by this trick, they would have got safely away. The Syracusans at daybreak dispatched the soldiers who were to seize in advance the narrow passes in the roads. And the Athenian generals, dividing the soldiers into two bodies, put the pack-animals and the sick and injured in the centre and stationed those who were in con-

---

[1] Thucydides (7. 72) states that Nicias agreed to this plan, but gave it up when the sailors, after their hard beating, refused to man the ships.

τες, τοὺς δὲ δυναμένους μάχεσθαι προηγεῖσθαι καὶ
οὐραγεῖν τάξαντες, προῄεσαν ἐπὶ Κατάνης, ὧν μὲν
Δημοσθένους, ὧν δὲ Νικίου καθηγουμένων.

19. Οἱ δὲ Συρακόσιοι πεντήκοντα μὲν τὰς κατα-
λειφθείσας ναῦς ἀναψάμενοι κατήγαγον εἰς τὴν
πόλιν, ἐκβιβάσαντες δ' ἐκ τῶν τριήρων ἅπαντας
καὶ καθοπλίσαντες, μετὰ πάσης τῆς δυνάμεως
ἠκολούθουν τοῖς Ἀθηναίοις, ἐξαπτόμενοι καὶ βαδί-
2 ζειν εἰς τοὔμπροσθεν διακωλύοντες. ἐπὶ τρεῖς δ'
ἡμέρας ἐπακολουθοῦντες καὶ πανταχόθεν περι-
λαμβάνοντες[1] ἀπεῖργον εὐθυπορεῖν πρὸς τὴν σύμμαχον Κατάνην, παλινοδίαν δὲ καταναγκάσαντες
ποιήσασθαι διὰ τοῦ Ἑλωρίου πεδίου, πρὸς τῷ
Ἀσινάρῳ ποταμῷ περικυκλώσαντες ἀπέκτειναν
μὲν μυρίους ὀκτακισχιλίους, ἐζώγρησαν δὲ[2] ἑπτα-
κισχιλίους, ἐν οἷς καὶ τοὺς στρατηγοὺς Δημοσθένην καὶ Νικίαν· οἱ δὲ λοιποὶ διηρπάσθησαν
3 ὑπὸ τῶν στρατιωτῶν. οἱ γὰρ Ἀθηναῖοι πάντοθεν ἀποκλειομένης τῆς σωτηρίας ἠναγκάσθησαν τὰ
ὅπλα καὶ ἑαυτοὺς παραδοῦναι τοῖς πολεμίοις. τούτων δὲ πραχθέντων οἱ Συρακόσιοι στήσαντες δύο
τρόπαια, καὶ τὰ τῶν στρατηγῶν ὅπλα πρὸς ἑκάτερον
προσηλώσαντες, ἀνέστρεψαν εἰς τὴν πόλιν.

4 Τότε μὲν οὖν τοῖς θεοῖς ἔθυσαν πανδημεί, τῇ
δ' ὑστεραίᾳ συναχθείσης ἐκκλησίας ἐβουλεύοντο
πῶς χρήσονται τοῖς αἰχμαλώτοις. Διοκλῆς δέ
τις, τῶν δημαγωγῶν ἐνδοξότατος ὤν, ἀπεφήνατο
γνώμην ὡς δέοι τοὺς μὲν στρατηγοὺς τῶν Ἀθη-

---

[1] So Madvig : προλαμβάνοντες.
[2] ὀκτακισχιλίους, ἐζώγρησαν δὲ omitted PF.

dition to fight in the van and the rear, and then set out for Catanê, Demosthenes commanding one group and Nicias the other.

19. The Syracusans took in tow the fifty ships left behind [1] and brought them to the city, and then, taking off all the crews of their triremes and providing them with arms, they followed after the Athenians with their entire armament, harassing them and hindering their forward progress. For three days following close on their heels and encompassing them on all sides they prevented them from taking a direct road toward Catanê, their ally ; instead they compelled them to retrace their steps through the plain of Elorium, and surrounding them at the Asinarus River, slew eighteen thousand and took captive seven thousand, among whom were also the generals Demosthenes and Nicias. The remainder were seized as their plunder by the soldiers [2] ; for the Athenians, since their escape was blocked in every direction, were obliged to surrender their weapons and their persons to the enemy. After this had taken place, the Syracusans set up two trophies, nailing to each of them the arms of a general, and turned back to the city.

Now at that time the whole city of Syracuse offered sacrifices to the gods, and on the next day, after the Assembly had gathered, they considered what disposition they should make of the captives. A man named Diocles, who was a most notable leader of the populace, declared his opinion that the Athenian

---

[1] By the Athenians.

[2] The seven thousand were formally surrendered and became prisoners of the state ; the others were taken by the soldiers as their individual captives, either before the formal surrender or after, as they were picked up over the countryside.

ναίων μετ' αἰκίας ἀνελεῖν, τοὺς δ' ἄλλους αἰχμαλώτους ἐν μὲν τῷ παρόντι τεθῆναι πάντας εἰς τὰς
λατομίας, μετὰ δὲ ταῦτα τοὺς μὲν συμμαχήσαντας
τοῖς Ἀθηναίοις λαφυροπωλῆσαι, τοὺς δ' Ἀθηναίους ἐργαζομένους ἐν τῷ δεσμωτηρίῳ λαμβάνειν
5 ἀλφίτων δύο κοτύλας.[1] ἀναγνωσθέντος δὲ τοῦ
ψηφίσματος Ἑρμοκράτης παρελθὼν εἰς τὴν ἐκκλησίαν ἐνεχείρει λέγειν, ὡς κάλλιόν ἐστι τοῦ νικᾶν
6 τὸ τὴν νίκην ἐνεγκεῖν ἀνθρωπίνως. θορυβοῦντος
δὲ τοῦ δήμου καὶ τὴν δημηγορίαν οὐχ ὑπομένοντος,
Νικόλαός τις, ἐστερημένος ἐν τῷ πολέμῳ δυεῖν
υἱῶν, ἀνέβαινεν ἐπὶ τὸ βῆμα κατεχόμενος ὑπὸ
τῶν οἰκετῶν διὰ τὸ γῆρας· ὃν ὡς εἶδεν ὁ δῆμος,
ἔληξε τοῦ θορύβου, νομίζων κατηγορήσειν τῶν
αἰχμαλώτων. γενομένης οὖν σιωπῆς ὁ πρεσβύτερος
ἐντεῦθεν ἤρξατο τῶν λόγων.

20. Τῶν κατὰ τὸν πόλεμον ἀτυχημάτων, ἄνδρες
Συρακόσιοι, μέρος οὐκ ἐλάχιστον ἐγὼ μετέσχηκα·
δυεῖν γὰρ υἱῶν γενόμενος πατὴρ ἐξέπεμψα μὲν
αὐτοὺς εἰς τὸν ὑπὲρ τῆς πατρίδος κίνδυνον, ὑπε-
δεξάμην δ' ἀντ'[2] αὐτῶν ἀγγελίαν ἣ τὸν ἐκείνων
2 θάνατον ἐμήνυεν. διὸ καὶ καθ' ἡμέραν ἐπιζητῶν
τὴν συμβίωσιν καὶ τὴν τελευτὴν ἀναλογιζόμενος,
ἐκείνους μὲν μακαρίζω, τὸν ἐμαυτοῦ δὲ βίον ἐλεῶ,
3 πάντων ἡγούμενος εἶναι δυστυχέστατος. ἐκεῖνοι
μὲν γὰρ τὸν ὀφειλόμενον τῇ φύσει θάνατον εἰς
πατρίδος σωτηρίαν ἀναλώσαντες ἀθάνατον ἑαυτῶν
δόξαν καταλελοίπασιν, ἐγὼ δ' ἐπὶ τῆς ἐσχάτης
ἡλικίας ἔρημος ὢν τῶν θεραπευσόντων τὸ γῆρας

---

[1] So Wesseling (cp. Thuc. 7. 87. 2 ; Plut. *Nic.* 29. 1) : χοίνικας.
[2] ἀντ' added by Reiske.

generals should be put to death under torture and 413 B.C. the other prisoners should for the present all be thrown into the quarries; but that later the allies of the Athenians should be sold as booty and the Athenians should labour as prisoners under guard, receiving two cotyls [1] of barley meal. When this motion had been read, Hermocrates took the floor and endeavoured to show that a fairer thing than victory is to bear the victory with moderation.[2] But when the people shouted their disapproval and would not allow him to continue, a man named Nicolaüs, who had lost two sons in the war, made his way, supported by his slaves because of his age, to the platform. When the people saw him, they stopped shouting, believing that he would denounce the prisoners. As soon, then, as there was silence, the old man began to speak.

20. " Of the misfortunes of the war, men of Syracuse, I have shared in a part, and not the least; for being the father of two sons, I sent them into the struggle on behalf of the fatherland, and I received back, in place of them, a message which announced their death. Therefore, as I miss their companionship each day and call to mind once more that they are dead, I deem them happy, but pity my own lot, believing myself to be the most unfortunate of men. For they, having expended for the salvation of their fatherland the death which mankind owes to Nature, have left behind them deathless renown for themselves, whereas I, bereft at the end of my days of those who were to minister to my old age, bear a

---

[1] An almost starvation fare of about one pint.

[2] His words in Plutarch, *Nicias*, 28. 2 are: τοῦ νικᾶν κρεῖττόν ἐστι τὸ καλῶς χρῆσθαι τῇ νίκῃ (" Better than victory is a noble use of victory ").

διπλοῦν ἔχω τὸ πένθος, τὴν συγγένειαν ἅμα καὶ
4 ἀρετὴν ἐπιζητῶν· ὅσῳ γὰρ εὐγενέστερον ἐτελεύτησαν, τοσούτῳ ποθεινοτέραν τὴν ὑπὲρ αὐτῶν
μνήμην καταλελοίπασιν. εἰκότως οὖν μισῶ τοὺς
Ἀθηναίους, δι' ἐκείνους οὐχ ὑπὸ τῶν τέκνων, ἀλλ'
5 ὑπὸ οἰκετῶν, ὡς ὁρᾶτε, χειραγωγούμενος. εἰ μὲν
οὖν ἑώρων, ὦ ἄνδρες Συρακόσιοι, τὴν παροῦσαν
ἐνεστηκέναι βουλὴν ὑπὲρ Ἀθηναίων, εἰκότως ἂν
καὶ διὰ τὰς κοινὰς τῆς πατρίδος συμφορὰς καὶ
διὰ τὰς ἰδίας ἀτυχίας πικρῶς ἂν αὐτοῖς προσ-
ηνέχθην· ἐπεὶ δ' ἅμα τῷ πρὸς τοὺς ἠτυχηκότας
ἐλέῳ κρίνεται τό τε κοινῇ συμφέρον καὶ ἡ πρὸς
ἅπαντας ἀνθρώπους ὑπὲρ τοῦ δήμου τῶν Συρακοσίων ἐξενεχθησομένη δόξα, ἀκέραιον ποιήσομαι
τὴν τοῦ συμφέροντος συμβουλίαν.

21. Ὁ μὲν οὖν δῆμος τῶν Ἀθηναίων τῆς ἰδίας
ἀνοίας ἀξίαν κεκόμισται τιμωρίαν, πρῶτον μὲν
παρὰ θεῶν, μετὰ δὲ ταῦτα παρ' ἡμῶν τῶν ἀδικη-
2 θέντων. ἀγαθὸν γάρ ἐστι τὸ θεῖον τοὺς ἀδίκου
πολέμου καταρχομένους καὶ τὴν αὐτῶν[1] ὑπεροχὴν
οὐκ ἐνεγκόντας ἀνθρωπίνως ἀνελπίστοις περιβα-
3 λεῖν συμφοραῖς. τίς γὰρ ἂν ἤλπισεν Ἀθηναίους,
μύρια μὲν εἰληφότας ἐκ Δήλου τάλαντα, τριήρεις
δὲ διακοσίας εἰς Σικελίαν ἀπεσταλκότας καὶ τοὺς
ἀγωνισομένους ἄνδρας πλείους τῶν τετρακισμυρίων, οὕτως μεγάλαις συμφοραῖς περιπεσεῖσθαι;
ἀπὸ γὰρ τῆς τηλικαύτης παρασκευῆς οὔτε ναῦς
οὔτ' ἀνὴρ οὐθεὶς ἐπανῆλθεν, ὥστε μηδὲ τὸν ἀγγε-
4 λοῦντα αὐτοῖς τὴν συμφορὰν περιλειφθῆναι. εἰδό-

---

[1] So Stephanus: αὐτήν.

twofold sorrow, in that it is both the children of my own body and their valour that I miss. For the more gallant their death, the more poignant the memory of themselves they have left behind. I have good reason, then, for hating the Athenians, since it is because of them that I am being guided here, not by my own sons, but, as you can see, by slaves. Now if I perceived, men of Syracuse, that the matter under discussion was merely a decision affecting the Athenians, I with good reason, both because of the misfortunes of our country, shared by all, and because of my personal afflictions, should have dealt bitterly with them ; but since, along with consideration of the pity which is shown to unfortunates, the question at issue concerns both the good of the State and the fame of the people of the Syracusans which will be spread abroad to all mankind, I shall direct my proposal solely to the question of expediency.

21. " The people of the Athenians have received a punishment their own folly deserved, first of all from the hands of the gods and then from us whom they had wronged. Good it is indeed that the deity involves in unexpected disasters those who begin an unjust war and do not bear their own superiority as men should. For who could have expected that the Athenians, who had removed ten thousand talents [1] from Delos to Athens and had dispatched to Sicily two hundred triremes and more than forty thousand men to fight, would ever suffer disasters of such magnitude ? for from the preparations they made on such a scale not a ship, not a man has returned home, so that not even a survivor is left to carry to them word of the disaster. Knowing, therefore, men

---

[1] Given as " some eight thousand " in Book 12. 38. 2.

τες οὖν, ἄνδρες Συρακόσιοι, τοὺς ὑπερηφανοῦντας[1]
παρὰ θεοῖς καὶ παρ' ἀνθρώποις μισουμένους, προσ-
κυνοῦντες τὴν τύχην μηθὲν ὑπὲρ ἄνθρωπον πρά-
ξητε. τί γὰρ σεμνὸν φονεῦσαι τὸν ὑποπεπτωκότα;
τί δ' ἔνδοξον τιμωρίᾳ περιβαλεῖν; ὁ γὰρ ἀμετάθετον ἔχων τὴν περὶ τῶν ἀτυχημάτων[2] ὠμότητα
5 συναδικεῖ τὴν κοινὴν ἀνθρώπων ἀσθένειαν. οὐθεὶς
γάρ ἐστιν οὕτω φρόνιμος ὥστε μεῖζον ἰσχῦσαι τῆς
τύχης, ἢ φύσει ταῖς ἀνθρωπίναις ἡδομένη συμφοραῖς ὀξείας τῆς εὐδαιμονίας ποιεῖ τὰς μεταβολάς.
Ἐροῦσί τινες ἴσως, ἠδίκησαν καὶ τῆς κατ' αὐ-
6 τῶν τιμωρίας ἔχομεν τὴν ἐξουσίαν. οὐκοῦν παρὰ
μὲν τοῦ δήμου πολλαπλασίαν εἰλήφατε τιμωρίαν,
παρὰ δὲ τῶν αἰχμαλώτων ἱκανὴν ἔχετε κόλασιν;
παρέδωκαν γὰρ ἑαυτοὺς μετὰ τῶν ὅπλων πιστεύσαντες τῇ τῶν κρατούντων εὐγνωμοσύνῃ· διόπερ
οὐκ ἄξιον αὐτοὺς τῆς ἡμετέρας ψευσθῆναι φιλ-
7 ανθρωπίας. οἱ μὲν οὖν ἀμετάθετον τὴν ἔχθραν
φυλάττοντες μαχόμενοι τετελευτήκασιν, οἱ δ' ἑαυτοὺς ἡμῖν ἐγχειρίσαντες ἀντὶ πολεμίων γεγόνασιν
ἱκέται. οἱ γὰρ ἐν ταῖς μάχαις τοῖς ἐναντίοις τὰ
σώματα ἐγχειρίζοντες ἐπ' ἐλπίδι σωτηρίας τοῦτο
πράττουσιν· εἰ δὲ πιστεύσαντες τιμωρίας τεύξονται
τηλικαύτης, οἱ μὲν παθόντες ἀναδέξονται τὴν συμφοράν, οἱ δὲ πράξαντες ἀγνώμονες ἂν κληθεῖεν.

---

[1] καὶ after ὑπερηφανοῦντας omitted PA.
[2] Vogel suggests ἠτυχηκότων.

---

[1] Literally "do an injustice to." The "weakness" of
mankind lies in their being subject to the whim of Fortune.
The conqueror of to-day may to-morrow be pleading for

of Syracuse, that the arrogant are hated among gods 413 B.C. and men, do you, humbling yourselves before Fortune, commit no act that is beyond man's powers. What nobility is there in slaying the man who lies at your feet? What glory is there in wreaking vengeance on him? He who maintains his savagery unalterable amid human misfortunes also fails to take proper account [1] of the common weakness of mankind. For no man is so wise that his strength can prevail over Fortune, which of its nature finds delight in the sufferings of men and works swift changes in prosperity.

" Some, perhaps, will say, ' They have committed a wrong, and we have the power to punish them.' But have you, then, not inflicted a many times greater punishment on the Athenian people, and are you not satisfied with your chastisement of the prisoners? For they have surrendered themselves together with their arms, trusting in the reasonableness of their conquerors; it is, therefore, not seemly that they should be cheated of our expected humaneness. For those who maintained unalterable their enmity toward us have died fighting, but these who delivered themselves into our hands have become suppliants, no longer enemies. For those who in battle deliver their persons into the hands of their opponents do so in the hope of saving their lives; and should the men who have shown this trust receive so severe a punishment, though the victims will accept their misfortune, yet the punishers would be called hard-hearted. But

mercy from to-day's conquered. We should not shut our eyes to the universal law that a turn of Fortune may make the weak strong, the unfortunate favoured of Fortune. The same thought recurs twice *infra*, chap. 24. 4 (ἀδικεῖν) and 6 (ὑπερφρονεῖν τὴν ἀνθρωπίνην ἀσθένειαν), where the rôle of Fortune in the affairs of men is specifically mentioned.

8 δεῖ δὲ τοὺς τῆς ἡγεμονίας ἀντιποιουμένους, ὦ ἄνδρες
Συρακόσιοι, μὴ οὕτως τοῖς ὅπλοις ἑαυτοὺς ἰσχυροὺς
κατασκευάζειν ὡς τοῖς τρόποις ἐπιεικεῖς παρέχεσθαι.

22. Οἱ γὰρ ὑποτεταγμένοι τοὺς μὲν φόβῳ κατ-
ισχύοντας καιροτηρήσαντες ἀμύνονται διὰ τὸ μῖσος, τοὺς δὲ φιλανθρώπως ἀφηγουμένους βεβαίως
ἀγαπῶντες ἀεὶ συναύξουσι τὴν ἡγεμονίαν. τί
καθεῖλε τὴν Μήδων ἀρχήν; ἡ πρὸς τοὺς ταπεινο-
2 τέρους ὠμότης. ἀποστάντων γὰρ Περσῶν καὶ
τὰ πλεῖστα τῶν ἐθνῶν συνεπέθετο. πῶς γὰρ Κῦρος
ἐξ ἰδιώτου τῆς Ἀσίας ὅλης ἐβασίλευσε; τῇ πρὸς
τοὺς κρατηθέντας εὐγνωμοσύνῃ. Κροῖσον γὰρ
τὸν βασιλέα λαβὼν αἰχμάλωτον οὐχ ὅπως ἠδί-
κησεν, ἀλλὰ καὶ προσευηργέτησεν· παραπλησίως
δὲ καὶ τοῖς ἄλλοις βασιλεῦσί τε καὶ δήμοις προσ-
3 ηνέχθη. τοιγαροῦν διαδοθείσης εἰς πάντα τόπον
τῆς ἡμερότητος ἅπαντες οἱ κατὰ τὴν Ἀσίαν ἀλλήλους φθάνοντες εἰς τὴν τοῦ βασιλέως συμμαχίαν
παρεγίνοντο.

4 Τί λέγω τὰ μακρὰν καὶ τόποις καὶ χρόνοις
ἀφεστηκότα; κατὰ γὰρ τὴν ἡμετέραν πόλιν οὐ
πάλαι Γέλων ἐξ ἰδιώτου τῆς Σικελίας ὅλης ἡγεμὼν
ἐγένετο, τῶν πόλεων ἑκουσίως εἰς τὴν ἐξουσίαν
ἐκείνου παραγενομένων· προσεκαλεῖτο γὰρ ἡ τἀνδρὸς ἐπιείκεια πάντας ἀνθρώπους, τὴν εἰς τοὺς
5 ἠτυχηκότας συγγνώμην[1] προσλαβοῦσα.[2] ἀπ᾽ ἐκείνων οὖν τῶν χρόνων τῆς κατὰ Σικελίαν ἡγεμονίας
ἀντιποιουμένης τῆς πόλεως, μὴ καταρρίψωμεν τὸν

---

[1] So Reiske: γνώμην.   [2] So Wesseling: προσβαλοῦσα.

---

[1] King of Persia, 550–529 B.C.
[2] " General " of Syracuse, 485–478 B.C. For his great
victory over the Carthaginians at Himera see Book 11. 22 ff.

those who lay claim to leadership, men of Syracuse, _{413 B.C.} should not strive to make themselves strong in arms so much as they should show themselves reasonable in their character.

22. " The fact is that subject peoples bide their time against those who dominate them by fear and, because of their hatred, retaliate upon them, but they steadfastly cherish those who exercise their leadership humanely and thereby always aid them in strengthening their supremacy. What destroyed the kingdom of the Medes ? Their brutality toward the weaker. For after the Persians revolted from them, their kingdom was attacked by most of the nations also. Else how did Cyrus [1] rise from private citizen to the kingship over all of Asia ? By his considerate treatment of the conquered. When, for example, he took King Croesus captive, far from doing him any injustice he actually became his benefactor ; and in much the same way did he also deal with all the other kings as well as peoples. As a consequence, when the fame of his clemency had been spread abroad to every region, all the inhabitants of Asia vied with one another in entering into alliance with the king.

" But why do I speak of things distant in both place and time ? In this our city, not long since, Gelon [2] rose from private citizen [3] to be lord of the whole of Sicily, the cities willingly putting themselves under his authority ; for the fairness of the man, combined with his sympathy for the unfortunate, drew all men to him. And since from those times our city has laid claim to the leadership in Sicily, let us not bring into disrepute the fair name our ancestors

[3] Not strictly true, since Gelon was tyrant of Gela when he was called to Syracuse by the aristocratic party.

ὑπὲρ τῶν προγόνων ἔπαινον, μηδ᾽ ἑαυτοὺς θηριώ-
δεις καὶ ἀπαραιτήτους πρὸς ἀνθρωπίνην ἀτυχίαν
παράσχωμεν. οὐ γὰρ προσήκει δοῦναι τῷ φθόνῳ
καθ᾽ ἡμῶν ἀφορμὴν εἰπεῖν ὡς ἀναξίως εὐτυχοῦμεν·
καλὸν γὰρ καὶ τὸ τῆς τύχης ἀντιπραττούσης ἔχειν
τοὺς συναλγήσοντας καὶ πάλιν ἐν τοῖς κατορθώ-
6 μασι τοὺς ἡδομένους. τὰ μὲν οὖν ἐν τοῖς ὅπλοις
πλεονεκτήματα τύχῃ καὶ καιρῷ κρίνεται πολλάκις,
ἡ δ᾽ ἐν ταῖς εὐπραξίαις ἡμερότης ἴδιόν ἐστι ση-
μεῖον τῆς τῶν εὐτυχούντων ἀρετῆς. διὸ μὴ φθο-
νήσητε τῇ πατρίδι περιβόητον γενέσθαι παρὰ
πᾶσιν ἀνθρώποις ὅτι τοὺς Ἀθηναίους ἐνίκησεν οὐ
μόνον τοῖς ὅπλοις, ἀλλὰ καὶ τῇ φιλανθρωπίᾳ.
7 φανήσονται γὰρ οἱ[1] τῶν ἄλλων ὑπερέχειν ἡμερό-
τητι σεμνυνόμενοι τῇ παρ᾽ ἡμῶν εὐγνωμοσύνῃ
πολυωρούμενοι, καὶ οἱ πρῶτοι βωμὸν ἐλέου καθ-
ιδρυσάμενοι τοῦτον ἐν τῇ πόλει τῶν Συρακοσίων
8 εὑρήσουσιν. ἐξ ὧν πᾶσιν ἔσται φανερὸν ὡς ἐκεῖνοι
μὲν δικαίως ἐσφάλησαν, ἡμεῖς δ᾽ ἀξίως ηὐτυ-
χήσαμεν, εἴπερ οἱ μὲν τοιούτους ἀδικεῖν ἐπεχείρησαν οἳ καὶ πρὸς τοὺς ἐχθροὺς εὐγνωμόνησαν,
ἡμεῖς δὲ τοιούτους ἐνικήσαμεν οἳ καὶ τοῖς πολε-
μιωτάτοις μερίζουσι τὸν ἔλεον ἐτόλμησαν ἐπιβου-
λεῦσαι· ὥστε μὴ μόνον ὑπὸ τῶν ἄλλων κατηγορίας
τυγχάνειν τοὺς Ἀθηναίους, ἀλλὰ καὶ αὐτοὺς ἑαυτῶν καταγινώσκειν, εἰ τοιούτους ἄνδρας ἀδικεῖν
ἐνεχείρησαν.
23. Καλόν, ὦ ἄνδρες Συρακόσιοι, κατάρξασθαι

----

[1] οἱ added by Rhodoman.

----

[1] It was a boast of the Athenians that their city had always

won nor show ourselves brutal and implacable toward 413 B.C. human misfortune. Indeed it is not fitting to give envy an occasion to criticize us by saying that we make an unworthy use of our good fortune ; for it is a fine thing to have those who will grieve with us when Fortune is adverse and rejoice in turn at our successes. The advantages which are won in arms are often determined by Fortune and opportunity, but clemency amid constant success is a distinctive mark of the virtue of men whose affairs prosper. Do not, therefore, begrudge our country the opportunity of being acclaimed by all mankind, because it has surpassed the Athenians not only in feats of arms but also in humanity. For it will be manifest that the people who vaunt their superiority to all others in civilization have received by our kindness all consideration, and they who were the first to raise an altar to Mercy [1] will find that mercy in the city of the Syracusans. From this it will be clear to all that they suffered a just defeat and we enjoyed a deserved success, if it so be that, although they sought to wrong men who had treated with kindness even their foes, we, on the contrary, defeated men who ventured treacherously to attack a people which shows mercy even to its bitterest enemies. And so the Athenians would not only stand accused by all the world, but even they themselves would condemn themselves, that they had undertaken to wrong such men.

23. " A fine thing it is, men of Syracuse, to take

been a refuge for the distressed, such as Orestes and Oedipus and the children of Heracles. The altar of Mercy and its grove were well known to the ancient world and are described at length in one of the more famous passages of the *Thebaid* (12. 481-511 ; tr. in the *L.C.L.*) of Statius, who calls it the altar of " gentle Clemency."

φιλίας, καὶ τῷ τῶν ἠτυχηκότων ἐλέῳ σπείσασθαι
τὴν διαφοράν. δεῖ γὰρ τὴν μὲν πρὸς τοὺς φίλους
εὔνοιαν ἀθάνατον φυλάττειν, τὴν δὲ πρὸς τοὺς
ἐναντίους ἔχθραν θνητήν· οὕτω γὰρ συμβήσεται
τοὺς μὲν συμμάχους γίνεσθαι πλείους, τοὺς δὲ
2 πολεμίους ἐλάττους. τὴν δὲ διαφορὰν αἰώνιον δια-
φυλάττοντας παραδιδόναι παισὶ παίδων οὔτ' εὔ-
γνωμον οὔτε ἀσφαλές· ἐνίοτε γὰρ οἱ δοκοῦντες
ὑπερέχειν ἐν ῥοπῇ καιροῦ τῶν πρότερον ὑποπεπτω-
3 κότων ἀσθενέστεροι γίνονται. μαρτυρεῖ δ' ὁ νῦν
γενόμενος πόλεμος· οἱ γὰρ ἐπὶ πολιορκίᾳ παραγενόμενοι καὶ διὰ τὴν ὑπεροχὴν ἀποτειχίσαντες
τὴν πόλιν ἐκ μεταβολῆς αἰχμάλωτοι γεγόνασιν,
ὡς ὁρᾶτε. καλὸν οὖν ἐν ταῖς τῶν ἄλλων ἀτυχίαις
ἡμέρους φανέντας ἕτοιμον ἔχειν τὸν παρὰ πάντων
ἔλεον ἐάν τι συμβαίνῃ τῶν ἀνθρωπίνων. πολλὰ
γὰρ ὁ βίος ἔχει παράδοξα, στάσεις πολιτικάς,
λῃστείας, πολέμους, ἐν οἷς οὐ ῥᾴδιον διαφεύγειν
4 τὸν κίνδυνον ἄνθρωπον ὄντα. διόπερ εἰ τὸν πρὸς
τοὺς ὑποπεπτωκότας ἔλεον ἀποκόψομεν, πικρὸν
καθ' ἑαυτῶν νόμον θήσομεν εἰς ἅπαντα τὸν αἰῶνα.
οὐ γὰρ δυνατὸν τοὺς ἄλλοις ἀνημέρως χρησαμένους
αὐτοὺς παρ' ἑτέρων τυχεῖν ποτε φιλανθρωπίας,
ἄλλους τε[1] πράξαντας δεινὰ παθεῖν εὐγνώμονα
καὶ παρὰ τοὺς τῶν Ἑλλήνων ἐθισμοὺς τοσούτους
ἄνδρας φονεύσαντας ἐν ταῖς τοῦ βίου μεταβολαῖς
5 ἐπιβοᾶσθαι τὰ κοινὰ πάντων νόμιμα. τίς γὰρ
Ἑλλήνων τοὺς παραδόντας ἑαυτοὺς καὶ τῇ τῶν

[1] ἄλλους τε Wesseling, οὐδὲ Rhodoman, καὶ Dindorf: ἀλλά.

186

the lead in establishing a friendship and, by showing mercy to the unfortunate, to make up the quarrel. For goodwill toward our friends should be kept imperishable, but hatred toward our enemies perishable, since by this practice it will come about that one's allies increase in number and one's enemies decrease. But for us to maintain the quarrel forever and to pass it on to children's children is neither kindly nor safe ; since it sometimes happens that those who appear to be more powerful turn out to be weaker by the decision of a moment than their former subjects. And a witness to this is the war which has just now ceased : The men who came here to lay siege to the city and, by means of their superior power, threw a wall about it have by a change in fortune become captives, as you can see. It is a fine thing, therefore, by showing ourselves lenient amid the misfortunes of other men, to have reserved for us the hope of mercy from all men, in case some ill befall us of such as come to mortal men. For many are the unexpected things life holds —civic strifes, robberies, wars, amid which one may not easily avoid the peril, being but human. Consequently, if we shall exclude the thought of mercy for the defeated, we shall be setting up, for all time to come, a harsh law against ourselves. For it is impossible that men who have shown no compassion for others should themselves ever receive humane treatment at the hands of another and that men who have outraged others should be treated indulgently, or that we, after murdering so many men contrary to the traditions of the Greeks, should in the reversals which attend life appeal to the usages common to all mankind. For what Greek has ever judged that those who have surrendered themselves and put

187

κρατούντων εὐγνωμοσύνῃ πιστεύσαντας ἀπαραιτή-
του τιμωρίας ἠξίωκεν,[1] ἢ τίς ἧττον τοῦ μὲν ὠμοῦ
τὸν ἔλεον, τῆς δὲ προπετείας τὴν εὐλάβειαν
ἔσχηκεν;

24. Πάντες δὲ ἀνατείνονται μὲν πρὸς τοὺς ἀντιταττομένους, εἴκουσι δὲ τοῖς ὑποπεπτωκόσιν, ὧν
μὲν τὴν τόλμαν καταπονοῦντες, ὧν δὲ τὴν ἀτυχίαν
οἰκτείροντες. θραύεται γὰρ ἡμῶν ὁ θυμὸς ὅταν
ὁ πρότερον ἐχθρὸς ὢν ἐκ μεταβολῆς ἱκέτης γενόμενος ὑπομένῃ παθεῖν ὅτι ἂν δοκῇ τοῖς κρατοῦσιν.
2 ἁλίσκονται δ', οἶμαι, τῶν ἡμέρων ἀνδρῶν αἱ ψυ-
χαὶ μάλιστά πως ἐλέῳ διὰ τὴν κοινὴν τῆς φύσεως
ὁμοπάθειαν. Ἀθηναῖοι γὰρ κατὰ τὸν Πελοποννη-
σιακὸν πόλεμον εἰς τὴν Σφακτηρίαν νῆσον πολλοὺς
τῶν Λακεδαιμονίων κατακλείσαντες καὶ λαβόντες
3 αἰχμαλώτους ἀπελύτρωσαν τοῖς Σπαρτιάταις. πάλιν Λακεδαιμόνιοι πολλοὺς τῶν Ἀθηναίων καὶ τῶν
συμμάχων αἰχμαλωτισάμενοι παραπλησίως ἐχρήσαντο. καὶ καλῶς ἀμφότεροι ταῦτ' ἔπραξαν. δεῖ
γὰρ τοῖς Ἕλλησι τὴν ἔχθραν εἶναι μέχρι τῆς νίκης,
4 καὶ κολάζειν μέχρι τοῦ κρατῆσαι τῶν ἐναντίων. ὁ
δὲ περαιτέρω τὸν ὑποπεσόντα καὶ πρὸς τὴν τοῦ
κρατοῦντος εὐγνωμοσύνην προσφεύγοντα τιμωρού-
μενος οὐκέτι τὸν ἐχθρὸν κολάζει, πολὺ δὲ μᾶλλον
5 ἀδικεῖ τὴν ἀνθρωπίνην ἀσθένειαν. εἴποι[2] γὰρ ἄν
τις πρὸς τὴν τοῦ τοιούτου σκληρότητα τὰς τῶν
πάλαι σοφῶν ἀποφάσεις, ἄνθρωπε, μὴ μέγα φρόνει,
γνῶθι σαυτόν, ἰδὲ τὴν τύχην ἁπάντων οὖσαν κυρίαν.
τίνος γὰρ χάριν οἱ πρόγονοι πάντων τῶν Ἑλλήνων

---

[1] So Hertlein : ἠξίωσεν.
[2] So Hertlein, εἶπεν P, εἶπε other MSS.

[1] Cp. Book 12. 61 ff.

their trust in the kindness of their conquerors are deserving of implacable punishment ? or who has ever
held mercy less potent than cruelty, precaution than
rashness ?

24. " All men sturdily oppose the enemy which is
lined up for battle but fall back when he has surrendered, wearing down the hardihood of the former
and showing pity for the misfortune of the latter.
For our ardour is broken whenever the former enemy,
having by a change of fortune become a suppliant,
submits to suffer whatever suits the pleasure of his
conquerors. And the spirits of civilized men are
gripped, I believe, most perhaps by mercy, because
of the sympathy which nature has planted in all.
The Athenians, for example, although in the Peloponnesian War they had blockaded many Lacedaemonians on the island of Sphacteria [1] and taken them
captive, released them to the Spartans on payment
of ransom. On another occasion the Lacedaemonians,
when they had taken prisoner many of the Athenians
and their allies, disposed of them in the same manner.
And in so doing they both acted nobly. For hatred
should exist between Greeks only until victory has
been won and punishment only until the enemy
has been overcome. And whoever goes farther and
wreaks vengeance upon the vanquished who flees for
refuge to the leniency of his conqueror is no longer
punishing his enemy but, far more, is guilty of
an offence against human weakness. For against
harshness such as this one may mention the adages
of the wise men of old : ' O man, be not high-
spirited '; ' Know thyself '; ' Observe how Fortune
is lord of all.' For what reason did the ancestors
of all the Greeks ordain that the trophies set up in

189

ἐν ταῖς κατὰ πόλεμον νίκαις κατέδειξαν οὐ διὰ λίθων,
διὰ δὲ τῶν τυχόντων ξύλων ἱστάναι τὰ τρόπαια;
6 ἆρ᾽ οὐχ ὅπως ὀλίγον χρόνον διαμένοντα ταχέως ἀφα-
νίζηται τὰ τῆς ἔχθρας ὑπομνήματα; καθόλου δ᾽
εἰ μὲν αἰώνιον ἵστασθαι τὴν διαφορὰν βούλεσθε,
μάθετε τὴν ἀνθρωπίνην ἀσθένειαν ὑπερφρονοῦντες·
εἷς γὰρ καιρὸς καὶ βραχεῖα ῥοπὴ τύχης ταπεινοῖ
πολλάκις τοὺς ὑπερηφάνους.

25. Εἰ δ᾽, ὅπερ εἰκός ἐστι, παύσεσθε πολεμοῦντες, τίνα καλλίω καιρὸν εὑρήσετε τοῦ νῦν
ὑπάρχοντος, ἐν ᾧ τὴν πρὸς τοὺς ἐπταικότας φιλαν-
θρωπίαν ἀφορμὴν τῆς φιλίας ποιήσεσθε; μὴ γὰρ
οἴεσθε τὸν τῶν Ἀθηναίων δῆμον τελέως ἐξησθενη-
κέναι διὰ τὴν ἐν Σικελίᾳ συμφοράν, ὃς κρατεῖ
σχεδὸν τῶν τε κατὰ τὴν Ἑλλάδα νήσων ἁπασῶν
καὶ τῆς παραλίου τῆς τε κατὰ τὴν Εὐρώπην καὶ
2 τὴν Ἀσίαν ἔχει τὴν ἡγεμονίαν. καὶ γὰρ πρότερον
περὶ τὴν Αἴγυπτον τριακοσίας τριήρεις αὐτάνδρους
ἀπολέσας τὸν δοκοῦντα κρατεῖν βασιλέα συνθήκας
ἀσχήμονας ποιεῖν ἠνάγκασε, καὶ πάλιν ὑπὸ Ξέρξου
τῆς πόλεως κατασκαφείσης μετ᾽ ὀλίγον κἀκεῖνον
ἐνίκησε καὶ τῆς Ἑλλάδος τὴν ἡγεμονίαν ἐκτήσατο.
3 ἀγαθὴ γὰρ ἡ πόλις ἐν τοῖς μεγίστοις ἀτυχήμασι
μεγίστην ἐπίδοσιν λαβεῖν καὶ μηδέποτε ταπεινὸν
μηδὲν βουλεύεσθαι. καλὸν οὖν ἀντὶ τοῦ τὴν ἔχθραν
ἐπαύξειν συμμάχους αὐτοὺς ἔχειν φεισαμένους τῶν
4 αἰχμαλώτων. ἀνελόντες μὲν γὰρ αὐτοὺς τῷ θυμῷ
μόνον χαριούμεθα, τὴν ἄκαρπον ἐπιθυμίαν ἐκπλη-
ροῦντες, φυλάξαντες δὲ παρὰ μὲν τῶν εὖ παθόντων

---

[1] Around Memphis ; cp. Book 11. 74-77 *passim*.

celebrating victories in war should be made, not of stone, but of any wood at hand ? Was it not in order that the memorials of the enmity, lasting as they would for a brief time, should quickly disappear ? Speaking generally, if you wish to establish the quarrel for all time, know that in doing so you are treating with disdain human weakness ; for a single moment, a slight turn of Fortune, often brings low the arrogant.

25. " If, as is likely, you will make an end of the war, what better time will you find than the present, in which you will make your humane treatment of the prostrate the occasion for friendship ? For do not assume that the Athenian people have become completely exhausted by their disaster in Sicily, seeing that they hold sway over practically all the islands of Greece and retain the supremacy over the coasts of both Europe and Asia. Indeed once before, after losing three hundred triremes together with their crews in Egypt,[1] they compelled the King,[2] who seemed to hold the upper hand, to accept ignominious terms of peace, and again, when their city had been razed to the ground by Xerxes, after a short time they defeated him also and won for themselves the leadership of Greece. For that city has a clever way, in the midst of the greatest misfortunes, of making the greatest growth in power and of never adopting a policy that is mean-spirited. It would be a fine thing, therefore, instead of increasing their enmity, to have the Athenians as allies after sparing the prisoners. For if we put them to death we shall merely be indulging our anger, sating a fruitless passion, whereas if we put them under guard, we

[2] Of Persia ; cp. Book 12. 4.

τὴν χάριν ἕξομεν παρὰ δὲ τῶν ἄλλων ἁπάντων τὴν εὐδοξίαν.

26. Ναί, ἀλλά τινες τῶν Ἑλλήνων ἀπέσφαξαν τοὺς αἰχμαλώτους. τί οὖν; εἰ μὲν αὐτοῖς ἐκ ταύτης τῆς πράξεως ἔπαινοι τυγχάνουσι, μιμησώμεθα τοὺς τῆς δόξης πεφροντικότας· εἰ δὲ παρὰ πρώτων ἡμῶν τυγχάνουσι κατηγορίας, μηδὲ αὐτοὶ πράξωμεν τὰ αὐτὰ τοῖς ὁμολογουμένως ἡμαρτηκόσι. 2 μέχρι μὲν γὰρ τοῦ μηδὲν ἀνήκεστον πεπονθέναι τοὺς εἰς τὴν ἡμετέραν πίστιν ἑαυτοὺς παραδόντας, ἅπαντες καταμέμψονται δικαίως τὸν¹ Ἀθηναίων δῆμον· ἐὰν δὲ ἀκούσωσι παρὰ τὰ κοινὰ νόμιμα τοὺς αἰχμαλώτους παρεσπονδημένους, ἐφ' ἡμᾶς μετοίσουσι τὴν κατηγορίαν. καὶ γὰρ εἴ τινων ἄλλων, Ἀθηναίων ἄξιόν ἐστιν ἐντραπῆναι μὲν τὸ τῆς πόλεως ἀξίωμα, χάριν δ' αὐτοῖς ἀπομερίσαι 3 τῶν εἰς ἄνθρωπον εὐεργετημάτων. οὗτοι γάρ εἰσιν οἱ πρῶτοι τροφῆς ἡμέρου τοῖς Ἕλλησι μεταδόντες, ἣν ἰδίᾳ παρὰ θεῶν λαβόντες τῇ χρείᾳ κοινὴν ἐποίησαν· οὗτοι νόμους εὗρον, δι' οὓς ὁ κοινὸς βίος ἐκ τῆς ἀγρίας καὶ ἀδίκου ζωῆς εἰς ἥμερον καὶ δικαίαν ἐλήλυθε συμβίωσιν· οὗτοι πρῶτοι τοὺς καταφυγόντας διασώσαντες τοὺς περὶ τῶν ἱκετῶν νόμους παρὰ πᾶσιν ἀνθρώποις ἰσχῦσαι παρεσκεύασαν· ὧν ἀρχηγοὺς γενομένους οὐκ ἄξιον αὐτοὺς ἀποστερῆσαι. καὶ ταῦτα μὲν πρὸς ἅπαντας· ἰδίᾳ δ' ἐνίους ὑπομνήσω τῶν φιλανθρώπων.

---

¹ τὸν] τῶν P, τὸν τῶν Vogel; cp. ch. 27. 2, 4.

---

[1] Reference is to the discovery of corn (wheat) ; although in Book 5. 4, 69 Diodorus states that wheat was first discovered in Sicily and from there passed to the Athenians.

shall have the gratitude of the men we succoured and 413 B.C. the approbation of all other peoples.

26. " Yes, some will answer, but there are Greeks who have executed their prisoners. What of it ? If praise accrues to them from that deed, let us nevertheless imitate those who have paid heed to their reputation ; but if we are the first by whom they are accused, let us not ourselves commit the same crimes as those who by their own admission have sinned. So long as the men who entrusted their lives to our good faith have suffered no irremediable punishment, all men will justly censure the Athenian people ; but if they hear that, contrary to the generally accepted customs of mankind, faith has been broken with the captives, they will shift their accusation against us. For in truth, if it can be said of any other people, the prestige of the city of the Athenians deserves our reverence, and we may well return to them our gratitude for the benefactions they have bestowed upon man. For it is they who first gave to the Greeks a share in a food ¹ gained by cultivation of the soil, which, though they had received it from the gods ² for their exclusive use, they made available to all. They it was who discovered laws, by the application of which the manner of men's living has advanced from the savage and unjust existence to a civilized and just society. It was they who first, by sparing the lives of any who sought refuge with them, contrived to cause the laws on suppliants to prevail among all men, and since they were the authors of these laws, we should not deprive them of their protection. So much to all of you ; but some among you I shall remind of the claims of human kindness.

² The " gift of Demeter."

27. Ὅσοι μὲν γὰρ λόγου καὶ παιδείας ἐν τῇ πόλει μετεσχήκατε, δότε τὸν ἔλεον τοῖς τὴν πατρίδα κοινὸν παιδευτήριον παρεχομένοις πᾶσιν ἀνθρώποις· ὅσοι δὲ τῶν ἁγνοτάτων μυστηρίων μετειλήφατε, σώσατε τοὺς μυήσαντας, οἱ μὲν ἤδη μετεσχηκότες τῶν φιλανθρωπιῶν[1] τὴν χάριν διδόντες τῆς εὐεργεσίας, οἱ δὲ μέλλοντες μεταλήψεσθαι μὴ παρ-
2 αιρούμενοι τῷ θυμῷ τὴν ἐλπίδα. ποῖος γὰρ τόπος τοῖς ξένοις βάσιμος εἰς παιδείαν ἐλευθέριον τῆς Ἀθηναίων πόλεως ἀνῃρημένης; βραχὺ τὸ διὰ τὴν ἁμαρτίαν μῖσος, μεγάλα δὲ καὶ πολλὰ τὰ πρὸς εὔνοιαν αὐτοῖς εἰργασμένα.

Χωρὶς δὲ τῆς περὶ τὴν πόλιν ἐντροπῆς καὶ κατ' ἰδίαν ἄν τις τοὺς αἰχμαλώτους ἐξετάζων εὕροι δικαίως ἐλέου τυγχάνοντας. οἱ μὲν γὰρ σύμμαχοι τῇ τῶν κρατούντων ὑπεροχῇ βιασθέντες ἠναγκά-
3 σθησαν συστρατεύειν. διόπερ εἰ τοὺς ἐξ ἐπιβολῆς ἀδικήσαντας δίκαιόν ἐστι τιμωρεῖσθαι, τοὺς ἀκουσίως ἐξαμαρτάνοντας προσῆκον ἂν εἴη συγγνώμης ἀξιοῦν. τί λέγω Νικίαν, ὃς ἀπ' ἀρχῆς τὴν πολιτείαν ὑπὲρ Συρακοσίων ἐνστησάμενος μόνος ἀντεῖπεν ὑπὲρ τῆς εἰς Σικελίαν στρατείας, ἀεὶ δὲ τῶν παρεπιδημούντων Συρακοσίων φροντίζων καὶ
4 πρόξενος ὢν διατετέλεκεν; ἄτοπον οὖν Νικίαν κολάζεσθαι τὸν ὑπὲρ ἡμῶν Ἀθήνησι πεπολιτευμένον καὶ διὰ μὲν τὴν εἰς ἡμᾶς εὔνοιαν μὴ τυχεῖν

---

[1] φιλανθρωπιῶν] φιλανθρώπων Dindorf.

[1] The Eleusinian Mysteries.
[2] On the position of proxenus see p. 45, n. 1. Nicias' speech in opposition to the expedition is given by Thucydides (6. 9-14); cp. also his second speech (*ibid.* 20-23 and Plutarch, *Nicias*, 12).

27. " All you who in that city have participated in 413 B.C. its eloquence and learning, show mercy to men who offer their country as a school for the common use of mankind ; and do all you, who have taken part in the most holy Mysteries,[1] save the lives of those who initiated you, some by way of showing gratitude for kindly services already received and others, who look forward to partaking of them, not in anger depriving yourselves of that hope. For what place is there to which foreigners may resort for a liberal education once the city of the Athenians has been destroyed ? Brief is the hatred aroused by the wrong they have committed, but important and many are their accomplishments which claim goodwill.

" But apart from consideration for the city, one might, in examining the prisoners individually, find those who would justly receive mercy. For the allies of Athens, being under constraint because of the superior power of their rulers, were compelled to join the expedition. It follows, then, that if it is just to take vengeance upon those who have done wrong from design, it would be fitting to treat as worthy of leniency those who sin against their will. What shall I say of Nicias, who from the first, after initiating his policy in the interest of the Syracusans, was the only man to oppose the expedition against Sicily, and who has continually looked after the interests of Syracusans resident in Athens and served as their proxenus ?[2] It would be extraordinary indeed that Nicias, who had sponsored our cause as a politician in Athens, should be punished, and that he should not be accorded humane treatment because of the goodwill he has shown toward us but because of his

195

φιλανθρωπίας, διὰ δὲ τὴν ἐν τοῖς κοινοῖς ὑπηρεσίαν
ἀπαραιτήτῳ περιπεσεῖν τιμωρίᾳ, καὶ τὸν μὲν ἐπ-
αγαγόντα[1] τὸν πόλεμον ἐπὶ Συρακοσίους Ἀλκιβιάδην ἅμα καὶ παρ' ἡμῶν καὶ παρ' Ἀθηναίων
ἐκφυγεῖν τὴν τιμωρίαν, τὸν δ' ὁμολογουμένως φιλ-
ανθρωπότατον Ἀθηναίων γεγενημένον μηδὲ τοῦ
5 κοινοῦ τυχεῖν ἐλέου. διόπερ ἔγωγε τὴν τοῦ βίου
μεταβολὴν θεωρῶν ἐλεῶ τὴν τύχην. πρότερον μὲν
γὰρ ἐν τοῖς ἐπισημοτάτοις τῶν Ἑλλήνων ὑπάρχων
καὶ διὰ τὴν καλοκἀγαθίαν ἐπαινούμενος μακαριστὸς
6 ἦν καὶ περίβλεπτος κατὰ πᾶσαν πόλιν· νυνὶ δ'
ἐξηγκωνισμένος ἐν ἀσχήμονι χιτῶνι[2] προσόψει τῶν
τῆς[3] αἰχμαλωσίας οἰκτρῶν πεπείραται, καθαπερεὶ
τῆς τύχης ἐν τῷ τούτου βίῳ τὴν ἑαυτῆς δύναμιν
ἐπιδείξασθαι βουλομένης. ἧς τὴν εὐημερίαν[4] ἀνθρωπίνως ἡμᾶς ὑπενεγκεῖν προσήκει καὶ μὴ
βάρβαρον ὠμότητα πρὸς ὁμοεθνεῖς ἀνθρώπους
ἐνδείξασθαι.

28. Νικόλαος μὲν οὖν πρὸς τοὺς Συρακοσίους
τοιούτοις χρησάμενος λόγοις κατέπαυσε τὴν δημηγορίαν, συμπαθεῖς ποιήσας τοὺς ἀκούοντας.
Γύλιππος δ' ὁ Λάκων, ἀπαραίτητον τὸ πρὸς Ἀθηναίους μῖσος διαφυλάττων, ἀναβὰς ἐπὶ τὸ βῆμα
2 τῶν λόγων τὴν ἀρχὴν ἐντεῦθεν ἐποιήσατο. θαυ-
μάζω μεγάλως, ἄνδρες Συρακόσιοι, θεωρῶν ὑμᾶς
οὕτως ταχέως, περὶ ὧν ἔργῳ κακῶς πεπόνθατε,
περὶ τούτων τῷ λόγῳ μεταδιδασκομένους. εἰ γὰρ

---

[1] So Dindorf: ἐπάγοντα.
[2] So Capps, καὶ ἐν ἀ. τινι Vogel: ἐν ἀσχήμονι καί τινι.
[3] So Rhodoman: τῆς τῶν.
[4] εὐημερίαν Madvig, εὔροιαν Bezzel: ἐλευθερίαν.

service in business of his country should meet with 413 b.c. implacable punishment, and that Alcibiades, the man who brought on the war against the Syracusans, should escape his deserved punishment both from us and from the Athenians, whereas he who has proved himself by common consent the most humane among Athenians should not even meet with the mercy accorded to all men. Therefore for my part, when I consider the change in his circumstances, I pity his lot. For formerly, as one of the most distinguished of all Greeks and applauded for his knightly character, he was one to be deemed happy and was admired in every city ; but now, with hands bound behind his back in a tunic squalid in appearance, he has experienced the piteous state of captivity, as if Fortune wished to give, in the life of this man, an example of her power. The prosperity which Fortune gives it behooves us to bear as human beings should and not show barbarous savagery toward men of our own race."

28. Such were the arguments used by Nicolaüs in addressing the people of Syracuse and before he ceased he had won the sympathy of his hearers. But the Laconian Gylippus,[1] who still maintained implacable his hatred of Athenians, mounting the rostrum began his argument with that topic. " I am greatly surprised, men of Syracuse, to see that you so quickly, on a matter in which you have suffered grievously by deeds, are moved to change your minds by words.[2] For if you who, in order to

[1] The general of the forces sent by the Lacedaemonians to the aid of Syracuse ; cp. chap. 7.

[2] Cp. " The world will little note nor long remember what we say here, but it can never forget what they did here " (Lincoln, *The Gettysburg Oration*).

ὑμεῖς[1] ὑπὲρ ἀναστάσεως κινδυνεύσαντες πρὸς τοὺς
ἐπὶ κατασκαφῇ τῆς πατρίδος ὑμῶν παραγεγενη-
μένους ἀνεῖσθε τοῖς θυμοῖς, τί χρὴ νῦν ἡμᾶς δια-
3 τείνεσθαι τοὺς μηδὲν ἠδικημένους; δότε δέ μοι,
πρὸς θεῶν, ἄνδρες Συρακόσιοι, συγγνώμην τὴν
συμβουλίαν ἐκτιθεμένῳ μετὰ παρρησίας· Σπαρτιάτης γὰρ ὢν καὶ τὸν λόγον ἔχω Σπαρτιάτην. καὶ
πρῶτον ἄν τις ἐπιζητήσειε πῶς Νικόλαος ἐλεῆσαί
φησι[2] τοὺς Ἀθηναίους, οἳ τὸ γῆρας αὐτοῦ διὰ
τὴν ἀπαιδίαν ἐλεεινὸν πεποιήκασι, καὶ παριὼν εἰς
ἐκκλησίαν ἐν ἐσθῆτι πενθίμῃ δακρύει καὶ λέγει
δεῖν οἰκτείρειν τοὺς φονεῖς τῶν ἰδίων τέκνων.
4 οὐκέτι γὰρ ἐπιεικής ἐστιν ὁ τῶν συγγενεστάτων
μετὰ τὴν τελευτὴν ἀμνημονῶν τοὺς δὲ πολεμι-
ωτάτους σῶσαι προαιρούμενος. ἐπεὶ πόσοι τῶν
ἐκκλησιαζόντων υἱοὺς ἀνηρημένους κατὰ τὸν πόλεμον ἐπενθήσατε; (πολλοὶ γοῦν[3] τῶν καθημένων
5 ἐθορύβησαν.) ὁ δ᾽ ἐπιβαλών, Ὁρᾷς,[4] φησί, τοὺς
τῷ θορύβῳ τὴν συμφορὰν ἐμφανίζοντας; πόσοι
δὲ ἀδελφοὺς ἢ συγγενεῖς ἢ φίλους ἀπολωλεκότες
ἐπιζητεῖτε; (καὶ[5] πολλῷ πλείους ἐπεσημήναντο.)
6 καὶ ὁ Γύλιππος, Θεωρεῖς, ἔφη, τὸ πλῆθος τῶν
δι᾽ Ἀθηναίους δυστυχούντων; οὗτοι πάντες οὐδὲν
εἰς ἐκείνους ἁμαρτάνοντες τῶν ἀναγκαιοτάτων
σωμάτων ἐστερήθησαν, καὶ τοσοῦτο μισεῖν τοὺς
Ἀθηναίους ὀφείλουσιν ὅσον τοὺς ἰδίους ἠγαπήκασι.
29. Πῶς οὖν οὐκ ἄτοπον, ἄνδρες Συρακόσιοι,
τοὺς μὲν τετελευτηκότας ἑκούσιον ὑπὲρ ὑμῶν
ἑλέσθαι θάνατον, ὑμᾶς δὲ ὑπὲρ ἐκείνων μηδὲ παρὰ

---

[1] ὑμεῖς added by Vogel. [2] So Dindorf: φήσει.
[3] γοῦν Capps: οὖν all MSS. except P.
[4] So Dindorf: ὁρῶ. [5] καὶ omitted P, Vogel.

save your city from desolation, faced peril against 418 B.C.
men who came to destroy your country, have become
relaxed in temper, why, then, should we who have
suffered no wrong exert ourselves ? Do you in
heaven's name, men of Syracuse, grant me pardon
as I set forth my counsel with all frankness ; for,
being a Spartan, I have also a Spartan's manner of
speech. And first of all one might inquire how
Nicolaüs can say, ' Show mercy to the Athenians,'
who have rendered his old age piteous because child-
less, and how, coming before the Assembly in
mourner's dress, he can weep and say that you
should show pity to the murderers of his own children.
For that man is no longer equitable who ceases to
think of his nearest of kin after their death but elects
to save the lives of his bitterest foes. Why how many
of you who are assembled here have mourned sons
who have been slain in the war ? " (Many of the
audience at least raised a great outcry.) And
Gylippus interrupting it said, " Do you see, Nicolaüs,
those who by their outcry proclaim their misfortune ?
And how many of you look in vain for brothers or
relatives or friends whom you have lost ? " (A far
greater number shouted agreement.) Gylippus then
continued : " Do you observe, Nicolaüs, the multitude
of those who have suffered because of Athenians ?
All these, though guilty of no wrong done to
Athenians, have been robbed of their nearest kinsmen, and they are bound to hate the Athenians in as
great a measure as they have loved their own.

29. " Will it not be strange, men of Syracuse, if
those who have perished chose death on your behalf of their own accord, but that you on their behalf

τῶν πολεμιωτάτων λαβεῖν τιμωρίαν, καὶ ἐπαινεῖν
μὲν τοὺς ὑπὲρ τῆς κοινῆς ἐλευθερίας τοὺς ἰδίους[1]
ἀναλώσαντας βίους, περὶ πλείονος δὲ τὴν τῶν
φονέων ποιεῖσθαι σωτηρίαν τῆς ἐκείνων τιμῆς;
2 κοσμεῖν ἐψηφίσασθε δημοσίᾳ τοὺς τάφους τῶν
μετηλλαχότων· καὶ τίνα καλλίονα κόσμον εὑρήσετε
τοῦ κολάσαι τοὺς ἐκείνων αὐτόχειρας; εἰ μὴ νὴ
Δία πολιτογραφήσαντες αὐτοὺς βούλεσθε καταλι-
3 πεῖν ἔμψυχα τρόπαια τῶν μετηλλαχότων. ἀλλὰ
μεταβαλόντες τὴν τῶν πολεμίων προσηγορίαν γεγόνασιν ἱκέται· πόθεν αὐτοῖς ταύτης τῆς φιλανθρωπίας
συγκεχωρημένης; οἱ γὰρ ἀπ' ἀρχῆς τὰ περὶ τούτων νόμιμα διατάξαντες τοῖς μὲν δυστυχοῦσι τὸν
ἔλεον, τοῖς δὲ διὰ πονηρίαν ἀδικοῦσιν ἔταξαν τι-
4 μωρίαν. ἐν ποτέρᾳ δὴ τάξει θῶμεν τοὺς αἰχμαλώτους; ἐν τῇ τῶν ἠτυχηκότων; καὶ τίς αὐτοὺς
τύχῃ μὴ προαδικηθέντας ἐβιάσατο πολεμεῖν Συρακοσίοις καὶ τὴν παρὰ πᾶσιν ἐπαινουμένην εἰρήνην
ἀφέντας ἐπὶ κατασκαφῇ παρεῖναι τῆς ὑμετέρας
5 πόλεως; διόπερ ἑκουσίως ἑλόμενοι πόλεμον ἄδικον
εὐψύχως ὑπομενόντων τὰ τούτου δεινά, καὶ μή,
κρατοῦντες μέν, ἀπαραίτητον ἐχόντων τὴν καθ'
ὑμῶν[2] ὠμότητα, σφαλέντες δέ, τοῖς τῆς ἱκεσίας
6 φιλανθρώποις παραιτείσθων[3] τὴν τιμωρίαν. εἰ δ'
ἐλέγχονται διὰ πονηρίαν καὶ πλεονεξίαν τοιούτοις
ἐλαττώμασι περιπεπτωκότες, μὴ καταμεμφέσθων
τὴν τύχην μηδ' ἐπικαλείσθων[4] τὸ τῆς ἱκεσίας

---

[1] περὶ πλείους after ἰδίους deleted by Rhodoman.
[2] So Eichstädt : ἡμῶν.
[3] So Wesseling : παραιτεῖσθαι.
[4] So Dindorf : καταμεμφέσθωσαν . . . ἐπικαλείσθωσαν.

shall not exact punishment from even your bitterest 413 b.c. enemies ? and that, though you praise those who gave their very lives to preserve their country's freedom, you shall make it a matter of greater moment to preserve the lives of the murderers than to safeguard the honour of these men ? You have voted to embellish at public expense the tombs of the departed ; yet what fairer embellishment will you find than the punishing of their slayers ? Unless, by Zeus, it would be by enrolling them among your citizens, you should wish to leave living trophies of the departed. But, it may be said, they have renounced the name of enemies and have become suppliants. On what grounds, pray, would this humane treatment have been accorded them ? For those who first established our ordinances regarding these matters prescribed mercy for the unfortunates, but punishment for those who from sheer depravity practise iniquity. In which category, now, are we to place the prisoners ? In that of unfortunates ? Why, what Fortune compelled them, who had suffered no wrong, to make war on Syracusans, to abandon peace, which all men praise, and to come here with the purpose of destroying your city ? Consequently let those who of their free will chose an unjust war bear its hard consequences with courage, and let not those who, if they had conquered, would have kept implacable their cruelty toward you, now that they have been thwarted in their purpose, beg off from punishment by appealing to the human kindness which is due to the prayer of a suppliant. And if they stand convicted of having suffered their serious defeats because of wickedness and greed, let them not blame Fortune for them nor summon to their aid

ὄνομα. τοῦτο γὰρ παρ' ἀνθρώποις φυλάττεται
τοῖς καθαρὰν μὲν τὴν ψυχὴν ἀγνώμονα δὲ τὴν
7 τύχην ἐσχηκόσιν. οὗτοι δ' ἁπάντων τῶν ἀδικημάτων[1] πλήρη τὸν βίον ἔχοντες οὐδένα τόπον
αὑτοῖς βάσιμον εἰς ἔλεον καὶ καταφυγὴν ἀπολε-
λοίπασι.

30. Τί γὰρ τῶν αἰσχίστων οὐκ ἐβουλεύσαντο, τί
δὲ τῶν δεινοτάτων οὐκ ἔπραξαν; πλεονεξίας ἴδιόν
ἐστι τὸ ταῖς ἰδίαις εὐτυχίαις οὐκ ἀρκούμενον τῶν
πόρρω κειμένων καὶ μηδὲν προσηκόντων ἐπιθυ-
μεῖν· οὗτοι ταῦτ' ἔπραξαν. εὐδαιμονέστατοι γὰρ
ὄντες τῶν Ἑλλήνων, τὴν εὐτυχίαν ὥσπερ βαρὺ
φορτίον οὐ φέροντες, τὴν πελάγει τηλικούτῳ διειρ-
γομένην Σικελίαν ἐπεθύμησαν κατακληρουχῆσαι,
2 τοὺς ἐνοικοῦντας ἐξανδραποδισάμενοι. δεινόν ἐστι
μὴ προαδικηθέντας πόλεμον ἐπιφέρειν· καὶ τοῦτ'
ἐνήργησαν. φίλοι γὰρ ὄντες τὸν ἔμπροσθεν χρόνον,
ἐξαίφνης ἀνελπίστως τηλικαύτῃ δυνάμει Συρακο-
3 σίους ἐπολιόρκησαν. ὑπερηφάνων ἐστὶ τὸ τῶν
μήπω κρατηθέντων προλαμβάνοντας[2] τὴν τύχην
καταψηφίζεσθαι τιμωρίαν· οὐδὲ τοῦτο παραλε-
λοίπασι. πρὸ τοῦ γὰρ ἐπιβῆναι τῆς Σικελίας
γνώμην ἐκύρωσαν Συρακοσίους μὲν καὶ Σελινουντίους ἐξανδραποδίσασθαι, τοὺς δὲ λοιποὺς διδόναι
φόρους ἀναγκάζειν. ὅταν οὖν περὶ τοὺς αὐτοὺς
ἀνθρώπους ὑπάρχῃ πλεονεξία, ἐπιβουλή, ὑπερη-
4 φανία, τίς ἂν νοῦν ἔχων αὐτοὺς ἐλεήσειεν; ἐπεί
τοί γε Ἀθηναῖοι πῶς ἐχρήσαντο Μιτυληναίοις;
κρατήσαντες γὰρ αὐτῶν, ἀδικῆσαι μὲν οὐδὲν βου-

---

[1] So Faber (cp. ch. 31. 1 *infra*): ἀτυχημάτων.
[2] So Vogel suggests: προλαμβάνοντα.

the name of 'supplication.' For that term is reserved among men for those who are pure in heart
but have found Fortune unkind. These men, however, whose lives have been crammed with every
malefaction, have left for themselves no place in the
world which will admit them to mercy and refuge.

30. " For what utterly shameful deed have they
not planned, what deed most shocking have they not
perpetrated ? It is a distinctive mark of greed that
a man, not being content with his own gifts of
Fortune, covets those which are distant and belong
to someone else ; and this these men have done. For
though the Athenians were the most prosperous of
all the Greeks, dissatisfied with their felicity as if it
were a heavy burden, they longed to portion out
to colonists Sicily, separated as it was from them by
so great an expanse of sea, after they had sold the
inhabitants into slavery. It is a terrible thing to
begin a war, when one has not first been wronged ;
yet that is what they did. For though they were
your friends until then, on a sudden, without warning,
with an armament of such strength they laid siege
to Syracusans. It is characteristic of arrogant men,
anticipating the decision of Fortune, to decree
the punishment of peoples not yet conquered ; and
this also they have not left undone. For before the
Athenians ever set foot on Sicily they approved a
resolution to sell into slavery the citizens of Syracuse
and Selinus and to compel the remaining Sicilians to
pay tribute. When there is to be found in the same
men greediness, treachery, arrogance, what person in
his right mind would show them mercy ? How then,
mark you, did the Athenians treat the Mitylenaeans ?
Why after conquering them, although the Mity-

λομένων, ἐπιθυμούντων δὲ τῆς ἐλευθερίας, ἐψηφίσαντο τοὺς ἐν τῇ πόλει κατασφάξαι. ὠμόν τε
5 καὶ βάρβαρον τὸ πεπραγμένον. καὶ ταῦτα ἐξήμαρτον εἰς Ἕλληνας, εἰς συμμάχους, εἰς εὐεργέτας
πολλάκις γεγενημένους. μὴ δὴ νῦν ἀγανακτούντων
εἰ τοιαῦτα πρὸς τοὺς ἄλλους πράξαντες αὐτοὶ
παραπλησίας τεύξονται τιμωρίας· δικαιότατον[1] γάρ
ἐστιν, ὃν καθ’ ἑτέρων νόμον τις ἔθηκε, τούτῳ
6 χρώμενον μὴ ἀγανακτεῖν. καὶ τί λέγω Μηλίους,
οὓς[2] ἐκπολιορκήσαντες ἡβηδὸν ἀπέκτειναν, καὶ
Σκιωναίους, οἳ συγγενεῖς ὄντες τῆς αὐτῆς Μηλίοις
τύχης ἐκοινώνησαν; ὥστε δύο δήμους πρὸς Ἀττικὴν ὀργὴν ἐπταικότας οὐδὲ τοὺς κηδεύσοντας[3]
7 ἔχειν τὰ τῶν τετελευτηκότων σώματα. οὐ Σκύθαι
τοῦτ’ ἔπραξαν, ἀλλ’ ὁ προσποιούμενος φιλανθρωπίᾳ
διαφέρειν δῆμος ψηφίσμασι τὰς πόλεις ἄρδην ἀν-
ῄρηκεν. ἤδη λογίζεσθε τί ἂν ἔπραξαν εἰ τὴν τῶν
Συρακοσίων πόλιν ἐξεπόρθησαν· οἱ γὰρ τοῖς οἰκείοις οὕτως ὠμῶς χρησάμενοι τοῖς μηδὲν προσ-
ήκουσι βαρυτέραν ἂν ἐξεῦρον τιμωρίαν.

31. Οὐκ ἔστιν οὖν τούτοις δίκαιος ἀποκείμενος
ἔλεος· αὐτοὶ γὰρ αὑτὸν ἐπὶ τῶν ἰδίων ἀκληρημάτων
ἀνῃρήκασι. ποῦ γὰρ ἄξιον τούτοις καταφυγεῖν;
πρὸς θεούς, ὧν τὰς πατρίους τιμὰς ἀφελέσθαι
προείλοντο; πρὸς ἀνθρώπους, οὓς δουλωσόμενοι
παρεγένοντο; Δήμητρα καὶ Κόρην καὶ τὰ τούτων
ἐπικαλοῦνται μυστήρια τὴν ἱερὰν αὐτῶν νῆσον

---

[1] So Wesseling : δικαιότερον.
[2] οὓς added by Dindorf.
[3] κηδεύσοντας] κηδεύσαντας PAFJK, Vogel.

---

[1] This decree was not actually carried out ; cp. Book 12.
55. 8 f.   [2] Cp. Book 12. 80. 5.   [3] Cp. Book 12. 76. 3.

lenaeans had no intention of doing them any wrong
but only desired their freedom, they voted to put to
the sword all the inhabitants of the city.[1] A cruel
and barbarous deed. And that crime too they committed against Greeks, against allies, against men
who had often been their benefactors. Let them not
now complain if, after having done such things to the
rest of mankind, they themselves shall receive like
punishment; for it is altogether just that a man
should accept his lot without complaint when he is
himself affected by the law he has laid down for
others. What shall I say also of the Melians,[2] whom
they reduced by siege and slew from the youth upward? and of the Scionaeans,[3] who, although their
kinsmen, shared the same fate as the Melians?
Consequently two peoples who had fallen foul of
Attic fury had left not even any of their number to
perform the rites over the bodies of their dead. It is
not Scythians who committed such deeds, but the
people who claim to excel in love of mankind have
by their decrees utterly destroyed these cities. Consider now what they would have done if they had
sacked the city of the Syracusans; for men who
dealt with their kinsmen with such savagery would
have devised a harsher punishment for a people with
whom they had no ties of blood.

31. " There is, therefore, no just measure of mercy
in store for them to call upon, since as for the use of
it on the occasion of their own mishaps they themselves have destroyed it. Where is it worth their
while to flee for safety? To gods, whom they have
chosen to rob of their traditional honours? To men,
whom they have visited only to enslave? Do they
call upon Demeter and Corê and their Mysteries now

2 πεπορθηκότες; ναί, ἀλλ᾽ οὐκ αἴτιον τὸ πλῆθος
τῶν Ἀθηναίων, ἀλλ᾽ Ἀλκιβιάδης ὁ ταῦτα συμ-
βουλεύσας. ἀλλ᾽ εὑρήσομεν τοὺς συμβούλους κατὰ
τὸ πλεῖστον στοχαζομένους τῆς τῶν ἀκουόντων
βουλήσεως, ὥσθ᾽ ὁ χειροτονῶν τῷ ῥήτορι λόγον
οἰκεῖον ὑποβάλλει τῆς ἑαυτοῦ προαιρέσεως. οὐ
γὰρ ὁ λέγων κύριος τοῦ πλήθους, ἀλλ᾽ ὁ δῆμος
ἐθίζει τὸν ῥήτορα τὰ βέλτιστα λέγειν χρηστὰ βου-
3 λευόμενος. εἰ δὲ τοῖς ἀδικοῦσιν ἀνήκεστα συγγνώμην δώσομεν, ἐὰν εἰς τοὺς συμβούλους τὴν
αἰτίαν ἀναφέρωσιν, εὐχερῆ τοῖς πονηροῖς τὴν
ἀπολογίαν παρεξόμεθα. ἁπλῶς δὲ πάντων ἐστὶν
ἀδικώτατον τῶν μὲν εὐεργεσιῶν μὴ τοὺς συμβούλους, ἀλλὰ τὸν δῆμον ἀπολαμβάνειν τὰς χάριτας
παρὰ τῶν εὖ παθόντων, τῶν δ᾽ ἀδικημάτων ἐπὶ
τοὺς ῥήτορας μεταφέρειν τὴν τιμωρίαν.

4 Καὶ ἐπὶ τοσοῦτόν τινες ἐξεστήκασι τῶν λο-
γισμῶν ὥστ᾽ Ἀλκιβιάδην, εἰς ὃν τὴν ἐξουσίαν οὐκ
ἔχομεν, φασὶ δεῖν τιμωρεῖσθαι, τοὺς δ᾽ αἰχμαλώτους ἀγομένους ἐπὶ τὴν προσήκουσαν τιμωρίαν
ἀφεῖναι, καὶ πᾶσιν ἐνδείξασθαι διότι τὴν δικαίαν
μισοπονηρίαν οὐκ ἔσχηκεν ὁ δῆμος τῶν Συρακο-
5 σίων. εἰ δὲ καὶ κατ᾽ ἀλήθειαν αἴτιοι γεγόνασιν
οἱ σύμβουλοι τοῦ πολέμου, μεμφέσθω τὸ μὲν
πλῆθος τοῖς ῥήτορσιν ὑπὲρ ὧν ἐξηπάτησαν, ὑμεῖς
δὲ δικαίως μετελεύσεσθε τὸ πλῆθος ὑπὲρ ὧν
ἠδίκησθε. καθόλου δ᾽ εἰ μὲν ἐπιστάμενοι σαφῶς
ἠδίκησαν, δι᾽ αὐτὴν τὴν προαίρεσιν ἄξιοι τιμωρίας,
εἰ δ᾽ εἰκῇ βουλευσάμενοι τὸν πόλεμον ἐξήνεγκαν,

---

[1] Sicily.

that they have laid waste the sacred island [1] of these 413 B.C. goddesses? Yes, some will say, but not the whole people of the Athenians are to blame, but only Alcibiades who advised this expedition. We shall find, however, that in most cases their advisers pay every attention to the wishes of their audience, so that the voter suggests to the speaker words that suit his own purpose. For the speaker is not the master of the multitude, but the people, by adopting measures that are honest, train the orator to propose what is best. If we shall pardon men guilty of irrevocable injustices when they lay the responsibility upon their advisers, we shall indeed be providing the wicked with an easy defence! It is clear that nothing in the world could be more unjust than that, while in the case of benefactions it is not the advisers but the people who receive the thanks of the recipients, in the matter of injustices the punishment is passed on to the speakers.

" Yet some have lost their reasoning powers to such a degree as to assert that it is Alcibiades, over whom we have no power, who should be punished, but that we should release the prisoners, who are being led to their deserved punishment, and thus make it known to the world that the people of the Syracusans have no righteous indignation against base men. But if the advocates of the war have in truth been the cause of it, let the people blame the speakers for the consequences of their deception, but you will with justice punish the people for the wrongs which you have suffered. And, speaking generally, if they committed the wrongs with full knowledge that they were so doing, because of their very intention they deserve punishment, but if they entered the war without a considered plan,

οὐδ' ὡς αὐτοὺς ἀφετέον, ἵνα μὴ σχεδιάζειν ἐν τοῖς
τῶν ἄλλων βίοις ἐθισθῶσιν. οὐ γὰρ δίκαιόν ἐστι
τὴν Ἀθηναίων ἄγνοιαν Συρακοσίοις φέρειν ἀπώλειαν οὐδ' ἐν οἷς τὸ πραχθὲν ἀνήκεστόν ἐστιν, ἐν
τούτοις ἀπολογίαν ὑπολείπεσθαι τοῖς ἁμαρτάνουσι.
32. Νὴ Δία, ἀλλὰ Νικίας ὑπὲρ Συρακοσίων ἐπο-
λιτεύσατο καὶ μόνος συνεβούλευσε μὴ πολεμεῖν.
τὸν μὲν ἐκεῖ γεγενημένον λόγον ἀκούομεν, τὰ δ'
2 ἐνταῦθα πεπραγμένα τεθεωρήκαμεν. ὁ γὰρ ἀντ-
ειπὼν ἐκεῖ περὶ τῆς στρατείας, ἐνταῦθα στρατηγὸς ἦν τῆς δυνάμεως· καὶ ὁ πολιτευόμενος ὑπὲρ
Συρακοσίων ἀπετείχισεν ὑμῶν τὴν πόλιν· καὶ ὁ
φιλανθρώπως διακείμενος πρὸς ὑμᾶς, Δημοσθένους
καὶ τῶν ἄλλων ἁπάντων βουλομένων λῦσαι τὴν
πολιορκίαν, μόνος ἐβιάσατο μένειν καὶ πολεμεῖν.
διόπερ ἔγωγε νομίζω μὴ δεῖν[1] παρ' ὑμῖν πλέον
ἰσχῦσαι τὸν μὲν λόγον τῶν ἔργων, τὴν δ' ἀπαγ-
γελίαν τῆς πείρας, τὰ δ' ἀφανῆ τῶν ὑπὸ πάντων
ἑωραμένων.
3 Νὴ Δί', ἀλλὰ καλὸν μὴ ποιεῖν τὴν ἔχθραν αἰώνιον. οὐκοῦν μετὰ τὴν τῶν ἠδικηκότων κόλασιν,
ἐὰν ὑμῖν δοκῇ, προσηκόντως διαλύσεσθε τὴν ἔχθραν. οὐ γὰρ δίκαιον, ὅταν μὲν κρατῶσιν, ὡς δού-
λοις χρῆσθαι τοῖς ἡλωκόσιν, ὅταν δὲ κρατηθῶσιν,
ὡς οὐδὲν ἠδικηκότας συγγνώμης τυγχάνειν. καὶ
τοῦ μὲν δοῦναι δίκην ὧν ἔπραξαν ἀφεθήσονται,
λόγῳ δ' εὐσχήμονι καθ' ὃν ἂν χρόνον αὐτοῖς συμ-
4 φέρῃ τῆς φιλίας μνημονεύσουσιν. ἐῶ[2] γὰρ ὅτι
τοῦτο πράξαντες σὺν πολλοῖς ἄλλοις καὶ τοὺς

[1] μὴ δεῖν Dindorf : μηδέν.
[2] So Wesseling : ἐν.

even so they should not be let off, in order that they 413 B.C.
may not grow accustomed to act offhand in matters
which affect the lives of other men. For it is not just
that the ignorance of the Athenians should bring
destruction to Syracusans or that in a case where the
crime is irremediable, the criminals should retain a
vestige of defence.

32. " Yet, by Zeus, someone will say, Nicias took
the part of the Syracusans in the debate and was the
only one who advised against making war. As for
what he said there we know it by hearsay, but what
has been done here we have witnessed with our own
eyes. For the man who there opposed the expedition
was here commander of the armament ; he who takes
the part of Syracusans in debate walled off your city ;
and he who is humanely disposed toward you, when
Demosthenes and all the others wished to break off
the siege, alone compelled them to remain and continue the war. Therefore for my part I do not believe that his words should have greater weight with
you than his deeds, report than experience, things un-
seen than things that have been witnessed by all.

" Yet, by Zeus, someone will say, it is a good thing
not to make our enmity eternal. Very well, then,
after the punishment of the malefactors you will, if
you so agree, put an end to your enmity in a suitable
manner. For it is not just that men who treat their
captives like slaves when they are the victors, should,
when they in turn are the vanquished, be objects of
pity as if they had done no wrong. And though they
will have been freed of paying the penalty for their
deeds, by specious pleas they will remember the friendship only so long as it is to their advantage. For I
omit to mention the fact that, if you take this course,

Λακεδαιμονίους ἀδικήσετε, ὑμῶν χάριν κἀκεῖ τὸν
πόλεμον ἐπανηρημένους καὶ ἐνταῦθα συμμαχίαν
ἀποστείλαντας· ἐξῆν γὰρ αὐτοῖς ἀγαπητῶς ἄγειν
εἰρήνην καὶ περιορᾶν τὴν Σικελίαν πορθουμένην.
5 διόπερ ἐὰν τοὺς αἰχμαλώτους ἀφέντες φιλίαν συν-
άπτησθε, προδόται φανήσεσθε τῶν συμμαχη-
σάντων, καὶ τοὺς κοινοὺς ἐχθροὺς δυνάμενοι
ταπεινῶσαι, τοσούτους στρατιώτας ἀποδόντες πάλιν
ἰσχυροὺς κατασκευάσετε. οὐ γὰρ ἄν¹ ποτ' ἔγωγε
πιστεύσαιμι ὡς Ἀθηναῖοι τηλικαύτην ἔχθραν ἐπ-
ανηρημένοι βεβαίαν φυλάξουσι τὴν φιλίαν, ἀλλ'
ἀσθενεῖς μὲν ὄντες ὑποκριθήσονται τὴν εὔνοιαν,
ἀναλαβόντες δ' αὑτοὺς τὴν ἀρχαίαν προαίρεσιν εἰς
6 τέλος ἄξουσιν. ἐγὼ μὲν οὖν, ὦ Ζεῦ καὶ πάντες
θεοί, μαρτύρομαι πάντας ὑμᾶς μὴ σώζειν τοὺς
πολεμίους, μὴ ἐγκαταλιπεῖν τοὺς συμμάχους, μὴ
πάλιν ἕτερον ἐπάγειν τῇ πατρίδι κίνδυνον. ὑμεῖς
δέ, ὦ ἄνδρες Συρακόσιοι, τούτους ἀφέντες, ἐὰν
ἀποβῇ τι δυσχερές, οὐδ' ἀπολογίαν ἑαυτοῖς εὐ-
σχήμονα καταλείψετε.

33. Τοιαῦτα διαλεχθέντος τοῦ Λάκωνος μετέπεσε
τὸ πλῆθος καὶ τὴν Διοκλέους γνώμην ἐκύρωσεν.
διόπερ οἱ μὲν στρατηγοὶ παραχρῆμα ἀνηρέθησαν
καὶ οἱ σύμμαχοι, οἱ δ' Ἀθηναῖοι παρεδόθησαν εἰς
τὰς λατομίας, ὧν ὕστερον οἱ μὲν ἐπὶ πλεῖον παι-

¹ ἄν added by Dindorf.

¹ At the first request of the Syracusans for aid the Lacedaemonians did no more than send their general Gylippus
(chap. 7), not wishing to break the peace with Athens. But
early in 413 they declared war on Athens, seized and fortified
Deceleia in Attica, and began sending troops on merchant
ships to Sicily.
² Plutarch (*Nicias*, 28. 2) and Thucydides (7. 86. 2) state

you will be wronging not only many others but also 413 B.C.
the Lacedaemonians, who for your sake both entered
upon the war over there and also sent you aid here ;
for they might have been well content to maintain
peace and look on while Sicily was being laid waste.[1]
Consequently, if you free the prisoners and thus enter
into friendly relations with Athens, you will be looked
upon as traitors to your allies and, when it is in your
power to weaken the common enemy, by releasing
so great a number of soldiers you will make our
enemy again formidable. For I could never bring
myself to believe that Athenians, after getting themselves involved in so bitter an enmity, will keep the
friendly relation unbroken ; on the contrary, while
they are weak they will feign goodwill, but when they
have recovered their strength, they will carry their
original purpose to completion. I therefore adjure
you all, in the name of Zeus and all the gods, not to
save the lives of your enemies, not to leave your allies
in the lurch, not again for a second time to bring peril
upon your country. You yourselves, men of Syracuse, if you let these men go and then some ill befalls
you, will leave for yourselves not even a respectable
defence." [2]

33. After the Laconian had spoken to this effect,
the multitude suddenly changed its mind and approved the proposal of Diocles.[3] Consequently the
generals [4] and the allies [5] were forthwith put to death,
and the Athenians were consigned to the quarries ;
and at a later time such of them as possessed a better

that Gylippus proposed that the lives of the generals be
spared, since he wished to take them back with him to Sparta.
[3] Cp. chap. 19. 4.   [4] Demosthenes and Nicias.
[5] Associated with the Athenians. But Diocles had proposed (chap. 19. 4) that the allies should be sold as booty.

δείας μετεσχηκότες ὑπὸ τῶν νεωτέρων ἐξαρπαγέν-
τες διεσώθησαν, οἱ δὲ λοιποὶ σχεδὸν ἅπαντες ἐν τῷ
δεσμωτηρίῳ κακούμενοι τὸν βίον οἰκτρῶς κατ-
έστρεψαν.

2 Μετὰ δὲ τὴν κατάλυσιν τοῦ πολέμου Διοκλῆς
τοὺς νόμους ἀνέγραψε τοῖς Συρακοσίοις, καὶ συνέβη
παράδοξον περὶ τὸν ἄνδρα τοῦτον γενέσθαι περι-
πέτειαν. ἀπαραίτητος γὰρ ἐν τοῖς ἐπιτιμίοις
γενόμενος καὶ σκληρῶς κολάζων τοὺς ἐξαμαρτάνοντας, ἔγραψεν ἐν τοῖς νόμοις, ἐάν τις ὅπλον ἔχων
εἰς τὴν ἀγορὰν παραγένηται, θάνατον εἶναι πρόσ-
τιμον, οὔτε ἀγνοίᾳ δοὺς οὔτε ἄλλῃ τινὶ περιστάσει
3 συγγνώμην. προσαγγελθέντων δὲ πολεμίων ἐπὶ
τῆς χώρας ἐξεπορεύετο ξίφος ἔχων· αἰφνιδίου δὲ
στάσεως καὶ ταραχῆς κατὰ τὴν ἀγορὰν γενομένης,
ἀγνοήσας μετὰ τοῦ ξίφους παρῆν εἰς τὴν ἀγοράν.
τῶν δὲ ἰδιωτῶν τινος κατανοήσαντος καὶ εἰπόντος
ὅτι τοὺς ἰδίους αὐτὸς καταλύει νόμους, ἀνεβόησε,
Μὰ Δία οὐ μὲν οὖν, ἀλλὰ καὶ[1] κυρίους ποιήσω.
καὶ σπασάμενος τὸ ξίφος ἑαυτὸν ἀπέκτεινεν.

Ταῦτα μὲν οὖν ἐπράχθη κατὰ τοῦτον τὸν ἐνιαυτόν.

34. Ἐπ᾿ ἄρχοντος δ᾿ Ἀθήνησι Καλλίου Ῥωμαῖοι μὲν ἀντὶ τῶν ὑπάτων χιλιάρχους κατέστησαν
τέτταρας, Πόπλιον Κορνήλιον[2] . . . Γάιον Φάβιον,
Ὀλυμπιὰς δ᾿ ἤχθη παρ᾿ Ἠλείοις δευτέρα πρὸς
ταῖς ἐνενήκοντα, καθ᾿ ἣν ἐνίκα στάδιον Ἐξαίνετος
Ἀκραγαντῖνος. ἐπὶ δὲ τούτων Ἀθηναίων περὶ
Σικελίαν ἐπταικότων συνέβη τὴν ἡγεμονίαν αὐτῶν
2 καταφρονηθῆναι· εὐθὺς γὰρ Χῖοι καὶ Σάμιοι καὶ

---

[1] ἀλλὰ καὶ PAFJK, ἀλλὰ cet.
[2] Κορνήλιον καὶ P, Vogel.

education were rescued from there by the younger 413 B.C. men and thus got away safe, but practically all the rest ended their lives pitiably amid the hardships of this place of confinement.

After the termination of the war Diocles set up the laws for the Syracusans, and it came to pass that this man experienced a strange reversal of fortune. For having become implacable in fixing penalties and severe in punishing offenders, he wrote in the laws that, if any man should appear in the market-place carrying a weapon, the punishment should be death, and he made no allowance for either ignorance or any other circumstance. And when word had been received that enemies were in the land, he set forth carrying a sword ; but since sudden civil strife had arisen and there was uproar in the market-place, he thoughtlessly entered the market-place with the sword. And when one of the ordinary citizens, noticing this, said that he himself was annulling his own laws, he cried out, " Not so, by Zeus, I will even uphold them." And drawing the sword he slew himself.[1]

These, then, were the events of this year.

34. When Callias was archon in Athens, the 412 B.C. Romans elected in place of consuls four military tribunes, Publius Cornelius . . . Gaius Fabius, and among the Eleians the Ninety-second Olympiad was celebrated, that in which Exaenetus of Acragas won the " stadion." In this year it came to pass that, after the Athenians had collapsed in Sicily, their supremacy was held in contempt ; for immediately the peoples of Chios, Samos, Byzantium, and many

---

[1] See Book 12. 19.

Βυζάντιοι καὶ πολλοὶ τῶν συμμάχων ἀπέστησαν
πρὸς τοὺς Λακεδαιμονίους. διόπερ ὁ δῆμος ἀθυμήσας ἐξεχώρησεν ἑκουσίως τῆς δημοκρατίας,
ἑλόμενος δὲ ἄνδρας τετρακοσίους, τούτοις τὴν
διοίκησιν ἐπέτρεψε τῶν κοινῶν. οἱ δὲ τῆς ὀλιγαρχίας προεστῶτες ναυπηγησάμενοι πλείους τριήρεις
3 ἀπέστειλαν τεσσαράκοντα καὶ στρατηγούς. οὗτοι
δὲ στασιάζοντες πρὸς ἀλλήλους εἰς Ὠρωπὸν ἐξ-
έπλευσαν· ἐκεῖ γὰρ ὥρμουν αἱ τῶν πολεμίων
τριήρεις. γενομένης οὖν ναυμαχίας ἐνίκων οἱ
Λακεδαιμόνιοι καὶ σκαφῶν εἴκοσι καὶ δυεῖν ἐκυρίευσαν.

4 Συρακόσιοι δὲ καταλελυκότες τὸν πρὸς Ἀθηναίους πόλεμον, τοὺς μὲν Λακεδαιμονίους συμμαχήσαντας, ὧν ἦρχε Γύλιππος, ἐτίμησαν τοῖς ἐκ
τοῦ πολέμου λαφύροις, συναπέστειλαν δ' αὐτοῖς εἰς
Λακεδαίμονα συμμαχίαν εἰς τὸν πρὸς Ἀθηναίους
πόλεμον τριάκοντα καὶ πέντε τριήρεις, ὧν ἦρχεν
5 Ἑρμοκράτης ὁ πρωτεύων τῶν πολιτῶν. αὐτοὶ δὲ
τὰς ἐκ τοῦ πολέμου γενομένας ὠφελείας ἀθροίσαντες τοὺς μὲν ναοὺς ἀναθήμασι καὶ σκύλοις
ἐκόσμησαν, τῶν δὲ στρατιωτῶν τοὺς ἀριστεύσαν-
6 τας ταῖς προσηκούσαις δωρεαῖς ἐτίμησαν. μετὰ
δὲ ταῦτα τῶν δημαγωγῶν ὁ πλεῖστον παρ' αὐτοῖς
ἰσχύσας Διοκλῆς ἔπεισε τὸν δῆμον μεταστῆσαι
τὴν πολιτείαν εἰς τὸ κλήρῳ τὰς ἀρχὰς διοικεῖσθαι,
ἑλέσθαι δὲ καὶ νομοθέτας εἰς τὸ τὴν πολιτείαν
διατάξαι καὶ νόμους καινοὺς ἰδίᾳ συγγράψαι.

---

[1] Diodorus is most sketchy at this point and in the repetitive
passage in chap. 36. A Peloponnesian fleet had been lying
off Salamis, possibly hoping to be able to attack the Peiraeus
in the midst of the political confusion in Athens ; it had then

of the allies revolted to the Lacedaemonians.   Conse- 412 B.C.
quently the Athenian people, being disheartened, of
their own accord renounced the democracy, and
choosing four hundred men they turned over to them
the administration of the state.   And the leaders of
the oligarchy, after building a number of triremes,
sent out forty of them together with generals.[1]
Although these were at odds with one another, they
sailed off to Oropus, for the enemy's triremes lay
at anchor there.   In the battle which followed the
Lacedaemonians were victorious and captured twenty-
two vessels.

After the Syracusans had brought to an end the
war with the Athenians, they honoured with the booty
taken in the war the Lacedaemonians who had fought
with them under the command of Gylippus, and they
sent back with them to Lacedaemon, to aid them
in the war against the Athenians, an allied force
of thirty-five triremes under the command of Hermocrates, their foremost citizen.   And as for themselves,
after gathering the spoil that accrued from the war,
they embellished their temples with dedications and
with arms taken from the enemy and honoured with
the appropriate gifts those soldiers who had fought
with distinction.   After this Diocles, who was the
most influental among them of the leaders of the
populace, persuaded the citizens to change their form
of government so that the administration would be
conducted by magistrates chosen by lot and that
lawgivers also should be elected for organizing the
polity and drafting new laws privately.

sailed on to Euboea, which was of the utmost importance to
Athens now that all Attica was exposed to the Spartan troops
stationed in Deceleia.   See Thucydides, 8. 94-95.

35. Διόπερ οἱ Συρακόσιοι τοὺς φρονήσει διαφέροντας τῶν πολιτῶν εἵλοντο νομοθέτας, ὧν ἦν
ἐπιφανέστατος Διοκλῆς. τοσοῦτο γὰρ τῶν ἄλλων
διήνεγκε συνέσει καὶ δόξῃ ὥστε τῆς νομοθεσίας ὑπὸ
πάντων κοινῇ γραφείσης ὀνομασθῆναι τοὺς νόμους
2 Διοκλέους. οὐ μόνον δὲ τὸν ἄνδρα τοῦτον ζῶντα
ἐθαύμασαν οἱ Συρακόσιοι, ἀλλὰ καὶ τελευτήσαντα
τιμαῖς ἡρωικαῖς ἐτίμησαν καὶ νεὼν ᾠκοδόμησαν
δημοσίᾳ τὸν ὕστερον ὑπὸ Διονυσίου κατὰ τὴν τει-
χοποιίαν καθαιρεθέντα. ἐθαυμάσθη δὲ ὁ ἀνὴρ
3 οὗτος καὶ παρὰ τοῖς ἄλλοις Σικελιώταις· πολλαὶ
γοῦν τῶν κατὰ τὴν νῆσον πόλεων χρώμεναι διε-
τέλεσαν τοῖς τούτου νόμοις, μέχρι ὅτου πάντες οἱ
Σικελιῶται τῆς Ῥωμαίων πολιτείας ἠξιώθησαν.
οἱ δ' οὖν Συρακόσιοι κατὰ τοὺς νεωτέρους χρόνους
κατὰ μὲν Τιμολέοντα νομοθετήσαντος αὐτοῖς Κε-
φάλου, κατὰ δὲ τὸν Ἱέρωνα τὸν βασιλέα Πολυδώρου, οὐδέτερον αὐτῶν ὠνόμασαν νομοθέτην, ἀλλ'
ἢ ἐξηγητὴν τοῦ νομοθέτου, διὰ τὸ τοὺς νόμους
γεγραμμένους ἀρχαίᾳ διαλέκτῳ δοκεῖν εἶναι δυσ-
4 κατανοήτους. μεγάλης δὲ οὔσης κατὰ τὴν νομο-
θεσίαν ἀναθεωρήσεως, μισοπόνηρος μὲν φαίνεται[1]
διὰ τὸ πάντων τῶν νομοθετῶν πικρότατα πρόστιμα
θεῖναι κατὰ πάντων τῶν ἀδικούντων, δίκαιος δ'
ἐκ τοῦ περιττότερον τῶν πρὸ αὐτοῦ κατ' ἀξίαν

───────

[1] φαίνεται] ὁ ἀνὴρ added by Suidas (s.v. ἀναθεώρησις),
Const. Exc. 2 (1), p. 232.

───────

[1] In 402 B.C. ; cp. Book 14. 18.
[2] Cicero (ad Att. 14. 12), writing in April, 43 B.C., states
that this was an act of Antony, based upon a law of Caesar's
presumably passed by the Roman people. Nothing can
have come of it, since Sextus Pompeius held the island by
late 43 B.C. and lost it to Augustus, who showed no interest in

35. Consequently the Syracusans elected lawgivers 412 b.c. from such of their citizens as excelled in judgement, the most distinguished of them being Diocles. For he so far excelled the rest in understanding and renown that, although the writing of the code was a task of all in common, they were called " The Laws of Diocles." And not only did the Syracusans admire this man during his lifetime, but also, when he died, they rendered him the honours accorded to heroes and built a temple in his honour at public expense— the one which was torn down by Dionysius at a later time when the walls of the city were being constructed.[1] And this man was held in high esteem among the other Sicilian Greeks as well ; indeed many cities of the island continued to use his laws down to the time when the Sicilian Greeks as a body were granted Roman citizenship.[2] Accordingly, when in later times laws were framed for the Syracusans by Cephalus [3] in the time of Timoleon and by Polydorus in the time of King Hiero,[4] they called neither one of these men a " lawgiver," but rather an " interpreter of the lawgiver," since men found the laws of Diocles, written as they were in an ancient style, difficult to understand. Profound reflection is displayed in his legislation, the lawmaker showing himself to be a hater of evil, since he sets heavier penalties against all wrongdoers than any other legislator, just, in that more precisely than by any

extending Roman citizenship to the provinces on such a wholesale scale. Pliny in his sketch of Sicily (3. 88-91) lists, shortly before A.D. 79, several different degrees of civic status for the cities of the island.

[3] In 339 B.C. ; cp. Book 16. 82.

[4] Hiero was given the title of " King " in 270 B.C. and probably bore it until his death in 216.

ἑκάστῳ τὸ ἐπιτίμιον ὑπάρξαι,[1] πραγματικὸς δὲ
καὶ πολύπειρος ἐκ τοῦ πᾶν ἔγκλημα καὶ πρᾶγμα
δημόσιόν τε καὶ ἰδιωτικὸν ἀμφισβητούμενον ὡρισ-
μένης ἀξιῶσαι τιμωρίας· ἔστι δὲ καὶ κατὰ τὴν
λέξιν σύντομος καὶ πολλὴν τοῖς ἀναγινώσκουσιν
5 ἀπολείπων ἀναθεώρησιν. ἐμαρτύρησε δ' αὐτοῦ τὴν
ἀρετὴν καὶ τὴν σκληρότητα τῆς ψυχῆς ἡ περὶ
τὴν τελευτὴν περιπέτεια.

Ταῦτα μὲν οὖν ἀκριβέστερον εἰπεῖν προήχθην διὰ
τὸ τοὺς πλείους τῶν συγγραφέων ὀλιγωρότερον[2]
περὶ αὐτοῦ διειλέχθαι.

36. Οἱ δ' Ἀθηναῖοι πυθόμενοι τὴν ἐν Σικελίᾳ
δύναμιν ἄρδην ἀνῃρημένην, βαρέως ἔφερον τὸ
πλῆθος τῆς συμφορᾶς. οὐ μὴν ἔληγόν γε διὰ τοῦτο
τῆς[3] φιλοτιμίας περὶ τῆς ἡγεμονίας, ἀλλὰ ναῦς
τε κατεσκεύαζον πλείους καὶ χρήματα ἐπορίζοντο,
ὅπως φιλονικῶσι μέχρι τῆς ἐσχάτης ἐλπίδος ὑπὲρ
2 τῶν πρωτείων. ἑλόμενοι δὲ τετρακοσίους ἄνδρας,
τούτοις ἔδωκαν τὴν ἐξουσίαν αὐτοκράτορα διοικεῖν
τὰ κατὰ τὸν πόλεμον· ὑπελάμβανον γὰρ τὴν ὀλιγαρχίαν εὐθετωτέραν εἶναι τῆς δημοκρατίας ἐν
3 ταῖς τοιαύταις περιστάσεσιν. οὐ μὴν[4] τὰ πράγματά γε κατὰ τὴν ἐκείνων ἠκολούθησε κρίσιν, ἀλλὰ
πολὺ χεῖρον τὸν πόλεμον διῴκησαν. ἀποστείλαντες
γὰρ τεσσαράκοντα ναῦς συνεξέπεμψαν τοὺς ἀφηγη-
σομένους δύο στρατηγοὺς ἀλλοτρίως ἔχοντας πρὸς
ἀλλήλους. τῶν δὲ περὶ τοὺς Ἀθηναίους πραγμάτων τεταπεινωμένων ὁ μὲν καιρὸς προσεδεῖτο πολ-

---

[1] ὑπάρξαι] cp. 14. 6. 3, ὑποδεῖξαι or ὑποτάξαι Reiske, τάξαι
(cp. 1. 78. 1 ; 12. 21. 1) Bezzel.
[2] So Reiske : ὀλίγῳ πρότερον.
[3] Λακεδαιμονίων after τῆς deleted by Vogel.

predecessor the punishment of each man is fixed ac- 412 B.C.
cording to his deserts, and both practical and widely
experienced, in that he judges every complaint and
every dispute, whether it concerns the state or the
individual, to be deserving of a fixed penalty. He is
also concise in his style and leaves much for the
readers to reflect upon. And the dramatic manner
of his death [1] bore witness to the uprightness and
austerity of his soul.

Now these qualities of Diocles I have been moved
to set forth in considerable detail by reason of the
fact that most historians have rather slighted him in
their treatises.

36. When the Athenians learned of the total destruction of their forces in Sicily, they were deeply
distressed at the magnitude of the disaster. Yet
they would not at all on that account abate their
ardent aspiration for the supremacy, but set about
both constructing more ships and providing themselves with funds wherewith they might contend to
the last hope for the primacy. Choosing four hundred
men they put in their hands the supreme authority to
direct the conduct of the war ; for they assumed that
an oligarchy was more suitable than a democracy
in critical circumstances like these. The events, however, did not turn out according to the judgement
of those who held that opinion, but the Four Hundred
conducted the war far less competently. For, although they dispatched forty ships, they sent along
to command them two generals who were at odds
with each other. Although, with the affairs of the
Athenians at such low ebb, the emergency called for

[1] Cp. chap. 33.

---

[4] καί after μήν deleted by Vogel.

λῆς ὁμονοίας, οἱ δὲ στρατηγοὶ πρὸς ἀλλήλους
4 ἐστασίαζον. καὶ τέλος ἐκπλεύσαντες εἰς Ὠρωπὸν
ἀπαράσκευοι πρὸς τοὺς Πελοποννησίους ἐναυμά-
χησαν· κακῶς δὲ καὶ τὴν μάχην ἐνστησάμενοι καὶ
τὸν κίνδυνον ἀγεννῶς ὑπομείναντες, ἀπέβαλον ναῦς
δύο πρὸς ταῖς εἴκοσι, τὰς δὲ λοιπὰς μόγις διέσωσαν
εἰς Ἐρέτριαν.
5 Τούτων δὲ πραχθέντων οἱ σύμμαχοι τῶν Ἀθηναίων διά τε τὰς περὶ Σικελίαν ἀτυχίας καὶ διὰ
τὰς τῶν ἡγεμόνων καχεξίας μεθίσταντο[1] πρὸς
Λακεδαιμονίους. συμμάχου δ' ὄντος τοῖς Λακεδαιμονίοις Δαρείου τοῦ Περσῶν βασιλέως, Φαρνάβαζος ὁ τῶν ἐπὶ θαλάττης τόπων ἔχων τὴν
στρατηγίαν ἐχορήγει χρήματα τοῖς Λακεδαιμονί-
οις· μετεπέμψατο δὲ καὶ τὰς ἐκ Φοινίκης τριήρεις
τριακοσίας, διαλογιζόμενος ἀποστεῖλαι τοῖς Λακεδαιμονίοις ἐπὶ τὴν βοήθειαν.[2]

37. Τοιούτων δ' ἐλαττωμάτων τοῖς Ἀθηναίοις
εἰς ἕνα καιρὸν συνδραμόντων[3] ἅπαντες καταλελύσθαι
τὸν πόλεμον διειλήφεισαν· οὐκέτι γὰρ τοὺς Ἀθηναίους οὐδὲ τὸν ἐλάχιστον χρόνον οὐδεὶς ἤλπιζε
τοιαῦτα ὑποστήσεσθαι. οὐ μὴν τὰ πράγματά γε
τῇ τῶν πολλῶν ὑπολήψει τέλος ἔσχεν ἀκόλουθον,
ἀλλ' εἰς τοὐναντίον πάντα διὰ τὰς τῶν διαπολεμούντων ὑπεροχὰς μεταπεσεῖν συνέβη διὰ τοιαύτας
αἰτίας.
2 Ἀλκιβιάδης φυγὰς ὢν ἐξ Ἀθηνῶν συνεπολέμησε
χρόνον τινὰ τοῖς Λακεδαιμονίοις, καὶ μεγάλας ἐν
τῷ πολέμῳ χρείας παρέσχετο· ἦν γὰρ καὶ λόγῳ
δυνατώτατος καὶ τόλμῃ πολὺ προέχων τῶν πολι-

---

[1] So Reiske: καθίσταντο.　　　[2] So Dindorf: Βοιωτίαν.
[3] So Dindorf: προσδραμόντων.

complete concord, the generals kept quarrelling with 412 B.C. each other. And finally they sailed to Oropus without preparation and met the Peloponnesians in a sea-battle; but since they made a wretched beginning of the battle and stood up to the fighting like churls, they lost twenty-two ships and barely got the rest safe over to Eretria.

After these events had taken place, the allies of the Athenians, because of the defeats they had suffered in Sicily as well as the estranged relations of the commanders, revolted to the Lacedaemonians. And since Darius, the king of the Persians, was an ally of the Lacedaemonians, Pharnabazus, who had the military command of the regions bordering on the sea, supplied money to the Lacedaemonians; and he also summoned the three hundred triremes supplied by Phoenicia, having in mind to dispatch them to the aid of the Lacedaemonians.

37. Inasmuch as the Athenians had experienced setbacks so serious at one and the same time, everyone had assumed that the war was at an end; for no one expected that the Athenians could possibly endure such reverses any longer, even for a moment. However, events did not come to an end that tallied with the assumption of the majority, but on the contrary it came to pass, such was the superiority of the combatants, that the whole situation changed for the following reasons.

Alcibiades, who was in exile from Athens, had for a time fought on the side of the Lacedaemonians and had rendered them great assistance in the war; for he was a most able orator and far the outstanding

τῶν, ἔτι[1] δ' εὐγενείᾳ καὶ πλούτῳ πρῶτος Ἀθη-
3 ναίων. οὗτος οὖν ἐπιθυμῶν τῆς εἰς τὴν πατρίδα
τυχεῖν καθόδου, πάντα ἐμηχανᾶτο πρὸς τὸ τοῖς
Ἀθηναίοις πρᾶξαί τι τῶν χρησίμων, καὶ μάλιστ'
ἐν οἷς καιροῖς ἐδόκουν τοῖς ὅλοις ἐλαττοῦσθαι.
4 ἔχων οὖν φιλίαν πρὸς Φαρνάβαζον τὸν Δαρείου
σατράπην, καὶ θεωρῶν αὐτὸν μέλλοντα τριακοσίας
ναῦς ἀποστέλλειν τοῖς Λακεδαιμονίοις εἰς συμμαχίαν, ἔπεισεν ἀποστῆναι τῆς πράξεως· ἐδίδασκε
γὰρ ὡς οὐ συμφέρει τῷ βασιλεῖ τοὺς Λακεδαιμονίους ποιεῖν ἄγαν ἰσχυρούς· οὐ γὰρ συνοίσειν
Πέρσαις· κρεῖττον οὖν εἶναι περιορᾶν τοὺς δια-
πολεμοῦντας ἴσους ὄντας, ὅπως πρὸς ἀλλήλους ὡς
5 πλεῖστον χρόνον διαφέρωνται. ὅθεν ὁ Φαρνάβαζος
διαλαβὼν εὖ λέγειν τὸν Ἀλκιβιάδην, πάλιν τὸν
στόλον ἀπέστειλεν εἰς Φοινίκην. τότε μὲν οὖν
τηλικαύτην τῶν Λακεδαιμονίων συμμαχίαν παρεί-
λατο· μετὰ δέ τινα χρόνον τυχὼν τῆς καθόδου καὶ
δυνάμεως ἡγησάμενος, πολλαῖς μὲν μάχαις ἐνίκησε
Λακεδαιμονίους, καὶ τελέως τὰ τῶν Ἀθηναίων
6 πράγματα πεσόντα πάλιν ἤγειρεν. ἀλλὰ περὶ μὲν
τούτων ἐν τοῖς οἰκείοις χρόνοις ἀκριβέστερον ἐροῦ-
μεν, ἵνα μὴ παρὰ φύσιν προλαμβάνωμεν τῇ γραφῇ
τοὺς καιρούς.

38. Τοῦ γὰρ ἐνιαυσιαίου χρόνου διεληλυθότος
Ἀθήνησι μὲν ἦρχε Θεόπομπος, Ῥωμαῖοι δ' ἀντὶ
τῶν ὑπάτων τέτταρας χιλιάρχους κατέστησαν, Τιβέ-

---

[1] So Dindorf: ἐν.

[1] Cp. chap. 36. 5.

citizen in daring, and, besides, he was in high 412 B.C.
birth and wealth first among the Athenians. Now
since Alcibiades was eager to be allowed to return to
his native city, he contrived every device whereby
he could do the Athenians some good turn, and in
particular at the crucial moments when the Athenians
seemed doomed to utter defeat. Accordingly, since
he was on friendly terms with Pharnabazus, the
satrap of Darius, and saw that he was on the point of
sending three hundred ships to the support of the
Lacedaemonians,[1] he persuaded him to give up the
undertaking; for he showed him that it would not
be to the advantage of the King to make the Lacedaemonians too powerful. That would not, he said,
help the Persians, and so a better policy would be to
maintain a neutral attitude toward the combatants
so long as they were equally matched, in order that
they might continue their quarrel as long as possible.
Thereupon Pharnabazus, believing that Alcibiades
was giving him good advice, sent the fleet back
to Phoenicia. Now on that occasion Alcibiades deprived the Lacedaemonians of so great an allied force;
and some time later, when he had been allowed to
return to Athens and been given command of a
military force, he defeated the Lacedaemonians in
many battles and completely restored again the
sunken fortunes of the Athenians. But we shall
discuss these matters in more detail in connection
with the appropriate period of time, in order that our
account may not by anticipation violate the natural
order of events.

38. After the close of the year Theopompus was 411 B.C.
archon in Athens and the Romans elected in place
of consuls four military tribunes, Tiberius Postumius,

ριον Ποστούμιον καὶ Γάιον Κορνήλιον, πρὸς δὲ τούτοις Γάιον Οὐαλέριον καὶ Καίσωνα Φάβιον. περὶ
δὲ τούτους τοὺς χρόνους Ἀθηναῖοι τὴν ἐκ τῶν τετρακοσίων ὀλιγαρχίαν κατέλυσαν καὶ τὸ σύστημα τῆς
2 πολιτείας ἐκ τῶν πολιτῶν[1] συνεστήσαντο. τούτων
δὲ πάντων ἦν εἰσηγητὴς Θηραμένης, ἀνὴρ καὶ τῷ
βίῳ κόσμιος καὶ φρονήσει δοκῶν διαφέρειν τῶν
ἄλλων· καὶ γὰρ τὸν Ἀλκιβιάδην οὗτος μόνος συνεβούλευσε κατάγειν, δι' ὃν πάλιν ἑαυτοὺς ἀνέλαβον,
καὶ πολλῶν ἄλλων εἰσηγητὴς γενόμενος ἐπ' ἀγαθῷ
τῆς πατρίδος οὐ μετρίας ἀποδοχῆς ἐτύγχανεν.
3 Ἀλλὰ ταῦτα μὲν μικρὸν ὕστερον ἐγενήθη, εἰς
δὲ τὸν πόλεμον Ἀθηναῖοι μὲν στρατηγοὺς κατέστησαν Θράσυλλον καὶ Θρασύβουλον, οἳ τὸν στόλον
εἰς Σάμον ἀθροίσαντες ἐγύμναζον τοὺς στρατιώτας
εἰς ναυμαχίαν καθ' ἡμέραν ἀναπείρας ποιούμενοι.
4 Μίνδαρος δ' ὁ τῶν Λακεδαιμονίων ναύαρχος χρόνον μέν τινα περὶ τὴν Μίλητον διέτριβε, προσδο-
κῶν τὴν παρὰ Φαρναβάζου βοήθειαν· τριακοσίας
γὰρ τριήρεις ἀκούων ἐκ Φοινίκης καταπεπλευκέναι
μετέωρος ἦν ταῖς ἐλπίσι, νομίζων τηλικούτῳ στόλῳ
5 καταλύσειν τὴν Ἀθηναίων ἡγεμονίαν· μετ' ὀλίγον
δὲ πυθόμενός τινων, ὅτι πεισθεὶς Ἀλκιβιάδῃ πάλιν
ἀπέστειλε τὸν στόλον εἰς Φοινίκην, τὰς μὲν παρὰ
Φαρναβάζου ἐλπίδας ἀπέγνω, αὐτὸς δὲ καταρτίσας
τάς τ' ἐκ Πελοποννήσου ναῦς καὶ τὰς παρὰ τῶν
ἔξωθεν συμμάχων, Δωριέα μὲν μετὰ τριῶν καὶ
δέκα νεῶν ἀπέστειλεν εἰς Ῥόδον, πυνθανόμενος
ἐπὶ νεωτερισμῷ τινας συνίστασθαι τῶν Ῥοδίων·
6 προσφάτως γὰρ τοῖς Λακεδαιμονίοις τινὲς τῶν

---

[1] ὁπλιτῶν Krüger.

---

[1] This step was the government of the Five Thousand in

Gaius Cornelius, Gaius Valerius, and Caeso Fabius. 411 B.C.
At this time the Athenians dissolved the oligarchy
of the Four Hundred and formed the constitution
of the government from the citizens at large.[1] The
author of all these changes was Theramenes, a man
who was orderly in his manner of life and was reputed to surpass all others in judgement; for he was
the only person to advise the recall from exile of
Alcibiades, through whom the Athenians recovered
themselves, and since he was the author of many
other measures for the benefit of his country, he was
the recipient of no small approbation.

But these events took place at a little later time,
and for the war the Athenians appointed Thrasyllus
and Thrasybulus generals, who collected the fleet at
Samos and trained the soldiers for battle at sea, giving
them daily exercises. But Mindarus, the Lacedaemonian admiral, was inactive for some time at
Miletus, expecting the aid promised by Pharnabazus;
and when he heard that three hundred triremes had
arrived from Phoenicia, he was buoyed up in his hopes,
believing that with so great a fleet he could destroy
the empire of the Athenians. But when a little later
he learned from sundry persons that Pharnabazus had
been won over by Alcibiades and had sent the fleet
back to Phoenicia, he gave up the hopes he had placed
in Pharnabazus, and by himself, after equipping both
the ships brought from the Peloponnesus and those
supplied by his allies from abroad, he dispatched
Dorieus with thirteen ships to Rhodes, since he had
learned that certain Rhodians were banding together
for a revolution.—The ships we have mentioned had

place of the oligarchy of the Four Hundred. The old
democracy was restored the following year.

ἀπὸ τῆς Ἰταλίας Ἑλλήνων ἀπεστάλκεισαν εἰς
συμμαχίαν τὰς προειρημένας ναῦς· αὐτὸς δὲ τὰς
ἄλλας πάσας ἀναλαβών, οὔσας ὀγδοήκοντα καὶ
τρεῖς, ἀπῆρεν εἰς Ἑλλήσποντον διὰ τὸ πυνθάνεσθαι
τὸν τῶν Ἀθηναίων στόλον ἐν Σάμῳ διατρίβειν.
7 καθ᾽ ὃν δὴ χρόνον οἱ τῶν Ἀθηναίων στρατηγοὶ
θεωροῦντες παραπλέοντας ἀνήχθησαν ἐπ᾽ αὐτοὺς
μετὰ νεῶν ἑξήκοντα. τῶν δὲ Λακεδαιμονίων κατ-
ενεχθέντων εἰς Χίον ἔδοξε τοῖς τῶν Ἀθηναίων
στρατηγοῖς προσπλεῦσαι τῇ Λέσβῳ, κἀκεῖ παρὰ
τῶν συμμάχων ἀθροῖσαι τριήρεις, ὅπως μὴ συμβαίνῃ τοὺς πολεμίους ὑπερέχειν τῷ πλήθει τῶν
νεῶν.

39. Οὗτοι μὲν οὖν περὶ ταῦτα διέτριβον. Μίνδαρος δ᾽ ὁ τῶν Λακεδαιμονίων ναύαρχος νυκτὸς μετὰ
τοῦ στόλου παντὸς ἐκπλεύσας εἰς Ἑλλήσποντον
ἐκομίζετο κατὰ σπουδήν, καὶ δευτεραῖος εἰς Σίγειον κατέπλευσεν. οἱ δ᾽ Ἀθηναῖοι πυθόμενοι τὸν
παράπλουν οὐκ ἀνέμειναν ἁπάσας τὰς παρὰ τῶν
συμμάχων τριήρεις, τριῶν δὲ μόνον προσγενο-
2 μένων αὐτοῖς, ἐδίωκον τοὺς Λακεδαιμονίους. ἐπεὶ
δ᾽ ἦλθον εἰς Σίγειον, εὗρον τὸν μὲν στόλον ἐκ-
πεπλευκότα, τρεῖς δὲ ναῦς ὑπολελειμμένας, ὧν
εὐθέως ἐκυρίευσαν· καὶ μετὰ ταῦτ᾽ εἰς Ἐλεοῦντα
καταπλεύσαντες τὰ περὶ τὴν ναυμαχίαν παρ-
3 εσκευάζοντο. Λακεδαιμόνιοι δὲ θεωροῦντες τοὺς
πολεμίους τὰ πρὸς τὴν μάχην ἑτοιμαζομένους,
καὶ αὐτοὶ πένθ᾽ ἡμέρας ἀναπείρας[1] ποιούμενοι καὶ
γυμνάσαντες τοὺς ἐρέτας, ἐξέταξαν τὸν στόλον εἰς
ναυμαχίαν, ὄντα νεῶν δυεῖν ἐλάττω τῶν ἐνενήκοντα.
οὗτοι μὲν οὖν ἐκ τοῦ πρὸς τὴν Ἀσίαν μέρους
ἔστησαν τὰς ναῦς, οἱ δ᾽ Ἀθηναῖοι τὸ πρὸς τὴν

recently been sent to the Lacedaemonians as an 411 B.C. allied force by certain Greeks of Italy.—And Mindarus himself took all the other ships, numbering eighty-three, and set out for the Hellespont, since he had learned that the Athenian fleet was tarrying at Samos. The moment the generals of the Athenians saw them sailing by, they put out to sea against them with sixty ships. But when the Lacedaemonians put in at Chios, the Athenian generals decided to sail on to Lesbos and there to gather triremes from their allies, in order that it should not turn out that the enemy surpassed them in number of ships.

39. Now the Athenians were engaged in gathering ships. But Mindarus, the Lacedaemonian admiral, setting out by night with his entire fleet, made in haste for the Hellespont and arrived on the second day at Sigeium.[1] When the Athenians learned that the fleet had sailed by them, they did not wait for all the triremes of their allies, but after only three had been added to their number they set out in pursuit of the Lacedaemonians. When they arrived at Sigeium, they found the fleet already departed, but three ships left behind they at once captured; after this they put in at Eleüs [2] and made preparations for the sea-battle. The Lacedaemonians, seeing the enemy rehearsing for the battle, did likewise, spending five days in proving their ships and exercising their rowers; then they drew up the fleet for the battle, its strength being eighty-eight ships. Now the Lacedaemonians stationed their ships on the Asian side of the channel, while the Athenians lined

---

[1] On the Asian side at the very entrance of the Hellespont.
[2] Directly opposite Sigeium.

---

[1] So Hertlein: ἀνάπειραν.

Εὐρώπην ἔχοντες ἀντανήγοντο, τῷ μὲν πλήθει
4 λειπόμενοι ταῖς δ' ἐμπειρίαις ὑπερέχοντες. Λακεδαιμόνιοι μὲν οὖν ἐπὶ τοῦ δεξιοῦ κέρατος ἔταξαν
τοὺς Συρακοσίους ὧν Ἑρμοκράτης ἀφηγεῖτο, τὸ
δ' εὐώνυμον αὐτοὶ¹ συνεπλήρουν Πελοποννήσιοι,
Μινδάρου τὴν ἡγεμονίαν ἔχοντος. τῶν δ' Ἀθηναίων ἐπὶ μὲν τὸ δεξιὸν ἐτάχθη Θράσυλλος, ἐπὶ
δὲ τὸ εὐώνυμον Θρασύβουλος. καὶ τὸ μὲν πρῶτον
ἔσπευδον ἀμφότεροι φιλοτιμούμενοι περὶ τοῦ τόπου
5 ὅπως μὴ τὸν ῥοῦν ἔχωσιν ἐναντίον. διὸ καὶ πολὺν
χρόνον ἀλλήλους περιέπλεον, διακλείοντες τὰ στενὰ
καὶ περὶ τῆς στάσεως τοπομαχοῦντες· μεταξὺ γὰρ
Ἀβύδου καὶ Σηστοῦ τῆς ναυμαχίας γινομένης συνέβαινε τὸν ῥοῦν οὐ μετρίως ἐμποδίζειν ἐν στενοῖς
τόποις. οὐ μὴν ἀλλ' οἱ τῶν Ἀθηναίων κυβερνῆται
πολὺ ταῖς ἐμπειρίαις προέχοντες πολλὰ πρὸς τὴν
νίκην συνεβάλοντο.

40. Τῶν γὰρ Πελοποννησίων ὑπερεχόντων τῷ
πλήθει τῶν νεῶν καὶ ταῖς τῶν ἐπιβατῶν ἀρεταῖς, ἡ
τέχνη τῶν κυβερνητῶν ἄχρηστον τὴν ὑπεροχὴν τῶν
ἐναντίων ἐποίει. ὁπότε γὰρ οἱ Πελοποννήσιοι κατὰ
σπουδὴν ἀθρόαις ταῖς ναυσὶν εἰς ἐμβολὴν ἐπιφέροιντο, τὰς ἑαυτῶν οὕτως φιλοτέχνως καθίστανον
ὥστε τοῦ μὲν ἄλλου μέρους αὐτὰς μὴ δύνασθαι
θιγεῖν,² τοῖς δὲ στόμασι τῶν ἐμβόλων μόνοις
2 ἀναγκάζεσθαι συμβάλλειν. διόπερ ὁ Μίνδαρος
ὁρῶν ἄπρακτον οὖσαν τὴν ἐκ τῶν ἐμβολῶν βίαν,
κατ' ὀλίγας καὶ κατὰ μίαν ἐκέλευσε συμπλέκεσθαι.
οὐ μὴν οὐδ' ἐνταῦθα τὴν τῶν κυβερνητῶν τέχνην

¹ αὐτοὶ suggested by Vogel (cp. Thuc. 8. 104. 3): αὐτοῖς.
² θιγεῖν] θήγειν PF.

up against them on the European side, being fewer 411 B.C.
in number but of superior training. The Lacedaemonians put on their right wing the Syracusans, whose
leader was Hermocrates, and the Peloponnesians
themselves formed the whole left wing with Mindarus
in command. For the Athenians Thrasyllus was
stationed on the right wing and Thrasybulus on the
left. At the outset both sides strove stubbornly for
position in order that they might not have the current
against them. Consequently they kept sailing around
each other for a long time, endeavouring to block off
the straits and struggling for an advantageous position; for the battle took place between Abydus and
Sestus [1] and it so happened that the current was of no
little hindrance where the strait was narrow. However, the pilots of the Athenian fleet, being far superior
in experience, contributed greatly to the victory.

40. For although the Peloponnesians had the advantage in the number of their ships and the valour
of their marines, the skill of the Athenian pilots
rendered the superiority of their opponents of no
effect. For whenever the Peloponnesians, with their
ships in a body, would charge swiftly forward to
ram, the pilots would manœuvre their own ships so
skilfully that their opponents were unable to strike
them at any other spot but could only meet them
bows on, ram against ram. Consequently Mindarus,
seeing that the force of the rams was proving ineffective, gave orders for his ships to come to grips
in small groups, or one at a time. But not by this
manœuvre either, as it turned out, was the skill of

[1] Some eight miles up the Hellespont from the entrance.

ἄπρακτον εἶναι συνέβαινεν, ἀλλ' εὐφυῶς ἐκκλίνοντες
τὰς τῶν νεῶν ἐπιφερομένας ἐμβολὰς πλαγίαις ἐν-
3 έσειον καὶ πολλὰς κατετίτρωσκον. φιλοτιμίας δ'
ἐμπεσούσης εἰς ἀμφοτέρους, οὐ μόνον ταῖς ἐμβολαῖς διεκινδύνευον, ἀλλὰ συμπλεκόμενοι τοῖς
ἐπιβάταις διηγωνίζοντο. πολλὰ δ' ὑπὸ τῆς τοῦ
ῥοῦ βίας διακωλυόμενοι πράττειν ἐφ' ἱκανὸν χρόνον
διεκινδύνευον, οὐδετέρων δυναμένων τυχεῖν τῆς
4 νίκης. ἰσορρόπου δὲ τῆς μάχης οὔσης, ἐπεφάνησαν
ὑπέρ τινος ἄκρας ναῦς εἴκοσι πέντε παρὰ τῶν
συμμάχων ἀπεσταλμέναι τοῖς Ἀθηναίοις. φοβηθέντες δὲ οἱ Πελοποννήσιοι πρὸς τὴν Ἄβυδον
ἔφυγον, ἐξαπτομένων τῶν Ἀθηναίων καὶ φιλοτιμότερον διωξάντων.

5   Τῆς δὲ ναυμαχίας τοιοῦτον τέλος λαβούσης,
Ἀθηναῖοι ναῦς ἔλαβον ὀκτὼ μὲν Χίων, πέντε δὲ
Κορινθίων, Ἀμβρακιωτῶν δὲ δύο, Συρακοσίων δὲ
καὶ Πελληνέων[1] καὶ Λευκαδίων μίαν ἐξ ἑκάστων·
αὐτοὶ δὲ πέντε[2] ναῦς ἀπέβαλον, ἃς πάσας βυθι-
6 σθῆναι συνέβη. μετὰ δὲ ταῦθ' οἱ περὶ τὸν Θρασύβουλον ἔστησαν τρόπαιον ἐπὶ τῆς ἄκρας, οὗ τὸ
τῆς Ἑκάβης ἐστὶ μνημεῖον, καὶ τοὺς ἀπαγγελοῦντας τὴν νίκην εἰς Ἀθήνας ἔπεμψαν, αὐτοὶ δὲ
μετὰ παντὸς τοῦ στόλου τὸν πλοῦν ἐπὶ Κύζικον
ἐποιήσαντο· αὕτη γὰρ πρὸ τῆς ναυμαχίας ἦν ἀφ-
εστηκυῖα πρὸς Φαρνάβαζον τὸν Δαρείου στρατηγὸν
καὶ Κλέαρχον τὸν Λακεδαιμονίων ἡγεμόνα. εὑρόντες δ' αὐτὴν ἀτείχιστον ῥᾳδίως τῆς ἐπιβολῆς ἐκρά-

[1] So Vogel: Παλληναίων.
[2] πέντε] πεντεκαίδεκα Thuc. 8. 106. 3.

the Athenian pilots rendered ineffective ; on the 411 B.C.
contrary, cleverly avoiding the on-coming rams of the
ships, they struck them on the side and damaged
many. And such a spirit of rivalry pervaded both
forces that they would not confine the struggle to
ramming tactics, but tangling ship with ship fought
it out with the marines. Although they were hindered by the strength of the current from achieving
great success, they continued the struggle for a
considerable time, neither side being able to gain
the victory. While the fighting was thus equally
balanced, there appeared beyond a cape twenty-five
ships which had been dispatched to the Athenians
from their allies. The Peloponnesians thereupon in
alarm turned in flight toward Abydus, the Athenians
clinging to them and pursuing them the more
vigorously.

Such was the end of the battle ; and the Athenians
captured eight ships of the Chians, five of the
Corinthians, two of the Ambraciotes, and one each
of the Syracusans, Pellenians, and Leucadians, while
they themselves lost five ships, all of them, as it
happened, having been sunk. After this Thrasybulus
set up a trophy on the cape where stands the memorial
of Hecabê [1] and sent messengers to Athens to carry
word of the victory, and himself made his way to
Cyzicus with the entire fleet. For before the sea-
battle this city had revolted to Pharnabazus, the
general of Darius, and to Clearchus, the Lacedaemonian commander. Finding the city unfortified the

---

[1] Also called " Hecabê's Monument " and " Bitch's
Monument " (Strabo, 7. 55 ; the Cynossema of the Romans,
modern Cape Volpo), because one account states that Hecabê
(Hecuba) was metamorphosed into a bitch (cp. Euripides,
Hec. 1273).

τησαν, καὶ χρήματα πραξάμενοι τοὺς Κυζικηνοὺς
ἀπέπλευσαν εἰς Σηστόν.

41. Μίνδαρος δ' ὁ τῶν Λακεδαιμονίων ναύαρχος
ἀπὸ τῆς ἥττης φυγὼν εἰς Ἄβυδον τάς τε πεπονηκυίας ναῦς ἐπεσκεύασε καὶ πρὸς τὰς ἐν Εὐβοίᾳ
τριήρεις ἀπέστειλεν Ἐπικλέα τὸν Σπαρτιάτην,
2 προστάξας ἄγειν τὴν ταχίστην. ὃς ἐπεὶ κατέπλευσεν εἰς Εὔβοιαν, ἀθροίσας τὰς ναῦς οὔσας πεντήκοντα κατὰ σπουδὴν ἀνήχθη· καὶ κατὰ τὸν Ἄθω
γενομένων τῶν τριήρων ἐπεγενήθη χειμὼν τηλι-
κοῦτος ὥστε τὰς μὲν ναῦς ἁπάσας ἀπολέσθαι τῶν
3 δὲ ἀνδρῶν δώδεκα μόνον[1] διασωθῆναι. δηλοῖ δὲ
τὰ[2] περὶ τούτων ἀνάθημα κείμενον ἐν τῷ περὶ
Κορώνειαν νεῷ, καθάπερ φησὶν Ἔφορος, τὴν ἐπιγραφὴν ἔχον ταύτην·

οἶδ' ἀπὸ πεντήκοντα νεῶν θάνατον προφυγόντες
   πρὸς σκοπέλοισιν Ἄθω σώματα γῇ πέλασαν
δώδεκα, τοὺς δ' ἄλλους ὄλεσεν μέγα λαῖτμα θα-
   λάσσης
νῆάς τε στυγεροῖς πνεύμασι χρησαμένας.

4 Περὶ δὲ τὸν αὐτὸν καιρὸν Ἀλκιβιάδης ἔχων
τρισκαίδεκα τριήρεις κατέπλευσε πρὸς τοὺς ἐν
Σάμῳ διατρίβοντας, οἳ πάλαι προακηκοότες ἦσαν
ὅτι πεπεικὼς εἴη τὸν Φαρνάβαζον μηκέτι ταῖς
τριακοσίαις ναυσὶ βοηθεῖν τοῖς Λακεδαιμονίοις.
5 φιλοφρόνως δ' αὐτὸν ἀποδεξαμένων τῶν ἐν τῇ
Σάμῳ, διελέγετο πρὸς αὐτοὺς περὶ τῆς καθόδου,
πολλὰ κατεπαγγελλόμενος χρήσιμος ἔσεσθαι τῇ
πατρίδι, ὁμοίως καὶ τὰ καθ' ἑαυτὸν ἀπολογησά-

---

[1] So Hertlein: μόνους.
[2] τὰ Vogel: τό.

Athenians easily achieved their end, and after exacting money of the Cyziceni they sailed off to Sestus.

41. Mindarus, the Lacedaemonian admiral, after
his flight to Abydus from the scene of his defeat
repaired the ships that had been damaged and also
sent the Spartan Epicles to the triremes at Euboea
with orders to bring them with all speed. When
Epicles arrived at Euboea, he gathered the ships,
which amounted to fifty, and hurriedly put out to
sea ; but when the triremes were off Mt. Athos there
arose a storm of such fury that all the ships were lost
and of their crews twelve men alone survived. These
facts are set forth by a dedication, as Ephorus states,
which stands in the temple at Coroneia and bears the
following inscription :

These from the crews of fifty ships, escaping de-
        struction,
    Brought their bodies to land hard by Athos' sharp
        crags ;
Only twelve, all the rest the yawning depth of the
        waters
    Took to their death with their ships, meeting with
        terrible winds.

At about the same time Alcibiades with thirteen
triremes came by sea to the Athenians who were
lying at Samos and had already heard that he had
persuaded Pharnabazus not to come, as he had
intended, with his three hundred ships to reinforce
the Lacedaemonians. And since the troops at Samos
gave him a friendly welcome, he discussed with
them the matter of his return from exile, offering
promises to render many services to the fatherland ;
and in like manner he defended his own conduct and

233

μενος καὶ πολλὰ τὴν ἑαυτοῦ δακρύσας τύχην, ὅτι
τὴν ἰδίαν ἀρετὴν ὑπὸ τῶν ἐχθρῶν ἠνάγκασται κατὰ
τῆς πατρίδος ἐνδείξασθαι.

42. Τῶν δὲ στρατιωτῶν ἀσμένως τοὺς λόγους
προσδεξαμένων καὶ περὶ τούτων διαπεμψαμένων
εἰς Ἀθήνας, ἔδοξε τῷ δήμῳ τὸν ἄνδρα τῶν ἐγκλημάτων ἀπολῦσαι καὶ μεταδοῦναι τῆς στρατηγίας·
θεωροῦντες γὰρ αὐτοῦ τὸ πρακτικὸν τῆς τόλμης
καὶ τὴν παρὰ τοῖς Ἕλλησι δόξαν, ὑπελάμβανον,
ὅπερ ἦν εἰκός, οὐ μικρὰν ῥοπὴν ἔσεσθαι τοῖς
2 σφετέροις πράγμασι τούτου προσγενομένου. καὶ
γὰρ ὁ τῆς πολιτείας ἀφηγούμενος τότε Θηραμένης, ἀνὴρ εἰ καί τις ἄλλος εἶναι δόξας συνετός,
τῷ δήμῳ συνεβούλευσε κατάγειν τὸν Ἀλκιβιάδην.
τούτων δ’ ἀπαγγελθέντων εἰς Σάμον, Ἀλκιβιάδης
πρὸς αἷς εἶχεν ἰδίαις ναυσὶ τρισκαίδεκα ἐννέα
προσέλαβε, καὶ μετὰ τούτων ἐκπλεύσας εἰς Ἁλι-
καρνασσὸν παρὰ τῆς πόλεως εἰσεπράξατο χρήματα.
3 μετὰ δὲ ταῦτα τὴν Μεροπίδα¹ πορθήσας μετὰ
πολλῆς λείας ἀνέπλευσεν εἰς Σάμον. πολλῶν δὲ
συναχθέντων λαφύρων, τοῖς τ’ ἐν Σάμῳ στρατιώταις καὶ τοῖς μεθ’ ἑαυτοῦ διελόμενος τὰς ὠφελείας
ταχὺ τοὺς εὖ παθόντας εὔνους ἑαυτῷ κατεσκεύασεν.
4 Περὶ δὲ τὸν αὐτὸν χρόνον Ἀντάνδριοι, φρουρὰν
ἔχοντες, μετεπέμψαντο παρὰ Λακεδαιμονίων στρατιώτας, μεθ’ ὧν ἐκβαλόντες τὴν φυλακὴν ἐλευθέραν
ᾤκουν τὴν πατρίδα· οἱ γὰρ Λακεδαιμόνιοι περὶ
τῆς εἰς Φοινίκην ἀποστολῆς τῶν τριακοσίων νεῶν

¹ So Palmer : Μεροδίπα.

---

¹ According to Thucydides (8. 81) this meeting between
Alcibiades and the Athenian fleet took place before the
naval battle. ² The Assembly in Athens.

shed many tears over his own fortune, because he 411 B.C. had been compelled by his enemies to give proof of his own valour at the expense of his native land.[1]

42. And since the soldiers heartily welcomed the offers of Alcibiades and sent messages to Athens regarding them, the people [2] voted to dismiss the charges against Alcibiades and to give him a share in the command ; for as they observed the efficiency of his daring and the fame he enjoyed among the Greeks, they assumed, and with good reason, that his adherence to them would add no little weight to their cause. Moreover, Theramenes, who at the time enjoyed the leadership in the government and who, if anyone, had a reputation of sagacity, advised the people to recall Alcibiades. When word of this action was reported to Samos, Alcibiades added nine ships to the thirteen he already had, and sailing with them to Halicarnassus he exacted money from that city. After this he sacked Meropis [3] and returned to Samos with much plunder. And since a great amount of booty had been amassed, he divided the spoils among the soldiers at Samos and his own troops, thereby soon causing the recipients of his benefactions to be well disposed toward himself.

About the same time the Antandrians,[4] who were held by a garrison,[5] sent to the Lacedaemonians for soldiers, with whose aid they expelled the garrison and thus made their country a free place to live in ; for the Lacedaemonians, finding fault with Pharnabazus for the sending of the three hundred ships back

[3] The island of Cos.
[4] Just outside the Troad to the south-east.
[5] Of Persians (Thucydides, 8. 108).

ἐγκαλοῦντες τῷ Φαρναβάζῳ τοῖς Ἄντανδρον οἰ-
κοῦσι συνεμάχησαν.

5 Τῶν δὲ συγγραφέων Θουκυδίδης μὲν τὴν ἱστορίαν κατέστροφε,[1] περιλαβὼν χρόνον ἐτῶν εἴκοσι
καὶ δυοῖν ἐν βύβλοις ὀκτώ· τινὲς δὲ διαιροῦσιν εἰς
ἐννέα· Ξενοφῶν δὲ καὶ Θεόπομπος ἀφ' ὧν ἀπέλιπε
Θουκυδίδης τὴν ἀρχὴν πεποίηνται, καὶ Ξενοφῶν
μὲν περιέλαβε χρόνον ἐτῶν τεσσαράκοντα καὶ
ὀκτώ, Θεόπομπος δὲ τὰς Ἑλληνικὰς πράξεις
διελθὼν ἐπ' ἔτη ἑπτακαίδεκα καταλήγει τὴν ἱστορίαν εἰς τὴν περὶ Κνίδον ναυμαχίαν ἐν βύβλοις
δώδεκα.

6 Τὰ μὲν οὖν κατὰ τὴν Ἑλλάδα καὶ τὴν Ἀσίαν
ἐν τούτοις ἦν. Ῥωμαῖοι δὲ πρὸς Αἴκους διαπολε-
μοῦντες ἐνέβαλον αὐτῶν εἰς τὴν χώραν μετὰ πολλῆς
δυνάμεως· περιστρατοπεδεύσαντες δὲ πόλιν Βώλας
ὀνομαζομένην ἐξεπολιόρκησαν.

43. Τῶν δὲ κατὰ τὸν ἐνιαυτὸν τοῦτον πράξεων
τέλος ἐχουσῶν Ἀθήνησι μὲν ἦρχε Γλαύκιππος, ἐν
δὲ τῇ Ῥώμῃ κατεστάθησαν ὕπατοι Μάρκος Κορνήλιος καὶ Λεύκιος Φούριος. περὶ δὲ τούτους τοὺς
χρόνους Αἰγεσταῖοι κατὰ τὴν Σικελίαν σύμμαχοι
γεγενημένοι τοῖς Ἀθηναίοις κατὰ Συρακοσίων,
καταλυθέντος τοῦ πολέμου περιδεεῖς καθεστήκει-
σαν· ἤλπιζον γάρ, ὅπερ ἦν εἰκός, τιμωρίαν δώσειν
τοῖς Σικελιώταις ὑπὲρ ὧν εἰς αὐτοὺς ἐξήμαρτον.

2 τῶν δὲ Σελινουντίων περὶ τῆς ἀμφισβητησίμου
χώρας πολεμούντων αὐτοὺς ἑκουσίως ἐξεχώρουν,
εὐλαβούμενοι μὴ διὰ ταύτην τὴν πρόφασιν οἱ
Συρακόσιοι συνεπιλάβωνται τοῦ πολέμου τοῖς
Σελινουντίοις, καὶ κινδυνεύσωσιν ἄρδην ἀπολέσαι

---

[1] So Dindorf: κατέστρεψε.

to Phoenicia, gave their aid to the inhabitants of 411 B.C. Antandrus.

Of the historians, Thucydides ended his history,[1] having included a period of twenty-two years in eight Books, although some divide it into nine [2]; and Xenophon and Theopompus have begun at the point where Thucydides left off. Xenophon embraced a period of forty-eight years, and Theopompus set forth the facts of Greek history for seventeen years and brings his account to an end with the sea-battle of Cnidus in twelve Books.[3]

Such was the state of affairs in Greece and Asia. The Romans were waging war with the Aequi and invaded their territory with a strong army; and investing the city named Bolae they took it by siege.

43. When the events of this year had come to an 410 B.C. end, in Athens Glaucippus was archon and in Rome the consuls elected were Marcus Cornelius and Lucius Furius. At this time in Sicily the Aegestaeans, who had allied themselves with the Athenians against the Syracusans, had fallen into great fear at the conclusion of the war; for they expected, and with good reason, to pay the penalty to the Sicilian Greeks for the wrongs they had inflicted upon them. And when the Selinuntians went to war with them over the land in dispute,[4] they withdrew from it of their free will, being concerned lest the Syracusans should use this excuse to join the Selinuntians in the war and they should thereby run the risk of utterly

---

[1] *i.e.* with this year.
[2] Modern editions recognize eight Books.
[3] The *Hellenica* of Xenophon covers the years 411–362 B.C., ending with the battle of Mantineia, and the *Hellenica* of Theopompus, which is not extant, included the years 410–394 B.C.   [4] Cp. Book 12. 82.

3 τὴν πατρίδα. ἐπεὶ δ' οἱ Σελινούντιοι χωρὶς τῆς
ἀμφισβητησίμου πολλὴν τῆς παρακειμένης ἀπετέ-
μοντο, τηνικαῦθ' οἱ τὴν Αἴγεσταν οἰκοῦντες πρέσβεις ἀπέστειλαν εἰς Καρχηδόνα, δεόμενοι βοηθῆσαι
4 καὶ τὴν πόλιν αὐτοῖς ἐγχειρίζοντες. καταπλευ-
σάντων δὲ τῶν πεμφθέντων, καὶ τῇ γερουσίᾳ τὰς·
παρὰ τοῦ δήμου δεδομένας ἐντολὰς εἰπόντων, οὐ
μετρίως διηπόρησαν οἱ Καρχηδόνιοι· ἅμα μὲν γὰρ
ἐπεθύμουν παραλαβεῖν πόλιν εὔκαιρον, ἅμα δ' ἐφο-
βοῦντο τοὺς Συρακοσίους, ἑωρακότες προσφάτως
καταπεπολεμημένας τὰς τῶν Ἀθηναίων δυνάμεις.
5 οὐ μὴν ἀλλὰ καὶ τοῦ παρ' αὐτοῖς πρωτεύοντος
Ἀννίβου συμβουλεύοντος[1] παραλαβεῖν τὴν πόλιν,
τοῖς μὲν πρεσβευταῖς ἀπεκρίθησαν βοηθήσειν, εἰς
δὲ τὴν τούτων διοίκησιν, ἂν ᾖ χρεία πολεμεῖν,
στρατηγὸν κατέστησαν τὸν Ἀννίβαν, κατὰ νόμους
τότε βασιλεύοντα. οὗτος δὲ ἦν υἱωνὸς μὲν τοῦ
πρὸς Γέλωνα πολεμήσαντος Ἀμίλκου καὶ πρὸς
Ἱμέρᾳ τελευτήσαντος, υἱὸς δὲ Γέσκωνος, ὃς διὰ
τὴν τοῦ πατρὸς ἧτταν ἐφυγαδεύθη καὶ κατεβίωσεν
ἐν τῇ Σελινοῦντι.
6 Ὁ δ' οὖν Ἀννίβας, ὢν μὲν καὶ φύσει μισέλλην,
ὁμοῦ[2] δὲ τὰς τῶν προγόνων ἀτιμίας διορθώσασθαι
βουλόμενος, ἔσπευδε δι' ἑαυτοῦ τι κατασκευάσαι
χρήσιμον τῇ πατρίδι. θεωρῶν οὖν τοὺς Σελινουντίους οὐκ ἀρκουμένους τῇ παραχωρήσει τῆς ἀμφισβητησίμου χώρας, πρέσβεις ἀπέστειλε μετὰ τῶν
Αἰγεσταίων πρὸς Συρακοσίους, ἐπιτρέπων αὐτοῖς

---

[1] Ἀννίβου συμβουλεύοντος added by Vogel, παρακαλοῦντος
by Reiske; τοῦ placed after πρωτεύοντος by Dindorf.
[2] So Dindorf: ὅμως.

---

[1] As one of the two annually elected suffetes, somewhat

destroying their country. But when the Selinuntians
proposed, quite apart from the territory in dispute,
to carve off for themselves a large portion of the
neighbouring territory, the inhabitants of Aegesta
thereupon dispatched ambassadors to Carthage,
asking for aid and putting their city in the hands
of the Carthaginians. When the envoys arrived and
laid before the Senate the instructions the people
had given them, the Carthaginians found themselves
in no little quandary ; for while they were eager to
acquire a city so strategically situated, at the same
time they stood in fear of the Syracusans, having
just witnessed their defeat of the armaments of the
Athenians. But when Hannibal, their foremost
citizen, also advised them to acquire the city, they
replied to the ambassadors that they would come to
their aid, and to supervise the undertaking, in case
it should lead to war, they selected as general
Hannibal, who at the time lawfully exercised sove-
reign powers.[1] He was the grandson of Hamilcar,
who fought in the war against Gelon and died at
Himera,[2] and the son of Gescon, who had been exiled
because of his father's defeat and had ended his
life in Selinus.

Now Hannibal, who by nature was a hater of the
Greeks and at the same time desired to wipe out
the disgraces which had befallen his ancestors, was
eager by his own efforts to achieve some advantage
for his country. Hence, seeing that the Selinuntians
were not satisfied with the cession of the territory
in dispute, he dispatched ambassadors together with
the Aegestaeans to the Syracusans, referring to them

similar to the Roman consuls. Evidently Diodorus preferred
not to use the unfamiliar title. [2] Cp. Book 11. 21-22.

τὴν κρίσιν τούτων, τῷ μὲν λόγῳ προσποιούμενος
δικαιοπραγεῖν, τῇ δ' ἀληθείᾳ νομίζων ἐκ τοῦ μὴ
βούλεσθαι τοὺς Σελινουντίους διακριθῆναι μὴ συμ-
7 μαχήσειν αὐτοῖς τοὺς Συρακοσίους. ἀποστειλάντων δὲ καὶ Σελινουντίων πρέσβεις, διακριθῆναι
μὲν μὴ βουλομένων, πολλὰ δὲ πρὸς τοὺς παρὰ
Καρχηδονίων καὶ τῶν Αἰγεσταίων πρέσβεις ἀντει-
πόντων, τέλος ἔδοξε τοῖς Συρακοσίοις ψηφίσασθαι
τηρεῖν πρὸς μὲν Σελινουντίους τὴν συμμαχίαν,
πρὸς δὲ Καρχηδονίους τὴν εἰρήνην.

44. Μετὰ δὲ τὴν ἐπάνοδον τῶν πρεσβευτῶν
Καρχηδόνιοι μὲν τοῖς Αἰγεσταίοις ἀπέστειλαν Λί-
βυάς τε πεντακισχιλίους καὶ τῶν Καμπανῶν ὀκτα-
2 κοσίους. οὗτοι δ' ἦσαν ὑπὸ τῶν Χαλκιδέων τοῖς
Ἀθηναίοις εἰς τὸν πρὸς Συρακοσίους πόλεμον με-
μισθωμένοι, καὶ μετὰ τὴν ἧτταν καταπεπλευκότες οὐκ εἶχον τοὺς μισθοδοτήσοντας· οἱ δὲ
Καρχηδόνιοι πᾶσιν ἵππους ἀγοράσαντες καὶ μισθοὺς ἀξιολόγους δόντες εἰς τὴν Αἴγεσταν κατέστησαν.

3 Οἱ δὲ Σελινούντιοι κατ' ἐκείνους τοὺς χρόνους
εὐδαιμονοῦντες καὶ τῆς πόλεως αὐτοῖς πολυανδρού-
σης,[1] κατεφρόνουν τῶν Αἰγεσταίων. καὶ τὸ μὲν
πρῶτον ἐν τάξει τὴν ὅμορον χώραν ἐπόρθουν, πολὺ
προέχοντες ταῖς δυνάμεσι, μετὰ δὲ ταῦτα καταφρονήσαντες κατὰ πᾶσαν τὴν χώραν ἐσκεδάσθησαν.
4 οἱ δὲ τῶν Αἰγεσταίων στρατηγοὶ παρατηρήσαντες
αὐτοὺς ἐπέθεντο μετὰ τῶν Καρχηδονίων καὶ τῶν
Καμπανῶν. ἀπροσδοκήτου δὲ τῆς ἐφόδου γενομένης ῥᾳδίως ἐτρέψαντο τοὺς Σελινουντίους, καὶ
τῶν μὲν στρατιωτῶν ἀνεῖλον περὶ χιλίους, τῆς

----

[1] So Dindorf: πολυάνδρου οὔσης.

the decision of the dispute ; and though ostensibly 410 B.C.
he pretended to be seeking that justice be done, in
fact he believed that, after the Selinuntians refused
to agree to arbitration, the Syracusans would not join
them as allies. Since the Selinuntians also dispatched
ambassadors, refusing the arbitration and answering
at length the ambassadors of the Carthaginians and
Aegestaeans, in the end the Syracusans decided to
vote to maintain their alliance with the Selinuntians
and their state of peace with the Carthaginians.

44. After the return of their ambassadors the
Carthaginians dispatched to the Aegestaeans five
thousand Libyans and eight hundred Campanians.
These troops had been hired by the Chalcidians [1] to
aid the Athenians in the war against the Syracusans,
and on their return after its disastrous conclusion they
found no one to hire their services ; but the Carthaginians purchased horses for them all, gave them high
pay, and sent them to Aegesta.

The Selinuntians, who were prosperous in those
days and whose city was heavily populated, held the
Aegestaeans in contempt. And at first, deploying
in battle order, they laid waste the land which touched
their border, since their armies were far superior, but
after this, despising their foe, they scattered everywhere over the countryside. The generals of the
Aegestaeans, watching their opportunity, attacked
them with the aid of the Carthaginians [2] and Campanians. Since the attack was not expected, they
easily put the Selinuntians to flight, killing about a
thousand of the soldiers and capturing all their loot.

[1] Of Sicily.
[2] More accurately, the Libyan mercenaries mentioned in
the preceding paragraph.

δὲ λείας πάσης ἐκυρίευσαν. μετὰ δὲ τὴν μάχην
εὐθέως ἀπέστειλαν πρέσβεις, οἱ μὲν Σελινούντιοι
πρὸς Συρακοσίους, οἱ δ' Αἰγεσταῖοι πρὸς Καρ-
5 χηδονίους περὶ βοηθείας. ἑκατέρων δ' ἐπαγ-
γειλαμένων συμμαχήσειν, ὁ μὲν Καρχηδονιακὸς
πόλεμος ταύτην ἔλαβεν ἀρχήν· οἱ δὲ Καρχηδόνιοι
προορώμενοι τὸ μέγεθος τοῦ πολέμου, τὴν ἐπι-
τροπὴν ἔδωκαν Ἀννίβᾳ τῷ στρατηγῷ περὶ τοῦ
μεγέθους τῆς δυνάμεως, καὶ πάντα προθύμως ὑπ-
6 ηρέτουν. ὁ δὲ Ἀννίβας τό τε θέρος ἐκεῖνο καὶ τὸν
συνάπτοντα χειμῶνα πολλοὺς μὲν ἐξ Ἰβηρίας ἐξε-
νολόγησεν, οὐκ ὀλίγους δὲ καὶ τῶν πολιτῶν κατ-
έγραφεν· ἐπῄει δὲ καὶ τὴν Λιβύην ἐπιλεγόμενος ἐξ
ἁπάσης πόλεως τοὺς κρατίστους, καὶ ναῦς παρ-
εσκευάζετο, διανοούμενος τῆς ἐαρινῆς ὥρας ἐνιστα-
μένης διαβιβάζειν τὰς δυνάμεις.

Τὰ μὲν οὖν κατὰ τὴν Σικελίαν ἐν τούτοις ἦν.

45. Κατὰ δὲ τὴν Ἑλλάδα Δωριεὺς ὁ Ῥόδιος,
ναύαρχος ὢν τῶν ἐξ Ἰταλίας τριήρων, ἐπειδὴ κατέστησε τὴν ἐν Ῥόδῳ ταραχήν, ἐξέπλευσεν ἐφ'
Ἑλλήσποντον, σπεύδων συμμῖξαι τῷ Μινδάρῳ·
οὗτος γὰρ ἐν Ἀβύδῳ διατρίβων συνῆγε πανταχόθεν
2 τὰς συμμαχούσας ναῦς τοῖς Πελοποννησίοις. ἤδη
δὲ τοῦ Δωριέως ὄντος περὶ τὸ Σίγειον τῆς Τρῳάδος,
οἱ περὶ Σηστὸν ὄντες Ἀθηναῖοι πυθόμενοι τὸν παράπλουν ἀνήχθησαν ἐπ' αὐτοὺς πάσαις ταῖς ναυσίν,
3 οὔσαις ἑβδομήκοντα καὶ τέσσαρσιν. ὁ δὲ Δωριεὺς
μέχρι μέν τινος ἀγνοήσας τὸ γινόμενον ἔπλει
μετέωρος· κατανοήσας δὲ τὸ μέγεθος τοῦ στόλου
κατεπλάγη, καὶ σωτηρίαν ἄλλην οὐδεμίαν ὁρῶν
4 κατέφυγεν εἰς Δάρδανον. ἐκβιβάσας δὲ τοὺς στρατιώτας καὶ τοὺς φρουροῦντας τὴν πόλιν προσλαβό-

And after the battle both sides straightway dispatched ambassadors, the Selinuntians to the Syracusans and the Aegestaeans to the Carthaginians,
asking for help. Both parties promised their assistance and the Carthaginian War thus had its beginning.
The Carthaginians, foreseeing the magnitude of the
war, entrusted the responsibility for the size of their
armament to Hannibal as their general and enthusiastically rendered him every assistance. And Hannibal during the summer and the following winter
enlisted many mercenaries from Iberia and also
enrolled not a few from among the citizens ; he
also visited Libya, choosing the stoutest men from
every city, and he made ready ships, planning to
convey the armies across with the opening of spring.
Such, then, was the state of affairs in Sicily.

45. In Greece Dorieus the Rhodian, the admiral
of the triremes from Italy, after he had quelled the
tumult in Rhodes,[1] set sail for the Hellespont, being
eager to join Mindarus ; for the latter was lying
at Abydus and collecting from every quarter the
ships of the Peloponnesian alliance. And when Dorieus was already in the neighbourhood of Sigeium
in the Troad, the Athenians who were at Sestus,
learning that he was sailing along the coast, put out
against him with their ships, seventy-four in all.
Dorieus held to his course for a time in ignorance of
what was happening ; but when he observed the
great strength of the fleet he was alarmed, and seeing
no other way to save his force he put in at Dardanus.
Here he disembarked his soldiers and took over the

---

[1] Cp. chap. 38. 5 ; Thucydides, 8. 44.

μενος, βέλη τε παμπληθῆ ταχέως παρεκόμισε καὶ
τῶν στρατιωτῶν οὓς μὲν ἐπὶ τὰς πρῴρας ἐπέστησεν,
5 οὓς δ' ἐπὶ τῆς γῆς εὐκαίρως ἔταξεν. οἱ δ' Ἀθηναῖοι κατὰ πολλὴν σπουδὴν καταπλεύσαντες ἐνεχείρησαν ἀποσπᾶν τὰς ναῦς, καὶ πανταχόθεν τῷ
πλήθει περιχυθέντες κατεπόνουν τοὺς ἐναντίους.
6 ἃ δὴ πυθόμενος Μίνδαρος ὁ τῶν Πελοποννησίων
ναύαρχος, εὐθέως ἐξ Ἀβύδου μετὰ παντὸς ἀνήχθη
τοῦ στόλου, καὶ κατέπλει πρὸς τὸ Δαρδάνειον μετὰ
νεῶν τεσσάρων πρὸς ταῖς ὀγδοήκοντα, βοηθήσων
τοῖς μετὰ τοῦ Δωριέως· συμπαρῆν δὲ καὶ τὸ πεζὸν
στράτευμα τοῦ Φαρναβάζου βοηθοῦν τοῖς Λακεδαιμονίοις.
7 Ὡς δ' ἐγγὺς ἀλλήλων ἐγενήθησαν οἱ στόλοι,
διέταξαν ἀμφότεροι τὰς τριήρεις εἰς ναυμαχίαν·
καὶ Μίνδαρος μὲν ἔχων ἑπτὰ πρὸς ταῖς ἐνενήκοντα
ναυσὶν ἐπὶ μὲν τὸ λαιὸν κέρας ἔταξε Συρακοσίους,
τοῦ δεξιοῦ δ' αὐτὸς εἶχε τὴν ἡγεμονίαν· τῶν δ'
Ἀθηναίων τοῦ μὲν δεξιοῦ μέρους Θρασύβουλος
8 ἡγεῖτο, τοῦ δ' ἑτέρου Θράσυλλος. τοῦτον δὲ τὸν
τρόπον αὐτῶν ἐξηρτυμένων, οἱ μὲν ἡγεμόνες αὐτῶν
ἦραν τὸ σύσσημον τῆς μάχης, οἱ σαλπικταὶ δὲ ἀφ'
ἑνὸς παραγγέλματος ἤρξαντο σημαίνειν τὸ πο-
λεμικόν· καὶ τῶν μὲν ἐρετῶν οὐθὲν ἐλλειπόντων
προθυμίας, τῶν δὲ κυβερνητῶν ἐντέχνως τοῖς
οἴαξι χρωμένων, καταπληκτικὸν συνέβαινε γίνεσθαι
9 τὸν ἀγῶνα. ὁπότε γὰρ αἱ τριήρεις εἰς ἐμβολὴν
ἐπιφέροιντο,[1] τηνικαῦτα οἱ κυβερνῆται πρὸς αὐτὴν
τὴν τοῦ καιροῦ ῥοπὴν ἐπέστρεφον τὰς ναῦς πραγ-
ματικῶς ὥστε τὰς πληγὰς γίνεσθαι κατ' ἐμβολήν.
10 οἱ μὲν οὖν ἐπιβάται θεωροῦντες πλαγίας τὰς ἑαυτῶν ναῦς συνεπιφερομένας ταῖς τῶν πολεμίων

troops who were guarding the city, and then he 410 B.C. speedily got in a vast supply of missiles and stationed his soldiers both on the fore-parts of the ships and in advantageous positions on the land. The Athenians, sailing in at full speed, set to work hauling the ships away from the shore, and they were wearing down the enemy, having crowded them on every side by their superior numbers. When Mindarus, the Peloponnesian admiral, learned of the situation, he speedily put out from Abydus with his entire fleet and sailed to the Dardanian Promontory [1] with eighty-four ships to the aid of the fleet of Dorieus; and the land army of Pharnabazus was also there, supporting the Lacedaemonians.

When the fleets came near one another, both sides drew up the triremes for battle; Mindarus, who had ninety-seven ships, stationed the Syracusans on his left wing, while he himself took command of the right; as for the Athenians, Thrasybulus led the right wing and Thrasyllus the other. After the forces had made ready in this fashion, their commanders raised the signal for battle and the trumpeters at a single word of command began to sound the attack; and since the rowers showed no lack of eagerness and the pilots managed their helms with skill, the contest which ensued was an amazing spectacle. For whenever the triremes would drive forward to ram, at that moment the pilots, at just the critical instant, would turn their ships so effectively that the blows were made ram on. As for the marines, whenever they would see their own ships borne along with their sides to the triremes of the enemy, they would be

[1] Some ten miles inside the Hellespont on the Asian side.

---

[1] So Hertlein (cp. ch. 40. 1): ἐπεφέροντο.

τριήρεσι, περιδεεῖς ἐγίνοντο, περὶ σφῶν ἀγωνιῶντες·
ὁπότε δ' οἱ κυβερνῆται ταῖς ἐμπειρίαις ἐκκρούσειαν
τὰς ἐπιφοράς, πάλιν ἐγίνοντο περιχαρεῖς καὶ μετέωροι ταῖς ἐλπίσιν.

46. Οὐ μὴν οὐδ' οἱ[1] τοῖς καταστρώμασιν ἐπιβε-
βηκότες ἄπρακτον εἶχον τὴν φιλοτιμίαν, ἀλλ' οἱ μὲν
ἐκ πολλοῦ διαστήματος ἐφεστηκότες ἐτόξευον κατὰ
τὸ συνεχὲς καὶ ταχὺ ὁ τόπος ἦν βελῶν πλήρης·
οἱ δ' ἀεὶ προσιόντες ἐγγυτέρω τὰς λόγχας ἠκόντιζον, οἱ μὲν ἐπὶ τοὺς ἀμυνομένους ἐπιβάτας οἱ
δ' ἐπ' αὐτοὺς βαλεῖν φιλοτιμούμενοι τοὺς κυβερ-
νήτας· ὁπότε δὲ συνερείσειαν αἱ ναῦς, τοῖς τε
δόρασιν ἠγωνίζοντο καὶ κατὰ τὰς προσαγωγὰς εἰς
τὰς τῶν πολεμίων τριήρεις μεθαλλόμενοι τοῖς
2 ξίφεσιν ἀλλήλους ἠμύνοντο. κατὰ δὲ τὰς γινο-
μένας ἐλαττώσεις τῶν νικώντων ἐπαλαλαζόντων
καὶ τῶν ἄλλων μετὰ βοῆς παραβοηθούντων,
κραυγὴ σύμμικτος ἐγίνετο παρ' ὅλον τὸν τῆς ναυμαχίας τόπον.

Ἐπὶ πολὺν οὖν χρόνον ἰσόρροπος ἦν ἡ μάχη διὰ
τὴν ὑπερβολὴν τῆς παρ' ἀμφοτέροις φιλοτιμίας·
μετὰ δὲ ταῦτα Ἀλκιβιάδης ἐκ Σάμου παραδόξως
ἐπεφάνη μετὰ νεῶν εἴκοσι, πλέων κατὰ τύχην εἰς
3 Ἑλλήσποντον. τούτων δὲ πόρρω μὲν οὐσῶν,
ἑκάτεροι σφίσι βοήθειαν ἐλπίζοντες παραγενέσθαι,
μετέωροι ταῖς ἐλπίσιν ἐγίνοντο καὶ πολὺ προθυ-
μότερον ταῖς τόλμαις διεκινδύνευον· ἐπεὶ δ' ἤδη
σύνεγγυς ἦν ὁ στόλος καὶ τοῖς μὲν Λακεδαιμονίοις
οὐδὲν ἐφαίνετο σύσσημον, τοῖς δ' Ἀθηναίοις
Ἀλκιβιάδης μετέωρον ἐποίησεν ἐπίσημον φοινι-
κοῦν ἀπὸ τῆς ἰδίας νεώς, ὅπερ ἦν σύσσημον αὐτοῖς
διατεταγμένον, οἱ μὲν Λακεδαιμόνιοι καταπλα-

terror-stricken, despairing of their lives ; but when- 410 B.C.
ever the pilots, employing the skill of practice, would
frustrate the attack, they would in turn be overjoyed
and elated in their hopes.

46. Nor did the men whose position was on the
decks fail to maintain the zeal which brooked no
failure ; but some, while still at a considerable distance from the enemy, kept up a stream of arrows and
soon the space was full of missiles, while others, each
time that they drew near, would hurl their javelins,
some doing their best to strike the defending marines
and others the enemy pilots themselves ; and whenever the ships would come close together, they would
not only fight with their spears but at the moment of
contact would also leap over on the enemy's triremes
and carry on the contest with their swords. And
since at each reverse the victors would raise the war-
cry and the others would rush to aid with shouting,
a mingled din prevailed over the entire area of the
battle.

For a long time the battle was equally balanced
because of the very high rivalry with which both
sides were inspired ; but later on Alcibiades unexpectedly appeared from Samos with twenty ships,
sailing by mere chance to the Hellespont. While
these ships were still at a distance, each side, hoping
that reinforcement had come for themselves, was
elated in its hopes and fought on with far greater
courage ; but when the fleet was now near and for
the Lacedaemonians no signal was to be seen, but
for the Athenians Alcibiades ran up a purple flag
from his own ship, which was the signal they had
agreed upon, the Lacedaemonians in dismay turned

---

[1] ἐν after οἱ deleted by Vogel.

γέντες ἐτράπησαν, οἱ δ' Ἀθηναῖοι τῷ προτερήματι
μετεωρισθέντες μετὰ σπουδῆς ἐπεδίωκον τὰς ὑπο-
4 φευγούσας. καὶ δέκα μὲν νεῶν εὐθὺς ἐκυρίευσαν,
μετὰ δὲ ταῦτα χειμῶνος ἐπιγενομένου καὶ πνευμάτων μεγάλων πολλὰ περὶ τὸν διωγμὸν αὐτοὺς
ἐμποδίζεσθαι συνέβαινε· διὰ γὰρ τὸ μέγεθος τῶν
κυμάτων τὰ μὲν σκάφη τοῖς οἴαξιν ἠπείθει τὰς
δ' ἐμβολὰς ἀπράκτους συνέβαινε γίνεσθαι, τῶν
5 τυπτομένων νεῶν ὑποχωρουσῶν. τέλος δ' οἱ μὲν
Λακεδαιμόνιοι πρὸς τὴν γῆν κατενεχθέντες ἔφυγον
πρὸς τὸ πεζὸν τοῦ Φαρναβάζου στρατόπεδον, οἱ
δ' Ἀθηναῖοι τὸ μὲν πρῶτον ἐπεχείρησαν ἀποσπᾶν
τὰς ναῦς ἀπὸ τῆς γῆς καὶ παραβόλως διεκινδύνευον,
ὑπὸ δὲ τοῦ Περσικοῦ στρατεύματος ἀνακοπέντες
6 ἀπέπλευσαν εἰς Σηστόν. ὁ γὰρ Φαρνάβαζος βουλόμενος τοῖς Λακεδαιμονίοις ὑπὲρ ὧν ἐνεκάλουν
ἀπολογεῖσθαι, βιαιότερον διηγωνίζετο πρὸς τοὺς
Ἀθηναίους· ἅμα δὲ καὶ περὶ τῶν εἰς Φοινίκην
ἀποσταλεισῶν νεῶν τριακοσίων ἐδίδαξεν, ὡς τοῦτο
ἔπραξε πυνθανόμενος τόν τε τῶν Ἀράβων βασιλέα
καὶ τὸν τῶν[1] Αἰγυπτίων ἐπιβουλεύειν τοῖς περὶ
Φοινίκην πράγμασιν.

47. Τῆς δὲ ναυμαχίας τοιοῦτον τὸ τέλος λαβούσης Ἀθηναῖοι τότε μὲν εἰς Σηστὸν ἀπέπλευσαν
ἤδη νυκτὸς οὔσης, ἅμα δ' ἡμέρα τά τε ναυάγια
συνήγαγον καὶ πρὸς τῷ προτέρῳ τροπαίῳ πάλιν
2 ἕτερον ἔστησαν. Μίνδαρος δὲ νυκτὸς περὶ πρώτην
φυλακὴν εἰς Ἄβυδον ἀναχθεὶς τάς τε πεπονηκυίας
ναῦς ἐπεσκεύαζε[2] καὶ πρὸς Λακεδαιμονίους δι-
επέμψατο περὶ βοηθείας πεζῆς τε καὶ ναυτικῆς·

---

[1] τὸν τῶν Vogel : τῶν P, τὸν other MSS.
[2] So Hertlein : κατεσκεύαζε.

in flight and the Athenians, elated by the advantage 410 B.C.
they now possessed, pressed eagerly upon the ships
trying to escape. And they speedily captured ten
ships, but then a storm and violent winds arose, as
a result of which they were greatly hindered in the
pursuit; for because of the high waves the boats
would not respond to the tillers, and the attempts
at ramming proved fruitless, since the ships were re-
ceding when struck. In the end the Lacedaemonians,
gaining the shore, fled to the land army of Pharnabazus, and the Athenians at first essayed to drag the
ships from the shore and put up a desperate battle,
but when they were checked in their attempts by the
Persian forces they sailed off to Sestus. For Pharnabazus, wishing to build a defence for himself before
the Lacedaemonians against the charges they were
bringing against him, put up all the more vigorous
fight against the Athenians; while at the same time,
with respect to his sending the three hundred triremes to Phoenicia,[1] he explained to them that he
had done so on receiving information that the king
of the Arabians and the king of the Egyptians had
designs upon Phoenicia.

47. When the sea-battle had ended as we have
related, the Athenians sailed off at the time to Sestus,
since it was already night, but when day came they
collected their ships which had been damaged and
set up another trophy near the former one.[2] And
Mindarus about the first watch of the night set out
to Abydus, where he repaired his ships that had been
damaged and sent word to the Lacedaemonians for
reinforcements of both soldiers and ships; for he

[1] Cp. chap. 37. 4 f.
[2] Cp. chap. 40. 6.

διενοεῖτο γὰρ ἐν ὅσῳ τὰ κατὰ τὸν στόλον ἕτοιμα
ἐγίνετο, πεζῇ μετὰ Φαρναβάζου τὰς συμμαχούσας
κατὰ τὴν Ἀσίαν πόλεις Ἀθηναίοις πολιορκήσειν.

3 Χαλκιδεῖς δὲ καὶ σχεδὸν οἱ λοιποὶ πάντες οἱ τὴν
Εὔβοιαν κατοικοῦντες ἀφεστηκότες ἦσαν Ἀθηναίων,
καὶ διὰ τοῦτο περιδεεῖς ἐγίνοντο, μήποτε νῆσον
οἰκοῦντες ἐκπολιορκηθῶσιν ὑπ᾽ Ἀθηναίων θαλασ-
σοκρατούντων· ἠξίουν οὖν Βοιωτοὺς κοινῇ χῶσαι
τὸν Εὔριπον, ὥστε συνάψαι τὴν Εὔβοιαν τῇ

4 Βοιωτίᾳ. συγκαταθεμένων δὲ τῶν Βοιωτῶν διὰ
τὸ κἀκείνοις συμφέρειν τὴν Εὔβοιαν εἶναι τοῖς
μὲν ἄλλοις νῆσον, ἑαυτοῖς δ᾽ ἤπειρον· διόπερ αἱ
πόλεις ἅπασαι πρὸς τὴν διάχωσιν ἐπερρώσθησαν
καὶ πρὸς ἀλλήλας ἡμιλλῶντο· οὐ γὰρ μόνον τοῖς
πολίταις ἐξιέναι πανδημεὶ προσέταξαν, ἀλλὰ καὶ
τοῖς παροικοῦσι ξένοις, ὥστε διὰ τὸ πλῆθος τῶν
τοῖς ἔργοις προσιόντων τὴν πρόθεσιν ταχέως λαβεῖν

5 συντέλειαν. τῆς μὲν οὖν Εὐβοίας κατεσκευάσθη
τὸ χῶμα κατὰ τὴν Χαλκίδα, τῆς δὲ Βοιωτίας
πλησίον Αὐλίδος· ἐνταῦθα γὰρ ὁ μεταξὺ τόπος ἦν[1]
στενώτατος. συνέβαινε μὲν οὖν καὶ πρότερον ἀεὶ
κατ᾽ ἐκεῖνον τὸν τόπον εἶναι ῥοῦν καὶ πυκνὰς
ποιεῖσθαι τροπὰς τὴν θάλατταν, τότε δὲ πολὺ
μᾶλλον ἦν ἐπιτείνοντα τὰ κατὰ τὸν ῥοῦν, ὡς ἂν
εἰς στενὸν ἄγαν συγκεκλεισμένης τῆς θαλάττης·
ὁ γὰρ διέκπλους ἀπελείφθη μιᾷ νηί. ᾠκοδόμησαν

---

[1] τόπος ἦν] προσῆν AH, πόρος ἦν Wesseling.

had in mind, while the fleet was being made ready, 410 B.C. to lay siege with the army together with Pharna-bazus to the cities in Asia which were allied with the Athenians.

The people of Chalcis and almost all the rest of the inhabitants of Euboea had revolted from the Athenians[1] and were therefore highly apprehensive lest, living as they did on an island, they should be forced to surrender to the Athenians, who were masters of the sea ; and they therefore asked the Boeotians to join with them in building a causeway across the Euripus and thereby joining Euboea to Boeotia.[2] The Boeotians agreed to this, since it was to their special advantage that Euboea should be an island to everybody else but a part of the mainland to them-selves. Consequently all the cities threw themselves vigorously into the building of the causeway and vied with one another ; for orders were issued not only to the citizens to report *en masse* but to the foreigners dwelling among them as well, so that by reason of the great number that came forward to the work the proposed task was speedily completed. On Euboea the causeway was built at Chalcis, and in Boeotia in the neighbourhood of Aulis, since at that place the channel was narrowest. Now it so happened that in former times also there had always been a current in that place and that the sea frequently reversed its course, and at the time in question the force of the current was far greater because the sea had been confined into a very narrow channel ; for passage was left for only a single ship. High towers were also

[1] Soon after the Athenian disaster at Syracuse (Thucy-dides, 8. 95).

[2] Strabo (9. 2. 2) quotes Ephorus to the effect that a bridge only two plethra (202 ft.) long spanned the Euripus at Chalcis.

δὲ καὶ πύργους ὑψηλοὺς ἐπ' ἀμφοτέρων τῶν ἄκρων,
καὶ ξυλίνας τοῖς διάρροις ἐπέστησαν γεφύρας.

6 Θηραμένης δ' ὑπ' Ἀθηναίων ἀποσταλεὶς μετὰ
νεῶν τριάκοντα τὸ μὲν πρῶτον ἐπεχείρησε κωλύειν
τοὺς ἐπὶ τῶν ἔργων, πολλοῦ δὲ πλήθους στρατιωτῶν συμπαρόντος τοῖς κατασκευάζουσι τὰ χώ-
ματα ταύτης μὲν τῆς ἐπιβολῆς ἀπέστη, τὸν δὲ
7 πλοῦν ἐπὶ τῶν¹ νήσων ἐποιήσατο. βουλόμενος
δὲ τούς τε πολίτας καὶ συμμάχους ἀναπαῦσαι τῶν
εἰσφορῶν, τήν τε τῶν πολεμίων χώραν ἐπόρθησε
καὶ πολλὰς ὠφελείας ἤθροισεν. ἐπῄει δὲ καὶ τὰς
συμμαχίδας πόλεις καὶ τοὺς ἐν αὐταῖς νεωτερί-
8 ζοντας εἰσεπράττετο χρήματα. καταπλεύσας δ'
εἰς Πάρον καὶ καταλαβὼν ὀλιγαρχίαν ἐν τῇ πόλει,
τῷ μὲν δήμῳ τὴν ἐλευθερίαν ἀποκατέστησε, παρὰ
δὲ τῶν ἁψαμένων τῆς ὀλιγαρχίας χρημάτων πλῆθος εἰσεπράξατο.

48. Συνέβη δὲ περὶ τοῦτον τὸν χρόνον ἐν τῇ
Κορκύρᾳ γενέσθαι μεγάλην στάσιν καὶ σφαγήν, ἣν
δι' ἑτέρας μὲν αἰτίας λέγεται γενέσθαι, μάλιστα δὲ
διὰ τὴν ὑπάρχουσαν αὐτοῖς πρὸς ἀλλήλους ἔχθραν.
2 ἐν οὐδεμιᾷ γάρ ποτε² πόλει τοιοῦτοι πολιτῶν φόνοι
συνετελέσθησαν οὐδὲ μείζων ἔρις καὶ φιλονεικία
πρὸς ὄλεθρον ἀνήκουσα. δοκοῦσι γὰρ οἱ μὲν ἀναι-
ρεθέντες ὑπ' ἀλλήλων πρὸ ταύτης τῆς στάσεως
γεγονέναι περὶ χιλίους καὶ πεντακοσίους, καὶ
3 πάντες οὗτοι πρωτεύοντες τῶν πολιτῶν. τούτων
δ' ἐπιγεγενημένων τῶν ἀτυχημάτων ἑτέραν αὐτοῖς
συμφορὰν ἐπέστησεν ἡ τύχη, τὴν πρὸς ἀλλήλους

¹ τῶν] omitted by Dindorf, Vogel.
² So Wesseling: τότε.

built on both ends and wooden bridges were thrown 410 B.C.
over the channel.

Theramenes, who had been dispatched by the
Athenians with thirty ships, at first attempted to stop
the workers, but since a strong body of soldiers was at
the side of the builders of the causeway, he abandoned
this design and directed his voyage toward the islands.[1]
And since he wished to relieve both the citizens and
the allies from their contributions,[2] he laid waste the
territory of the enemy and collected great quantities
of booty. He visited also the allied cities and exacted
money of such inhabitants as were advocating a
change in government. And when he put in at Paros
and found an oligarchy in the city, he restored their
freedom to the people and exacted a great sum of
money of the men who had participated in the
oligarchy.

48. It happened at this time that a serious civil strife
occurred in Corcyra accompanied by massacre, which
is said to have been due to various causes but most of
all to the mutual hatred that existed between its own
inhabitants. For never in any state have there taken
place such murderings of citizens nor have there been
greater quarrelling and contentiousness which cul-
minated in bloodshed.[3] For it would seem that the
number of those who were slain by their fellow
citizens before the present civil strife was some fifteen
hundred, and all of these were leading citizens. And
although these misfortunes had already befallen them,
Fortune brought upon them a second disaster, in that
she increased once more the disaffection which pre-

[1] *i.e.* of the Athenian Confederacy.

[2] Toward the cost of the war with the Lacedaemonians.

[3] Thucydides (3. 70 ff.) describes the earlier civil strife on
the island.

πάλιν αὐξήσασα διαφοράν. οἱ μὲν γὰρ προέχοντες
τοῖς ἀξιώμασι τῶν Κορκυραίων ὀρεγόμενοι τῆς
ὀλιγαρχίας ἐφρόνουν τὰ Λακεδαιμονίων, ὁ δὲ δημοτικὸς ὄχλος ἔσπευδε τοῖς Ἀθηναίοις συμμα-
4 χεῖν. καὶ γὰρ διαφερούσας τὰς σπουδὰς εἶχον οἱ
περὶ τῆς ἡγεμονίας διαγωνιζόμενοι δῆμοι· Λακεδαιμόνιοι γὰρ τοὺς πρωτεύοντας ἐν ταῖς συμμαχίσι
πόλεσιν ἐποίουν ἐπὶ τῆς διοικήσεως τῶν κοινῶν,
Ἀθηναῖοι δὲ δημοκρατίας ἐν ταῖς πόλεσι καθίστα-
5 νον. οἱ δ' οὖν Κορκυραῖοι θεωροῦντες τοὺς δυνατωτάτους τῶν πολιτῶν ὄντας πρὸς τῷ τὴν πόλιν
ἐγχειρίζειν Λακεδαιμονίοις, μετεπέμψαντο παρ'
Ἀθηναίων δύναμιν τὴν παραφυλάξουσαν τὴν πόλιν.
6 Κόνων δ' ὁ στρατηγὸς τῶν Ἀθηναίων πλεύσας εἰς
Κόρκυραν, ἑξακοσίους μὲν τῶν ἐκ Ναυπάκτου
Μεσσηνίων κατέλιπεν ἐν τῇ πόλει, αὐτὸς δὲ μετὰ
τῶν νεῶν παρέπλευσε καὶ καθωρμίσθη πρὸς τῷ
7 τῆς Ἥρας τεμένει. οἱ δὲ ἑξακόσιοι μετὰ τῶν
δημοτικῶν ὁρμήσαντες ἐπὶ τοὺς τὰ Λακεδαιμονίων
φρονοῦντας ἐξαίφνης ἀγορᾶς πληθούσης οὓς μὲν
συνελάμβανον, οὓς δ' ἐφόνευον, πλείους δὲ τῶν
χιλίων ἐφυγάδευσαν· ἐποιήσαντο δὲ τοὺς μὲν δού-
λους ἐλευθέρους, τοὺς δὲ ξένους πολίτας, εὐλαβούμενοι τό τε πλῆθος καὶ τὴν δύναμιν τῶν φυγάδων.
8 οἱ μὲν οὖν ἐκπεσόντες ἐκ τῆς πατρίδος εἰς τὴν
καταντίον ἤπειρον ἔφυγον· μετὰ δέ τινας ἡμέρας
τῶν ἐν τῇ πόλει τινὲς φρονοῦντες τὰ τῶν φυγάδων
κατελάβοντο τὴν ἀγορὰν καὶ μεταπεμψάμενοι τοὺς

vailed among them.   For the foremost Corcyraeans, 410 B.C.
who desired the oligarchy, favoured the cause of the
Lacedaemonians, whereas the masses which favoured
the democracy were eager to ally themselves with
the Athenians.   For the peoples who were struggling for leadership in Greece were devoted to
opposing principles ; the Lacedaemonians, for example, made it their policy to put the control of the
government in the hands of the leading citizens of
their allied states, whereas the Athenians regularly
established democracies in their cities.   Accordingly
the Corcyraeans, seeing that their most influential
citizens were planning to hand the city over to the
Lacedaemonians, sent to the Athenians for an army
to protect their city.   And Conon, the general of the
Athenians, sailed to Corcyra and left in the city six
hundred men from the Messenians in Naupactus,[1]
while he himself sailed on with his ships and cast
anchor off the sacred precinct of Hera.   And the six
hundred, setting out unexpectedly with the partisans
of the people's party at the time of full market [2]
against the supporters of the Lacedaemonians,
arrested some of them, slew others, and drove more
than a thousand from the state ; they also set the
slaves free and gave citizenship to the foreigners living
among them as a precaution against the great number
and influence of the exiles.   Now the men who had
been exiled from their country fled to the opposite
mainland ; but a few days later some people still in
the city who favoured the cause of the exiles seized
the market-place, called back the exiles, and essayed

[1] These Messenians had been allowed by the Spartans to
leave their country and had been settled in Naupactus by the
Athenian general Tolmides in 456 B.C. (cp. Book 11. 84).

[2] In the middle of the morning.

φυγάδας περὶ τῶν ὅλων διηγωνίζοντο. τέλος δὲ νυκτὸς καταλαβούσης εἰς ὁμολογίας ἦλθον πρὸς ἀλλήλους, καὶ τῆς φιλονεικίας παυσάμενοι κοινῶς ᾤκουν τὴν πατρίδα.

Ἡ μὲν οὖν ἐν Κορκύρᾳ σφαγὴ[1] τοιοῦτον ἔσχε τὸ τέλος.

49. Ἀρχέλαος δ' ὁ τῶν Μακεδόνων βασιλεύς, τῶν Πυδναίων ἀπειθούντων, πολλῇ δυνάμει τὴν πόλιν περιεστρατοπέδευσεν. παρεβοήθησε δ' αὐτῷ καὶ Θηραμένης ἔχων στόλον· ὃς χρονιζούσης τῆς πολιορκίας ἀπέπλευσεν εἰς Θρᾴκην πρὸς Θρασύ-
2 βουλον τὸν ἀφηγούμενον τοῦ στόλου παντός. ὁ μὲν οὖν Ἀρχέλαος φιλοτιμότερον πολιορκήσας τὴν Πύδναν καὶ κρατήσας μετῴκισεν αὐτὴν ἀπὸ θαλάττης ὡς εἴκοσι στάδια.

Ὁ δὲ Μίνδαρος, ἤδη τοῦ χειμῶνος λήγοντος, συνήγαγε τὰς πανταχόθεν τριήρεις· ἔκ τε γὰρ τῆς Πελοποννήσου πολλαὶ παρεγενήθησαν καὶ παρὰ τῶν ἄλλων συμμάχων ὁμοίως. οἱ δ' ἐν Σηστῷ τῶν Ἀθηναίων στρατηγοί, πυνθανόμενοι τὸ μέγεθος τοῦ συναγομένου τοῖς πολεμίοις στόλου, περιδεεῖς ἦσαν μήποτε πάσαις ταῖς τριήρεσιν ἐπιπλεύσαντες οἱ πολέμιοι κυριεύσωσι τῶν νεῶν.
3 ὅθεν αὐτοὶ μὲν καθελκύσαντες τὰς οὔσας ἐν Σηστῷ ναῦς περιέπλευσαν τὴν Χερρόνησον καὶ καθωρμίσθησαν εἰς Καρδίαν· εἰς δὲ Θρᾴκην πρὸς Θρασύβουλον καὶ Θηραμένην ἔπεμψαν τριήρεις, παρακαλοῦντες μετὰ τοῦ στόλου τὴν ταχίστην ἥκειν· μετεπέμψαντο δὲ καὶ τὸν Ἀλκιβιάδην ἐκ Λέσβου μεθ' ὧν εἶχε νεῶν, καὶ συνήχθη πᾶς ὁ στόλος

----
[1] So Krüger: φυγή.

a final decision of the struggle. When night brought 410 B.C. an end to the fighting they came to an agreement with each other, stopped their quarrelling, and resumed living together as one people in their fatherland.

Such, then, was the end of the massacre in Corcyra.

49. Archelaüs, the king of the Macedonians,[1] since the people of Pydna would not obey his orders, laid siege to the city with a great army. He received reinforcement also from Theramenes, who brought a fleet; but he, as the siege dragged on, sailed to Thrace, where he joined Thrasybulus who was commander of the entire fleet. Archelaüs now pressed the siege of Pydna more vigorously, and after reducing it he removed the city some twenty stades distant from the sea.

Mindarus, when the winter had come to an end, collected his triremes from all quarters, for many had come to him from the Peloponnesus as well as from the other allies. But the Athenian generals in Sestus, when they learned of the great size of the fleet that was being assembled by the enemy, were greatly alarmed lest the enemy, attacking with all their triremes, should capture their ships. Consequently the generals on their side hauled down the ships they had at Sestus, sailed around the Chersonesus, and moored them at Cardia[2]; and they sent triremes to Thrasybulus and Theramenes in Thrace, urging them to come with their fleet as soon as possible, and they summoned Alcibiades also from Lesbos with what ships he had. And the whole fleet was gathered into

[1] 413–399 B.C. He was a great admirer of Greek culture and Euripides was but one of many distinguished Greeks whom he invited to his kingdom.

[2] On the north side of the Chersonesus on the Gulf of Melas.

εἰς ἕνα τόπον, σπευδόντων τῶν στρατηγῶν περὶ
4 τῶν ὅλων διακινδυνεῦσαι. Μίνδαρος δ᾽ ὁ τῶν Λακεδαιμονίων ναύαρχος πλεύσας εἰς Κύζικον πᾶσαν
τὴν δύναμιν ἐξεβίβασε καὶ τὴν πόλιν περιεστρατοπέδευσεν. παρεγενήθη δὲ καὶ Φαρνάβαζος μετὰ
πολλῆς στρατιᾶς, μεθ᾽ οὗ πολιορκήσας Μίνδαρος
εἷλε τὴν Κύζικον κατὰ κράτος.
5 Οἱ δὲ[1] τῶν Ἀθηναίων στρατηγοὶ κρίναντες ἐπὶ
Κύζικον πλεῖν, ἀνήχθησαν μετὰ πασῶν τῶν νεῶν
καὶ τὴν Χερρόνησον περιέπλεον. καὶ πρῶτον μὲν
εἰς Ἐλεοῦντα παρεγένοντο· μετὰ δὲ ταῦτα ἐφιλο-
τιμήθησαν νυκτὸς τὴν τῶν Ἀβυδηνῶν πόλιν παρα-
πλεῦσαι πρὸς τὸ μὴ κατανοηθῆναι τὸ πλῆθος τῶν
6 νεῶν ὑπὸ τῶν πολεμίων. ἐπεὶ δ᾽ ἦλθον εἰς Προι-
κόννησον, τὴν μὲν νύκτα κατηυλίσθησαν ἐν ταύτῃ,
τῇ δ᾽ ὑστεραίᾳ τοὺς μὲν ἐπιβεβηκότας στρατιώτας
διεβίβασαν εἰς τὴν τῶν Κυζικηνῶν χώραν, καὶ τῷ
στρατηγοῦντι τούτων Χαιρέᾳ προσέταξαν ἄγειν τὸ
στρατόπεδον ἐπὶ τὴν πόλιν.
50. Αὐτοὶ δ᾽ εἰς τρία μέρη διείλαντο τὸ ναυτικόν,
καὶ τοῦ μὲν ἦρχεν Ἀλκιβιάδης, τοῦ δὲ Θηραμένης,
τοῦ δὲ τρίτου Θρασύβουλος. Ἀλκιβιάδης μὲν οὖν
μετὰ τοῦ καθ᾽ αὑτὸν μέρους πολὺ προέπλευσε τῶν
ἄλλων, βουλόμενος προκαλέσασθαι τοὺς Λακεδαιμονίους εἰς ναυμαχίαν· Θηραμένης δὲ καὶ
Θρασύβουλος ἐφιλοτέχνουν εἰς τὸ κυκλώσασθαι
καὶ τῆς εἰς τὴν πόλιν ἐπανόδου τοὺς ἐκπλεύσαντας
2 εἶρξαι. Μίνδαρος δὲ τὰς μὲν Ἀλκιβιάδου ναῦς
εἴκοσι[2] μόνας ὁρῶν προσφερομένας, τὰς δ᾽ ἄλλας
ἀγνοῶν, κατεφρόνησε, καὶ ναυσὶν ὀγδοήκοντα
θρασέως ἐκ τῆς πόλεως τὸν ἐπίπλουν ἐποιήσατο.

[1] μετὰ after δὲ deleted by Dindorf.

one place, the generals being eager for a decisive 410 B.C.
battle.   Mindarus, the Lacedaemonian admiral, sailing to Cyzicus, disembarked his whole force and invested the city.   Pharnabazus was also there with a
large army and with his aid Mindarus laid siege to
Cyzicus and took it by storm.

The Athenian generals, having decided to sail to
Cyzicus, put out to sea with all their ships and sailed
around the Chersonesus.   They arrived first at Eleüs ;
and after that they made a special point of sailing past
the city of Abydus at night, in order that the great
number of their vessels might not be known to the
enemy.   And when they had arrived at Proconnesus,[1]
they spent the night there and the next day they disembarked the soldiers who had shipped with them
on the territory of the Cyzicenes and gave orders to
Chaereas, their commander, to lead the army against
the city.

50. As for the generals themselves, they divided
the naval force into three squadrons, Alcibiades commanding one, Theramenes another, and Thrasybulus
the third.   Now Alcibiades with his own squadron
advanced far ahead of the others, wishing to draw the
Lacedaemonians out to a battle, whereas Theramenes
and Thrasybulus planned the manœuvre of encircling
the enemy and, if they sailed out, of blocking their
retreat to the city.   Mindarus, seeing only the ships
of Alcibiades approaching, twenty in number, and
having no knowledge of the others, held them in contempt and boldly set sail from the city with eighty

---

[1] The island of Marmora.

---

[2] εἴκοσι (κ′) Vogel (cp. Xen. *Hell.* 1. 1. 18) ; καὶ MSS.
except AHLM which omit.

ὡς δὲ πλησίον ἐγένετο τῶν περὶ τὸν Ἀλκιβιάδην,
οἱ μὲν Ἀθηναῖοι, καθάπερ ἦν αὐτοῖς παρηγγελμένον, προσεποιοῦντο φεύγειν, οἱ δὲ Πελοποννήσιοι
περιχαρεῖς ὄντες ἠκολούθουν κατὰ σπουδὴν ὡς
3 νικῶντες. ὁ δὲ Ἀλκιβιάδης ἐπειδὴ τῆς πόλεως
αὐτοὺς ἀπέσπασε πορρωτέρω, τὸ σύσσημον ἦρεν·
οὗ γενηθέντος αἱ μετ' Ἀλκιβιάδου τριήρεις ἐξαίφνης πρὸς ἕνα καιρὸν ἐπέστρεψαν ἀντίπρωροι τοῖς
πολεμίοις, Θηραμένης δὲ καὶ Θρασύβουλος ἔπλεον
ἐπὶ τὴν πόλιν καὶ τὸν ἀπόπλουν[1] τῶν Λακεδαι-
4 μονίων ὑπετέμοντο. οἱ δὲ μετὰ τοῦ Μινδάρου
καθορῶντες ἤδη τὸ πλῆθος τῶν πολεμίων νεῶν
καὶ μαθόντες ἑαυτοὺς κατεστρατηγημένους, περί-
φοβοι καθειστήκεισαν. τέλος δὲ τῶν Ἀθηναίων
πανταχόθεν ἐπιφαινομένων καὶ τῆς εἰς τὴν πόλιν
ἐφόδου τοὺς Πελοποννησίους ἀποκλεισάντων, ὁ
Μίνδαρος ἠναγκάσθη καταφυγεῖν τῆς χώρας πρὸς
τοὺς καλουμένους Κλήρους, ὅπου καὶ Φαρνάβαζος
5 εἶχε τὴν δύναμιν. Ἀλκιβιάδης δὲ κατὰ σπουδὴν
διώκων ἃς μὲν κατέδυεν, ἃς δὲ κατατιτρώσκων
ὑποχειρίους ἐλάμβανε, τὰς δὲ πλείστας πρὸς αὐτῇ
τῇ γῇ καθωρμισμένας καταλαβὼν ἐπέβαλλε σιδηρᾶς
χεῖρας, καὶ ταύταις[2] ἀποσπᾶν ἀπὸ τῆς γῆς ἐπει-
6 ρᾶτο. παραβοηθούντων δὲ τῶν πεζῶν ἀπὸ τῆς
γῆς τοῖς Πελοποννησίοις πολὺς ἐγένετο φόνος, ὡς
ἂν τῶν μὲν Ἀθηναίων διὰ τὸ προτέρημα θρα-
σύτερον ἢ συμφορώτερον ἀγωνιζομένων, τῶν δὲ
Πελοποννησίων πολὺ τοῖς πλήθεσιν ὑπεραγόντων·
καὶ γὰρ τὸ τοῦ Φαρναβάζου στρατόπεδον παρεβοήθει τοῖς Λακεδαιμονίοις, καὶ τὴν μάχην ἐκ τῆς

---

[1] So Wesseling : ἐπίπλουν.
[2] So Dindorf: ταύτας.

ships to attack him. Then, when he had come near 410 B.C.
the ships of Alcibiades, the Athenians, as they had
been commanded, pretended to flee, and the Peloponnesians, in high spirits, pursued after them
vigorously in the belief they were winning the victory.
But after Alcibiades had drawn them a considerable
distance from the city, he raised the signal ; and when
this was given, the ships of Alcibiades suddenly at
the same time turned about to face the enemy, and
Theramenes and Thrasybulus sailed toward the city
and cut off the retreat of the Lacedaemonians. The
troops of Mindarus, when they now observed the
multitude of the enemy ships and realized that they
had been outgeneralled, were filled with great fear.
And finally, since the Athenians were appearing from
every direction and had shut off the Peloponnesians
from their line of approach to the city, Mindarus was
forced to seek safety on land near Cleri, as it is called,
where also Pharnabazus had his army. Alcibiades,
pursuing him vigorously, sank some ships, damaged
and captured others, and the largest number, which
were moored on the land itself, he seized and threw
grappling-irons on, endeavouring by this means to
drag them from the land. And when the infantry of
Pharnabazus rushed to the aid of the Lacedaemonians, there was great bloodshed, inasmuch as the
Athenians because of the advantage they had won
were fighting with greater boldness than expediency,
while the Peloponnesians were in number far superior ;
for the army of Pharnabazus was supporting the Lacedaemonians and fighting as it was from the land the

---

[3] ὑπεραγόντων PA, ὑπερεχόντων cet.

γῆς ποιούμενον τὴν στάσιν εἶχεν ἀσφαλεστέραν.
7 Θρασύβουλος δὲ θεωρῶν τοὺς πεζοὺς τοῖς πολεμίοις βοηθοῦντας, καὶ τοὺς λοιποὺς τῶν ἐπιβατῶν
ἀπεβίβασεν εἰς τὴν γῆν, σπεύδων βοηθῆσαι τοῖς
περὶ τὸν Ἀλκιβιάδην· τῷ δὲ Θηραμένει παρεκε-
λεύσατο τοῖς περὶ Χαιρέαν[1] πεζοῖς συνάψαντα τὴν
ταχίστην ἥκειν, ὅπως πεζῇ διαγωνίσωνται.

51. Τῶν δὲ Ἀθηναίων περὶ ταῦτα γινομένων
Μίνδαρος ὁ τῶν Λακεδαιμονίων ἀφηγούμενος αὐτὸς
μὲν πρὸς Ἀλκιβιάδην ὑπὲρ τῶν ἀφελκομένων νεῶν[2]
διηγωνίζετο, Κλέαρχον δὲ τὸν Σπαρτιάτην μετὰ
μέρους τῶν Πελοποννησίων ἀπέστειλε πρὸς τοὺς
περὶ Θρασύβουλον· συναπέστειλε δ' αὐτῷ καὶ τοὺς
2 παρὰ Φαρναβάζῳ στρατευομένους μισθοφόρους. ὁ
δὲ Θρασύβουλος μετὰ τῶν ἐπιβατῶν καὶ τῶν τοξο-
τῶν τὸ μὲν πρῶτον εὐρώστως ὑπέστη τοὺς πολεμίους καὶ πολλοὺς μὲν ἀνεῖλεν, οὐκ ὀλίγους δὲ
καὶ τῶν ἰδίων ἑώρα πίπτοντας· τῶν δὲ μετὰ τοῦ
Φαρναβάζου μισθοφόρων κυκλούντων τοὺς Ἀθηναίους καὶ τῷ πλήθει πανταχόθεν περιχεομένων,[3]
ἐπεφάνη Θηραμένης τούς τε ἰδίους καὶ τοὺς μετὰ
3 Χαιρέου ἄγων πεζούς. οἱ δὲ μετὰ τοῦ Θρασυβούλου καταπεπονημένοι καὶ τὰς τῆς σωτηρίας ἐλπίδας
ἀπεγνωκότες πάλιν ἐξαίφνης ταῖς ψυχαῖς διηγεί-
4 ροντο τηλικαύτης βοηθείας παραγεγενημένης. ἐπὶ
πολὺν δὲ χρόνον καρτερᾶς μάχης γενομένης, τὸ
μὲν πρῶτον οἱ τοῦ Φαρναβάζου μισθοφόροι φεύγειν
ἤρξαντο καὶ τὸ συνεχὲς ἀεὶ τῆς τάξεως παρερρή-
γνυτο· τέλος δὲ οἱ Πελοποννήσιοι μετὰ Κλεάρχου
καταλειφθέντες καὶ πολλὰ δράσαντες καὶ παθόντες
ἐξεώσθησαν.
5 Τούτων δὲ καταπεπονημένων οἱ περὶ τὸν Θηρα-

position it had was more secure. But when Thrasy- 410 B.C.
bulus saw the infantry aiding the enemy, he put the
rest of his marines on the land with intent to assist
Alcibiades and his men, and he also urged Theramenes
to join up with the land troops of Chaereas and come
with all speed, in order to wage a battle on land.

51. While the Athenians were busying themselves
with these matters, Mindarus, the Lacedaemonian
commander, was himself fighting with Alcibiades for
the ships that were being dragged off, and he dispatched Clearchus the Spartan with a part of the
Peloponnesians against the troops with Thrasybulus ;
and with him he also sent the mercenaries in the
army of Pharnabazus. Thrasybulus with the marines
and archers at first stoutly withstood the enemy, and
though he slew many of them, he also saw not a few of
his own men falling ; but when the mercenaries of Pharnabazus were surrounding the Athenians and were
crowding about them in great numbers from every
direction, Theramenes appeared, leading both his
own troops and the infantry with Chaereas. Although
the troops of Thrasybulus were exhausted and had
given up hope of rescue, their spirits were suddenly
revived again when reinforcements so strong were at
hand. An obstinate battle which lasted a long time
ensued ; but at first the mercenaries of Pharnabazus
began to withdraw and the continuity of their battle
line was broken ; and finally the Peloponnesians who
had been left behind with Clearchus, after having
both inflicted and suffered much punishment, were
expelled.

Now that the Peloponnesians had been defeated,

---

[1] So Krüger : Χάρητα. [2] νεῶν added by Rhodoman.
[3] So Wesseling, περιερχομένων PAFJL.

μένην ὥρμησαν τοῖς μετ' Ἀλκιβιάδου κινδυνεύσασι
βοηθῆσαι. συνδραμουσῶν δὲ τῶν δυνάμεων εἰς
ἕνα τόπον, ὁ μὲν[1] Μίνδαρος οὐ κατεπλάγη τὴν
ἔφοδον τῶν περὶ Θηραμένην, ἀλλὰ διελόμενος
τοὺς Πελοποννησίους τοῖς μὲν ἡμίσεσιν ἀπήντα
τοῖς ἐπιοῦσι, τοὺς δ' ἡμίσεις αὐτὸς ἔχων, καὶ δεό-
μενος ἑκάστου μὴ καταισχῦναι τὸ τῆς Σπάρτης
ἀξίωμα, καὶ ταῦτα πεζομαχοῦντας, ἀντετάχθησαν[2]
6 τοῖς περὶ τὸν Ἀλκιβιάδην. περὶ δὲ τῶν νεῶν
ἡρωικὴν συστησάμενος μάχην, καὶ πρὸ πάντων
αὐτὸς κινδυνεύων, πολλοὺς μὲν ἀνεῖλε τῶν ἀντιτεταγμένων, τὸ δὲ τελευταῖον ἀξίως τῆς πατρίδος
ἀγωνισάμενος ὑπὸ τῶν περὶ τὸν Ἀλκιβιάδην ἀνῃρέθη. τούτου δὲ πεπτωκότος οἵ τε Πελοποννήσιοι
καὶ πάντες οἱ σύμμαχοι συνέδραμον καὶ καταπλα-
7 γέντες εἰς φυγὴν ὥρμησαν. οἱ δ' Ἀθηναῖοι μέχρι
μέν τινος ἐπεδίωξαν τοὺς πολεμίους, πυνθανόμενοι
δὲ τὸν Φαρνάβαζον μετὰ πολλῆς ἵππου κατὰ
σπουδὴν ἐπειγόμενον,[3] ἀνέκαμψαν ἐπὶ τὰς ναῦς,
καὶ τὴν μὲν πόλιν παρέλαβον, δύο δὲ τρόπαια
κατέστησαν ἀφ' ἑκατέρας νίκης, τὸ μὲν τῆς ναυμαχίας ἐν τῇ νήσῳ τῇ Πολυδώρου καλουμένῃ, τὸ
δὲ τῆς πεζομαχίας οὗ τὴν τροπὴν ἐποιήσαντο τὴν
8 πρώτην. οἱ μὲν οὖν ἐν τῇ πόλει Πελοποννήσιοι
καὶ πάντες οἱ διαφυγόντες ἐκ τῆς μάχης ἔφυγον
ἐπὶ τὸ[4] τοῦ Φαρναβάζου στρατόπεδον· οἱ δὲ τῶν
Ἀθηναίων στρατηγοὶ τῶν τε νεῶν ἁπασῶν ἐγκρατεῖς ἐγενήθησαν καὶ πολλοὺς μὲν αἰχμαλώτους,

---

[1] ὁ μὲν] ὅμως or ὁ Vogel.
[2] ἔχων . . . ἀντετάχθησαν is ungrammatical. ἀντετάχθη
Reiske.   [3] So Vogel: ἐπιγινόμενον.

the troops of Theramenes rushed to give aid to the 410 B.C.
soldiers who had been fighting under Alcibiades.
Although the forces had rapidly assembled at one
point, Mindarus was not dismayed at the attack of
Theramenes, but, after dividing the Peloponnesians,
with half of them he met the advancing enemy, while
with the other half which he himself commanded, first
calling upon each soldier not to disgrace the fair name
of Sparta, and that too in a fight on land, he formed
a line against the troops of Alcibiades. He put up
a heroic battle about the ships, fighting in person
before all his troops, but though he slew many of the
opponents, in the end he was killed by the troops of
Alcibiades as he battled nobly for his fatherland.
When he had fallen, both the Peloponnesians and all
the allies banded together and broke into terror-
stricken flight. The Athenians pursued the enemy
for a distance, but when they learned that Pharnabazus was hurrying up at full speed with a strong force
of cavalry, they returned to the ships, and after they
had taken the city [1] they set up two trophies for the
two victories, one for the sea-battle at the island of
Polydorus, as it is called, and one for the land-battle
where they forced the first flight of the enemy. Now
the Peloponnesians in the city and all the fugitives
from the battle fled to the camp of Pharnabazus ; and
the Athenian generals not only captured all the ships
but they also took many prisoners and an immeasur-

---

[1] Cyzicus.

---

[4] So Rhodoman : ὑπὸ PAK, ὑπὸ τὸ *cet.*

ἀναρίθμητον δὲ πλῆθος λαφύρων ἤθροισαν, ὡς ἂν
δύο δυνάμεις ἅμα τηλικαύτας νενικηκότες.

52. Ἀπενεχθείσης δὲ τῆς νίκης εἰς Ἀθήνας, ὁ
μὲν δῆμος ἐκ τῶν προτέρων συμφορῶν ἀνελπίστους
εὐτυχίας ὁρῶν τῇ πόλει προσγεγενημένας μετέωρος
ἦν ἐπὶ τοῖς εὐημερήμασι καὶ τοῖς μὲν θεοῖς πανδημεὶ θυσίας καὶ πανηγύρεις ἐποιήσατο, εἰς δὲ τὸν
πόλεμον ἐπέλεξε χιλίους τῶν ὁπλιτῶν[1] τοὺς κρατίστους, ἱππεῖς δ' ἑκατόν, πρὸς δὲ τούτοις τριάκοντα
τριήρεις ἀπέστειλε τοῖς περὶ τὸν Ἀλκιβιάδην,
ὅπως τὰς περὶ Λακεδαιμονίους πόλεις ἀδεῶς
2 πορθῶσι κρατοῦντες τῆς θαλάττης. οἱ δὲ Λακεδαιμόνιοι ὡς ἤκουσαν τὴν περὶ Κύζικον αὐτοῖς
γενομένην συμφοράν, πρέσβεις ἐξέπεμψαν εἰς Ἀθήνας ὑπὲρ εἰρήνης, ὧν ἦν ἀρχιπρεσβευτὴς Ἔνδιος.
ἐξουσίας δ' αὐτῷ δοθείσης παρελθὼν συντόμως
καὶ λακωνικῶς διελέχθη· διόπερ ἔκρινα μὴ παρα-
λιπεῖν τοὺς ῥηθέντας λόγους.

3 Βουλόμεθα πρὸς ὑμᾶς ἄγειν εἰρήνην, ἄνδρες
Ἀθηναῖοι, καὶ τὰς μὲν πόλεις ἔχειν ἃς ἑκάτεροι
κρατοῦμεν, τὰ δὲ φρούρια τὰ παρ' ἀλλήλοις καταλῦσαι, τῶν δ' αἰχμαλώτων λυτροῦντες ἀνθ' ἑνὸς
Ἀθηναίου λαβεῖν ἕνα Λάκωνα. οὐ γὰρ ἀγνοοῦμεν
τὸν πόλεμον ἀμφοτέροις μὲν βλαβερόν, πολὺ δὲ
4 μᾶλλον ὑμῖν. παραπέμψαντες δὲ τὸν ἐμὸν λόγον
ἐκ τῶν πραγμάτων μάθετε. ἡμεῖς μὲν ἅπασαν

[1] So Dindorf, cp. Xen. Hell. 1. 1. 34 : πολιτῶν.

[1] The despair of the Lacedaemonians after such a disaster
is portrayed in the letter from the vice-admiral to Sparta

able quantity of booty, since they had won the victory 410 B.C. at the same time over two armaments of such size.[1]

52. When the news of the victory came to Athens, the people, contemplating the unexpected good fortune which had come to the city after their former disasters, were elated over their successes and the populace in a body offered sacrifices to the gods and gathered in festive assemblies ; and for the war they selected from their most stalwart men one thousand hoplites and one hundred horsemen, and in addition to these they dispatched thirty triremes to Alcibiades, in order that, now that they dominated the sea, they might lay waste with impunity the cities which favoured the Lacedaemonians. The Lacedaemonians, on the other hand, when they heard of the disaster they had suffered at Cyzicus, sent ambassadors to Athens to treat for peace, the chief of whom was Endius.[2] When permission was given him, he took the floor and spoke succinctly and in the terse fashion of Laconians, and for this reason I have decided not to omit the speech as he delivered it.

" We want to be at peace with you, men of Athens, and that each party should keep the cities which it now possesses and cease to maintain its garrisons in the other's territory, and that our captives be ransomed, one Laconian for one Athenian. We are not unmindful that the war is hurtful to both of us, but far more to you. Never mind the words I use but learn from the facts. As for us, we till the entire

which is given by Xenophon (*Hell.* 1. 1. 23) and ran as follows : " The ships are gone. Mindarus is dead. The men are starving. We know not what to do."

[2] Endius, an ex-ephor, was an hereditary friend of Alcibiades and had served before on such a mission (Thuc. 5. 44. 3 ; 8. 6. 3).

τὴν Πελοπόννησον γεωργοῦμεν, ὑμεῖς δὲ βραχὺ
μέρος τῆς Ἀττικῆς· καὶ Λάκωσι μὲν ὁ πόλεμος
πολλοὺς συνέθηκε συμμάχους, Ἀθηναίων δὲ τοσούτους ἀφείλατο ὅσους τοῖς πολεμίοις ἔδωκε·
καὶ ἡμῖν μὲν ὁ πλουσιώτατος τῶν κατὰ τὴν οἰκουμένην βασιλέων χορηγός ἐστι τοῦ πολέμου, ὑμῖν
δὲ οἱ πενιχρότατοι τῶν κατὰ τὴν οἰκουμένην·
5 διόπερ οἱ μὲν ἡμέτεροι κατὰ τὸ μέγεθος τῶν
μισθῶν προθύμως στρατεύονται, οἱ δὲ ὑμέτεροι,
τὰς εἰσφορὰς ἀπὸ τῶν ἰδίων διδόντες οὐσιῶν, ἅμα
καὶ τὰς κακοπαθείας φεύγουσι καὶ τὰς δαπάνας.
6 ἔπειθ' ἡμεῖς μὲν κατὰ θάλατταν πολεμοῦντες
σκάφεσι πολιτικοῖς μόνον[1] κινδυνεύομεν, ὑμεῖς δὲ
πολίτας ἔχετε τοὺς πλείστους ἐν ταῖς ναυσίν. τὸ
δὲ μέγιστον, ἡμεῖς μὲν κἂν κρατηθῶμεν ἐν τοῖς
κατὰ θάλατταν πράγμασι, τήν γε κατὰ γῆν ἡγεμονίαν ὁμολογουμένως ἔχομεν· οὐδὲ γὰρ οἶδε τὸ[2]
φυγεῖν πεζὸς Σπαρτιάτης· ὑμεῖς δὲ τῆς θαλάττης
ἐκβληθέντες[3] οὐχ ὑπὲρ ἡγεμονίας πεζῆς, ἀλλ' ὑπὲρ
ἀναστάσεως ἀγωνιᾶτε.
7 Καταλείπεταί μοι διδάξαι, πῶς τοσαῦτα καὶ
τηλικαῦτα πλεονεκτοῦντες ἐν τῷ πολεμεῖν εἰρήνην
ἄγειν παρακαλοῦμεν. ἐγὼ δ' ὠφελεῖσθαι μὲν ἐκ
τοῦ πολεμεῖν οὔ φημι τὴν Σπάρτην, βλάπτεσθαι
μέντοι γε ἔλαττον τῶν Ἀθηναίων. ἀποπλήκτων
δὲ εὐδοκεῖν συνατυχοῦντας τοῖς πολεμίοις, παρὸν
μηδ' ὅλως ἀτυχίας λαβεῖν πεῖραν· οὐ τοσαύτην γὰρ
ἡ τῶν πολεμίων ἀπώλεια φέρει χαρὰν ἡλίκην ἔχει

[1] πολεμοῦντες σ. π. μόνον Dindorf : πέμποντες σ. π. μᾶλλον.
[2] τὸ added by Capps.
[3] ἐκβληθέντες added by Reiske.

268

Peloponnesus, but you only a small part [1] of Attica. 410 B.C.
While to the Laconians the war has brought many
allies, from the Athenians it has taken away as
many as it has given to their enemies. For us the
richest king to be found in the inhabited world [2]
defrays the cost of the war, for you the most poverty-
stricken folk of the inhabited world. Consequently
our troops, in view of their generous pay, make war
with spirit, while your soldiers, because they pay the
war-taxes out of their own pockets, shrink from both
the hardships and the costs of war. In the second
place, when we make war at sea, we risk losing only
hulls among resources of the state, while you have on
board crews most of whom are citizens. And, what
is the most important, even if we meet defeat in our
actions at sea, we still maintain without dispute the
mastery on land—for a Spartan foot-soldier does not
even know what flight means—but you, if you are
driven from the sea, contend, not for the supremacy
on land, but for survival.

" It remains for me to show you why, despite so
many and great advantages we possess in the fighting,
we urge you to make peace. I do not affirm that
Sparta is profiting from the war, but only that she
is suffering less than the Athenians. Only fools find
satisfaction in sharing the misfortunes of their enemies,
when it is in their power to make no trial whatsoever
of misfortune. For the destruction of the enemy
brings no joy that can balance the grief caused by

---

[1] From Deceleia, some 13 miles north and a little east of
Athens, which the Lacedaemonians had seized and fortified,
they could raid the larger part of Attica.
[2] The king of Persia, who was contributing to the maintenance of the Peloponnesian fleet, but not as yet so generously
as toward the end of the war.

8 λύπην ἡ τῶν ἰδίων ταλαιπωρία. οὐ μόνον δὲ τούτων ἕνεκα διαλυθῆναι σπεύδομεν, ἀλλὰ καὶ τὸ
πάτριον ἔθος τηροῦντες· θεωροῦντες γὰρ τὰς ἐν
τῷ πολέμῳ φιλονεικίας πολλὰ καὶ δεινὰ πάθη ποιού-
σας, οἰόμεθα δεῖν φανερὸν ποιῆσαι πᾶσι καὶ θεοῖς
καὶ ἀνθρώποις, ὅτι τούτων ἥκιστα πάντων ἐσμὲν
αἴτιοι.

53. Τοιαῦτα δὲ καὶ τούτοις παραπλήσια τοῦ
Λάκωνος διαλεχθέντος, οἱ μὲν ἐπιεικέστατοι τῶν
Ἀθηναίων ἔρρεπον ταῖς γνώμαις πρὸς τὴν εἰρήνην,
οἱ δὲ πολεμοποιεῖν εἰωθότες καὶ τὰς δημοσίας
ταραχὰς ἰδίας ποιούμενοι προσόδους ᾑροῦντο τὸν
2 πόλεμον. συνεπελάβετο δὲ τῆς γνώμης ταύτης
καὶ Κλεοφῶν, μέγιστος ὢν τότε δημαγωγός. ὃς
παρελθὼν καὶ πολλὰ πρὸς τὴν ὑπόθεσιν οἰκείως
διαλεχθεὶς ἐμετεώρισε τὸν δῆμον, τὸ μέγεθος τῶν
εὐημερημάτων προφερόμενος, ὥσπερ τῆς τύχης
οὐκ ἐναλλὰξ εἰθισμένης βραβεύειν τὰ κατὰ πόλεμον
3 προτερήματα. Ἀθηναῖοι μὲν οὖν κακῶς βουλευσάμενοι μετενόησαν ὅτε οὐδὲν ὄφελος, καὶ λόγοις
πρὸς ἀρέσκειαν εἰρημένοις ἐξαπατηθέντες οὕτως
ἔπταισαν τοῖς ὅλοις, ὥστε μηκέτι δύνασθαι πώποτε
4 αὐτοὺς γνησίως ἀναλαβεῖν. ἀλλὰ ταῦτα μὲν ὕστερον πραχθέντα τεύξεται λόγου κατὰ τοὺς ἰδίους
χρόνους· τότε δὲ οἱ Ἀθηναῖοι τοῖς τε εὐημερήμασιν ἐπαρθέντες καὶ πολλὰς καὶ μεγάλας ἐλπίδας ἔχοντες ἐν τῷ τὸν Ἀλκιβιάδην ἀφηγεῖσθαι τῶν
ἰδίων δυνάμεων, ταχέως ᾤοντο τὴν ἡγεμονίαν ἀνα-
κτήσασθαι.[1]

54. Τῶν δὲ κατὰ τοῦτον τὸν ἐνιαυτὸν πράξεων

---

[1] ἀνακτήσασθαι] ἀνακτήσεσθαι Dindorf.

the distress of one's own people. And not for these 410 B.C.
reasons alone are we eager to come to terms, but because we hold fast to the custom of our fathers ; for
when we consider the many terrible sufferings which
are caused by the rivalries which accompany war, we
believe we should make it clear in the sight of all gods
and men that we are least responsible of all men for
such things."

53. After the Laconian had made these and similar
representations, the sentiments of the most reasonable men among the Athenians inclined toward the
peace, but those who made it their practice to foment
war and to turn disturbances in the state to their
personal profit chose the war. A supporter of this
sentiment was, among others, Cleophon, who was the
most influential leader of the populace at this time.
He, taking the floor and arguing at length on the
question in his own fashion, buoyed up the people,
citing the magnitude of their military successes, as
if indeed it is not the practice of Fortune to adjudge
the advantages in war now to one side and now to the
other. Consequently the Athenians, after taking un-
wise counsel, repented of it when it could do them no
good, and, deceived as they were by words spoken in
flattery, they made a blunder so vital that never again
at any time were they able truly to recover. But
these events, which took place at a later date, will be
described in connection with the period of time to
which they belong ; at the time we are discussing the
Athenians, being elated by their successes and enter-
taining many great hopes because they had Alcibiades
as the leader of their armed forces, thought that they
had quickly won back their supremacy.

54. When the events of this year had come to an 409 B.C.

τέλος ἐχουσῶν Ἀθήνησι μὲν παρέλαβε τὴν ἀρχὴν
Διοκλῆς, ἐν Ῥώμῃ δὲ τὴν ὕπατον εἶχον ἀρχὴν
Κόιντος Φάβιος καὶ Γάιος Φούριος. περὶ δὲ
τούτους τοὺς καιροὺς Ἀννίβας ὁ τῶν Καρχηδονίων
στρατηγὸς τούς τ' ἐξ Ἰβηρίας ξενολογηθέντας καὶ
τοὺς ἐκ τῆς Λιβύης καταγραφέντας στρατιώτας
συνήγαγε, καὶ μακρὰς μὲν ἑξήκοντα ναῦς ἐπλήρωσε,
τὰ δὲ φορτηγὰ πλοῖα περὶ χίλια πεντακόσια παρ-
2 εσκευάσατο. ἐν τούτοις τήν τε δύναμιν διεκόμιζε
καὶ τὰ πρὸς τὰς πολιορκίας μηχανήματα καὶ βέλη
καὶ τὴν ἄλλην παρασκευὴν ἅπασαν. περαιωθεὶς
δὲ μετὰ τοῦ στόλου τὸ Λιβυκὸν πέλαγος, κατέπλευσε τῆς Σικελίας ἐπὶ τὴν ἄκραν τὴν ἀπέναντι
3 τῆς Λιβύης, καλουμένην Λιλύβαιον· καθ' ὃν δὴ
χρόνον τῶν Σελινουντίων τινὲς ἱππέων περὶ τοὺς
τόπους διατρίβοντες καὶ τὸ μέγεθος τοῦ κατα-
πλέοντος στόλου θεασάμενοι, ταχέως τοῖς πολίταις
τὴν τῶν πολεμίων παρουσίαν ἐδήλωσαν. καὶ οἱ
μὲν Σελινούντιοι τοὺς βιβλιαφόρους παραχρῆμα
πρὸς τοὺς Συρακοσίους ἀπέστειλαν, δεόμενοι βοη-
4 θεῖν· ὁ δ' Ἀννίβας ἐκβιβάσας τὴν δύναμιν κατεστρατοπέδευσεν, ἀρξάμενος ἀπὸ τοῦ φρέατος, ὃ
κατ' ἐκείνους μὲν τοὺς καιροὺς ὠνομάζετο Λιλύ-
βαιον, μετὰ δὲ ταῦτα πολλοῖς ἔτεσι πρὸς αὐτῷ
κτισθείσης πόλεως αἴτιον ἐγενήθη τῇ πόλει τῆς
5 ἐπωνυμίας. εἶχε δὲ τοὺς σύμπαντας Ἀννίβας,
ὡς μὲν Ἔφορος ἀνέγραψε, πεζῶν μυριάδας εἴκοσι,
ἱππεῖς δὲ τετρακισχιλίους, ὡς δὲ Τίμαιός φησιν,
οὐ πολλῷ πλείους τῶν δέκα μυριάδων. τὰς μὲν
οὖν ναῦς ἐν τῷ περὶ Μοτύην κόλπῳ πάσας ἐνεώλκησε, βουλόμενος ἔννοιαν διδόναι τοῖς Συρακοσίοις,
ὡς οὐ πάρεστιν ἐκείνοις πολεμήσων οὐδὲ ναυτικῇ

end, in Athens Diocles took over the chief office,[1] and 409 B.C.
in Rome Quintus Fabius and Gaius Furius held the
consulship. At this time Hannibal, the general of the
Carthaginians, gathered together both the mercenaries he had collected from Iberia and the soldiers he
had enrolled from Libya, manned sixty ships of war,
and made ready some fifteen hundred transports. On
these he loaded the troops, the siege-engines, missiles,
and all the other accessories. After crossing with the
fleet the Libyan Sea he came to land in Sicily on the
promontory which lies opposite Libya and is called
Lilybaeum ; and at that very time some Selinuntian
cavalry were tarrying in those regions, and having
seen the great size of the fleet as it came to land, they
speedily informed their fellow citizens of the presence
of the enemy. The Selinuntians at once dispatched
their letter-carriers to the Syracusans, asking their
aid; and Hannibal disembarked his troops and pitched
a camp, beginning at the well which in those times had
the name Lilybaeum, and many years after these
events, when a city was founded near it,[2] the presence
of the well occasioned the giving of the name to the
city.[3] Hannibal had all told, as Ephorus has recorded,
two hundred thousand infantry and four thousand
cavalry, but as Timaeus says, not many more than one
hundred thousand men. His ships he hauled up on
land in the bay about Motyê,[4] every one of them,
wishing to give the Syracusans the impression that he
had not come to make war upon them or to sail along

[1] Of archon.　　　　　　　　[2] In 396 B.C.
[3] The city of Lilybaeum.
[4] The bay and island of the same name lie a little north
of Lilybaeum.

---

[1] ὡς δὲ Stephanus : ὁ δέ.

6 δυνάμει παραπλεύσων ἐπὶ Συρακούσας. παραλαβὼν δὲ τοὺς παρ' Αἰγεσταίων στρατιώτας καὶ
τοὺς παρὰ τῶν ἄλλων συμμάχων ἀνέζευξεν ἀπὸ
τοῦ Λιλυβαίου τὴν πορείαν ποιούμενος ἐπὶ Σελινοῦντος. ὡς δ' ἐπὶ τὸν Μάζαρον ποταμὸν παρεγενήθη, τὸ μὲν παρ' αὐτὸν ἐμπόριον κείμενον
εἷλεν ἐξ ἐφόδου, πρὸς δὲ τὴν πόλιν παραγενηθεὶς
εἰς δύο μέρη διεῖλε τὴν δύναμιν· περιστρατοπε-
δεύσας δ' αὐτὴν καὶ τὰς μηχανὰς ἐπιστήσας μετὰ
7 πάσης σπουδῆς τὰς προσβολὰς ἐποιεῖτο. ἓξ μὲν
γὰρ πύργους ὑπερβάλλοντας τοῖς μεγέθεσιν ἐπέστησε, τοὺς ἴσους δὲ κριοὺς κατασεσιδηρωμένους
προσήρεισε τοῖς τείχεσι· χωρὶς δὲ τούτων τοῖς
τοξόταις καὶ σφενδονήταις πολλοῖς χρώμενος ἀν-
έστελλε τοὺς ἐπὶ τῶν ἐπάλξεων μαχομένους.

55. Οἱ δὲ Σελινούντιοι ἐκ πολλῶν ὄντες ἄπειροι
πολιορκίας, καὶ Καρχηδονίοις ἐν τῷ πρὸς Γέλωνα
πολέμῳ συνηγωνισμένοι μόνοι τῶν Σικελιωτῶν,
οὔποτ' ἤλπιζον ὑπὸ τῶν εὐεργετηθέντων εἰς τοιού-
2 τους φόβους συγκλεισθήσεσθαι. θεωροῦντες δὲ τὰ
μεγέθη τῶν μηχανημάτων καὶ τὰ πλήθη τῶν
πολεμίων, περιδεεῖς ἦσαν καὶ κατεπλήττοντο τὸ
3 μέγεθος τοῦ περιεστῶτος κινδύνου. οὐ μὴν κατὰ
πᾶν γε τὴν σωτηρίαν ἀπεγίνωσκον, ἀλλὰ προσδοκῶντες συντόμως ἥξειν τοὺς Συρακοσίους καὶ τοὺς
ἄλλους συμμάχους, πανδημεὶ τοὺς πολεμίους ἀπὸ
4 τῶν τειχῶν ἠμύνοντο. οἱ μὲν γὰρ ἀκμάζοντες
ταῖς ἡλικίαις ἐν τοῖς ὅπλοις ὄντες διεκινδύνευον,
οἱ δὲ πρεσβύτεροι περί τε τὰς παρασκευὰς ἦσαν
καὶ περιπορευόμενοι τὸ τεῖχος ἐδέοντο τῶν νέων
μὴ περιδεῖν αὐτοὺς ὑποχειρίους τοῖς πολεμίοις

the coast with his naval force against Syracuse. And
after adding to his army the soldiers supplied by the
Aegestaeans and by the other allies he broke camp
and made his way from Lilybaeum towards Selinus.
And when he came to the Mazarus River, he took at
the first assault the trading-station situated by it, and
when he arrived before the city, he divided his army
into two parts ; then, after he had invested the city
and put his siege-engines in position, he began the
assaults with all speed. He set up six towers of
exceptional size and advanced an equal number of
battering-rams plated with iron against the walls ;
furthermore, by employing his archers and slingers
in great numbers he beat back the fighters on the
battlements.

55. The Selinuntians, who had for a long time been
without experience in sieges and had been the only
Sicilian Greeks to fight on the side of the Carthaginians in the war against Gelon,[1] had never conceived
that they would be brought to such a state of fear
by the people whom they had befriended. But
when they saw the great size of the engines of war
and the hosts of the enemy, they were filled with
dread and dismayed at the magnitude of the danger
threatening them. However, they did not totally
despair of their deliverance, but in the expectation
that the Syracusans and their other allies would soon
arrive, the whole populace fought off the enemy from
the walls. Indeed all the men in the prime of life
were armed and battled desperately, while the older
men busied themselves with the supplies and, as they
made the rounds of the wall, begged the young men
not to allow them to fall under subjection to the

Cp. Book 11. 21.

γινομένους· γυναῖκες δὲ καὶ παῖδες τάς τε τροφὰς καὶ[1] βέλη τοῖς ὑπὲρ τῆς πατρίδος ἀγωνιζομένοις παρεκόμιζον, τὴν αἰδῶ καὶ τὴν ἐπὶ τῆς
5 εἰρήνης αἰσχύνην παρ' οὐδὲν ἡγούμεναι. τοσαύτη
κατάπληξις καθειστήκει[2] ὥστε τὸ μέγεθος τῆς
περιστάσεως δεῖσθαι καὶ τῆς παρὰ τῶν γυναικῶν
βοηθείας.

Ὁ δ' Ἀννίβας ἐπαγγειλάμενος τοῖς στρατιώταις
εἰς διαρπαγὴν δώσειν τὴν πόλιν, τάς τε μηχανὰς
προσήρεισε καὶ τοῖς κρατίστοις στρατιώταις ἐκ
6 διαδοχῆς προσέβαλλε τοῖς τείχεσιν. ὁμοῦ δὲ αἵ
τε σάλπιγγες τὸ πολεμικὸν ἐσήμαινον καὶ πρὸς
ἓν παράγγελμα πᾶν ἐπηλάλαξε τὸ τῶν Καρχηδονίων στράτευμα, καὶ τῇ βίᾳ μὲν τῶν κριῶν
ἐσαλεύετο τὰ τείχη, τῷ δ' ὕψει τῶν πύργων οἱ
μαχόμενοι πολλοὺς τῶν Σελινουντίων ἀνήρουν.
7 ἐν πολυχρονίῳ γὰρ εἰρήνῃ γεγονότες καὶ τῶν τειχῶν οὐδ' ἡντινοῦν ἐπιμέλειαν πεποιημένοι ῥᾳδίως κατεπονοῦντο, τῶν ξυλίνων πύργων πολὺ τοῖς
ὕψεσιν ὑπερεχόντων. πεσόντος δὲ τοῦ τείχους οἱ
μὲν Καμπανοὶ σπεύδοντες ἐπιφανές τι πρᾶξαι,
8 ταχέως εἰσέπεσον εἰς τὴν πόλιν. τὸ μὲν οὖν
πρῶτον κατεπλήξαντο τοὺς ὑποστάντας, ὀλίγους
ὄντας· μετὰ δὲ ταῦτα πολλῶν συνδραμόντων ἐπὶ
τὴν βοήθειαν ἐξεώσθησαν καὶ συχνοὺς ἑαυτῶν
ἀπέβαλον· οὔπω γὰρ τελέως ἀνακεκαθαρμένου τοῦ
τείχους βιασάμενοι καὶ κατὰ τὴν ἔφοδον εἰς
δυσχωρίας ἐμπίπτοντες ῥᾳδίως ἡλαττοῦντο. νυκτὸς δ' ἐπιγενομένης οἱ μὲν Καρχηδόνιοι τὴν
πολιορκίαν ἔλυσαν.

56. Οἱ δὲ Σελινούντιοι τῶν ἱππέων τοὺς κρατίστους ἐπιλέξαντες διὰ νυκτὸς εὐθέως ἀπέστειλαν

enemy ; and women and girls supplied the food and 409 B.C.
missiles to the defenders of the fatherland, counting
as naught the modesty and the sense of shame which
they cherished in time of peace.   Such consternation
prevailed that the magnitude of the emergency called
for even the aid of their women.

Hannibal, who had promised the soldiers that he
would give them the city to pillage, pushed the siege-
engines forward and assaulted the walls in waves with
his best soldiers.   And all together the trumpets
sounded the signal for attack and at one command the
army of the Carthaginians as a body raised the war-
cry, and by the power of the rams the walls were
shaken, while by reason of the height of the towers
the fighters on them slew many of the Selinuntians.
For in the long period of peace they had enjoyed they
had given no attention whatever even to their walls
and so they were easily subdued, since the wooden
towers far exceeded the walls in height.   When the
wall fell the Campanians, being eager to accomplish
some outstanding feat, broke swiftly into the city.
Now at the outset they struck terror into their
opponents, who were few in number ; but after that,
when many gathered to the aid of the defenders, they
were thrust out with heavy losses among their own
soldiers ; for since they had forced a passage when the
wall had not yet been completely cleared and in their
attack had fallen foul of difficult terrain, they were
easily overcome.   At nightfall the Carthaginians
broke off the assault.

56. The Selinuntians, picking out their best horsemen, dispatched them at once by night, some to

---

¹ τὰ after καὶ omitted PA, Vogel.
² So Hertlein : εἰστήκει.

τοὺς μὲν εἰς Ἀκράγαντα, τοὺς δ᾽ εἰς Γέλαν καὶ
Συρακούσας, δεόμενοι τὴν ταχίστην βοηθεῖν, ὡς
οὐ δυναμένης πλείω χρόνον τῆς πόλεως ὑποστῆναι
2 τῶν πολεμίων τὴν δύναμιν. οἱ μὲν οὖν Ἀκραγαντῖνοι καὶ Γελῷοι περιέμενον τοὺς Συρακοσίους,
βουλόμενοι τὴν δύναμιν ἀθρόαν ἄγειν ἐπὶ τοὺς
Καρχηδονίους· οἱ δὲ Συρακόσιοι πυθόμενοι τὰ
περὶ τὴν πολιορκίαν, πρὸς μὲν Χαλκιδεῖς πόλεμον
ἔχοντες διελύσαντο, τὰς δ᾽ ἀπὸ τῆς χώρας δυνάμεις
ἀθροίζοντες, μεγάλην ποιούμενοι παρασκευὴν ἐχρό-
νιζον, νομίζοντες ἐκπολιορκηθήσεσθαι[1] τὴν πόλιν,
ἀλλ᾽ οὐκ ἀναρπασθήσεσθαι.
3 Ἀννίβας δὲ τῆς νυκτὸς διελθούσης ἅμα ἡμέρᾳ
πανταχόθεν μὲν προσέβαλε, τὸ δὲ κατὰ τὴν πόλιν
πεπτωκὸς μέρος τοῦ τείχους καὶ τὸ συνάπτον
4 τούτῳ κατέβαλε ταῖς μηχαναῖς. ἀνακαθάρας δὲ
τὸν πεσόντα τόπον τοῦ τείχους, καὶ τοῖς κρατίστοις
ἐκ διαδοχῆς ἀγωνιζόμενος, ἐπ᾽ ὀλίγον ἐξέωσε τοὺς
Σελινουντίους· οὐ μήν γε βιάσασθαι δυνατὸν ἦν
5 τοὺς ὑπὲρ τῶν ὅλων διαγωνιζομένους. πολλῶν δ᾽
ἀναιρουμένων παρ᾽ ἀμφοτέροις, τοῖς μὲν Καρχηδονίοις νεαλεῖς διεδέχοντο τὴν μάχην, τοῖς δὲ
Σελινουντίοις οὐκ ἦν τὸ βοηθῆσον. τῆς δὲ πολιορκίας ἐφ᾽ ἡμέρας ἐννέα γενομένης μετὰ φιλοτιμίας
ἀνυπερβλήτου, πολλὰ συνέβη τοὺς Καρχηδονίους
6 κακοπαθεῖν καὶ δρᾶσαι δεινά. κατὰ δὲ τὸ πεπτωκὸς τεῖχος ἀναβάντων τῶν Ἰβήρων, αἱ μὲν ἐπὶ
τῶν οἰκιῶν οὖσαι γυναῖκες ἀνεβόησαν, οἱ δὲ
Σελινούντιοι νομίζοντες ἁλίσκεσθαι τὴν πόλιν
κατεπλάγησαν, καὶ τὰ τείχη λιπόντες κατὰ τὰς

---

[1] So Wurm, ἀπολιορκηθήσεσθαι P¹, πολιορκήσεσθαι F, πολιορ-
κηθήσεσθαι cet.

Acragas, and others to Gela and Syracuse, asking 409 B.C. them to come to their aid with all speed, since their city could not withstand the strength of the enemy for any great time.   Now the Acragantini and Geloans waited for the Syracusans, since they wished to lead their troops as one body against the Carthaginians ; and the Syracusans, on learning the facts about the siege, first stopped the war they were engaged in with the Chalcidians and then spent some time in gathering the troops from the countryside and making great preparations, thinking that the city might be forced by siege to surrender but would not be taken by storm.

Hannibal, when the night had passed, at daybreak launched assaults from every side, and the part of the city's wall which had already fallen and the portion of the wall next the breach he broke down with the siege-engines.   He then cleared the area of the fallen part of the wall and, attacking in relays of his best troops, gradually forced out the Selinuntians ; it was not possible, however, to overpower by force men who were fighting for their very existence.   Both sides suffered heavy losses, but for the Carthaginians fresh troops kept taking over the fighting, while for the Selinuntians there was no reserve to come to their support.   The siege continued for nine days with unsurpassed stubbornness, and in the event the Carthaginians suffered and inflicted many terrible injuries. When the Iberians mounted where the wall had fallen, the women who were on the house-tops raised a great cry, whereupon the Selinuntians, thinking that the city was being taken, were struck with terror, and

εἰσβολὰς τῶν στενωπῶν¹ ἀθρόοι συνίσταντο, καὶ
τὰς μὲν ὁδοὺς διοικοδομεῖν ἐνεχείρησαν, τοὺς δὲ
7 πολεμίους ἐπὶ πολὺν χρόνον ἠμύνοντο. βιαζομένων δὲ τῶν Καρχηδονίων, τὰ πλήθη τῶν γυναικῶν καὶ παίδων ἔφευγον ἐπὶ τὰς οἰκίας, καὶ
τούς τε λίθους καὶ τὰς κεραμίδας ἔβαλλον ἐπὶ τοὺς
πολεμίους. ἐπὶ πολὺν δὲ χρόνον οἱ Καρχηδόνιοι
κακῶς ἀπήλλαττον, οὔτε περιστῆναι δυνάμενοι
τοὺς ἐν τοῖς στενωποῖς διὰ τοὺς τῶν οἰκιῶν τοί-
χους, οὔτ' ἐπ' ἴσης διαγωνίσασθαι διὰ τοὺς ἀπὸ
8 τῶν στεγῶν βάλλοντας. οὐ μὴν ἀλλὰ τοῦ κινδύνου
μέχρι δείλης παρεκτείνοντος, τοῖς μὲν ἀπὸ τῶν
οἰκιῶν ἀγωνιζομένοις ἐνέλιπε τὰ βέλη, τοῖς δὲ
Καρχηδονίοις οἱ διαδεχόμενοι τοὺς κακοπαθοῦντας
ἀκέραιοι διηγωνίζοντο. τέλος δὲ τῆς μὲν ἔνδον
δυνάμεως ἀφαίρεσιν λαμβανούσης, τῶν δὲ πολεμίων ἀεὶ πλειόνων εἰς τὴν πόλιν ἐμπιπτόντων,
ἐξεώσθησαν ἐκ τῶν στενωπῶν οἱ Σελινούντιοι.

57. Διὸ καὶ τῆς πόλεως καταλαμβανομένης παρὰ
μὲν τοῖς Ἕλλησιν ἦν ὀδυρμοὺς καὶ δάκρυα θεωρεῖν,
παρὰ δὲ τοῖς βαρβάροις ἀλαλαγμὸς ἦν καὶ βοὴ
σύμμικτος· οἱ μὲν γὰρ τὸ μέγεθος τῆς περιεστώσης
συμφορᾶς ἐν ὀφθαλμοῖς ἔχοντες περιδεεῖς ἦσαν,
οἱ δὲ τοῖς εὐημερήμασιν ἐπηρμένοι σφάττειν παρ-
2 εκελεύοντο. εἰς δὲ τὴν ἀγορὰν συνδραμόντων τῶν
Σελινουντίων, οὗτοι μὲν ἐνταῦθα μαχόμενοι πάντες
ἀνῃρέθησαν· οἱ δὲ βάρβαροι σκεδασθέντες καθ'
ὅλην τὴν πόλιν τὴν μὲν ἐν ταῖς οἰκίαις εὐδαιμονίαν
συνήρπασαν, τῶν δὲ ἐγκαταληφθέντων² σωμάτων

---

¹ So Reiske: στενῶν τόπων.
² So Wurm: ἐγκαταλειφθέντων.

leaving the walls they gathered in bands at the en- 409 B.C.
trances of the narrow alleys, endeavoured to barricade
the streets, and held off the enemy for a long time.
And as the Carthaginians pressed the attack, the
multitudes of women and children took refuge on the
housetops whence they threw both stones and tiles
on the enemy. For a long time the Carthaginians
came off badly, being unable either, because of the
walls of the houses, to surround the men in the alleys
or, because of those hurling at them from the roofs, to
fight it out on equal terms. However, as the struggle
went on until the afternoon, the missiles of the
fighters from the houses were exhausted, whereas the
troops of the Carthaginians, which constantly relieved
those which were suffering heavily, continued the
fighting in fresh condition. Finally, since the troops
within the walls were being steadily reduced in
number and the enemy entered the city in ever-
increasing strength, the Selinuntians were forced
out of the alleys.

57. And so, while the city was being taken, there
was to be observed among the Greeks lamentation and
weeping, and among the barbarians there was cheer-
ing and commingled outcries ; for the former, as
their eyes looked upon the great disaster which surrounded them, were filled with terror, while the latter,
elated by their successes, urged on their comrades
to slaughter. The Selinuntians gathered into the
market-place and all who reached it died fighting
there ; and the barbarians, scattering throughout the
entire city, plundered whatever of value was to be
found in the dwellings, while of the inhabitants they

281

ἃ μὲν[1] ταῖς οἰκίαις συγκατέκαιον, τῶν δ' εἰς τὰς
ὁδοὺς βιαζομένων οὐ διακρίνοντες οὔτε φύσιν οὔθ'
ἡλικίαν, ἀλλ' ὁμοίως παῖδας νηπίους, γυναῖκας,
πρεσβύτας ἐφόνευον, οὐδεμίαν συμπάθειαν λαμ-
3 βάνοντες. ἠκρωτηρίαζον δὲ καὶ τοὺς νεκροὺς
κατὰ τὸ πάτριον ἔθος, καί τινες μὲν χεῖρας ἀθρόας
περιέφερον τοῖς σώμασι, τινὲς δὲ κεφαλὰς ἐπὶ
τῶν γαίσων καὶ τῶν σαυνίων ἀναπείροντες ἔφερον.
ὅσας δὲ τῶν γυναικῶν μετὰ τέκνων εἰς τοὺς ναοὺς
συμπεφευγυίας κατελάμβανον, παρεκελεύοντο μὴ
4 φονεύειν, καὶ ταύταις μόναις πίστιν ἔδοσαν. τοῦτο
δ' ἔπραξαν οὐ τοὺς ἀκληροῦντας ἐλεοῦντες, ἀλλ'
εὐλαβούμενοι, μήποτε τὴν σωτηρίαν αἱ γυναῖκες
ἀπογνοῦσαι κατακαύσωσι τοὺς ναούς, καὶ μὴ
δυνηθῶσι συλῆσαι τὴν ἐν αὐτοῖς καθιερωμένην
5 πολυτέλειαν. τοσοῦτο γὰρ ὠμότητι διέφερον οἱ
βάρβαροι τῶν ἄλλων, ὥστε τῶν λοιπῶν ἕνεκα τοῦ
μηδὲν ἀσεβεῖν εἰς τὸ δαιμόνιον διασωζόντων τοὺς
εἰς τὰ ἱερὰ καταπεφευγότας Καρχηδόνιοι τοὐναντίον ἀπέσχοντο τῶν πολεμίων, ὅπως τοὺς τῶν
6 θεῶν ναοὺς συλήσειαν. ἤδη δὲ νυκτὸς οὔσης ἡ μὲν
πόλις διήρπαστο, τῶν δ' οἰκιῶν αἱ μὲν κατεκαύ-
θησαν, αἱ δὲ κατεσκάφησαν, πᾶς δ' ἦν τόπος αἵματος καὶ νεκρῶν πλήρης. ἑξακισχίλια μὲν πρὸς
τοῖς μυρίοις εὑρέθη σώματα πεπτωκότα, καὶ χωρὶς αἰχμάλωτα συνήχθη πλείω τῶν πεντακισχιλίων.
58. Θεωροῦντες δὲ τὴν τοῦ βίου μεταβολὴν οἱ
τοῖς Καρχηδονίοις Ἕλληνες συμμαχοῦντες ἠλέουν
τὴν τῶν ἀκληρούντων τύχην. αἱ μὲν γυναῖκες ἐστε-

---

[1] ἐν after μὲν deleted by Hertlein.

[1] Cp. Book 5. 29 for the custom of the Gauls of preserving
the heads of warriors they had conquered.

found in them some they burned together with their _{409 B C.}
homes and when others struggled into the streets,
without distinction of sex or age but whether infant
children or women or old men, they put them to the
sword, showing no sign of compassion. They mutilated
even the dead according to the practice of their people,
some carrying bunches of hands about their bodies
and others heads which they had spitted upon their
javelins and spears.[1] Such women as they found to
have taken refuge together with their children in the
temples they called upon their comrades not to kill,
and to these alone did they give assurance of their
lives. This they did, however, not out of pity for the
unfortunate people, but because they feared lest
the women, despairing of their lives, would burn down
the temples, and thus they would not be able to make
booty of the great wealth which was stored up in them
as dedications. To such a degree did the barbarians
surpass all other men in cruelty, that whereas the rest
of mankind spare those who seek refuge in the sanctuaries from the desire not to commit sacrilege against
the deity, the Carthaginians, on the contrary, would
refrain from laying hands on the enemy in order that
they might plunder the temples of their gods. By
nightfall the city had been sacked, and of the dwellings some had been burned and others razed to the
ground, while the whole area was filled with blood and
corpses. Sixteen thousand was the sum of the inhabitants who were found to have fallen, not counting
the more than five thousand who had been taken
captive.

58. The Greeks serving as allies of the Carthaginians, as they contemplated the reversal in the lives
of the hapless Selinuntians, felt pity at their lot. The

ρημέναι τῆς συνήθους τρυφῆς[1] ἐν πολεμίων ὕβρει
διενυκτέρευον, ὑπομένουσαι δεινὰς ταλαιπωρίας·
ὧν ἔνιαι θυγατέρας ἐπιγάμους ὁρᾶν ἠναγκάζοντο
2 πασχούσας οὐκ οἰκεῖα τῆς ἡλικίας. ἡ γὰρ βαρβάρων ὠμότης οὔτε παίδων ἐλευθέρων οὔτε παρθένων φειδομένη δεινὰς τοῖς ἠτυχηκόσι παρίστα
συμφοράς. διόπερ αἱ γυναῖκες ἀναλογιζόμεναι
μὲν τὴν ἐν τῇ Λιβύῃ μέλλουσαν αὐταῖς ἔσεσθαι
δουλείαν, θεωροῦσαι δ' αὐτὰς ἅμα τοῖς τέκνοις ἐν
ἀτιμίᾳ καὶ προπηλακισμῷ δεσποτῶν ἀναγκαζομένας
ὑπακούειν, τούτους δ' ὁρῶσαι ἀσύνετον μὲν τὴν
φωνήν, θηριώδη δὲ τὸν τρόπον ἔχοντας, τὰ μὲν
ζῶντα τῶν τέκνων ἐπένθουν, καὶ καθ' ἕκαστον
τῶν εἰς ταῦτα παρανομημάτων οἰονεὶ νυγμοὺς εἰς
τὴν ψυχὴν λαμβάνουσαι περιπαθεῖς ἐγίνοντο καὶ
πολλὰ τὴν ἑαυτῶν τύχην κατωδύροντο· τοὺς δὲ
πατέρας, ἔτι δὲ ἀδελφούς, οἳ διαγωνιζόμενοι περὶ
τῆς πατρίδος ἐτετελευτήκεισαν,[2] ἐμακάριζον, οὐθὲν
3 ἀνάξιον ἑωρακότας τῆς ἰδίας ἀρετῆς. οἱ δὲ τὴν
αἰχμαλωσίαν διαφυγόντες Σελινούντιοι, τὸν ἀριθμὸν
ὄντες ἑξακόσιοι πρὸς τοῖς δισχιλίοις, διεσώθησαν
εἰς Ἀκράγαντα καὶ πάντων ἔτυχον τῶν φιλαν-
θρώπων· οἱ γὰρ Ἀκραγαντῖνοι σιτομετρήσαντες
αὐτοῖς δημοσίᾳ διέδωκαν κατὰ τὰς οἰκίας, παρακελευσάμενοι τοῖς ἰδιώταις καὶ αὐτοῖς προθύμοις
οὖσι χορηγεῖν τὰ πρὸς τὸ ζῆν ἅπαντα.

59. Ἅμα δὲ τούτοις πραττομένοις εἰς τὸν Ἀκράγαντα κατήντησαν στρατιῶται τρισχίλιοι παρὰ
Συρακοσίων ἐπίλεκτοι, προαπεσταλμένοι κατὰ σπουδὴν ἐπὶ τὴν βοήθειαν. πυθόμενοι δὲ τὴν πόλιν

---

[1] So Dindorf : τροφῆς.
[2] So Dindorf : τετελευτήκασιν.

women, deprived now of the pampered life they had 409 B.C.
enjoyed, spent the nights in the very midst of the
enemies' lasciviousness, enduring terrible indignities,
and some were obliged to see their daughters of
marriageable age suffering treatment improper for
their years. For the savagery of the barbarians spared
neither free-born youths nor maidens, but exposed
these unfortunates to dreadful disasters. Consequently, as the women reflected upon the slavery that
would be their lot in Libya, as they saw themselves
together with their children in a condition in which
they possessed no legal rights and were subject to in-
solent treatment and thus compelled to obey masters,
and as they noted that these masters used an unintelligible speech and had a bestial character, they
mourned for their living children as dead, and receiving
into their souls as a piercing wound each and every
outrage committed against them, they became frantic
with suffering and vehemently deplored their own
fate ; while as for their fathers and brothers who had
died fighting for their country, them they counted
blessed, since they had not witnessed any sight unworthy of their own valour. The Selinuntians who
had escaped capture, twenty-six hundred in number,
made their way in safety to Acragas and there received all possible kindness ; for the Acragantini,
after portioning out food to them at public expense,
divided them for billeting among their homes, urging
the private citizens, who were indeed eager enough,
to supply them with every necessity of life.

59. While these events were taking place there
arrived at Acragas three thousand picked soldiers
from the Syracusans, who had been dispatched in
advance with all speed to bring aid. On learning of

ἡλωκυῖαν, πρέσβεις ἀπέστειλαν παρακαλοῦντες τὸν
Ἀννίβαν τούς τε αἰχμαλώτους ἀπολυτρῶσαι καὶ
2 τῶν θεῶν τοὺς ναοὺς ἐᾶσαι. ὁ δ' Ἀννίβας ἀπ-
εκρίθη, τοὺς μὲν Σελινουντίους μὴ δυναμένους
τηρεῖν τὴν ἐλευθερίαν πεῖραν τῆς δουλείας λήψεσθαι,
τοὺς δὲ θεοὺς ἐκτὸς Σελινοῦντος οἴχεσθαι προσ-
3 κόψαντας τοῖς ἐνοικοῦσιν. ὅμως δὲ τῶν πεφευ-
γότων Ἐμπεδίωνα πρεσβευτὴν ἀποστειλάντων,
τούτῳ μὲν ὁ Ἀννίβας τὰς οὐσίας ἀποκατέστησεν·
ἀεὶ γὰρ τὰ Καρχηδονίων ἦν πεφρονηκὼς καὶ πρὸ
τῆς πολιορκίας τοῖς πολίταις συμβεβουλευκὼς[1] μὴ
πολεμεῖν Καρχηδονίους· ἐχαρίσατο δ' αὐτῷ τοὺς
συγγενεῖς τοὺς ὄντας ἐν τοῖς αἰχμαλώτοις, καὶ
τοῖς ἐκπεφευγόσι Σελινουντίοις ἔδωκεν ἐξουσίαν
τὴν πόλιν οἰκεῖν καὶ τὴν χώραν γεωργεῖν τελοῦντας
φόρον τοῖς Καρχηδονίοις.
4   Αὕτη μὲν οὖν ἡ πόλις ἀπὸ τῆς κτίσεως οἰκη-
θεῖσα χρόνον ἐτῶν διακοσίων τεσσαράκοντα δύο
ἑάλω. ὁ δὲ Ἀννίβας περιελὼν τὰ τείχη τῆς
Σελινοῦντος ἀνέζευξε μετὰ πάσης τῆς δυνάμεως
ἐπὶ τὴν Ἱμέραν, ἐπιθυμῶν μάλιστα ταύτην κατα-
5 σκάψαι τὴν πόλιν. διὰ ταύτην γὰρ ὁ μὲν πατὴρ
αὐτοῦ φυγὰς ἦν, ὁ δὲ προπάτωρ Ἀμίλκας πρὸς
ταύτῃ καταστρατηγηθεὶς ὑπὸ Γέλωνος ἀνῃρέθη,
καὶ μετ' αὐτοῦ πεντεκαίδεκα μυριάδες στρατιωτῶν
ἀνῃρέθησαν, ἄλλαι δὲ οὐκ ἐλάττους τούτων ἠχμα-
6 λωτίσθησαν. ὑπὲρ ὧν σπεύδων τιμωρίαν λαβεῖν
Ἀννίβας τέτρασι μυριάσιν οὐκ[2] ἄπωθεν τῆς πόλεως
ἐπί τινων λόφων κατεστρατοπέδευσε, τῇ δ' ἄλλῃ
δυνάμει πάσῃ περιεστρατοπέδευσε τὴν πόλιν, προσγενομένων ἄλλων παρά τε Σικελῶν καὶ Σικανῶν

---

[1] So Reiske : συμπεφωνηκώς.   [2] οὐκ added by Hertlein.

the fall of Selinus, they sent ambassadors to Hannibal 409 B.C. urging him both to release the captives on payment of ransom and to spare the temples of the gods. Hannibal replied that the Selinuntians, having proved incapable of defending their freedom, would now undergo the experience of slavery, and that the gods had departed from Selinus, having become offended with its inhabitants. However, since the fugitives had sent Empedion as an ambassador, to him Hannibal restored his possessions; for Empedion had always favoured the cause of the Carthaginians and before the siege had counselled the citizens not to go to war against the Carthaginians. Hannibal also graciously delivered up to him his kinsmen who were among the captives and to the Selinuntians who had escaped he gave permission to dwell in the city and to cultivate its fields upon payment of tribute to the Carthaginians.

Now this city was taken after it had been inhabited from its founding for a period of two hundred and forty-two years. And Hannibal, after destroying the walls of Selinus, departed with his whole army to Himera, being especially bent upon razing this city to the ground. For it was this city which had caused his father to be exiled and before its walls his grandfather Hamilcar had been out-generalled by Gelon and then met his end,[1] and with him one hundred and fifty thousand soldiers had perished and no fewer than these had been taken captive. These were the reasons why Hannibal was eager to exact punishment, and with forty thousand men he pitched camp upon some hills not far from the city, while with the rest of his entire army he invested the city, twenty thousand additional soldiers from both Siceli and

[1] Cp. Book 11. 21 f.

7 δισμυρίων στρατιωτῶν. στήσας δὲ μηχανὰς τὸ
τεῖχος κατὰ πλείονας τόπους ἐσάλευε, καὶ πολλῷ
πλήθει διαγωνιζόμενος ἐκ διαδοχῆς κατεπόνει τοὺς
πολιορκουμένους, ἅτε καὶ τῶν στρατιωτῶν ἐπηρ-
8 μένων ταῖς εὐτυχίαις. ὑπώρυττε δὲ καὶ τὰ τείχη,
καὶ ξύλοις ὑπήρειδεν, ὧν ἐμπρησθέντων ταχὺ πολὺ
μέρος τοῦ τείχους ἔπεσεν. ἔνθα δὴ συνέβαινε καρ-
τερωτάτην μάχην γίνεσθαι, τῶν μὲν βιαζομένων
ἐντὸς τοῦ τείχους παρεισπεσεῖν, τῶν δὲ φοβου-
9 μένων μὴ ταὐτὰ πάθωσι τοῖς Σελινουντίοις. διὸ
καὶ τὸν ἔσχατον ἀγῶνα τιθεμένων αὐτῶν ὑπὲρ
τέκνων καὶ γονέων καὶ τῆς περιμαχήτου πᾶσι
πατρίδος, ἐξεώσθησαν οἱ βάρβαροι καὶ ταχὺ τὸ
μέρος τοῦ τείχους ἀνῳκοδόμησαν. παρεγενήθησαν
δ' αὐτοῖς εἰς τὴν βοήθειαν οἵ τ' ἐξ Ἀκράγαντος
Συρακόσιοι καί τινες τῶν ἄλλων συμμάχων, οἱ
πάντες εἰς τετρακισχιλίους, ὧν Διοκλῆς ὁ Συρακόσιος εἶχε τὴν ἡγεμονίαν.

60. Τότε μὲν οὖν νυκτὸς ἀφελομένης τὴν ἐπὶ τὸ
πλέον[1] φιλονεικίαν ἔλυσαν τὴν πολιορκίαν· ἅμα δ'
ἡμέρᾳ τοῖς Ἱμεραίοις ἔδοξε μὴ περιορᾶν αὐτοὺς
συγκεκλεισμένους ἀγεννῶς, καθάπερ τοὺς Σελινουντίους, ἐπὶ δὲ τῶν τειχῶν φύλακας κατέταττον,
τοὺς δ' ἄλλους στρατιώτας σὺν τοῖς παραγεγονόσι
2 συμμάχοις ἐξήγαγον, ὄντας περὶ μυρίους. ἀπροσδοκήτως δὲ τοῖς πολεμίοις ἀπαντήσαντες εἰς
ἔκπληξιν ἤγαγον τοὺς βαρβάρους, νομίζοντας
ἥκειν τοὺς συμμάχους τοῖς πολιορκουμένοις. πολὺ
δὲ ταῖς τόλμαις ὑπερέχοντες καὶ ταῖς εὐχειρίαις,
καὶ τὸ μέγιστον, μιᾶς ἐλπίδος εἰς σωτηρίαν ὑπο-

---

[1] So Reiske: τῷ πλέονι P, τῷ πλείονι cet.

Sicani having joined him. Setting up his siege-engines 409 B.C.
he shook the walls at a number of points, and since
he pressed the battle with waves of troops in great
strength, he wore down the defenders, especially since
his soldiers were elated by their successes. He also
set about undermining the walls, which he then shored
up with wooden supports, and when these were set on
fire, a large section of the wall soon fell. Thereupon
there ensued a most bitter battle, one side struggling
to force its way inside the wall and the other fearing lest
they should suffer the same fate as the Selinuntians.
Consequently, since the defenders put up a struggle
to the death on behalf of children and parents and
the fatherland which all men fight to defend, the
barbarians were thrust out and the section of the wall
quickly restored. To their aid came also the Syracusans from Acragas and troops from their other
allies, some four thousand in all, who were under the
command of Diocles the Syracusan.

60. At that juncture, when night brought an end
to all further striving for victory, the Carthaginians
abandoned the attack. And when day came, the
Himeraeans decided not to allow themselves to be
shut in and surrounded in this ignominious manner, as
were the Selinuntians, and so they stationed guards
on the walls and led out of the city the rest of their
soldiers together with the allies who had arrived,
some ten thousand men. And by engaging the enemy
thus unexpectedly, they threw the barbarians into
consternation, thinking as they did that allied forces
had arrived to aid those who were penned in by
the siege. And because the Himeraeans were far
superior in deeds of daring and of skill, and especially
because their single hope of safety lay in their pre-

κειμένης εἰ τῇ μάχῃ κρατήσειαν,[1] εὐθὺ τοὺς
3 πρώτους ὑποστάντας ἀνεῖλον. τοῦ δὲ πλήθους
τῶν βαρβάρων συντρέχοντος ἐν ἀταξίᾳ πολλῇ διὰ
τὸ μηδέποτ' ἂν ἐλπίσαι τοὺς συγκεκλεισμένους
τηλικαῦτα τολμήσειν, οὐ μετρίως ἠλαττοῦντο· εἰς
ἕνα γὰρ τόπον ὀκτὼ μυριάδων συνδραμουσῶν ἀτάκτως συνέβαινε τοὺς βαρβάρους ἀλλήλοις ἐμπί-
πτειν καὶ πλείονα πάσχειν ὑφ' ἑαυτῶν ἤπερ ὑπὸ
4 τῶν πολεμίων. οἱ δ' Ἱμεραῖοι θεατὰς ἔχοντες ἀπὸ
τῶν τειχῶν γονεῖς καὶ παῖδας, ἔτι δὲ τοὺς οἰκείους
ἅπαντας, ἀφειδῶς ἐχρῶντο τοῖς ἰδίοις σώμασιν
5 εἰς τὴν κοινὴν σωτηρίαν. λαμπρῶς δ' αὐτῶν
ἀγωνιζομένων οἱ βάρβαροι τάς τε τόλμας καὶ τὸ
παράδοξον καταπλαγέντες πρὸς φυγὴν ἐτράπησαν.
τούτων δ' οὐδενὶ κόσμῳ φευγόντων πρὸς τοὺς ἐπὶ
τῶν λόφων στρατοπεδεύοντας, ἐπηκολούθουν ἀλλήλοις παρακελευόμενοι μηδένα ζωγρεῖν, καὶ πλείους
ἀνεῖλον τῶν ἑξακισχιλίων, ὡς Τίμαιος, ὡς δ'
6 Ἔφορός φησι, δισμυρίων. ὁ δ' Ἀννίβας ὁρῶν
τοὺς ἰδίους καταπονουμένους, κατεβίβασε τοὺς ἐπὶ
τῶν λόφων κατεστρατοπεδευκότας, καὶ παρα-
βοηθήσας τοῖς ἐλαττουμένοις κατέλαβε τοὺς Ἱμεραίους ἐν οὐδεμιᾷ τάξει τὸν διωγμὸν ποιουμένους.
7 γενομένης δὲ μάχης καρτερᾶς τὸ μὲν πλῆθος
τῶν Ἱμεραίων πρὸς φυγὴν ὥρμησε,[2] τρισχίλιοι δ'
αὐτῶν ὑποστάντες τὴν τῶν Καρχηδονίων δύναμιν,
καὶ πολλὰ δράσαντες, ἅπαντες ἀνηρέθησαν.

61. Τῆς δὲ μάχης ταύτης ἤδη τέλος ἐχούσης
κατέπλευσαν πρὸς τὴν Ἱμέραν πέντε πρὸς ταῖς
εἴκοσι τριήρεις παρὰ τῶν Σικελιωτῶν, ἃς πρότερον

---

[1] ἂν after κρατήσειαν deleted by Reiske.
[2] ὥρμησε] ὥρμησαν PFJ, ὥρμησεν cet.

vailing in the battle, at the outset they slew the first
opponents. And since the multitude of the barbarians thronged together in great disorder because
they never would have expected that the besieged
would dare such a move, they were under no little
disadvantage ; for when eighty thousand men
streamed together without order into one place, the
result was that the barbarians clashed with each other
and suffered more heavily from themselves than from
the enemy. The Himeraeans, having as spectators
on the walls parents and children as well as all their
relatives, spent their own lives unsparingly for the
salvation of them all. And since they fought brilliantly, the barbarians, dismayed by their deeds of
daring and unexpected resistance, turned in flight.
They fled in disorder to the troops encamped on the
hills, and the Himeraeans pressed hard upon them,
crying out to each other to take no man captive, and
they slew more than six thousand of them, according
to Timaeus, or, as Ephorus states, more than twenty
thousand. But Hannibal, seeing that his men were
becoming exhausted, brought down his troops who
were encamped on the hills, and reinforcing his beaten
soldiers caught the Himeraeans in disorder as they
were pushing the pursuit. In the fierce battle which
ensued the main body of the Himeraeans turned in
flight, but three thousand of them who tried to oppose
the Carthaginian army, though they accomplished
great deeds, were slain to a man.

61. This battle had already come to an end when
there arrived at Himera from the Sicilian Greeks the
twenty-five triremes which had previously been sent

μὲν ἀπεστάλκεισαν τοῖς Λακεδαιμονίοις ἐπὶ συμμαχίαν, τότε δ' ἀνέστρεψαν ἀπὸ τῆς στρατείας.
2 διεδόθη δὲ καὶ φήμη τις κατὰ τὴν πόλιν ὅτι
Συρακόσιοι μὲν πανδημεὶ μετὰ τῶν συμμάχων
πορεύονται τοῖς Ἱμεραίοις βοηθεῖν, Ἀννίβας δὲ
μέλλοι τὰς ἐν Μοτύῃ τριήρεις πληροῦν τῶν κρατίστων ἀνδρῶν καὶ περιπλεύσας ἐπὶ Συρακούσας
ἔρημον τὴν πόλιν τῶν ἀμυνομένων καταλαβέσθαι.
3 διόπερ Διοκλῆς ὁ τῶν ἐν Ἱμέρᾳ στρατηγὸς συνεβούλευσε τοῖς ναυάρχοις τὴν ταχίστην ἐκπλεῖν εἰς
Συρακούσας, ἵνα μὴ συμβῇ κατὰ κράτος ἁλῶναι
τὴν πόλιν, ἀπόντων[1] ἐν τῇ μάχῃ τῶν κρατίστων
4 ἀνδρῶν. διόπερ ἐφαίνετο συμφέρειν αὐτοῖς ἐκλιπεῖν τὴν πόλιν καὶ τοὺς μὲν ἡμίσεις εἰς τὰς τριήρεις
ἐμβιβάσαι—ταύτας γὰρ κατακομεῖν αὐτούς, μέχρι
ἂν ἐκτὸς τῆς Ἱμεραίας γένωνται χώρας—, τοῖς
δ' ἡμίσεσι τηρεῖν, ἕως ἂν πάλιν αἱ τριήρεις ἐπι-
5 στρέψωσιν. τῶν δ' Ἱμεραίων σχετλιαζόντων μὲν
ἐπὶ τοῖς λεγομένοις, οὐκ ἐχόντων δὲ ὃ πράξειαν
ἕτερον, αἱ μὲν τριήρεις νυκτὸς ἐπληροῦντο κατὰ
σπουδὴν ἀναμὶξ γυναικῶν τε καὶ παίδων, ἔτι δὲ
τῶν ἄλλων σωμάτων,[2] ἐπὶ τούτων ἀποπλεόντων
6 ὡς ἐπὶ Μεσσήνην· Διοκλῆς δὲ τοὺς ἰδίους στρατιώτας ἀναλαβὼν καὶ τοὺς πεσόντας ἐν τῇ μάχῃ
καταλιπών, ὥρμησεν ἐπ' οἴκου τὴν πορείαν ποιούμενος. πολλοὶ δὲ τῶν Ἱμεραίων μετὰ τέκνων
καὶ γυναικῶν ἐξώρμησαν σὺν τοῖς περὶ τὸν Διοκλῆν,
μὴ δυναμένων χωρῆσαι τῶν τριήρων τὸν ὄχλον.

62. Οἱ δ' ἐν τῇ πόλει καταλειφθέντες διενυκτέρευον μὲν ἐν τοῖς ὅπλοις ἐπὶ τῶν τειχῶν· ἅμα δ'

---

[1] ἀπόντων Wurm : ἀπολωλότων. Vogel suggests πόλιν.
ἀπολωλότων δ' ἐν τῇ μ. τ. κ. ἀνδρῶν ἐφαίνετο κτλ.

to aid the Lacedaemonians [1] but at this time had re- 409 B.C.
turned from the campaign.   And a report also spread
through the city that the Syracusans *en masse* together with their allies were on the march to the aid
of the Himeraeans and that Hannibal was preparing
to man his triremes in Motyê with his choicest troops
and, sailing to Syracuse, seize that city while it was
stripped of its defenders.   Consequently Diocles, who
commanded the forces in Himera, advised the admirals of the fleet to set sail with all speed for
Syracuse, in order that it might not happen that the
city should be taken by storm while its best troops
were fighting a war abroad.   They decided, therefore,
that their best course was to abandon the city, and
that they should embark half the populace on the
triremes (for these would convey them until they had
got beyond Himeraean territory) and with the other
half keep guard until the triremes should return.
Although the Himeraeans complained indignantly at
this conclusion, since there was no other course they
could take, the triremes were hastily loaded by night
with a mixed throng of women and children and of
other inhabitants also, who sailed on them as far as
Messenê ;   and Diocles, taking his own soldiers and
leaving behind the bodies of those who had fallen in
the fighting, set forth upon the journey home.[2]   And
many Himeraeans with children and wives set out
with Diocles, since the triremes could not carry the
whole populace.

62. Those who had been left behind in Himera
spent the night under arms on the walls ;   and when

---

[1] Cp. chaps. 34. 4 ; 40. 5 ; 63. 1.   [2] To Syracuse.

[2] καὶ after σωμάτων PFK, omitted *cet.*   Vogel suggests
καὶ . . . ἀπέπλεον.

ἡμέρᾳ τῶν Καρχηδονίων περιστρατοπεδευσάντων
τὴν πόλιν καὶ πυκνὰς προσβολὰς ποιουμένων, οἱ
καταλειφθέντες τῶν Ἱμεραίων ἀφειδῶς ἠγωνίζοντο,
2 προσδοκῶντες τὴν τῶν νεῶν παρουσίαν. ἐκείνην
μὲν οὖν τὴν ἡμέραν διεκαρτέρησαν, τῇ δ' ὑστεραίᾳ
τῶν τριήρων ἐπιφαινομένων ἤδη συνέβαινε τὸ μὲν
τεῖχος πεσεῖν ὑπὸ τῶν μηχανῶν, τοὺς δ' Ἴβηρας
ἀθρόους παρεισπεσεῖν εἰς τὴν πόλιν. τῶν δὲ βαρβάρων οἱ μὲν ἠμύνοντο τοὺς παραβοηθοῦντας τῶν
Ἱμεραίων, οἱ δὲ καταλαμβανόμενοι τὰ τείχη παρ-
3 εδέχοντο τοὺς ἰδίους. κατὰ κράτος οὖν ἁλούσης τῆς
πόλεως, ἐπὶ πολὺν χρόνον οἱ βάρβαροι πάντας ἐφόνευον τοὺς καταλαμβανομένους ἀσυμπαθῶς. τοῦ δ'
Ἀννίβα ζωγρεῖν παραγγείλαντος ὁ μὲν φόνος ἔλη-
4 ξεν, ἡ δ' ἐκ τῶν οἰκιῶν εὐδαιμονία διεφορεῖτο. ὁ δ'
Ἀννίβας τὰ μὲν ἱερὰ συλήσας καὶ τοὺς καταφυγόντας ἱκέτας ἀποσπάσας ἐνέπρησε, καὶ τὴν πόλιν εἰς
ἔδαφος κατέσκαψεν, οἰκισθεῖσαν ἔτη διακόσια τεσ-
σαράκοντα· τῶν δ' αἰχμαλώτων γυναῖκας καὶ[1] παῖδας διαδοὺς εἰς τὸ στρατόπεδον παρεφύλαττε, τῶν
δ' ἀνδρῶν τοὺς ἁλόντας εἰς τρισχιλίους ὄντας παρ-
ήγαγεν ἐπὶ τὸν τόπον ἐν ᾧ πρότερον Ἀμίλκας ὁ
πάππος αὐτοῦ ὑπὸ Γέλωνος ἀνῃρέθη, καὶ πάντας
5 αἰκισάμενος κατέσφαξεν. μετὰ δὲ ταῦτα διαλύσας
τὸ στρατόπεδον, τοὺς μὲν ἀπὸ Σικελίας συμμάχους
ἀπέστειλεν εἰς τὰς πατρίδας, μεθ' ὧν καὶ Καμπανοὶ
συνηκολούθησαν ἐγκαλοῦντες[2] τοῖς Καρχηδονίοις
ὡς αἰτιώτατοι μὲν τῶν εὐημερημάτων γεγενημένοι,
οὐκ ἀξίας δὲ χάριτας εἰληφότες τῶν πεπραγμένων·

[1] καὶ PAF, τε καὶ cet.
[2] μὲν after ἐγκαλοῦντες deleted by Dindorf; Wurm suggests μέντοι.

294

with the coming of day the Carthaginians surrounded 409 B.C.
the city and launched repeated attacks, the remaining
Himeraeans fought with no thought for their lives,
expecting the arrival of the ships. For that day,
therefore, they continued to hold out, but on the next,
even when the triremes were already in sight, it so
happened that the wall began to fall before the blows
of the siege-engines and the Iberians to pour in a
body into the city. Some of the barbarians thereupon
would hold off the Himeraeans who rushed up to bring
aid, while others, gaining command of the walls, would
help their comrades get in. Now that the city had
been taken by storm, for a long time the barbarians
continued, with no sign of compassion, to slaughter
everyone they seized. But when Hannibal issued
orders to take prisoners, although the slaughter
stopped, the wealth of the dwellings now became
the objects of plunder. Hannibal, after sacking the
temples and dragging out the suppliants who had fled
to them for safety, set them afire, and the city he
razed to the ground, two hundred and forty years
after its founding. Of the captives the women and
children he distributed among the army and kept
them under guard, but the men whom he took
captive, some three thousand, he led to the spot where
once his grandfather Hamilcar had been slain by
Gelon [1] and after torturing them put them all to death.
After this, breaking up his army, he sent the Sicilian
allies back to their countries, and accompanying them
also were the Campanians, who bitterly complained
to the Carthaginians that, though they had been the
ones chiefly responsible for the Carthaginian successes,
the rewards they had received were not a fair return

[1] Cp. Book 11. 22.

6 ὁ δ' Ἀννίβας εἰς τὰς μακρὰς ναῦς καὶ φορτηγοὺς ἐμβιβάσας τὴν δύναμιν, καὶ τοὺς ἱκανοὺς τοῖς συμμάχοις ἀπολιπὼν στρατιώτας, ἐξέπλευσεν ἐκ τῆς Σικελίας. ἐπεὶ δ' εἰς Καρχηδόνα κατέπλευσε μετὰ πολλῶν λαφύρων, ἀπήντων αὐτῷ πάντες δεξιούμενοι καὶ τιμῶντες ὡς ἐν ὀλίγῳ χρόνῳ μείζονα πράξαντα τῶν πρότερον στρατηγῶν.

63. Εἰς δὲ τὴν Σικελίαν κατέπλευσεν Ἑρμοκράτης ὁ Συρακόσιος. οὗτος δ' ἐν μὲν τῷ πρὸς Ἀθηναίους πολέμῳ στρατηγήσας καὶ πολλὰ τῇ πατρίδι χρήσιμος γενόμενος πλεῖστον ἴσχυσε παρὰ τοῖς Συρακοσίοις, μετὰ δὲ ταῦτα ναύαρχος πεμφθεὶς σὺν τριάκοντα πέντε τριήρεσι Λακεδαιμονίοις συμμαχήσων ὑπὸ τῶν ἀντιπολιτευομένων κατεστασιάσθη, καὶ φυγῆς μὲν ἐγενήθη κατάδικος, τὸν δὲ στόλον παρέδωκεν ἐν Πελοποννήσῳ[1] τοῖς ἐπὶ τὴν

2 διαδοχὴν ἀποσταλεῖσιν. αὐτὸς δ' ἐκ τῆς στρατείας φιλίαν ἔχων πρὸς Φαρνάβαζον τὸν τῶν Περσῶν σατράπην ἔλαβε παρ' αὐτοῦ πολλὰ χρήματα, μεθ' ὧν εἰς Μεσσήνην καταπλεύσας πέντε μὲν ἐναυπήγησε τριήρεις, χιλίους δ' ἐμισθώσατο στρατιώτας.

3 παραλαβὼν δὲ καὶ τῶν ἐκπεπτωκότων Ἱμεραίων ὡς χιλίους, ἐπεχείρησε μὲν εἰς Συρακούσας κατελθεῖν συναγωνιζομένων αὐτῷ τῶν φίλων, ἀποτυχὼν δὲ τῆς ἐπιβολῆς ὥρμησε διὰ τῆς μεσογείου, καὶ καταλαβόμενος τὸν Σελινοῦντα[2] τῆς πόλεως μέρος ἐτείχισε καὶ πανταχόθεν κατεκάλει τοὺς διασωζο-

---

[1] Πελοποννήσῳ] Ἑλλησπόντῳ (cp. Xen. Hell. 1. 1. 31) Wesseling.   [2] καὶ after Σελινοῦντα deleted by Reiske.

for their accomplishments. Then Hannibal embarked 409 B.C.
his army on the warships and merchant vessels, and
leaving behind sufficient troops for the needs of his
allies he set sail from Sicily.   And when he arrived at
Carthage with much booty, the whole city came out to
meet him, paying him homage and honour as one who
in a brief time had performed greater deeds than any
general before him.

63. Hermocrates the Syracusan arrived in Sicily.
This man, who had served as general in the war
against the Athenians and had been of great service
to his country, had acquired the greatest influence
among the Syracusans, but afterwards, when he had
been sent as admiral in command of thirty-five triremes to support the Lacedaemonians,[1] he was overpowered by his political opponents and, upon being
condemned to exile, he handed over the fleet in
the Peloponnesus [2] to the men who had been dispatched to succeed him.   And since he had struck
up a friendship with Pharnabazus, the satrap of the
Persians, as a result of the campaign, he accepted
from him a great sum of money with which, after he
had arrived at Messenê, he had five triremes built and
hired a thousand soldiers.   Then, after adding to this
force also about a thousand of the Himeraeans who
had been driven from their home, he endeavoured
with the aid of his friends to make good his return to
Syracuse ; but when he failed in this design, he set
out through the middle of the island and seizing
Selinus he built a wall about a part of the city and
called to him from all quarters the Selinuntians who

[1] Cp. chap. 34. 4.
[2] Xenophon (*Hell.* 1. 1. 31) states that the new commanders took over the Syracusan ships and troops at Miletus.

4 μένους τῶν Σελινουντίων. πολλοὺς δὲ καὶ ἄλλους
ὑποδεχόμενος εἰς τὸν τόπον συνήγαγε δύναμιν ἐπιλέκτων ἀνδρῶν ἑξακισχιλίων. ἐντεῦθεν δ' ὁρμώ-
μενος πρῶτον μὲν τὴν τῶν Μοτυηνῶν ἐπόρθησε
χώραν, καὶ τοὺς ἐπεξελθόντας ἐκ τῆς πόλεως
μάχῃ[1] κρατήσας πολλοὺς μὲν ἀνεῖλε, τοὺς δ'
ἄλλους συνεδίωξεν ἐντὸς τοῦ τείχους. μετὰ δὲ
ταῦτα τὴν[2] τῶν Πανορμιτῶν χώραν λεηλατήσας
ἀναριθμήτου λείας ἐκυρίευσε, τῶν δὲ Πανορμιτῶν
πανδημεὶ παραταξαμένων πρὸ τῆς πόλεως εἰς
πεντακοσίους μὲν αὐτῶν ἀνεῖλε τοὺς δ' ἄλλους
5 συνέκλεισεν ἐντὸς τῶν τειχῶν. παραπλησίως δὲ
καὶ τὴν ἄλλην χώραν ἅπασαν τὴν ὑπὸ Καρχηδονίους οὖσαν πορθῶν ἐπαίνου παρὰ τοῖς Σικελιώταις ἐτύγχανεν. εὐθὺ δὲ καὶ τῶν Συρακοσίων οἱ
πλεῖστοι μετεμελήθησαν, ἀναξίως τῆς ἰδίας ἀρετῆς
6 ὁρῶντες πεφυγαδευμένον τὸν Ἑρμοκράτην. διὸ
καὶ περὶ αὐτοῦ πολλῶν λόγων γινομένων ἐν ταῖς
ἐκκλησίαις, ὁ μὲν δῆμος φανερὸς ἦν βουλόμενος
καταδέχεσθαι τὸν ἄνδρα, ὁ δ' Ἑρμοκράτης ἀκούων
τὴν περὶ αὐτοῦ φήμην ἐν ταῖς Συρακούσαις παρ-
εσκευάζετο πρὸς τὴν αὐτοῦ[3] κάθοδον ἐπιμελῶς,
εἰδὼς τοὺς ἀντιπολιτευομένους ἀντιπράξοντας.

Καὶ τὰ μὲν κατὰ Σικελίαν ἐν τούτοις ἦν.

64. Κατὰ δὲ τὴν Ἑλλάδα Θρασύβουλος πεμφθεὶς παρ' Ἀθηναίων μετὰ νεῶν τριάκοντα καὶ
πολλῶν ὁπλιτῶν σὺν ἱππεῦσιν ἑκατὸν κατέπλευσεν
εἰς τὴν Ἔφεσον· ἐκβιβάσας δὲ τὴν δύναμιν κατὰ
δύο τόπους προσβολὰς ἐποιήσατο. τῶν δ' ἔνδον

---

[1] So Reiske : μάχῃ τε.   [2] So Eichstädt : τήν τε.
[3] So Dindorf : αὐτοῦ FJK, αὐτῆς P, αὐτὴν cet.

were still alive.[1] He also received many others into ^{409 B.C.} the place and thus gathered a force of six thousand picked warriors. Making Selinus his base he first laid waste the territory of the inhabitants of Motyê [2] and defeating in battle those who came out from the city against him he slew many and pursued the rest within the wall of the city. After this he ravaged the territory of the people of Panormus [3] and acquired countless booty, and when the inhabitants offered battle *en masse* before the city he slew about five hundred of them and shut up the rest within their walls. And since he also laid waste in like fashion all the rest of the territory in the hands of the Carthaginians, he won the commendation of the Sicilian Greeks. And at once the majority of the Syracusans also repented of their treatment of him, realizing that Hermocrates had been banished contrary to the merits of his valour. Consequently, after much discussion of him in meetings of the assembly, it was evident that the people desired to receive the man back from exile, and Hermocrates, on hearing of the talk about himself that was current in Syracuse, laid careful plans regarding his return from exile, knowing that his political opponents would work against it.

Such was the course of events in Sicily.

64. In Greece Thrasybulus,[4] who had been sent out by the Athenians with thirty ships and a strong force of hoplites as well as a hundred horsemen, put in at Ephesus ; and after disembarking his troops at two points he launched assaults upon the city. The in-

---

[1] Hermocrates is carrying on his own war against that part of Sicily held by the Carthaginians.
[2] Cp. chap. 54. 5.   [3] Modern Palermo.
[4] Thrasyllus, according to Xenophon, *Hell.* 1. 2. 6 ff. The account is resumed from the end of chapter 53.

ἐπεξελθόντων καρτερὰν συνέβη μάχην συστῆναι·
πανδημεὶ δὲ τῶν Ἐφεσίων ἀγωνισαμένων τετρα-
κόσιοι μὲν τῶν Ἀθηναίων ἔπεσον, τοὺς δ᾽ ἄλλους
ὁ Θρασύβουλος ἀναλαβὼν εἰς τὰς ναῦς ἐξέπλευ-
2 σεν εἰς Λέσβον. οἱ δὲ περὶ Κύζικον ὄντες τῶν
Ἀθηναίων στρατηγοὶ πλεύσαντες ἐπὶ Χαλκηδόνα,
Χρυσόπολιν ᾤκισαν φρούριον καὶ τὴν ἱκανὴν αὐτῷ
κατέλιπον δύναμιν· τοῖς δ᾽ ἐπὶ τούτων καταστα-
θεῖσι προσέταξαν δεκάτην πράττεσθαι τοὺς ἐκ τοῦ
3 Πόντου πλέοντας. μετὰ δὲ ταῦτα διελομένων
αὐτῶν τὰς δυνάμεις, Θηραμένης μὲν μετὰ πεντήκοντα νεῶν κατελείφθη πολιορκήσων Χαλκηδόνα
καὶ Βυζάντιον, Θρασύβουλος δὲ περὶ Θράκην
πεμφθεὶς τὰς ἐν τούτοις τοῖς τόποις πόλεις προσ-
4 ηγάγετο. Ἀλκιβιάδης δὲ τὸν Θρασύβουλον μετὰ
τῶν τριάκοντα νεῶν ἀπολύσας[1] ἔπλευσεν εἰς τὴν
ὑπὸ Φαρνάβαζον χώραν, καὶ κοινῇ πολλὴν αὐτῆς πορθήσαντες τούς τε στρατιώτας ἐνέπλησαν
ὠφελείας καὶ αὐτοὶ χρήματα συνήγαγον ἐκ τῶν
λαφύρων, βουλόμενοι κουφίσαι τὸν δῆμον τῶν
εἰσφορῶν.
5 Λακεδαιμόνιοι δὲ πυνθανόμενοι περὶ τὸν Ἑλλήσποντον ὑπάρχειν ἁπάσας τὰς τῶν Ἀθηναίων
δυνάμεις, ἐστράτευσαν ἐπὶ Πύλον, ἣν Μεσσήνιοι

---

[1] ἀπολύσας] ἀπολήψας Palmer, ἀποκαλέσας Reiske.

---

[1] Cp. p. 299, n. 4.
[2] On the Hellespont opposite Byzantium.
[3] Editors have been troubled by ἀπολύσας (cp. critical note),
here translated as " give a separate command," by pressing
the meaning of the word in the sense of " dismiss," whereas
both Alcibiades and Thrasyllus were later engaged together

habitants came out of the city against them and a
fierce battle ensued ; and since the entire populace
of the Ephesians joined in the fighting, four hundred
Athenians were slain and the remainder Thrasybulus [1] took aboard his ships and sailed off to Lesbos.
The Athenian generals who were in the neighbourhood of Cyzicus, sailing to Chalcedon,[2] established
there the fortress of Chrysopolis and left an adequate
force behind ; and the officers in charge they ordered
to collect a tenth from all merchants sailing out of
the Pontus. After this they divided their forces and
Theramenes was left behind with fifty ships with
which to lay siege to Chalcedon and Byzantium, and
Thrasybulus was sent to Thrace, where he brought the
cities in those regions over to the Athenians. And
Alcibiades, after giving Thrasybulus [1] a separate command [3] with the thirty ships, sailed to the territory
held by Pharnabazus, and when they had conjointly
laid waste a great amount of that territory, they not
only sated the soldiers with plunder but also themselves realized money from the booty, since they
wished to relieve the Athenian people of the property-
taxes imposed for the prosecution of the war.

When the Lacedaemonians learned that all the
armaments of the Athenians were in the region of the
Hellespont, they undertook a campaign against Pylos,
which the Messenians held with a garrison ; on the

in the raiding of Persian territory. But the word can also
mean no more than " separate," as when a man " separates "
(divorces) his wife. Xenophon (*Hell.* 1. 2. 15 ff.) states that
the troops of Alcibiades refused at first to join with those of
Thrasyllus because the latter had just suffered defeat before
Ephesus, but later agreed to the union of the two armies after
the successful raids. What Alcibiades probably did was to
send Thrasyllus ahead, and the generals operated separately
for a time.

φρουρᾷ κατεῖχον, κατὰ μὲν θάλατταν ἕνδεκα ναυσίν, ὧν ἦσαν αἱ μὲν ἀπὸ Σικελίας πέντε, ἓξ δὲ¹
ἐκ τῶν πολιτῶν πεπληρωμέναι· πεζῇ δὲ παρ-
ήγαγον ἱκανὴν δύναμιν, καὶ περιστρατοπεδεύσαντες
τὸ φρούριον ἐπόρθουν² ἅμα καὶ κατὰ γῆν καὶ κατὰ
6 θάλατταν. ἃ δὴ πυθόμενος ὁ τῶν Ἀθηναίων
δῆμος ἐξαπέστειλε τοῖς πολιορκουμένοις εἰς βοήθειαν ναῦς τριάκοντα καὶ στρατηγὸν Ἄνυτον τὸν
Ἀνθεμίωνος. οὗτος μὲν οὖν ἐκπλεύσας, καὶ διά
τινας χειμῶνας οὐ δυνηθεὶς τὸν Μαλέαν κάμψαι,
ἀνέπλευσεν³ εἰς Ἀθήνας. ἐφ᾽ οἷς ὁ μὲν δῆμος
ὀργισθεὶς καὶ καταιτιασάμενος αὐτοῦ προδοσίαν,
μετέστησεν εἰς κρίσιν· ὁ δ᾽ Ἄνυτος ἰσχυρῶς κινδυνεύων ἐρρύσατο χρήμασι τὴν ἰδίαν ψυχήν, καὶ
πρῶτος Ἀθηναίων δοκεῖ δικαστήριον δωροδοκῆσαι.
7 οἱ δ᾽ ἐν τῇ Πύλῳ Μεσσήνιοι μέχρι μέν τινος ἀντεῖχον, προσδοκῶντες παρὰ τῶν Ἀθηναίων βοή-
θειαν· ὡς δ᾽ οἱ μὲν πολέμιοι τὰς προσβολὰς ἐκ
διαδοχῆς ἐποιοῦντο τῶν δὲ ἰδίων οἱ μὲν ἐκ τῶν
τραυμάτων ἀπέθνησκον, οἱ δ᾽ ἐκ τῆς σιτοδείας
κακῶς ἀπήλλαττον, ὑπόσπονδοι τὸν τόπον ἐξέλιπον. Λακεδαιμόνιοι μὲν οὖν ἐγκρατεῖς ἐγένοντο
τῆς Πύλου, πεντεκαίδεκα ἔτη τῶν Ἀθηναίων αὐτὴν κατεσχηκότων, ἀφ᾽ ὅτου Δημοσθένης αὐτὴν
ἐτείχισεν.

65. Τούτων δὲ πραττομένων Μεγαρεῖς μὲν Νίσαιαν ὑπ᾽ Ἀθηναίους οὖσαν εἷλον, Ἀθηναῖοι δ᾽ ἐπ᾽
αὐτοὺς ἀπέστειλαν Λεωτροφίδην καὶ Τίμαρχον μετὰ
μὲν πεζῶν χιλίων, ἱππέων δὲ τετρακοσίων. οἷς οἱ
Μεγαρεῖς ἀπαντήσαντες μετὰ τῶν ὅπλων πανδημεὶ

¹ πέντε, ἓξ δὲ Wesseling, ἐκ PF, πέντε ἐκ cet.
² ἐπόρθουν] Capps suggests ἐπώθουν, Post ἐπολιόρκουν.

sea they had eleven ships, of which five were from
Sicily and six were manned by their own citizens,
while on land they had gathered an adequate army,
and after investing the fortress they began to wreak
havoc [1] both by land and by sea. As soon as the
Athenian people learned of this they dispatched to
the aid of the besieged thirty ships and as general
Anytus [2] the son of Anthemion. Now Anytus sailed
out on his mission, but when he was unable to round
Cape Malea because of storms he returned to Athens.
The people were so incensed at this that they accused
him of treason and brought him to trial ; but Anytus,
being in great danger, saved his own life by the use
of money, and he is reputed to have been the first
Athenian to have bribed a jury. Meanwhile the
Messenians in Pylos held out for some time, awaiting
aid from the Athenians ; but since the enemy kept
launching successive assaults and of their own number
some were dying of wounds and others were reduced
to sad straits for lack of food, they abandoned the
place under a truce. And so the Lacedaemonians
became masters of Pylos, after the Athenians had
held it fifteen years from the time Demosthenes had
fortified it.[3]

65. While these events were taking place, the
Megarians seized Nisaea, which was in the hands
of Athenians, and the Athenians dispatched against
them Leotrophides and Timarchus with a thousand
infantry and four hundred cavalry. The Megarians
went out to meet them *en masse* under arms, and after

---

[1] Or " to press the Messenians hard " (cp. critical note).
[2] Later one of the accusers of Socrates.
[3] Cp. Book 12. 63. 5.

---

[3] So Hertlein : ἀπέπλευσεν.

καὶ παραλαβόντες τινὰς τῶν ἐκ Σικελίας, παρετά-
ξαντο πρὸς τοῖς λόφοις τοῖς Κέρασι καλουμένοις·
2 τῶν δ' Ἀθηναίων λαμπρῶς ἀγωνισαμένων, καὶ
πολλαπλασίους ὄντας τοὺς πολεμίους τρεψαμένων,
Μεγαρέων ἔπεσον μὲν πολλοί, τῶν δὲ Λακεδαι-
μονίων¹ εἴκοσι μόνον· οἱ γὰρ Ἀθηναῖοι βαρέως
φέροντες ἐπὶ τῷ τὴν Νίσαιαν κατειλῆφθαι τοὺς
μὲν Λακεδαιμονίους¹ οὐκ ἐδίωξαν, πρὸς δὲ τοὺς
Μεγαρεῖς χαλεπῶς διακείμενοι παμπληθεῖς ἀνεῖλον.
3 Λακεδαιμόνιοι δὲ Κρατησιππίδαν ἑλόμενοι ναύαρχον, καὶ παρὰ τῶν συμμάχων ναῦς αὐτῶν πληρώσαντες εἴκοσι πέντε, προσέταξαν παραβοηθεῖν
τοῖς συμμάχοις. οὗτος δὲ χρόνον μέν τινα περὶ
τὴν Ἰωνίαν διέτριψεν οὐθὲν ἄξιον λόγου πράξας·
μετὰ δὲ ταῦτα παρὰ τῶν ἐκ Χίου φυγάδων λαβὼν
χρήματα κατήγαγεν αὐτοὺς καὶ τὴν ἀκρόπολιν τῶν
4 Χίων κατελάβετο. οἱ δὲ κατελθόντες τῶν Χίων
τοὺς ἀντιπολιτευομένους αὐτοῖς καὶ τῆς ἐκπτώσεως αἰτίους ὄντας² εἰς ἑξακοσίους τὸν ἀριθμὸν ὄντας ἐφυγάδευσαν. οὗτοι δὲ τῆς ἀντιπέραν ἠπείρου
χωρίον Ἀταρνέα καλούμενον κατελάβοντο, σφόδρα
τῇ φύσει καθεστηκὸς ὀχυρόν, καὶ τὸ λοιπὸν ἐκ
τούτου τὰς ἀφορμὰς ἔχοντες ἐπολέμουν τοῖς Χίον³
ἔχουσιν.
66. Τούτων δὲ πραττομένων Ἀλκιβιάδης καὶ
Θρασύβουλος Λάμψακον⁴ τειχίσαντες, ἐν μὲν ταύτῃ
τὴν ἱκανὴν φυλακὴν κατέλιπον, αὐτοὶ δὲ μετὰ τῆς

¹ For Λακεδαιμονίων and Λακεδαιμονίους Vogel suggests
Σικελιωτῶν and Σικελιώτας respectively.
² τοὺς ἀντιπολιτευομένους Dindorf, αἰτίους ὄντας H, τῶν ἀντιπολιτευομένων αὐτοῖς κ. τ. ἐκπτώσεως εἰς ἑξακοσίους cet.
³ τοῖς Χίον Rhodoman, τὸ ἴσχιον PA, τοῖς τὸ ἴσχιον cet.
⁴ So Palmer (cp. ch. 104. 8): λάβδακον.

adding to their number some of the troops from Sicily ^{409 B.C.} they drew up for battle near the hills called " The Cerata." [1]   Since the Athenians fought brilliantly and put to flight the enemy, who greatly outnumbered them, many of the Megarians were slain but only twenty Lacedaemonians [2] ; for the Athenians, made angry by the seizure of Nisaea, did not pursue the Lacedaemonians but slew great numbers of the Megarians with whom they were indignant.

The Lacedaemonians, having chosen Cratesippidas as admiral and manned twenty-five of their own ships with troops furnished by their allies, ordered them to go to the aid of their allies.   Cratesippidas spent some time near Ionia without accomplishing anything worthy of mention ; but later, after receiving money from the exiles of Chios, he restored them to their homes and seized the acropolis of the Chians.   And the returned exiles of the Chians banished the men who were their political opponents and had been responsible for their exile to the number of approximately six hundred.   These men then seized a place called Atarneus on the opposite mainland, which was by nature extremely rugged, and henceforth, from that as their base, continued to make war on their opponents who held Chios.

66. While these events were taking place Alcibiades and Thrasybulus,[3] after fortifying Lampsacus, left a strong garrison in that place and themselves sailed

[1] " The Horns," lying opposite Salamis on the border between Attica and Megara (cp. Strabo, 9. 1. 11).

[2] Perhaps here and just below " Sicilian Greeks " should be read for " Lacedaemonians," since the latter have not been mentioned as being present (cp. critical note).

[3] Thrasyllus (cp. p. 299, n. 4).

δυνάμεως ἐξέπλευσαν πρὸς Θηραμένην, ὃς ἐπόρθει
τὴν Χαλκηδόνα ναῦς μὲν ἔχων ἑβδομήκοντα, στρατιώτας δὲ πεντακισχιλίους. ἀθροισθεισῶν δὲ τῶν
δυνάμεων εἰς ἕνα τόπον ἀπετείχισαν τὴν πόλιν ἀπὸ
2 θαλάττης εἰς θάλατταν ξυλίνῳ τείχει. ὁ δ' ἐν τῇ
πόλει καθεσταμένος[1] ὑπὸ Λακεδαιμονίων Ἱπποκράτης ἡγεμών, ὃν οἱ Λάκωνες ἁρμοστὴν ἐκάλουν,
τούς τ' ἰδίους στρατιώτας προσήγαγε καὶ τοὺς
Χαλκηδονίους ἅπαντας. γενομένης δὲ καρτερᾶς
μάχης, καὶ τῶν περὶ τὸν Ἀλκιβιάδην ἐρρωμένως
ἀγωνισαμένων, ὅ τε Ἱπποκράτης ἔπεσε καὶ τῶν
λοιπῶν οἱ μὲν ἀνῃρέθησαν, οἱ δὲ κατατρωθέντες
3 συνέφυγον εἰς τὴν πόλιν. μετὰ δὲ ταῦτα Ἀλκιβιάδης μὲν εἰς Ἑλλήσποντον καὶ Χερρόνησον ἐξέπλευσε, βουλόμενος ἀθροῖσαι χρήματα, οἱ δὲ περὶ
τὸν Θηραμένην ὁμολογίαν ἐποιήσαντο πρὸς Χαλκηδονίους φόρον λαμβάνειν παρ' αὐτῶν ὅσον καὶ
πρότερον. ἐντεῦθεν δὲ τὰς δυνάμεις ἀπαγαγόντες πρὸς Βυζάντιον ἐπολιόρκουν τὴν πόλιν καὶ
μετὰ πολλῆς σπουδῆς ἀποτειχίζειν ἐπεχείρησαν.
4 Ἀλκιβιάδης δὲ ἀθροίσας χρήματα πολλοὺς αὑτῷ
τῶν Θρακῶν ἔπεισε συστρατεῦσαι, παρέλαβε δὲ
καὶ τοὺς Χερρόνησον οἰκοῦντας πανδημεί, καὶ μετὰ
πάσης τῆς[2] δυνάμεως ἀναζεύξας πρῶτον μὲν Ση-
λυβρίαν διὰ προδοσίας εἷλεν, ἐξ ἧς πολλὰ χρήματα
πραξάμενος ἐν μὲν ταύτῃ φρουρὰν κατέλιπεν, αὐτὸς δὲ διὰ τάχους ἧκε πρὸς τοὺς περὶ Θηραμένην
5 εἰς Βυζάντιον. ἀθροισθεισῶν δὲ τῶν δυνάμεων,
οὗτοι μὲν τὰ πρὸς πολιορκίαν ἡτοιμάζοντο· ἤμελλον γὰρ νικήσειν πόλιν βάρος ἔχουσαν καὶ γέμουσαν τῶν ὑπὲρ αὐτῆς ἀμυνομένων· χωρὶς γὰρ τῶν

---

[1] So Dindorf: καθιστάμενος.

with their force to Theramenes, who was laying waste Chalcedon with seventy ships and five thousand soldiers. And when the armaments had been brought together into one place they threw a wooden stockade about the city from sea to sea.[1] Hippocrates, who had been stationed by the Lacedaemonians in the city as commander (the Laconians call such a man a " harmost "), led against them both his own soldiers and all the Chalcedonians. A fierce battle ensued, and since the troops of Alcibiades fought stoutly, not only Hippocrates fell but of the rest of the soldiers some were slain, and the others, disabled by wounds, took refuge in a body in the city. After this Alcibiades sailed out into the Hellespont and to Chersonesus, wishing to collect money, and Theramenes concluded an agreement with the Chalcedonians whereby the Athenians received from them as much tribute as before. Then leading his troops from there to Byzantium he laid siege to the city and with great alacrity set about walling it off. And Alcibiades, after collecting money, persuaded many of the Thracians to join his army and he also took into it the inhabitants of Chersonesus *en masse*; then, setting forth with his entire force, he first took Selybria[2] by betrayal, in which, after exacting from it much money, he left a garrison, and then himself came speedily to Theramenes at Byzantium. When the armaments had been united, the commanders began making the preparations for a siege; for they were setting out to conquer a city of great wealth which was crowded with defenders, since, not counting the

---

[1] " From sea to sea," *i.e.* from Bosporus to Propontis.
[2] Or Selymbria, modern Silivri, on the Propontis.

---

[2] τῆς added by Dindorf.

Βυζαντίων, πολλῶν ὄντων, Κλέαρχος ὁ Λακεδαιμόνιος ἁρμοστὴς εἶχε πολλοὺς ἐν τῇ πόλει τῶν
6 Πελοποννησίων καὶ μισθοφόρους. μέχρι μὲν οὖν
τινος προσβολὰς ποιούμενοι, κακὸν οὐδὲν ἀξιόλογον δρῶντες τοὺς ἔνδον διετέλουν· ἐπεὶ δ᾽ ὁ τῆς
πόλεως ἐπιστάτης ἀπῆλθε πρὸς Φαρνάβαζον, ὅπως
λάβῃ χρήματα, τηνικαῦτά τινες τῶν Βυζαντίων,
μισοῦντες τὸ βάρος τῆς ἐπιστασίας—ἦν γὰρ ὁ
Κλέαρχος χαλεπός—, προύδωκαν τὴν πόλιν τοῖς
περὶ τὸν Ἀλκιβιάδην.

67. Οὗτοι δὲ ὡς λύσοντες τὴν πολιορκίαν καὶ τὰς
δυνάμεις ἀπάξοντες εἰς Ἰωνίαν δείλης ταῖς ναυσὶ
πάσαις ἐξέπλευσαν, καὶ τὸ πεζὸν στράτευμα μέχρι
τινὸς ἀπαγαγόντες, ὡς ἐπέλαβεν ἡ νύξ, πάλιν
ὑπέστρεψαν καὶ περὶ μέσας[1] νύκτας προσέμιξαν
τῇ πόλει, καὶ τὰς μὲν τριήρεις ἀπέστειλαν προστάξαντες ἀφέλκειν τὰ πλοῖα καὶ κραυγὴν ποιεῖν, ὡς
ἁπάσης ἐκεῖ τῆς δυνάμεως οὔσης, αὐτοὶ δὲ μετὰ
τοῦ πεζοῦ στρατεύματος πρὸς τοῖς τείχεσιν ἐτή-
ρουν τὸ συντεταγμένον παρὰ τῶν ἐνδιδόντων σύσ-
2 σημον. τῶν δ᾽ ἐν ταῖς τριήρεσι ποιησάντων τὸ
προσταχθέν, καὶ τῶν πλοίων τὰ μὲν συντριβόντων[2]
ταῖς ἐμβολαῖς, τὰ δ᾽ ἀποσπᾶν πειρωμένων[3] ταῖς
σιδηραῖς χερσίν, ἔτι δὲ βοὴν ἐξαίσιον ποιούντων,
οἱ μὲν κατὰ τὴν πόλιν ὄντες Πελοποννήσιοι καὶ
πάντες οἱ τὴν ἀπάτην ἀγνοοῦντες ἐξεβοήθουν ἐπὶ
3 τοὺς λιμένας. διόπερ οἱ τὴν πόλιν προδιδόντες
ἦραν τὸ σύσσημον ἀπὸ τοῦ τείχους καὶ παρεδέ-
χοντο τοὺς περὶ τὸν Ἀλκιβιάδην διὰ τῶν κλιμά-

---

[1] τὰς after μέσας deleted by Dindorf.
[2] So Wesseling : συντριβόμενα.
[3] ἀποσπᾶν πειρωμένων Vogel : ἀπὸ τῶν χρωμένων.

Byzantines, who were many, Clearchus, the Lacedaemonian harmost, had in the city many Peloponnesians and mercenaries. Consequently, though they
kept launching assaults for some time, they continued
to inflict no notable damage on the defenders ; but
when the governor [1] left the city to visit Pharnabazus
in order to get money, thereupon certain Byzantines,
hating the severity of his administration (for Clearchus
was a harsh man), agreed to deliver up the city to
Alcibiades and his colleagues.

67. The Athenian generals, giving the impression
that they intended to raise the siege and take their
armaments to Ionia, sailed out in the afternoon with
all their ships and withdrew the land army some
distance ; but when night came, they turned back
again and about the middle of the night drew near
the city, and they dispatched the triremes with orders
to drag off the boats [2] and to raise a clamour as if the
entire force were at that point, while they themselves,
holding the land army before the walls, watched for
the signal which had been agreed upon with those
who were yielding the city. And when the crews of
the triremes set about carrying out their orders, shattering some of the boats with their rams, trying to
haul off others with their grappling irons, and all
the while raising a tremendous outcry,[3] the Peloponnesians in the city and everyone who was unaware of
the trickery rushed out to the harbours to bring aid.
Consequently the betrayers of the city raised the
signal from the wall and admitted Alcibiades' troops

---

[1] Clearchus. [2] *i.e.* the boats of the Byzantines.
[3] Xenophon (*Hell.* 1. 3. 14 ff.) does not mention this
action in the harbour.

κων κατὰ πολλὴν ἀσφάλειαν, ὡς ἂν τοῦ πλήθους
4 ἐπὶ τὸν λιμένα συνδεδραμηκότος. οἱ δὲ Πελοποννήσιοι πυθόμενοι τὸ γεγονὸς τὸ μὲν πρῶτον
τοὺς ἡμίσεις ἐπὶ τοῦ λιμένος ἀπέλιπον, τοῖς δὲ
λοιποῖς κατὰ σπουδὴν ἐξεβοήθουν ἐπὶ τὰ κατει-
5 λημμένα τείχη. ἤδη δὲ[1] σχεδὸν πάσης τῆς δυνάμεως τῶν Ἀθηναίων παρεισπεπτωκυίας, ὅμως οὐ
κατεπλάγησαν ἀλλὰ πολὺν χρόνον ἀντιστάντες
εὐρώστως τοὺς Ἀθηναίους ἠμύνοντο συναγωνιζομένων τῶν Βυζαντίων. καὶ πέρας οὐκ ἂν ἐκράτησαν Ἀθηναῖοι τῆς πόλεως διὰ μάχης, εἰ μὴ
συννοήσας τὸν καιρὸν Ἀλκιβιάδης ἐκήρυξε μηδὲν ἀδίκημα ποιεῖν τοῖς Βυζαντίοις· οὕτω γὰρ
οἱ πολιτικοὶ μεταβαλλόμενοι τοὺς Πελοποννησίους
6 ἠμύνοντο. ὅθεν οἱ πλεῖστοι μὲν αὐτῶν ἀνηρέθησαν
εὐγενῶς ἀγωνισάμενοι, οἱ δὲ περιλειφθέντες εἰς
πεντακοσίους κατέφυγον πρὸς τοὺς ἐν τοῖς ἱεροῖς
7 βωμούς. οἱ δ᾽ Ἀθηναῖοι τοῖς μὲν Βυζαντίοις
ἀπέδωκαν τὴν πόλιν, συμμάχους αὐτοὺς ποιησάμενοι, πρὸς δὲ τοὺς ἐπὶ τοῖς βωμοῖς ὄντας ἱκέτας
ὁμολογίας ἔθεντο, τὰ μὲν ὅπλα παραλαβεῖν, τὰ
δὲ σώματα εἰς Ἀθήνας κομίσαντες[2] ἐπιτρέψαι τῷ
δήμῳ περὶ αὐτῶν.

68. Τοῦ δ᾽ ἔτους[3] διελθόντος Ἀθηναῖοι μὲν Εὐ-
κτήμονι παρέδωκαν τὴν ἀρχήν, Ῥωμαῖοι δ᾽ ὑπάτους κατέστησαν Μάρκον Παπίριον καὶ Σπόριον
Ναύτιον, Ὀλυμπιὰς δ᾽ ἐγένετο τρίτη πρὸς ταῖς
ἐνενήκοντα, καθ᾽ ἣν ἐνίκα στάδιον Εὔβατος[4] Κυρη-
ναῖος. περὶ δὲ τούτους τοὺς χρόνους οἱ τῶν Ἀθηναίων στρατηγοὶ Βυζαντίου κυριεύσαντες ἐπῆλθον

---

[1] δὲ added by Reiske.   [2] κομίσαντες PA, κομίσαντας cet.
[3] τούτου after ἔτους added by Dindorf, Vogel.

by means of ladders in complete safety, since the 409 B.C. multitude had thronged down to the harbour. When the Peloponnesians learned what had happened, at first they left half their troops at the harbour and with the rest speedily rushed back to attack the walls which had been seized. And although practically the entire force of the Athenians had already effected an entrance, they nonetheless were not panic-stricken but resisted stoutly for a long while and battled the Athenians with the help of the Byzantines. And in the end the Athenians would not have conquered the city by fighting, had not Alcibiades, perceiving his opportunity, had the announcement made that no wrong should be done to the Byzantines ; for at this word the citizens changed sides and turned upon the Peloponnesians. Thereupon the most of them were slain fighting gallantly, and the survivors, about five hundred, fled for refuge to the altars of the temples. The Athenians returned the city to the Byzantines, having first made them allies, and then came to terms with the suppliants at the altars : the Athenians would take away their arms and carrying their persons to Athens turn them over to the decision of the Athenian people.

68. At the end of the year the Athenians bestowed 408 B.C. the office of archon upon Euctemon and the Romans elected as consuls Marcus Papirius and Spurius Nautius, and the Ninety-third Olympiad was celebrated, that in which Eubatus of Cyrenê won the "stadion." About this time the Athenian generals, now that they had taken possession of Byzantium

---

⁴ Εὔβατος] Εὐβώτας Xen. *Hell.* 1. 2. 1.

τὸν Ἑλλήσποντον καὶ τὰς ἐν αὐτῷ πόλεις πλὴν
2 Ἀβύδου πάσας εἷλον. μετὰ δὲ ταῦτα Διόδωρον
καὶ Μαντίθεον ἐπιμελητὰς μετὰ τῆς ἱκανῆς δυνάμεως κατέλιπον, αὐτοὶ δὲ μετὰ τῶν νεῶν καὶ τῶν
λαφύρων ἔπλεον εἰς Ἀθήνας, πολλὰ καὶ μεγάλα
κατειργασμένοι τῇ πατρίδι. ὡς δ' ἐγγὺς ἦσαν,
ὁ δῆμος ἅπας ἀπήντα περιχαρὴς ἐπὶ τοῖς εὐημερή-
μασι· συνέδραμον δ' εἰς τὸν Πειραιέα πολλοὶ καὶ
3 τῶν ξένων, ἔτι δὲ παίδων καὶ γυναικῶν. εἶχε γὰρ
πολλὴν κατάπληξιν τῶν στρατηγῶν ὁ κατάπλους·
ἦγον γὰρ τῶν ἡλωκυιῶν νεῶν οὐκ ἐλάττους διακοσίων, αἰχμαλώτων δὲ ἀνδρῶν καὶ λαφύρων
πλῆθος· εἶχον δὲ τὰς ἰδίας τριήρεις ὅπλοις ἐπι-
χρύσοις καὶ στεφάνοις, ἔτι δὲ λαφύροις καὶ τοῖς
ἄλλοις ἅπασιν ἐπιμελῶς κεκοσμημένας. πλεῖστοι
δ' ἐπὶ τὴν Ἀλκιβιάδου θέαν συνέδραμον ἐπὶ τοὺς
λιμένας, ὥστε παντελῶς ἐρημωθῆναι τὴν πόλιν,
συμφιλοτιμουμένων τοῖς ἐλευθέροις τῶν δούλων.
4 κατ' ἐκείνους γὰρ τοὺς χρόνους οὕτω συνέβη
θαυμασθῆναι τὸν ἄνδρα τοῦτον, ὥσθ' οἱ μὲν
ὑπερέχοντες τῶν Ἀθηναίων μόγις ἐνόμιζον εὑρηκέναι δυνατὸν ἄνδρα τὸν[1] φανερῶς καὶ θρασέως
ἀντιτάξασθαι τῷ δήμῳ δυνάμενον, οἱ δ' ἄποροι
ὑπειλήφεισαν συναγωνιστὴν ἕξειν ἄριστον τὸν ἀπο-
νενοημένον συνταράξοντα τὴν πόλιν καὶ τὴν ἑαυτῶν
5 ἐπανορθώσοντα πενίαν. θράσει γὰρ πολὺ διέφερε
τῶν ἄλλων, καὶ δεινότατος ἦν εἰπεῖν, καὶ κατὰ μὲν
τὴν στρατηγίαν[2] ἄριστος, κατὰ δὲ τὴν τόλμαν
πρακτικώτατος· ἦν δὲ καὶ τὴν ὄψιν καθ' ὑπερβολὴν
εὐπρεπὴς καὶ τὴν ψυχὴν λαμπρὸς καὶ μεγαλεπί-

---

[1] τὸν Hertlein : τοῦτον.
[2] So Dobraeus, στρατειὰν P, στρατείαν cet.

proceeded against the Hellespont and took every one 408 B.C.
of the cities of that region with the exception of
Abydus.[1] Then they left Diodorus and Mantitheüs
in charge with an adequate force and themselves
sailed to Athens with the ships and the spoils, having
performed many great deeds for the fatherland.
When they drew near the city, the populace in a body,
overjoyed at their successes, came out to meet them,
and great numbers of the aliens, as well as children
and women, flocked to the Peiraeus.   For the return
of the generals gave great cause for amazement, in
that they brought no less than two hundred captured
vessels, a multitude of captive soldiers, and a great
store of spoils ; and their own triremes they had gone
to great care to embellish with gilded arms and gar-
lands and, besides, with spoils and all such decora-
tions.   But most men thronged to the harbours to
catch sight of Alcibiades, so that the city was entirely
deserted, the slaves vying with the free.   For at that
time it had come to pass that this man was such
an object of admiration that the leading Athenians
thought that they had at long last found a strong
man capable of opposing the people openly and
boldly, while the poor had assumed that they would
have in him an excellent supporter who would recklessly throw the city into confusion and relieve their
destitute condition.   For in boldness he far excelled all other men, he was a most eloquent speaker,
in generalship he was unsurpassed, and in daring he
was most successful ; furthermore, in appearance he
was exceedingly handsome and in spirit brilliant and

[1] The Lacedaemonian base.

6 βολος. καθόλου δὲ τηλικαύτην ὑπόληψιν εἶχον ὑπὲρ αὐτοῦ σχεδὸν ἅπαντες, ὥσθ' ἅμα τῇ κείνου καθόδῳ καὶ τὴν τῶν πραγμάτων εὐτυχίαν εἰς τὴν πόλιν ἥκειν διελάμβανον. πρὸς δὲ τούτοις, ὥσπερ Λακεδαιμόνιοι τούτου συναγωνιζομένου προετέρουν, οὕτως ἑαυτοὺς πάλιν κατορθώσειν ἤλπιζον σύμμαχον ἔχοντες τὸν ἄνδρα τοῦτον.

69. Ἐπεὶ δ' οὖν κατέπλευσεν ὁ στόλος, ἐπέστρεψε τὸ πλῆθος ἐπὶ τὴν Ἀλκιβιάδου ναῦν, ἐξ ἧς ἐκβάντα τὸν ἄνδρα πάντες ἐδεξιοῦντο, τοῖς εὐημερήμασιν ἅμα καὶ τῇ καθόδῳ συγχαίροντες. ὁ δ' ἀσπασάμενος τὰ πλήθη φιλανθρώπως ἐκκλησίαν συνήγαγε, καὶ πολλὰ τῶν καθ' ἑαυτὸν ἀπολογησάμενος εἰς τοσαύτην εὔνοιαν τοὺς ὄχλους ἤγαγεν ὥστε ὁμολογεῖν πάντας τὴν πόλιν αἰτίαν γεγονέναι τῶν κατ'

2 ἐκείνου ψηφισμάτων. διόπερ αὐτῷ τήν τε οὐσίαν ἀπέδωκαν ἣν ἐδήμευσαν, ἔπειτα δὲ τὰς στήλας[1] κατεπόντισαν ἐν αἷς ἦν ἡ[2] καταδίκη καὶ τἆλλα τὰ κατ' ἐκείνου κυρωθέντα· ἐψηφίσαντο δὲ καὶ τοὺς Εὐμολπίδας ἆραι τὴν ἀρὰν ἣν ἐποιήσαντο κατ' αὐτοῦ καθ' ὃν καιρὸν ἔδοξεν ἀσεβεῖν περὶ τὰ μυ-

3 στήρια. τὸ δὲ τελευταῖον αὐτὸν στρατηγὸν καταστήσαντες αὐτοκράτορα καὶ κατὰ γῆν καὶ κατὰ θάλατταν, ἀπάσας τὰς δυνάμεις ἐνεχείρισαν αὐτῷ. εἵλαντο[3] δὲ καὶ στρατηγοὺς ἑτέρους οὓς ἐκεῖνος[4] ἤθελεν, Ἀδείμαντον καὶ Θρασύβουλον.

4 Ὁ δ' Ἀλκιβιάδης ἑκατὸν ναῦς πληρώσας ἐξέπλευσεν εἰς Ἄνδρον, καὶ καταλαβόμενος Γαύριον[5] φρούριον ἐτείχισεν. ἐξελθόντων δὲ τῶν Ἀνδρίων

---

[1] So Reiske : δίκας.   [2] ἐν αἷς ἦν ἡ Dobraeus : ἐν δ' ἴσῃ.
[3] So Vogel, εἵλοντο Dindorf, εἵλατο P, εἵλετο cet.
[4] So Dindorf : ἐκεῖνος οὕς.

intent upon great enterprises.   In a word, practically 408 B.C.
all men had conceived such assumptions regarding him
that they believed that along with his return from
exile good fortune in their undertakings had also come
again to the city.   Furthermore, just as the Lacedaemonians enjoyed success while he was fighting on
their side, so they expected that they in turn would
again prosper when they had this man as an ally.

69. So when the fleet came to land the multitude
turned to the ship of Alcibiades, and as he stepped
from it all gave their welcome to the man, congratu-
lating him on both his successes and his return from
exile.   He in turn, after greeting the crowds kindly,
called a meeting of the Assembly, and offering a long
defence of his conduct he brought the masses into
such a state of goodwill to him that all agreed that the
city had been to blame for the decrees issued against
him.   Consequently they not only returned to him
his property, which they had confiscated, but went
farther and cast into the sea the stelae on which were
written his sentence and all the other acts passed
against him ; and they also voted that the Eumol-
pidae[1] should revoke the curse they had pronounced
against him at the time when men believed he had
profaned the Mysteries.   And to cap all they appointed him general with supreme power both on land
and on sea and put in his hands all their armaments.
They also chose as generals others whom he wished,
namely, Adeimantus and Thrasybulus.

Alcibiades manned one hundred ships and sailed
to Andros, and seizing Gaurium, a stronghold, he
strengthened it with a wall.   And when the Andrians,

---

[1] The sacerdotal family which presided over the Mysteries.

[5] So Rhodoman (cp. Xen. *Hell.* 1. 4. 22) : Κάτριον.

πανδημεὶ μετὰ τῶν παραφυλαττόντων τὴν πόλιν
Πελοποννησίων ἐγενήθη μάχη, καθ᾽ ἣν ἐνίκησαν
Ἀθηναῖοι· τῶν δ᾽ ἐκ τῆς πόλεως πολλοὶ μὲν ἀνῃρέθησαν, τῶν δὲ διασωθέντων οἱ μὲν κατὰ τὴν
χώραν διεσκεδάσθησαν, οἱ δ᾽ ἐντὸς τῶν τειχῶν
5 συνέφυγον. αὐτὸς δ᾽ Ἀλκιβιάδης προσβολὰς ποιησάμενος τῇ πόλει, ἐν μὲν τῷ πεφρουρημένῳ τείχει
τὴν ἱκανὴν φυλακὴν κατέλιπε καὶ Θρασύβουλον
ἡγεμόνα κατέστησεν, αὐτὸς δὲ μετὰ τῆς δυνάμεως
ἐκπλεύσας τήν τε Κῶν καὶ Ῥόδον ἐδῄωσε, καὶ
συχνὰς ὠφελείας ἤθροισε πρὸς τὰς τῶν στρατιωτῶν διατροφάς.

70. Λακεδαιμόνιοι δὲ τήν τε ναυτικὴν δύναμιν
ἄρδην[1] ἀπολωλεκότες καὶ μετ᾽ αὐτῆς Μίνδαρον τὸν
ἡγεμόνα, ταῖς ψυχαῖς ὅμως οὐκ ἐνέδωκαν, ἀλλὰ
ναύαρχον εἵλαντο Λύσανδρον, δοκοῦντα στρατηγίᾳ
διαφέρειν τῶν ἄλλων καὶ τόλμαν ἔμπρακτον ἔχοντα
πρὸς πᾶσαν περίστασιν· ὃς παραλαβὼν τὴν ἀρχὴν
ἐκ τῆς Πελοποννήσου στρατιώτας τε κατέγραφε
τοὺς ἱκανοὺς καὶ ναῦς ἐπλήρωσεν ὅσας ἐδύνατο
2 πλείστας. ἐκπλεύσας δὲ εἰς Ῥόδον καὶ προσλαβόμενος ἐκεῖθεν ναῦς ὅσας εἶχον αἱ πόλεις,[2] ἔπλευσεν εἰς Ἔφεσον καὶ Μίλητον. καταρτίσας δὲ καὶ
τὰς ἐν ταύταις ταῖς[3] πόλεσι τριήρεις μετεπέμψατο
τὰς ἐκ Χίου, καὶ στόλον ἐξήρτυεν ἐξ Ἐφέσου νεῶν
3 ὑπάρχοντα σχεδὸν ἑβδομήκοντα. ἀκούσας δὲ

---

[1] ἄρδην De la Barre, ἀρχὴν AL, καὶ ἀρχὴν PF, καὶ τὴν ἀρχὴν
cet.   [2] παραλαβὼν after πόλεις omitted by M.
[3] So Reiske: καὶ ταύτας τὰς ἐν ταῖς.

---

[1] Cyrus the Younger, whose later attempt to win the
Persian throne is told in Xenophon's *Anabasis*. Persia had
finally decided to throw its power behind the combatant

together with the Peloponnesians who were guarding 408 B.C.
the city, came out against him *en masse*, a battle
ensued in which the Athenians were the victors ; and
of the inhabitants of the city many were slain, and of
those who escaped some were scattered throughout the countryside and the rest found safety within
the walls. As for Alcibiades, after having launched
assaults upon the city he left an adequate garrison
in the fort he had occupied, appointing Thrasybulus
commander, and himself sailed away with his force
and ravaged both Cos and Rhodes, collecting abundant booty to support his soldiers.

70. Although the Lacedaemonians had entirely lost
not only their sea force but Mindarus, the commander,
together with it, nevertheless they did not let their
spirits sink, but they chose as admiral Lysander, a
man who was believed to excel all others in skill
as a general and who possessed a daring that was
ready to meet every situation. As soon as Lysander
assumed the command he enrolled an adequate
number of soldiers from the Peloponnesus and also
manned as many ships as he was able. Sailing to
Rhodes he added to his force the ships which the cities
of Rhodes possessed, and then sailed to Ephesus and
Miletus. After equipping the triremes in these cities
he summoned those which were supplied by Chios and
thus fitted out at Ephesus a fleet of approximately
seventy ships. And hearing that Cyrus,[1] the son of

which could not support a fleet without Persian assistance.
Cyrus was sent down as " caranus (lord) of all those whose
mustering-place is Castolus " (a plain probably near Sardis),
i.e. as governor-general of Asia Minor (Xenophon, *Hell.*
1. 4. 3) with abundant funds and orders to support the
Lacedaemonians in the war. This decision of the Great
King was the death-knell of the Athenian Empire.

Κῦρον τὸν Δαρείου τοῦ βασιλέως υἱὸν ὑπὸ τοῦ
πατρὸς ἀπεσταλμένον συμπολεμεῖν τοῖς Λακεδαιμονίοις, ἧκεν εἰς Σάρδεις πρὸς αὐτόν, καὶ παροξύ-
νας τὸν νεανίσκον εἰς τὸν κατὰ τῶν Ἀθηναίων
πόλεμον μυρίους μὲν δαρεικοὺς παραχρῆμα ἔλαβεν
εἰς τὸν τῶν στρατιωτῶν μισθόν, καὶ εἰς¹ τὸ λοιπὸν
δὲ ὁ Κῦρος ἐκέλευσεν αἰτεῖν μηδὲν ὑποστελλό-
μενον· ἐντολὰς γὰρ ἔχειν παρὰ τοῦ πατρός, ὅπως
ὅσα ἂν προαιρῶνται Λακεδαιμόνιοι χορηγῆσαι αὐ-
4 τοῖς. ἀνακάμψας δὲ εἰς Ἔφεσον ἀπὸ τῶν πόλεων
μετεπέμπετο τοὺς δυνατωτάτους, πρὸς οὓς ἑται-
ρίας συντιθέμενος ἐπηγγέλλετο τῶν πραγμάτων
κατορθωθέντων κυρίους ἑκάστους τῶν πόλεων
ποιήσειν. δι’ ἣν αἰτίαν συνέβη τούτους πρὸς ἀλλήλους ἁμιλλωμένους ὑπηρετεῖν πλείονα τῶν ἐπι-
ταττομένων, καὶ ταχὺ παραδόξως εὐπορεῖν τὸν
Λύσανδρον πάντων τῶν εἰς πόλεμον χρησίμων.
71. Ἀλκιβιάδης δὲ πυθόμενος ἐν Ἐφέσῳ τὸν
Λύσανδρον ἐξαρτύειν τὸν στόλον, ἀνήχθη μετὰ
πασῶν τῶν νεῶν εἰς Ἔφεσον. ἐπιπλεύσας δὲ τοῖς
λιμέσιν, ὡς οὐδεὶς ἀντανήγετο, τὰς μὲν πολλὰς²
ναῦς καθώρμισε περὶ τὸ Νότιον, τὴν ἡγεμονίαν
αὐτῶν παραδοὺς Ἀντιόχῳ τῷ ἰδίῳ κυβερνήτῃ, δια-
κελευσάμενος αὐτῷ μὴ ναυμαχεῖν ἕως ἂν αὐτὸς
παραγένηται, τὰς δὲ στρατιώτιδας ναῦς ἀνέλαβε
καὶ κατὰ σπουδὴν ἔπλευσεν εἰς Κλαζομενάς· αὕτη
γὰρ ἡ πόλις σύμμαχος Ἀθηναίων οὖσα κακῶς
2 ἔπασχεν ὑπό τινων φυγάδων πορθουμένη. ὁ δ’
Ἀντίοχος ὢν τῇ φύσει πρόχειρος καὶ σπεύδων δι’
ἑαυτοῦ τι πρᾶξαι λαμπρόν, τῶν μὲν Ἀλκιβιάδου

¹ εἰς deleted by Vogel, but cp. Kallenberg ad loc.
² πολλὰς] Vogel would prefer ἄλλας.

King Darius, had been dispatched by his father to aid
the Lacedaemonians in the war, he went to him at
Sardis, and stirring up the youth's [1] enthusiasm for
the war against the Athenians he received on the spot
ten thousand darics [2] for the pay of his soldiers ; and
for the future Cyrus told him to make requests without reserve, since, as he stated, he carried orders from
his father to supply the Lacedaemonians with whatever they should want.   Then Lysander, returning to
Ephesus, called to him the most influential men of the
cities, and arranging with them to form cabals he
promised that if his undertakings were successful he
would put each group in control of its city.   And it
came to pass for this reason that these men, vying
with one another, gave greater aid than was required
of them and that Lysander was quickly supplied in
startling fashion with all the equipment that is useful
in war.

71. When Alcibiades learned that Lysander was
fitting out his fleet in Ephesus, he set sail for there
with all his ships.   He sailed up to the harbours, but
when no one came out against him, he had most of
his ships cast anchor at Notium,[3] entrusting the command of them to Antiochus, his personal pilot, with
orders not to accept battle until he should be present,
while he took the troop-ships and sailed in haste to
Clazomenae ; for this city, which was an ally of the
Athenians, was suffering from forays by some of its
exiles.   But Antiochus, who was by nature an im-
petuous man and was eager to accomplish some
brilliant deed on his own account, paid no attention

[1] Cyrus was seventeen years of age.
[2] A Persian coin containing about 125 grains of gold,
worth approximately one pound sterling or five dollars.
[3] On the north side of the large bay before Ephesus.

DIODORUS OF SICILY

λόγων ἠμέλησε, δέκα δὲ ναῦς τὰς¹ ἀρίστας πληρώσας, καὶ τὰς ἄλλας τοῖς τριηράρχοις παραγγείλας
ἑτοίμας ἔχειν ἂν ᾖ χρεία ναυμαχεῖν, ἐπέπλευσε
3 τοῖς πολεμίοις προκαλεσόμενος² εἰς ναυμαχίαν. ὁ
δὲ Λύσανδρος πεπυσμένος παρά τινων αὐτομόλων
τὴν ἄφοδον Ἀλκιβιάδου καὶ τῶν ἀρίστων μετ’ αὐτοῦ στρατιωτῶν, καιρὸν εἶναι διέλαβε πρᾶξαί τι
τῆς Σπάρτης ἄξιον. διόπερ πάσαις ταῖς ναυσὶν
ἀνταναχθεὶς μίαν μὲν τὴν προπλέουσαν τῶν δέκα,
καθ’ ἣν Ἀντίοχος ἦν ἀντιτεταγμένος, κατέδυσε,
τὰς δ’ ἄλλας τρεψάμενος ἐδίωξε, μέχρις οὗ τὰς
ἄλλας πληρώσαντες οἱ τριήραρχοι τῶν Ἀθηναίων
4 παρεβοήθησαν ἐν οὐδεμιᾷ τάξει. γενομένης δὲ
ναυμαχίας ἀθρόαις ταῖς ναυσὶν οὐ μακρὰν τῆς
γῆς, Ἀθηναῖοι διὰ τὴν ἀταξίαν ἠλαττώθησαν καὶ
ναῦς ἀπέβαλον δύο πρὸς ταῖς εἴκοσι, τῶν δ’ ἐν αὐταῖς ἀνδρῶν ὀλίγοι μὲν ἐζωγρήθησαν, οἱ δὲ λοιποὶ
πρὸς τὴν γῆν διενήξαντο. Ἀλκιβιάδης δὲ πυθόμενος τὸ γεγενημένον διὰ σπουδῆς ἀνέκαμψεν εἰς τὸ
Νότιον καὶ πάσας τὰς τριήρεις πληρώσας ἐπέπλευσε
τοῖς λιμέσι τῶν πολεμίων· οὐ τολμῶντος δ’ ἀντ-
αναχθῆναι³ τοῦ Λυσάνδρου τὸν πλοῦν εἰς Σάμον
ἐποιήσατο.

72. Τούτων δὲ πραττομένων Θρασύβουλος ὁ
τῶν Ἀθηναίων στρατηγὸς μετὰ νεῶν πεντεκαίδεκα πλεύσας ἐπὶ Θάσον ἐνίκησε μάχῃ τοὺς ἐκ
τῆς πόλεως καὶ περὶ διακοσίους αὐτῶν ἀνεῖλεν·
ἐγκλείσας δ’ αὐτοὺς εἰς πολιορκίαν ἠνάγκασε
τοὺς φυγάδας τοὺς τὰ τῶν Ἀθηναίων φρονοῦντας
καταδέχεσθαι, καὶ φρουρὰν λαβόντας συμμάχους

¹ τὰς added by Dindorf.
² So Eichstädt: προσ- or προκαλεσάμενος.

320

to the orders of Alcibiades, but manning ten of the 408 B.C.
best ships and ordering the captains to keep the others
ready in case they should need to accept battle, he
sailed up to the enemy in order to challenge them to
battle. But Lysander, who had learned from certain
deserters of the departure of Alcibiades and his best
soldiers, decided that the favourable time had come
for him to strike a blow worthy of Sparta. Accordingly, putting out to sea for the attack with all his
ships, he encountered the leading one of the ten ships,
the one on which Antiochus had taken his place for
the attack, and sank it, and then, putting the rest to
flight, he chased them until the Athenian captains
manned the rest of their vessels and came to the
rescue, but in no battle order at all. In the sea-battle
which followed between the two entire fleets not far
from the land the Athenians, because of their disorder, were defeated and lost twenty-two ships, but
of their crews only a few were taken captive and the
rest swam to safety ashore. When Alcibiades learned
what had taken place, he returned in haste to Notium
and manning all the triremes sailed to the harbours
which were held by the enemy ; but since Lysander
would not venture to come out against him, he
directed his course to Samos.

72. While these events were taking place Thrasybulus, the Athenian general, sailing to Thasos with
fifteen ships defeated in battle the troops who came
out from the city and slew about two hundred of them;
then, having bottled them up in a siege of the city, he
forced them to receive back their exiles, that is the
men who favoured the Athenians, to accept a garri-

---

³ So Wesseling: ἀναχθῆναι.

2 Ἀθηναίων εἶναι. μετὰ δὲ ταῦτα πλεύσας εἰς
Ἄβδηρα προσηγάγετο πόλιν ἐν ταῖς δυνατωτάταις
οὖσαν τότε τῶν ἐπὶ Θρᾴκης.

Οἱ μὲν οὖν στρατηγοὶ τῶν Ἀθηναίων ταῦτα
3 ἔπραξαν μετὰ τὸν οἴκοθεν ἔκπλουν. Ἄγις δ' ὁ
τῶν Λακεδαιμονίων βασιλεὺς ἔτυχε μὲν ἐν τῇ
Δεκελείᾳ διατρίβων μετὰ τῆς δυνάμεως, πυνθανόμενος δὲ τοὺς κρατίστους τῶν Ἀθηναίων μετ'
Ἀλκιβιάδου στρατευομένους, νυκτὸς ἀσελήνου τὸ
4 στρατόπεδον ἤγαγεν ἐπὶ τὰς Ἀθήνας. εἶχε δὲ
πεζοὺς δισμυρίους ὀκτακισχιλίους, ὧν ἦσαν οἱ μὲν
ἡμίσεις ὁπλῖται κατ' ἐκλογήν, οἱ δ' ἡμίσεις ψιλοί·
κατηκολούθουν δ' αὐτῷ καὶ τῶν ἱππέων εἰς χιλίους
διακοσίους, ὧν ἐννακοσίους μὲν Βοιωτοὶ παρείχοντο, τοὺς δὲ λοιποὺς Πελοποννήσιοι συνεξέπεμψαν. ὡς δ' ἐγγὺς ἐγενήθη τῆς πόλεως, ἔλαθε
ταῖς προφυλακαῖς ἐγγίσας, καὶ ῥᾳδίως αὐτοὺς
τρεψάμενος διὰ τὸ παράδοξον, ὀλίγους μὲν ἀνεῖλε,
5 τοὺς δ' ἄλλους συνεδίωξεν ἐντὸς τῶν τειχῶν. οἱ
δ' Ἀθηναῖοι μαθόντες τὸ γεγενημένον ἅπασι
παρήγγειλαν τοῖς πρεσβυτέροις καὶ τοῖς μεγίστοις
παισὶν ἀπαντᾶν μετὰ τῶν ὅπλων· ὧν ταχὺ τὸ
προσταχθὲν ποιησάντων, ὁ μὲν κύκλος τοῦ τείχους
πλήρης ἐγένετο τῶν ἐπὶ τὸν κοινὸν κίνδυνον συνδε-
6 δραμηκότων, οἱ δὲ στρατηγοὶ τῶν Ἀθηναίων ἅμ'
ἡμέρᾳ θεωροῦντες ἐκτεταγμένην[1] τὴν τῶν πολεμίων
δύναμιν εἰς φάλαγγα τὸ μὲν βάθος εἰς τέτταρας
ἄνδρας, τὸ δὲ μῆκος ἐπὶ σταδίους ὀκτώ, τότε
πρῶτον κατεπλάγησαν, θεωροῦντες τὰ δύο μέρη
σχεδὸν τοῦ τείχους ὑπὸ τῶν πολεμίων περιει-

---

[1] So Dindorf: ἐκτεταμένην.

son, and to be allies of the Athenians. After this, 408 B.C. sailing to Abdera,[1] he brought that city, which at that time was among the most powerful in Thrace, over to the side of the Athenians.

Now the foregoing is what the Athenian generals had accomplished since they sailed from Athens. But Agis, the king of the Lacedaemonians, as it happened, was at the time in Deceleia [2] with his army, and when he learned that the best Athenian troops were engaged in an expedition with Alcibiades, he led his army on a moonless night to Athens. He had twenty-eight thousand infantry, one-half of whom were picked hoplites and the other half light-armed troops ; there were also attached to his army some twelve hundred cavalry, of whom the Boeotians furnished nine hundred and the rest had been sent with him by Peloponnesians. As he drew near the city, he came upon the outposts before they were aware of him, and easily dispersing them because they were taken by surprise he slew a few and pursued the rest within the walls. When the Athenians learned what had happened, they issued orders for all the older men and the sturdiest of the youth to present themselves under arms. Since these promptly responded to the call, the circuit of the wall was manned with those who had rushed together to meet the common peril ; and the Athenian generals, when in the morning they surveyed the army of the enemy extended in a line four men deep and eight stades in length, at the moment were at first dismayed, seeing as they did that approximately two-thirds of the wall was surrounded by the enemy.

[1] The birthplace of the great Greek physical philosopher Democritus.
[2] The fortress in Attica which the Lacedaemonians, on the advice of Alcibiades (cp. chap. 9. 2), had permanently occupied.

DIODORUS OF SICILY

7 λημμένα. μετὰ δὲ ταῦτα τοὺς ἱππεῖς ἐξαπέστειλαν,
ὄντας παραπλησίους τὸν ἀριθμὸν τοῖς ἐναντίοις·
ὧν πρὸ τῆς πόλεως συστησαμένων ἱππομαχίαν ἐπί
τινα χρόνον ἐγένετο καρτερὰ μάχη. ἡ μὲν γὰρ
φάλαγξ περὶ πέντε σταδίους ἀπεῖχε τοῦ τείχους,
οἱ δ' ἱππεῖς συμπλακέντες ἀλλήλοις πρὸς αὐτοῖς
8 τοῖς τείχεσι διηγωνίζοντο. οἱ μὲν οὖν Βοιωτοὶ
καθ' αὑτοὺς προνενικηκότες ἐπὶ Δηλίῳ τοὺς Ἀθηναίους, δεινὸν ἡγοῦντο τῶν ἡττημένων[1] φανῆναι
καταδεέστεροι· οἱ δ' Ἀθηναῖοι θεατὰς ἔχοντες τῆς
ἀρετῆς τοὺς ἐπὶ τῶν τειχῶν ἐφεστῶτας καὶ κατὰ
ἄνδρα γνωριζόμενοι, πᾶν ὑπέμενον ὑπὲρ τῆς νίκης.
9 τέλος δὲ βιασάμενοι τοὺς ἀντιτεταγμένους, συχνοὺς
μὲν αὐτῶν ἀνεῖλον, τοὺς δ' ἄλλους κατεδίωξαν
μέχρι τῆς τῶν πεζῶν φάλαγγος. μετὰ δὲ ταῦτα
οὗτοι μὲν ἐπιπορευομένων τῶν πεζῶν ἀνεχώρησαν
εἰς τὴν πόλιν.

73. Ἆγις δὲ τότε μὲν οὐ κρίνας πολιορκεῖν ἐν
Ἀκαδημίᾳ κατεστρατοπέδευσε, τῇ δ' ὑστεραίᾳ τῶν
Ἀθηναίων στησάντων τρόπαιον ἐξέταξε τὴν δύναμιν καὶ προεκαλεῖτο τοὺς ἐν τῇ πόλει περὶ τοῦ
2 τροπαίου διαγωνίσασθαι.[2] τῶν δ' Ἀθηναίων ἐξ-
αγαγόντων τοὺς στρατιώτας καὶ παρὰ τὸ τεῖχος
παραταττομένων, τὸ μὲν πρῶτον οἱ Λακεδαιμόνιοι
πρὸς μάχην ὥρμησαν, ἀπὸ δὲ τῶν τειχῶν πολλοῦ
πλήθους βελῶν ἐπ' αὐτοὺς ῥιφέντος ἀπήγαγον τὴν
δύναμιν ἀπὸ τῆς πόλεως· μετὰ δὲ ταῦτα τὸ λοιπὸν
τῆς Ἀττικῆς δῃώσαντες εἰς Πελοπόννησον ἀπηλλάγησαν.

[1] ἡττημένων M, ἡττωμένων cet.
[2] So Hertlein : ἐξαγωνίσασθαι.

[1] Cp. Book 12. 70.

324

After this, however, they sent out their cavalry, who ^{408 B.C.} were about equal in number to the opposing cavalry, and when the two bodies met in a cavalry-battle before the city, sharp fighting ensued which lasted for some time. For the line of the infantry was some five stades from the wall, but the cavalry which had engaged each other were fighting at the very walls. Now the Boeotians, who by themselves alone had formerly defeated the Athenians at Delium,[1] thought it would be a terrible thing if they should prove to be inferior to the men they had once conquered, while the Athenians, since they had as spectators of their valour the populace standing upon the walls and were known every one to them, were ready to endure everything for the sake of victory. Finally, overpowering their opponents they slew great numbers of them and pursued the remainder as far as the line of the infantry. After this when the infantry advanced against them, they withdrew within the city.

73. Agis, deciding for the time not to lay siege to the city, pitched camp in the Academy,[2] but on the next day, after the Athenians had set up a trophy, he drew up his army in battle order and challenged the troops in the city to fight it out for the possession of the trophy. The Athenians led forth their soldiers and drew them up along the wall, and at first the Lacedaemonians advanced to offer battle, but since a great multitude of missiles was hurled at them from the walls, they led their army away from the city. After this they ravaged the rest of Attica and then departed to the Peloponnesus.

[2] The grove of olive-trees, where Plato later had his school, six stades north-west of the Dipylon Gate.

3 Ἀλκιβιάδης δὲ ἐκ Σάμου μετὰ πασῶν τῶν νεῶν
πλεύσας εἰς Κύμην ψευδεῖς αἰτίας ἐπέρριψε τοῖς
Κυμαίοις, βουλόμενος αὐτῶν μετὰ προφάσεως δι-
αρπάσαι τὴν χώραν. καὶ τὸ μὲν πρῶτον πολλῶν
αἰχμαλώτων σωμάτων κυριεύσας ἀπῆγεν[1] ἐπὶ τὰς
4 ναῦς· ἐκβοηθησάντων δὲ τῶν ἐκ τῆς πόλεως πανδημεὶ καὶ προσπεσόντων ἀπροσδοκήτως, χρόνον μέν
τινα διεκαρτέρουν οἱ περὶ τὸν Ἀλκιβιάδην, μετὰ
δὲ ταῦτα τοῖς Κυμαίοις προσγενομένων πολλῶν
τῶν ἐκ τῆς πόλεως καὶ τῆς χώρας ἠναγκάσθησαν καταλιπόντες τοὺς αἰχμαλώτους καταφυγεῖν
5 ἐπὶ τὰς ναῦς. ὁ δ᾽ Ἀλκιβιάδης ἐπὶ τοῖς ἐλαττώμασι περιαλγὴς γενόμενος ἐκ Μιτυλήνης μετεπέμψατο τοὺς ὁπλίτας, καὶ πρὸ τῆς πόλεως
ἐκτάξας τὴν δύναμιν προεκαλεῖτο τοὺς Κυμαίους
εἰς μάχην· οὐδενὸς δ᾽ ἐξιόντος δῃώσας τὴν χώραν
6 ἀπέπλευσεν ἐπὶ Μιτυλήνην. Κυμαίων δὲ πεμψάντων εἰς Ἀθήνας πρεσβείαν καὶ κατηγορούντων
Ἀλκιβιάδου, διότι σύμμαχον πόλιν οὐδὲν ἀδική-
σασαν ἐπόρθησεν· ἐγίνοντο δὲ καὶ ἄλλαι πολλαὶ
διαβολαὶ κατ᾽ αὐτοῦ· τῶν γὰρ ἐν Σάμῳ τινὲς
στρατιωτῶν ἀλλοτρίως τὰ πρὸς αὐτὸν ἔχοντες
ἔπλευσαν εἰς Ἀθήνας, καὶ κατηγόρησαν ἐν ἐκκλησίᾳ κατ᾽ Ἀλκιβιάδου, ὅτι τὰ Λακεδαιμονίων
φρονεῖ καὶ πρὸς Φαρνάβαζον ἔχει φιλίαν, δι᾽ ἧς
ἐλπίζει καταλυθέντος τοῦ πολέμου καταδυναστεύ-
σειν τῶν πολιτῶν.

74. Ταχὺ δὲ τοῦ πλήθους πιστεύοντος ταῖς διαβολαῖς, ἡ μὲν περὶ[2] Ἀλκιβιάδην ἐθραύετο δόξα διὰ
τὸ περὶ τὴν ναυμαχίαν ἐλάττωμα καὶ τὰ περὶ τὴν
Κύμην ἡμαρτημένα, ὁ δὲ τῶν Ἀθηναίων δῆμος
ὑφορώμενος τὴν τἀνδρὸς τόλμαν δέκα στρατηγοὺς

Alcibiades, having sailed with all his ships from 408 B.C.
Samos to Cymê,[1] hurled false charges against the
Cymaeans, since he wished to have an excuse for
plundering their territory. And at the outset he
gained possession of many captives and was taking
them to his ships ; but when the men of the city came
out *en masse* to the rescue and fell unexpectedly on
Alcibiades' troops, for a time they stood off the attack,
but as later many from the city and countryside rein-
forced the Cymaeans, they were forced to abandon
their prisoners and flee for safety to their ships.
Alcibiades, being greatly distressed by his reverses,
summoned his hoplites from Mitylenê, and drawing up
his army before the city he challenged the Cymaeans
to battle ; but when no one came out of the city, he
ravaged its territory and sailed off to Mitylenê. The
Cymaeans dispatched an embassy to Athens and denounced Alcibiades for having laid waste an allied city
which had done no wrong ; and there were also many
other charges brought against him ; for some of the
soldiers at Samos, who were at odds with him, sailed
to Athens and accused Alcibiades in the Assembly of
favouring the Lacedaemonian cause and of forming
ties of friendship with Pharnabazus whereby he hoped
that at the conclusion of the war he should lord it over
his fellow citizens.

74. Since the multitude soon began to believe these
accusations, not only was the fame of Alcibiades
damaged because of his defeat in the sea-battle and
the wrongs he had committed against Cymê, but the
Athenian people, viewing with suspicion the boldness

---

[1] In Lydia.

---

[1] ἀπῆγεν PM, ἀπήγαγεν cet.
[2] So Dindorf: πρός.

εἴλατο, Κόνωνα, Λυσίαν,[1] Διομέδοντα, Περικλέα,
πρὸς δὲ τούτοις Ἐρασινίδην, Ἀριστοκράτην, Ἀρχέ-
στρατον, Πρωτόμαχον, Θρασύβουλον, Ἀριστο-
γένην· ἐκ δὲ τούτων προκρίνας Κόνωνα ταχέως
ἐξέπεμψε παρ᾽ Ἀλκιβιάδου τὸ ναυτικὸν παραληψό-
2 μενον. Ἀλκιβιάδης δὲ τῆς ἀρχῆς ἐκχωρήσας τῷ
Κόνωνι καὶ τὰς δυνάμεις παραδούς, τὴν μὲν εἰς
Ἀθήνας ἐπάνοδον ἀπέγνω, μετὰ δὲ τριήρους μιᾶς
εἰς Πακτύην τῆς Θράκης ἀπεχώρησε· χωρὶς γὰρ
τῆς τοῦ πλήθους ὀργῆς καὶ τὰς ἐπενηνεγμένας
3 αὐτῷ δίκας εὐλαβεῖτο. πολλοὶ γὰρ θεωροῦντες αὐτὸν κακῶς φερόμενον ἐπενηνόχεισαν ἐγκλήματα
πολλά· μέγιστον δ᾽ ἦν τὸ περὶ τῶν ἵππων, τετιμη-
μένον ταλάντων ὀκτώ. Διομήδους γάρ τινος τῶν
φίλων συμπέμψαντος αὐτῷ τέθριππον εἰς Ὀλυμπίαν,
ὁ Ἀλκιβιάδης κατὰ τὴν ἀπογραφὴν[2] τὴν εἰωθυῖαν
γίνεσθαι τοὺς ἵππους ἰδίους ἀπεγράψατο,[3] καὶ
νικήσας[4] τὸ τέθριππον τήν τ᾽ ἐκ τῆς νίκης δόξαν
αὐτὸς ἀπηνέγκατο καὶ τοὺς ἵππους οὐκ ἀπέδωκε
4 τῷ πιστεύσαντι. ταῦτα δὴ πάντα διανοούμενος
ἐφοβεῖτο, μήποτε καιρὸν λαβόντες Ἀθηναῖοι τιμωρίαν ἐπιθῶσι περὶ πάντων ὧν εἰς αὐτοὺς ἐξήμαρτεν·
αὐτὸς οὖν[5] αὐτοῦ κατέγνω φυγήν.

[1] So Palmer (cp. ch. 101. 5) : Λυσανίαν.
[2] So Schäfer : ὑπογραφήν.
[3] So Schäfer (cp. Const. Exc. 2 (1), p. 233 ; Plut. Alc. 12) :
ὑπεγράψατο.
[4] νικήσας Const. Exc. l.c., Stephanus, νικήσαντος P, νικήσαντας cet. Vogel suggests νικήσαντος τοῦ τεθρίππου.
[5] οὖν added by Stephanus.

---

[1] This should be Thrasyllus.
[2] Alcibiades had acquired castles here and at Bisanthê
against some such contingency as this.
[3] Cp. Isocrates, On the Team of Horses.

of the man, chose as the ten generals Conon, Lysias, 408 B.C. Diomedon, and Pericles, and in addition Erasinides, Aristocrates, Archestratus, Protomachus, Thrasybulus,[1] and Aristogenes. Of these they gave first place to Conon and dispatched him at once to take over the fleet from Alcibiades. After Alcibiades had relinquished his command to Conon and handed over his armaments, he gave up any thought of returning to Athens, but with one trireme withdrew to Pactyê [2] in Thrace, since, apart from the anger of the multitude, he was afraid of the law-suits which had been brought against him. For there were many who, on seeing how he was hated, had filed numerous complaints against him, the most important of which was the one about the horses, involving the sum of eight talents. Diomedes, it appears, one of his friends, had sent in his care a four-horse team to Olympia ; and Alcibiades, when entering it in the usual way, listed the horses as his own ; and when he was the victor in the four-horse race, Alcibiades took for himself the glory of the victory and did not return the horses to the man who had entrusted them to his care.[3] As he thought about all these things he was afraid lest the Athenians, seizing a suitable occasion, would inflict punishment upon him for all the wrongs he had committed against them. Consequently he himself condemned himself to exile.[4]

[4] " Feared and distrusted in Athens, Sparta, and Persia alike, the most brilliant man of action of his generation, whose judgment of public policies was as unerring as his personal aims, methods, and conduct were wrong, found outlet for his restless energy only in waging private war on the ' kingless ' Thracians. Had Athens been able to trust him he might have saved her Empire and destroyed her liberty." (W. S. Ferguson in *Camb. Anc. Hist.* 5, p. 354.)

75. Προσετέθη δὲ καὶ συνωρὶς κατὰ τὴν αὐτὴν Ὀλυμπιάδα· καὶ παρὰ Λακεδαιμονίοις Πλειστῶναξ ὁ βασιλεὺς ἐτελεύτησεν ἄρξας ἔτη πεντήκοντα, διαδεξάμενος δὲ τὴν ἀρχὴν Παυσανίας ἦρξεν ἔτη τετταρακαίδεκα. οἱ δὲ τὴν Ῥόδον νῆσον κατοικοῦντες καὶ Ἰηλυσὸν καὶ Λίνδον καὶ Κάμειρον μετῳκίσθησαν εἰς μίαν πόλιν τὴν νῦν καλουμένην Ῥόδον.

2 Ἑρμοκράτης δ' ὁ Συρακόσιος ἀναλαβὼν τοὺς μετ' αὐτοῦ στρατεύοντας ὥρμησεν ἐκ Σελινοῦντος, καὶ παραγενόμενος πρὸς τὴν Ἱμέραν κατεστρατοπέδευσεν ἐν τοῖς προαστείοις τῆς ἀνατετραμμένης πόλεως. διαπυθόμενος δ' ἐν ᾧ τόπῳ παρετάχθησαν οἱ Συρακόσιοι, τὰ τῶν τετελευτηκότων ὀστᾶ συνήθροιζε, παρασκευάσας δ' ἁμάξας πολυτελῶς κεκοσμημένας, ἐπὶ τούτων παρεκόμισεν

3 αὐτὰ ἐπὶ τὴν Συράκουσαν. αὐτὸς μὲν οὖν ἐπὶ τῶν ὅρων[1] κατέμεινε διὰ τὸ κωλύεσθαι τοὺς φυγάδας ὑπὸ τῶν νόμων συνιέναι,[2] τῶν δὲ μετ' αὐτοῦ τινας ἀπέστειλεν, οἳ τὰς ἁμάξας παρεκό-

4 μισαν εἰς τὰς Συρακούσας. ὁ δ' Ἑρμοκράτης ταῦτα ἔπραττεν ὅπως ὁ μὲν Διοκλῆς ἀντιπράττων αὐτῷ περὶ τῆς καθόδου δοκῶν δ' αἴτιος εἶναι τοῦ περιεωρᾶσθαι[3] τοὺς τετελευτηκότας ἀτάφους, προσκόψαι τοῖς πλήθεσιν, αὐτὸς δὲ φιλανθρώπως τούτοις προσενεχθεὶς ἐπαγάγοι[4] τὸ πλῆθος εἰς τὴν προτέ-

5 ραν εὔνοιαν. τῶν οὖν ὀστῶν παρακομισθέντων ἐνέπεσεν εἰς τὰ πλήθη στάσις, τοῦ μὲν Διοκλέους

---

[1] So Wesseling: ὁρῶν.   [2] συνιέναι] εἰσιέναι Wesseling.
[3] So Reiske, περιεωρακότος PL, περιεωρακέναι cet.

75. The two-horse chariot race [1] was added in this 408 B.C. same Olympic Festival [2]; and among the Lacedaemonians Pleistonax, their king, died after a reign of fifty years, and Pausanias succeeded to the throne and reigned for fourteen years. Also the inhabitants of the island of Rhodes left the cities of Ielysus, Lindus, and Cameirus and settled in one city, that which is now called Rhodes.

Hermocrates,[3] the Syracusan, taking his soldiers set out from Selinus, and on arriving at Himera he pitched camp in the suburbs of the city, which lay in ruins. And finding out the place where the Syracusans had made their stand, he collected the bones of the dead [4] and putting them upon wagons which he had constructed and embellished at great cost he conveyed them to Syracuse. Now Hermocrates himself stopped at the border of Syracusan territory, since the exiles were forbidden by the laws from accompanying the bones farther, but he sent on some of his troops who brought the wagons to Syracuse. Hermocrates acted in this way in order that Diocles, who opposed his return and was generally believed to be responsible for the lack of concern over the failure to bury the dead, should fall out with the masses, whereas he, by his humane consideration for the dead, would win the multitude back to the feeling of goodwill in which they had formerly held him. Now when the bones had been brought into the city, civil discord arose among the masses, Diocles objecting to their burial

[1] Until this time the only chariot race had been that with teams of four horses (cp. Pausanias, 5. 8. 10).
[2] The ninety-third, 408 B.C.
[3] The narrative is resumed from the end of chap. 63.
[4] Cp. chap. 61. 6.

---

[4] So Dindorf: ἐπαγάγῃ.

κωλύοντος θάπτειν, τῶν δὲ πολλῶν συγκατατιθεμένων. τέλος δ' οἱ Συρακόσιοι ἔθαψάν τε¹ τὰ
λείψανα τῶν τετελευτηκότων καὶ πανδημεὶ τὴν
ἐκφορὰν ἐτίμησαν. καὶ ὁ μὲν Διοκλῆς ἐφυγαδεύθη, τὸν δ' Ἑρμοκράτην οὐδ' ὡς προσεδέξαντο·
ὑπώπτευον γὰρ τὴν τἀνδρὸς τόλμαν, μήποτε τυχὼν
6 ἡγεμονίας ἀναδείξῃ ἑαυτὸν τύραννον. ὁ μὲν οὖν
Ἑρμοκράτης τότε τὸν καιρὸν οὐχ ὁρῶν εὔθετον
εἰς τὸ βιάσασθαι, πάλιν ἀνεχώρησεν εἰς Σελινοῦντα.
μετὰ δέ τινα χρόνον τῶν φίλων αὐτὸν μεταπεμπο-
μένων ὥρμησε μετὰ τρισχιλίων στρατιωτῶν, καὶ
πορευθεὶς διὰ τῆς Γελῴας ἧκε νυκτὸς ἐπὶ τὸν
7 συντεταγμένον τόπον. οὐ δυνηθέντων δὲ ἁπάντων ἀκολουθῆσαι τῶν στρατιωτῶν, ὁ μὲν Ἑρμοκράτης μετ' ὀλίγων προσελθὼν τῷ κατὰ τὴν
Ἀχραδινὴν πυλῶνι, καὶ τῶν φίλων τινὰς εὑρὼν
προκατειλημμένους τοὺς τόπους, ἀνελάμβανε τοὺς
8 ἀφυστεροῦντας· οἱ δὲ Συρακόσιοι τὸ γεγενημένον
ἀκούσαντες σὺν τοῖς ὅπλοις ἦλθον εἰς τὴν ἀγοράν,
καθ' ἣν μετὰ πολλοῦ πλήθους ἐπιφανέντες τόν τε
Ἑρμοκράτην καὶ τῶν συμπραττόντων αὐτῷ τοὺς
πλείστους ἀπέκτειναν. τοὺς δὲ ἀπὸ τῆς μάχης
διασωθέντας μεθιστάντες εἰς κρίσιν φυγῇ κατεδί-
9 καζον· διόπερ τινὲς αὐτῶν πολλοῖς περιπεσόντες
τραύμασιν ὡς τετελευτηκότες ὑπὸ τῶν συγγενῶν
παρεδόθησαν, ὅπως μὴ τῇ τοῦ πλήθους ὀργῇ παρα-
δοθῶσιν, ὧν² ἦν καὶ Διονύσιος ὁ μετὰ ταῦτα τῶν
Συρακοσίων τυραννήσας.

76. Τῶν δὲ κατὰ τὸν ἐνιαυτὸν τοῦτον πράξεων
τέλος ἐχουσῶν Ἀθήνησι μὲν Ἀντιγένης τὴν ἀρχὴν

---

¹ ἔθαψάν τε Dindorf : θάψαντες.

and the majority favouring it.   Finally the Syracusans 408 B.C.
not only buried the remains of the dead but also by
turning out *en masse* paid honour to the burial procession.   Diocles was exiled ; but even so they did
not receive Hermocrates back, since they were wary
of the daring of the man and feared lest, once he had
gained a position of leadership, he should proclaim
himself tyrant. Accordingly Hermocrates, seeing that
the time was not opportune for resorting to force,
withdrew again to Selinus.   But some time later,
when his friends sent for him, he set out with three
thousand soldiers, and making his way through the
territory of Gela he arrived at night at the place
agreed upon.   Although not all his soldiers had been
able to accompany him, Hermocrates with a small
number of them came to the gate on Achradinê, and
when he found that some of his friends had already
occupied the region, he waited to pick up the late-
comers.   But when the Syracusans heard what had
happened, they gathered in the market-place under
arms, and here, since they appeared accompanied by
a great multitude, they slew both Hermocrates and
most of his supporters.   Those who had not been
killed in the fighting were brought to trial and sen-
tenced to exile ; consequently some of them who had
been severely wounded were reported by their relatives as having died, in order that they might not be
given over to the wrath of the multitude.   Among
their number was also Dionysius, who later became
tyrant of the Syracusans.[1]

76. When the events of this year came to an end, 407 B.C.
in Athens Antigenes took over the office of archon and

---

[1] 405–367 B.C.

---

[2] ὧν] ἐν οἶς Vogel, εἰς Cobet.

παρέλαβε, Ῥωμαῖοι δ' ὑπάτους κατέστησαν Γάιον
Μάνιον Αἰμίλιον καὶ Γάιον Οὐαλέριον. περὶ δὲ
τούτους τοὺς χρόνους Κόνων ὁ τῶν Ἀθηναίων στρατηγός, ἐπειδὴ παρέλαβε τὰς δυνάμεις ἐν Σάμῳ,
τάς τε παρούσας τῶν νεῶν ἐξηρτύετο καὶ τὰς
παρὰ τῶν συμμάχων ἤθροιζε, σπεύδων ἐφάμιλ-
λον κατασκευάσαι τὸν στόλον ταῖς τῶν πολεμίων
2 ναυσίν. οἱ δὲ Σπαρτιᾶται, τῷ Λυσάνδρῳ διεληλυθότος ἤδη τοῦ τῆς ναυαρχίας χρόνου, Καλλι-
κρατίδην ἐπὶ τὴν διαδοχὴν ἀπέστειλαν. οὗτος δὲ
νέος μὲν ἦν παντελῶς, ἄκακος δὲ καὶ τὴν ψυχὴν
ἁπλοῦς, οὔπω τῶν ξενικῶν ἠθῶν πεπειραμένος,
δικαιότατος δὲ Σπαρτιατῶν· ὁμολογουμένως δὲ
καὶ κατὰ¹ τὴν ἀρχὴν οὐδὲν ἔπραξεν ἄδικον οὔτ'
εἰς πόλιν οὔτ' εἰς ἰδιώτην, ἀλλὰ καὶ τοῖς ἐπιχει-
ροῦσιν αὐτὸν διαφθείρειν χρήμασι χαλεπῶς ἔφερε
3 καὶ δίκην παρ' αὐτῶν ἐλάμβανεν. οὗτος καταπλεύσας εἰς Ἔφεσον παρέλαβε τὰς ναῦς, μεταπεμψάμενος δὲ² καὶ τὰς παρὰ τῶν συμμάχων
ναῦς³ τὰς πάσας σὺν ταῖς παρὰ Λυσάνδρου παρ-
έλαβεν ἑκατὸν τεσσαράκοντα. ἐν δὲ τῇ Χίων
χώρᾳ Δελφίνιον κατεχόντων Ἀθηναίων, ἐπὶ τούτους
ἔπλευσε μετὰ πασῶν τῶν νεῶν, καὶ πολιορκεῖν
4 ἐπεχείρησεν. οἱ δ' Ἀθηναῖοι περὶ πεντακοσίους
ὄντες κατεπλάγησαν τὸ μέγεθος τῆς δυνάμεως,
καὶ διεξελθόντες ἐξέλιπον τὸ χωρίον ὑπόσπονδοι.⁴
Καλλικρατίδας δὲ τὸ μὲν φρούριον παραλαβὼν
κατέσκαψεν, ἐπὶ δὲ Τηΐους πλεύσας καὶ νυκτὸς

¹ καὶ κατὰ AFK, καὶ P, κατὰ cet.
² δὲ P, omitted cet.
³ καὶ τὰς παρὰ τῶν συμμάχων ναῦς added by Oldfather from
suggestions of Stroth and Vogel.

the Romans elected as consuls Gaius Manius Aemilius and Gaius Valerius. About this time Conon, the Athenian general, now that he had taken over the armaments in Samos,[1] fitted out the ships which were in that place and also collected those of the allies, since he was intent upon making his fleet a match for the ships of the enemy. And the Spartans, when Lysander's period of command as admiral had expired, dispatched Callicratidas to succeed him. Callicratidas was a very young man, without guile and straightforward in character, since he had had as yet no experience of the ways of foreign peoples, and was the most just man among the Spartans; and it is agreed by all that also during his period of command he committed no wrong against either a city or a private citizen but dealt summarily with those who tried to corrupt him with money and had them punished. He put in at Ephesus and took over the fleet, and since he had already sent for the ships of the allies, the sum total he took over, including those of Lysander, was one hundred and forty. And since the Athenians held Delphinium in the territory of the Chians, he sailed against them with all his ships and undertook to lay siege to it. The Athenians, who numbered some five hundred, were dismayed at the great size of his force and abandoned the place, passing through the enemy under a truce. Callicratidas took over the fortress and levelled it to the ground, and then, sailing against the Teïans, he stole inside the walls of the city

---

[1] Cp. chap. 74. 1.

---

[4] So Wesseling: ὑπόσπονδον.

παρεισπεσὼν ἐντὸς τῶν τειχῶν διήρπασε τὴν πόλιν.
5 μετὰ δὲ ταῦτα πλεύσας εἰς Λέσβον, τῇ Μηθύμνῃ
προσέβαλε μετὰ τῆς δυνάμεως παρ' Ἀθηναίων
ἐχούσῃ φρουράν. ποιησάμενος δὲ συνεχεῖς προσβολὰς ἐν ἀρχῇ μὲν οὐδὲν ἤνυε, μετ' ὀλίγον δέ
τινων ἐνδόντων αὐτῷ τὴν πόλιν παρεισέπεσεν ἐντὸς
τῶν τειχῶν, καὶ τὰς μὲν κτήσεις διήρπασε, τῶν
δ' ἀνδρῶν φεισάμενος ἀπέδωκε τοῖς Μηθυμναίοις
6 τὴν πόλιν. τούτων δὲ πραχθέντων ἐπὶ τὴν Μιτυλήνην ὥρμησε, καὶ τοὺς μὲν ὁπλίτας Θώρακι
τῷ Λακεδαιμονίῳ παραδοὺς ἐκέλευσε πεζῇ κατὰ
σπουδὴν ἐπείγεσθαι, ταῖς δὲ ναυσὶν αὐτὸς παρέπλευσεν.

77. Κόνων δ' ὁ τῶν Ἀθηναίων στρατηγὸς εἶχε
μὲν ἑβδομήκοντα ναῦς οὕτως ἐξηρτυμένας τὰ[1] πρὸς
ναυμαχίαν ὡς οὐδεὶς ἕτερος τῶν πρότερον στρατηγῶν ἦν κατεσκευακώς. ἔτυχε μὲν οὖν ἁπάσαις
2 ἀνηγμένος ἐπὶ τὴν βοήθειαν τῆς Μηθύμνης· εὑρὼν
δὲ αὐτὴν ἡλωκυῖαν τότε μὲν ηὐλίσθη πρός τινι
νήσῳ τῶν Ἑκατὸν καλουμένων, ἅμα δ' ἡμέρᾳ
κατανοήσας τὰς τῶν πολεμίων ναῦς προσπλεούσας,
τὸ[2] μὲν αὐτοῦ[3] διαναυμαχεῖν ἔκρινεν ἐπισφαλὲς
εἶναι πρὸς διπλασίας τριήρεις, διενοεῖτο δὲ ἔξω
πλέων φυγεῖν καὶ προσεπισπασάμενός τινας τῶν
πολεμίων τριήρων ναυμαχῆσαι πρὸς τῇ Μιτυλήνῃ[4]·
οὕτως γὰρ ὑπελάμβανε νικῶν μὲν ἕξειν ἀναστροφὴν
εἰς τὸ διώκειν, ἡττώμενος δ' εἰς τὸν λιμένα κατα-
3 φεύξεσθαι. ἐμβιβάσας[5] οὖν τοὺς στρατιώτας ἔπλει
σχολαίως ταῖς εἰρεσίαις χρώμενος, ὅπως αἱ τῶν

---

[1] τὰ] δὲ Vogel.   [2] τὸ Dindorf: τότε.
[3] So Wesseling: αὐτούς.
[4] So Reiske: τὴν Μιτυλήνην.

by night and plundered it.   After this he sailed to
Lesbos and with his force attacked Methymnê, which
held a garrison of Athenians.   Although he launched
repeated assaults, at first he accomplished nothing,
but soon afterward, with the help of certain men who
betrayed the city to him, he broke inside its walls,
and although he plundered its wealth, he spared the
lives of the inhabitants and returned the city to the
Methymnaeans.   After these exploits he made for
Mitylenê ; and assigning the hoplites to Thorax, the
Lacedaemonian, he ordered him to advance by land
with all speed and himself sailed on past Thorax with
his fleet.

77. Conon, the Athenian general, had seventy ships
which he had fitted out with everything necessary for
making war at sea more carefully than any other
general had ever done by way of preparation.   Now
it so happened that he had put out to sea with all his
ships when he went to the aid of Methymnê ; but on
discovering that it had already fallen, at the time he
had bivouacked at one of the Hundred Isles, as they
are called, and at daybreak, when he observed that the
enemy's ships were bearing down on him, he decided
that it would be dangerous for him to join battle in
that place with triremes double his in number, but he
planned to avoid battle by sailing outside the Isles
and, drawing some of the enemy's triremes after him,
to engage them off Mitylenê.   For by such tactics, he
assumed, in case of victory he could turn about and
pursue and in case of defeat he could withdraw for
safety to the harbour.   Consequently, having put his
soldiers on board ship, he set out with the oars at a
leisurely stroke in order that the ships of the Pelopon-

---

⁵ So Rhodoman : ἐκβιβάσας.

Πελοποννησίων ἐγγίσωσιν. οἱ δὲ Λακεδαιμόνιοι
προσιόντες ἀεὶ μᾶλλον ἤλαυνον τὰς ναῦς, ἐλπίζον-
4 τες αἱρήσειν τὰς ἐσχάτας τῶν πολεμίων. τοῦ δὲ
Κόνωνος ὑποχωροῦντος οἱ τὰς ἀρίστας ἔχοντες
ναῦς τῶν Πελοποννησίων κατὰ σπουδὴν ἐδίωκον,
καὶ τοὺς μὲν ἐρέτας διὰ τὴν συνέχειαν τῆς εἰρεσίας
ἐξέλυσαν, αὐτοὶ δὲ πολὺ τῶν ἄλλων ἀπεσπάσθησαν.
ἃ δὴ συνιδὼν ὁ Κόνων, ὡς ἤδη τῆς Μιτυλήνης
ἤγγιζον, ἦρεν ἀπὸ τῆς ἰδίας νεὼς φοινικίδα· τοῦτο
5 γὰρ σύσσημον ἦν τοῖς τριηράρχοις. διόπερ αἱ μὲν
ναῦς, τῶν πολεμίων ἐξαπτομένων, ἐξαίφνης πρὸς
ἕνα καιρὸν ἐπέστρεψαν, καὶ τὸ μὲν πλῆθος ἐπαι-
άνισεν, οἱ δὲ σαλπικταὶ τὸ πολεμικὸν ἐσήμηναν·
οἱ δὲ Πελοποννήσιοι καταπλαγέντες ἐπὶ τῷ γε-
γονότι ταχέως ἐπεχείρουν ἀντιπαρατάττειν[1] τὰς
ναῦς, τοῦ καιροῦ δ' ἀναστροφὴν οὐ διδόντος οὗτοι μὲν ἐν πολλῷ θορύβῳ καθειστήκεισαν διὰ τὸ
τὰς ἀφυστερούσας ναῦς τὴν εἰθισμένην λελοιπέναι
τάξιν.
78. Ὁ δὲ Κόνων δεξιῶς τῷ καιρῷ χρησάμενος
εὐθὺς ἐνέκειτο καὶ τὴν παράταξιν αὐτῶν διεκώλυεν,
ἃς μὲν τιτρώσκων, ὧν δὲ τοὺς ταρσοὺς παρασύρων.
τῶν μὲν οὖν κατὰ τὸν Κόνωνα ταχθεισῶν οὐδεμία
πρὸς φυγὴν ἐπέστρεψεν, ἀλλὰ πρύμναν ἀνακρουό-
μεναι διεκαρτέρουν, προσδεχόμεναι τὰς ἀφυστε-
2 ρούσας· οἱ δὲ τὴν εὐώνυμον ἔχοντες τάξιν Ἀθηναῖοι
τρεψάμενοι τοὺς καθ' αὑτοὺς ἐπέκειντο φιλοτιμότερον ἐπὶ πολὺν χρόνον διώκοντες. ἤδη δὲ πασῶν
τῶν νεῶν τοῖς Πελοποννησίοις ἠθροισμένων, ὁ
μὲν Κόνων εὐλαβηθεὶς τὸ πλῆθος τῶν πολεμίων
τοῦ μὲν διώκειν ἀπέστη, μετὰ τεσσαράκοντα δὲ
3 νεῶν ἀπέπλευσεν εἰς Μιτυλήνην. τοὺς δὲ διώ-

nesians might draw near him. And the Lacedae- 407 B.C.
monians, as they approached, kept driving their
ships faster and faster in the hope of seizing the hind-
most ships of the enemy. As Conon withdrew, the
commanders of the best ships of the Peloponnesians
pushed the pursuit hotly, and they wore out the rowers
by their continued exertion at the oars and were
themselves separated a long distance from the others.
Conon, noticing this, when his ships were already near
Mitylenê, raised from his flagship a red banner, for
this was a signal for the captains of the triremes. At
this his ships, even as the enemy was overhauling
them, suddenly turned about at the same moment,
and the crews raised the battle-song and the trumpeters sounded the attack. The Peloponnesians, dismayed at the turn of events, hastily endeavoured to
draw up their ships to repel the attack, but as there
was not time for them to turn about they had fallen
into great confusion because the ships coming up after
them had left their accustomed position.

78. Conon, making clever use of the opportunity, at
once pressed upon them, and prevented their establishing any order, damaging some ships and shearing
off the rows of oars of others. Of the ships opposing
Conon not one turned to flight, but they continued to
back water while waiting for the ships which tarried
behind ; but the Athenians who held the left wing,
putting to flight their opponents, pressed upon them
with increasing eagerness and pursued them for a long
time. But when the Peloponnesians had brought all
their ships together, Conon, fearing the superior
numbers of the enemy, stopped the pursuit and sailed
off to Mitylenê with forty ships. As for the Athenians

---

[1] So Wesseling : ἀντιπράττειν.

DIODORUS OF SICILY

ξαντας Ἀθηναίους αἱ τῶν Πελοποννησίων ναῦς
ἅπασαι περιχυθεῖσαι κατεπλήξαντο, καὶ τῆς ἐπὶ
τὴν πόλιν ἐπανόδου διακλείσασαι φυγεῖν πρὸς τὴν
γῆν ἐβιάσαντο. ἐπικειμένων δὲ τῶν Πελοποννησίων πάσαις ταῖς ναυσίν, Ἀθηναῖοι θεωροῦντες
μηδεμίαν σωτηρίαν ἄλλην ὑποκειμένην, κατέφυγον
πρὸς τὴν γῆν, καὶ καταλιπόντες τὰ σκάφη διεσώθησαν εἰς Μιτυλήνην.

4 Καλλικρατίδας δὲ τριάκοντα νεῶν κυριεύσας τὸ
μὲν ναυτικὸν ἐθεώρει τῶν πολεμίων καταλελυ-
μένον, πεζῇ δὲ τοὺς ἀγῶνας ἤλπιζεν ὑπολείπεσθαι.
διόπερ οὗτος μὲν ἐπὶ τὴν πόλιν διέπλει, Κόνων δ᾽
ἅμα τῷ καταπλεῦσαι προσδεχόμενος τὴν πολιορκίαν, τὰ περὶ τὸν εἴσπλουν τοῦ λιμένος κατ-
εσκεύαζεν· εἰς μὲν γὰρ τὰ βράχη τοῦ λιμένος πλοῖα
μικρὰ πληρώσας λίθων κατεπόντισε, πρὸς δὲ τοῖς
βάθεσιν ὁλκάδας καθώρμιζεν οὔσας λιθοφόρους.
5 οἱ μὲν οὖν Ἀθηναῖοι καὶ τῶν Μιτυληναίων ὄχλος
πολὺς ἐκ τῶν ἀγρῶν διὰ τὸν πόλεμον συνεληλυθὼς[1]
ταχέως κατεσκεύασε τὰ πρὸς τὴν πολιορκίαν. ὁ δὲ
Καλλικρατίδας ἐκβιβάσας τοὺς στρατιώτας εἰς τὸν
πλησίον τῆς πόλεως αἰγιαλὸν ἐποιήσατο παρεμβολήν, καὶ τρόπαιον ἀπὸ τῆς ναυμαχίας ἔστησεν.
τῇ δ᾽ ὑστεραίᾳ τὰς κρατίστας τῶν νεῶν ἐπιλέξας
καὶ παρακελευσάμενος μὴ ἀπολείπεσθαι τῆς ἰδίας
νεώς, ἀνήχθη, σπεύδων εἰς τὸν λιμένα πλεῦσαι
6 καὶ λῦσαι τὸ διάφραγμα τῶν πολεμίων. ὁ δὲ
Κόνων τοὺς μὲν εἰς τὰς τριήρεις ἐνεβίβασε[2] καὶ
κατὰ τὸν διέκπλουν ἀντιπρώρους κατέστησε, τοὺς
δ᾽ ἐπὶ τὰ μεγάλα πλοῖα διέταξε, τινὰς δ᾽ ἐπὶ τὰς
χηλὰς τοῦ λιμένος παρέπεμψεν ὅπως πανταχόθεν

---

[1] So Eichstädt: διεληλυθώς.

who had set out in pursuit, all the Peloponnesian ships, swarming around them, struck terror into them, and cutting them off from return to the city compelled them to turn in flight to the land. And since the Peloponnesians pressed upon them with all their ships, the Athenians, seeing no other means of deliverance, fled for safety to the land and deserting their vessels found refuge in Mitylenê.

Callicratidas, by the capture of thirty ships, was aware that the naval power of the enemy had been destroyed, but he anticipated that the fighting on land remained. Consequently he sailed on to the city, and Conon, who was expecting a siege when he arrived, began upon preparations about the entrance to the harbour; for in the shallow places of the harbour he sank small boats filled with rocks and in the deep waters he anchored merchantmen armed with stones.[1] Now the Athenians and a great throng of the Mitylenaeans who had gathered from the fields into the city because of the war speedily completed the preparations for the siege. Callicratidas, disembarking his soldiers on the beach near the city, pitched a camp, and then he set up a trophy for the sea-battle. And on the next day, after choosing out his best ships and commanding them not to get far from his own ship, he put out to sea, being eager to sail into the harbour and break the barrier constructed by the enemy. Conon put some of his soldiers on the triremes, which he placed with their prows facing the open passage, and some he assigned to the large vessels,[2] while others he sent to the breakwaters of the harbour in order that

---

[1] Carried on the yard-arms.
[2] Presumably the merchantmen mentioned above.

---

[2] So Dindorf: ἀνεβίβασεν.

ᾗ πεφραγμένος καὶ κατὰ γῆν καὶ κατὰ θάλατταν.
7 αὐτὸς μὲν οὖν ὁ Κόνων τὰς τριήρεις ἔχων ἐναυ-
μάχει, πληρώσας τὸν μεταξὺ τόπον τῶν διαφραγ-
μάτων· οἱ δ᾽ ἐπὶ τῶν μεγάλων πλοίων ἐφεστῶτες
ἐπέρριψαν ταῖς τῶν πολεμίων ναυσὶ τοὺς ἀπὸ τῶν
κεραιῶν λίθους· οἱ δ᾽ ἐπὶ ταῖς χηλαῖς τοῦ λιμένος
τεταγμένοι διεκώλυον τοὺς ἀποτολμῶντας εἰς τὴν
γῆν ἀποβαίνειν.

79. Οἱ δὲ Πελοποννήσιοι τῆς τῶν Ἀθηναίων
φιλοτιμίας ἐλείποντο οὐδέν. ταῖς γὰρ ναυσὶν
ἀθρόαις ἐπιπλεύσαντες, καὶ τοὺς ἀρίστους ἄνδρας
ἐπὶ τὰ καταστρώματα τάξαντες, τὴν ναυμαχίαν ἅμα
καὶ πεζὴν ἐποιοῦντο μάχην· βιαζόμενοι γὰρ[1] εἰς τὰς
τῶν ἀντιτεταγμένων ναῦς ταῖς πρῴραις ἐπέβαινον
τετολμηκότως,[2] ὡς οὐχ ὑποστησομένων τὸ δεινὸν
2 τῶν προηττημένων. οἱ δ᾽ Ἀθηναῖοι καὶ Μιτυλη-
ναῖοι μίαν ὁρῶντες ἀπολειπομένην σωτηρίαν τὴν
ἐκ τῆς νίκης, εὐγενῶς ἀποθνήσκειν ἔσπευδον ὑπὲρ
τοῦ μὴ λιπεῖν τὴν τάξιν. κατεχούσης δὲ φιλοτιμίας
ἀνυπερβλήτου τὰ στρατόπεδα πολὺς ἐγένετο φόνος,[3]
ἁπάντων ἀφειδῶς τὰ σώματα τοῖς κινδύνοις παραρ-
3 ριπτόντων. οἱ μὲν γὰρ ἐπὶ[4] τῶν καταστρωμάτων
ὑπὸ τοῦ πλήθους τῶν εἰς αὐτοὺς φερομένων βελῶν
κατετιτρώσκοντο, καὶ τινὲς μὲν ἐπικαίρως πλη-
γέντες ἔπιπτον εἰς τὴν θάλατταν, τινὲς δ᾽ οὐκ
αἰσθανόμενοι θερμῶν ἔτι τῶν πληγῶν οὐσῶν δι-
ηγωνίζοντο· πλεῖστοι δ᾽ ὑπὸ τῶν λιθοφόρων κεραιῶν
ἔπιπτον, ὡς ἂν ἐξ ὑπερδεξίων τόπων βαλλόντων
4 λίθους ὑπερμεγέθεις τῶν Ἀθηναίων. οὐ μὴν ἀλλὰ
τῆς μάχης ἐπὶ πολὺν χρόνον γενομένης καὶ πολλῶν

[1] βιαζόμενοι μὲν γὰρ ἅμα MSS.; μὲν deleted by Bekker,
ἅμα by Wesseling.

the harbour might be fenced in on every side, both by land and by sea. Then Conon himself with his triremes joined the battle, filling with his ships the space lying between the barriers ; and the soldiers stationed on the large ships hurled the stones from the yardarms upon the ships of the enemy, while those drawn up on the breakwaters of the harbour held off those who might have ventured to disembark on the land.

79. The Peloponnesians were not a whit outdone by the emulation displayed by the Athenians. Advancing with their ships in mass formation and with their best soldiers lined up on the decks they made the sea-battle also a fight between infantry ; for as they pressed upon their opponents' ships they boldly boarded their prows, in the belief that men who had once been defeated would not stand up to the terror of battle. But the Athenians and Mitylenaeans, seeing that the single hope of safety left to them lay in their victory, were resolved to die nobly rather than leave their station. And so, since an unsurpassable emulation pervaded both forces, a great slaughter ensued, all the participants exposing their bodies, without regard of risk, to the perils of battle. The soldiers on the decks were wounded by the multitude of missiles which flew at them, and some of them, who were mortally struck, fell into the sea, while some, so long as their wounds were fresh, fought on without feeling them ; but very many fell victims to the stones that were hurled by the stone-carrying yardarms, since the Athenians kept up a shower of huge stones from these commanding positions. The fighting had continued, none the less, for a long while and many

---

² So Dindorf: τετολμηκότες.

³ So Madvig: πόλεμος.   ⁴ So Dindorf: ἀπό.

παρ' ἀμφοτέροις ἀπολλυμένων, ὁ Καλλικρατίδας
ἀνεκαλέσατο τῇ σάλπιγγι τοὺς στρατιώτας, βου-
5 λόμενος αὐτοὺς διαναπαῦσαι. μετὰ δέ τινα καιρὸν
πάλιν πληρώσας τὰς ναῦς, καὶ πολὺν διαγωνισά-
μενος χρόνον, μόγις τῷ¹ τε πλήθει τῶν νεῶν καὶ
τῇ ῥώμῃ τῶν ἐπιβατῶν ἐξέωσε τοὺς Ἀθηναίους.
ὧν συμφυγόντων εἰς τὸν ἐν τῇ πόλει λιμένα, διέ-
πλευσε τὰ διαφράγματα καὶ καθωρμίσθη πλησίον
6 τῆς πόλεως τῶν Μιτυληναίων. ὁ γὰρ εἴσπλους
ὑπὲρ οὗ διηγωνίζοντο λιμένα μὲν εἶχε² καλόν,
ἐκτὸς δὲ τῆς πόλεώς ἐστιν. ἡ μὲν γὰρ ἀρχαία
πόλις μικρὰ νῆσός ἐστιν, ἡ δ' ὕστερον προσοι-
κισθεῖσα τῆς ἀντιπέραν ἐστὶ Λέσβου· ἀνὰ μέσον
δ' αὐτῶν ἐστιν εὔριπος στενὸς καὶ ποιῶν τὴν πόλιν
7 ὀχυράν. ὁ δὲ Καλλικρατίδας ἐκβιβάσας τὴν δύναμιν περιεστρατοπέδευσε τὴν πόλιν καὶ πανταχόθεν προσβολὰς ἐποιεῖτο.

Καὶ τὰ μὲν κατὰ τὴν Μιτυλήνην ἐν τούτοις ἦν.
8 Κατὰ δὲ Σικελίαν Συρακόσιοι πέμψαντες εἰς
Καρχηδόνα πρέσβεις περί τε τοῦ πολέμου κατ-
εμέμφοντο καὶ³ τὸ λοιπὸν ἠξίουν παύσασθαι τῆς
διαφορᾶς. οἷς οἱ Καρχηδόνιοι τὰς ἀποκρίσεις
ἀμφιβόλους δόντες, ἐν μὲν τῇ Λιβύῃ μεγάλας παρεσκευάζοντο δυνάμεις, ἐπιθυμοῦντες ἁπάσας τὰς ἐν
τῇ νήσῳ πόλεις καταδουλώσασθαι· πρὶν ἢ δὲ τὰ
στρατόπεδα διαβιβάζειν, καταλέξαντες τῶν πολιτῶν τινας καὶ τῶν ἄλλων Λιβύων τοὺς βουλομένους
ἔκτισαν ἐν τῇ Σικελίᾳ πρὸς αὐτοῖς τοῖς θερμοῖς
ὕδασι πόλιν, ὀνομάσαντες Θέρμα.

¹ μόγις τῷ Dindorf : μεγίστῳ.
² εἶχε] Vogel suggests ἔχει.
³ εἰς after καὶ deleted by Vogel.

had met death on both sides, when Callicratidas, wish- 407 B.C.
ing to give his soldiers a breathing-spell, sounded the
recall. After some time he again manned his ships
and continued the struggle over a long period, and
with great effort, by means of the superior number of
his ships and the strength of the marines, he thrust
out the Athenians. And when the Athenians fled for
refuge to the harbour within the city, he sailed
through the barriers and brought his ships to anchor
near the city of the Mitylenaeans. It may be explained that the entrance for whose control they had
fought had a good harbour, which, however, lies outside the city. For the ancient city is a small island,
and the later city, which was founded near it, is opposite it on the island of Lesbos ; and between the two
cities is a narrow strait which also adds strength to
the city. Callicratidas now, disembarking his troops,
invested the city and launched assaults upon it from
every side.

Such was the state of affairs at Mitylenê.

In Sicily ¹ the Syracusans, sending ambassadors to
Carthage, not only censured them for the war but required that for the future they cease from hostilities.
To them the Carthaginians gave ambiguous answers
and set about assembling great armaments in Libya,
since their desire was fixed on enslaving all the cities
of the island ; but before sending their forces across
to Sicily they picked out volunteers from their citizens
and the other inhabitants of Libya and founded in
Sicily right at the warm (*therma*) springs a city which
they named Therma.²

---

¹ The narrative is resumed from the end of chap. 62.
² It was near Himera (Cicero, *In Verr.* 2. 35) ; the springs
are mentioned in Book 4. 23.

80. Τῶν δὲ κατὰ τοῦτον τὸν ἐνιαυτὸν πράξεων τέλος ἐχουσῶν Ἀθήνησι μὲν παρέλαβε τὴν ἀρχὴν Καλλίας, ἐν δὲ τῇ Ῥώμῃ κατεστάθησαν ὕπατοι Λεύκιος Φούριος καὶ Γναῖος Πομπήιος. περὶ δὲ τούτους τοὺς χρόνους Καρχηδόνιοι τοῖς περὶ Σικελίαν εὐτυχήμασι μετεωριζόμενοι καὶ σπεύδοντες ἁπάσης τῆς νήσου κυριεῦσαι, μεγάλας δυνάμεις ἐψηφίσαντο παρασκευάζεσθαι· ἑλόμενοι δὲ στρατηγὸν Ἀννίβαν τὸν κατασκάψαντα τήν τε τῶν Σελινουντίων καὶ τὴν τῶν Ἱμεραίων πόλιν, ἅπασαν αὐτῷ τὴν κατὰ τὸν πόλεμον ἐξουσίαν

2 ἐπέτρεψαν. παραιτουμένου δὲ διὰ τὸ γῆρας, προσκατέστησαν καὶ ἄλλον στρατηγὸν Ἱμίλκωνα τὸν Ἄννωνος, ἐκ τῆς αὐτῆς ὄντα συγγενείας. οὗτοι δὲ κοινῇ συνεδρεύσαντες ἔπεμψάν τινας τῶν ἐν ἀξιώματι παρὰ τοῖς Καρχηδονίοις ὄντων μετὰ πολλῶν χρημάτων, τοὺς μὲν εἰς Ἰβηρίαν, τοὺς δ᾽ εἰς τὰς Βαλιαρίδας νήσους, παρακελευσάμενοι

3 ξενολογεῖν ὡς πλείστους. αὐτοὶ δ᾽ ἐπῄεσαν τὴν Λιβύην καταγράφοντες στρατιώτας Λίβυας καὶ Φοίνικας καὶ τῶν πολιτικῶν τοὺς κρατίστους. μετεπέμποντο δὲ καὶ παρὰ τῶν συμμαχούντων αὐτοῖς ἐθνῶν καὶ βασιλέων στρατιώτας Μαυρουσίους καὶ Νομάδας καί τινας τῶν οἰκούντων τὰ

4 πρὸς τὴν Κυρήνην κεκλιμένα μέρη. ἐκ δὲ τῆς Ἰταλίας μισθωσάμενοι Καμπανοὺς διεβίβασαν εἰς Λιβύην· ᾔδεισαν γὰρ τὴν μὲν χρείαν αὐτῶν μεγάλα συμβαλλομένην, τοὺς δ᾽ ἐν Σικελίᾳ καταλελειμ-

---

[1] Gnaeus Cornelius (Livy, 4. 54). The Pompeys were a plebeian house and the consulship was not yet open to plebeians.

[2] A recently discovered inscription from Athens, a decree

346

80. When the events of this year came to an end, 406 B.C. in Athens Callias succeeded to the office of archon and in Rome the consuls elected were Lucius Furius and Gnaeus Pompeius.[1] At this time the Carthaginians, being elated over their successes in Sicily and eager to become lords of the whole island, voted to prepare great armaments ; and electing as general Hannibal, who had razed to the ground both the city of the Selinuntians and that of the Himeraeans, they committed to him full authority over the conduct of the war. When he begged to be excused because of his age, they appointed besides him another general, Himilcon, the son of Hanno and of the same family.[2] These two, after full consultation, dispatched certain citizens who were held in high esteem among the Carthaginians with large sums of money, some to Iberia and others to the Baliarides Islands, with orders to recruit as many mercenaries as possible. And they themselves canvassed Libya, enrolling as soldiers Libyans and Phoenicians and the stoutest from among their own citizens. Moreover they summoned soldiers also from the nations and kings who were their allies, Maurusians and Nomads and certain peoples who dwell in the regions toward Cyrenê. Also from Italy they hired Campanians and brought them over to Libya ; for they knew that their aid would be of great assistance to them and that the Campanians who had

of the Council mentioning Hannibal and Himilcon, has been published by B. D. Meritt, " Athens and Carthage," *Harvard Studies in Classical Philology*, Supplementary Volume I (1940), pp. 247-253. Although the inscription is most fragmentary, it would appear that heralds from Carthage had come to Athens in connection with this invasion, and it is certain that the Athenians had sent a mission to confer with Hannibal and Himilcon in Sicily.

DIODORUS OF SICILY

μένους Καμπανοὺς διὰ τὸ προσκεκοφέναι τοῖς
Καρχηδονίοις¹ μετὰ τῶν Σικελιωτῶν ταχθησο-
5 μένους. τέλος δὲ τῶν δυνάμεων ἀθροισθεισῶν
εἰς Καρχηδόνα συνήχθησαν αὐτοῖς οἱ πάντες σὺν
ἱππεῦσιν οὐ πολλῷ πλείους, ὡς μὲν Τίμαιος, τῶν
δώδεκα μυριάδων, ὡς δ' Ἔφορος, τριάκοντα
μυριάδες.²

Καρχηδόνιοι μὲν οὖν τὰ πρὸς τὴν διάβασιν
ἑτοιμάζοντες τάς τε τριήρεις πάσας κατήρτιζον
καὶ φορτηγὰ πλοῖα συνήγαγον πλείω τῶν χιλίων·
6 προαποστειλάντων δ' αὐτῶν εἰς Σικελίαν τεσσαράκοντα τριήρεις, οἱ Συρακόσιοι κατὰ τάχος ταῖς
παραπλησίαις ναυσὶν ἐπεφάνησαν ἐν τοῖς περὶ τὸν
Ἔρυκα τόποις. γενομένης δὲ ναυμαχίας ἐπὶ
πολὺν χρόνον πεντεκαίδεκα μὲν τῶν Φοινισσῶν
νεῶν διεφθάρησαν, αἱ δ' ἄλλαι νυκτὸς ἐπιγενο-
7 μένης ἔφυγον εἰς τὸ πέλαγος. ἀπαγγελθείσης δὲ
τῆς ἥττης τοῖς Καρχηδονίοις, Ἀννίβας ὁ στρατηγὸς
ἐξέπλευσε μετὰ νεῶν πεντήκοντα· ἔσπευδε γὰρ
τοὺς μὲν Συρακοσίους κωλῦσαι χρήσασθαι τῷ
προτερήματι, ταῖς δὲ ἰδίαις δυνάμεσιν ἀσφαλῆ
παρασκευάσαι τὸν κατάπλουν.

81. Διαβοηθείσης δὲ τῆς Ἀννίβα βοηθείας κατὰ
τὴν νῆσον, ἅπαντες προσεδόκων καὶ τὰς δυνάμεις
εὐθέως διαβιβασθήσεσθαι. αἱ δὲ πόλεις τὸ μέγεθος τῆς παρασκευῆς ἀκούουσαι καὶ συλλογι-
ζόμεναι τὸν ἀγῶνα περὶ τῶν ὅλων ἐσόμενον, οὐ
2 μετρίως ἠγωνίων. οἱ μὲν οὖν Συρακόσιοι πρός
τε τοὺς κατ' Ἰταλίαν Ἕλληνας καὶ πρὸς Λακεδαιμονίους περὶ συμμαχίας διεπέμποντο· ἀπ-

¹ So Wesseling : τοὺς Καρχηδονίους.
² So Wurm : μυριάδων.

348

been left behind in Sicily, because they had fallen out with the Carthaginians,[1] would fight on the side of the Sicilian Greeks. And when the armaments were finally assembled at Carthage, the sum total of the troops collected together with the cavalry was a little over one hundred and twenty thousand, according to Timaeus, but three hundred thousand, according to Ephorus.

The Carthaginians, in preparation for their crossing over to Sicily, made ready and equipped all their triremes and also assembled more than a thousand cargo ships, and when they dispatched in advance forty triremes to Sicily, the Syracusans speedily appeared with about the same number of warships in the region of Eryx. In the long sea-battle which ensued fifteen of the Phoenician ships were destroyed and the rest, when night fell, fled for safety to the open sea. And when word of the defeat was brought to the Carthaginians, Hannibal the general set out to sea with fifty ships, since he was eager both to prevent the Syracusans from exploiting their advantage and to make the landing safe for his own armaments.

81. When news of the reinforcements which Hannibal was bringing was noised throughout Sicily, everyone expected that his armaments would also be brought over at once. And the cities, as they heard of the great scale of the preparations and came to the conclusion that the struggle was to be for their very existence, were distressed without measure. Accordingly the Syracusans set about negotiating alliances both with the Greeks of Italy and with the Lacedae-

---

[1] Cp. chap. 62. 5.

ἔστελλον¹ δὲ καὶ πρὸς τὰς ἐν Σικελίᾳ πόλεις² τοὺς
παρορμήσοντας τὰ πλήθη πρὸς τὸν ὑπὲρ τῆς
3 κοινῆς ἐλευθερίας κίνδυνον. ᾿Ακραγαντῖνοι δέ,
ὁμοροῦντες τῇ τῶν Καρχηδονίων ἐπικρατείᾳ,³
διελάμβανον, ὅπερ ἦν, ἐπ᾿ αὐτοὺς πρώτους ἥξειν
τὸ τοῦ πολέμου βάρος. ἔδοξεν οὖν αὐτοῖς τόν τε
σῖτον καὶ τοὺς ἄλλους καρπούς, ἔτι δὲ τὰς κτήσεις
ἁπάσας, ἀπὸ τῆς χώρας κατακομίζειν ἐντὸς τῶν
4 τειχῶν. κατ᾿ ἐκείνους δὲ τοὺς καιροὺς τήν τε
πόλιν καὶ τὴν χώραν τῶν ᾿Ακραγαντίνων συνέβαινεν εὐδαιμονίας ὑπάρχειν πλήρη· περὶ ἧς οὐκ
ἀνάρμοστόν μοι φαίνεται διελθεῖν. καὶ γὰρ ἀμπε-
λῶνες τοῖς μεγέθεσι καὶ τῷ κάλλει διαφέροντες,⁴
καὶ τὸ πλεῖστον τῆς χώρας ἐλαίαις κατάφυτον,
ἐξ ἧς παμπληθῆ κομιζόμενοι καρπὸν ἐπώλουν εἰς
5 Καρχηδόνα· οὔπω γὰρ κατ᾿ ἐκείνους τοὺς χρόνους
τῆς Λιβύης πεφυτευμένης οἱ τὴν ᾿Ακραγαντίνην
νεμόμενοι τὸν ἐκ τῆς Λιβύης ἀντιφορτιζόμενοι
πλοῦτον οὐσίας ἀπίστους τοῖς μεγέθεσιν ἐκέκτηντο.
πολλὰ δὲ τοῦ πλούτου παρ᾿ αὐτοῖς διαμένει σημεῖα,
περὶ ὧν οὐκ ἀνοίκειόν ἐστι βραχέα διελθεῖν.

82. Ἥ τε γὰρ τῶν ἱερῶν κατασκευὴ καὶ μάλιστα
ὁ τοῦ Διὸς νεὼς ἐμφαίνει τὴν μεγαλοπρέπειαν τῶν
τότε ἀνθρώπων· τῶν μὲν οὖν⁵ ἄλλων ἱερῶν τὰ μὲν
κατεκαύθη, τὰ δὲ τελείως κατεσκάφη διὰ τὸ πολλάκις ἡλωκέναι τὴν πόλιν, τὸ δ᾿⁶ Ὀλύμπιον μέλλον
λαμβάνειν τὴν ὀροφὴν ὁ πόλεμος ἐκώλυσεν· ἐξ

¹ So Rhodoman : ἐπέστελλον.
² πρὸς after πόλεις deleted by Rhodoman.
³ ὁμοροῦντες τῇ . . . ἐπικρατείᾳ Dindorf: ὁρῶντες τὴν . . .
ἐπικράτειαν.
⁴ Reiske would add ἦσαν or ὑπῆρχον; Vogel suggests
εἶχον γὰρ ἀμπελῶνας . . . διαφέροντας.

350

monians ; and they also continued to dispatch emis-
saries to the cities of Sicily to arouse the masses to
fight for the common freedom. The Acragantini,
because they were the nearest to the empire of the
Carthaginians, assumed what indeed took place, that
the weight of the war would fall on them first. They
decided, therefore, to gather not only their grain and
other crops but also all their possessions from the
countryside within their walls. At this time, it so
happened, both the city and the territory of the
Acragantini enjoyed great prosperity, which I think it
would not be out of place for me to describe. Their
vineyards excelled in their great extent and beauty
and the greater part of their territory was planted in
olive-trees from which they gathered an abundant
harvest and sold to Carthage ; for since Libya at that
time was not yet planted in fruit-trees,[1] the inhabitants of the territory belonging to Acragas took
in exchange for their products the wealth of Libya and
accumulated fortunes of unbelievable size. Of this
wealth there remain among them many evidences,
which it will not be foreign to our purpose to discuss
briefly.

82. Now the sacred buildings which they constructed, and especially the temple of Zeus, bear
witness to the grand manner of the men of that day.
Of the other sacred buildings some have been burned
and others completely destroyed because of the many
times the city has been taken in war, but the completion of the temple of Zeus, which was ready to
receive its roof, was prevented by the war ; and after

[1] But cp. Book 4. 17. 4 where we are told that Heracles
planted much of Libya in vineyards and olive orchards.

---

[5] οὖν Vogel: γάρ.   [6] τὸ δ' Vogel: τὸ δ' οὖν.

οὗ τῆς πόλεως κατασκαφείσης οὐδέποτε ὕστερον
ἴσχυσαν Ἀκραγαντῖνοι τέλος ἐπιθεῖναι τοῖς οἰκο-
2 δομήμασιν. ἔστι δὲ ὁ νεὼς ἔχων τὸ μὲν μῆκος
πόδας τριακοσίους τεσσαράκοντα, τὸ δὲ πλάτος
ἑξήκοντα, τὸ δὲ ὕψος ἑκατὸν εἴκοσι χωρὶς τοῦ
κρηπιδώματος. μέγιστος δ' ὢν τῶν ἐν Σικελίᾳ
καὶ τοῖς ἐκτὸς οὐκ ἀλόγως ἂν συγκρίνοιτο κατὰ
τὸ μέγεθος τῆς ὑποστάσεως· καὶ γὰρ εἰ μὴ τέλος
λαβεῖν συνέβη τὴν ἐπιβολήν, ἥ γε προαίρεσις[1]
3 ὑπάρχει φανερά. τῶν δ' ἄλλων ἢ μετὰ περιτειχῶν[2]
τοὺς νεὼς οἰκοδομούντων ἢ κύκλῳ κίοσι[3] τοὺς
σηκοὺς[4] περιλαμβανόντων, οὗτος ἑκατέρας τούτων
μετέχει τῶν ὑποστάσεων· συνῳκοδομοῦντο γὰρ
τοῖς τοίχοις οἱ κίονες,[5] ἔξωθεν μὲν στρογγύλοι,
τὸ δ' ἐντὸς τοῦ νεὼ ἔχοντες τετράγωνον· καὶ τοῦ
μὲν ἐκτὸς μέρους ἐστὶν αὐτῶν ἡ περιφέρεια ποδῶν
εἴκοσι, καθ' ἣν εἰς τὰ διαξύσματα δύναται ἀνθρώ-
πινον ἐναρμόζεσθαι σῶμα, τὸ[6] δ' ἐντὸς ποδῶν δώ-
4 δεκα. τῶν δὲ στοῶν τὸ μέγεθος καὶ τὸ ὕψος
ἐξαίσιον ἐχουσῶν, ἐν μὲν τῷ πρὸς ἕω μέρει τὴν
γιγαντομαχίαν ἐποιήσαντο γλυφαῖς καὶ τῷ μεγέθει
καὶ τῷ κάλλει διαφερούσαις,[7] ἐν δὲ τῷ πρὸς δυσμὰς
τὴν ἅλωσιν τῆς Τροίας, ἐν ᾗ τῶν ἡρώων ἕκαστον
ἰδεῖν ἔστιν οἰκείως τῆς περιστάσεως δεδημιουργη-
5 μένον. ἦν δὲ καὶ λίμνη κατ' ἐκεῖνον τὸν χρόνον

---

[1] So Reiske : προδιαίρεσις.
[2] μετὰ περιτειχῶν Capps, μετὰ τοίχων Reiske, μετὰ θριγκῶν Dindorf, μέχρι τεγῶν or συνεχεῖ τοίχῳ Vogel : μέχρι τοίχων.
[3] ἢ κύκλῳ κίοσι Wesseling : ἡ κύκλωσις.
[4] So Reiske : οἴκους.
[5] So Dindorf : οἱ τοῖχοι τοῖς κίοσιν.
[6] τὸ] τοῦ Dindorf.
[7] So Dindorf, διαφερούσας PAK, διαφέρουσαν cet.

the war, since the city had been completely destroyed, 406 B.C. never in the subsequent years did the Acragantini find themselves able to finish their buildings. The temple has a length of three hundred and forty feet, a width of sixty, and a height of one hundred and twenty not including the foundation.[1] And being as it is the largest temple in Sicily, it may not unreasonably be compared, so far as the magnitude of its substructure is concerned, with the temples outside of Sicily ; for even though, as it turned out, the design could not be carried out, the scale of the undertaking at any rate is clear. And though all other men build their temples either with walls forming the sides or with rows of columns, thus enclosing their sanctuaries, this temple combines both these plans; for the columns were built in with the walls,[2] the part extending outside the temple being rounded and that within square ; and the circumference of the outer part of the column which extends from the wall is twenty feet and the body of a man may be contained in the fluting, while that of the inner part is twelve feet. The porticoes were of enormous size and height, and in the east pediment they portrayed The Battle between the Gods and the Giants in sculptures which excelled in size and beauty, and in the west The Capture of Troy, in which each one of the heroes may be seen portrayed in a manner appropriate to his rôle. There was at that

---

[1] The actual dimensions of this great Olympieum are in English feet (c. 5 mm. longer than the Attic foot) : length excluding steps 361 ft. ; breadth $173\frac{1}{2}$; height of columns with capitals $62\frac{1}{2}$ (?) ; diameter of columns at bottom 14.

[2] i.e. they were engaged or half-columns ; see the frontispiece of this Volume.

ἐκτὸς τῆς πόλεως χειροποίητος, ἔχουσα τὴν περί-
μετρον σταδίων ἑπτά, τὸ δὲ βάθος εἴκοσι πηχῶν·
εἰς ἣν ἐπαγομένων ὑδάτων ἐφιλοτέχνησαν πλῆθος
ἰχθύων ἐν αὐτῇ ποιῆσαι παντοίων εἰς τὰς δημοσίας
ἑστιάσεις, μεθ' ὧν συνδιέτριβον κύκνοι καὶ τῶν
ἄλλων ὀρνέων πολὺ πλῆθος, ὥστε μεγάλην τέρψιν
6 παρασκευάζειν τοῖς θεωμένοις. δηλοῖ δὲ τὴν τρυφὴν αὐτῶν καὶ ἡ πολυτέλεια τῶν μνημείων, ἃ τινὰ
μὲν τοῖς ἀθληταῖς ἵπποις κατεσκεύασαν, τινὰ δὲ
τοῖς ὑπὸ τῶν παρθένων καὶ παίδων ἐν οἴκῳ τρεφο-
μένοις ὀρνιθαρίοις, ἃ Τίμαιος ἑωρακέναι φησὶ μέχρι
7 τοῦ καθ' ἑαυτὸν βίου διαμένοντα. καὶ κατὰ τὴν
προτέραν δὲ ταύτης Ὀλυμπιάδα, δευτέραν ἐπὶ ταῖς
ἐνενήκοντα, νικήσαντος Ἐξαινέτου Ἀκραγαντίνου,
κατήγαγον αὐτὸν εἰς τὴν πόλιν ἐφ' ἅρματος· συν-
επόμπευον δ' αὐτῷ χωρὶς τῶν ἄλλων συνωρίδες
τριακόσιαι λευκῶν ἵππων, πᾶσαι παρ' αὐτῶν τῶν
8 Ἀκραγαντίνων. καθόλου δὲ καὶ τὰς ἀγωγὰς εὐθὺς
ἐκ παίδων ἐποιοῦντο τρυφεράς, τήν τ' ἐσθῆτα
μαλακὴν φοροῦντες καθ' ὑπερβολὴν καὶ χρυσοφο-
ροῦντες, ἔτι δὲ στλεγγίσι[1] καὶ ληκύθοις ἀργυραῖς
τε καὶ χρυσαῖς χρώμενοι.

83. Ἦν[2] δὲ τῶν Ἀκραγαντίνων σχεδὸν πλουσιώτατος κατ' ἐκεῖνον τὸν χρόνον Τελλίας,[3] ὃς κατὰ
τὴν οἰκίαν ξενῶνας ἔχων πλείους πρὸς ταῖς πύλαις
ἔταττεν οἰκέτας, οἷς παρηγγελμένον ἦν ἅπαντας
τοὺς ξένους καλεῖν ἐπὶ ξενίᾳ. πολλοὶ δὲ καὶ τῶν
ἄλλων Ἀκραγαντίνων ἐποίουν τὸ παραπλήσιον,

---

[1] στλεγγίσι Α, στήγεσιν Ρ, στεγίσι cet.
[2] ἦν Madvig: ὁ.   [3] So Dindorf: Γελλίας and below.

time also an artificial pool outside the city, seven stades 406 B.C. in circumference and twenty cubits deep ; into this they brought water and ingeniously contrived to produce a multitude of fish of every variety for their public feastings, and with the fish swans spent their time and a vast multitude of every other kind of bird, so that the pool was an object of great delight to gaze upon. And witness to the luxury of the inhabitants is also the extravagant cost of the monuments which they erected, some adorned with sculptured race-horses and others with the pet birds kept by girls and boys in their homes, monuments which Timaeus says he had seen extant even in his own lifetime.[1] And in the Olympiad previous to the one we are discussing, namely, the Ninety-second, when Exaenetus of Acragas won the " stadion,"[2] he was conducted into the city in a chariot and in the procession there were, not to speak of the other things, three hundred chariots each drawn by two white horses, all the chariots belonging to citizens of Acragas. Speaking generally, they led from youth onward a manner of life which was luxurious, wearing as they did exceedingly delicate clothing and gold ornaments and, besides, using strigils and oil-flasks made of silver and even of gold.

83. Among the Acragantini of that time perhaps the richest man was Tellias, who had in his mansion a considerable number of guest-chambers and used to station servants before his gates with orders to invite every stranger to be his guest. There were also many other Acragantini who did something of this kind,

[1] Timaeus died c. 250 B.C.

[2] He was victor not only in the Ninety-second Olympiad (412 B.C.; chap. 34) but also in the Ninety-first (416 B.C.; Book 12. 82).

ἀρχαϊκῶς καὶ φιλανθρώπως ὁμιλοῦντες· διόπερ
καὶ Ἐμπεδοκλῆς λέγει περὶ αὐτῶν,

ξείνων αἰδοῖοι λιμένες, κακότητος ἄπειροι.

2 καὶ δή ποτε πεντακοσίων ἱππέων παραγενομένων
ἐκ Γέλας χειμερίου περιστάσεως οὔσης, καθάπερ
φησὶ Τίμαιος ἐν τῇ πεντεκαιδεκάτῃ βίβλῳ, πάντας
αὐτὸς[1] ὑπεδέξατο, καὶ παραχρῆμα πᾶσιν ἱμάτια
3 καὶ χιτῶνας ἔνδοθεν προενέγκας ἔδωκεν. καὶ
Πολύκλειτος ἐν ταῖς ἱστορίαις ἐξηγεῖται περὶ τοῦ
κατὰ τὴν οἰκίαν πιθεῶνος, λέγων ὡς διαμείναντος
αὐτοῦ τε[2] στρατευομένου ἐν Ἀκράγαντι τεθεωρη-
κότος[3]· εἶναι δ' ἐν αὐτῷ τριακοσίους μὲν πίθους
ἐξ αὐτῆς τῆς πέτρας τετμημένους, ἕκαστον ἑκατὸν
ἀμφορεῖς χωροῦντα· κολυμβήθραν δὲ παρ' αὐτοῖς
ὑπάρχειν κεκονιαμένην, χωροῦσαν ἀμφορεῖς χιλίους,
4 ἐξ ἧς τὴν ῥύσιν εἰς τοὺς πίθους γίνεσθαι. γεγονέναι δέ φασι τὸν Τελλίαν τὸ μὲν εἶδος εὐτελῆ
παντελῶς, τὸ δὲ ἦθος θαυμαστόν. ἀποσταλέντος
οὖν αὐτοῦ πρὸς Κεντοριπίνους κατὰ πρεσβείαν,
καὶ παρεληλυθότος εἰς τὴν ἐκκλησίαν, τὸ μὲν
πλῆθος προέπεσεν[4] εἰς ἄκαιρον γέλωτα, θεωρῶν

---

[1] So Sintenis : αὐτούς.
[2] τε added by Capps.
[3] So Capps : τεθεωρηκέναι. The text after πιθεῶνος has
been variously emended.
[4] So Dindorf : προσέπεσεν.

---

[1] The famous fifth-century physical philosopher, a native
of Acragas.

mingling with others in an old-fashioned and friendly 406 B.C. manner; consequently also Empedocles [1] speaks of them as

> Havens of mercy for strangers, unacquainted with evil.[2]

Indeed once when five hundred cavalry from Gela arrived there during a wintry storm, as Timaeus says in his Fifteenth Book, Tellias entertained all of them by himself and provided them all forthwith from his own stores with outer and under garments. And Polycleitus [3] in his *Histories* describes the wine-cellar in the house as still existing and as he had himself seen it when in Acragas as a soldier; there were in it, he states, three hundred great casks hewn out of the very rock, each of them with a capacity of one hundred amphoras,[4] and beside them was a wine-vat, plastered with stucco and with a capacity of one thousand amphoras, from which the wine flowed into the casks. And we are told that Tellias was quite plain in appearance but wonderful in character. So once when he had been dispatched on an embassy to the people of Centoripa and came forward to speak before the Assembly, the multitude broke into unseemly laughter

---

[2] The third line of the opening lines of his work *On Purifications* which run (Frag. 112 Diels[5]):

> ὦ φίλοι, οἳ μέγα ἄστυ κατὰ ξανθοῦ Ἀκράγαντος
> ναίετ' ἀν' ἄκρα πόλεος, ἀγαθῶν μελεδήμονες ἔργων,
> ξείνων κτλ.

(" My friends, who make your homes in the great settlement which forms golden Acragas, up on the heights of the city, ye who are careful to perform good deeds," then the line Diodorus quotes.)

[3] A native of Larissa and probably of the generation of Alexander the Great.

[4] An amphora was about nine gallons.

καταδεέστερον τῆς περὶ αὐτοῦ δόξης· ὁ δ' ὑπο-
λαβὼν εἶπε μὴ θαυμάζειν· ἐν ἔθει γὰρ εἶναι τοῖς
Ἀκραγαντίνοις πρὸς μὲν τὰς ἐπιδόξους πόλεις ἀποστέλλειν τοὺς κρατίστους τῷ κάλλει, πρὸς δὲ τὰς
ταπεινὰς καὶ λίαν εὐτελεῖς ὁμοίους.

84. Οὐ μόνον δὲ περὶ τὸν Τελλίαν συνέβαινεν
εἶναι τοῦ πλούτου μεγαλοπρέπειαν, ἀλλὰ καὶ περὶ
πολλοὺς ἄλλους Ἀκραγαντίνους. Ἀντισθένης γοῦν
ὁ ἐπικαλούμενος Ῥόδος γάμους ἐπιτελῶν τῆς θυγα-
τρὸς εἱστίασε τοὺς πολίτας ἐπὶ τῶν στενωπῶν ὧν
ᾤκουν ἕκαστοι, καὶ ζεύγη τῇ νύμφῃ συνηκολούθησε
πλείω τῶν ὀκτακοσίων· πρὸς δὲ τούτοις οὐ μόνον
οἱ κατ' αὐτὴν τὴν πόλιν ἱππεῖς, ἀλλὰ καὶ τῶν ἀστυγειτόνων πολλοὶ κληθέντες ἐπὶ τὸν γάμον συμ-
2 προέπεμψαν τὴν νύμφην. περιττότατον δέ φασι
γενέσθαι τὸ περὶ τὴν τοῦ φωτὸς κατασκευήν· τούς
τε γὰρ βωμοὺς τοὺς ἐν πᾶσι τοῖς ἱεροῖς καὶ τοὺς ἐν
τοῖς στενωποῖς καθ' ὅλην τὴν πόλιν ἐπλήρωσε ξύλων, καὶ τοῖς ἐπὶ τῶν ἐργαστηρίων ἔδωκε[1] σχίδακας
καὶ κληματίδας, παραγγείλας, ὅταν ἀπὸ τῆς ἀκρο-
πόλεως ἀναφθῇ πῦρ, ἅπαντας ἐπιτελεῖν τὸ παρα-
3 πλήσιον· ὧν ποιησάντων τὸ προσταχθέν, καθ' ὃν
καιρὸν ἤγετο ἡ νύμφη, προηγουμένων πολλῶν τῶν
τὰς δᾷδας φερόντων, ἡ μὲν πόλις ἔγεμε φωτός, τὸ
δὲ συνακολουθοῦν πλῆθος οὐκ ἐχώρουν αἱ δημό-
σιαι κατὰ τὸ ἑξῆς ὁδοί, πάντων συμφιλοτιμουμένων τῇ τἀνδρὸς μεγαλοπρεπείᾳ. κατ' ἐκεῖνον
γὰρ τὸν χρόνον Ἀκραγαντῖνοι μὲν ἦσαν πλείους
τῶν δισμυρίων, σὺν δὲ τοῖς κατοικοῦσι ξένοις οὐκ
4 ἐλάττους τῶν εἴκοσι μυριάδων. φασὶ δὲ τὸν Ἀντι-
σθένην, ἐπειδὴ τὸν υἱὸν ἑώρα πολεμοῦντά τινα τῶν

---

[1] ἔδωκε M, omitted cet.

as they saw how much he fell short of their expecta- tion. But he, interrupting them, said, " Don't be surprised, for it is the practice of the Acragantini to send to famous cities their most handsome citizens, but to insignificant and most paltry cities men of their sort."

84. It was not in the case of Tellias only that such magnificence of wealth occurred, he says, but also of many other inhabitants of Acragas. Antisthenes at any rate, who was called Rhodus, when celebrating the marriage of his daughter, gave a party to all the citizens in the courtyards where they all lived and more than eight hundred chariots followed the bride in the procession ; furthermore, not only the men on horseback from the city itself but also many from neighbouring cities who had been invited to the wedding joined to form the escort of the bride. But most extraordinary of all, we are told, was the provision for the lighting : the altars in all the temples and those in the courtyards throughout the city he had piled high with wood, and to the shopkeepers he gave firewood and brush with orders that when a fire was kindled on the acropolis they should all do the same ; and when they did as they were ordered, at the time when the bride was brought to her home, since there were many torch-bearers in the procession, the city was filled with light, and the main streets through which the procession was to pass could not contain the accompanying throng, all the inhabitants zealously emulating the man's grand manner. For at that time the citizens of Acragas numbered more than twenty thousand, and when resident aliens were included, not less than two hundred thousand. And men say that once when Antisthenes saw his son quarrelling with a

ἀγρογειτόνων[1] πένητα καὶ βιαζόμενον ἑαυτῷ τὸ
ἀγρίδιον πωλῆσαι, μέχρι μέν τινος ἐπιπλήττειν,[2]
τῆς δ' ἐπιθυμίας ἐπίτασιν λαμβανούσης, φῆσαι δεῖν
μὴ σπεύδειν πῶς ἄπορον ποιήσῃ τὸν γείτονα, ἀλλὰ
τοὐναντίον ὅπως πλούσιος ὑπάρχῃ· οὕτως γὰρ
αὐτὸν ἐπιθυμήσειν μὲν ἀγροῦ μείζονος, οὐ δυνάμενον δὲ παρὰ τοῦ γείτονος προσαγοράσαι τὸν
ὑπάρχοντα πωλήσειν.

5   Διὰ δὲ τὸ μέγεθος τῆς κατὰ τὴν πόλιν εὐπορίας
τοσαύτην συνέβαινε τρυφὴν εἶναι παρὰ τοῖς Ἀκραγαντίνοις ὥστε μετ' ὀλίγον τῆς πολιορκίας γινομένης ποιῆσαι ψήφισμα περὶ τῶν ἐν τοῖς φυλακείοις
διανυκτερευόντων, ὅπως μή τις ἔχῃ πλεῖον τύλης
καὶ περιστρώματος καὶ κωδίου καὶ δυεῖν προσκε-
6 φαλαίων. τοιαύτης δὲ τῆς σκληροτάτης στρωμνῆς
ὑπαρχούσης, ἔξεστι λογίζεσθαι τὴν κατὰ τὸν
λοιπὸν βίον τρυφήν. περὶ μὲν οὖν τούτων οὔτε
παραδραμεῖν ἠθελήσαμεν οὔτ' ἐπὶ πλεῖον μακρο-
λογεῖν, ἵνα μὴ τῶν ἀναγκαιοτέρων ἀποπίπτωμεν.

85. Οἱ δὲ Καρχηδόνιοι τὰς δυνάμεις διαβιβάσαντες εἰς τὴν Σικελίαν ἀνέζευξαν ἐπὶ τὴν πόλιν
τῶν Ἀκραγαντίνων καὶ δύο παρεμβολὰς ἐποιήσαντο,
μίαν μὲν ἐπί τινων λόφων, ἐφ' ὧν[3] τούς τε Ἴβηρας
καί τινας τῶν Λιβύων ἔταξαν εἰς τετρακισμυρίους·
τὴν δ' ἄλλην οὐκ ἄπωθεν τῆς πόλεως ποιησάμενοι
2 τάφρῳ βαθείᾳ καὶ χάρακι περιέλαβον.[4] καὶ πρῶτον μὲν ἀπέστειλαν πρέσβεις πρὸς τοὺς Ἀκραγαντίνους ἀξιοῦντες μάλιστα μὲν συμμαχεῖν αὐτοῖς,
εἰ δὲ μή γε, ἡσυχίαν ἔχειν καὶ φίλους εἶναι Καρχηδονίοις ἐν εἰρήνῃ μένοντας· οὐ προσδεξαμένων δὲ

---

[1] So Wurm: ἀπὸ γειτόνων.
[2] So Eichstädt; ἐπέπληττεν PA, ἐπέπληττε cet.

neighbouring farmer, a poor man, and pressing him to 406 B.C. sell him his little plot of land, for a time he merely reproved his son ; but when his son's cupidity grew more intense, he said to him that he should not be doing his best to make his neighbour poor but, on the contrary, to make him rich ; for then the man would long for more land, and when he would be unable to buy additional land from his neighbour he would sell what he now had.

Because of the immense prosperity prevailing in the city the Acragantini came to live on such a scale of luxury that a little later, when the city was under siege, they passed a decree about the guards who spent the nights at their posts, that none of them should have more than one mattress, one cover, one sheepskin, and two pillows. When such was their most rigorous kind of bedding, one can get an idea of the luxury which prevailed in their living generally. Now it was our wish neither to pass these matters by nor yet to speak of them at greater length, in order that we may not fail to record the more important events.

85. The Carthaginians, after transporting their armaments to Sicily, marched against the city of the Acragantini and made two encampments, one on certain hills where they stationed the Iberians and some Libyans to the number of about forty thousand, and the other they pitched not far from the city and surrounded it with a deep trench and a palisade. And first they dispatched ambassadors to the Acragantini, asking them, preferably, to become their allies, but otherwise to stay neutral and be friends with the Carthaginians, thereby remaining in peace; and when

---

³ ἐφ' ὧν M, omitted *cet.*   ⁴ So Wesseling : περιέβαλον.

τῶν ἐν τῇ πόλει τοὺς λόγους, εὐθὺς τὰ τῆς πολιορ-
3 κίας ἐνηργεῖτο. οἱ μὲν οὖν Ἀκραγαντῖνοι τοὺς
ἐν ἡλικίᾳ πάντας καθώπλισαν, καὶ καταστήσαντες
εἰς τάξιν τοὺς μὲν ἐπὶ τῶν τειχῶν ἔστησαν, τοὺς
δὲ ἐφέδρους πρὸς τὰς τῶν καταπονουμένων δια-
δοχάς. συνεμάχει δ' αὐτοῖς Δέξιππός τε ὁ Λακεδαιμόνιος προσφάτως ἐκ Γέλας παρὼν μετὰ ξένων
χιλίων πεντακοσίων· οὗτος γὰρ κατ' ἐκεῖνον τὸν
χρόνον, ὡς Τίμαιός φησιν, ἐν Γέλᾳ διέτριβεν, ἔχων
4 ἀξίωμα διὰ τὴν πατρίδα. διόπερ ἠξίωσαν αὐτὸν
οἱ Ἀκραγαντῖνοι μισθωσάμενον στρατιώτας ὡς
πλείστους ἐλθεῖν εἰς Ἀκράγαντα· ἅμα δὲ τούτοις
ἐμισθώθησαν[1] καὶ οἱ πρότερον Ἀννίβᾳ[2] συμμα-
χήσαντες Καμπανοί, περὶ ὀκτακοσίους ὄντες.
οὗτοι δὲ κατέσχον τὸν ὑπὲρ τῆς πόλεως λόφον,
τὸν Ἀθήναιον μὲν ὀνομαζόμενον, κατὰ δὲ τῆς
5 πόλεως εὐφυῶς κείμενον. Ἰμίλκας δὲ καὶ Ἀννίβας οἱ τῶν Καρχηδονίων στρατηγοὶ διασκεψά-
μενοι τὰ τείχη, καὶ καθ' ἕνα τόπον θεωροῦντες,
εὐέφοδον οὖσαν τὴν πόλιν, δύο πύργους προσ-
ήγαγον τοῖς τείχεσιν ὑπερμεγέθεις. τὴν μὲν οὖν
πρώτην ἡμέραν ἐπὶ τούτων τειχομαχήσαντες καὶ
συχνοὺς ἀνελόντες ἀνεκαλέσαντο τῇ σάλπιγγι τοὺς
μαχομένους· τῆς δὲ νυκτὸς ἐπιγενομένης οἱ κατὰ
τὴν πόλιν ἐπεξελθόντες ἐνεπύρισαν τὰς μηχανάς.
86. Οἱ δὲ περὶ τὸν Ἀννίβαν σπεύδοντες κατὰ
πλείονα μέρη τὰς προσβολὰς ποιεῖσθαι, παρήγγειλαν
τοῖς στρατιώταις καθαιρεῖν[3] τὰ μνήματα καὶ χώ-
ματα κατασκευάζειν μέχρι τῶν τειχῶν. ταχὺ δὲ
τῶν ἔργων διὰ τὴν πολυχειρίαν συντελουμένων ἐν-

---

[1] ἐμισθώθησαν M, ἐμίσθωσαν cet.
[2] Ἀννίβᾳ Wesseling, ἱμίλκα PA, Ἀμίλκα cet.

the inhabitants of the city would not entertain these 406 B.C.
terms, the siege was begun at once. The Acragantini
thereupon armed all those of military age, and forming
them in battle order they stationed one group upon the
walls and the other as a reserve to replace the soldiers
as they became worn out. Fighting with them was
also Dexippus the Lacedaemonian, who had lately
arrived there from Gela with fifteen hundred mercenaries ; for at that time, as Timaeus says, Dexippus
was tarrying in Gela, enjoying high regard by reason
of the city of his birth. Consequently the Acragantini
invited him to recruit as many mercenaries as he could
and come to Acragas ; and together with them the
Campanians who had formerly fought with Hannibal,[1]
some eight hundred, were also hired. These mercenaries held the height above the city which is called
the Hill of Athena and is strategically situated over-
hanging the city. Himilcar and Hannibal, the Carthaginian generals, noting, after they had surveyed the
walls, that in one place the city was easily assailable,
advanced two enormous towers against the walls.
During the first day they pressed the siege from these
towers, and after inflicting many casualties then
sounded the recall for their soldiers ; but when night
had fallen the defenders of the city launched a
counter-attack and burned the siege-engines.

86. Hannibal, being eager to launch assaults in an
increasing number of places, ordered the soldiers to
tear down the monuments and tombs and to build
mounds extending to the walls. But when these
works had been quickly completed because of the
united labour of many hands, a deep superstitious fear

[1] Cp. chaps. 44. 1 ; 62. 5.

---

[3] So Wesseling : καθαίρειν.

ἔπεσεν[1] εἰς τὸ στρατόπεδον πολλὴ δεισιδαιμονία.
2 τὸν γὰρ τοῦ Θήρωνος τάφον ὄντα καθ' ὑπερβολὴν
μέγαν συνέβαινεν ὑπὸ κεραυνοῦ διασεῖσθαι· διόπερ αὐτοῦ καθαιρουμένου[2] τῶν τε μάντεών τινες
προνοήσαντες διεκώλυσαν, εὐθὺ δὲ καὶ λοιμὸς
ἐνέπεσεν εἰς τὸ στρατόπεδον, καὶ πολλοὶ μὲν ἐτε-
λεύτων, οὐκ ὀλίγοι δὲ στρέβλαις καὶ δειναῖς ταλαι-
3 πωρίαις περιέπιπτον. ἀπέθανε δὲ καὶ Ἀννίβας ὁ
στρατηγός, καὶ τῶν ἐπὶ τὰς φυλακὰς προπεμπο-
μένων ἤγγελλόν τινες διὰ νυκτὸς εἴδωλα φαίνεσθαι
τῶν τετελευτηκότων. Ἱμίλκας δὲ θεωρῶν τὰ
πλήθη δεισιδαιμονοῦντα πρῶτον μὲν ἐπαύσατο
καθαιρῶν[3] τὰ μνημεῖα, μετὰ δὲ ταῦτα ἱκέτευε
τοὺς θεοὺς κατὰ τὸ πάτριον ἔθος τῷ μὲν Κρόνῳ
παῖδα σφαγιάσας, τῷ δὲ Ποσειδῶνι πλῆθος ἱερείων
καταποντίσας. οὐ μὴν ἀπέστη γε τῶν ἔργων,
ἀλλὰ χώσας τὸν παρὰ τὴν πόλιν ποταμὸν μέχρι
τῶν τειχῶν ἐπέστησε πάσας τὰς μηχανὰς καὶ καθ'
ἡμέραν προσβολὰς ἐποιεῖτο.
4 Οἱ δὲ Συρακόσιοι θεωροῦντες τὴν Ἀκράγαντος
πολιορκίαν, καὶ φοβούμενοι μὴ τῆς αὐτῆς τοῖς
Σελινουντίοις καὶ τοῖς Ἱμεραίοις τύχωσιν οἱ πολιορκούμενοι τύχης, πάλαι μὲν ἔσπευδον ἐκπέμψαι
τὴν βοήθειαν, τότε δὲ παραγενομένων τῶν ἐξ
Ἰταλίας καὶ Μεσσήνης συμμάχων στρατηγὸν
5 Δαφναῖον εἵλαντο. τὴν δὲ δύναμιν ἀθροίσαντες
παρέλαβον κατὰ τὴν ὁδὸν Καμαριναίους καὶ Γε-
λῴους· ἔτι[4] δὲ τῶν ἐκ τῆς μεσογείου μεταπεμψά-
μενοί τινας ἐπ' Ἀκράγαντος τὴν πορείαν ἐποιοῦντο,

---

[1] So Dindorf: συνέπεσεν.   [2] So Wesseling: καθαιρομένου.
[3] So Wesseling: καθαίρων.
[4] ἔτι] ἐπὶ P, ἐπεὶ AFJ.

fell upon the army. For it happened that the tomb 406 B.C.
of Theron,[1] which was exceedingly large, was shaken
by a stroke of lightning ; consequently, when it was
being torn down, certain soothsayers, presaging what
might happen, forbade it, and at once a plague broke
out in the army, and many died of it while not a few
suffered tortures and grievous distress. Among the
dead was also Hannibal the general, and among the
watch-guards who were sent out there were some who
reported that in the night spirits of the dead were to
be seen. Himilcar, on seeing how the throng was
beset with superstitious fear, first of all put a stop to
the destruction of the monuments, and then he suppli-
cated the gods after the custom of his people by
sacrificing a young boy to Cronus and a multitude of
cattle to Poseidon by drowning them in the sea. He
did not, however, neglect the siege works, but filling
up the river which ran beside the city as far as the
walls, he advanced all his siege-engines against them
and launched daily assaults.

The Syracusans, seeing that Acragas was under
siege and fearing lest the besieged might suffer the
same fate as befell the Selinuntians and Himeracans,[2]
had long been eager to send them their aid, and when
at this juncture allied troops arrived from Italy and
Messenê they elected Daphnaeus [3] general. Collecting their forces they added along the way soldiers
from Camarina and Gela, and summoning additional
troops from the peoples of the interior they made their

---

[1] Tyrant of Acragas, 488–472 B.C. ; cp. Book 11. 53.
[2] Cp. chaps. 57 and 62 respectively.
[3] A Syracusan, later executed by Dionysius (*infra*,
chap. 96. 3).

συμπαραπλεουσῶν αὐτοῖς καὶ τῶν νεῶν τριάκοντα. εἶχον¹ δὲ τοὺς πάντας πεζοὺς μὲν πλείους τῶν τρισμυρίων, ἱππεῖς δ' οὐκ ἐλάττους τῶν πεντακισχιλίων.

87. Ἰμίλκων δὲ πυθόμενος τὴν τῶν πολεμίων ἔφοδον, ἀπέστειλεν αὐτοῖς ἀπαντᾶν τούς τε Ἴβηρας καὶ Καμπανοὺς καὶ τῶν ἄλλων οὐκ ἐλάττους τετρακισμυρίων. ἤδη δὲ τῶν Συρακοσίων τὸν Ἱμέραν ποταμὸν διαβεβηκότων ἀπήντησαν οἱ βάρβαροι, καὶ παρατάξεως γενομένης ἐπὶ πολὺν χρόνον ἐνίκησαν οἱ Συρακόσιοι καὶ πλείους τῶν ἑξακισχιλίων 2 ἀνεῖλον. τελέως δὲ ὅλον τὸ στρατόπεδον διέφθειραν ἂν² καὶ μέχρι τῆς πόλεως κατεδίωξαν, ἀλλὰ τῶν στρατιωτῶν ἀτάκτως διωκόντων ὁ στρατηγὸς εὐλαβήθη μήποτε μετὰ τοῦ λοιποῦ στρατεύματος Ἰμίλκας ἐπιφανεὶς ἀναλάβῃ τὴν ἧτταν. καὶ γὰρ τοὺς Ἱμεραίους ἐγίνωσκε παρὰ τὴν αὐτὴν αἰτίαν τοῖς ὅλοις ἐπταικότας. οὐ μὴν ἀλλὰ τῶν βαρβάρων φευγόντων εἰς τὴν πρὸς Ἀκράγαντι παρεμβολήν, οἱ κατὰ τὴν πόλιν στρατιῶται θεωροῦντες τὴν τῶν Καρχηδονίων ἧτταν ἐδέοντο τῶν στρατηγῶν ἐξάγειν αὐτούς, καιρὸν εἶναι φάσκοντες τοῦ φθεῖραι 3 τὴν τῶν πολεμίων δύναμιν. οἱ δ', εἴτε χρήμασιν ἐφθαρμένοι, καθάπερ ἦν λόγος, εἴτε φοβηθέντες μὴ τῆς πόλεως ἐρημωθείσης Ἰμίλκων αὐτὴν καταλάβηται, τῆς ὁρμῆς ἐπέσχον τοὺς στρατιώτας. οἱ μὲν οὖν φεύγοντες μετὰ πάσης ἀσφαλείας διεσώθησαν εἰς τὴν πρὸς τῇ πόλει παρεμβολήν. ὁ δὲ Δαφναῖος μετὰ τῆς δυνάμεως παραγενηθεὶς εἰς τὴν ὑπὸ τῶν βαρβάρων ἐκλελειμμένην στρατο- 4 πεδείαν, ἐν ταύτῃ παρενέβαλεν. εὐθὺ δὲ καὶ τῶν ἐκ τῆς πόλεως στρατιωτῶν ἐπιμιχθέντων καὶ τοῦ

way towards Acragas, while thirty of their ships sailed ^{406 B.C.} along beside them. The forces which they had numbered in all more than thirty thousand infantry and not less than five thousand cavalry.

87. When Himilcon learned of the approach of the enemy, he dispatched to meet them both his Iberians and his Campanians and more than forty thousand other troops. The Syracusans had already crossed the Himera River when the barbarians met them, and in the long battle which ensued the Syracusans were victorious and slew more than six thousand men. They would have crushed the whole army completely and pursued it all the way to the city, but since the soldiers were pressing the pursuit without order, the general was concerned lest Himilcar should appear with the rest of his army and retrieve the defeat. For he remembered also how the Himeraeans had been utterly destroyed for the same reason.[1] However, when the barbarians were in flight to their camp before Acragas, the soldiers in the city, seeing the defeat of the Carthaginians, begged their generals to lead them out, saying that the opportunity had come to destroy the host of the enemy. But the generals, whether they had been bribed, as the report ran, or feared that Himilcon would seize the city if it were stripped of defenders, checked the ardour of their men. So the fleeing men quite safely made good their escape to the camp before the city. When Daphnaeus with his army arrived at the encampment which the barbarians had deserted, he took up his quarters there. At once both the soldiers from the city mingled with his troops and Dexippus

---

[1] By a disorderly pursuit; cp. chap. 60 *ad fin.*

---

[1] εἶχον Wurm, εἶχεν P, εἶχε *cet.* [2] ἂν added by Post.

Δεξίππου συγκαταβάντος αὐτοῖς, ἀπὸ συνδρομῆς
εἰς ἐκκλησίαν τὰ πλήθη συνῆλθεν, πάντων δ'
ἀγανακτούντων ἐπὶ τῷ παρεῖσθαι τὸν καιρὸν καὶ
κεκρατηκότας τῶν βαρβάρων τὴν προσήκουσαν
τιμωρίαν παρ' αὐτῶν μὴ λαβεῖν, ἀλλὰ δυναμένους
τοὺς ἐκ τῆς πόλεως στρατηγοὺς ἐπεξελθεῖν καὶ
διαφθεῖραι τὴν τῶν πολεμίων δύναμιν ἀφεικέναι
5 τοσαύτας μυριάδας. θορύβου δὲ καὶ πολλῆς κραυγῆς ἐπεχούσης τὴν ἐκκλησίαν, παρελθὼν Μένης
ὁ Καμαριναῖος ἐφ' ἡγεμονίας τεταγμένος κατηγό-
ρησε τῶν Ἀκραγαντίνων στρατηγῶν καὶ πάντας
οὕτω παρώξυνεν, ὥστε τῶν κατηγορουμένων ἐγχει-
ρούντων ἀπολογεῖσθαι μηδένα προσδέχεσθαι τοὺς
λόγους καὶ τὸ πλῆθος ὁρμῆσαν ἐπὶ τὸ βάλλειν τοῖς
λίθοις τέσσαρας αὐτῶν καταλεῦσαι, τὸν δὲ πέμπτον,
Ἀργεῖον καλούμενον, τὴν δ' ἡλικίαν παντελῶς
ὄντα νεώτερον, ἀφεθῆναι· βλασφημίας δὲ τυγχάνειν καὶ τὸν Λακεδαιμόνιον Δέξιππον, ὅτι τεταγμένος ἐφ' ἡγεμονίας καὶ δοκῶν εἶναι τῶν
πολεμικῶν ἔργων οὐκ ἄπειρος τοῦτ' ἔπραξε προδοσίας ἕνεκα.

88. Μετὰ δὲ τὴν ἐκκλησίαν οἱ περὶ τὸν Δαφναῖον
προαγαγόντες τὰς δυνάμεις ἐπεχείρουν μὲν πολιορκεῖν τὴν παρεμβολὴν τῶν Καρχηδονίων, πολυτελῶς
δ' αὐτὴν ὁρῶντες ὠχυρωμένην ταύτης μὲν τῆς
ἐπιβολῆς ἀπέστησαν, τὰς δ' ὁδοὺς ἱππαζόμενοι
τούς τ' ἐν ταῖς προνομαῖς αὐτῶν κατελάμβανον
καὶ τῶν σιτοπομπιῶν ἀποκλείοντες εἰς πολλὴν
2 ἀπορίαν ἦγον. οἱ δὲ Καρχηδόνιοι παρατάττεσθαι
μὲν οὐ τολμῶντες, τῇ δὲ σιτοδείᾳ δεινῶς πιεζού-
μενοι, μεγάλοις ἀτυχήμασι περιέπιπτον. τῶν μὲν
γὰρ στρατιωτῶν πολλοὶ διὰ τὴν σπάνιν ἀπέθνησκον,

accompanied his men, and the multitude gathered in a tumultuous throng in an assembly, everyone being vexed that the opportunity had been let slip and that although they had the barbarians in their power, they had not inflicted on them the punishment they deserved, but that the generals in the city, although able to lead them forth to attack and destroy the host of the enemy, had let so many myriads of men off scot-free. While great uproar and tumult prevailed in the assembly, Menes of Camarina, who had been put in command, came forward and lodged an accusation against the Acragantine generals and so incited all who were present that, when the accused tried to offer a defence, no one would let them speak and the multitude began to throw stones and killed four of them, but the fifth, Argeius by name, who was very much younger, they spared. Dexippus the Lacedaemonian, we are told, also was the object of abuse on the ground that, although he held a position of command and was reputed to be not inexperienced in warfare, he had acted as he did treacherously.

88. After the assembly Daphnaeus led forth his forces and undertook to lay siege to the camp of the Carthaginians, but when he saw that it had been fortified with great outlay, he gave up that design; however, by covering the roads with his cavalry he seized such as were foraging, and by cutting off the transport of supplies brought them into serious straits. The Carthaginians, not daring to wage a pitched battle and being hard pinched by lack of food, were enduring great misfortunes. For many of the soldiers were dying of want, and the Campanians together with the

369

οἱ δὲ Καμπανοὶ μετὰ τῶν ἄλλων μισθοφόρων σχεδὸν
ἅπαντες ἐπὶ τὴν Ἰμίλκα σκηνὴν ὠθούμενοι τὰς
σιτομετρίας τὰς προτεταγμένας ᾔτουν· εἰ δὲ μή,
διηπειλοῦντο μεταβάλλεσθαι πρὸς τοὺς πολεμίους.
3 ὁ δ᾽ Ἰμίλκας ἦν ἀκηκοώς τινος, ὅτι Συρακόσιοι
πλῆθος σίτου παρακομίζοιεν εἰς Ἀκράγαντα κατὰ
θάλατταν. διόπερ ταύτην μόνην ἔχων ἐλπίδα σωτηρίας, τοὺς μὲν στρατιώτας ἔπεισεν ὀλίγας ἐπισχεῖν
ἡμέρας, ἐνέχυρα δοὺς τὰ παρὰ τῶν ἐκ Καρχηδόνος
4 στρατευομένων ποτήρια. καὶ αὐτὸς μὲν ἐκ Πανόρ-
μου καὶ Μοτύης μεταπεμψάμενος τεσσαράκοντα
τριήρεις ἐπέθετο τοῖς τὴν ἀγορὰν παρακομίζουσιν·
οἱ δὲ Συρακόσιοι, τὸν ἔμπροσθεν χρόνον τῶν βαρβάρων τῆς θαλάττης παρακεχωρηκότων καὶ τοῦ
χειμῶνος ἐνεστηκότος ἤδη, κατεφρόνουν τῶν Καρχηδονίων, ὡς[1] οὐκέτι τολμησόντων πληροῦν τὰς
5 τριήρεις. διόπερ ὀλιγώρως αὐτῶν παραπεμψάντων
τὴν ἀγοράν, Ἰμίλκας ἐκπλεύσας τεσσαράκοντα
τριήρεσιν ἄφνω κατέδυσε μὲν τῶν μακρῶν νεῶν
ὀκτώ, τὰς δ᾽ ἄλλας εἰς τὸν αἰγιαλὸν κατεδίωξεν·
τῶν δ᾽ ἄλλων πλοίων ἁπάντων κυριεύσας, τοσοῦτον
εἰς τοὐναντίον τὰς ἑκατέρων ἐλπίδας μεταπεσεῖν
ἐποίησεν ὥστε τοὺς παρὰ τοῖς Ἀκραγαντίνοις
Καμπανοὺς καταγνόντας τῆς τῶν Ἑλλήνων ὑποθέσεως πεντεκαίδεκα ταλάντοις φθαρῆναι καὶ μετα-
βαλέσθαι πρὸς τοὺς Καρχηδονίους.
6 Οἱ δὲ Ἀκραγαντῖνοι τὸ μὲν πρῶτον κακῶς
ἀπαλλαττόντων τῶν Καρχηδονίων ἀφθόνως ἀπ-
ήλαυον τοῦ τε σίτου καὶ τῶν ἄλλων ἐπιτηδείων,
ἀεὶ προσδοκῶντες[2] ταχέως λυθήσεσθαι τὴν πολι-
ορκίαν· ἐπεὶ δ᾽ αἱ τῶν βαρβάρων ἐλπίδες ἀνέκυψαν

---

[1] ὡς added by M and Stephanus.

other mercenaries, almost in a body, forced their way 406 B.C.
to the tent of Himilcar and demanded the rations
which had been agreed upon ; and if these were not
given them, they threatened to go over to the enemy.
But Himilcar had learned from some source that the
Syracusans were conveying a great amount of grain
to Acragas by sea.   Consequently, since this was the
only hope he had of salvation, he persuaded the
soldiers to wait a few days, giving them as a pledge
the goblets belonging to the troops from Carthage.
He then summoned forty triremes from Panormus and
Motyê and planned an attack upon the ships which
were bringing the supplies ; and the Syracusans, because up to this time the barbarians had retired from
the sea and winter had already set in, held the Carthaginians in contempt, feeling assured that they would
not again have the courage to man their triremes.
Consequently, since they gave little concern to the
convoying of the supplies, Himilcar, sailing forth unawares with forty triremes, sank eight of their warships and pursued the rest to the beach ; and by
capturing all the remaining vessels he effected such
a reversal in the expectations of both sides that the
Campanians who were in the service of the Acragantini, considering the position of the Greeks to be
hopeless, were bought off for fifteen talents and went
over to the Carthaginians.

The Acragantini at first, when the Carthaginians
were faring badly, had enjoyed their grain and other
supplies without stint, expecting all the while that the
siege would be quickly lifted ; but when the hopes of
the barbarians began to rise and so many myriads of

---

[2] So Wesseling : προσδοκώντων.

καὶ τοσαῦται μυριάδες εἰς μίαν ἠθροίσθησαν πόλιν,
7 ἔλαθεν αὐτοὺς ὁ σῖτος ἐξαναλωθείς. λέγεται δὲ
καὶ Δέξιππος ὁ Λακεδαιμόνιος πεντεκαίδεκα ταλάντοις διαφθαρῆναι· εὐθὺ γὰρ ἀπεκρίνατο πρὸς τοὺς
τῶν Ἰταλιωτῶν στρατηγούς, ὅτι συμφέρει τὸν
πόλεμον ἐν ἄλλῳ συστήσασθαι τόπῳ· τὴν γὰρ
τροφὴν ἐκλιπεῖν. διόπερ οἱ στρατηγοὶ πρόφασιν
ἐνέγκαντες ὡς διεληλύθασιν οἱ ταχθέντες τῆς στρατηγίας χρόνοι, τὰς δυνάμεις ἀπήγαγον ἐπὶ τὸν
8 πορθμόν. μετὰ δὲ τὴν τούτων ἀπαλλαγὴν συνελθόντες οἱ στρατηγοὶ μετὰ τῶν ἐφ' ἡγεμονίας
τεταγμένων διέγνωσαν ἐξετάσαι τὸν ἐν τῇ πόλει
σῖτον· ὃν εὑρόντες παντελῶς ὀλίγον ἐθεώρουν
ἀναγκαῖον ὑπάρχειν ἐκλιπεῖν τὴν πόλιν. εὐθὺς
οὖν ἐπιγινομένης τῆς νυκτὸς παρήγγειλαν ἀνα-
ζευγνύειν ἅπαντας.

89. Τοσούτου δὲ πλήθους ἀνδρῶν γυναικῶν παίδων ἐκλιπόντων[1] τὴν πόλιν ἄφνω πολὺς οἶκτος καὶ
δάκρυα κατεῖχε τὰς οἰκίας. ἅμα γὰρ ὁ τῶν πολεμίων ἐξέπληττε φόβος, ἅμα δὲ διὰ τὴν σπουδὴν
ἠναγκάζοντο καταλιπεῖν εἰς διαρπαγὴν τοῖς βαρβάροις ταῦτ' ἐφ' οἷς ἑαυτοὺς ἐμακάριζον· ἀφαι-
ρουμένης γὰρ τῆς τύχης τὴν ἐξουσίαν τῶν οἴκοι
καλῶν, ἀγαπητὸν ἡγοῦντο τὰ σώματα γοῦν αὑ-
2 τῶν διασῶσαι. οὐ μόνον δὲ τῆς τοιαύτης πόλεως
εὐδαιμονίαν παρῆν ὁρᾶν ἀπολειπομένην, ἀλλὰ καὶ
σωμάτων πλῆθος. οἱ μὲν γὰρ ἐν ἀρρωστίαις ὑπὸ
τῶν οἰκείων περιεωρῶντο, τῆς καθ' ἑαυτὸν σωτηρίας ἑκάστου φροντίζοντος, οἱ δὲ ταῖς ἡλικίαις ἤδη
προβεβηκότες ὑπὸ τῆς τοῦ γήρως ἀσθενείας κατ-

---

[1] ἐκλιπόντων MSS., ἐκλιπόντος Vogel.

[1] Presumably of Messina.

human beings were gathered into one city, the grain 406 B.C. was exhausted before they were aware of it. And the story is told that also Dexippus the Lacedaemonian was corrupted by a bribe of fifteen talents ; for without hesitation he replied to a question of the generals of the Italian Greeks, "Yes, it's better if the war is settled somewhere else, for our provisions have failed." Consequently the generals, offering as their excuse that the time agreed upon for the campaign had elapsed, led their troops off to the Strait.[1] After the departure of these troops the generals met with the commanders and decided to make a survey of the supply of grain in the city, and when they discovered that it was quite low, they perceived that they were compelled to desert the city. At once, then, they issued orders that all should leave on the next night.

89. With such a throng of men, women, and children deserting the city, at once endless lamentation and tears pervaded all homes. For while they were panic-stricken from fear of the enemy, at the same time they were also under necessity, because of their haste, of leaving behind as booty for the barbarians the possessions on which they had based their happiness ; for when Fortune was robbing them of the comforts they enjoyed in their homes, they thought that they should be content that at least they were preserving their lives. And one could see the abandonment not only of the opulence of so wealthy a city but also of a multitude of human beings. For the sick were neglected by their relatives, everyone taking thought for his own safety, and those who were already far advanced in years were abandoned because of the weakness of old age ; and many, reckon-

ἐλείποντο· πολλοὶ δὲ καὶ τὴν ἀλλαγὴν τῆς πατρίδος
θανάτου τιμώμενοι τὰς χεῖρας ἑαυτοῖς προσήνεγ-
καν ὅπως ταῖς πατρῴαις οἰκίαις ἐναποπνεύσωσιν.
3 οὐ μὴν ἀλλὰ τὸ μὲν ἐκ τῆς πόλεως ἐξιὸν πλῆθος
οἱ στρατιῶται μετὰ τῶν ὅπλων παρέπεμπον εἰς
τὴν Γέλαν· ἡ δ' ὁδὸς καὶ πάντα τὰ πρὸς τὴν
Γελῴαν[1] ἀποκεκλιμένα τῆς χώρας μέρη ἔγεμε
γυναικῶν καὶ παίδων ἀναμὶξ παρθένοις, αἳ τὴν
συνήθη τρυφὴν εἰς ὁδοιπορίαν σύντονον καὶ κακοπάθειαν ὑπεράγουσαν μεταβαλλόμεναι διεκαρτέρουν
4 τοῦ φόβου τὰς ψυχὰς ἐντείνοντος.[2] οὗτοι μὲν οὖν
ἀσφαλῶς διασωθέντες εἰς Γέλαν ὕστερον εἰς Λεοντίνους κατῴκησαν, Συρακοσίων αὐτοῖς δόντων τὴν
πόλιν ταύτην οἰκητήριον.

90. Ὁ δ' Ἰμίλκας ἅμα τῷ φωτὶ[3] τὴν[4] δύναμιν
ἐντὸς τῶν τειχῶν παρεισαγαγὼν σχεδὸν ἅπαντας
τοὺς ἐγκαταλειφθέντας[5] ἀνεῖλεν· ὅτε δὴ[6] καὶ τοὺς
ἐν τοῖς ναοῖς καταπεφευγότας ἀποσπῶντες οἱ Καρ-
2 χηδόνιοι ἀνήρουν. λέγεται δὲ τὸν Τελλίαν τὸν
πρωτεύοντα τῶν πολιτῶν πλούτῳ καὶ καλοκἀγαθίᾳ
συνατυχῆσαι τῇ πατρίδι, βουληθέντα καταφυγεῖν
σύν τισιν ἑτέροις εἰς τὸ τῆς Ἀθηνᾶς ἱερόν, νομί-
ζοντα τῆς εἰς θεοὺς παρανομίας ἀφέξεσθαι τοὺς
Καρχηδονίους· θεωροῦντα δὲ αὐτῶν τὴν ἀσέβειαν,
ἐμπρῆσαι τὸν νεὼν καὶ μετὰ τῶν ἐν τούτῳ ἀνα-
θημάτων ἑαυτὸν συγκατακαῦσαι. μιᾷ γὰρ πράξει
διελάμβανεν ἀφελέσθαι θεῶν ἀσέβειαν, πολεμίων
ἁρπαγὰς πολλῶν χρημάτων, μέγιστον ἑαυτοῦ τὴν

[1] Γελῴαν PAFK, Γέλαν cet.
[2] So Reiske, Madvig, ἐκτείνοντος Dindorf, ἐγείροντος suggested by Vogel: ἐκτέμνοντος.
[3] φωτὶ Reiske: φόβῳ.
[4] τὴν added by Dindorf.

ing even separation from their native city to be the 406 B.C. equivalent of death, laid hands upon themselves in order that they might breathe their last in the dwellings of their ancestors. However, the multitude which left the city was given armed escort by the soldiers to Gela; and the highway and all parts of the countryside which led away toward the territory of the Geloans were crowded with women and children intermingled with maidens, who, changing from the pampered life to which they had been accustomed to a strenuous journey by foot and extreme hardship, held out to the end, since fear nerved their souls. Now these got safely to Gela [1] and at a later time made their home in Leontini, the Syracusans having given them this city for their dwelling-place.

90. Himilcar, leading his army at dawn within the walls, put to death practically all who had been left behind; yes, even those who had fled for safety to the temples the Carthaginians hauled out and slew. And we are told that Tellias, who was the foremost citizen in wealth and honourable character, shared in the misfortune of his country: He had decided to take refuge with certain others in the temple of Athena, thinking that the Carthaginians would refrain from acts of lawlessness against the gods, but when he saw their impiety, he set fire to the temple and burned himself together with the dedications in it. For by one deed, he thought, he would withhold from the gods impiety, from the enemy a vast store of plunder, and from himself, most important of all, certain

---

[1] A little over 40 miles from Acragas.

---

[5] ἐγκαταλειφθέντας] ἐγκαταληφθέντας Hertlein, Vogel.
[6] δὴ Eichstädt: δέ.

3 εἰς τὸ σῶμα ἐσομένην ὕβριν. ὁ δὲ Ἰμίλκας τὰ
ἱερὰ καὶ τὰς οἰκίας συλήσας καὶ φιλοτίμως ἐρευ-
νήσας, τοσαύτην ὠφέλειαν συνήθροισεν ὅσην εἰκός
ἐστιν ἐσχηκέναι πόλιν οἰκουμένην ὑπὸ ἀνδρῶν
εἴκοσι μυριάδων, ἀπόρθητον δὲ ἀπὸ τῆς κτίσεως
γεγενημένην, πλουσιωτάτην δὲ σχεδὸν τῶν τότε
Ἑλληνίδων πόλεων γεγενημένην, καὶ ταῦτα τῶν
ἐν αὐτῇ φιλοκαλησάντων εἰς παντοίων[1] κατα-
4 σκευασμάτων πολυτέλειαν· καὶ γὰρ γραφαὶ παμπληθεῖς ηὑρέθησαν εἰς ἄκρον ἐκπεπονημέναι καὶ
παντοίων ἀνδριάντων[2] φιλοτέχνως δεδημιουργη-
μένων ὑπεράγων ἀριθμός. τὰ μὲν οὖν πολυτελέστατα τῶν ἔργων ἀπέστειλεν εἰς Καρχηδόνα, ἐν
οἷς καὶ τὸν Φαλάριδος συνέβη κομισθῆναι ταῦρον,
5 τὴν δ᾽ ἄλλην ὠφέλειαν ἐλαφυροπώλησεν. τοῦτον
δὲ τὸν ταῦρον ὁ Τίμαιος ἐν ταῖς ἱστορίαις διαβε-
βαιωσάμενος μὴ γεγονέναι τὸ σύνολον, ὑπ᾽ αὐτῆς
τῆς τύχης ἠλέγχθη· Σκιπίων γὰρ ὕστερον ταύτης
τῆς ἁλώσεως σχεδὸν ἑξήκοντα καὶ διακοσίοις ἔτεσιν ἐκπορθήσας Καρχηδόνα τοῖς Ἀκραγαντίνοις
μετὰ τῶν ἄλλων τῶν διαμεινάντων παρὰ τοῖς Καρχηδονίοις ἀποκατέστησε τὸν ταῦρον, ὃς καὶ τῶνδε
τῶν ἱστοριῶν γραφομένων ἦν ἐν Ἀκράγαντι.

6 Περὶ δὲ τούτου φιλοτιμότερον εἰπεῖν προήχθην,
διότι Τίμαιος ὁ τῶν πρό γε αὐτοῦ συγγραφέων
πικρότατα κατηγορήσας καὶ συγγνώμην οὐδεμίαν
τοῖς ἱστοριογράφοις ἀπολιπὼν αὐτὸς εὑρίσκεται
σχεδιάζων, ἐν οἷς μάλιστα ἑαυτὸν ἀποπέφαγκεν
7 ἀκριβολογούμενον. δεῖ γάρ, οἶμαι, τοὺς συγγρα-
φεῖς ἐν μὲν τοῖς ἀγνοήμασι τυγχάνειν συγγνώμης,
ὡς ἂν ἀνθρώπους ὄντας καὶ τῆς ἐν τοῖς παροιχο-

[1] So Dindorf: παντοίαν.

physical indignity. But Himilcar, after pillaging and 406 B.C.
industriously ransacking the temples and dwellings,
collected as great a store of booty as a city could
be expected to yield which had been inhabited by
two hundred thousand people, had gone unravaged
since the date of its founding, had been well-nigh the
wealthiest of the Greek cities of that day, and whose
citizens, furthermore, had shown their love of the
beautiful in expensive collections of works of art of
every description. Indeed a multitude of paintings
executed with the greatest care was found and an
extraordinary number of sculptures of every description and worked with great skill. The most valuable
pieces, accordingly, Himilcar sent to Carthage, among
which, as it turned out, was the bull of Phalaris,[1] and
the rest of the pillage he sold as booty. As regards
this bull, although Timaeus in his *History* has maintained that it never existed at all, he has been refuted
by Fortune herself; for some two hundred and sixty
years after the capture of Acragas, when Scipio sacked
Carthage,[2] he returned to the Acragantini, together
with their other possessions still in the hands of the
Carthaginians, the bull, which was still in Acragas at
the time this history was being written.

I have been led to speak of this matter rather
copiously because Timaeus, who criticized most bitterly
the historians before his time and left the writers
of history bereft of all forgiveness, is himself caught
improvising in the very province where he most pro-
claims his own accuracy. For historians should, in
my opinion, be granted charity in errors that come of
ignorance, since they are human beings and since the

[1] Cp. Book 9. 18-19.   [2] In 146 B.C.

---

[2] παντοίων ἀνδριάντων] παντοίαν ἀνδρείαν τῶν P.

μένοις χρόνοις ἀληθείας οὔσης δυσευρέτου, τοὺς
μέντοι γε κατὰ προαίρεσιν οὐ τυγχάνοντας τοῦ
ἀκριβοῦς προσηκόντως κατηγορίας τυγχάνειν, ὅταν
κολακεύοντές τινας ἢ δι' ἔχθραν πικρότερον προσβάλλοντες ἀποσφάλλωνται τῆς ἀληθείας.

91. Ἰμίλκας δὲ ὀκτὼ μῆνας πολιορκήσας τὴν
πόλιν καὶ μικρὸν πρὸ τῆς χειμερινῆς τροπῆς
κυριεύσας αὐτῆς, οὐκ εὐθὺς κατέσκαψεν, ὅπως αἱ
δυνάμεις ἐν ταῖς οἰκίαις παραχειμάσωσιν. τῆς δὲ
περὶ τὸν Ἀκράγαντα συμφορᾶς διαγγελθείσης τοσ-
οῦτος τὴν νῆσον κατέσχε φόβος, ὥστε τῶν Σικελιωτῶν τοὺς μὲν εἰς Συρακούσας μεθίστασθαι, τοὺς
δὲ εἰς τὴν Ἰταλίαν τέκνα καὶ γυναῖκας καὶ τὴν
2 ἄλλην κτῆσιν ἀποσκευάζεσθαι. οἱ δὲ διαφυγόντες
τὴν αἰχμαλωσίαν Ἀκραγαντῖνοι παραγενηθέντες εἰς
Συρακούσας κατηγόρουν τῶν στρατηγῶν, φάσκοντες διὰ τὴν ἐκείνων προδοσίαν¹ ἀπολωλέναι τὴν πατρίδα. συνέβαινε δὲ καὶ ὑπὸ τῶν ἄλλων Σικελιωτῶν ἐπιτιμήσεως τυγχάνειν τοὺς Συρακοσίους, ὅτι
τοιούτους προστάτας αἱροῦνται, δι' οὓς ἀπολέσθαι
3 κινδυνεύει πᾶσα Σικελία. οὐ μὴν ἀλλὰ συναχθείσης
ἐκκλησίας ἐν Συρακούσαις, καὶ μεγάλων φόβων
ἐπικρεμαμένων, οὐθεὶς ἐτόλμα περὶ τοῦ πολέμου
συμβουλεύειν. ἀπορουμένων δὲ πάντων παρελθὼν
Διονύσιος ὁ Ἑρμοκράτους τῶν μὲν στρατηγῶν
κατηγόρησεν ὡς προδιδόντων τὰ πράγματα τοῖς
Καρχηδονίοις, τὰ δὲ πλήθη παρώξυνε πρὸς τὴν
αὐτῶν τιμωρίαν, παρακαλῶν μὴ περιμεῖναι τὸν
κατὰ τοὺς νόμους λῆρον,² ἀλλ' ἐκ χειρὸς³ ἐπι-

---

¹ So Rhodoman : παρουσίαν.
² λῆρον Post : κλῆρον.
³ εὐθέως after χειρὸς deleted by Kallenberg.

truth of ages past is hard to discover, but historians 406 B.C.
who deliberately do not give the exact facts should
properly be open to censure, whenever in flattering
one man or another or in attacking others from hatred
too bitterly, they stray from the truth.

91. Since Himilcar, after besieging the city for eight
months, had taken it shortly before the winter solstice,[1] he did not destroy it at once, in order that his
forces might winter in the dwellings. But when the
misfortune that had befallen Acragas was noised
abroad, such fear took possession of the island that
of the Sicilian Greeks some removed to Syracuse
and others transferred their children and wives and all
their possessions to Italy. The Acragantini who had
escaped being taken captive, when they arrived in
Syracuse, lodged accusations against their generals,
asserting that it was due to their treachery that their
country had perished. And it so happened that the
Syracusans also came in for censure by the rest of the
Sicilian Greeks, because, as they charged, they elected
the kind of leaders through whose fault the whole of
Sicily ran the risk of destruction. Nevertheless, even
though an assembly of the people was held in Syracuse and great fears hung over them, not a man would
venture to offer any counsel respecting the war.
While everyone was at a loss what to do, Dionysius,
the son of Hermocrates, taking the floor, accused the
generals of betraying their cause to the Carthaginians
and stirred up the assemblage to exact punishment of
them, urging them not to await the futile procedure
prescribed by the laws but to pass judgement upon

[1] December 22.

4 θεῖναι τὴν δίκην. τῶν δ᾽ ἀρχόντων ζημιούντων
τὸν Διονύσιον κατὰ τοὺς νόμους ὡς θορυβοῦντα,
Φίλιστος ὁ τὰς ἱστορίας ὕστερον συγγράψας, οὐσίαν ἔχων μεγάλην, ἐξέτισε τὰ πρόστιμα καὶ τῷ
Διονυσίῳ παρεκελεύετο λέγειν ὅσα προῄρητο. καὶ
προσεπειπόντος[1] ὅτι καθ᾽ ὅλην τὴν ἡμέραν ἂν
ζημιοῦν θέλωσιν, ἐκτίσει τἀργύριον ὑπὲρ αὐτοῦ,
τὸ λοιπὸν θαρρήσας ἀνέσειε τὰ πλήθη, καὶ τὴν
ἐκκλησίαν συνταράττων διέβαλλε τοὺς στρατηγούς,
ὅτι χρήμασι πεισθέντες ἐγκατέλιπον τὴν τῶν Ἀκραγαντίνων σωτηρίαν. συγκατηγόρησε δὲ καὶ τῶν
ἄλλων τῶν ἐπισημοτάτων πολιτῶν, συνιστὰς αὐτοὺς
5 οἰκείους ὄντας ὀλιγαρχίας. διόπερ συνεβούλευεν
αἱρεῖσθαι στρατηγοὺς μὴ τοὺς δυνατωτάτους, ἀλλὰ
τοὺς εὐνουστάτους καὶ δημοτικοὺς μᾶλλον· ἐκείνους μὲν γὰρ δεσποτικῶς ἄρχοντας τῶν πολιτῶν
καταφρονεῖν τῶν πολλῶν, καὶ τὰς τῆς πατρίδος
συμφορὰς ἰδίας ἡγεῖσθαι προσόδους, τοὺς δὲ τα-
πεινοτέρους οὐδὲν πράξειν τῶν τοιούτων, δεδιότας
τὴν περὶ αὐτοὺς ἀσθένειαν.

92. Πάντα δὲ πρὸς τὴν τῶν ἀκουόντων προαίρεσιν καὶ τὴν ἰδίαν ἐπιβολὴν δημηγορήσας οὐ μετρίως ἐξῆρε τὸν τῶν ἐκκλησιαζόντων θυμόν· ὁ γὰρ
δῆμος καὶ πάλαι μισῶν τοὺς στρατηγοὺς διὰ τὸ
δοκεῖν κακῶς[2] προΐστασθαι τοῦ πολέμου, τότε διὰ
τῶν λόγων παροξυνθεὶς παραυτίκα τοὺς μὲν ἔλυσε
τῆς ἀρχῆς, ἑτέρους δ᾽ εἵλατο στρατηγούς, ἐν οἷς
καὶ τὸν Διονύσιον, ὃς ἐν ταῖς πρὸς Καρχηδονίους

---

[1] So Dindorf: προῃρεῖτο. καὶ προσέτι εἰπόντος.
[2] κακῶς added by Rhodoman.

them at once. And when the archons, in accordance 406 B.C.
with the laws, laid a fine upon Dionysius on the
charge of raising an uproar, Philistus, who later composed his *History*,[1] a man of great wealth, paid the
fine and urged Dionysius to speak out whatever
he had had in his mind to say. And when Philistus
went on to say that if they wanted to fine Dionysius
throughout the whole day he would provide the
money for him, from then on Dionysius, full of con-
fidence, kept stirring up the multitude, and throwing
the assembly into confusion he accused the generals
of taking bribes to put the security of the Acragantini in jeopardy. And he also denounced the
rest of the most renowned citizens, presenting them
as friends of oligarchy. Consequently he advised
them to choose as generals not the most influential
citizens, but rather those who were the best disposed
and most favourable to the people ; for the former, he
maintained, ruling the citizens as they do in a despotic
manner, hold the many in contempt and consider the
misfortunes of their own country their own source of in-
come, whereas the more humble will do none of such
things, since they fear their own weakness.

92. Dionysius, by suiting every word of his har-
angue to the people to the predilection of his hearers
and his own personal design, stirred the anger of the
assembly to no small degree ; for the people, which
for some time past had hated the generals for what
they considered to be their bad conduct of the war
and at the moment were spurred on by what was being
said to them, immediately dismissed some of them
from office and chose other generals, among whom
was also Dionysius, who enjoyed the reputation of

[1] Of Sicily, in thirteen Books (cp. *infra*, chap. 103. 3).

μάχαις ἀνδρείᾳ δόξας διενηνοχέναι περίβλεπτος ἦν
2 παρὰ τοῖς Συρακοσίοις. διὸ καὶ μετεωρισθεὶς ταῖς
ἐλπίσι πᾶν ἐμηχανήσατο πρὸς τὸ γενέσθαι τῆς
πατρίδος τύραννος. μετὰ γὰρ τὴν παράληψιν τῆς
ἀρχῆς οὔτε συνήδρευσεν ἅμα τοῖς στρατηγοῖς οὔθ'
ὅλως συνῆν· ταῦτα δὲ πράττων διεδίδου λόγον ὡς
διαπεμπομένων αὐτῶν πρὸς τοὺς πολεμίους. οὕτω
γὰρ μάλιστ' ἤλπιζεν ἐκείνων μὲν περιαιρήσεσθαι[1]
τὴν ἐξουσίαν, ἑαυτῷ δὲ μόνῳ περιστήσειν τὴν
στρατηγίαν.
3   Ταῦτα δ' αὐτοῦ πράττοντος οἱ μὲν χαριέστατοι
τῶν πολιτῶν ὑπώπτευον τὸ γινόμενον, καὶ κατὰ
πάσας τὰς συνόδους ἐβλασφήμουν αὐτόν, ὁ δὲ
δημοτικὸς ὄχλος, ἀγνοῶν τὴν ἐπιβουλήν, ἐπῄνει
καὶ μόγις[2] ἔφασκε τὴν πόλιν προστάτην εὑρηκέναι
4 βέβαιον. οὐ μὴν ἀλλὰ πολλάκις ἐκκλησίας συν-
αγομένης περὶ τῆς εἰς τὸν πόλεμον παρασκευῆς,
θεωρήσας τοὺς Συρακοσίους καταπεπληγμένους
τὸν ἀπὸ τῶν πολεμίων φόβον, συνεβούλευε κατ-
5 άγειν τοὺς φυγάδας· ἄτοπον γὰρ ὑπάρχειν ἐκ μὲν
Ἰταλίας καὶ Πελοποννήσου μεταπέμπεσθαι βοήθειαν παρὰ τῶν ἀλλοτρίων, τοὺς δὲ πολίτας μὴ
βούλεσθαι πρὸς τοὺς ἰδίους κινδύνους συμπαρα-
λαμβάνειν, οὕς—τῶν πολεμίων μεγάλας δωρεὰς
ὑπισχνουμένων, ἂν συστρατεύσωσιν—προαιρεῖσθαι
μᾶλλον ἐπὶ ξένης ἀλωμένους ἀποθανεῖν ἤπερ ἀλλό-
6 τριόν τι κατὰ τῆς πατρίδος βουλεύσασθαι. καὶ
γὰρ[3] διὰ τὰς γεγενημένας ἐν τῇ πόλει στάσεις
φυγόντας, νῦν γε τυχόντας ταύτης τῆς εὐεργεσίας
προθύμως ἀγωνιεῖσθαι, τοῖς εὖ ποιήσασιν ἀπο-

---

[1] So Reiske : περιαιρεθήσεσθαι.   [2] μόγις Dindorf : μόλις.
[3] εἰ after γὰρ deleted by Reiske.

having shown unusual bravery in the battles against ^{406 B.} the Carthaginians and was admired of all the Syracusans. Having become elated, therefore, in his hopes, he tried every device to become tyrant of his country. For example, after assuming office he neither participated in the meetings of the generals nor associated with them in any way; and while acting in this manner he spread the report that they were carrying on negotiations with the enemy. For in this way he hoped that he could most effectively strip them of their power and clothe himself alone with the office of general.

While Dionysius was acting in this fashion, the most respectable citizens suspected what was taking place and in every gathering spoke disparagingly of him, but the common crowd, being ignorant of his scheme, gave him their approbation and declared that at long last the city had found a steadfast leader. However, when the assembly convened time and again to consider preparations for the war, Dionysius, observing that fear of the enemy had struck the Syracusans with terror, advised them to recall the exiles; for it was absurd, he said, to seek aid from peoples of other states in Italy and the Peloponnesus and to be unwilling to enlist the assistance of their fellow citizens in facing their own dangers, citizens who, although the enemy kept promising them great rewards for their military co-operation, chose rather to die as wanderers on foreign soil than plan some hostile act against their native land. And in fact, he declared, men who were now in exile because of past civil strife in the city, if at this time they were the recipients of this benefaction, would fight with eagerness, showing in this way their appreciation to their benefactors.

διδόντας χάριτας. πρὸς δὲ τὴν ὑπόθεσιν ταύτην
πολλὰ διαλεχθεὶς οἰκεῖα τοῖς πράγμασι συμψήφους
ἔλαβε τοὺς Συρακοσίους· οὐδὲ γὰρ τῶν συναρχόντων οὐδεὶς ἐτόλμα περὶ τούτων ἀντειπεῖν διά τε
τὴν τοῦ πλήθους ὁρμὴν καὶ διὰ τὸ θεωρεῖν ἑαυτῷ
μὲν περιεσομένην τὴν ἀπέχθειαν, ἐκείνῳ δὲ τὴν
7 παρὰ τῶν εὐεργετηθέντων χάριν. τοῦτο δ᾿ ἔπραξεν ὁ Διονύσιος ἐλπίζων ἰδίους ἕξειν τοὺς φυγάδας, ἀνθρώπους μεταβολῆς ἐπιθυμοῦντας καὶ πρὸς
τὴν ἐπίθεσιν τῆς τυραννίδος εὐθέτως διακειμένους·
ἤμελλον γὰρ ἡδέως ὄψεσθαι τῶν ἐχθρῶν φόνους.
δημεύσεις τῶν οὐσιῶν, ἑαυτοῖς ἀποκαθεσταμένα τὰ
χρήματα. καὶ τέλος κυρωθείσης τῆς περὶ τῶν
φυγάδων γνώμης, οὗτοι μὲν εὐθὺς εἰς τὴν πατρίδα
κατῆλθον.

93. Ἐκ δὲ τῆς Γέλας ἐνεχθέντων γραμμάτων,
ὅπως ἀποσταλῶσι στρατιῶται πλείους, ἔλαβεν ὁ
Διονύσιος οἰκείαν ἔφοδον τῆς ἰδίας προαιρέσεως.
ἀποσταλεὶς γὰρ μετὰ στρατιωτῶν πεζῶν μὲν δισχιλίων, ἱππέων δὲ τετρακοσίων, ἦλθε συντόμως
εἰς τὴν πόλιν τῶν Γελῴων, ἣν τότε παρεφύλαττε
Δέξιππος ὁ Λακεδαιμόνιος, κατασταθεὶς ὑπὸ Συρα-
2 κοσίων. ὁ δ᾿ οὖν Διονύσιος καταλαβὼν τοὺς εὐπορωτάτους στασιάζοντας πρὸς τὸν δῆμον, καὶ
κατηγορήσας αὐτῶν ἐν ἐκκλησίᾳ καὶ κατακρίνας,
αὐτοὺς μὲν ἀπέκτεινε, τὰς δ᾿ οὐσίας αὐτῶν ἐδή-
μευσεν, ἐκ δὲ τῶν χρημάτων τούτων τοῖς μὲν φρου-
ροῦσι τὴν πόλιν, ὧν ἡγεῖτο Δέξιππος, ἀπέδωκε
τοὺς ὀφειλομένους μισθούς· τοῖς δὲ μετ᾿ αὐτοῦ
παραγεγονόσιν ἐκ Συρακουσῶν ἐπηγγείλατο διπλοῦς
3 ποιήσειν τοὺς μισθοὺς ὧν ἡ πόλις ἔταξε. διὰ δὲ

After reciting many arguments for this proposal that 406 B.C.
bore on the situation, he won the votes of the
Syracusans to his view; for no one of his colleagues
in office dared oppose him in the matter both because
of the eagerness shown by the multitude and because
each observed that he himself would gain only enmity,
while Dionysius would reap a reward of gratitude
from those who had received kindness from him.
Dionysius took this course in the hope that he would
win the exiles for himself, men who wished a change
and would be favourably disposed toward the estab-
lishment of a tyranny; for they would be happy to
witness the murder of their enemies, the confiscation
of their property, and the restoration to themselves of
their possessions. And when finally the resolution regarding the exiles was passed, these returned at once
to their native land.

93. When messages were brought from Gela re-
questing the dispatch of additional troops, Dionysius
got a favourable means of accomplishing his own
purpose. Having been dispatched with two thousand
infantry and four hundred cavalry, he arrived speedily
at the city of the Geloans, which at that time was
under the eye of Dexippus, the Lacedaemonian, who
had been put in charge by the Syracusans. And when
Dionysius on arrival found the wealthiest citizens
engaged in strife with the people, he accused them
in an assembly and secured their condemnation,
whereupon he put them to death and confiscated their
possessions. With the money thus gained he paid the
guards of the city under the command of Dexippus the
wages which were owing them, while to his own troops
who had come with him from Syracuse he promised he
would pay double the wages which the city had deter-

385

τούτου τοῦ τρόπου τούς τ᾽ ἐν Γέλᾳ στρατιώτας καὶ
τοὺς μετ᾽ αὐτοῦ ταῖς εὐνοίαις ἰδίους κατεσκεύασεν.
ἐπῃνεῖτο δὲ καὶ ὑπὸ τοῦ δήμου τῶν Γελῴων ὡς αἴτιος αὐτοῖς γεγενημένος τῆς ἐλευθερίας· τοῖς γὰρ
δυνατωτάτοις φθονοῦντες τὴν ἐκείνων ὑπεροχὴν
4 δεσποτείαν αὐτῶν ἀπεκάλουν. διόπερ ἐξέπεμψαν
πρέσβεις τοὺς ἐπαινοῦντας ἐν Συρακούσαις καὶ
τὰ ψηφίσματα φέροντας, ἐν οἷς¹ αὐτὸν μεγάλαις
δωρεαῖς ἐτίμησαν. ὁ δὲ Διονύσιος ἐπεβάλετο μὲν
τὸν Δέξιππον πείθειν κοινωνῆσαι τῆς ἐπιβολῆς·
ἐπεὶ δ᾽ οὐ συγκατετίθετο, μετὰ τῶν ἰδίων στρατιωτῶν ἕτοιμος ἦν ἀνακάμπτειν εἰς Συρακούσας.
5 οἱ δὲ Γελῷοι πυνθανόμενοι τοὺς Καρχηδονίους μέλ-
λειν μετὰ πάσης τῆς δυνάμεως ἐπὶ πρώτην στρατεύειν τὴν Γέλαν, ἐδέοντο τοῦ Διονυσίου μεῖναι
καὶ μὴ περιιδεῖν αὐτοὺς τὰ αὐτὰ τοῖς Ἀκραγαντίνοις παθόντας. οἷς ἐπαγγειλάμενος ὁ Διονύσιος
συντόμως ἥξειν μετὰ πλείονος δυνάμεως, ἐξώρμη-
σεν ἐκ τῆς Γέλας μετὰ τῶν ἰδίων στρατιωτῶν.

94. Θέας δ᾽ οὔσης ἐν ταῖς Συρακούσαις, κατὰ²
τὴν ὥραν τῆς ἀπαλλαγῆς τῶν ἐκ τοῦ θεάτρου παρῆν
εἰς τὴν πόλιν. συνδραμόντων δὲ τῶν ὄχλων ἐπ᾽
αὐτὸν καὶ πυνθανομένων περὶ τῶν Καρχηδονίων,
ἀγνοεῖν αὐτούς, ἔφη, διότι τῶν ἔξωθεν πολεμιω-
τέρους ἔχουσι τοὺς ἔνδον τῶν κοινῶν προεστῶτας,
οἷς οἱ μὲν πολῖται πιστεύοντες ἑορτάζουσιν, αὐτοὶ
δὲ διαφοροῦντες τὰ δημόσια τοὺς στρατιώτας ἀμί-
σθους πεποιήκασι, καὶ τῶν πολεμίων ἀνυπερβλή-
τους ποιουμένων τὰς εἰς τὸν πόλεμον παρασκευὰς
καὶ μελλόντων ἐπὶ Συρακούσας τὴν δύναμιν ἄγειν,

¹ οἷς Eichstädt: αἷς.
² κατὰ added by Rhodoman.

mined. In this manner he won over to himself the
loyalty not only of the soldiers in Gela but also of those
whom he had brought with him. He also gained the
approval of the populace of the Geloans, who believed
him to be responsible for their liberation ; for in their
envy of the most influential citizens they stigmatized
the superiority these men possessed as a despotism
over themselves. Consequently they dispatched ambassadors who sang his praises in Syracuse and reported
decrees in which they honoured him with rich gifts.
Dionysius also undertook to persuade Dexippus to
associate himself with his design, and when Dexippus
would not join with him, he was on the point of returning with his own troops to Syracuse. But the
Geloans, on learning that the Carthaginians with their
entire host were going to make Gela the first object
of attack, besought Dionysius to remain and not to
stand idly by while they suffered the same fate as the
Acragantini. Dionysius replied to them that he would
return speedily with a larger force and set forth from
Gela with his own soldiers.

94. A play was being presented in Syracuse and
Dionysius arrived in the city at the time when the
people were leaving the theatre. When the populace
rushed in throngs to him and were questioning him
about the Carthaginians, they were unaware, he said,
that they had more dangerous enemies than their
foreign foes—the men within the city in charge of the
public interests ; these men the citizens trusted while
they held public festivals, but these very men, while
plundering the public funds, had let the soldiers go
unpaid, and although the enemy was making their preparations for the war on a scale which could not be
surpassed and were about to lead their forces upon

2 τούτων[1] οὐδ' ἡντινοῦν ποιοῦνται[2] φροντίδα. δι' ἣν
δ' αἰτίαν ταῦτα πράττουσιν, εἰδέναι μὲν καὶ πρότερον, νῦν δὲ σαφέστερον ἀνεγνωκέναι[3]· Ἰμίλκωνα
γὰρ πρὸς αὐτὸν ἀπεσταλκέναι κήρυκα, πρόφασιν
μὲν ὑπὲρ τῶν αἰχμαλώτων, παρακαλεῖν δέ—πλῆθος τῶν συναρχόντων περιποιησάμενον μηδὲν τῶν
πραττομένων πολυπραγμονεῖν—μή γ'[4] ἀντιπράτ-
3 τειν, ἐπειδὴ συνεργεῖν οὐ προαιρεῖται. μηκέτ' οὖν
βούλεσθαι στρατηγεῖν, ἀλλὰ παρεῖναι τὴν ἀρχὴν
ἀποθησόμενος· οὐ γὰρ ἀνεκτὸν εἶναι, τῶν ἄλλων
πωλούντων τὴν πατρίδα, μόνον[5] κινδυνεύειν μετὰ
τῶν πολιτῶν ἅμα[6] καὶ δόξειν μετεσχηκέναι τῆς
προδοσίας.

4 Παροξυνθέντων δὲ ἐπὶ τοῖς ῥηθεῖσι καὶ τοῦ λόγου διὰ πάσης τῆς δυνάμεως ῥυέντος, τότε μὲν
εἷς ἕκαστος ἀγωνιῶν εἰς οἶκον ἐχωρίσθη· τῇ δ'
ὑστεραίᾳ συναχθείσης ἐκκλησίας ἐν ᾗ[7] τῶν ἀρχόντων πολλὰ κατηγορήσας οὐ μετρίως εὐδοκίμησε,
τὸν δὲ[8] δῆμον κατὰ τῶν στρατηγῶν παρώξυνε,
5 τέλος[9] τῶν καθημένων τινὲς ἀνεβόησαν στρατηγὸν
αὐτὸν αὐτοκράτορα καθιστάναι καὶ μὴ περιμένειν
ἄχρις ἂν οἱ πολέμιοι τοῖς τείχεσιν ἐπεισίωσι·
χρείαν γὰρ ἔχειν τὸ μέγεθος τοῦ πολέμου τοιούτου στρατηγοῦ, δι' οὗ δυνατὸν εἶναι εὐπορεῖν τοῖς
πράγμασιν· τὰ δὲ περὶ τῶν προδοτῶν ἐν ἐκκλησίᾳ

---

[1] τούτων Reiske : τούτων δ'.
[2] So Dindorf : ποιούμενοι.
[3] ἀνεγνωκέναι] ἐγνωκέναι Dindorf.
[4] μή γ' Vogel : μήδ'.
[5] μὴ added by Eichstädt, οὐ by Reiske before μόνον with
ἀλλὰ for ἅμα. [6] ἅμα Vogel : ἀλλά.
[7] ἐν ᾗ deleted by Reiske. [8] δὲ deleted by Eichstädt.
[9] δὲ after τέλος deleted by Bekker.

406 B.C.

Syracuse, the generals were giving these matters no concern whatsoever. The reason for such conduct, he continued, he had been aware of before, but now he had got fuller information. For Himilcon had sent a herald to him, ostensibly to treat about the captives, but in fact to urge him, now that Himilcon had induced a large number of Dionysius' colleagues not to bother themselves with what was taking place, at least to offer no opposition, since he, Dionysius, did not choose to co-operate with him. Consequently, Dionysius continued, he did not wish to serve longer as general, but was present in Syracuse to lay down his office ; for it was intolerable for him, while the other generals were selling out their country, to be the only one to fight together with the citizens and yet be at the same time destined to be thought in after years to have shared in their betrayal.[1]

Although the populace had been stirred by what Dionysius had said and his words spread through the whole army, at the time every man departed to his home full of anxiety. But on the following day, when an assembly had been convened in which Dionysius won no small approval when he lodged many accusations against the magistrates and stirred up the populace against the generals, finally some of the members cried out to appoint him general with supreme power and not to wait until the enemy were storming their walls ; for the magnitude of the war, they urged, made necessary such a general, through whose leadership their cause could prosper ; as for the traitors, their case would be debated in another

[1] Or, following Eichstädt and Reiske, "for it was intolerable for him, while the rest of the generals were selling out the state, not only to fight together with the citizens but also to be thought in after years to have shared in the betrayal."

ἑτέρᾳ βουλεύεσθαι· τῶν γὰρ ἐνεστώτων καιρῶν
ἀλλότριον εἶναι· καὶ πρότερον δὲ Καρχηδονίων τὰς
τριάκοντα μυριάδας περὶ τὴν Ἱμέραν νενικῆσθαι
στρατηγοῦντος Γέλωνος αὐτοκράτορος. 95. ταχὺ
δὲ τῶν πολλῶν, ὥσπερ εἰώθασιν, ἐπὶ τὸ χεῖρον
ῥεπόντων, ὁ Διονύσιος ἀπεδείχθη στρατηγὸς αὐτο-
κράτωρ. ἐπεὶ δ' οὖν αὐτῷ τὰ πράγματα κατὰ
νοῦν ἠκολούθει, ψήφισμα ἔγραψε τοὺς μισθοὺς δι-
πλασίους εἶναι· πάντας γὰρ ἔφησε τούτου γενομένου προθυμοτέρους ἔσεσθαι πρὸς τὸν ἀγῶνα,
καὶ περὶ τῶν χρημάτων παρεκάλει μηθὲν ἀγωνιᾶν·
ἔσεσθαι γὰρ αὐτῶν τὸν πόρον ῥᾴδιον.

2 Διαλυθείσης δὲ τῆς ἐκκλησίας οὐκ ὀλίγοι τῶν
Συρακοσίων κατηγόρουν τῶν πραχθέντων, ὥσπερ
οὐκ αὐτοὶ ταῦτα κεκυρωκότες[1]· τοῖς γὰρ λογισμοῖς
εἰς ἑαυτοὺς ἐρχόμενοι τὴν ἐσομένην δυναστείαν ἀν-
εθεώρουν. οὗτοι μὲν οὖν βεβαιῶσαι βουλόμενοι
τὴν ἐλευθερίαν ἔλαθον ἑαυτοὺς δεσπότην τῆς πα-
3 τρίδος καθεστακότες· ὁ δὲ Διονύσιος τὴν μετάνοιαν
τῶν ὄχλων φθάσαι βουλόμενος, ἐπεζήτει δι' οὗ
τρόπου δύναιτο φύλακας αἰτήσασθαι τοῦ σώματος·
τούτου γὰρ συγχωρηθέντος ῥᾳδίως ἤμελλε κυριεύ-
σειν τῆς τυραννίδος. εὐθὺς οὖν παρήγγειλε τοὺς
ἐν ἡλικίᾳ πάντας ἕως ἐτῶν τεσσαράκοντα λαβόντας ἐπισιτισμὸν ἡμερῶν τριάκοντα καταντᾶν μετὰ
τῶν ὅπλων εἰς Λεοντίνους. αὕτη δ' ἡ πόλις τότε
φρούριον ἦν τῶν Συρακοσίων, πλῆρες ὑπάρχον φυγάδων καὶ ξένων ἀνθρώπων. ἤλπιζε γὰρ τούτους συναγωνιστὰς ἕξειν, ἐπιθυμοῦντας μεταβολῆς,
τῶν δὲ Συρακοσίων τοὺς πλείστους οὐδ' ἥξειν εἰς

---

[1] ταῦτα κεκυρωκότες] Vogel suggests τὰ κεκυρωμένα πεποιη-
κότες ταῦτα.

assembly, since it was foreign to the present situation; indeed at a former time three hundred thousand Carthaginians had been conquered at Himera when Gelon was general with supreme power.[1] 95. And soon the multitude, as is their wont, swung to the worse decision and Dionysius was appointed general with supreme power. And now, since the situation corresponded to his desires, he proposed a decree that the pay of the mercenaries be doubled; for they would all, he said, if this were done, be more eager for the coming contest, and he urged them not to worry at all about the funds, since it would be an easy task to raise them.

After the assembly was adjourned no small number of the Syracusans condemned what had been done, as if they themselves had not had their way in the matter; for as their thoughts turned to their own state they could imagine the tyrannical power which was to follow. Now these men, in their desire to insure their freedom, had unwittingly established a despot over their country; Dionysius, on the other hand, wishing to forestall the change of mind on the part of the populace, kept seeking a means whereby he could ask for a guard for his person, for if this were granted him he would easily establish himself in the tyranny. At once, then, he issued orders that all men of military age up to forty years should provide themselves with rations for thirty days and report to him under arms at Leontini. This city was at that time an outpost of the Syracusans, being full of exiles and foreigners.[2] For Dionysius hoped that he would have these men on his side, desiring as they did a change of government, and that the majority of the Syracusans would

---

[1] Cp. Book 11. 22.   [2] *i.e.* non-Syracusans.

4 Λεοντίνους. οὐ μὴν ἀλλὰ νυκτὸς ἐπὶ τῆς χώρας
στρατοπεδεύων, καὶ προσποιηθεὶς ἐπιβουλεύεσθαι,
κραυγὴν ἐποίησε καὶ θόρυβον διὰ τῶν ἰδίων οἰκε-
τῶν· τοῦτο δὲ πράξας συνέφυγεν εἰς τὴν ἀκρόπολιν,
καὶ διενυκτέρευσε πυρὰ καίων καὶ τοὺς γνωριμω-
5 τάτους τῶν στρατιωτῶν μεταπεμπόμενος. ἅμα δ'
ἡμέρᾳ τοῦ πλήθους ἀθροισθέντος εἰς Λεοντίνους,
πολλὰ πρὸς τὴν τῆς ἐπιβολῆς ὑπόθεσιν πιθανολο-
γήσας ἔπεισε τοὺς ὄχλους δοῦναι φύλακας αὐτῷ
τῶν στρατιωτῶν ἑξακοσίους, οὓς ἂν προαιρῆται.
λέγεται δὲ τοῦτο πρᾶξαι τὸν Διονύσιον ἀπομιμού-
6 μενον¹ Πεισίστρατον τὸν Ἀθηναῖον· καὶ γὰρ ἐκεῖ-
νόν φασιν ἑαυτὸν κατατραυματίσαντα προελθεῖν
εἰς τὴν ἐκκλησίαν ὡς ἐπιβεβουλευμένον, καὶ διὰ
τοῦτο φυλακὴν λαβεῖν παρὰ τῶν πολιτῶν, ᾗ χρη-
σάμενον τὴν τυραννίδα περιπεποιῆσθαι. καὶ τότε
Διονύσιος τῇ παραπλησίᾳ μηχανῇ τὸ πλῆθος ἐξαπατήσας ἐνήργει τὰ τῆς τυραννίδος.

96. Εὐθὺ γὰρ τοὺς χρημάτων μὲν ἐνδεεῖς, τῇ
δὲ ψυχῇ θρασεῖς ἐπιλέξας, ὑπὲρ τοὺς χιλίους,
ὅπλοις τε πολυτελέσι καθώπλισε καὶ ταῖς μεγίσταις ἐπαγγελίαις ἐμετεώρισε, τοὺς δὲ μισθοφόρους
ἀνακαλούμενος καὶ φιλανθρώποις λόγοις χρώμενος
ἰδίους κατεσκεύαζεν. μετετίθει δὲ καὶ τὰς τάξεις,
τοῖς πιστοτάτοις τὰς ἡγεμονίας παραδιδούς, καὶ
Δέξιππον τὸν Λακεδαιμόνιον ἀπέλυσεν εἰς τὴν Ἑλ-
λάδα· ὑφεωρᾶτο γὰρ τὸν ἄνδρα τοῦτον, μὴ καιροῦ
λαμβανόμενος ἀνακτήσηται τοῖς Συρακοσίοις
2 τὴν ἐλευθερίαν. μετεπέμψατο δὲ καὶ τοὺς ἐν

not even come to Leontini. However, while he was 406 B.C. encamped at night in the countryside, he pretended that he was the object of a plot and had his personal servants raise a tumult and uproar ; and after doing this he took refuge on the acropolis, where he passed the night, keeping fires burning and summoning to him his most trustworthy soldiers. And at daybreak, when the common people were gathered into Leontini, he delivered a long plausible speech to further his design and persuaded the populace to give him a guard of six hundred soldiers whomsoever he should select. It is said that Dionysius did this in imitation of Peisistratus the Athenian ; for he, we are told, after wounding himself, appeared before the assembly alleging that he had been the victim of a plot, and because of this he received a guard at the hands of the citizens, by means of which he established the tyranny.[1] And at this time Dionysius, having deceived the multitude by a similar device, put into effect the structure of his tyranny.

96. For instance Dionysius at once selected such citizens as were without property but bold in spirit, more than a thousand in number, provided them with costly arms, and buoyed them up with extravagant promises ; the mercenaries also he won to himself by calling them to him and conversing with them in friendly fashion. He made changes also in the military posts, conferring their commands upon his most faithful followers ; and Dexippus the Lacedaemonian he dismissed to Greece, for he was suspicious of this man lest he should seize a favourable opportunity and restore to the Syracusans their liberty. He also called

---

[1] Cp. Herodotus, 1. 59 ; Plutarch, *Solon*, 30.

---

[1] So Reiske : ὑπομιμούμενον.

Γέλα μισθοφόρους, καὶ πανταχόθεν συνῆγε τοὺς
φυγάδας καὶ ἀσεβεῖς, ἐλπίζων διὰ τούτων βεβαιό-
τατα τηρηθήσεσθαι τὴν τυραννίδα. οὐ μὴν ἀλλὰ
παραγενόμενος εἰς Συρακούσας κατεσκήνωσεν ἐν
τῷ ναυστάθμῳ, φανερῶς αὑτὸν ἀναδείξας τύραννον.
οἱ δὲ Συρακόσιοι βαρέως φέροντες ἠναγκάζοντο
τὴν ἡσυχίαν ἔχειν· οὐδὲν γὰρ ἔτι περαίνειν ἠδύ-
ναντο· ἥ τε γὰρ πόλις ἔγεμεν ὅπλων ξενικῶν, τούς
τε Καρχηδονίους ἐδεδοίκεισαν τηλικαύτας ἔχοντας
3 δυνάμεις. ὁ δ᾽ οὖν Διονύσιος εὐθέως ἔγημε τὴν
Ἑρμοκράτους θυγατέρα τοῦ καταπολεμήσαντος
Ἀθηναίους, καὶ τὴν ἀδελφὴν ἔδωκε Πολυξένῳ
τῆς Ἑρμοκράτους γυναικὸς ἀδελφῷ· τοῦτο δ᾽
ἔπραξε βουλόμενος οἰκίαν ἐπίσημον εἰς οἰκειότητα
προσλαβέσθαι πρὸς τὸ τὴν τυραννίδα ποιῆσαι βεβαίαν. μετὰ δὲ ταῦτα συναγαγὼν ἐκκλησίαν τῶν
ἀντιπραξάντων αὐτῷ τοὺς δυνατωτάτους[1] ὄντας,
Δαφναῖον καὶ Δήμαρχον, ἀνεῖλεν.

4 Διονύσιος μὲν οὖν ἐκ γραμματέως καὶ τοῦ
τυχόντος ἰδιώτου τῆς μεγίστης πόλεως τῶν Ἑλληνίδων ἐγενήθη τύραννος· διετήρησε δὲ τὴν
δυναστείαν ἄχρι τῆς τελευτῆς, τυραννήσας ἔτη δύο
λείποντα τῶν τεσσαράκοντα. τὰς δὲ κατὰ μέρος
αὐτοῦ πράξεις καὶ τὴν αὔξησιν τῆς ἀρχῆς ἐν τοῖς
οἰκείοις χρόνοις διέξιμεν· δοκεῖ γὰρ οὗτος μεγίστην τῶν ἱστορουμένων τυραννίδα περιπεποιῆσθαι
δι᾽ ἑαυτοῦ καὶ πολυχρονιωτάτην.

5 Οἱ δὲ Καρχηδόνιοι μετὰ τὴν ἅλωσιν τῆς πόλεως
τὰ μὲν ἀναθήματα καὶ τοὺς ἀνδριάντας καὶ τἄλλα
τὰ πολυτελέστατα μετήνεγκαν εἰς Καρχηδόνα, τὰ
δ᾽ ἱερὰ κατακαύσαντες καὶ τὴν πόλιν διαρπάσαντες

---

[1] So Reiske: τοὺς ἀντιπράξαντας αὐτῷ τῶν δυνατωτάτων.

to himself the mercenaries in Gela and gathered from 406 B.C. all quarters the exiles and impious, hoping that in these men the tyranny would find its strongest support. While in Syracuse, however, he took up his quarters in the naval station, having openly proclaimed himself tyrant. Although the Syracusans were offended, they were compelled to keep quiet; for they were unable to effect anything now, since not only was the city thronged with mercenary soldiers but the people were filled with fear of the Carthaginians who possessed such powerful armaments. Now Dionysius straightway married the daughter of Hermocrates, the conqueror of the Athenians,[1] and gave his sister in marriage to Polyxenus, the brother of Hermocrates' wife. This he did out of a desire to draw a distinguished house into relationship with him in order to make firm the tyranny. After this he summoned an assembly and had his most influential opponents, Daphnaeus and Demarchus, put to death.

Now Dionysius, from a scribe and ordinary private citizen, had become tyrant of the largest city of the Greek world[2]; and he maintained his dominance until his death, having ruled as tyrant for thirty-eight years.[3] But we shall give a detailed account of his deeds and of the expansion of his rule in connection with the appropriate periods of time; for it seems that this man, single-handed, established the strongest and longest tyranny of any recorded by history.

The Carthaginians, after their capture of the city,[4] transferred to Carthage both the votive offerings and statues and every other object of greatest value, and when they had burned down the temples and plun-

[1] Cp. chaps. 18. 3; 34. 4.
[2] Probably Syracuse grew to be such before the death of Dionysius.   [3] 405–367 B.C.   [4] Acragas.

αὐτοῦ παρεχείμασαν. ἐπὶ δὲ τὴν ἐαρινὴν ὥραν παρεσκευάζοντο μηχανήματα καὶ βέλη παντοδαπά, διανοούμενοι πρώτην πολιορκῆσαι τὴν τῶν Γελῴων πόλιν.

97. Τούτων δὲ πραττομένων Ἀθηναῖοι μὲν κατὰ τὸ συνεχὲς ἐλαττώμασι περιπίπτοντες, ἐποιήσαντο πολίτας τοὺς μετοίκους καὶ τῶν ἄλλων ξένων τοὺς βουλομένους συναγωνίσασθαι· ταχὺ δὲ πολλοῦ πλήθους πολιτογραφηθέντος, οἱ στρατηγοὶ κατέγραφον τοὺς εὐθέτους εἰς τὴν στρατείαν.[1] παρεσκευάσαντο δὲ ναῦς ἑξήκοντα, καὶ ταύτας πολυτελῶς καταρτίσαντες ἐξέπλευσαν εἰς Σάμον, ἐν ᾗ κατέλαβον τοὺς ἄλλους στρατηγοὺς ἀπὸ τῶν ἄλ-
2 λων νήσων ὀγδοήκοντα τριήρεις ἠθροικότας. δεηθέντες δὲ καὶ τῶν Σαμίων προσπληρῶσαι δέκα τριήρεις, ἀνήχθησαν ἁπάσαις ταῖς ναυσὶν οὔσαις ἑκατὸν πεντήκοντα καὶ κατέπλευσαν εἰς τὰς Ἀργινούσας νήσους, σπεύδοντες λῦσαι τὴν Μιτυλήνης
3 πολιορκίαν. ὁ δὲ τῶν Λακεδαιμονίων ναύαρχος Καλλικρατίδας πυθόμενος τὸν κατάπλουν τῶν νεῶν, ἐπὶ μὲν τῆς πολιορκίας κατέλιπεν Ἐτεόνικον μετὰ τῆς πεζῆς δυνάμεως, αὐτὸς δὲ πληρώσας ναῦς ἑκατὸν τεσσαράκοντα κατὰ σπουδὴν ἀνήχθη[2] τῶν Ἀργινουσῶν περὶ θάτερα μέρη· αἳ νῆσοι τότ' ἦσαν οἰκούμεναι καὶ πολισμάτιον Αἰολικὸν ἔχουσαι, κείμεναι μεταξὺ Μιτυλήνης καὶ Κύμης, ἀπέχουσαι τῆς ἠπείρου βραχὺ παντελῶς καὶ τῆς ἄκρας τῆς Κανίδος.[3]
4 Οἱ δ' Ἀθηναῖοι τὸν μὲν κατάπλουν τῶν πολεμίων εὐθέως ἔγνωσαν, οὐ μακρὰν ὁρμοῦντες, διὰ δὲ τὸ

---

[1] στρατείαν] στρατιὰν Vogel.
[2] καὶ (κατὰ P) after ἀνήχθη deleted by Wesseling.

dered the city, they spent the winter there. And in 406 B.C.
the springtime they made ready every kind of engine
of war and of missile, planning to lay siege first to the
city of the Geloans.

97. While these events were taking place, the
Athenians,[1] who had suffered a continued series of
reverses, conferred citizenship upon the metics and
any other aliens who were willing to fight with them ;
and when a great multitude was quickly enrolled
among the citizens, the generals kept mustering for
the campaign all who were in fit condition. They
made ready sixty ships, and after fitting them out at
great expense they sailed forth to Samos, where they
found the other generals who had assembled eighty
triremes from the rest of the islands. They also had
asked the Samians to man and equip ten additional
triremes, and with one hundred and fifty ships in all
they set out to sea and put in at the Arginusae Islands,
being eager to raise the siege of Mitylenê. When
Callicratidas, the admiral of the Lacedaemonians,
learned of the approach of the ships, he left Eteonicus
with the land troops in charge of the siege, while he
himself manned one hundred and forty ships and
hurriedly put out to sea on the other side of the
Arginusae. These islands, which were inhabited at
that time and contained a small settlement of
Aeolians, lie between Mitylenê and Cymê and are
but a very small distance from the mainland and the
headland of Canis.

The Athenians learned at once of the approach of
the enemy, since they lay at anchor no small distance

---

[1] The narrative is resumed from chap. 79.

---

[3] So Casaubon : κατάνιδος.

μέγεθος τῶν πνευμάτων τὸ μὲν ναυμαχεῖν ἀπέγνω-
σαν, εἰς δὲ τὴν ἐχομένην ἡμέραν ἡτοιμάζοντο τὰ
πρὸς τὴν ναυμαχίαν, τὸ αὐτὸ ποιούντων καὶ τῶν
Λακεδαιμονίων, καίπερ[1] ἀμφοτέροις ἀπαγορευόν-
5 των τῶν μάντεων. τοῖς μὲν γὰρ Λακεδαιμονίοις
ἡ τοῦ θύματος κεφαλὴ κειμένη παρὰ τὸν αἰγιαλὸν
ἀφανὴς ἐγεγόνει, προσκλύζοντος τοῦ κύματος· διόπερ ὁ μάντις προύλεγε διότι τελευτήσει ναυμαχῶν
ὁ ναύαρχος· οὗ ῥηθέντος φασὶ τὸν Καλλικρατίδαν
εἰπεῖν, ὅτι τελευτήσας κατὰ τὴν μάχην οὐδὲν ἀδο-
6 ξοτέραν ποιήσει τὴν Σπάρτην. τῶν δ' Ἀθηναίων
ὁ στρατηγὸς Θρασύβουλος, ὃς ἦν ἐπὶ τῆς ἡγεμονίας
ἐκείνην τὴν ἡμέραν, εἶδε κατὰ τὴν νύκτα τοιαύ-
την ὄψιν· ἔδοξεν Ἀθήνησι τοῦ θεάτρου πλήθοντος
αὐτός τε καὶ τῶν ἄλλων στρατηγῶν ἓξ ὑποκρί-
νεσθαι τραγῳδίαν Εὐριπίδου Φοινίσσας· τῶν δ'
ἀντιπάλων ὑποκρινομένων τὰς Ἱκέτιδας δόξαι τὴν
Καδμείαν νίκην αὐτοῖς περιγενέσθαι,[2] καὶ πάντας ἀποθανεῖν μιμουμένους τὰ πράγματα τῶν ἐπὶ
7 τὰς Θήβας στρατευσάντων. ἀκούσας δ' ὁ μάντις
ταῦτα διεσάφει τοὺς ἑπτὰ τῶν στρατηγῶν ἀν-
αιρεθήσεσθαι. τῶν δ' ἱερῶν φερόντων νίκην, οἱ
στρατηγοὶ περὶ μὲν τῆς ἑαυτῶν ἀπωλείας ἐκώλυον
ἑτέροις ἀπαγγέλλειν, περὶ δὲ τῆς ἐν τοῖς ἱεροῖς
νίκης ἀνήγγειλαν καθ' ὅλην τὴν δύναμιν.

98. Καλλικρατίδας δ' ὁ ναύαρχος συναγαγὼν τὰ
πλήθη καὶ παραθαρσύνας τοῖς οἰκείοις λόγοις, τὸ
τελευταῖον εἶπεν· εἰς τὸν ὑπὲρ τῆς πατρίδος
κίνδυνον οὕτως εἰμὶ[3] πρόθυμος αὐτός, ὥστε τοῦ

---

[1] καίπερ P, καὶ παρ' cet., καίπερ παρ' Wurm.
[2] So Hertlein : προσγενέσθαι.
[3] εἰμὶ Wesseling : ἐστὶν P, ἐστὶ cet.

away, but refused battle because of the strong winds 406 B.C.
and made ready for the conflict on the following day,
the Lacedaemonians also doing likewise, although the
seers on both sides forbade it. For in the case of the
Lacedaemonians the head of the victim, which lay on
the beach, was lost to sight when the waves broke on
it, and the seer accordingly foretold that the admiral
would die in the fight. At this prophecy Callicratidas,
we are told, remarked, " If I die in the fight, I shall
not have lessened the fame of Sparta." And in the
case of the Athenians Thrasybulus [1] their general,
who held the supreme command on that day, saw in
the night the following vision. He dreamed that he
was in Athens and the theatre was crowded, and that
he and six of the other generals were playing the
Phoenician Women of Euripides, while their com-
petitors were performing the *Suppliants* [2] ; and that
it resulted in a " Cadmean victory " [3] for them and
they all died, just as did those who waged the campaign against Thebes. When the seer heard this, he
disclosed that seven of the generals would be slain.
Since the omens revealed victory, the generals forbade any word going out to the others about their
own death but they passed the news of the victory
disclosed by the omens throughout the whole army.

98. The admiral Callicratidas, having assembled his
whole force, encouraged them with the appropriate
words and concluded his speech as follows. "So eager
am I myself to enter battle for my country that,

---

[1] This should be Thrasyllus.
[2] Also by Euripides. Both plays are on the theme of the
war of the seven Argive chiefs against Thebes.
[3] Cp. Book 11. 12. 1.

μάντεως λέγοντος διὰ τῶν ἱερείων[1] ὑμῖν μὲν προ-
σημαίνεσθαι νίκην, ἐμοὶ δὲ θάνατον, ὅμως ἕτοιμός
εἰμι τελευτᾶν. εἰδὼς οὖν μετὰ τὸν τῶν ἡγεμόνων
θάνατον[2] ἐν θορύβῳ τὰ στρατόπεδα γινόμενα, νῦν
ἀναδεικνύω ναύαρχον, ἂν ἐγώ τι πάθω, τὸν δια-
δεξόμενον Κλέαρχον, ἄνδρα πεῖραν δεδωκότα τῶν
2 κατὰ τὸν πόλεμον ἔργων. ὁ μὲν οὖν Καλλικρατίδας ταῦτ᾽ εἰπὼν οὐκ ὀλίγους ἐποίησε ζηλῶσαι τὴν
ἀρετὴν αὐτοῦ καὶ προθυμοτέρους γενέσθαι πρὸς
τὴν μάχην. καὶ Λακεδαιμόνιοι μὲν παρακαλοῦντες
ἀλλήλους ἀνέβαινον εἰς τὰς ναῦς· οἱ δ᾽ Ἀθηναῖοι,
παρακληθέντες ὑπὸ τῶν στρατηγῶν εἰς τὸν ἀγῶνα,
κατὰ σπουδὴν ἐπλήρουν τὰς τριήρεις καὶ πάντες
3 εἰς τάξιν καθίσταντο. τοῦ μὲν οὖν δεξιοῦ κέρατος
Θράσυλλος ἡγεῖτο καὶ Περικλῆς ὁ Περικλέους τοῦ
προσαγορευθέντος κατὰ τὴν δύναμιν Ὀλυμπίου·
συμπαρέλαβε δὲ καὶ Θηραμένην εἰς τὸ δεξιὸν
κέρας, ἐφ᾽ ἡγεμονίας τάξας· ὃς ἰδιώτης ὢν μὲν
συνεστράτευε[3] τότε, πρότερον[4] δὲ πολλάκις ἦν
ἀφηγημένος δυνάμεων· τοὺς δ᾽ ἄλλους στρατηγοὺς
παρ᾽ ὅλην τὴν φάλαγγα διέταξε, καὶ τὰς καλουμένας Ἀργινούσας νήσους συμπεριέλαβε τῇ τάξει,
4 σπεύδων ὅτι πλεῖστον παρεκτεῖναι τὰς ναῦς. ὁ δὲ
Καλλικρατίδας ἀνήχθη τὸ μὲν δεξιὸν μέρος αὐτὸς
ἔχων, τὸ δ᾽ εὐώνυμον παρέδωκε Βοιωτοῖς, ὧν
Θρασώνδας ὁ Θηβαῖος τὴν ἡγεμονίαν ἔσχεν. οὐ
δυνάμενος δὲ τὴν τάξιν ἐξισῶσαι τοῖς πολεμίοις
διὰ τὸ τὰς νήσους πολὺν ἐπέχειν τόπον, διείλατο
τὴν δύναμιν, καὶ δύο ποιήσας στόλους πρὸς ἑκά-

---

[1] ἱερείων] ἱερῶν Vogel.
[2] καὶ after θάνατον omitted by M; Vogel suggests κατὰ
θόρυβον.

although the seer declares that the victims foretell 406 B.C.
victory for you but death for me, I am none the less
ready to die. Accordingly, knowing that after the
death of commanders forces are thrown into confusion, I designate at this time as admiral to succeed me,
in case I meet with some mishap, Clearchus, a man
who has proved himself in deeds of war." By these
words Callicratidas led not a few to emulate his valour
and to become more eager for the battle. The Lacedaemonians, exhorting one another, entered their
ships, and the Athenians, after hearing the exhorta-
tions of their generals summoning them to the
struggle, manned the triremes in haste and all took
their positions. Thrasyllus commanded the right
wing and also Pericles, the son of the Pericles who,
by reason of his influence, had been dubbed " The
Olympian " ; and he associated with himself on the
right wing also Theramenes, giving him a command.
At the time Theramenes was on the campaign as a
private citizen, although formerly he had often been
in command of armaments. The rest of the generals
he stationed along the entire line, and the Arginusae
Islands, as they are called, he enclosed by his battle
order, since he wished to extend his ships as far as
possible. Callicratidas put out to sea holding himself
the right flank, and the left he entrusted to the
Boeotians, who were commanded by Thrasondas the
Theban. And since he was unable to make his line
equal to that of the enemy by reason of the large space
occupied by the islands, he divided his force, and forming two fleets fought two battles separately, one on

---

³ So Vogel : συνεστρατεύετο.
⁴ τότε, πρότερον Stroth : πρότερον, τότε.

5 τερον μέρος δίχα διηγωνίζετο. διὸ καὶ παρείχετο
μεγάλην κατάπληξιν πολλαχῇ τοῖς θεωμένοις, ὡς
ἂν τεττάρων μὲν στόλων ναυμαχούντων, τῶν δὲ
νεῶν συνηθροισμένων εἰς ἕνα τόπον οὐ πολλαῖς
ἐλάττω τῶν τριακοσίων· μεγίστη γὰρ αὕτη μνη-
μονεύεται ναυμαχία γεγενημένη[1] Ἕλλησι πρὸς
Ἕλληνας.

99. Ἅμα δ᾽ οἵ τε ναύαρχοι τοῖς σαλπιγκταῖς
παρεκελεύοντο σημαίνειν καὶ τὸ παρ᾽ ἑκατέροις
πλῆθος ἐναλλὰξ ἐπαλαλάζον ἐξαίσιον ἐποίει βοήν·
πάντες δὲ μετὰ σπουδῆς ἐλαύνοντες τὸ ῥόθιον ἐφιλοτιμοῦντο πρὸς ἀλλήλους, ἑκάστου σπεύδοντος
2 πρώτου κατάρξασθαι τῆς μάχης. ἔμπειροί τε γὰρ
ἦσαν τῶν κινδύνων οἱ πλεῖστοι διὰ τὸ μῆκος τοῦ
πολέμου καὶ σπουδὴν ἀνυπέρβλητον εἰσεφέροντο[2]
διὰ τὸ[3] τοὺς κρατίστους εἰς[4] τὸν ὑπὲρ τῶν ὅλων
ἀγῶνα συνηθροῖσθαι· πάντες γὰρ ὑπελάμβανον τοὺς
ταύτῃ τῇ μάχῃ νικήσαντας πέρας ἐπιθήσειν τῷ
3 πολέμῳ. οὐ μὴν ἀλλ᾽ ὁ Καλλικρατίδας ἀκηκοὼς
τοῦ μάντεως τὴν περὶ αὐτὸν ἐσομένην τελευτήν,
ἔσπευδεν ἐπιφανέστατον ἑαυτῷ περιποιήσασθαι
θάνατον. διόπερ πρῶτος ἐπὶ τὴν Λυσίου[5] τοῦ
στρατηγοῦ ναῦν ἐπιπλεύσας καὶ σὺν ταῖς ἅμα
πλεούσαις τριήρεσιν ἐξ ἐφόδου τρώσας, κατέδυσε·
τῶν δ᾽ ἄλλων τὰς μὲν τοῖς ἐμβόλοις τύπτων ἄπλους
ἐποίει, τῶν δὲ τοὺς ταρσοὺς παρασύρων[6] ἀχρή-
4 στους ἀπετέλει πρὸς τὴν μάχην. τὸ δὲ τελευταῖον
δοὺς ἐμβολὴν[7] τῇ τοῦ Περικλέους τριήρει βιαιότερον, τῆς μὲν τριήρους ἐπὶ πολὺν ἀνέρρηξε τόπον,
τοῦ δὲ στόματος ἐναρμοσθέντος εἰς τὴν λακίδα[8]

---

[1] τοῖς after γεγενημένη deleted by Dindorf.
[2] So Hertlein : ἐπεφέροντο.

each wing. Consequently he aroused great amazement in the spectators on many sides, since there were four fleets engaged and the ships that had been gathered into one place did not lack many of being three hundred. For this is the greatest sea-battle on record of Greeks against Greeks.

99. At the very moment when the admirals gave orders to sound the trumpets the whole host on each side, raising the war-cry in turn, made a tremendous shout ; and all, as they enthusiastically struck the waves, vied with one another, every man being anxious to be the first to begin the battle. For the majority were experienced in fighting, because the war had endured so long, and they displayed insuperable enthusiasm, since it was the choicest troops who had been gathered for the decisive contest ; for all took it for granted that the conquerors in this battle would put an end to the war. But Callicratidas especially, since he had heard from the seer of the end awaiting him, was eager to compass for himself a death that would be most renowned. Consequently he was the first to drive at the ship of Lysias the general, and shattering it at the first blow together with the triremes accompanying it, he sank it ; and as for the other ships, some he rammed and made unseaworthy and from others he tore away the rows of oars and rendered them useless for the fighting. Last of all he rammed the trireme of Pericles with a rather heavy blow and broke a great hole in the trireme ; then, since the beak of his ship stuck tight in the gap and they

---

[3] τὸ added by Stephanus.
[4] εἰς added by M, Stephanus.
[5] So Palmer (infra, ch. 101. 5): Ναυσίου.
[6] παρασύρων added by Wurm and Cobet.
[7] So Dindorf: ἔμβολον. [8] So Dobraeus: ἀκίδα.

καὶ μὴ δυναμένων αὐτῶν ἀνακρούσασθαι, Περικλῆς
μὲν ἐπέβαλε τῇ τοῦ Καλλικρατίδα νηὶ σιδηρᾶν
χεῖρα, προσαφθείσης[1] δ' αὐτῆς οἱ μὲν Ἀθηναῖοι
περιστάντες τὴν ναῦν εἰσήλλοντο, καὶ περιχυθέντες
5 τοὺς ἐν αὐτῇ πάντας ἀπέσφαξαν. τότε δή φασι τὸν
Καλλικρατίδαν λαμπρῶς ἀγωνισάμενον καὶ πολὺν
ἀντισχόντα χρόνον, τὸ τελευταῖον ὑπὸ τοῦ πλήθους
πανταχόθεν τιτρωσκόμενον καταπονηθῆναι.[2] ὡς δὲ
τὸ περὶ τὸν ναύαρχον ἐλάττωμα συμφανὲς ἐγένετο,
συνέβη τοὺς Πελοποννησίους δείσαντας ἐγκλῖναι.
6 τοῦ δὲ δεξιοῦ μέρους τῶν Πελοποννησίων φυγόντος,[3]
οἱ τὸ λαιὸν ἔχοντες Βοιωτοὶ χρόνον μέν τινα
διεκαρτέρουν εὐρώστως ἀγωνιζόμενοι· εὐλαβοῦντο
γὰρ αὐτοί τε καὶ[4] οἱ συγκινδυνεύοντες Εὐβοεῖς
καὶ πάντες οἱ τῶν Ἀθηναίων ἀφεστηκότες, μήποτε
Ἀθηναῖοι τὴν ἀρχὴν ἀνακτησάμενοι τιμωρίαν παρ'
αὐτῶν λάβωσιν ὑπὲρ τῆς ἀποστάσεως· ἐπειδὴ δὲ
τὰς πλείστας ναῦς ἑώρων τετρωμένας καὶ τὸ
πλῆθος τῶν νικώντων ἐπ' αὐτοὺς ἐπιστραφέν,
ἠναγκάσθησαν φυγεῖν. τῶν μὲν οὖν Πελοποννησίων οἱ μὲν εἰς Χίον, οἱ δ' εἰς Κύμην διεσώθησαν.
100. Οἱ δ' Ἀθηναῖοι διώξαντες ἐφ' ἱκανὸν τοὺς
ἡττημένους πάντα τὸν σύνεγγυς τόπον τῆς θαλάττης
ἐπλήρωσαν νεκρῶν καὶ ναυαγίων. μετὰ δὲ ταῦτα
τῶν στρατηγῶν οἱ μὲν ᾤοντο δεῖν τοὺς τετελευτηκότας ἀναιρεῖσθαι διὰ τὸ χαλεπῶς διατίθεσθαι τοὺς
Ἀθηναίους ἐπὶ τοῖς ἀτάφους περιορῶσι τοὺς τε-

---

[1] So Reiske : προσαχθείσης.
[2] Warmington suggests καταποντωθῆναι.
[3] φυγόντος Eichstädt : φυγόντων.
[4] αὐτοί τε καὶ Wurm : αὐτούς.

could not withdraw it, Pericles threw an iron hand[1] 406 B.C. on the ship of Callicratidas, and when it was fastened tight, the Athenians, surrounding the ship, sprang upon it, and pouring over its crew put them all to the sword. It was at this time, we are told, that Callicratidas, after fighting brilliantly and holding out for a long time, finally was worn down by numbers, as he was struck from all directions.[2] As soon as the defeat of the admiral became evident, the result was that the Peloponnesians gave way in fear. But although the right wing of the Peloponnesians was in flight, the Boeotians, who held the left, continued to put up a stout fight for some time ; for both they and the Euboeans who were fighting by their side as well as all the other Greeks who had revolted from the Athenians feared lest the Athenians, if they should once regain their sovereignty, would exact punishment of them for their revolt. But when they saw that most of their ships had been damaged and that the main body of the victors was turning against them, they were compelled to take flight. Now of the Peloponnesians some found safety in Chios and some in Cymê.

100. The Athenians, while they pursued the defeated foe for a considerable distance, filled the whole area of the sea in the neighbourhood of the battle with corpses and the wreckage of ships. After this some of the generals thought that they should pick up the dead, since the Athenians are incensed at those who

[1] A grappling-iron, first introduced in the fighting in the harbour of Syracuse (cp. Thucydides, 7. 62). Called the " crow " by the Romans, it was used by them with great effectiveness against the Carthaginians in 260 B.C.

[2] Xenophon (*Hell.* 1. 6. 33) says that he " fell overboard into the sea and disappeared."

τελευτηκότας, οἱ δ᾽ ἔφασαν δεῖν ἐπὶ τὴν Μιτυλήνην πλεῖν καὶ τὴν ταχίστην λῦσαι τὴν πολιορκίαν.
2 ἐπεγενήθη δὲ καὶ χειμὼν μέγας, ὥστε σαλεύεσθαι
τὰς τριήρεις καὶ τοὺς στρατιώτας διά τε τὴν ἐκ
τῆς μάχης κακοπάθειαν καὶ διὰ τὸ μέγεθος τῶν
κυμάτων ἀντιλέγειν πρὸς τὴν ἀναίρεσιν τῶν νε-
3 κρῶν. τέλος δὲ τοῦ χειμῶνος ἐπιτείνοντος οὔτε
ἐπὶ τὴν Μιτυλήνην ἔπλευσαν οὔτε τοὺς τετελευτηκότας ἀνείλαντο, βιασθέντες δὲ ὑπὸ τῶν πνευμάτων εἰς Ἀργινούσας κατέπλευσαν. ἀπώλοντο
δὲ ἐν τῇ ναυμαχίᾳ τῶν μὲν Ἀθηναίων ναῦς εἴκοσι
πέντε καὶ τῶν ἐν αὐταῖς οἱ πλεῖστοι, τῶν δὲ Πελο-
4 ποννησίων ἑπτὰ πρὸς ταῖς ἑβδομήκοντα· διόπερ
τοσούτων νεῶν καὶ τῶν ἐν αὐταῖς γεγενημένων
ἀνδρῶν ἀπολωλότων ἐπλήσθη τῆς Κυμαίων καὶ
Φωκαέων ἡ παραθαλάττιος χώρα νεκρῶν καὶ ναυαγίων.
5 Ὁ δὲ τὴν Μιτυλήνην πολιορκῶν Ἐτεόνικος
πυθόμενός τινος τὴν τῶν Πελοποννησίων ἧτταν,
τὰς μὲν ναῦς εἰς Χίον ἔπεμψε, τὴν δὲ πεζὴν
δύναμιν αὐτὸς ἔχων εἰς τὴν Πυρραίων[1] πόλιν
ἀπεχώρησεν, οὖσαν σύμμαχον· ἐδεδοίκει γάρ, μήποτε τῷ στόλῳ πλευσάντων τῶν Ἀθηναίων ἐπ᾽
αὐτοὺς καὶ τῶν ἐκ τῆς πόλεως ἐπεξελθόντων κιν-
6 δυνεύσῃ τὴν δύναμιν ἀποβαλεῖν ἅπασαν. οἱ δὲ
τῶν Ἀθηναίων στρατηγοὶ πλεύσαντες εἰς Μιτυλήνην καὶ τὸν Κόνωνα μετὰ τῶν τεσσαράκοντα νεῶν
παραλαβόντες εἰς Σάμον κατέπλευσαν, κἀκεῖθεν
ὁρμώμενοι τὴν τῶν πολεμίων χώραν ἐπόρθουν.
7 μετὰ δὲ ταῦτα οἱ περὶ τὴν Αἰολίδα καὶ τὴν Ἰωνίαν
καὶ τὰς νήσους τὰς συμμαχούσας Λακεδαιμονίοις

[1] So Palmer: Τυρραίων.

allow the dead to go unburied,[1] but others of them said they should sail to Mitylenê and raise the siege with all speed. But in the meantime a great storm arose, so that the ships were tossed about and the soldiers, by reason both of the hardships they had suffered in the battle and the heavy waves, opposed picking up the dead. And finally, since the storm increased in violence, they neither sailed to Mitylenê nor picked up the dead but were forced by the winds to put in at the Arginusae. The losses in the battle were twenty-five ships of the Athenians together with most of their crews and seventy-seven of the Peloponnesians ; and as a result of the loss of so many ships and of the sailors who manned them the coastline of the territory of the Cymaeans and Phocaeans was strewn with corpses and wreckage.

When Eteonicus, who was besieging Mitylenê, learned from someone of the defeat of the Peloponnesians, he sent his ships to Chios and himself retreated with his land forces to the city of the Pyrrhaeans,[2] which was an ally ; for he feared lest, if the Athenians should sail against his troops with their fleet and the besieged make a sortie from the city, he should run the risk of losing his entire force. And the generals of the Athenians, after sailing to Mitylenê and picking up Conon and his forty ships, put in at Samos, and from there as their base they set about laying waste the territory of the enemy. After this the inhabitants of Aeolis and Ionia and of the islands which were allies

---

[1] Aelian (*Var. Hist.* 5. 14) states that the Athenians had a law requiring anyone who happened upon an unburied human body to cast earth upon it.

[2] Some fifteen miles west of Mitylenê.

συνῆλθον εἰς Ἔφεσον, καὶ βουλευομένοις αὐτοῖς
ἔδοξεν ἀποστέλλειν εἰς Σπάρτην καὶ Λύσανδρον
αἰτεῖσθαι ναύαρχον· οὗτος γὰρ ἔν τε τῷ τῆς ναυαρχίας χρόνῳ κατωρθωκὼς ἦν πολλὰ καὶ ἐδόκει
8 διαφέρειν στρατηγίᾳ τῶν ἄλλων. οἱ δὲ Λακεδαιμόνιοι νόμον ἔχοντες δὶς τὸν αὐτὸν μὴ πέμπειν καὶ
τὸ πάτριον ἔθος μὴ θέλοντες καταλύειν, Ἄρακον[1]
μὲν εἵλοντο ναύαρχον, τὸν δὲ Λύσανδρον ἰδιώτην
αὐτῷ συνεξέπεμψαν, προστάξαντες ἀκούειν ἅπαντα
τούτου. οὗτοι μὲν ἐκπεμφθέντες ἐπὶ τὴν ἡγεμονίαν
ἔκ τε τῆς Πελοποννήσου καὶ παρὰ τῶν συμμάχων
τριήρεις ἤθροιζον ὅσας ἠδύναντο πλείστας.

101. Ἀθηναῖοι δὲ πυθόμενοι τὴν ἐν ταῖς Ἀργινούσαις εὐημερίαν ἐπὶ μὲν τῇ νίκῃ τοὺς στρατηγοὺς
ἐπῄνουν, ἐπὶ δὲ τῷ περιιδεῖν ἀτάφους τοὺς ὑπὲρ
τῆς ἡγεμονίας τετελευτηκότας χαλεπῶς διετέθησαν.
2 Θηραμένους δὲ καὶ Θρασυβούλου προαπεληλυθότων
εἰς Ἀθήνας, ὑπολαβόντες οἱ στρατηγοὶ τούτους
εἶναι τοὺς διαβαλόντας πρὸς τὰ πλήθη περὶ[2] τῶν
τελευτησάντων, ἀπέστειλαν κατ' αὐτῶν ἐπιστολὰς
πρὸς τὸν δῆμον, διασαφοῦντες ὅτι τούτοις ἐπέταξαν
ἀνελέσθαι τοὺς τελευτήσαντας· ὅπερ μάλιστ' αὐτοῖς
3 αἴτιον ἐγενήθη τῶν κακῶν. δυνάμενοι γὰρ ἔχειν
συναγωνιστὰς εἰς τὴν κρίσιν τοὺς περὶ Θηραμένην,
ἄνδρας καὶ λόγῳ δυνατοὺς καὶ φίλους πολλοὺς
ἔχοντας, καὶ τὸ μέγιστον, συμπαραγεγονότας τοῖς

---

[1] So Wesseling : Ἄρατον.
[2] περὶ added by Wurm. Wesseling would read πρὸς τοὺς
συγγενεῖς τῶν τελευτησάντων or delete τῶν τελευτησάντων;
Palmer would read πλήθη ὡς ἀμελήσαντας.

of the Lacedaemonians gathered in Ephesus, and as 406 B.C. they counselled together they resolved to send to Sparta and to ask for Lysander as admiral ; for during the time Lysander had been in command of the fleet he had enjoyed many successes and was believed to excel all others in skill as a general. The Lacedaemonians, however, having a law not to send the same man twice and being unwilling to break the custom of their fathers, chose Aracus as admiral but sent Lysander with him as an ordinary citizen,[1] commanding Aracus to follow the advice of Lysander in every matter. These leaders, having been dispatched to assume the command, set about assembling the greatest possible number of triremes from both the Peloponnesus and their allies.

101. When the Athenians learned of their success at the Arginusae, they commended the generals for the victory but were incensed that they had allowed the men who had died to maintain their supremacy to go unburied. Since Theramenes and Thrasybulus had gone off to Athens in advance of the others, the generals, having assumed that it was they who had made accusations before the populace with respect to the dead, dispatched letters against them to the people stating that it was they whom the generals had ordered to pick up the dead. But this very thing turned out to be the principal cause of their undoing. For although they could have had the help of Theramenes and his associates in the trial, men who both were able orators and had many friends and, most important of all, had been participants in the events

[1] Xenophon's statement (*Hell*. 2. 1. 7) is more precise and credible. He says that the law forbade a man " to hold the office of admiral twice " and that Lysander was sent as " vice-admiral."

εἰς[1] τὴν ναυμαχίαν πράγμασιν, ἐκ τῶν ἐναντίων
4 ἔσχον ἀντιδίκους καὶ πικροὺς κατηγόρους. ἀνα-
γνωσθεισῶν γὰρ ἐν τῷ δήμῳ τῶν ἐπιστολῶν εὐθὺς
μὲν τοῖς περὶ Θηραμένην ὠργίζετο τὰ πλήθη,
τούτων δὲ ἀπολογησαμένων συνέβη τὴν ὀργὴν
5 πάλιν μεταπεσεῖν εἰς τοὺς στρατηγούς. διόπερ ὁ
δῆμος προέθηκεν αὐτοῖς κρίσιν, καὶ Κόνωνα μὲν
ἀπολύσας τῆς αἰτίας προσέταξε τούτῳ τὰς δυνάμεις παραδίδοσθαι, τοὺς δ' ἄλλους ἐψηφίσατο τὴν
ταχίστην ἥκειν. ὧν Ἀριστογένης μὲν καὶ Πρωτό-
μαχος φοβηθέντες τὴν ὀργὴν τοῦ πλήθους ἔφυγον,
Θράσυλλος δὲ καὶ Καλλιάδης, ἔτι δὲ Λυσίας καὶ
Περικλῆς καὶ Ἀριστοκράτης μετὰ τῶν πλείστων
νεῶν κατέπλευσαν εἰς τὰς Ἀθήνας, ἐλπίζοντες
τοὺς ἐν ταῖς ναυσὶ πολλοὺς ὄντας βοηθοὺς ἕξειν
6 ἐν τῇ κρίσει. ὡς δ' εἰς τὴν ἐκκλησίαν τὰ πλήθη
συνῆλθον, τῆς μὲν κατηγορίας καὶ τῶν πρὸς χάριν
δημηγορούντων ἤκουον, τοὺς δ' ἀπολογουμένους
συνθορυβοῦντες οὐκ ἠνείχοντο τῶν λόγων. οὐκ ἐλά-
χιστα δ' αὐτοὺς ἔβλαψαν οἱ συγγενεῖς τῶν τετελευτηκότων, παρελθόντες μὲν εἰς τὴν ἐκκλησίαν
ἐν πενθίμοις, δεόμενοι δὲ τοῦ δήμου τιμωρήσασθαι
τοὺς περιεωρακότας ἀτάφους τοὺς ὑπὲρ τῆς πατρί-
7 δος προθύμως τετελευτηκότας. τέλος δ' οἵ τε
τούτων φίλοι καὶ οἱ τοῖς περὶ Θηραμένην συναγωνιζόμενοι πολλοὶ καθεστῶτες ἐνίσχυσαν, καὶ
συνέβη καταδικασθῆναι τοὺς στρατηγοὺς θανάτῳ
καὶ δημεύσει τῶν οὐσιῶν.

102. Τούτων δὲ κυρωθέντων καὶ μελλόντων αὐτῶν ὑπὸ τῶν δημοσίων ἐπὶ τὸν θάνατον ἄγεσθαι,
Διομέδων εἷς τῶν στρατηγῶν παρῆλθεν εἰς τὸ

[1] εἰς] κατὰ Capps.

relative to the battle, they had them, on the contrary, as adversaries and bitter accusers. For when the letters were read before the people, the multitude was at once angered at Theramenes and his associates, but after these had presented their defence, it turned out that their anger was directed again on the generals. Consequently the people served notice on them of their trial and ordered them to turn over the command of the armaments to Conon, whom they freed of the responsibility, while they decreed that the others should report to Athens with all speed. Of the generals Aristogenes and Protomachus, fearing the wrath of the populace, sought safety in flight, but Thrasyllus and Calliades and, besides, Lysias and Pericles and Aristocrates sailed home to Athens with most of their ships, hoping that they would have their crews, which were numerous, to aid them in the trial. When the populace gathered in the assembly, they gave attention to the accusation and to those who spoke to gratify them, but any who entered a defence they unitedly greeted with clamour and would not allow to speak. And not the least damaging to the generals were the relatives of the dead, who appeared in the assembly in mourning garments and begged the people to punish those who had allowed men who had gladly died on behalf of their country to go unburied. And in the end the friends of these relatives and the partisans of Theramenes, being many, prevailed and the outcome was that the generals were condemned to death and their property confiscated.

102. After this action had been taken and while the generals were about to be led off by the public executioners to death, Diomedon, one of the generals,

μέσον, ἀνὴρ καὶ τὰ περὶ τὸν πόλεμον ἔμπρακτος
καὶ δικαιοσύνη τε καὶ ταῖς ἄλλαις ἀρεταῖς δοκῶν
2 διαφέρειν. σιωπησάντων δὲ πάντων εἶπεν· Ἄνδρες Ἀθηναῖοι, τὰ μὲν περὶ ἡμῶν κυρωθέντα συν-
ενέγκαι τῇ πόλει· τὰς δὲ ὑπὲρ τῆς νίκης εὐχὰς
ἐπειδήπερ ἡ τύχη κεκώλυκεν ἡμᾶς ἀποδοῦναι, καλῶς ἔχον ὑμᾶς φροντίσαι,[1] καὶ τῷ Διὶ τῷ σωτῆρι
καὶ Ἀπόλλωνι καὶ ταῖς σεμναῖς θεαῖς ἀπόδοτε·
τούτοις γὰρ εὐξάμενοι τοὺς πολεμίους κατεναυ-
3 μαχήσαμεν. ὁ μὲν οὖν Διομέδων ταῦτα διαλεχθεὶς
ἐπὶ τὸν κυρωθέντα θάνατον ἀπήγετο μετὰ τῶν
ἄλλων στρατηγῶν, τοῖς ἀγαθοῖς τῶν πολιτῶν πολὺν
οἶκτον παραστήσας καὶ δάκρυα· τὸν γὰρ ἀδίκως
τελευτᾶν μέλλοντα τοῦ μὲν καθ' αὑτὸν πάθους μηδ'
ἡντινοῦν ποιεῖσθαι μνείαν, ὑπὲρ δὲ τῆς ἀδικούσης
πόλεως ἀξιοῦν τὰς εὐχὰς ἀποδιδόναι τοῖς θεοῖς,
ἐφαίνετ' ἀνδρὸς εὐσεβοῦς ἔργον καὶ μεγαλοψύχου
4 καὶ τῆς περὶ αὐτὸν τύχης ἀναξίου. τούτους μὲν
οὖν οἱ ταχθέντες ὑπὸ τῶν νόμων ἔνδεκα ἄρχοντες
ἀπέκτειναν, οὐχ οἷον ἠδικηκότας τι τὴν πόλιν,
ἀλλὰ ναυμαχίαν μεγίστην τῶν Ἕλλησι πρὸς Ἕλληνας γεγενημένων νενικηκότας καὶ ἐν ἄλλαις
μάχαις λαμπρῶς ἠγωνισμένους καὶ διὰ τὰς ἰδίας
ἀρετὰς τρόπαια κατὰ τῶν πολεμίων ἑστακότας.
5 οὕτως δ' ὁ δῆμος τότε παρεφρόνησε, καὶ παροξυνθεὶς ἀδίκως ὑπὸ τῶν δημαγωγῶν τὴν ὀργὴν

---

[1] So Hemsterhuis and Cobet: φρονῆσαι.

---

[1] The Erinyes (Furies).
[2] A Board which had charge of condemned prisoners and

412

406 B.C.

took the floor before the people, a man who was both vigorous in the conduct of war and thought by all to excel both in justice and in the other virtues. And when all became still, he said : " Men of Athens, may the action which has been taken regarding us turn out well for the state ; but as for the vows which we made for the victory, inasmuch as Fortune has prevented our paying them, since it is well that you give thought to them, do you pay them to Zeus the Saviour and Apollo and the Holy Goddesses [1] ; for it was to these gods that we made vows before we overcame the enemy." Now after Diomedon had made this request he was led off to the appointed execution together with the other generals, though among the better citizens he had aroused great compassion and tears ; for that the man who was about to meet an unjust death should make no mention whatsoever of his own fate but on behalf of the state which was wronging him should request it to pay his vows to the gods appeared to be an act of a man who was god-fearing and magnanimous and undeserving of the fate that was to befall him. These men, then, were put to death by the eleven [2] magistrates who are designated by the laws, although far from having committed any crime against the state, they had won the greatest naval battle that had ever taken place of Greeks against Greeks and fought in splendid fashion in other battles and by reason of their individual deeds of valour had set up trophies of victories over their enemies. To such an extent were the people beside themselves at that time, and provoked unjustly as they were by their political leaders, they vented their rage upon

of the execution of the death sentence. They are more commonly referred to simply as " The Eleven."

ἀπέσκηψεν εἰς ἄνδρας οὐ τιμωρίας, ἀλλὰ πολλῶν
ἐπαίνων καὶ στεφάνων ἀξίους.

103. Ταχὺ δὲ καὶ τοῖς πείσασι καὶ τοῖς πεισθεῖσι
μετεμέλησεν, οἱονεὶ νεμεσήσαντος τοῦ δαιμονίου·
οἱ μὲν γὰρ ἐξαπατηθέντες ἐπίχειρα τῆς ἀγνοίας
ἔλαβον μετ' οὐ πολὺν χρόνον καταπολεμηθέντες οὐχ
2 ὑφ' ἑνὸς δεσπότου μόνον ἀλλὰ τριάκοντα· ὁ δ'
ἐξαπατήσας καὶ τὴν γνώμην εἰπὼν Καλλίξενος
εὐθὺ τοῦ πλήθους μεταμεληθέντος εἰς αἰτίαν ἦλθεν
ὡς τὸν δῆμον ἐξηπατηκώς· οὐκ ἀξιωθεὶς δ' ἀπο-
λογίας ἐδέθη, καὶ καταβληθεὶς εἰς τὴν δημοσίαν
φυλακὴν ἔλαθε μετά τινων διορύξας τὸ δεσμωτήριον
καὶ διαδρὰς πρὸς τοὺς πολεμίους εἰς Δεκέλειαν
ὅπως διαφυγὼν τὸν θάνατον μὴ μόνον Ἀθήνησιν
ἀλλὰ καὶ παρὰ τοῖς ἄλλοις Ἕλλησι δακτυλοδεικ-
τουμένην ἔχῃ τὴν πονηρίαν παρ' ὅλον τὸν βίον.

3 Τὰ μὲν οὖν κατὰ τοῦτον τὸν ἐνιαυτὸν πραχθέντα
σχεδὸν ταῦτ' ἐστίν. τῶν δὲ συγγραφέων Φίλιστος
τὴν πρώτην σύνταξιν τῶν Σικελικῶν εἰς τοῦτον τὸν
ἐνιαυτὸν κατέστροφεν[1] εἰς τὴν Ἀκράγαντος ἅλωσιν,
ἐν βύβλοις ἑπτὰ διελθὼν χρόνον ἐτῶν πλείω τῶν
ὀκτακοσίων, τῆς δὲ δευτέρας συντάξεως τὴν μὲν
ἀρχὴν ἀπὸ τῆς[2] τῆς προτέρας τελευτῆς πεποίηται,
γέγραφε δὲ βύβλους τέσσαρας.

4 Περὶ δὲ τὸν αὐτὸν χρόνον ἐτελεύτησε Σοφοκλῆς
ὁ Σοφίλου,[3] ποιητὴς τραγῳδιῶν, ἔτη βιώσας ἐνενήκοντα, νίκας δ' ἔχων ὀκτωκαίδεκα. φασὶ δὲ τὸν

---

[1] So Dindorf: κατέστρεφεν.
[2] τῆς added by Eichstädt.
[3] ὁ Σοφίλου Meursius : Θεοφίλου.

---

[1] The " Thirty Tyrants " (cp. Book 14. 3 ff.).

men who were deserving, not of punishment, but of ^{406 B.C.} many praises and crowns.

103. Soon, however, both those who had urged this action and those whom they had persuaded repented, as if the deity had become wroth with them ; for those who had been deceived got the wages of their error when not long afterwards they fell before the power of not one despot only but of thirty [1] ; and the deceiver, who had also proposed the measure, Callixenus, when once the populace had repented, was brought to trial on the charge of having deceived the people, and without being allowed to speak in his defence he was put in chains and thrown into the public prison ; and secretly burrowing his way out of the prison with certain others he managed to make his way to the enemy at Deceleia, to the end that by escaping death he might have the finger of scorn pointed at his turpitude not only in Athens but also wherever else there were Greeks throughout his entire life.

Now these, we may say, were the events of this year. And of the historians Philistus [2] ended his first History of Sicily with this year and the capture of Acragas, treating a period of more than eight hundred years in seven Books, and he began his second History where the first leaves off and wrote four Books.[3]

At this same time Sophocles the son of Sophilus, the writer of tragedies, died at the age of ninety years, after he had won the prize eighteen [4] times. And we

---

[2] Of Syracuse (cp. *supra*, chap. 91. 4).

[3] Philistus also wrote two more Books on the younger Dionysius (cp. Book 15. 89. 3), a total of thirteen Books on Sicily.

[4] The eighteen firsts are confirmed by the " Victory " inscription (*I.G.* ii. 977a).

ἄνδρα τοῦτον τὴν ἐσχάτην τραγῳδίαν εἰσαγαγόντα
καὶ νικήσαντα χαρᾷ περιπεσεῖν ἀνυπερβλήτῳ, δι'
5 ἣν καὶ τελευτῆσαι. Ἀπολλόδωρος δ' ὁ τὴν χρο-
νικὴν σύνταξιν πραγματευσάμενός φησι καὶ τὸν
Εὐριπίδην κατὰ τὸν αὐτὸν ἐνιαυτὸν τελευτῆσαι·
τινὲς δὲ λέγουσι παρ' Ἀρχελάῳ τῷ βασιλεῖ
Μακεδόνων κατὰ τὴν χώραν ἐξελθόντα κυσὶ περιπεσεῖν καὶ διασπασθῆναι μικρῷ πρόσθεν τούτων
τῶν χρόνων.

104. Τοῦ δ' ἔτους τούτου διελθόντος Ἀθήνησι
μὲν ἦρχεν Ἀλεξίας, ἐν δὲ τῇ Ῥώμῃ ἀντὶ τῶν ὑπάτων τρεῖς χιλίαρχοι κατεστάθησαν, Γάιος Ἰούλιος,
Πούπλιος Κορνήλιος, Γάιος Σερουίλιος. τούτων
δὲ τὴν ἀρχὴν παραλαβόντων Ἀθηναῖοι μετὰ τὴν ἀναίρεσιν τῶν στρατηγῶν ἐπὶ τὴν ἡγεμονίαν ἔταξαν
Φιλοκλέα, καὶ τὸ ναυτικὸν αὐτῷ παραδόντες ἐξέπεμψαν πρὸς Κόνωνα, προστάξαντες κοινῶς ἀφ-
2 ηγεῖσθαι τῶν δυνάμεων. ὃς ἐπεὶ κατέπλευσε πρὸς
Κόνωνα εἰς Σάμον, τὰς ναῦς ἁπάσας ἐπλήρωσεν
οὔσας τρεῖς πρὸς ταῖς ἑκατὸν ἑβδομήκοντα. τούτων εἴκοσι μὲν ἔδοξεν αὐτοῦ καταλιπεῖν, ταῖς δ'
ἄλλαις ἁπάσαις ἀνήχθησαν εἰς Ἑλλήσποντον, ἡγουμένου Κόνωνος καὶ Φιλοκλέους.

3 Λύσανδρος δ' ὁ τῶν Λακεδαιμονίων ναύαρχος
ἐκ Πελοποννήσου παρὰ τῶν ἐγγὺς συμμάχων
τριάκοντα πέντε ναῦς ἀθροίσας κατέπλευσεν εἰς
Ἔφεσον· μεταπεμψάμενος[1] δὲ καὶ τὸν ἐκ Χίου
στόλον ἐξήρτυεν· ἀνέβη δὲ καὶ πρὸς Κῦρον τὸν
Δαρείου τοῦ βασιλέως υἱόν, καὶ χρήματα πολλὰ

are told of this man that when he presented his last 406 B.C.
tragedy and won the prize, he was filled with insuperable jubilation which was also the cause of his death.
And Apollodorus,[1] who composed his *Chronology*,
states that Euripides also died in the same year;
although others say that he was living at the court of
Archelaüs, the king of Macedonia, and that once when
he went out in the countryside, he was set upon by
dogs and torn to pieces a little before this time.

104. At the end of this year Alexias was archon in 405 B.C.
Athens and in Rome in the place of consuls three
military tribunes were elected, Gaius Julius, Publius
Cornelius, and Gaius Servilius. When these had
entered office, the Athenians, after the execution of
the generals, put Philocles in command, and turning
over the fleet to him, they sent him to Conon with
orders that they should share the leadership of the
armaments in common. After he had joined Conon in
Samos, he manned all the ships which numbered one
hundred and seventy-three. Of these it was decided
to leave twenty at Samos, and with all the rest they
set out for the Hellespont under the command of
Conon and Philocles.

Lysander, the admiral of the Lacedaemonians,
having collected thirty-five ships from his neighbouring allies of the Peloponnesus, put in at Ephesus; and
after summoning also the fleet from Chios he made it
ready. He also went inland to Cyrus, the son of King
Darius, and received from him a great sum of money

---

[1] A philosopher and historian of Athens of the second
century B.C. (cp. Book 1. 5. 1). His *Chronology* covered
the years 1184–119 B.C.

---

[1] μεταπεμψάμενος K and all editors before Vogel; μετεπέμψατο other MSS., and Vogel with lacuna after στόλον.

παρέλαβε πρὸς τὰς τῶν στρατιωτῶν διατροφάς.
4 ὁ δὲ Κῦρος, μεταπεμπομένου τοῦ πατρὸς αὐτὸν
εἰς Πέρσας, τῷ Λυσάνδρῳ τῶν ὑφ' αὐτὸν πόλεων τὴν ἐπιστασίαν[1] παρέδωκε καὶ τοὺς φόρους
τούτῳ τελεῖν συνέταξεν. ὁ δὲ Λύσανδρος πάντων τῶν εἰς πόλεμον εὐπορήσας εἰς Ἔφεσον ἀν-
έστρεψεν.
5 Καθ' ὃν δὴ χρόνον ἐν τῇ Μιλήτῳ τινὲς ὀλιγαρχίας ὀρεγόμενοι κατέλυσαν τὸν δῆμον, συμπραξάν-
των αὐτοῖς Λακεδαιμονίων. καὶ τὸ μὲν πρῶτον
Διονυσίων ὄντων ἐν ταῖς οἰκίαις τοὺς μάλιστα
ἀντιπράττοντας συνήρπασαν καὶ περὶ τεσσαράκοντα
ὄντας ἀπέσφαξαν, μετὰ δέ, τῆς ἀγορᾶς πληθούσης,
τριακοσίους ἐπιλέξαντες τοὺς εὐπορωτάτους ἀν-
6 εῖλον. οἱ δὲ χαριέστατοι τῶν τὰ τοῦ δήμου φρο-
νούντων, ὄντες οὐκ ἐλάττους χιλίων, φοβηθέντες
τὴν περίστασιν ἔφυγον πρὸς Φαρνάβαζον τὸν
σατράπην· οὗτος δὲ φιλοφρόνως αὐτοὺς δεξάμενος,
καὶ στατῆρα χρυσοῦν ἑκάστῳ δωρησάμενος, κατ-
ῴκισεν εἰς Βλαῦδα,[2] φρούριόν τι τῆς Λυδίας.
7 Λύσανδρος δὲ μετὰ τῶν πλείστων νεῶν ἐπὶ
Ἴασον[3] τῆς Καρίας πλεύσας κατὰ κράτος αὐτὴν
εἷλεν Ἀθηναίοις συμμαχοῦσαν, καὶ τοὺς μὲν ἡβῶν-
τας ὀκτακοσίους ὄντας ἀπέσφαξε, παῖδας δὲ καὶ
γυναῖκας λαφυροπωλήσας κατέσκαψε τὴν πόλιν.
8 μετὰ δὲ ταῦτ' ἐπὶ τὴν Ἀττικὴν καὶ πολλοὺς τόπους
πλεύσας μέγα μὲν οὐδὲν οὐδ' ἄξιον μνήμης ἔπραξε·
διὸ καὶ ταῦτα μὲν οὐκ ἀναγράφειν ἐσπουδάσαμεν·
τὸ δὲ τελευταῖον Λάμψακον ἑλὼν τὴν μὲν Ἀθη-

---

[1] So Dindorf: ἐπίστασιν.
[2] So Wesseling: κλαῦδα.
[3] Ἴασον Palmer: Θάσσων P, Θάσον cet.

with which to maintain his soldiers. And Cyrus, since 405 B.C. his father was summoning him to Persia, turned over to Lysander the authority over the cities under his command and ordered them to pay the tribute to him. Lysander, then, after being thus supplied with every means for making war, returned to Ephesus.

At the same time certain men in Miletus, who were striving for an oligarchy, with the aid of the Lacedaemonians put an end to the government of the people. First of all, while the Dionysia was being celebrated, they seized in their homes and carried off their principal opponents and put some forty of them to the sword, and then, at the time when the market-place was full, they picked out three hundred of the wealthiest citizens and slew them. The most respectable citizens among those who favoured the people, not less than one thousand, fearing the situation they were in, fled to Pharnabazus the satrap, who received them kindly and giving each of them a gold stater [1] settled them in Blauda, a fortress of Lydia.

Lysander, sailing with the larger part of his ships to Iasus in Caria, took the city, which was an ally of the Athenians, by storm, put to the sword the males of military age to the number of eight hundred, sold the children and women as booty, and razed the city to the ground. After this he sailed against Attica and many places, but accomplished nothing of importance or worthy of record; consequently we have not taken pains to recount these events. Finally, capturing Lampsacus,[2] he let the Athenian garrison depart

[1] Probably the Persian daric, whose bullion worth was about \$5.40 or £1 : 3s.

[2] In the Troad about thirty-five miles up the Hellespont.

ναίων φρουρὰν ἀφῆκεν ὑπόσπονδον, τὰς δὲ κτήσεις
ἁρπάσας τοῖς Λαμψακηνοῖς ἀπέδωκε τὴν πόλιν.

105. Οἱ δὲ τῶν Ἀθηναίων στρατηγοὶ πυθόμενοι
τοὺς Λακεδαιμονίους πάσῃ τῇ δυνάμει πολιορκεῖν
Λάμψακον, συνήγαγόν τε πανταχόθεν τριήρεις καὶ
κατὰ σπουδὴν ἀνήχθησαν ἐπ' αὐτοὺς ναυσὶν ἑκατὸν
2 ὀγδοήκοντα. εὑρόντες δὲ τὴν πόλιν ἡλωκυῖαν,
τότε μὲν ἐν Αἰγὸς ποταμοῖς καθώρμισαν τὰς ναῦς,
μετὰ δὲ ταῦτ' ἐπιπλέοντες τοῖς πολεμίοις καθ'
ἡμέραν εἰς ναυμαχίαν προεκαλοῦντο. οὐκ ἀντ-
αναγομένων δὲ τῶν Πελοποννησίων, οἱ μὲν Ἀθηναῖοι διηπόρουν ὅτι χρήσωνται τοῖς πράγμασιν, οὐ
δυνάμενοι τὸν πλείω χρόνον ἐκεῖ διατρέφειν[1] τὰς
3 δυνάμεις. Ἀλκιβιάδου δὲ πρὸς αὐτοὺς ἐλθόντος
καὶ λέγοντος, ὅτι Μήδοκος καὶ Σεύθης οἱ τῶν
Θρακῶν βασιλεῖς εἰσιν αὐτῷ φίλοι, καὶ δύναμιν
πολλὴν ὡμολόγησαν δώσειν, ἐὰν βούληται διαπολεμεῖν τοῖς Λακεδαιμονίοις· διόπερ αὐτοὺς ἠξίου
μεταδοῦναι τῆς ἡγεμονίας, ἐπαγγελλόμενος αὐτοῖς
δυεῖν θάτερον, ἢ ναυμαχεῖν τοὺς πολεμίους ἀναγ-
κάσειν ἢ πεζῇ μετὰ Θρακῶν πρὸς αὐτοὺς δι-
4 αγωνιεῖσθαι. ταῦτα δὲ ὁ Ἀλκιβιάδης ἔπραττεν
ἐπιθυμῶν δι' ἑαυτοῦ τῇ πατρίδι μέγα τι κατεργά-
σασθαι καὶ διὰ τῶν εὐεργεσιῶν τὸν δῆμον ἀπο-
καταστῆσαι εἰς τὴν ἀρχαίαν εὔνοιαν. οἱ δὲ τῶν
Ἀθηναίων στρατηγοί, νομίσαντες τῶν μὲν ἐλαττωμάτων ἑαυτοῖς τὴν μέμψιν ἀκολουθήσειν, τὰ
δ' ἐπιτεύγματα προσάψειν ἅπαντας[2] Ἀλκιβιάδῃ,

---

[1] So Wesseling : διατρίβειν.
[2] ἅπαντας Wesseling : ἅπαντα.

---

[1] The "Goat-rivers," about five miles across the strait
from Lampsacus.

under a truce, but seized the property of the in- 405 B.C. habitants and then returned the city to them.

105. The generals of the Athenians, on learning that the Lacedaemonians in full force were besieging Lampsacus, assembled their triremes from all quarters and put forth against them in haste with one hundred and eighty ships. But finding the city already taken, at the time they stationed their ships at Aegospotami [1] but afterward sailed out each day against the enemy and offered battle. When the Peloponnesians persisted in not coming out against them, the Athenians were at a loss what to do in the circumstances, since they were unable to find supplies for their armaments for any further length of time where they were. Alcibiades [2] now came to them and said that Medocus and Seuthes, the kings of the Thracians, were friends of his and had agreed to give him a large army if he wished to make war to a finish on the Lacedaemonians ; he therefore asked them to give him a share in the command, promising them one of two things, either to compel the enemy to accept battle or to contend with them on land with the aid of the Thracians.[3] This offer Alcibiades made from a desire to achieve by his own efforts some great success for his country and through his benefactions to bring the people back to their old affection for him. But the generals of the Athenians, considering that in case of defeat the blame would attach to them and that in case of success all men would attribute it to Alcibiades,

[2] He had retired to two castles in Thrace, one of which was at Pactyê, only some twenty miles from where the Athenians were anchored (cp. *supra*, chap. 74. 2).

[3] Xenophon (*Hell.* 2. 1. 25 f.) says nothing about this demand of Alcibiades, but only that he urged the generals to base upon Sestus.

ταχέως αὐτὸν ἐκέλευσαν ἀπιέναι καὶ μηκέτι προσεγγίζειν τῷ στρατοπέδῳ.

106. Ἐπεὶ δ᾽ οἱ μὲν πολέμιοι ναυμαχεῖν οὐκ ἤθελον, τὸ δὲ[1] στρατόπεδον σιτοδείᾳ κατεῖχε, Φιλοκλῆς ἐκείνην τὴν ἡμέραν ἀφηγούμενος τοῖς μὲν ἄλλοις τριηράρχοις προσέταξε πληρώσαντας τὰς τριήρεις ἀκολουθεῖν, αὐτὸς δ᾽ ἑτοίμας ἔχων
2 ναῦς τριάκοντα τάχιον ἐξέπλευσεν. ὁ δὲ Λύσανδρος παρά τινων αὐτομόλων ταῦτ᾽ ἀκούσας, μετὰ πασῶν τῶν νεῶν ἀναχθεὶς καὶ τὸν Φιλοκλέα τρεψάμενος
3 πρὸς τὰς ἄλλας ναῦς κατεδίωξεν. οὔπω δὲ τῶν τριήρων τοῖς Ἀθηναίοις πεπληρωμένων θόρυβος κατεῖχεν ἅπαντας διὰ τὴν ἀπροσδόκητον ἐπιφά-
4 νειαν τῶν πολεμίων. ὁ δὲ Λύσανδρος συνιδὼν τὴν τῶν ἐναντίων ταραχήν, Ἐτεόνικον μὲν μετὰ τῶν εἰωθότων πεζῇ μάχεσθαι ταχέως ἀπεβίβασεν· ὁ δὲ ὀξέως τῇ τοῦ καιροῦ ῥοπῇ χρησάμενος μέρος κατελάβετο τῆς παρεμβολῆς· αὐτὸς δ᾽ ὁ Λύσανδρος ἁπάσαις ταῖς τριήρεσιν ἐξηρτυμέναις ἐπιπλεύσας καὶ σιδηρᾶς ἐπιβαλὼν χεῖρας, ἀπέσπα τὰς ὁρμούσας
5 ἐπὶ τῇ γῇ[2] ναῦς. Ἀθηναῖοι δὲ τὸ παράδοξον ἐκπεπληγμένοι καὶ μήτ᾽ ἀναχθῆναι ταῖς ναυσὶν ἀναστροφὴν ἔχοντες μήτε πεζῇ διαγωνίζεσθαι δυνάμενοι, βραχὺν ἀντισχόντες χρόνον ἐτράπησαν, εὐθὺ δ᾽ οἱ μὲν τὰς ναῦς, οἱ δὲ τὴν παρεμβολὴν ἐκλιπόντες ἔφυγον, ὅπου ποθ᾽ ἕκαστος ἤλπιζε
6 σωθήσεσθαι. τῶν μὲν οὖν τριήρων δέκα μόνον διεξέπεσον, ὧν μίαν ἔχων Κόνων ὁ στρατηγὸς τὴν μὲν εἰς Ἀθήνας ἐπάνοδον ἀπέγνω φοβηθεὶς τὴν ὀργὴν τοῦ δήμου, πρὸς Εὐαγόραν δὲ τὸν ἀφηγούμενον τῆς Κύπρου κατέφυγεν, ἔχων πρὸς αὐτὸν

---

[1] δὲ Wurm : τε.   [2] τῇ γῇ Reiske : τὴν γῆν.

quickly bade him to be gone and not come near the camp ever again.

106. Since the enemy refused to accept battle at sea and famine gripped the army, Philocles, who held the command on that day, ordered the other captains to man their triremes and follow him, while he with thirty triremes which were ready set out in advance. Lysander, who had learned of this from some deserters, set out to sea with all his ships, and putting Philocles to flight, pursued him toward the other ships.[1] The triremes of the Athenians had not yet been manned and confusion pervaded them all because of the unexpected appearance of the enemy. And when Lysander perceived the tumult among the enemy, he speedily put ashore Eteonicus and the troops who were practised in fighting on land. Eteonicus, quickly turning to his account the opportunity of the moment, seized a part of the camp, while Lysander himself, sailing up with all his triremes in trim for battle, after throwing iron hands on the ships which were moored along the shore began dragging them off. The Athenians, panic-stricken at the unexpected move, since they neither had respite for putting out to sea with their ships nor were able to fight it out by land, held out for a short while and then gave way, and at once, some deserting the ships, others the camp, they took to flight in whatever direction each man hoped to find safety. Of the triremes only ten escaped. Conon the general, who had one of them, gave up any thought of returning to Athens, fearing the wrath of the people, but sought safety with Evagoras, who was in control of Cyprus

---

[1] This account of the battle differs radically from that in Xenophon (*Hell.* 2. 1. 27-28), which is more credible.

φιλίαν· τῶν δὲ στρατιωτῶν οἱ πλεῖστοι μὲν κατὰ
7 γῆν φυγόντες εἰς Σηστὸν διεσώθησαν. Λύσανδρος
δὲ τὰς λοιπὰς ναῦς παραλαβὼν αἰχμαλώτους, καὶ
ζωγρήσας Φιλοκλέα τὸν στρατηγόν, ἀπαγαγὼν εἰς
Λάμψακον ἀπέσφαξεν.

Μετὰ δὲ ταῦτ᾽ εἰς Λακεδαίμονα τοὺς τὴν νίκην
ἀπαγγελοῦντας ἀπέστειλεν ἐπὶ τῆς κρατίστης τριήρους, κοσμήσας τοῖς πολυτελεστάτοις τὴν ναῦν
8 ὅπλοις καὶ λαφύροις. ἐπὶ δὲ τοὺς εἰς Σηστὸν
καταφυγόντας Ἀθηναίους στρατεύσας τὴν μὲν
πόλιν εἷλε, τοὺς δ᾽ Ἀθηναίους ὑποσπόνδους
ἀφῆκεν. εὐθὺς δὲ τῇ δυνάμει πλεύσας ἐπὶ Σάμον
αὐτὸς μὲν ταύτην ἐπολιόρκει, Γύλιππον δὲ τὸν εἰς
Σικελίαν τοῖς Συρακοσίοις τῷ ναυτικῷ συμπο-
λεμήσαντα ἀπέστειλεν εἰς Σπάρτην τά τε λάφυρα
κομίζοντα καὶ μετὰ τούτων ἀργυρίου τάλαντα
9 χίλια καὶ πεντακόσια. ὄντος δὲ τοῦ χρήματος
ἐν σακίοις, καὶ ταῦτ᾽ ἔχοντος ἑκάστου σκυτάλην
ἔχουσαν τὴν ἐπιγραφὴν τὸ πλῆθος τοῦ χρήματος
δηλοῦσαν, ταύτην ἀγνοήσας ὁ Γύλιππος τὰ μὲν
σακία παρέλυσεν, ἐξελόμενος δὲ τάλαντα τριακόσια,
καὶ διὰ τῆς ἐπιγραφῆς γνωσθεὶς ὑπὸ τῶν ἐφόρων,
10 ἔφυγε καὶ κατεδικάσθη θανάτῳ. παραπλησίως δὲ
καὶ τὸν πατέρα τοῦ Γυλίππου Κλέαρχον συνέβη
φυγεῖν ἐν τοῖς ἔμπροσθεν χρόνοις, ὅτι δόξας παρὰ
Περικλέους λαβεῖν χρήματα περὶ[1] τοῦ τὴν εἰσβο-
λὴν εἰς τὴν Ἀττικὴν μὴ ποιήσασθαι κατεδικάσθη

---

[1] περὶ] ὑπὲρ Capps.

---

[1] Some eight miles down the Hellespont from Aegospotami.
[2] Cp. chaps. 7 ; 8 ; 28 ff.
[3] The σκυτάλη was a staff used for writing in code. The

and with whom he had relations of friendship; and
of the soldiers the majority fled by land to Sestus[1] and
found safety there. The rest of the ships Lysander
captured, and taking prisoner Philocles the general,
he took him to Lampsacus and had him executed.

After this Lysander dispatched messengers by the
swiftest tireme to Lacedaemon to carry news of the
victory, first decking the vessel out with the most
costly arms and booty. After this, advancing against
the Athenians who had found refuge in Sestus, he took
the city but let the Athenians depart under a truce.
Then he sailed at once to Samos with his troops and
himself began the siege of the city, but Gylippus, who
with a flotilla had fought in aid of the Syracusans in
Sicily,[2] he dispatched to Sparta to take there both the
booty and with it fifteen hundred talents of silver.
The money was in small bags, each of which contained
a *skytalê*[3] which carried the notation of the amount
of the money. Gylippus, not knowing of the *skytalê*,
secretly undid the bags and took out three hundred
talents, and when, by means of the notation, Gylippus
was detected by the ephors, he fled the country and
was condemned to death. Similarly it happens that
Clearchus[4] also, the father of Gylippus, fled the
country at an earlier time, when he was believed to
have accepted a bribe from Pericles not to make the
planned raid into Attica, and was condemned to

Lacedaemonians had two round staves of identical size, the
one kept at Sparta, the other in possession of commanders
abroad. A strip of paper was rolled slantwise around the
staff and the dispatch written lengthwise on it; when un-
rolled the dispatch was unintelligible, but rolled slantwise
round the commander's *skytalê* it could be read. Even if
Gylippus had found the dispatch he could not have read it.

[4] Called Cleandridas by Thucydides (6. 93. 2).

θανάτῳ, καὶ φυγὼν ἐν Θουρίοις τῆς Ἰταλίας διέτριβεν. οὗτοι μὲν οὖν, ἄνδρες ἱκανοὶ τἆλλα δόξαντες εἶναι, ταῦτα πράξαντες τὸν ἄλλον βίον
αὐτῶν κατήσχυναν.

107. Ἀθηναῖοι δὲ τὴν τῶν δυνάμεων φθορὰν
ἀκούσαντες τοῦ μὲν ἀντέχεσθαι τῆς θαλάττης
ἀπέστησαν, περὶ δὲ τὴν τῶν τειχῶν κατασκευὴν
ἐγίνοντο καὶ τοὺς λιμένας ἀπεχώννυον,[1] ἐλπίζοντες,
ὅπερ ἦν εἰκός, εἰς πολιορκίαν καταστήσεσθαι.
2 εὐθὺ γὰρ οἱ μὲν τῶν Λακεδαιμονίων βασιλεῖς
Ἆγις καὶ Παυσανίας μετὰ πολλῆς δυνάμεως ἐμβαλόντες εἰς τὴν Ἀττικὴν πρὸς τοῖς τείχεσιν ἐστρα-
τοπέδευον, Λύσανδρος δὲ πλέον ἢ διακοσίαις
τριήρεσιν εἰς τὸν Πειραιέα κατέπλευσεν. οἱ δ᾽
Ἀθηναῖοι τηλικούτοις περιεχόμενοι κακοῖς ὅμως
ἀντεῖχον καὶ ῥᾳδίως τὴν πόλιν παρεφύλαττον ἐπί
3 τινα χρόνον. τοῖς δὲ Πελοποννησίοις ἔδοξεν,
ἐπείπερ δυσχερὴς ἦν ἡ πολιορκία, τὰς μὲν δυνάμεις
ἀπαγαγεῖν ἐκ τῆς Ἀττικῆς, ταῖς δὲ ναυσὶ μακρὰν
ἐφεδρεύειν, ὅπως αὐτοῖς μὴ παρακομισθῇ σῖτος.
4 οὗ συντελεσθέντος, οἱ μὲν Ἀθηναῖοι εἰς δεινὴν
σπάνιν ἐνέπεσον ἁπάντων μέν, μάλιστα δὲ τροφῆς
διὰ τὸ ταύτην ἀεὶ κατὰ θάλατταν αὐτοῖς κομί-
ζεσθαι. ἐπιτείνοντος δὲ τοῦ δεινοῦ καθ᾽ ἡμέραν,
ἡ μὲν πόλις ἔγεμε νεκρῶν, οἱ δὲ λοιποὶ διαπρεσβευσάμενοι πρὸς Λακεδαιμονίους συνέθεντο τὴν εἰρήνην, ὥστε τὰ μακρὰ σκέλη καὶ τὰ τείχη τοῦ
Πειραιέως περιελεῖν, καὶ μακρὰς ναῦς μὴ πλεῖον
ἔχειν δέκα, τῶν δὲ πόλεων πασῶν ἐκχωρῆσαι καὶ

[1] So Reiske: ἐπεχώννυον.

---

[1] Xenophon (*Hell.* 2. 2. 3), who was in Athens on the

death, spending his life as an exile in Thurii in Italy. 405 B.C. And so these men, who in all other affairs were looked upon as individuals of ability, by such conduct brought shame upon the rest of their lives.

107. When the Athenians heard [1] of the destruction of their armaments, they abandoned the policy of control of the sea, but busied themselves with putting the walls in order and with blocking the harbours, expecting, as well they might, that they would be besieged. For at once the kings of the Lacedaemonians, Agis and Pausanias, invaded Attica with a large army and pitched their camp before the walls, and Lysander with more than two hundred triremes put in at the Peiraeus. Although they were in the grip of such hard trials, the Athenians nevertheless held out and had no trouble defending their city for some time. And the Peloponnesians decided, since the siege was offering difficulties, to withdraw their armies from Attica and to conduct a blockade at a distance with their ships, in order that no grain should come to the inhabitants. When this was done, the Athenians came into dire want of everything, but especially of food, because this had always come to them by sea. Since the suffering increased day by day, the city was filled with dead, and the survivors sent ambassadors and concluded peace with the Lacedaemonians on the terms that they should tear down the two long walls and those of the Peiraeus, keep no more than ten ships of war, withdraw from all the cities, and recognize the

occasion, tells how the news came. " It was at night that the Paralus arrived at Athens with tidings of the disaster, and a sound of wailing ran from Piraeus through the long walls to the city, one man passing on the news to another ; and during that night no one slept. . . ." (Tr. of Brownson in the *L.C.L.*)

427

5 Λακεδαιμονίοις ἡγεμόσι χρῆσθαι. ὁ μὲν οὖν Πελοποννησιακὸς πόλεμος, μακρότατος γενόμενος ὧν
ἴσμεν, τοιοῦτον ἔσχε τὸ τέλος, ἔτη διαμείνας ἑπτὰ
πρὸς τοῖς εἴκοσι.

108. Μικρὸν δὲ τῆς εἰρήνης ὕστερον ἐτελεύτησε
Δαρεῖος ὁ τῆς Ἀσίας βασιλεύς, ἄρξας ἔτη ἐννεα-
καίδεκα, τὴν δ' ἡγεμονίαν διεδέξατο τῶν υἱῶν ὁ
πρεσβύτατος Ἀρταξέρξης καὶ ἦρξεν ἔτη τρία πρὸς
τοῖς τεσσαράκοντα. καθ' ὃν δὴ χρόνον καὶ Ἀντί-
μαχον τὸν ποιητὴν Ἀπολλόδωρος ὁ Ἀθηναῖός
φησιν ἠνθηκέναι.

2 Κατὰ δὲ τὴν Σικελίαν Ἱμίλκων ὁ τῶν Καρχηδονίων ἀφηγούμενος ἀρχομένου τοῦ θέρους τὴν μὲν
τῶν Ἀκραγαντίνων πόλιν κατέσκαψε, τῶν δ' ἱερῶν,
ὅσα μηδ' ἱκανῶς[1] ὑπὸ τοῦ πυρὸς ἐδόκει διεφθάρθαι,
τὰς γλυφὰς καὶ τὰ περιττοτέρως εἰργασμένα περι-
έκοψεν· αὐτόθε[2] δ' ἀναλαβὼν ἅπασαν τὴν δύνα-
3 μιν ἐνέβαλεν εἰς τὴν τῶν Γελώων χώραν. ἐπελθὼν
δὲ ταύτην πᾶσαν καὶ τὴν Καμαριναίαν,[3] πλῆρες
ἐποίησε τὸ στράτευμα παντοίας ὠφελείας. μετὰ
δὲ ταῦτα ἐπὶ Γέλαν πορευθεὶς παρὰ τὸν ὁμώνυμον
4 ποταμὸν τῇ πόλει κατεστρατοπέδευσεν. ἐχόντων
δὲ τῶν Γελώων ἐκτὸς τῆς πόλεως Ἀπόλλωνος ἀν-
δριάντα χαλκοῦν σφόδρα μέγαν, συλήσαντες αὐτὸν
ἀπέστειλαν εἰς τὴν Τύρον. τοῦτον μὲν οἱ Γελῷοι κατὰ τὸν τοῦ θεοῦ χρησμὸν ἀνέθηκαν, οἱ
δὲ Τύριοι καθ' ὃν καιρὸν ὕστερον ὑπ' Ἀλεξάνδρου

---

[1] μηδ' ἱκανῶς Post: μὴ καλῶς.
[2] So Capps: αὐτός.   [3] So Wesseling: Καμάριναν.

---

[1] Cp. p. 417, n. 1.
[2] Antimachus of Colophon wrote an epic poem entitled
Thebaïs and an elegiac poem *Lydê*.

hegemony of the Lacedaemonians. And so the Peloponnesian War, the most protracted of any of which we have knowledge, having run for twenty-seven years, came to the end we have described.

108. Not long after the peace Darius, the King of Asia, died after a reign of nineteen years, and Artaxerxes, his eldest son, succeeded to the throne and reigned for forty-three years. During this period, as Apollodorus the Athenian [1] says, the poet Antimachus [2] flourished.

In Sicily [3] at the beginning of summer Himilcon, the commander of the Carthaginians, razed to the ground the city of the Acragantini, and in the case of the temples which did not appear to have been sufficiently destroyed even by the fire he mutilated the sculptures and everything of rather exceptional workmanship ; he then at once with his entire army invaded the territory of the Geloans. In his attack upon all this territory and that of Camarina he enriched his army with booty of every description. After this he advanced to Gela and pitched his camp along the river of the same name as the city. The Geloans had, outside the city, a bronze statue of Apollo of colossal size ; this the Carthaginians seized as spoil and sent to Tyre.[4] The Geloans had set up the statue in accordance with an oracular response of the god, and the Tyrians at a later time, when they were being besieged by Alexander of Macedon, treated the god

---

[3] The narrative is resumed from the end of chap. 96.

[4] Tyre was the mother-city of the colony of Carthage. The Apollo of Tyre, as well as the Apollo who is mentioned in the treaty between the Carthaginians and Philip of Macedon (Polybius, 7. 9), is generally considered to have been the god Reshef (variously spelled), originally a flame or lightning god of Syria.

τοῦ Μακεδόνος ἐπολιορκοῦντο, καθύβριζον ὡς
συναγωνιζόμενον τοῖς πολεμίοις· Ἀλεξάνδρου δ᾽
ἑλόντος τὴν πόλιν, ὡς Τίμαιός φησι, κατὰ τὴν
ὁμώνυμον ἡμέραν καὶ τὴν αὐτὴν ὥραν ἐν ᾗ Καρχηδόνιοι τὸν Ἀπόλλωνα περὶ Γέλαν ἐσύλησαν,
συνέβη τιμηθῆναι θυσίαις καὶ προσόδοις ταῖς
μεγίσταις ὑπὸ τῶν Ἑλλήνων, ὡς αἴτιον γεγενη-
5 μένον τῆς ἁλώσεως. ταῦτα μὲν οὖν, καίπερ ἐν
ἄλλοις πραχθέντα χρόνοις, οὐκ ἀνεπιτήδειον ἡγη-
σάμεθα παρ᾽ ἄλληλα θεῖναι διὰ τὸ παράδοξον.

Οἱ δ᾽ οὖν Καρχηδόνιοι δενδροτομοῦντες τὴν
χώραν τάφρον περιεβάλοντο τῇ στρατοπεδείᾳ·
προσεδέχοντο γὰρ τὸν Διονύσιον ἥξειν μετὰ δυνά-
6 μεως πολλῆς βοηθήσοντα τοῖς κινδυνεύουσιν. οἱ
δὲ Γελῷοι τὸ μὲν πρῶτον ἐψηφίσαντο τέκνα καὶ
γυναῖκας εἰς Συρακούσας ὑπεκθέσθαι διὰ τὸ μέγεθος
τοῦ προσδοκωμένου κινδύνου· τῶν δὲ γυναικῶν ἐπὶ
τοὺς κατὰ τὴν ἀγορὰν βωμοὺς καταφυγουσῶν καὶ
δεομένων τῆς αὐτῆς τοῖς ἀνδράσι τύχης κοινω-
7 νῆσαι, συνεχώρησαν. μετὰ δὲ ταῦτα τάξεις ποιησάμενοι πλείστας, κατὰ μέρος τοὺς στρατιώτας
ἀπέστελλον ἐπὶ τὴν χώραν· οὗτοι δ᾽ ἐμπειρίαν
ἔχοντες ἐπετίθεντο τοῖς πλανωμένοις τῶν πολεμίων,
καὶ πολλοὺς μὲν αὐτῶν καθ᾽ ἡμέραν ἀνῆγον ζῶντας,
8 οὐκ ὀλίγους δὲ ἀνῄρουν. τῶν δὲ Καρχηδονίων
ἀπὸ μέρους προσβαλλόντων τῇ πόλει καὶ τοῖς
κριοῖς καταβαλλόντων τὰ τείχη γενναίως ἠμύνοντο·
τά τε γὰρ ἐφ᾽ ἡμέρας πίπτοντα τῶν τειχῶν νυκτὸς
ἀνῳκοδόμουν,[1] συνυπηρετουσῶν τῶν γυναικῶν καὶ

disrespectfully on the ground that he was fighting on 405 B.C.
the side of the enemy.[1] But when Alexander took the
city, as Timaeus says, on the day with the same name
and at the same hour on which the Carthaginians
seized the Apollo at Gela, it came to pass that the god
was honoured by the Greeks with the greatest sacrifices
and processions as having been the cause of its capture. Although these events took place at different
times, we have thought it not inappropriate to bring
them together because of their astonishing nature.

Now the Carthaginians cut down the trees of the
countryside and threw a trench [2] about their encampment, since they were expecting Dionysius to come
with a strong army to the aid of the imperilled inhabitants. The Geloans at first voted to remove their
children and women out of danger to Syracuse because
of the magnitude of the expected danger, but when
the women fled to the altars about the market-place
and begged to share the same fortune as the men, they
yielded to them. After this, forming a very large
number of detachments, they sent the soldiers in turn
over the countryside ; and they, because of their
knowledge of the land, attacked wandering bands of
the enemy, daily brought back many of them alive, and
slew not a few. And although the Carthaginians kept
launching assaults in relays upon the city and breach-
ing the walls with their battering-rams, the Geloans
defended themselves gallantly ; for the portions of
the walls which fell during the day they built up again
at night, the women and children assisting. For those

[1] Cp. Book 17. 41. 7.
[2] And also a palisade built from the timbers (*infra*, chap.
110. 3).

---

[1] ἀνῳκοδόμουν Vogel (from 17. 43. 5): ᾠκοδόμουν.

παίδων· οἱ μὲν γὰρ ἀκμάζοντες ταῖς ἡλικίαις ἐν
τοῖς ὅπλοις ὄντες διετέλουν μαχόμενοι, τὸ δ' ἄλλο
πλῆθος τοῖς ἔργοις καὶ ταῖς ἄλλαις παρασκευαῖς
9 προσήδρευε μετὰ πάσης προθυμίας· τὸ δὲ σύνολον
οὕτως ἐδέξαντο τὴν ἔφοδον τῶν Καρχηδονίων εὐρώστως, ὥστε καὶ πόλιν ἀνώχυρον ἔχοντες καὶ
συμμάχων ὄντες ἔρημοι, πρὸς δὲ τούτοις τὰ τείχη
θεωροῦντες πίπτοντα κατὰ πλείονας τόπους, οὐ
κατεπλάγησαν τὸν περιεστῶτα κίνδυνον.

109. Διονύσιος δ' ὁ τῶν Συρακοσίων τύραννος
μεταπεμψάμενος παρὰ τῶν ἐξ Ἰταλίας Ἑλλήνων
βοήθειαν ἐξῆγε καὶ παρὰ τῶν ἄλλων συμμάχων
δύναμιν· ἐπέλεξε δὲ καὶ τῶν Συρακοσίων τοὺς
πλείστους τῶν ἐν ἡλικίᾳ καὶ τοὺς μισθοφόρους
2 κατέλεξεν εἰς τὸ στρατόπεδον. εἶχε δὲ τοὺς ἅπαντας, ὡς μέν τινες, πεντακισμυρίους, ὡς δὲ Τίμαιος
ἀνέγραψε, πεζοὺς μὲν τρισμυρίους, ἱππεῖς δὲ χιλίους, ναῦς δὲ καταφράκτους πεντήκοντα. μετὰ
δὲ τοσαύτης δυνάμεως ἐξορμήσας ἐπὶ τὴν βοήθειαν
τοῖς Γελῴοις,[1] ὡς ἤγγισε τῆς πόλεως, κατεστρα-
3 τοπέδευσε παρὰ τὴν θάλατταν. ἔσπευδε γὰρ μὴ
διασπᾶν τὴν στρατιάν, ἀλλ' ἐκ τοῦ αὐτοῦ τόπου
τὴν ὁρμὴν ποιούμενος κατὰ γῆν ἅμα καὶ κατὰ
θάλατταν ἀγωνίζεσθαι· τοῖς μὲν γὰρ ψιλοῖς ἠγω-
νίζετο καὶ τὴν χώραν οὐκ εἴα προνομεύεσθαι, τοῖς
δ' ἱππεῦσι καὶ ταῖς ναυσὶν ἐπειρᾶτο τὰς ἀγορὰς
ἀφαιρεῖσθαι τὰς κομιζομένας τοῖς Καρχηδονίοις ἐκ
4 τῆς ἰδίας ἐπικρατείας. ἐφ' ἡμέρας μὲν οὖν εἴκοσι
διέτριβον οὐδὲν ἄξιον λόγου πράττοντες· μετὰ δὲ
ταῦτα Διονύσιος τοὺς πεζοὺς εἰς τρία μέρη διεῖλεν,
ἐν μὲν τάγμα ποιήσας τῶν Σικελιωτῶν, οἷς προσ-
έταξεν ἐν[2] ἀριστερᾷ τὴν πόλιν ἔχοντας ἐπὶ τὸν

who were in the bloom of their physical strength were 405 B.C. under arms and constantly in battle, and the rest of the multitude stood by to attend to the defences and the rest of the tasks with all eagerness. In a word, they met the attack of the Carthaginians so stoutly that, although their city lacked natural defences and they were without allies and they could, besides, see the walls falling in a number of places, they were not dismayed at the danger which threatened them.

109. Dionysius, the tyrant of the Syracusans, summoning aid from the Greeks of Italy and his other allies, led forth his army ; and he also enlisted the larger part of the Syracusans of military age and enrolled the mercenaries in the army. He had in all, as some record, fifty thousand soldiers, but according to Timaeus, thirty thousand infantry, a thousand cavalry, and fifty decked vessels. With a force of such size he set out to the aid of the Geloans, and when he drew near the city, he pitched camp by the sea. For his intent was not to divide his army but to use the same base for the fighting by land as well as by sea ; and with his light armed troops he engaged the enemy and did not allow them to forage over the countryside, while with his cavalry and ships he attempted to deprive the Carthaginians of the supplies which they got from the territory of which they were masters. Now for twenty days they were inactive, doing nothing worthy of mention. But after this Dionysius divided his infantry into three groups, and one division, which he formed of the Sicilian Greeks, he ordered to advance against the entrenched camp of

---

[1] τοῖς Γελῴοις Reiske, Madvig, omitted L, τοῖς τόποις cet.
[2] ἐν added by Reiske.

χάρακα τῶν ἐναντίων πορεύεσθαι· τὸ δ' ἕτερον
τάγμα συμμάχων καταστήσας ἐκέλευσεν[1] ἐν[2] δεξιᾷ
τὴν πόλιν ἔχοντας ἐπείγεσθαι παρ' αὐτὸν τὸν
αἰγιαλόν· αὐτὸς δ' ἔχων τὸ τῶν μισθοφόρων σύν-
ταγμα διὰ τῆς πόλεως ὥρμησεν ἐπὶ τὸν τόπον, οὗ
5 τὰ μηχανήματα τῶν Καρχηδονίων ἦν. καὶ τοῖς
μὲν ἱππεῦσι παρήγγειλεν, ἐπειδὰν ἴδωσι τοὺς πεζοὺς
ὡρμημένους, διαβῆναι τὸν ποταμὸν καὶ τὸ πεδίον
καθιππάζεσθαι, κἂν μὲν ὁρῶσι τοὺς ἰδίους προτε-
ροῦντας, συνεπιλαμβάνεσθαι τῆς μάχης, ἂν δ' ἐλατ-
τωμένους, δέχεσθαι τοὺς θλιβομένους· τοῖς δ' ἐν
ταῖς ναυσὶ παρήγγειλε πρὸς τὴν τῶν Ἰταλιωτῶν
ἔφοδον τῇ παρεμβολῇ τῶν πολεμίων ἐπιπλεῦ-
σαι.

110. Εὐκαίρως δ' αὐτῶν ποιησάντων τὸ παραγ-
γελθέν, οἱ μὲν Καρχηδόνιοι πρὸς ἐκεῖνο τὸ μέρος
παρεβοήθουν, ἀνείργοντες τοὺς ἐκ τῶν νεῶν ἀπο-
βαίνοντας· καὶ γὰρ οὐδ' ὠχυρωμένον τῆς στρατοπεδείας[3] τὸ μέρος εἶχον, ἅπαν τὸ παρὰ τὸν αἰγιαλόν·
2 οἱ δ' Ἰταλιῶται κατὰ τοῦτον τὸν καιρὸν παρὰ τὴν
θάλατταν τὸ πᾶν διανύσαντες ἐπέθεντο τῇ παρεμβολῇ τῶν Καρχηδονίων, τοὺς πλείστους εὑρόντες
παραβεβοηθηκότας ἐπὶ τὰς ναῦς· τοὺς δ' ἐπὶ τούτου τοῦ μέρους ὑπολελειμμένους τρεψάμενοι παρεισ-
3 έπεσον εἰς τὴν στρατοπεδείαν. οὗ γενηθέντος οἱ
Καρχηδόνιοι τῷ πλείστῳ μέρει τῆς δυνάμεως ἐπι-
στρέψαντες καὶ πολὺν διαγωνισάμενοι χρόνον μόγις
ἐξέωσαν τοὺς ἐντὸς τῆς τάφρου βιασαμένους. οἱ
δὲ Ἰταλιῶται τῷ πλήθει τῶν βαρβάρων κατα-

---

[1] ἐκέλευε A, ἐκέλευσε cet.   [2] ἐν added by Reiske.

[3] τῆς στρατοπεδείας placed here by Reiske from after αἰγιαλόν.

their adversaries with the city on their left flank ; the 405 B.C.
second division, which he formed of allies, he com-
manded to drive along the shore with the city on their
right ; and he himself with the contingent of mercenaries advanced through the city against the place
where the Carthaginian engines of war were stationed.
And to the cavalry he gave orders that, as soon as they
saw the infantry advancing, they should cross the
river and overrun the plain, and if they should see
their comrades winning, they should join in the fighting, but in case they were losing, they should receive
any who were in distress ; and to the troops on the
ships his orders were, so soon as the Italian Greeks
made their attack, to sail against the camp of the
enemy.

110. When the fleet carried out their orders at the
proper time, the Carthaginians rushed to the aid of
that sector in an attempt to keep back the attackers
disembarking from the ships ; and in fact that portion
of the camp which the Carthaginians occupied was
unfortified, all the part which lay along the beach.
And at this very time the Italian Greeks, who had
covered the entire distance along the sea, attacked
the camp of the Carthaginians, having found that
most of the defenders had gone to give aid against the
ships, and putting to flight the troops which had been
left behind at this place, they forced their way into
the encampment. At this turn of affairs the Carthaginians, turning about with the greater part of their
troops, after a sustained fight, thrust out with difficulty the men who had forced their way within the
trench. The Italian Greeks, overcome by the multi-

πονούμενοι κατὰ τὴν ἀναχώρησιν εἰς τὸ τοῦ
χάρακος ἀπωξυμμένον¹ ἐνέπιπτον, οὐκ ἔχοντες
4 βοήθειαν· οἵ τε γὰρ Σικελιῶται διὰ τοῦ πεδίου
πορευόμενοι καθυστέρουν τῶν καιρῶν, οἵ τε μετὰ
Διονυσίου μισθοφόροι μόγις² διεπορεύοντο τὰς
κατὰ τὴν πόλιν ὁδούς, οὐ δυνάμενοι κατὰ τὴν
ἰδίαν προαίρεσιν ἐπισπεῦσαι. οἱ δὲ Γελῷοι μέχρι
τινὸς ἐπεξιόντες ἐπεβοήθουν κατὰ βραχὺν τόπον
τοῖς Ἰταλιώταις, εὐλαβούμενοι λιπεῖν τὴν τῶν
τειχῶν φυλακήν· διόπερ ὑστέρουν τῆς βοηθείας.
5 οἱ δὲ Ἴβηρες καὶ Καμπανοὶ μετὰ τῶν Καρχηδονίων
στρατευόμενοι καὶ βαρεῖς ἐπικείμενοι τοῖς ἀπὸ
τῆς Ἰταλίας Ἕλλησι, κατέβαλον αὐτῶν πλείους
τῶν χιλίων. τῶν δ' ἐν ταῖς ναυσὶν ἀνειργόντων
τοξεύμασι τοὺς διώκοντας, οἱ λοιποὶ μετ' ἀσφα-
6 λείας διεσώθησαν πρὸς τὴν πόλιν. ἐκ δὲ θατέρου
μέρους οἱ Σικελιῶται πρὸς τοὺς ἀπαντήσαντας
Λίβυας διαγωνισάμενοι συχνοὺς μὲν αὐτῶν ἀνεῖλον,
τοὺς δ' ἄλλους εἰς τὴν στρατοπεδείαν συνεδίωξαν·
τῶν δὲ Ἰβήρων καὶ Καμπανῶν, ἔτι δὲ Καρχηδονίων, παραβοηθησάντων τοῖς Λίβυσι, περὶ ἑξακοσίους ἀποβαλόντες πρὸς τὴν πόλιν ἀπεχώρησαν.
7 οἱ δ' ἱππεῖς ὡς εἶδον τοὺς ἰδίους ἡττημένους, καὶ
αὐτοὶ πρὸς τὴν πόλιν ἀπῆλθον, ἐπικειμένων αὐτοῖς
τῶν πολεμίων. Διονύσιος δὲ μόγις διελθὼν τὴν
πόλιν ὡς κατέλαβε τὸ στρατόπεδον ἠλαττωμένον,
τότε μὲν ἐντὸς τῶν τειχῶν ἀνεχώρησεν.

111. Μετὰ δὲ ταῦτα τῶν φίλων συναγαγὼν
συνέδριον ἐβουλεύετο περὶ τοῦ πολέμου. πάντων
δὲ λεγόντων ἀνεπιτήδειον εἶναι τὸν τόπον περὶ τῶν

¹ ἀπωξυμμένον] ἀποξυμμένον PA, ἀπωχυρωμένον Reiske.
² μόγις Dindorf: μόλις.

tude of the barbarians, encountered as they withdrew _{405 B.C.} the acute angle of the palisade and no help came to them ; for the Sicilian Greeks, advancing through the plain, came too late and the mercenaries with Dionysius encountered difficulties in making their way through the streets of the city and thus were unable to make such haste as they had planned. The Geloans, advancing for some distance from the city, gave aid to the Italian Greeks over only a short space of the area, since they were afraid to abandon the guarding of the walls, and as a result they were too late to be of any assistance. The Iberians and Campanians, who were serving in the army of the Carthaginians, pressing hard upon the Italian Greeks, slew more than a thousand of them. But since the crews of the ships held back the pursuers with showers of arrows, the rest of them got back in safety to the city. In the other part the Sicilian Greeks, who had engaged the Libyans who opposed them, slew great numbers of them and pursued the rest into the encampment ; but when the Iberians and Campanians and, besides, the Carthaginians came up to the aid of the Libyans, they withdrew to the city, having lost some six hundred men. And the cavalry, when they saw the defeat of their comrades, likewise withdrew to the city, since the enemy pressed hard upon them. Dionysius, having barely got through the city, found his army defeated and for the time being withdrew within the walls.

111. After this Dionysius called a meeting of his friends and took counsel regarding the war. When they all said that his position was unfavourable for a

ὅλων διακρίνεσθαι τοῖς πολεμίοις,[1] πρὸς τὴν ἑσπέ-
ραν ἀπέστειλε κήρυκα περὶ τῆς εἰς αὔριον ἀν-
αιρέσεως τῶν νεκρῶν, καὶ τὸν μὲν ἐκ τῆς πόλεως
ὄχλον περὶ πρώτην φυλακὴν τῆς νυκτὸς ἐξαπέστειλεν, αὐτὸς δὲ περὶ μέσας νύκτας ἀφώρμησε, κατα-
2 λιπὼν τῶν ψιλῶν περὶ δισχιλίους. τούτοις δ' ἦν
παρηγγελμένον πυρὰ καίειν δι' ὅλης τῆς νυκτὸς
καὶ θορυβοποιεῖν πρὸς τὸ δόξαν ἐμποιῆσαι τοῖς
Καρχηδονίοις ὡς μένοντος ἐν τῇ πόλει. οὗτοι μὲν
οὖν ἤδη τῆς ἡμέρας ὑποφωσκούσης ἀφώρμησαν
πρὸς τοὺς περὶ τὸν Διονύσιον, οἱ δὲ Καρχηδόνιοι
διαισθόμενοι τὸ γεγονὸς μετεστρατοπέδευσαν εἰς
τὴν πόλιν καὶ τὰ περιλειφθέντα κατὰ τὰς οἰκίας
διήρπασαν.
3 Διονύσιος δὲ παραγενόμενος εἰς τὴν Καμάριναν
ἠνάγκασε καὶ τοὺς ἐκεῖ μετὰ τέκνων καὶ γυναικῶν
εἰς Συρακούσας ἀπιέναι. τοῦ φόβου δ' οὐδεμίαν
ἀναβολὴν διδόντος τινὲς μὲν ἀργύριον καὶ χρυσίον
καὶ τὰ ῥᾳδίως φέρεσθαι δυνάμενα συνεσκευάζοντο,
τινὲς δὲ γονεῖς καὶ τέκνα[2] τὰ νήπια λαβόντες
ἔφευγον, οὐδεμίαν ἐπιστροφὴν χρημάτων ποιού-
μενοι· ἔνιοι δὲ γεγηρακότες ἢ νόσῳ βαρυνόμενοι
δι' ἐρημίαν συγγενῶν ἢ φίλων ὑπελείποντο, προσ-
δοκωμένων ὅσον οὔπω παρέσεσθαι τῶν Καρχη-
4 δονίων· ἢ γὰρ περὶ Σελινοῦντα καὶ Ἱμέραν, ἔτι
δὲ Ἀκράγαντα, γενομένη συμφορὰ τοὺς ἀνθρώπους
ἐξέπληττε, πάντων καθάπερ ὑπὸ τὴν ὅρασιν λαμ-
βανόντων τὴν τῶν Καρχηδονίων δεινότητα. οὐδεμία γὰρ ἦν παρ' αὐτοῖς φειδὼ τῶν ἁλισκομένων,

---

[1] διακρίνεσθαι τοῖς πολεμίοις Vogel: κρίνεσθαι διὰ τοὺς
πολεμίους.
[2] καὶ after τέκνα deleted by Wesseling.

decisive battle with the enemy, he dispatched a herald
toward evening to arrange for the taking up of the
dead on the next day, and about the first watch of the
night he sent out of the city the mass of the people,
while he himself set out about the middle of the night,
leaving behind some two thousand of his light-armed
troops. These had been given orders to keep fires
burning through the entire night and to make an
uproar in order to cause the Carthaginians to believe
that he was still in the city. Now these troops, as the
day was beginning to break, set out to join Dionysius,
and the Carthaginians, on learning what had taken
place, moved their quarters into the city and plundered what had been left of the contents of the
dwellings.

When Dionysius arrived at Camarina, he compelled
the residents of that city also to depart with their
children and wives to Syracuse. And since their fear
admitted of no delay, some gathered together silver
and gold and whatever could be easily carried, while
others fled with only their parents and infant children,
paying no attention to valuables ; and some, who
were aged or suffering from illness, were left behind
because they had no relatives or friends, since the
Carthaginians were expected to arrive almost immediately. For the fate that had befallen Selinus
and Himera and Acragas [1] as well terrified the populace, all of whom felt as if they had actually been eye-
witnesses of the savagery of the Carthaginians. For
among them there was no sparing their captives, but

[1] Cp. chaps. 57 f., 62, and 90 respectively.

ἀλλ' ἀσυμπαθῶς τῶν ἠτυχηκότων οὓς μὲν ἀν-
5 εσταύρουν, οἷς δ' ἀφορήτους ἐπῆγον ὕβρεις. οὐ
μὴν ἀλλὰ δυεῖν πόλεων ἐξοριζομένων ἔγεμεν ἡ
χώρα[1] γυναικῶν καὶ παίδων καὶ τῶν ἄλλων ὄχλων·
ἃ θεωροῦντες οἱ στρατιῶται δι' ὀργῆς μὲν εἶχον
τὸν Διονύσιον, ἠλέουν δὲ τὰς τῶν ἀκληρούντων
6 τύχας· ἑώρων γὰρ παῖδας ἐλευθέρους καὶ παρθένους
ἐπιγάμους ἀναξίως τῆς ἡλικίας ὡς ἔτυχε κατὰ τὴν
ὁδὸν ὡρμημένας, ἐπειδὴ τὴν σεμνότητα καὶ τὴν
πρὸς τοὺς ἀλλοτρίους ἐντροπὴν ὁ καιρὸς ἀφῃρεῖτο.
παραπλησίως δὲ καὶ τοῖς πρεσβυτέροις συνήλγουν,
βλέποντες παρὰ φύσιν ἀναγκαζομένους ἅμα τοῖς
ἀκμάζουσιν ἐπισπεύδειν.

112. Ἐφ' οἷς ἐξεκάετο τὸ κατὰ τοῦ Διονυσίου
μῖσος· καὶ γὰρ ὑπελάμβανον αὐτὸν ἐκ συνθέσεως
τοῦτο πεποιηκέναι πρὸς τὸ τῷ[2] Καρχηδονίων φόβῳ
2 τῶν ἄλλων πόλεων ἀσφαλῶς δυναστεύειν. ἀνελογί-
ζοντο γὰρ τὴν βραδυτῆτα τῆς βοηθείας, τὸ μηδένα
πεπτωκέναι τῶν μισθοφόρων, τὸ μηδενὸς ἁδροῦ
πταίσματος γεγενημένου φυγεῖν ἀλόγως, τὸ δὲ
μέγιστον, τὸ μηδένα τῶν πολεμίων ἐπηκολου-
θηκέναι· ὥστε τοῖς πρότερον ἐπιθυμοῦσι καιρὸν
λαβεῖν τῆς ἀποστάσεως καθάπερ θεῶν προνοίᾳ
πάντα[3] ὑπουργεῖν πρὸς τὴν κατάλυσιν τῆς δυ-
ναστείας.

3 Οἱ μὲν οὖν Ἰταλιῶται καταλιπόντες αὐτὸν ἐπ'
οἴκου διὰ τῆς μεσογείου τὴν πορείαν ἐποιήσαντο,
οἱ δὲ τῶν Συρακοσίων ἱππεῖς τὸ μὲν πρῶτον

---

[1] ἔγεμεν ἡ χώρα Wurm : ἐν τῇ χώρᾳ.
[2] τὸ τῷ Dindorf : τῷ τῶν PA, τὸ τῶν cet.
[3] So Reiske : πάντας.

---

[1] To Gela.

they were without compassion for the victims of _{405 B.C.} Fortune of whom they would crucify some and upon others inflict unbearable outrages. Nevertheless, now that two cities had been driven into exile, the country-side teemed with women and children and the rabble in general. And when the soldiers witnessed these conditions, they were not only enraged against Dionysius but also filled with pity at the lot of the unfortunate victims; for they saw free-born boys and maidens of marriageable years rushing pell-mell along the road in a manner improper for their age, since the stress of the moment had done away with the dignity and respect which are shown before strangers. Similarly they sympathized also with the elderly, as they watched them being forced to push onward beyond their strength while trying to keep up with those in the prime of life.

112. It was for these reasons that the hatred against Dionysius was flaring up, since men assumed that he had so acted from this definite plan : by using the dread of the Carthaginians to be lord of the remaining cities of Sicily without risk. For they reckoned up his delay in bringing aid [1] ; the fact that none of his mercenaries had fallen ; that he had retreated without reason, since he had suffered no serious reverse ; and, most important of all, that not a single one of the Carthaginians had pursued them. Consequently, for those who before this were eager to seize an opportunity to revolt, all things, as if by the foreknowledge of the gods, were working toward the overthrow of the tyrannical power.

Now the Italian Greeks, deserting Dionysius, made their way home through the interior of the island, and the Syracusan cavalry at first kept watch in the hope

ἐπετήρουν, εἰ δύναιντο κατὰ τὴν ὁδὸν ἀνελεῖν τὸν
τύραννον· ὡς δὲ ἑώρων οὐκ ἀπολείποντας αὐτὸν
τοὺς μισθοφόρους, ὁμοθυμαδὸν ἀφίππευσαν εἰς
4 τὰς Συρακούσας. καταλαβόντες δὲ τοὺς ἐν τοῖς
νεωρίοις ἀγνοοῦντας τὰ περὶ τὴν Γέλαν, εἰσῆλθον
οὐδενὸς κωλύσαντος, καὶ τὴν μὲν οἰκίαν τοῦ Διονυσίου διήρπασαν γέμουσαν ἀργύρου τε καὶ χρυσοῦ
καὶ τῆς ἄλλης πολυτελείας ἁπάσης, τὴν δὲ γυναῖκα
συλλαβόντες οὕτω διέθεσαν κακῶς ὥστε καὶ τὸν
τύραννον βαρέως ἐνέχειν[1] τὴν ὀργήν, νομίζοντες
τὴν ταύτης τιμωρίαν μεγίστην εἶναι πίστιν τῆς
5 πρὸς ἀλλήλους κοινωνίας κατὰ τὴν ἐπίθεσιν. ὁ
δὲ Διονύσιος κατὰ τὴν ὁδοιπορίαν τὸ γεγονὸς
καταστοχαζόμενος, ἐπέλεξε τῶν ἱππέων καὶ τῶν
πεζῶν τοὺς πιστοτάτους, μεθ᾽ ὧν ἠπείγετο πρὸς
τὴν πόλιν σπουδῆς οὐδὲν ἐλλείπων· ἐλογίζετο γὰρ
οὐκ ἂν ἄλλως δυνατὸν ἐπικρατῆσαι τῶν ἱππέων,
εἰ μὴ σπεύδοι[2]· ὅπερ ἐποίησεν. εἰ γὰρ παρα-
δοξότερον[3] ἐκείνων ποιήσαιτο τὴν ἄφιξιν, ἤλπιζε
ῥᾳδίως κρατήσειν τῆς ἐπιβολῆς· ὅπερ καὶ συν-
6 έπεσεν. οἱ γὰρ ἱππεῖς οὔτ᾽ ἂν ἔτ᾽[4] ἀπελθεῖν οὔτε
μεῖναι κατὰ τὸ στρατόπεδον τὸν Διονύσιον ὑπ-
ελάμβανον· διόπερ κεκρατηκέναι τῆς ἐπιβολῆς
νομίσαντες, ἔφασαν αὐτὸν ἐκ μὲν Γέλας προσποιη-
θῆναι τοὺς Φοίνικας ἀποδιδράσκειν, νυνὶ δὲ ὡς
ἀληθῶς ἀποδεδρακέναι τοὺς Συρακοσίους.

113. Διονύσιος δὲ διανύσας σταδίους περὶ τετρακοσίους παρῆν περὶ μέσας νύκτας πρὸς τὴν πύλην

----

[1] So Post : ἐνεγκεῖν.
[2] So Reiske : πειθοῖ.
[3] παραδοξότερον] παρὰ δόξαν Reiske.
[4] ἂν ἔτ᾽ added by Post.

that they might be able to slay the tyrant along the 405 B.C.
road ; but when they saw that the mercenaries were
not deserting him, they rode off with one accord to
Syracuse. And finding the guards of the dockyards [1]
knew nothing of the events at Gela, they entered
these without hindrance, plundered the house of
Dionysius which was filled with silver and gold and all
other costly things, and seizing his wife left her so
ill-used [2] as to ensure the tyrant's keeping his anger
fiercely alive, acting as they did in the belief that
the vengeance they wreaked on Dionysius' wife
would be the surest guarantee of their holding by
each other in their attack upon him. And Dionysius,
guessing while on the way what had taken place,
picked out the most trustworthy of his cavalry and
infantry, with whom he pressed toward the city
without checking speed ; for he reasoned that he
could overcome the cavalry by no other means than
by speedy action, and he acted accordingly. For if
he should make his arrival even more of a surprise
than theirs had been, he had hope that he would
easily carry out his design ; and that is what happened. For the cavalry assumed that Dionysius
would now neither return to Syracuse nor remain
with his army ; consequently, in the belief that they
had carried out their design, they said that he had
pretended that in leaving Gela he was giving the slip
to the Carthaginians whereas the truth in fact was
that he had given the slip to the Syracusans.

113. Dionysius covered a distance of four hundred
stades [3] and arrived at the gates of Achradinê about

[1] Where Dionysius had taken up his residence (chap.
96. 2).
[2] According to Plutarch (*Dion*, 3. 1), she subsequently
committed suicide.   [3] About 46 miles.

τῆς Ἀχραδινῆς μεθ᾽ ἱππέων ἑκατὸν καὶ πεζῶν ἑξα-
κοσίων· ἣν καταλαβὼν κεκλεισμένην, προσέθηκεν
αὐτῇ τὸν κατακεκομισμένον ἐκ τῶν ἑλῶν κάλαμον,
ᾧ χρῆσθαι νομίζουσιν οἱ Συρακόσιοι πρὸς τὴν τῆς
κονίας σύνδεσιν. ἐν ὅσῳ δὲ συνέβαινε τὰς πύλας
κατακαίεσθαι, προσανελάμβανε τοὺς ἀφυστεροῦν-
2 τας. ἐπειδὴ δὲ τὸ πῦρ κατέφθειρε τὰς πύλας,
οὗτος μὲν μετὰ τῶν ἠκολουθηκότων εἰσήλαυνε διὰ
τῆς Ἀχραδινῆς, τῶν δ᾽ ἱππέων οἱ δυνατώτατοι τὸ
γεγονὸς ἀκούσαντες, τὸ μὲν πλῆθος οὐκ ἀνέμενον,
εὐθὺς δ᾽ ἐξεβοήθουν ὄντες ὀλίγοι παντελῶς—ἦσαν
δὲ περὶ τὴν ἀγοράν—καὶ κυκλωθέντες ὑπὸ τῶν
3 μισθοφόρων ἅπαντες κατηκοντίσθησαν. ὁ δὲ Διονύσιος ἐπελθὼν τὴν πόλιν τούς τε σποράδην ἐκβοη-
θοῦντας ἀνεῖλε, καὶ τῶν ἀλλοτρίως[1] διακειμένων
ἐπῄει τὰς οἰκίας, ὧν τοὺς μὲν ἀπέκτεινε, τοὺς δ᾽
ἐκ τῆς πόλεως ἐξέβαλε. τὸ δὲ λοιπὸν πλῆθος τῶν
ἱππέων ἐκπεσὸν ἐκ τῆς πόλεως κατελάβετο τὴν νῦν
4 καλουμένην Αἴτνην.[2] ἅμα δ᾽ ἡμέρᾳ τὸ μὲν πλῆθος
τῶν μισθοφόρων καὶ τὸ στράτευμα τῶν Σικελιωτῶν κατήντησεν εἰς τὰς Συρακούσας, Γελῷοι δὲ
καὶ Καμαριναῖοι τῷ Διονυσίῳ διαφόρως ἔχοντες
εἰς Λεοντίνους ἀπηλλάγησαν.

114. . . . Διόπερ ὑπὸ τῶν πραγμάτων ἀναγκαζό-
μενος Ἰμίλκας ἔπεμψεν εἰς Συρακούσας κήρυκα,
παρακαλῶν τοὺς ἡττημένους διαλύσασθαι. ἀσμένως
δ᾽ ὑπακούσαντος τοῦ Διονυσίου τὴν εἰρήνην ἐπὶ
τοῖσδε ἔθεντο· Καρχηδονίων εἶναι μετὰ[3] τῶν ἐξ
ἀρχῆς ἀποίκων Ἐλύμους[4] καὶ Σικανούς· Σελινουν-

---

[1] τῇ πόλει after ἀλλοτρίως deleted by Vogel.
[2] So Wesseling : Ἀχραδινήν.   [3] μετὰ Madvig : μέν.
[4] So Madvig, Unger : ἄλλους.

the middle of the night with a hundred cavalry and 405 B.C.
six hundred infantry, and finding the gate closed, he
piled upon it reeds brought from the marshes such as
the Syracusans are accustomed to use to bind their
stucco. While the gates were being burned down, he
gathered to his troops the laggards. And when the
fire had consumed the gates, Dionysius with his followers made their way through Achradinê, and the
stoutest soldiers among the cavalry, when they heard
what had happened, without waiting for the main
body, and although they were very few in number,
rushed forth at once to aid in the resistance. They
were gathered in the market-place, and there they
were surrounded by the mercenaries and shot down
to a man. Then Dionysius, ranging through the city,
slew any who came out here and there to resist him,
and entering the houses of those who were hostile
toward him, some of them he killed and others he
banished from the city. The main body of the cavalry
which was left fled from the city and occupied Aetnê,
as it is now called. At daybreak the main body of the
mercenaries and the army of the Sicilian Greeks
arrived at Syracuse, but the Geloans and Camarinaeans, who were at odds with Dionysius, left him and
departed to Leontini.

114. . . .[1] Consequently Himilcar, acting under
the stress of circumstances, dispatched a herald to
Syracuse urging the vanquished to make up their
differences. Dionysius was glad to comply and they
concluded peace on the following terms : To the
Carthaginians shall belong, together with their original
colonists, the Elymi and Sicani ; the inhabitants of

---

[1] Here there was probably an account of the plague which
visited the Carthaginian army.

445

τίους δὲ καὶ ᾿Ακραγαντίνους, ἔτι δ᾽ ᾿Ιμεραίους,
πρὸς δὲ τούτοις Γελῴους καὶ Καμαριναίους οἰκεῖν
μὲν ἐν ἀτειχίστοις ταῖς πόλεσι, φόρον δὲ τελεῖν
τοῖς Καρχηδονίοις· Λεοντίνους δὲ καὶ Μεσσηνίους
καὶ Σικελοὺς ἅπαντας αὐτονόμους εἶναι, καὶ Συρακοσίους μὲν ὑπὸ Διονύσιον τετάχθαι· τὰ δὲ αἰχμάλωτα καὶ τὰς ναῦς ἀποδοῦναι τοὺς[1] ἔχοντας τοῖς
ἀποβαλοῦσι.

2 Τῶν συνθηκῶν δὲ γενομένων Καρχηδόνιοι μὲν
εἰς Λιβύην ἐξέπλευσαν, πλεῖον ἢ τὸ ἥμισυ μέρος
τῶν στρατιωτῶν ἀποβαλόντες ὑπὸ τῆς νόσου·
οὐδὲν δ᾽ ἧττον καὶ κατὰ Λιβύην διαμείναντος τοῦ
λοιμοῦ, παμπληθεῖς αὐτῶν τε τῶν Καρχηδονίων,
ἔτι δὲ τῶν συμμάχων διεφθάρησαν.

3 ῾Ημεῖς δὲ παραγενηθέντες ἐπὶ τὴν κατάλυσιν
τῶν πολέμων, κατὰ μὲν τὴν ῾Ελλάδα τοῦ Πελοποννησιακοῦ, κατὰ δὲ τὴν Σικελίαν τοῦ Καρχηδονίοις
πρὸς Διονύσιον πρώτου συστάντος, ἡγούμεθα δεῖν
ἐπιτετελεσμένης τῆς προθέσεως τὰς ἑξῆς πράξεις
εἰς[2] τὴν ἐχομένην βίβλον καταχωρίσαι.

---

[1] τοὺς added by Reiske.
[2] τὰς ἑξῆς π. ε. Wesseling : εἰς τὰς ἑξῆς πράξεις.

Selinus, Acragas, and Himera as well as those of Gela 405 B.C. and Camarina may dwell in their cities, which shall be unfortified, but shall pay tribute to the Carthaginians; the inhabitants of Leontini and Messenê and the Siceli shall all live under laws of their own making, and the Syracusans shall be subject to Dionysius; and whatever captives and ships are held shall be returned to those who lost them.

As soon as this treaty had been concluded, the Carthaginians sailed off to Libya, having lost more than half their soldiers from the plague; but the pestilence continued to rage no less in Libya also and great numbers both of the Carthaginians themselves and of their allies were struck down.

But for our part, now that we have arrived at the conclusion of the wars, in Greece the Peloponnesian and in Sicily the first between the Carthaginians and Dionysius, and our proposed task has been completed,[1] we think that we should set down the events next in order in the following Book.

[1] Cp. chap. 1. 3.

A PARTIAL INDEX OF PROPER NAMES [1]

---

[1] A complete Index will appear in the last volume.

A PARTIAL INDEX OF PROPER NAMES

450

A PARTIAL INDEX OF PROPER NAMES

451

A PARTIAL INDEX OF PROPER NAMES

A PARTIAL INDEX OF PROPER NAMES

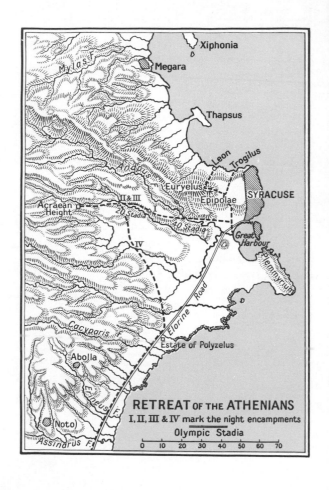

RETREAT OF THE **ATHENIANS**
I, II, III & IV mark the night encampments
Olympic Stadia

| 0 | 10 | 20 | 30 | 40 | 50 | 60 | 70 |

Leon

Trogilus

Labdalum

Three fortified camps of the Syracusans

Euryelus

Third Syracusan Counter-wall Parateichismal

E p i p o l a e

Cyclus

Syce

Syracusan Counter-wall

Hypoteichismal

Temenites

Outworks

O u t e r   C i t y   (Achradina)

Syracusan Counter-wall (center of 45-44 Proteichisma)

Circumvallation of 45-44

Lesser Harbour

Syracusan Counter-wall (center of 45-44 Proteichisma)

Marsh
Lysimeleïa

New Wall

The Acropolis

Mole

Inner
City
(Ortygia I)

Anapus F.

Fountain of Cyane

Elorine Road

Olympieum

Dascon

The

Great

Harbour

Plemmyrium

SIEGE OF SYRACUSE

Olympic Stadia

0   5   10   20

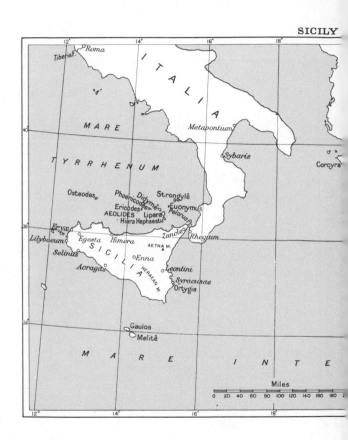

Maroneia

MACEDONIA

Samothrace

Peneius F.

Hellespont Troia (Dardanus)
IDA M.
Lemnos Tenedos Scamandrus F.

THESSALIA PELION M. Methymna
Iolcus Mytilene

Peparethos Scyros Lesbos

Cymé Phocaea

AETOLIA DORIS LOCRIS
Ithaka HELLAS BOEOTIA Chalcis Chios Erythrae
Thebes
Elis Sicyon Eleusis Tanagra
Olympia Phlius Athenae Andros Samos
PHOLOE M. Corinth
Alpheus F. ARCADIA Argos Aegina Ceos
Pisa Troezen CYCLADES Delos Miletus
Messené Sparta Ptyissa Calymna Cnidus
Naxos Cos
Nisyros Syme Ialysus
Malea Pr. Triopium Pr.
Rhodus Lindus

NUM

CRETA
IDA M.